Family Law
Second Edition

Frances Burton

Routledge
Taylor & Francis Group

LONDON AND NEW YORK

Second edition first published 2015
by Routledge
2 Park Square, Milton Park, Abingdon, Oxon OX14 4RN

and by Routledge
711 Third Avenue, New York, NY 10017

Routledge is an imprint of the Taylor & Francis Group, an informa business

First edition published by Routledge in 2012

Trademark notice: Product or corporate names may be trademarks or registered
trademarks, and are used only for identification and explanation without intent
to infringe.

British Library Cataloguing in Publication Data
A catalogue record for this book is available from the British Library

Library of Congress Cataloging in Publication Data
Burton, Frances (Frances R.), 1941– author.
  Family law / Frances Burton. — 2nd edition.
    pages cm
  ISBN 978-0-415-73358-8 (hbk) — ISBN 978-0-415-73357-1 (pbk) —
  ISBN 978-1-315-84828-0 (ebk)   1. Domestic relations—England.
  2. Children—Legal status, laws, etc.—England.   I. Title.
  KD750.B87 2015
  346.4201'5—dc23   2014035404

ISBN: 978-0-415-73358-8 (hbk)
ISBN: 978-0-415-73357-1 (pbk)
ISBN: 978-1-315-84828-0 (ebk)

Typeset in Joanna MT
by RefineCatch Limited, Bungay, Suffolk

MIX
Paper from
responsible sources
FSC® C013056
www.fsc.org

Printed and bound in Great Britain by
TJ International Ltd, Padstow, Cornwall

Contents

Preface

An earlier edition of a previous textbook by this author aimed to bridge the gap between traditional academic texts and the vocational course manuals used on the Legal Practice and Bar Vocational Courses, in the hope of providing some grasp of the procedural impact on substantive law which is essential to understanding the academic issues in Family Law, and also in seeking a working knowledge of this distinct discipline which is accepted to be 'different' from other civil litigation.

The present title continues in this new edition to aim to take this holistic approach much further by not only looking at the rapidly moving (and constantly widening) subject area in the same inclusive manner, but now doing so in the context of the radical modernisation which has been taking place in family justice in the past couple of years, which the President of the Family Division has described as 'the largest reform of the family justice system any of us have seen or will see in our professional lifetimes'. As he said in his 'Eleventh View from the President's Chambers',[1] 'we stand on the cusp of history', and he added that the introduction of the unified Family Court on 22 April 2014 amounted to 'a revolution . . . central to which has been – has had to be – a fundamental change in the culture of the family courts'.

For this reason, this edition of the book is inevitably 'work in progress' as there will be more change, continuing to hone and polish the system in every respect for at least the next legal and academic year. Fortunately we have a companion website which can not only add updates but also find room for more detailed treatment of key topics as this becomes possible while the new systems bed down.

As well as identifying the current debates and, where possible, going some way to addressing the contemporary academic and practitioner criticisms, the book aims to give those new to the subject as simple an introduction as possible to the various upheavals that have taken place, and to provide some signposting towards how the new systems may provide a better basis for the resolution of family disputes.

It is fashionable to claim that Family Law has been and still is 'in meltdown' and/or is 'a shambles' and in need of much more reform. There is something in each of these comments, and certainly the current cuts in public spending and economic constraints on the administration of justice in general (besides on operation of the courts in particular) pose problems for Family Law in practice. This is especially the case where resources are scarce to manage some changes, such as the lack of legal aid, which could have been better handled with more and earlier information for the public, many of whom have been left adrift as litigants in person.

However, on closer analysis there is much in Family Law that has been steadily developed over time (i.e. along the timeline from the 1950s when the subject area noticeably ceased to comprise only divorce and allied matters, with a little rudimentary child protection thrown in). Within the current modernisation there is still much that can be relied on and which does not really need any more radical change. Even the much maligned (i.e. apparent lack of) system of financial provision – which used to be called ancillary relief – is beginning to achieve coherence and, despite the wails of practitioners and clients that the outcome of any contested financial provision action cannot be predicted, so everyone must have a 'pre-nup', is not now beyond clear articulation – which in any

---

1 (2014) 44 *Family Law* 587.

case is coming, from the Family Justice Council (FJC), from the working group led by Cobb J (devising the new Money Arrangements Programme for the new Family Court), and possibly also from the government if they implement the Law Commission's recommendations on Qualifying Nuptial Agreements.

We also have (since the last edition of this book) same-sex marriage – together with potential in the 2014 Act for conversion from civil partnership for those who want it – a new child maintenance system in the apparently more steady hands (than its predecessors') of the Department for Work and Pensions (DWP), and a new Public Law Outline 2014 which aims to meet the criticisms of the Family Justice Review (FJR) and the implementation in private law cases of the new Child Arrangements Programme.

The only real 'running sores' which remain are the (perhaps) unsatisfactory lack of reform of the ground for divorce (which still troubles the theorist minority because it is said to be 'hypocritical', even though it works in practice), and the (certainly) complete disregard of the highly unsatisfactory state of the law relating to cohabitants, which requires definition of the legal effect of their relationship and property rights; happily their children were long ago separated out from these problems by the Children Act, Child Support Acts and allied legislation. Nearly 30 years after Mrs Burns' debacle and with marriage statistics at their lowest for nearly 35 years (and lower predicted) this is a serious matter worthy of academic, practitioners' and reformers' attention – especially at a time of economic constraint on resources for administration of justice, since the lack of a legal framework for family units forming such a large section of the community (and their being forced to use the complexity of trusts litigation at great expense when their partnerships break up) does not make legal, economic or social welfare sense.

In view of the importance of the developmental background in the continuing change to all areas of Family Law I have included in the text a date for each case selected for citation or comment (as well as giving the usual full library references in the footnotes) so that the reader can be constantly and conveniently orientated along the timeline of conceptual thought and underlying theory which has brought about the ongoing changes of the last 60 years.

This is an introductory book though, aiming to instil a grasp of the shape of the subject and an appreciation of its themes, and as such it aims to provide basic principles without the complication of too much detail (especially as many currently reported cases quickly become of transitory interest, being more graphic examples rather than really adding to the principles). For readers seeking a wider and deeper understanding and more detail the suggested further reading flags up some of the more probing literature which may perform that function, since of course a book of this length can only scratch the surface, especially as academic Family Law syllabuses are often customised to the interests of the course leader and may not include every one of the generally mainstream topics which have been chosen for coverage. For full-time, part-time or distance learning students all these resources should be readily available electronically through institutional libraries or more generally on the internet (even through Google Scholar) as well as in hard copy.

However, these are not the only current debates by any means, as indicated at the end of each chapter, and anyone with some existing knowledge will find the impact of some change or other on every page, so the website will have to do duty for any more. Of all the subject areas routinely studied in the academy. Family Law is the least static and has nothing in common with a dead language.

Frances Burton
Associate Lecturer in Family Law and Dispute Resolution
Buckinghamshire New University
Co-Director, International Centre for Family Law, Policy and Practice
www.famlawandpractice.com
January 2015

Table of Cases

S

Table of Statutes

Table of Statutory Instruments

Table of EU Legislation

Table of Abbreviations

AA 1976	Adoption Act 1976
AA 1996	Arbitration Act 1996
ACA 2002	Adoption and Children Act 2002
ADR	Alternative Dispute Resolution
AEA 1971	Attachment of Earnings Act 1971
AID	artificial insemination by donor
AIH	artificial insemination by husband
BPTC	Bar Practical Training Course
CA 1989	Children Act 1989
CAA 1984	Child Abduction Act 1984
CACA 1985	Child Abduction and Custody Act 1985
CAFA 2014	Children and Families Act 2014
CAFCASS	Children and Family Court Advice and Support Service
CAO	Child Arrangements Order (under the amendment to CA 1989 s 8 effected by CAFA 2014)
CAO	Child Assessment Order (under CA 1989 Part IV)
CAP	Child Arrangements Programme
CETV	cash equivalent transfer value
CFLQ	Child and Family Law Quarterly
CIArb	Chartered Institute of Arbitrators
CJC	Civil Justice Council
CMEC	Child Maintenance and Enforcement Commission
CMOPA 2008	Child Maintenance and Other Payments Act 2008
CMS	Child Maintenance Service
COTS	Childlessness Overcome Through Surrogacy
CPA 2004	Civil Partnership Act 2004
CPAG	Child Poverty Action Group
CPR	Civil Procedure Rules 1998
CSA 1991	Child Support Act 1991
CSA 1991–1995	Child Support Acts 1991–1995
CSA	Child Support Agency
CYPA 1933	Children and Young Persons Act 1933
DJ	District Judge
DMPA 1973	Domicile and Matrimonial Proceedings Act 1973
DPMCA 1978	Domestic Proceedings and Magistrates Court Act 1978
DR	Dispute Resolution
DRA 1969	Divorce Reform Act 1969
DSS	Department of Social Security
DWP	Department for Work and Pensions
ECHR	European Convention on Human Rights and Fundamental Freedoms 1950
ECtHR	European Court of Human Rights

EPO	Emergency Protection Order
FAO	Family Assistance Order
FCO	Foreign and Commonwealth Office
FDR	Financial Dispute Resolution
FJC	Family Justice Council
FJR	Family Justice Review
FLA 1996	Family Law Act 1996
FLBA	Family Law Bar Association
FLRA 1969	Family Law Reform Act 1969
FLRA 1987	Family Law Reform Act 1987
FMA	Family Mediators Association
FMC	Family Mediation Council
FMPA 2007	Forced Marriage Protection Act 2007
FMPO	Forced Marriage Protection Order
FMU	Forced Marriage Unit
FPC	Family Proceedings Court
FPI	Family and Parenting Institute
FPR 1991	Family Proceedings Rules 1991
FPR 2010	Family Procedure Rules 2010
GIFT	Gamete Intra-Fallopian Transfer
GRA 2004	Gender Recognition Act 2004
HAR	Human Assisted Reproduction
HFEA 1990	Human Fertilisation and Embryology Act 1990
HFEA	Human Fertilisation and Embryology Authority
HFEA 2008	Human Fertilisation and Embryology Act 2008
HMCTS	Her Majesty's Courts and Tribunals Service
HRA 1998	Human Rights Act 1998
IACP	International Academy of Collaborative Professionals
IAML	International Academy of Matrimonial Lawyers
IFLA	Institute of Family Law Arbitrators
IPFDA 1975	Inheritance (Provision for Families and Dependants) Act 1975
ISCO	Independent Schools Career Organisation
IVF	In Vitro Fertilisation
JS	Judicial Separation
LAA	Legal Aid Agency
LASPO 2012	Legal Aid, Sentencing and Punishment of Offenders Act 2012
LIP	Litigant in Person
LPA 1925	Law of Property Act 1925
LPC	Legal Practical Course
LSC	Legal Services Commission
MCA 1857	Matrimonial Causes Act 1857
MCA 1973	Matrimonial Causes Act 1973
MEA 1991	Maintenance Enforcement Act 1991
MFPA 1984	Matrimonial and Family Proceedings Act 1984
MHA 1967	Matrimonial Homes Act 1967
MHA 1983	Matrimonial Homes Act 1983
MHAs	Matrimonial Homes Acts
MIAM	Mediation information and assessment meeting
MOJ	Ministry of Justice
MPPA 1970	Matrimonial Proceedings and Property Act 1970

MPS	maintenance pending suit
MWPA 1882	Married Women's Property Act 1882
N-CDR	Non-Court Dispute Resolution
NRP	Non-Resident Parent
NSPCC	National Society for the Prevention of Cruelty to Children
OAPA 1861	Offences Against the Person Act 1861
PA 1995	Pensions Act 1995
PACS	Pacte Civile de Solidarite
PHA 1997	Protection from Harassment Act 1997
PLO	Public Law Outline
PR	Parental Responsibility
PSO	Prohibited Steps Order
PWC	Person with Care
QNP	Qualifying Nuptial Agreement
RSC	Rules of the Supreme Court
SAA 1985	Surrogacy Arrangements Act 1985
SCA 1981	Senior Courts Act 1981
SFLA	Solicitors Family Law Association
SIO	Specific Issue Order
SPIP	Separated Parents Information Programme
SSA 1986	Social Security Act 1986
SSA 1990	Social Security Act 1990
TOLATA 1996	Trusts of Land and Appointment of Trustees Act 1996
TRI form	TRI form (Land Registry for transfer of registered land)
UKCLE	UK Centre for Legal Education
UNCRC	UN Convention on the Rights of the Child

Chapter 1

Introduction: What is Contemporary Family Law?

Chapter Contents

Learning outcomes for this chapter

An understanding of the heavily discretionary based nature of English Family Law including:

(i) An awareness of the dramatic changes in family law in (a) the past dozen years, in particular in the current modernisation project following the Family Justice Review and other catalysts; and (b) the preceding 60 years, specifically in the following, in no particular order:

- financial provision on relationship breakdown;
- legal recognition of atypical adult partnerships (i.e. transsexuals in their acquired gender for all purposes, and both genders in relation to marriage);
- the alternatives to traditional opposite sex marriage of registered civil partnership, same-sex marriage and same-sex informal partnerships;
- the atypical shape of families, particularly owing to human assisted reproduction and the modernisation of adoption practice;
- government steering towards out-of-court dispute resolution, encouraging greater cooperation between separating parties, particularly parents of children;
- a culture of living with cost cutting and self reliance on information gathering without legal advice, including if necessary litigants in person before the court.

(ii) An overview of the areas of family law requiring reform and the underlying reasons for this perception.

(iii) An ability to analyse family law problems in the knowledge that a combination of professional practice and the court's discretion has developed the law in practice beyond the black letter provision in recent statutes.

1.1 Introduction

1.1.1 Social change and public perception

Before beginning any academic study of family law it is essential to understand the context in which this area of law now operates, the origins from which it has come and to disregard – and firmly shed – any preconceptions: the former 'traditional' conceptions, based in a general morality appropriate in earlier times, now bear little relation to the position at the present day.

Family law as a separate discipline, and especially as an academic subject of study, is of fairly recent invention: credit for this usually goes to the late Professor Peter Bromley, who published the first edition of his well known textbook in 1957. Naturally, there was a corpus of family law before that date, in the Matrimonial Causes Acts from 1857 and various child protection statutes, including the Guardianship of Infants Act 1925 from which the concept of the paramountcy of the welfare of the child originates: the separate discipline of Child Law had not then developed as such, and in practice did not until the 1980s.

In the same decade as Bromley, a practical text on 'Divorce', as the general subject of family law was then called, was published by Dmitri Tolstoy, an expatriate Russian aristocrat practising common law at the English Bar. At this time, only three generations ago, 'family law' consisted mostly of lengthy oral hearings of divorces, and the late Sir John Mortimer QC had not elevated to literary fame nor classic television the career of his father, the blind divorce lawyer Clifford Mortimer, the core of whose practice, like that of Tolstoy, was divorce, divorce and moreover mostly only divorce, as the wife in those days seldom received much money and often none at all if she had been adulterous or was in any way to blame for the parties' separation; and neither family law in general nor divorce (its best-known feature) in particular appeared in serious academic programmes.

Newspapers of the time show that any public interest was confined to the sensational details of these cases, whereas contemporary students are often now aware of far more fundamental current issues in family law – such as adoption, cohabitants' and gay rights and the tension between family autonomy and state intervention – from both the popular press and the more serious media. Nowadays an aware student recognises current topics long before beginning to study family law in structured academic or vocational programmes, or reading textbooks, specialist journals and law reports. Indeed this early exposure to family law issues of general interest is often the reason for a contemporary student's interest in the subject as an option in degree programmes.

The general public also now tends to take an interest in the key family law issues on which the courts daily make decisions. This interest has been encouraged by the broadsheets, e.g. in *The Times'* relentless campaign against what is their erroneous perception of the 'secret determinations' made 'behind closed doors' in family disputes relating to children, including those between the family and the state which can result in children being taken from their birth families, either into the care of the local authority or permanently removing them by adoption. This in turn has led to the decision of the present President of the Family Division, Sir James Munby, to tackle this syndrome by building on the earlier transparency initiatives of a former President, the distinguished commercial lawyer Sir Mark Potter, in allowing greater access by the press to courts hearing family cases: Sir James has already issued a Practice Direction now making most family judgments available for publication, subject to safeguards.[1]

1.1.2 Contemporary practice: litigants in person and modern perspectives

The President's initiative has also coincided with a concentration of greater numbers of litigants in person ('LIP's) in the family courts, since following the implementation in April 2014 of the **Legal Aid, Sentencing and Punishment of Offenders Act ('LASPO') 2012** these self-represented parties are perforce now obliged to learn enough about the general principles of family law to handle their own cases without lawyers, a much steeper learning curve for any ordinary member of the public than previously, when they could rely for information as well as advice on their legal advisers whose work could, for most ordinary clients, be funded by legal aid. This is because, in April 2013, LASPO removed legal aid from practically all private family law disputes, although it is still available in most more complex public law cases, e.g. care and supervision order proceedings, and in international cases, e.g. child abduction where the UK's treaty obligations require this in Hague Convention summary proceedings.

The nature and content of family law has also changed and continue to do so. For much of the past two to three years a more extensive and concentrated modernisation of family justice than for around six decades has been ongoing, and is still potentially continuing until at least 2015.

This has been generated partly by fundamental changes in the underlying principles on which family law is based (which can mostly be traced to equality measures[2]), and partly by cost cutting in litigation and also of the public's opportunities to engage in legal proceedings by statutorily requiring recourse to out-of-court dispute resolution (a policy of the government following the economic crisis caused by recent banking scandals and the ensuing recession). While this family justice project has, on the one hand, been presented as modernisation in step with changing social values (e.g. the contemporary acceptance of the concept of same-sex marriage), on the other, more frank government sources concede that the key is cost cutting, albeit designed to keep family litigation in step with both social thought and cuts in all public-funded budgets, not just in the law. For this reason undefended divorce, for example, is to become purely administrative, not involving

---

1 Available at www.flba.co.uk/wp-content/uploads/2013/06/pgtransparencyfam.doc.
2 Such as the Marriage (Same-Sex Couples} Act 2013, which has rewritten the traditional concept of marriage as a heterosexual legal relationship: this was presented not as a family law reform but as an equality measure. See further Chapter 2 for the detail.

any judicial participation. In other private law cases the **Children and Families Act (CAFA) 2014**[3] now requires all parties to attend a mediation information and assessment meeting (a 'MIAM') before they are permitted to start *any* private law family proceedings, publicly funded or not, unless the case involves an emergency, or some other exception can be certified by the mediator conducting the MIAM; cuts are also required even of court running costs and of the judiciary themselves, quite apart from cuts in legal aid.

Consequently, not only is the scope and extent of family law now much more extensive than in the middle of the last century when Bromley began his seminal first edition, but members of the public have perforce become more aware of their rights (e.g. in the campaigns of organisations like Families Need Fathers in seeking more meaningful contact with their children than a former partner will agree). With so little legal aid available this is clearly more difficult for ordinary people, who are now obliged as LIPs to self-inform before they self-represent if they want to apply to the new Family Court, as not only has the law grown in volume but its complexity has increased, not least because of the demands of the multicultural society in which we now live in England and Wales.

1.1.3 New content of contemporary family law

This is completely different from the post World War II period in which family law was last significantly developed: the sweeping extent of the current modernisation project has proved a shock to judiciary and public alike; frustrated litigants in person have even resorted to physical violence, e.g. where one, not receiving the order desired, and not restrained as previously litigants routinely were by their lawyers, punched the judge in the face, and was of course then most obviously in contempt of court.

The problems include the fact that the current legal landscape bears no relation to the context of those last significant reforms of the 1960s, a period not long after the late Lord Shawcross (then Sir Hartley Shawcross, the post-war Labour Attorney General) commented that family law was a 'very simple branch of the law' which required 'no study or thought at all'. This was mostly true until the major reforms of Divorce in the 1960s and Child Law in the 1980s, not least because the law of that time (albeit itself demanding to contemporary practitioners) lacked the volume and complexity of current family law and practice, which has created such a gloss on original concept and theory that even a lawyer can struggle to understand its more specialist provision (e.g. in the successive statutory schemes for child support maintenance), thus certainly taxing the LIP.

Moreover, the precise scope of Family Law (now developed to separate the distinct field of Child Law from that of general Family Law concerning adults' relationships) has over the years not been as settled as other mainstream core or optional subjects of the qualifying law degree, either in terms of the perceived extent of the subject area for academic or vocational purposes, or within the undergraduate curriculum, where it is now usually a popular second- or third-year optional subject, although specific coverage varies enormously from law school to law school. Consequently specialisms have developed which have split professional expertise, so that it is common to find both practitioners and academics who work solely in either Child Law or aspects of Family Law such as financial provision: in public law cases concerning children (e.g. care and supervision orders where a guardian must be appointed for the child in the proceedings) a specialist solicitor from the Child Law panel must be selected to advise the guardian (and the child, if of sufficient age to give instructions).

Thus other aspects of Lord Shawcross's late 1940s comment are no longer true. First, it is not 'simple' but is now a bulky subject involving close contact with a number of relevant peripheral

---

3 CFA 2014 s 10.

disciplines, such as those of psychologists, who have contributed significantly to the law of domestic violence protection and child contact. Second, some parts of it are now of moderate difficulty, for instance the complexity of the statutory child support legislation, in which parents are now expected to cooperate to adopt private ordering rather than to rely on state assistance in either calculating or collecting what each should pay towards the cost of their children's upbringing, and cohabitants' property rights, which still have no discrete scheme at all.

Disputes in this latter area of law must notoriously still be resolved (in default of agreement by the parties) by strict property law within the field of Equity and Trusts, although informed comment repeatedly points out that cohabitants' rights is now an important section of the law affecting families, which should thus in reality be brought within the family law fold, under the **Family Procedure Rules 2010** and within the jurisdiction of the new unified Family Court, since these are not suitable disputes to be referred to the Trusts jurisdiction of the **Chancery Division and the Civil Procedure Rules** (the 'CPR') for which that Chancery jurisdiction was never intended, still less for LIPs to litigate them there unaided.

The 'bulk' which has accumulated around the once 'very simple branch of the law' comes from the fact that new expertise is called for as new problems arise, as in child contact cases where the carer parent resists contact for the child with the violent non-resident parent because there has been domestic violence. Until the seminal cases of *Re L, Re V, Re M, Re H* in 2000[4] little attention had been given to the impact of prior experience of violence on children and their carers: the significant impact on this position was the Sturge and Glaser report[5] for the Children Act Sub-Committee of the Lord Chancellor's Advisory Board on Family Law, following which there was a sea change in the court's approach to contact with violent parents. Thus differing judicial views led to the increased influence of psychology studies on law and practice, and an increase in the participation of psychologists and other professionals in the application of the law to individual circumstances of the parties until an army of professionals associated with the child's file is now likely to attend a local authority investigation under s 47 of the **Children Act 1989** when a child is seen to be at risk, so that it must be determined whether s/he is or will suffer harm if action is not taken by the local authority (and if so which action in particular).[6]

Moreover, so great is the outward spread of the circle of those who may become involved in the administration of family justice that even the perceived extent of the subject areas for academic or vocational study has similarly spread. Thus some academic courses look at the family's whole life experience and adopt a 'cradle to grave' approach, even including succession to property on death (on the basis that more relationships statistically end on death than on divorce or dissolution of other relationships). However, others have adopted a more Child Law centred approach (on the basis that it has long been accepted that 'the family' is no longer necessarily defined by the status of the adults at its head). About the only consensus is that, within the undergraduate degree, family law is now usually a popular subject in which students, having developed some acquaintance with legal language in their introductory first year, find a consuming interest as each brings some background knowledge from experience of their own families and friends to what they perceive as 'the family' and how it should be treated in law and policy.

1.1.4 Impact of changes in content *and* legal practice

Nevertheless, even the role of students' academic interest in family law must now be queried because of the changes in legal practice following the LASPO legal aid cuts, causing many high

---

4 [2000] 2 FLR 334, CA.
5 Sturge, C and Glaser, D, 'Contact and Domestic Violence, The Expert Court Report' [2000] Fam Law 615.
6 See further Chapters 19 and 20.

street firms to close their family departments as being uneconomic to maintain, in turn discouraging students from studying family law in preference to other optional modules which might support a more sure start in the practising profession. There is undoubtedly less demand for specialist family law practitioners, in turn reducing the numbers of vocational course[7] students choosing family law electives or options.

The better view is, of course, that at least a working knowledge of family law is highly desirable for whatever area of practice in which an academic or vocational law graduate expects to work, since it is highly arguable that any lawyer (and in particular the commercial lawyer or general practitioner) who has no knowledge of family law is a potential danger to clients unless there is effective cross-referral between departments in a firm. Recent research has shown that in small jurisdictions, such as Scotland (where specialist law circles are small, so that practitioners all know one another), such a lack of background might not be a hazard as information is passed round, but that in the much larger jurisdiction of England and Wales such cross-referral is only likely in the larger firms where, for instance, a conveyancing or business law transaction in one department may result in the fee earner being alert to the fact that the client should take advice on the family law impact of that transaction; but this may be missed in smaller firms where the same range of specialist knowledge may not be available. It was no doubt for the reason that this synthesis could be crucial that the pre-LPC Final Examination of the Law Society up to 1993 made family law a compulsory module.

The 'moderate difficulty and complexity' of family law in some subject areas of course comes from the ever-increasing complexity of modern life, which generates profuse and constantly changing legislative needs. The 2013–14 Parliamentary session included the following public Bills: Divorce (Financial Provision) Bill, Cohabitants' Rights Bill, Abortion Act (Amendment) Bill, Modern Slavery Bill, Pension Schemes Bill, Assisted Dying Bill and the Criminal Justice and Courts Bill; and this is after the Marriage (Same-Sex Couples) Act 2013, the Crime and Courts Act 2013 and the CAFA 2014 have already made fundamental changes which have been described as the most radical for 60 years, including, in the case of the Children and Families Bill, major changes in the orders available for care of and contact with children following separation of their parents, who are now expected to cooperate in achieving such agreement, with or without mediation (for which legal aid is still available for mediation costs to those who qualify). This seems to demand an optimistic level of cooperation and self-reliance from separating couples, given that they have presumably separated as they could not live together in harmony.

1.1.5 The historical, cultural and conceptual timeline: 1957 to 2014

The position of family law today therefore presents a stark contrast with the initial post-World War II reforms of 60 years ago. Moreover, the dramatic social changes which have taken place since the end of the war and the present modernisation are only matched by the speed and nature of change since the millennium. The timeline and detail of development from the perspective of marriage as the normal adult relationship, rare divorce and simplistic child protection[8] of the pre-World War II period may be seen in Cretney's historical study *Family Law in the 20th Century* and in Probert's review of Douglas and Lowe's 2009 *Evolution of Family Law* for *Child and Family Law Quarterly*,[9] which looks back to an earlier such title, coincidentally published in 1957, by Graveson and Crane.[10] A mere

---

7 Unfortunately significant numbers of Legal Practice Course (LPC) and Bar Practical Training Course (BPTC) places have not been taken up in the past two years and within those some have not been able to run Family electives or options, making the reduction in numbers of Family practitioners a self-fulfilling prophecy. Nevertheless, even large commercial firms do have a requirement for family law knowledge, so study of the subject is seldom wasted.

8 Mostly only against what was termed 'cruelty' and which bore no relation to the extensive state intervention of today.

9 (2011) 23 CFLQ 1, p 144.

10 Graveson, R, and Crane, F, *A Century of Family Law 1857–1957*, London, Sweet & Maxwell, 1957.

comparison of the contents demonstrates better than any other method how family law has changed, since the very topics which now form the content of a standard Family Law syllabus are *absent* in the 1957 monograph.

The comparison is equally valuable with Cretney's 2003 work, since in the short period of a dozen years since the publication of his survey of the twentieth century, the entire landscape of financial provision and property division on divorce was changed out of all recognition by the case of *White v White* (2001)[11] and the subsequent line of 'sharing', 'compensation' and equality cases, as has the shape of the family, of which it is hard to say that there is now a typical example; and, as mentioned above, the way of *resolving* family disputes has changed radically even since the April 2011 introduction of the updated **Family Procedure Rules (FPR) 2010** with which came the protocol requiring *any* party to be assessed, before commencing any but emergency family proceedings, for suitability for Alternative Dispute Resolution (ADR), specifically at the first instance mediation.

This provision, although honoured until recently more in the breach than the observance while it remained only in the FPR rather than with the force of primary legislation in Parliament under CAFA 2014, appears now to be going to be enforced, so as to impose an MIAM on *all* potential litigants, not only on those seeking legal aid but also those paying privately, with very few exceptions,[12] since the new form of application to the unified Family Court now unites two former forms, one of application and the other of the mediator's MIAM certificate, into one new form: as a result, it is unlikely that any application will get past either the court counter staff or the first judge before whom the case is listed unless the parties' dispute has been certified as unsuitable for mediation because the new form will not be complete without the MIAM section being signed off.[13] It is clear that this is because the prior hope that the culture would be changed by the FPR requirement[14] for a MIAM form to accompany each application had not succeeded in many cases, since it was well known that some judges waived the production of the MIAM form when the application reached their lists. This will no longer be possible since the new form combines the two. In theory, this is one of the most fundamental steps to have been taken in the modernisation process, since it in effect throws the onus back on to the parties to attempt agreement in family disputes before starting proceedings, whereas previously 'see you in court' was often the first step.

1.1.6 New methods of resolving family disputes

There are other indications that mediation or other forms of ADR are set for a new role in family justice, such that the years of attempting to change the culture from litigation to settlement appear to be likely suddenly to come to fruition for the simple reason of the 'sudden death' nature of the lack of resources for litigation brought about by simply cutting off legal aid.

Following LASPO and the CAFA 2014, most of which came into force on 22 April 2014 (and following the inauguration of the unified Family Court created by the **Crime and Courts Act 2013** which began work on the same date), mediation or other alternative dispute resolution is now not only the government's preferred method of family dispute resolution, but, having statutory force,[15] can no longer be ignored or 'skipped' by either or both of determined parties and lenient judges not insisting on seeing the mediator's certificate (as was reportedly happening before April 2014, regardless of r 3A and the Protocol of the FPR).

As a result of these provisions, there have been two further developments in the concentrated promotion of mediation as an integral part of the post-2014 landscape of family justice.

---

11 [2001] 1 AC 596.
12 FPR 2010, r 3A and Protocol.
13 See further Chapter 6.
14 FPR 2101 r 3A and Protocol.
15 In the provisions of the former rule and protocol now being included in s 10 of the 2014 Act.

First, the government has adopted the more mainstream description of the out-of-court settlement processes they encourage by renaming ADR as Dispute Resolution or 'DR'. This was on the grounds that it is part of, and not an alternative or bolt-on to, litigation and is also presented as a policy decision for any family's benefit on the basis that agreement (even with inevitable compromise) is better than adversarial litigation.

Second, the President of the Family Division has adopted his own renaming for the desired out-of-court settlement processes now necessarily adopted by the Rule Committee which routinely amends the Family Procedure Rules 2010, as 'N-CDR' ('Non-Court Dispute Resolution'), which he then details in the successive 'Views from the President's Chambers' which he produces regularly for the profession, setting out his vision for the operation of family justice within the modernisation programme culminating in the new unified Family Court[16] and in the Practice Directions which he issues to supplement the FPR.

These Directions are also supported by new forms designed to effect the modernising changes introduced in the most efficient and speedy manner possible. For example, these are now to include a form for expediting consent orders based on the Award of an Arbitrator who has determined a financial provision case using the new tool of Family Arbitration under the Rules of the Institute of Family Law Arbitrators ('IFLA'), bringing those determinations into line with other consent orders expedited following a settlement achieved through collaborative law.[17]

Indeed much of the modernisation of family justice has been concerned with speeding up and simultaneously simplifying processes, so that the delays, inconsistency of treatment by different judges at each appointment, and costs which have been criticised in the past can be circumvented where possible. So now that all judges of the former three tiers of family courts – the Family Proceedings Court (FPC), the county court level and the High Court – sit together in one court and one building, it is no longer necessary for practitioners to start their cases in the appropriate court, as they simply apply to the Family Court and the court staff will allocate the case to the appropriate level of judge.

With legal aid withdrawn in most family cases, simultaneously with the apparently blind government reliance on mediation to fill the gap, neither profession nor public has been particularly happy, as without recourse to funded legal advice many members of the public have not been sufficiently signposted to mediation and have therefore failed to find such resources themselves, and as a result have decided to start proceedings as LIPs, when they will have finally been steered towards the necessary MIAM; which may, however, at that stage be too late if positions are already entrenched, although they might have been resolved by mediation in the first place if the parties had known about its existence – which (had there been legal aid for advice from solicitors, historically the main mediation gatekeepers) might have meant the case need never have gone to court except for a consent order to formalise the mediation settlement agreement!

In the circumstances this change has not been well managed since it is clear from the significant drop in funded mediation[18] that the cart has been before the horse here. Had the government managed to provide the information services promised when LASPO was driven through Parliament in 2012, and spent some time and resources on adequate publicity before implementing almost wholesale withdrawal of legal aid in family cases, the picture might have been quite different.

---

16 These twelve successive documents may be accessed at and downloaded from www.judiciary.gov.uk/publications/view-from-presidents-chambers.

17 See Chapter 6.

18 As much as 68 per cent down from previous levels on the basis of the most recent MOJ figures up to the end of 2013. The Family Law Bar Association (supported by the Bar Council) and other interested stakeholders campaigned against the LASPO legal aid cuts in their joint Manifesto in October 2011 on the grounds of hardship to many vulnerable people in the abrupt cuts in funded legal advice and representation, but secured only a delay in implementation to April 2014.

This is particularly sad in that the Jackson Review of costs in civil cases.[19] Lord Justice Jackson recommends in Chapter 7 no further cuts in eligibility or availability of legal aid as essential for access to justice, and the preparation of an authoritative ADR Handbook, which was duly produced[20] but obviously targeted at solicitors, not the general public – which should have indicated the need for adequate general preparation for the ordinary person of such a fundamental legal aid withdrawal as has afflicted family justice in 2013 and 2014.

1.1.7 The twenty-first-century family

With regard to fundamental change in the shape of the family, this is because *all* models are atypical in comparison to the typical pre-millenium nuclear family, although the most unusual is perhaps the two-parent same-sex family with a child or children conceived by IVF or surrogacy in accordance with the provisions for same-sex parenthood of the **Human Fertilisation and Embryology Act (HFEA) 2008**, especially if the parents are now not simply in a civil partnership pursuant to the **Civil Partnership Act (CPA) 2004**, but actually *married* pursuant to the **Marriage (Same-Sex Couples) Act 2013**, which came into force on 29 March 2014.

On the introduction of the earliest of these changes, commentators contrasted the previously typical nuclear family with 'cohabitation' and 'same-sex relationships', but now it is the former nuclear family which is itself in the minority, as marriage rates have fallen, cohabitation figures have escalated[21] and same-sex relationships (whether or not formalised as civil partnerships or marriage or kept informal) are constantly visible in the media, although actually numbers involved seem to remain small.

Consequently, the earlier recognition of transsexuals in their new gender for all purposes (which started this serial fundamental change with the **Gender Recognition Act 2004**) and of the impact of these advances in human assisted reproduction (HAR) culminating in the HFEA 2008, have fundamentally changed the characters in the plot and the actors in the drama, so that agreement as to whether traditional legal marriage or cohabitation is a better basis for raising children seems to be pure semantics; at various times government statements have supported both and statistics appear to support an all-time fall in the incidence of marriage (though figures were in fact steady in the latest year's available in 2013) and a steady rise in cohabitation.

Against this background there is a renewed movement to introduce no-fault divorce[22] (last attempted in Part II of the **Family Law Act 1996**, which has finally just been repealed by s 18 of the **Children and Families Act 2014**). Such a campaign, which has been on the back burner for some years, may perhaps now ultimately succeed contemporaneously with the projected change to administrative undefended divorce, which it is clear the President of the Family Division supports, since it would clearly relieve pressure on the new unified Family Court, which already has enough to do uniting the work of three levels of court – the former FPC, Divorce County Court and County Court Care Centres, also with the presence of High Court judges sitting in the new Court as required.

1.1.8 Defining family law

It is thus difficult in modern times to define 'family law'. First, one must define 'the family', a task hard enough in itself, since contemporary human rights law has accepted that a mere two persons

---

19 *Review of Civil Litigation Costs: Final report*, published 14 January 2010.
20 Blake, S, Brown, J and Sime, S, *Jackson ADR Handbook*, Oxford, OUP, 2013.
21 See the predictions of the Government Actuary of projected figures by 2030, Jordans' *Family Law Newswatch*, September 2009.
22 Long supported by the Law Society and Resolution (the business name of the Solicitors Family Law Association) and a head in the conclusions of the 2014 Interdisciplinary Conference at Dartington Hall: see [2014] 44 Fam Law which contains the collected papers and conclusions of that conference held in February 2014.

who have never met but are linked by blood – such as the unmarried father and his child found to be a *de facto* family in the case of *Keegan v Ireland* (1994)[23] – may comprise 'a family' sufficient to enable a breach of the right to 'family life'.

Moreover, family law now operates in an international dimension, bringing into the ever-widening concept of family law norms and traditions different from those which in the UK, and more specifically the jurisdiction of England and Wales, we take for granted. Article 8(1) of the **European Convention on Human Rights and Fundamental Freedoms (ECHR)** does not define the family life for which it guarantees a right to respect, although *Keegan* makes clear that 'the notion of "the family".. . is not confined solely to marriage-based relationships and may encompass other *de facto* "family" where the parties are living together outside of marriage'.

Family law is therefore a law of relationships, between adults *inter se*, between adults and children, and between both adults and children and the state, as continually influenced by social and demographic changes. It is a body of rules of different types (some rules being so loose that they are basically discretions, a distinguishing feature of family law) and defines and alters status, provides specific machinery for regulating property, protects both individuals and groups and attempts in so doing to support the family structure of our society.

Recent editions of Bromley's *Family Law* suggest that the family is almost impossible to define. Cretney, on the other hand, thinks that the 'key factor' running through family law is parentage, with a consequent focus on the child. Eekelaar and Maclean approach family law as a socio-legal study, and Barton and Hibbs examine the various family members (primary, secondary and tertiary) in order to define whether family law is 'interested' in them or not. Diduck and Kaganas look at the American feminist perspective, which seems to centre on the mother and child, although it is apparently accepted that a man could perform the 'mother' parenting role. After cantering through the philosophy, they conclude sensibly that, as there is no statutory or common law definition of 'the family', then 'a family is what the ordinary man on the street thinks it is', and cite a series of cases in support, beginning with the housing case of *Sefton Holdings and Cairns* (1998),[24] per Lloyd LJ, and ending with the more recent *Fitzpatrick v Sterling Housing Association Ltd* (1999)[25] and *Burden v UK* (2008).[26]

❖ CASE EXAMPLES

These cases, dating from 1988 to 2008, aptly demonstrate the development line which has changed contemporary thinking about what is 'a family'.

Sefton Holdings v Cairns was a tenancy succession case in which it was necessary to decide whether two unrelated unmarried women (not apparently in any form of lesbian relationship) were 'a family' so that the survivor could succeed to the deceased's statutory tenancy. They could of course form a civil partnership today, or even be legally married, as they were unrelated, and modern equality thinking has now shaped policy both to give civil partners virtually the same rights as married couples, and indeed to permit such same-sex partners actually to marry, so that they could have been 'a family' either as civil partners or spouses. This must now be compared with the case of the Burden sisters, who were clearly 'family' in the sense that they were sisters, but could not establish that they were eligible for the same inheritance tax benefits as spouses or civil partners

---

23 (1994) 18 EHRR 342.
24 [1988] 2 FLR 109.
25 [1999] 3 WLR 115 (HL). [1998] 1 FLR 6 (CA).
26 [2008] ECHR 357.

because, being sisters, they were related by blood, so fell foul of the tables of affinity and consanguinity which prevented their entering into a civil partnership or marriage. Professor Ruth Deech[27] criticised this, challenging the logicality, in her 2009 Gresham Lectures,[28] on the grounds that in considering whether the UK was discriminating against siblings living together in a family house, but who do not receive the same inheritance tax ('IHT') benefits as spouses or civil partners, the court had not considered what ordinary people might look for in a 'family' context, i.e. the very essence of the 'family' being founded on blood relationships and often a common residence.

Fitzpatrick v Sterling Housing Association Ltd was an overt same-sex couple case in which in the Court of Appeal Ward LJ, dissenting, wanted to find that the cohabitants were either the equivalent of persons living together as husband and wife or alternatively were simply 'a family', a view which was upheld in the House of Lords and has subsequently been developed in the case of *Mendoza v Ghaidan* (2002)[29] to accept same-sex couples as the equivalent of husband and wife. This was clearly a watershed case in the contemporary thinking which has accepted same-sex marriage.

The truth of the matter is that family law in modern times can be whatever a course designer wants it to be. Moreover, to spend much time debating what is the precise extent of family law will only waste time, which will already be pressing if any family course is to encompass a fraction of the peripheral influences which now impact upon the core topics, without some coverage of which those parts of the family course studied in detail will be somewhat sparse and dry. This is because of the fast-changing nature of those influences, and of the finite nature of the time available to study any topic. Each year, parts of courses must be removed to accommodate new material or the course becomes unmanageable.

Contemporary academic family courses tend to include some sociological, political and procedural background to the law because of the impact of those peripheral areas of study on the way in which the black letter law operates. What the student of a modern family law course is therefore likely to gain from study is an understanding of how the modern family, however composed, works in law and practice. From a study of specific parts of the syllabus an appreciation will be gained of the interrelation of the governing black letter law and the judicial discretion which is a key feature of English family law.[30] This is also the approach of this book, explaining the basic law, but directing the reader to further sources where greater depth may be plumbed once the principles have been discovered; and in view of the ongoing modernisation, where further developments are expected in legislation or practitioner guidance but are as yet not detailed, updates may be found on the accompanying website.

In this respect the reader should, however, be aware that the huge explosion of peripheral writing, while interesting and absorbing, only comprises an influence on the development of family law, which in the absence of further legislation remains to be found solely in existing statute and case law, and that at present the political will is to reduce the costs of family litigation, and family litigation itself, by steering family disputes towards the President's 'N-CDR' and thus away from the courts.

---

27 Formerly Law Fellow, later Principal, of St Anne's College, Oxford, Gresham Professor of Family Law and now sitting in the House of Lords as Baroness Deech of Cumnor, where she has introduced a Bill reforming financial provision in divorce.
28 'Sisters, sisters', available on the Gresham College website, www.gresham.ac.uk, and republished in (2010) 40 Fam Law 375.
29 [2002] EWCA Civ 1533.
30 See, for example, Chapter 7, Financial Provision on Divorce or Dissolution, and Chapter 12, the Children Act 1989, which explain the discretionary approach to these two key areas of family law.

This approach has been further supported by the Final Report of the Family Justice Review (FJR)[31] and the Government's Response[32] to it, which has, on the one hand, addressed the topic with a view to contextualising the key sections within the contemporary social situation[33] while also, inevitably, looking at it from the perspective of current government policy of making savings in delivering family justice. The committee was also clearly shocked by the delay, particularly in child cases, which has become inherent in the system which they called

> a system which is not a system, characterised by mutual distrust and a lack of leadership, by incoherence and without solid evidence-based knowledge about how it really works. The consequence for children is unconscionable delay that has continued to increase since we began our work.

In general terms the Family Law Bar Association (FLBA) welcomed the Report, although it has not been entirely happy with the resulting measures (as shown by its stance against the legal aid cuts, which everyone agrees have gone too far), but was particularly pleased that the Review recognised the contribution that practitioners make to family justice (a key plank of its Manifesto calling for reconsideration of the legal aid cuts) commenting

> the Review rightly recognises the vital role that family barristers and solicitors play in the speedy resolution of cases. This will, however, count for little if the government pursues these cuts. In that event the pool of talented family barristers will be significantly diminished at the expense of children, families and the family justice system.[34]

The government did pursue the cuts, the pool of the talented family barristers has been diminished as some of them have left the Bar (just as firms of high street solicitors have closed their family departments) owing to the removal of practically all family legal aid, and children, families and the family justice system are clearly significantly worse off. There is, however, news of some positive features, such as the availability of some funding to support the Family Mediation Council (FMC)[35] and thus possibly improvements in the uptake of family mediation, but this is also clearly an important area of family justice which will repay watching for further developments. Discussion of all such changes during the lifetime of this edition of the book will appear on the accompanying website but should also be found announced online on *Family Law Newswatch*,[36] an email resource which is free to subscribe to, and in *Family Law Week*,[37] both of which are regularly contributed to and read by the profession, and carry updating news faster than the monthly journal *Family Law*, the specialist journal which should be the academic law student's first journal resource.

1.2 The changing face of family law

Family law, in both academic and practical contexts, is an especially fast-moving subject because it reflects life as it exists rather than making abstract rules for observance by society – a trend first

---

31 Published November 2011, available at www.gov.uk.
32 Cm 8273, February 2012.
33 For example, by suggesting reforms in private Child Law which the committee considered would better reflect the contemporary social context and thus 'work better'.
34 Stephen Cobb QC, then Chair FLBA, 'Time up on child delays' in *Counsel*, December 2011, London, Bar Council, now Cobb J, in the Family Division of the High Court, and leader of the President's working groups on the new Child Arrangements Programme (see Chapter 12) and Money Arrangements Programme (see Chapter 7).
35 Which regulates family mediators' training and acceptance for legal aid work.
36 Jordan Publishing, Bristol; email info@jordanpublishing.co.uk for free subscription direct to your mailbox.
37 This may be freely read on www.familylawweek.co.uk, no subscription required.

identified in Maine's classic text, *Ancient Law*. Thus, any family law student or teacher must have a sound grasp of the basic principles of law and practice, and while the design and delivery of a well-balanced family law course will usually benefit from a good deal of planning and skilful execution, the course leader's own subjective views and preferences will naturally play a part.

Yet there is a basic common core of black letter law that every student family lawyer will need to acquire before any of the now extensive interdisciplinary influences, such as socio-legal studies and the wealth of empirical research around family law concepts, can be understood. One reason for this is that while family law is necessarily a human subject – because of its subject matter – and all students therefore bring human experience to its study which should help them in applying the discretionary rules that family law consists of, they do now need to develop the new skill of looking at family law in a different way from more traditional modules such as contract or land law. It is the development of this practical as well as academic approach which this book aims to impart, by explaining how the law works in practice and, where possible, why it is as it is. The concept is not new: Cretney, himself a solicitor, has been looking at the practical impact of the black letter law in his textbooks through several editions. It was doubtless this approach which rendered so successful his critical guides to the **Family Law Act 1996**, which were instrumental in highlighting the impractical features of Part II of that Act and the extreme likelihood that they would simply not work in practice in delivering a new system for dissolving marriages.[38]

The new student of family law should therefore first be encouraged not to fall for the general assertion that family law is not really law at all, but to look at it in a different light from other law modules. Family law is definitely 'law', but there is no doubt that it is 'different', and not only in academic terms. Among practitioners, even dedicated litigators long ago[39] discovered that the practice of family law demanded a different approach[40] from the aggressively adversarial system common in all civil litigation in earlier times; in this respect the non-confrontational culture of contemporary family law has had some influence on civil litigation generally.

Second, those new to family law should be encouraged to absorb the culture of this distinct breed of law so as to see themselves from first base as family lawyers, who must constantly remind themselves of its difference from other substantive law, thus continually honing their practice of its culture. Some undergraduates find this difficult, instinctively clinging to the black letter law of statute and precedent alone. Indeed, it is not so long since family law was approached in a much more legalistic way than is the fashion today. The watershed for this sea change was when the **Divorce Reform Act (DRA) 1969** was passed, replacing the former entirely fault-based divorce law with provisions more attuned to modern life – still partially fault-based but also recognising the complex nature of marriage and the interaction of other family relationships. From within this statutory watershed also emerged the multidisciplinary influences that generated the concept of family law in a different category from other litigation.

Students who have difficulty grasping the nature of modern family law can often profit from a study of some of the early 1970s cases, from which it is obvious that the older judges of the period

---

38 See Chapters 4 and 5 for the contemporary process which it is now intended should be replaced by administrative undefended divorce, and presumably by some form of defended divorce in the rare situations in which a defence is likely to be feasible at all, although for a long time even those cases starting out as defended – and perhaps ending with cross decrees – have been less than 1 per cent.

39 In the early 1980s when the Solicitors Family Law Association (now called Resolution) was formed for precisely this reason. See further below.

40 But it should be noted that when the Woolf reforms were later developed in civil litigation generally in the 1990s (requiring alternatives to litigation to be sought first before issuing proceedings, and then again at the earliest case management stage) this was probably inspired by the first ten years of the SFLA's code, following which the formerly exclusive family law approach was no longer unique. In turn it should also be noted that the FPR 2010, in force from April 2011, which replaced the former Family Proceedings Rules 1991 (which had in turn replaced the Divorce parts of the old – highly adversarial – Rules of the Supreme Court) then took much from the Civil Procedure Rules (CPR) which accompanied the Woolf reforms, so the two systems now to that extent run along similar lines of protocols and DR being preferred to litigation (although this is not compulsory under the CPR as it now is under the FPR and the CAFA 2014, despite the power of the court to make costs orders against litigants under the CPR who do not respond to the call to DR where not inappropriate).

also had difficulty in making the necessary conceptual changes. Examples may be seen in Chapter 5, where there are several instances of judicial wrestling with the new concept of adultery as being a symptom, not a *cause*, of marriage breakdown. Similar problems have been experienced with relating the new 1969 basis of 'behaviour' (in that it may be 'unreasonable' for the spouse to tolerate by continuing to cohabit with the offender) to the pre-1969 ground of 'cruelty', an altogether simpler concept which most people had little difficulty understanding. So students need not be alone in growing into the ethos of modern family law and the culture of its application in the round.

Nor are undergraduate students alone in finding difficulty in grasping the profound impact that the reformed law of divorce and children has had on the law in practice. It is unusual today to find any generalist practitioner, even one who does not practise much in family law, still displaying that old-fashioned pre-1969 approach which treated marriage breakdown as a contest which had to be 'won' by an 'innocent' party and 'lost' by the guilty. Such a practitioner, usually of a certain age, may occasionally still be found fighting a case brought under the **Inheritance (Provision for Family and Dependants) Act 1975** where a divorced wife who has not remarried, and received ongoing periodical payments which usually die with a former husband, seeks the provision she might have had had there been a clean break on her divorce.

This type of practitioner usually relies, albeit apparently under the modern law, on all the old pre-1969 ideas: often the fossilised view of guilt and innocence that an older practitioner retains provides the stark contrast which the student needs to understand how family law has achieved its 'different' character when compared with the approach of the younger practitioner who, having studied and worked under the reformed law, knows no other. Similar stark contrasts arise in child cases where, in an era of joint parental responsibility, any mud-slinging against each other by the parents is now actively discouraged: the pre-1969 lawyer, academic and practitioner alike, knew no other way to obtain an order but by character assassination of the child's other parent. Now the academic student is often confused by the apparently mutually exclusive nature of the law as read in the statute, and the practice, which the contemporary lecturer or tutor will explain is not at all as it sounds in the books.

For this reason, some older cases, even those decided by distinguished judges, may need to be treated with caution, because as well as the changes in the law there has inevitably been significant social change in the intervening years, so that the norms on the basis of which such decisions were made will also have changed. Further, the student should also be cautioned that precedent often has a limited use in family law, either because a statute expressly says so, or because, as family law has a highly discretionary element, it is rare that a case will ever be precisely on all fours with an apparent precedent, which may therefore only offer useful guidance for consistency rather than a rule.

It follows that this constant honing of modern themes means that while there is a place in the study of family law for the latest cases, the basic underlying principles are really what matters, because any recent decisions, unless in the Supreme Court (and even there their Lordships can rapidly change their mind), may only indicate how some judges are thinking, or were at the time they decided the cases in question. All this may indicate why, nearly a decade after the Divorce Reform Act 1969 had been consolidated in the **Matrimonial Causes Act (MCA) 1973**, a group of family solicitors decided that the time had come to recognise the way in which family law had grown away from other litigation, and to lay down some principles of practice, and thus in 1982 founded the Solicitors Family Law Association (SFLA), now 'Resolution', to which it made the change some years ago.

1.3 How family law differs from other civil litigation

It is now over a quarter of a century since it was realised by practitioners that family law in general, and paradoxically divorce law in particular, could not be regarded as just another aspect of civil litigation, although for the first 130 years since the initial **Matrimonial Causes Act (MCA) 1857** there were few lawyers who realised this and fewer still who adopted an approach to family law work which reflected such a view. The founders of the SFLA, a well-known group of specialist practitioners of the early 1980s, must be credited with taking the significant step of introducing a constructive and civilised approach to the legal aspects of matrimonial breakdown.

Innovative as this was at the time, it is now universally accepted that the resolution of family problems is not conveniently achieved by a predominantly litigious approach, even where a firm has no specialist family department. The SFLA was initially established to take family matters, as far as possible, out of the atmosphere of contentious litigation, with the aim of achieving agreed solutions which, while not substantially different from what the court would order if the matter were acrimoniously contested, might with cooperation be achieved at less cost, emotionally as well as financially.

As time has passed, this philosophy has become much more important since, for example, the passing of the **Children Act (CA) 1989**, which established the relatively innovative concept of parental responsibility (PR) and encouraged divorcing parents to continue good parenting regardless of the end of their marriage. However, whether or not a solicitor joins the now around 6,500-strong membership of what is now Resolution, the Law Society recommends that all solicitors practising family law observe the SFLA's principles and Code of Practice, adherence to which is made clear not to be a sign of weakness and not in any way to place the client at a disadvantage.

Of course, there are still solicitors who do not observe the Code, and who still insist on conducting matters in an aggressive and acrimonious manner, but the SFLA philosophy is now so well established that the majority do stick firmly to its principles even when encountering an aggressive opponent of the old-fashioned disposition, not giving in to the obvious temptation to retaliate in kind. This is probably made easier now there is a statutory requirement to go to a MIAM, unless one of the few exceptions applies, as a solicitor with the badge of the Resolution logo will be likely to be inclined, as well as obliged, to do. There are in fact now few such aggressive solicitors; where they do still exist they are well known in the profession, and their approach is well recognised as one unfortunately still rooted in the pre-1969 divorce and child law which was entirely adversarial and fault based.

Experience has shown the bulk of the profession that the best response to the few diehards is one of increased politeness and courtesy, backed up where necessary by immediate and decisive court action, which is in no way precluded or inhibited by the Code. The SFLA's principles merely require that litigation should not be the first resort where matters may instead be conveniently negotiated to start with and then formalised procedurally afterwards. This approach necessarily influences judges at every level and is to be easily identified in contemporary Court of Appeal judgments. It should also influence the approach of academic students to the interpretation of black letter family law.

1.4 The function of family law

With the change in the philosophy of family practitioners has come a widening of the range of sub-divisions of family law, so now the modern family lawyer has an increasingly unwieldy portfolio of topics to service. In academic terms, as a survey for the National Centre for Legal Education's manual *Teaching Family Law*[41] showed, this has meant that undergraduate courses now either embrace one (so called 'long thin') family course spread over one academic year, or two or more (so called

---

41 Burton, F, Martin Clement, N, Standley, K and Williams, C, which was available on the website of the former UK Centre for Legal Education (UKCLE) at Warwick University. The Centre was unfortunately a victim of the 2010–11 coalition government and the website has been taken down, but a mirror source may still be found at http://78.158.56.101/archive/law/.

'short fat') modules studied over two semesters. The long thin course usually covers marriage, divorce and other decrees, including financial provision and, increasingly, mediation, other DR, child law and the unmarried family. The short fat modules course usually consists of one module covering marriage, divorce and allied topics, while child law – including children's rights, child abduction, adoption, human assisted reproduction and termination of pregnancy – makes up a separate course. However, as mentioned above, some courses look at the family in a wider context, including a study of the termination of marriage by death, and give greater space to the study of the consequences of cohabitation, and of the wider concepts of the family, such as in homosexual and extended family relationships, and this is now likely to increase owing to the statutory recognition of same-sex marriage. Some universities actually identify this imaginative type of course quite separately with labels such as 'the Law of Relationships'.

Inevitably, in this way the function of family law comes under scrutiny, and the influence of the socio-legal dimension increases in direct proportion to the introduction of such innovative topics, depending on the space and weight given to them. This is, in practice, not only inevitable, but probably pragmatic and desirable. Even the President of the Family Division, Dame Elizabeth Butler-Sloss, upon taking office as Head of Division in the late summer of 1999, expressly commented in her first statements to the media on the changing shape and nature of the family which could be noted during the 40 years since she had commenced practice at the Bar.

It was only shortly afterwards that the House of Lords, in the context of succession to a tenancy by a member of a deceased tenant's family, accepted that the definition of 'the family' was now to be construed in a contemporary light: *Fitzpatrick v Sterling Housing Association*, above.

However, the House did stop short of recognising such a family member as a 'spouse', despite the claim of the survivor of the homosexual relationship, which had given rise to his recognition as a member of the deceased's family, that they were non-married partners in all other respects on the same footing as married persons. Addressing this point, Lord Slynn said that a 'spouse' was not to be interpreted 'at the present time' (i.e. in 1999) as including two persons of the same sex who were intimately linked in a settled relationship, having all the characteristics of a marriage except for the fact that the parties could not have children.[42] He based this view on the fact that, in that particular case, the successful claim of the appellant to be a 'family member' depended on a 1988 amendment of the **Rent Act 1977**, into which could not, in his view, be read the words 'same-sex partner' in lieu of 'spouse'. This was no doubt a convenient peg on which to hang this particular decision, since same-sex partners are of course (without resorting to adoption) able to have their own genetic children in the same way as heterosexual couples, by means of human assisted reproduction, as well-publicised surrogacy arrangements in the case of a famous singer and his partner have shown, and in which it was said that sperm from both male partners was used in artificial insemination (a case only reported in the popular press), but see the further development of this evolving concept of the family in the *Mendoza* case (CA) above at 1.1.8.

It seems, therefore, that it is accepted that in the law of adult relationships marriage alone no longer defines the family, and nor does heterosexual cohabitation. Precisely how widely the family extends is uncertain, as the contemporary concept has spread through both blood and marriage *and* cohabitation (and perhaps *formerly* cohabitation-linked) relationships, including quasi-relationships by marriage which in the case of marriages are called the 'in laws'. Certainly the concept of 'associated persons' envisaged in relation to domestic violence protection by Part IV of the **Family Law Act 1996** has thrown the net very wide.

In the practitioner context the concept of 'elder abuse', and the relatively new idea that there should be some protection for the elder relative akin to that afforded to children by the CA 1989, suggests that the family has an existence under the umbrella of the law that now regulates

---

42 Which now, of course, they could, pursuant to HFEA 2008; see Chapter 13.

relationships from cradle to grave. In this context, the statement of Neuberger J in *Re The Estate of John Watson (Decd)* (1998),[43] that the court 'should not ignore the multifarious nature of marital relations', would appear to be more in tune with current social trends than the approach of the Crown (in that case claiming the whole estate as *bona vacantia*), for whom the Treasury Solicitor said that the relationship of a couple in their fifties, who had given up sexual relations but otherwise shared financial and domestic responsibilities, was merely a house-sharing arrangement at arm's length. Such an approach certainly seems legalistic at a time when all cohabitants are constantly being urged to make clear financial arrangements, precisely because in the absence of a marriage certificate (giving rights on divorce under ss 23 and 24 of the **Matrimonial Causes Act (MCA) 1973**) or a similar situation in respect of civil partnership (under the **Civil Partnership Act 2004**), cohabitants who have provided the 'sweat capital' in a relationship are at risk of having few or no rights if a separation occurs during their joint lives (although the position is usually a little better on the death of a partner in such circumstances). The **Inheritance (Provision for Families and Dependants) Act 1975** provides for persons living 'as the wife' of the deceased, as Mr Watson's partner was held by Neuberger J to be doing.

The student should nevertheless not be discouraged by the wider spread of topics potentially to be covered as a result of this expansion of the subject, nor be suspicious of the validity of the interdisciplinary dimension. Family Law has come a long way since the first MCA 1857 (as the background explained in Chapter 6 shows). The concept of unity in the arts, developed not long after the 1857 Act by the philosopher and reformer William Morris, is now taken for granted; perhaps when a future President of the Family Division (now probably still at law school) takes office in the 2040s, the unity of sources of family law will not only be taken for granted, but will be seen in the same informative light as the crucial developments of the past 40 years commented upon by Dame Elizabeth Butler-Sloss[44] in 1999.

Since family law is so wide and diffuse in scope, it is in the interests of students to keep abreast of changing trends and of trends within trends as shown in the decided cases. Besides the online legal databases and www.bailii.org, for the full text of case judgments and other important documents, the journal *Family Law* is useful for this, since it summarises and comments on cases in each issue and offers articles on currently controversial topics and points of interest. It guides critical thinking in a way which may be useful to the student who does not have time to seek out and read all the potentially interesting or impacting peripheral texts. The student is in good company in reading it as all the Family Division judges, the FLBA membership and most practitioners and academics involved in family law will be reading it too.

1.5 Family law and human rights

The greatest changes to family law are probably yet to come. The **Human Rights Act (HRA) 1998** came into force in October 2000, enabling the ECHR to be enforced directly against the state as part of English law. The articles of the Convention most likely to impact upon family law are as follows:

- Article 6 (right to a fair trial);
- Article 8 (right to respect for private and family life);
- Article 9 (right to freedom of thought);
- Article 12 (right to marry);
- Article 14 (prohibition of discrimination).

---

43 (1998) *The Times*, 31 December.
44 Now Baroness Butler-Sloss, recently speaking on family law in the CAFA 2014 debates in the House of Lords.

It will be clear from 1.4, above, that Art 8 does not refer solely to marriage-based relationships, and the existing Strasbourg case law already indicates that a very slight relationship between a father and his child will be enough to invoke the concept of 'family'. Those whose sole contact has been to provide sperm for artificial insemination will clearly not be able to show a sufficient connection to establish a familial relationship, but (especially as the Convention is a living, legal organism and not a static body of rules) anything more, however temporary, may well be sufficient to create the necessary relationship. It should be noted that the Court of Appeal has already sounded a warning about using common sense in invoking human rights arguments: in *Daniels v Walker* (2000)[45] Lord Woolf, the Master of the Rolls, called for a 'responsible attitude' from lawyers raising such arguments, so as not to clog the courts with an unnecessary workload generated by meretricious points. He also expressed the hope that judges would take a robust attitude with inappropriate arguments, which he categorised as any which take 'the court down blind alleys'. There has already been some practitioner consideration of whether this might lead to adverse costs orders.

1.6 Current debates

Ideas for research on these current discussion questions can be accessed on the companion website updates.

- Reform of the law of divorce, almost certainly necessary for a non-judicial administrative process.
- To what extent can DR or N-CDR in its various forms resolve family disputes?
- How, in an era of government-imposed continuing economic restraint, could some public funding or alternative assistance for family law court proceedings be provided where such access to justice is essential?

1.7 Summary of Chapter 1
What is contemporary family law?

- Family law is a young academic subject, having been recognised as such only since the 1950s, when the first textbooks appeared.
- Previously there were Matrimonial Causes Acts since 1857 and some rudimentary child protection, but the nature of family law either side of the Divorce Reform Act 1969 is significantly different, and its practical application even more so: the nature of family law since 2003 has also become significantly different from the preceding 30 years since the MCA 1973, and each period demonstrates a distinct departure from the 1940s concept of a senior law officer of the time that family law was 'simple' requiring 'no study or thought at all'.
- Socially there has been much change since the last major reforms (1960s and 1980s).
- There is no statutory or common law definition of 'the family', nor any clear boundaries to the topics and issues to be studied on a family law course.
- The shape of the family has changed completely from the former marriage base of heterosexual partners with children.
- The subject area divides naturally into, first, a law of adult relationships and, second, child law: the former tends to cover marriage nullity, divorce and judicial separation (and financial provision following, or without, decree) and some introduction to the law of unmarried

---

45 (2000) *The Times*, 17 May.

relationships and civil partnerships; and the latter a study of the CA 1989, wardship, children's rights, child abduction, adoption and human assisted reproduction.

- Family law defines and alters status (except for cohabitants who have no discrete normative regime giving them rights as they remain single persons in law), protects individuals and groups, provides mechanisms to divide property, and attempts to support the family as a desirable social unit.
- Family law is heavily influenced by the process of family justice and procedure and is developing an out-of-court DR culture which is said to be a cultural advantage but is also a cost-cutting mechanism for a government policy which is based on the impossibility of affording the previous level of in-court determinations.

The changing face of family law

- Family law is often claimed not to contain much 'law' but is interdisciplinary and supplemented by socio-legal studies; it certainly requires thought, and is often not simple, since it is heavily discretionarily based.

How family law differs from other civil litigation

- Family law is not conducted in the same adversarial manner as other litigation except by a few old-fashioned practitioners.
- The contemporary approach is cooperative, putting the welfare of the family first, and seeking alternatives to litigation before resorting to court proceedings, the initiative of the SFLA in 1982.
- This is not seen as a weak approach but as one which facilitates the resolution of family disputes in a timely and constructive manner particularly since the CA 1989 promoted the concept of PR, enduring on the part of both parents in relation to their children even after divorce.
- Cooperation is now even more expected following the passage of LASPO 2012 and the CAFA 2014, both of which encourage parental cooperation, since post-LASPO only mediation still receives public funding and CAFA 2014 emphasises shared parenting as well as shared PR for children in new Child Arrangements Orders (CAOs) or through agreements without orders, facilitated by funded mediation where the parties qualify financially. The statutory child support maintenance schemes also encourage private ordering.

The function of family law

- The academic study of family law is no longer confined to one type of family law course, as the potential field of study is so wide that individual law schools now assemble their own menu of preferred topics, usually in one family law course over an academic year, or two or more shorter single semester courses, the basic two roughly divided into marriage, divorce and cohabitation (and the attendant topics such as financial provision) in one module and child law in a second, thus approximately covering the main corpus of contemporary family and child law which through the various provisions of statute and common law regulates the relationships of parents and children and the family and the state.
- Some courses are actually identified as a study of Law and Relationships, keeping child law largely out of that module. Academic writers increasingly accept that family law is either what

the ordinary person thinks it is, or (since teaching time and resources are finite) what the course leader has selected to teach.

- The concept of the family has changed over time and is now recognised as not restricted to married families or heterosexual cohabitation, but to include the extended family, possibly even after divorce and dissolution of cohabitation, and even to include a law of 'elder abuse' requiring statutory protection.
- Family law therefore now includes relationships between adults, children, the family and the state.
- The HRA 1998 is still likely to continue to impact significantly on family law.

 ## 1.8 Further reading

Barton, C and Hibbs, M, 'In which members of the family is family law interested?' in *Questions and Answers on Family Law*, 2nd edn, London, Blackstones, Chapter 2, 1998. (There are also later editions of this book.)

Bottomley, A and Wong, S, *Changing Contours of Domestic Life, Family and Law*, Oxford, Hart, 2009.

Bridgman, A, Keating, H and Lind, C, *Responsibility, Law and the Family*, London, Ashgate, 2008.

Choudry, S and Herring, J, *European Human Rights and Family Law*, Oxford, Hart, 2010.

Collier, R, 'Fathers' rights, gender and welfare: some questions for family law', (2009) *Journal of Social Welfare and Family Law* 31: 237.

Cretney, S, *Family Law in the 20th Century*, Oxford, OUP, 2003.

Diduck, A, *Law's Families*, London, Butterworths, 2003.

Diduck, A and Donovan, K (eds), *Feminine Perspectives on Family Law*, London, Routledge, 2007.

Douglas, G and Lowe, N (eds), *The Continuing Evolution of Family Law*, Bristol, Family Law, Jordan's Publishing, 2009.

Eekelaar, J, *Family Life and Personal Life*, Oxford, OUP, 2006.

Freeman, M (Michael), *Understanding Family Law*, London, Sweet & Maxwell, 2007.

Herring, J, *Family Law*, 6th edn, Harlow, Pearson Longman, Chapter 1, 2013.

Roberts, S, *Mediation in Family Disputes*, 3rd edn, Aldershot, Ashgate, 2008.

Ryder, Hon Mr Justice, 'The Family Courts of the Future', (2008) Fam Law 38: 854.

Walsh, E, *Working in the Family Justice System: The Official Handbook of the Family Justice Council*, 3rd edn, Bristol, Family Law, 2010.

Chapter 2

Marriage

Chapter Contents

Learning outcomes for this chapter

A sound understanding of the legal and philosophical theory of the marriage relationship in English law including:

(i)   An appreciation of the historical and theoretical background to the acceptance of the recognition of transsexuals in their new gender by the Gender Recognition Act (GRA) 2004.
(ii) An ability to determine whether a marriage is likely to be valid in English law, and if so whether it is void, voidable 'non-marriage' or valid.
(iii) An ability to synthesise the key points in relation to marriage as a relationship 'embedded in our culture' and to compare it with other relationships which will be explained in later chapters.
(iv) An understanding of the impact of the Marriage (Same-Sex Couples) Act 2013.

2.1 Introduction

According to the perception of the Family and Parenting Institute (FPI) as recently as 2009, the shape of the family in 2030 was already officially envisaged, for example by the Government Actuary, to be vastly different from that of today, and in particular the numbers of opposite-sex unions were viewed as likely to have shifted by that date towards unmarried cohabitation and away from traditional marriage.[1] Statistics showed that numbers of marriages were dropping[2] as in 2007 there was the lowest number since 1895, civil ceremonies outstripping religious ones by nearly 70 per cent. What, it seems, no one foresaw at that time in advancing these predictions, was that marriage would by March 2014 have included same-sex relationships. The flurry of articles in the broadsheets as the **Marriage (Same-Sex Couples) Act 2013** was brought into force at the end of that month, including by such routine Parliamentary commentators as Matthew Parris, indicated the extent of the surprise even of the gay marriage lobby.[3]

Whether this is a valid prognosis on the part of the Government Actuary, the institution of marriage is one that has always been said to be 'deeply embedded in the religious and social culture of this country' and also 'deeply embedded as a relationship between two persons of the opposite sex'.[4] As such it has always been thought probably likely to endure in English law, irrespective of the percentages of marriages as opposed to the alternative forms of adult relationships which are projected in any given timescale, although there have, alongside, been respectable academic arguments for considering whether marriage would endure at all in its present form in the Marriage Acts, in view of the strong trend towards cohabitation as an alternative. It is probably best to leave this speculation and the reasons for it until the literature on cohabitation is considered at a later stage in the book[5] so that the two alternatives can be compared, especially as same-sex couples now have the alternative of marriage to their previous limitation to registered civil partnership or an informal cohabiting arrangement, since it appears that what no one chose to speculate on at the time that the future of marriage versus cohabitation was discussed five years ago (at a time when the CPA 2004 was still relatively new and had been in force only since 2005) was when and if there would ultimately be full marriage for gays. With minor adjustments this is exactly the relationship that they are now able to contract, with precisely the same consequences for dissolution as their heterosexual compatriots.

---

1   See their 2009 report, *Family Trends*, Family Newswatch, Jordans, 3 December 2009.
2   See the up-to-date figures at www.gov.uk/government/statistics, which indicate that in the last published figures there was still no proportionate increase to indicate that marriage was gaining back ground, although for once figures were not actually falling.
3   Parris, M, *The Times*, 22 March 2014.
4   Per Lord Nicholls of Birkenhead in *Bellinger v Bellinger (Lord Chancellor Intervening)* [2003] UKHL 21.
5   For which see Chapter 9.

Meanwhile, owing to the change in our national law, marriage as we have always known it – and now available to same-sex partners – appears to continue also to be recognised as a right to be protected by Article 12 of the **European Convention on Human Rights**, which provides that 'Men and women of marriageable age have the right to marry and to found a family according to the national laws governing the exercise of this right.'

These 'national laws' in England and Wales have in the past caused some collision between English law and the ECHR in respect of transsexuals[6] because of the 'deeply embedded' culture of marriage in English law referred to by Lord Birkenhead in *Bellinger v Bellinger*[7] in the House of Lords in 2002, the very year in which the division between the ECHR and English law came to a head.

It is therefore important to understand the incidences of marriage, which include various rights and obligations,[8] so that it must be distinguished from alternative relationships, such as unmarried cohabitation, but in fact causes no problems in relation to gay marriage since Parliament has changed the law and in doing so altered the definition of marriage which used, in s 11(c) of the **Matrimonial Causes Act 1973**, to exclude same-sex couples, but owing to the amendment to the MCA 1973 effected by the Marriage (Same-Sex Couples) Act 2013, no longer does so.

Thus the debate has shifted back towards marriage versus cohabitation, which will only affect gays in so far as any gay couple has objections to contracting a marriage or civil partnership, in which case their union will be as informal as any opposite-sex cohabitation.

Accordingly, the discussion about what, if anything, should be done about the continuing informal status of cohabitants is one of the most hotly debated distinctions between marriage and the contemporary alternative of a stable cohabiting relationship, since cohabitants of the same or opposite sex (having no discrete normative regime of rights affecting their partnership) now form the only partnership where the parties remain single in the eyes of the law. The lack of any status for cohabitants is therefore perhaps one of the most difficult hurdles to surmount in arguing for a discrete property (and personal?) regime for those adults heading family units who choose to cohabit rather than to marry, even where there are children of the relationship.[9]

The legal consequences of marriage include that the parties retain separate legal as well as social personalities, making separate decisions about their medical treatment,[10] having financial obligations to each other,[11] and privileges in relation to criminal law, taxation and protection of their home rights and against domestic violence and harassment.[12]

2.2 Marriage: a status

Despite the fact that neither marriage nor civil partnership (nor heterosexual nor same-sex cohabitation without formalities) now alone defines the family, it is still usually important to discover whether there is a marriage or whether another partnering relationship is established, since such differing statuses are at present still crucial to much statutory family law.[13] This may change in the foreseeable future, as increasing claims are made with regard to parentage as the core status relationship.[14] Owing to the many changes in legislation that have occurred in the last decade and

---

6 See below at 2.3.3.
7 See n 4 above.
8 Such as in relation to property and finance during and on dissolution of the relationship: see Chapters 10 and 7 respectively.
9 See Deech, R, 'The Case Against Legal Recognition of Cohabitation' in Eekelaar, J and Katz, S (eds), *Marriage and Cohabitation in Contemporary Societies*, Toronto, Butterworths, 1980 and Deech, R, 'Cohabitation', (2010) Fam Law 40: 39.
10 See Chapter 13.
11 See Chapters 6, 7 and 10.
12 See Chapter 11.
13 Civil partnership and cohabitation are examined in Chapters 8 and 9, and have their own individual impacts on contemporary statutes, e.g. in relation to home and property rights and domestic violence.
14 See Chapter 1.

which, it seems, are essential in an inclusive society, the government is no longer realistically able explicitly to support the institution of marriage as the best environment in which to bring up children, although the influence of the current Conservative-led coalition government, as reported by the media, tends as much towards supporting traditional marriage as the previous Labour government appeared to tend towards a more inclusive approach.

Consequently, confusing messages are coming out from this source, which also espouses the principle that children's interests should be paramount and identifies this as the 'first principle' of modern family law (see the Home Office's consultation document, *Supporting Families*, 1998). Thus has Tolstoy's *Divorce*, which alone constituted the family law of half a century ago, been overtaken by wider views?

2.2.1 The essential validity of a marriage: 'valid', 'void', 'voidable' or non-marriage

The first essential point is that no 'marriage' can either be dissolved by divorce or annulled pursuant to the law of nullity if no valid marriage has been contracted in the first place. See, for example, *Hall v Jagger* (1999),[15] where the 'divorce' suit of the model and actress Jerry Hall against rock star Mick Jagger was nevertheless settled on the basis that Ms Hall received a financial package such as might have been ordered on decree of divorce or nullity. However, the court appears not actually to have pronounced either decree since the 'marriage', celebrated on a beach in Bali, but without the necessary formalities even in that jurisdiction, appears not to have been valid and moreover to have been *void* (as opposed to *voidable*) from the start. Mr Jagger may have been inspired by the earlier case of *Gereis v Yacoub*.[16] Since these two cases, however, there has also been a more recent one in which Mr Justice Bodey identified the further status of 'non-marriage' when in *Hudson v Leigh* (*Status of Non-Marriage*)[17] he found that there had been so little resemblance to a traditional marriage that it was not just a question of defective formalities, but such an absence of the traditional identifying factors of a marriage ceremony that the transaction could be distinguished from marriage in all essential respects. Similar cases have continued to occur from time to time, and the approach is to treat each on its own facts and to determine whether there has been a sufficient attempt to contract a valid marriage for a marriage to be recognised.

❖ CASE EXAMPLES

In *Gereis v Yacoub*, a Coptic marriage in a Coptic church in London which was not registered for marriages, the husband robustly argued that as the church was unregistered there was no marriage, but as the ceremony appeared to be merely an ordinary Christian marriage in an unregistered building, this defence failed, since defective formalities are not necessarily fatal to validity of a marriage unless the parties have avoided the formalities knowingly and wilfully; however, as this is precisely what the parties had done, since they had been advised by the priest to have a civil marriage ceremony and had not done so, the judge decided that they *had* 'knowingly and wilfully' married in disregard of the formalities required by the Marriage Act: see below at 2.3.

---

15 Unreported, 13 September 1999.
16 [1997] 1 FLR 854.
17 [2009] 3 FCR 401.

> This must be contrasted with *Hudson v* Leigh, where Mr Justice Bodey found that neither the parties nor the celebrant intended the ceremony to amount to a legal marriage and the traditional wording of the ceremony had been altered. The ceremony was therefore a 'non-marriage' not a 'void' marriage.

It is interesting that this distinction between a void and a 'non' marriage has apparently been recently re-analysed, as this is not the first time that marriages which do not resemble the traditional Christian marriage have been found to be inadequate to engage the usual consequential incidences of the validly married status.[18] It is important to understand the difference of status, depending on whether a marriage is 'valid', 'void' or 'voidable'; or, it seems, a non-marriage, since despite the fact that both a void and a 'non' marriage are similarly ineffective the distinction is not superfluous (especially as civil marriages – although not religious ones – may now be contracted in duly licensed premises, so that there is no immediately obvious significance in the fact that a ceremony has not been conducted in an obviously religious or other apparently official building). The importance of establishing the precise status of the marriage is because, even if a marriage is void, English law will still have jurisdiction to pronounce a decree of nullity, whereas if no recognisable marriage has taken place at all – as in the case of the Hall–Jagger union – there will be no jurisdiction to make financial provision orders following a nullity decree.

However, there is a further issue disclosed by the case of *Muñoz Diaz v Spain* (2010),[19] in which an invalid marriage in Spain was referred to the European Court of Human Rights (ECtHR) because the state had apparently misled the wife into believing that the marriage according to Roma rights would be valid (when a civil marriage was required to make it so for all purposes), and this had led to their refusing the wife rights to her husband's pension, which the Court found a breach of her rights under Article 14 and the first protocol, although not of Article 12 (the right to marry). This was because a civil ceremony would have been open to her and it was presumed to be her choice not to undergo this formality. In view of the importance of status in relation, for example, to pensions, as in this case, it does underline the significance of English law's being clear about the approach to the range of adult relationships now available, especially in view of the fact that while there now is a legal right for gay partners to marry or contract a civil partnership, there is as yet no similar choice for opposite-sex cohabitants if they have not married, even where they erroneously – as many people do – believe themselves to be parties to a 'common law marriage'. In the meantime the distinction between void and voidable marriages remains, for a number of purposes.

(1)   A 'valid' marriage is one which complies with the relevant law and practice in all respects: the parties will be man and wife (or in the case of gay parties the equivalent), it can be ended only by divorce or death, and on death the survivor will be a widow or widower.

(2)   A 'void' marriage is one which has some incurable defect, so that it could never be valid, whatever the parties wished. This type of defective marriage requires the parties who wish to maintain the relationship to start again from scratch, with a new effective ceremony, this time complying with the law and practice of any jurisdiction which has a matrimonial regime, and if in the meantime one of the parties dies, it will be too late to achieve the status of marriage, as the deceased will have died single and the surviving party is a single person.

---

18 See *A-M v A-M (Divorce: Jurisdiction: Validity of Marriage)* [2001] 2 FLR 6 (Islamic marriage on private premises) and *Ghandi v Patel* [2002] 1 FLR 603 (Hindu marriage in a restaurant) both involving leading world religions.

19 [2010] 1 FLR 1421.

(3) A 'voidable' marriage is one which is valid for all purposes until 'avoided', a process which can only be undertaken by the parties to the marriage who may affirm it instead if they wish (and no other person may attack its status). Such a marriage will usually be ended if the parties wish by an 'annulment' on a nullity decree, but might subsist until death, after which it is too late for a nullity decree, as it will have already been ended by death and the surviving party will be a widow or widower.

Marriage is, therefore, a definable status which requires to be established by proof of the marriage in due form before the court can entertain a suit for divorce in order to dissolve it: in the case of apparently void marriages where a declaration of nullity is sought, whether there is actually a marriage to annul or not will depend on whether the marriage is in fact void or merely voidable.

In the former case *where the marriage is void*

● while a declaration may be sought for any necessary purpose, in truth the marriage may be treated as void from the start and the declaration is only evidence of that fact.

In the latter case *where the marriage is only voidable*

● a decree is actually required to annul the union, which will otherwise be treated as valid until any decree of nullity is obtained.[20]

Marriage is also a contract and has been defined as 'a voluntary union for life of one man and one woman to the exclusion of all others': per Lord Penzance in *Hyde v Hyde* (1866).[21] It is a contract which creates a legal relationship with mutual rights and duties. This is particularly important in the era of European and human rights law, as the approach to marriage in English law has always been that marriage is

● voluntary;
● for life;
● heterosexual; and
● monogamous.

Since English law continues not to embrace the contemporary amendments to those traditional qualities of Christian marriage which are accepted in some other jurisdictions, the ECtHR has until recently always upheld our right to sustain this stance and treated our core beliefs that these concepts are central to our understanding of marriage in English law as part of our margin of appreciation: see further at 2.3.3, below. Nevertheless, clearly this has had to change now legislation is in place to permit legal marriage to same-sex relationships, a significant change to Lord Penzance's definition.

It must be asked, therefore, whether this will also change the perception of traditional marriage, which in practice is now viewed as a partnership: see Chapter 7, Financial Provision on Divorce or Dissolution, where the relative earning and homemaking contributions of the spouses have since *Lambert v Lambert* (2002)[22] been regarded as of equal worth, and in particular the *dicta* of Baroness Hale on the nature of modern marriage in the case of *Radmacher v Granatino* (2010).[23]

---

20 See Chapter 3.
21 (1866) LR 1 P & D 130 at p 133.
22 [2002] 3 FCR 673.
23 [2010] UKSC 42.

2.2.2 Essential formalities of marriage

In view of the practical consequences described above, formalities are important, and this includes demonstrable capacity to marry. Until **Lord Hardwicke's Act** (also called the **Clandestine Marriages Act**) of 1753, there were few formalities for marriage, which could be effected *inter alia* by simple declaration. The background to this Act is rooted in one of the above four central concepts, namely that marriage must be *voluntary*.

Prior to 1753, marriage in effect was left to the canon law of the church, and the common law recognised such marriages as proceeding from consent of the parties and their declaration that they took each other as husband and wife, a situation which subsisted in Scotland until 1940 and is still recognised in some American States (such as the Carolinas, where spouses spending the 'honeymoon' in that state might still cure any ceremonial defect elsewhere – a fact obviously not known to Jerry Hall). In Scotland it was until the **Family Law (Scotland) Act 2006** still possible to establish marriage by 'cohabitation with habit and repute' unless the parties had specifically rejected the institution of marriage, of which Ms Hall was perhaps similarly unaware since none of the numerous Hall/Jagger homes was located in Scotland.

In the Middle Ages, the emphasis was on the contract of marriage, largely for property purposes, which was therefore the origin of the requirement that marriages needed to be demonstrably consensual. It is worth looking back at this rationale in view of the contemporary trend towards pre-marital agreements, which practitioners tell us have increased in popularity since *Radmacher v Granatino* since, in view of the grant of married status to same-sex couples, discussion will inevitably sooner or later be once more generated as to the theoretical basis of contemporary marriage, which clearly will no longer meet Lord Penzance's criteria in law, whatever the parties choose to think about it.

Alongside this change, increased cross-border unions generate interest in whether English law should adopt matrimonial regimes as in the Civil Code based jurisdictions on the continent of Europe, and the trend towards pre-marital agreements already nods in that direction since if upheld (as *Radmacher* indicates they may in principle now be but no legislation yet confirms this) such agreements would bring marriage under English law much closer to the European models where the disposition of what is seen as 'family' property is of central importance.

The Law Commission has recently published the report of their investigations into marital agreements, needs and marital property[24] in which they have recommended that qualifying[25] marital agreements should be binding, providing the Commission's conditions are met, which fairly closely follow the *Radmacher* recommendations, namely no vitiating factors and no contracting out of needs, since the draft Nuptial Agreements Bill which is proposed in the Report, amends the **Matrimonial Causes Act 1973** so as to require a judge when dealing with financial provision to observe the terms of any qualifying marital agreement except in so far as it is necessary not to do so in order to address 'needs' of a party or in the interests of any child of the family.

Accordingly it seems that property could once more be the central issue in marriage under English law, thus turning back the clock to earlier times, as in these cases the pattern of contemporary marriage, while now departing from Lord Penzance's analysis in at least two respects, will have some similarities with the medieval approach, which was only coincidentally of a religious nature (since that period was an age of superstition) rather than the overtly Christian nature which inhibited the development of divorce during the ninteenth and much of the twentieth centuries (and in the sixteenth led to the establishment of the Church of England). Indeed there are other similarities between the contemporary position and that of medieval – property-driven – marriage, since the Law Commission's 2006–7 work on Cohabitation identified further similar patterns: a

---

24 Law Com 343, *Matrimonial Property, Needs and Agreements*, published 26 February 2014.
25 See further Chapter 7.

trend for a period of cohabitation before formal marriage was decided upon, often involving a pregnancy or even the birth of a first (or sometimes second) child as the trigger for the formal union, and a formal ceremony (not necessarily religious) to mark the transition from the original cohabitation to the more formal state of matrimony.

The only difference in effect appears to be that while in medieval times all such ceremonies were necessarily religious, the twenty-first century equivalent is clearly not: while there may for social purposes be an outwardly religious celebration, perhaps in a parish church. or another religious ceremony (whether the parties are practising members of their religious persuasion or not) it is just as common for there to be only a civil ceremony with no religious features whatever, and frequently without even the subsequent religious blessing which was often a fashionable extra during the decades following the post-1973 increase in divorce rates which inevitably led to remarriages which could not be celebrated in church. While that trend was dictated by the principal Christian churches' firm adherence to Lord Penzance's perception of marriage being for life it is clear that they have all, albeit slowly, retreated from this position over the subsequent lengthy period so that religious marriage is no longer virtually impossible for the previously divorced who want it.

In these circumstances the essential contemporary core feature appears to be not the nature of the marriage ceremony itself but that there is some definable rite of passage to mark the transition from the contemporary social acceptability of cohabitation before marriage[26] (which was not the case even twenty or thirty years ago but which the Law Commission identified in their cohabitation research is now practically the norm before the parties proceed to the greater commitment of marriage).

Indeed, this is very similar to the custom in the Middle Ages, which was to agree a marriage contract and then to have the ceremony blessed in church, although before the Council of Trent in 1563 no religious ceremony as such was required: there was a simple declaration *per verba de praesenti* or *de futuro* ('I take you' – or 'I shall take you' – 'as my wife/husband') and the marriage was binding as soon as consummated, which remains the position following a civil or religious ceremony today (save that in the case of same-sex marriage there is no requirement for consummation).

It was then even common for the religious ceremony to take place only when the bride had proved that she could become pregnant, because marriages were often important for providing an heir to property. In due course, however, a custom developed of exchanging the vows before a priest or (after the Reformation) a clerk in holy orders, and eventually there were three ways of contracting a marriage, either as above, or 'clandestinely' (i.e. speaking the words in private without the presence of the priest or clerk and subsequently consummating the marriage by sexual intercourse), or in church after publication of banns or with a licence (and after obtaining any necessary consents for minors).

The only reason that marriages came to be celebrated in church was to tackle this clandestine marriage option, which was sufficiently valid as to make any subsequent marriage void, and was a problem because it meant that no one could safely marry without fear that there might be already in existence an earlier clandestine marriage which made the subsequent union void. Moreover, as a woman's property passed under even a clandestine marriage to her husband, there were predictable abuses, especially as the consent of a parent was not required for a minor to contract a clandestine marriage, although a priest was sometimes used to conduct the ceremony – for example, in the Fleet Prison marriages, where priests incarcerated there would preside over a ceremony for a fee, so that the parties could say that they had made their vows before a priest.

To tackle this abuse, Lord Hardwicke's Act therefore required that all marriages should be in church according to the rites of the Church of England, in a parish where one of the parties resided

---

26 Two of the Queen's grandchildren having openly lived with their spouses for substantial periods before marriage.

and following publication of banns there and in the other party's parish. Moreover, the marriage had to be performed by a clergyman in the presence of two witnesses. If either party was under the age of 21, parental consent was required, or dispensation of parental consent had to be sought elsewhere, at first from the Lord Chancellor and later by application to the court.

While the result was the growth of a marriage trade at Gretna Green in Scotland, where some parties fled in order to avoid the new stringent requirements, particularly that of parental consent, the true position in English law is that there has never been an essential requirement that marriages should be religious and the Act was subsequently amended, and then replaced by later nineteenth-century statutes, which enabled those who were not members of the Church of England (and therefore unwilling to use its rites) to marry in other ceremonies; moreover from 1836, the **Marriage Acts** and **Births and Deaths Registrations Acts** enabled other religious buildings to be registered for marriages and also enabled civil marriage to take place on a Registrar's certificate as an alternative to banns. By 1898, ministers of all religions could perform marriages and there was a civil alternative. These Acts, which had become somewhat diffuse, were all consolidated respectively in 1949 and 1953.

In short, although great deference has always been accorded to Lord Penzance's definition of marriage in English law, this status appears to be merely a creature of statute and may be altered at the will of Parliament, including extending that status to same-sex couples if Parliament so wishes, as has been done in the **Marriage (Same-Sex Couples) Act 2013**, although for the time being marriage remains regulated by the modern Marriage Acts, most recently that of 1949 'as amended', including in 1970 and 1994. The latter Act now permits civil marriage in a wide range of licensed venues, although it is clear many couples still opt for a religious ceremony, whether or not they are themselves religious observers, and that many have far other concerns in relation to their marriage as a successful social occasion, as identified by Hibbs, Barton and Beswick in their 2001 article 'Why Marry? Perceptions of the Affianced'.[27]

In short, while the Marriage Act 1949 as amended is supposed to consolidate the law of marriage now, failure to observe proper formalities can, but does not necessarily, make a marriage void. The law has twice been reviewed in the past 40 years, first by the Law Commission Working Party in 1973 and by Green and White Papers in 1988, 1990 and 2002, none of which has so far achieved a thorough overhaul.

2.3 Grounds on which a marriage will be void

Both capacity and formalities are at the root of this question of validity where the marriage is claimed to be void. There are various distinct situations to be considered here.

2.3.1 Where the marriage is not valid under the Marriage Act 1949 as amended

Pursuant to s 11(a) of the **Matrimonial Causes Act (MCA) 1973**, this would be because:

(1)   The parties are within prohibited degrees (of blood relations and relations by marriage pursuant to the traditional tables of 'kindred and affinity' as established by the medieval Christian churches). The **Marriage Act 1949 (Remedial Order) 2007** amended Schedule 1 to the 1949 Act to remove the restriction on marriage between former parent in law and child in law, following the case of B and L v UK (No 36536/02)[28] where the divorced parties,

---

27   Hibbs, M, Barton, C and Beswick, J. (2001) Fam Law 31: 197.
28   [2006] 1 FLR 35.

with previous spouses still alive, were obliged to take their case to the ECtHR in order to secure a declaration that the UK policy not to allow such marriages was irrational and illogical and served no useful purpose.

(2)   Either party is under age 16: two cases illustrate the operation of this rule.

❖ CASE EXAMPLES

In *Alhaji Mohamed v Knott* (1968),[29] the parties were both domiciled Nigerians. The wife was only 13 years old; however, as the marriage was recognised in Nigeria, their domicile, it was still valid when they came to this country.

In *Pugh v Pugh* (1951),[30] the marriage was between a 15-year-old Hungarian girl and a British-domiciled soldier. The marriage took place in Austria and was recognised both there and in Hungary, but not in England, and as this was the law of the husband's domicile it was fatal to the validity of the marriage.

(3)   The formalities are defective, which may occur because the marriage is:

- not by the rites of the Church of England (i.e. after banns duly called, not by common licence from the bishop, or by special licence from the Archbishop of Canterbury);
- not by Superintendent Registrar's certificate;
- not in a Quaker or Jewish ceremony for which special arrangements pertain;
- not conducted by a proper clergyman or without the presence of the Registrar;
- not in a civil ceremony;
- not in a registered building; or
- not in the building specified in the certificate.

These defects will only render a marriage *void* if the marriage is entered into *knowingly and wilfully* by both parties: Marriage Act 1949.

Under (3), above, false information to obtain a Superintendent Registrar's certificate does not make the marriage void, but the opposite is true in the case of banns. The reason is that the banns procedure is to obtain *publicity* for the proposed marriage – a procedure developed due to the historical incidence of forced marriages in earlier centuries as explained above – but the Register Office procedure is not, so misdescription in that situation does not invalidate the marriage. Three cases illustrate this point.

❖ CASE EXAMPLES

In *Puttick v Attorney General* (1979)[31] the terrorist Astrid Proll, who had married while on the run in England, used the name of another German and a false passport, as her visa

---

29 [1968] 2 WLR 1446; [1968] 2 All ER 563.
30 [1951] 2 All ER 680.
31 [1979] 3 WLR 542; [1979] 3 All ER 463.

was about to expire. It was held that the marriage was not void in spite of the false particulars she gave.

In *Small v Small* (1923)[32] a deserter from the British Army, who had taken a false name to conceal his identity, sought to marry by banns. It was held that the banns were not duly published because the false name was given with fraudulent intent.

In *Dancer v Dancer* (1948)[33] a bride's innocent use of an incorrect name in publication of the banns was immaterial as the banns were held duly published. The reason was that she had always been known by the name of Jessamine Roberts, Roberts being her mother's cohabitant with whom the mother had had five further children. The mother had then assumed his name for herself and the three-year-old Jessamine, whom she had taken into the relationship. The real name of Jessamine and her mother was actually Knight. The truth was discovered on the death of the mother but the daughter continued to use the name Jessamine Roberts. Clearly there had been no intention to deceive in this case.

Some foreign marriages can be valid despite defective formalities, even though they do not comply with either local law or English law. An example of this is marriages in wartime.

❖ CASE EXAMPLE

In the case of *Taczanowska v Taczanowska* (1957)[34] a marriage between a Polish soldier serving in Italy and a Polish civilian refugee was conducted in Rome by a Roman Catholic priest. As both parties were theoretically domiciled in Poland, the marriage was void by that law, the law of their domicile, and also by Italian law as it had not complied with the local regulations. However the Court of Appeal held that its validity was saved by common law because it was a marriage celebrated by exchange of words before an episcopally ordained priest, and as a member of the conquering allied army the husband could not be expected to submit to the local law of the country where it was celebrated. Moreover the marriage did not need to comply with the law of their domicile as that was relevant only to capacity to marry.

2.3.2 Where the marriage is not valid because either party is already lawfully married

This is pursuant to Matrimonial Causes Act 1973 s 11(b) and is illustrated by the following cases.

---

32 (1923) 67 SJ 277.
33 [1948] 2 All ER 731.
34 [1957] 2 All ER 563.

❖ **CASE EXAMPLES**

In *Baindall v Baindall* (1946)[35] there was a valid (albeit potentially polygamous) first marriage in India of a Hindu man who subsequently purported to marry an English-domiciled wife in England. As the first marriage was clearly valid in India and therefore had to be recognised, but in England we do not practise polygamy, the second marriage was void.

In *Padolecchia v Padolecchia* (1967)[36] a first marriage by an Italian was from the point of view of Italian law ineffectively dissolved in Mexico, thus making his second marriage in London void.

In *Maples v Maples* (1987)[37] there was a Jewish divorce obtained in a religious ceremony not recognised in England by Israelis who had settled here. The wife's second marriage was void as she was still married to the first husband.

The second marriage may not be a criminal offence, e.g. as in R v Gould[38] where the accused honestly and reasonably believed that there was no subsisting first marriage, and R v Sagoo[39] where the first polygamous marriage was a potential defence to criminal liability.

2.3.3 The effect of the amendment to the MCA 1973 s 11

This is achieved for same-sex marriage by omitting s 11(c), which formerly provided that the marriage would be invalid where the parties are not respectively male and female. The result is that while but for the Marriage (Same-Sex Couples) Act 2013 the marriage would not have been valid because the parties are not respectively male and female, s 1(1) of the 2013 Act first makes such a marriage 'lawful' (notwithstanding s 11(c), which is not explicitly repealed at this stage, but pursuant to Part 2 of Schedule 7 of the 2013 Act s 11(c) is now to be omitted from the MCA 1973).

The position of transgender persons is not affected since the GRA 2004 provides for their full recognition in their new gender subject to the satisfaction of the various conditions required to achieve that recognition. The only situation in which a transgender person might not be able to marry or remarry would therefore only arise in the case of incomplete recognition.

Corbett v Corbett (1970)[40] was for many years the leading case on this point in English law, where the court concluded that in England and Wales a person's biological sex was fixed at birth according to his or her chromosomes and could not subsequently be changed by the artificial intervention of surgery to change the external appearance. But this was not the case in other jurisdictions, including some states of the USA, and it was heavily criticised in Australia long before subsequent cases in the ECtHR indicated a growing trend among European judges to regard the UK stance on sex and gender as a potential breach of the European Convention on Human Rights and Fundamental

---

35 [1946] 1 All ER 342.
36 [1967] 3 All ER 863.
37 [1987] 3 All ER 188.
38 [1968] 2 WLR 643.
39 [1975] 2 All ER 926.
40 [1970] 2 WLR 1306.

Freedoms. This was because a transsexual was unable to marry at all under English law unless marrying a person of the (originally) opposite sex, which such a transsexual would be unlikely to want to do.

It was long thought before the *volte face* finally came in *Goodwin* (2002)[41] that there would in due course be scope for a realignment of the law in this respect to create a valid status for transsexuals, following successive judgments in the ECtHR. It was always recognised that there would be problems in the short term because of the consequential legislation which would be required. The cases of *Rees v UK* (1986),[42] *Cossey v UK* (1993)[43] and *Sheffield and Horsham v UK* (1998)[44] indicated that in most post-operative transsexual cases the Court supported the English view that sexual identity was not thus changed, and that the detriment suffered was not sufficient to override the state's margin of appreciation, despite the guarantee of respect for private and family life under Article 8 of the Convention which has been imported into English law by the Human Rights Act 1998. Similarly, the above cases did not establish a right pursuant to Article 12 for transsexuals to marry, as it was accepted that in English law that meant traditional marriage between parties of the opposite sex within the long-established definition in *Hyde v Hyde*.[45] However, successive ECtHR and English decisions went further than the strong dissenting judgments in the earlier cases, and after 2002 the UK was finally obliged to enable transsexuals to be recognised in their new gender for the purpose of contracting a valid marriage under English law. This was then achieved by the **Gender Recognition Act 2004**.

The traditional stance of English law ignored the fact that transsexuals usually regard themselves as 'philosophically, psychologically and socially' aligned to their new sexual attribution, have been living in that state since the pressure for sexual reorientation resulted in their change of sex, and as a result of surgery and often extensive other treatment have lost all or most of the external attributes of their former sex by the time they want to change their gender officially. This theme, which was identified as long ago as the *Corbett* case (where it was held to be irrelevant), resurfaced in every succeeding attempt to secure acceptance of re-gendering to support their practical reorientation, and was in any case recognised by legal theorists as sometimes producing anomalous results.

❖ CASE EXAMPLE

In *R v Tan* (1983)[46] the issue was whether a transsexual was a 'man' for the purposes of ss 5 and 30 of the **Sexual Offences Act 1967**, i.e. living off immoral earnings, and the Court of Appeal accepted that 'both common sense and the desirability of certainty and consistency' required the *Corbett* approach to be followed.

The crux of the matter in English law (and why the UK held out so long against change) seemed to be registration.

---

41 See below.
42 (1986) 9 EHRR 56.
43 [1993] 2 FCR 97; (1991) 13 EHRR 622.
44 [1998] 2 FLR 928; (1998) 27 EHRR 163.
45 See 2.2.1 above.
46 [1983] QB 1053.

> ❖ **CASE EXAMPLE**
>
> In *Re P and G (Transsexuals)* (1996)[47] two transsexuals lost their judicial review applications of the Registrar General's refusal to alter the sex on their birth certificates.
>
> In *X, Y and Z v UK* (1997)[48] the female-to-male transsexual 'father' of a child conceived by artificial insemination by donor (AID) was refused registration as the father of his partner's child because that could be allowed only to a 'man', although the court did point out that the father could act as such in a social sense and could apply for a joint residence order with his partner so as to acquire parental responsibility.[49] Further it was made clear that there was no protection of family life under the Convention for a relationship with a transsexual partner: this was because while the European Court had found in *B v France* (1993)[50] that re-registration of civil papers to reflect a change of sex could be done in France without changing the law, and basically was essential to any quality of life for the applicant due to French bureaucracy, so failure to do this in the UK (where such re-registration was not possible) was found not to be a breach of Article 8.

Although the applicant's case in *Rees* (in 1986) was mainly about the inability of a transsexual to marry (because of the inability to marry a person of the transsexual's post-operative sex, and obvious lack of desire to marry a person legally considered to be of the opposite sex), the embarrassment caused by the mismatch between the original birth certificate and apparent post-operative gender was also an issue, and raised exactly the same principles as those found to warrant re-registration in *B v France*.

Although the ECtHR said that English law should clearly remain under review because of ongoing scientific developments, this not only did not happen until 2004, but in the subsequent case of *Cossey* (in 1991) little significant progress appears to have been made, despite a strong dissenting judgment by three members of the Court. Moreover, even seven years later, in 1998, the *Sheffield and Horsham* case appears to have been similarly trapped in a time warp, since the issue was still basically re-registration – Miss Horsham wanted to marry a male partner in the Netherlands but realised that her valid marriage there would not be recognised in the UK. In the era of harmonisation of law in Europe, as well as of EU cooperation on many fronts and of ease of travel and the right to relocation between the countries involved, this was clearly an area of law which required urgent holistic reappraisal long before 2004 and which surely should not have sheltered as long as it did behind a margin of appreciation which, in common sense terms, belongs to a much earlier period of European integration, especially once the HRA 1998 was in force in 2000. It is really surprising that resolution did not finally arrive until 2002, when the *Goodwin* case forced the English government to rethink, and (at last) to act, since the traditional view within English law that marriage was only for opposite-sex individuals in their original biological sex could no longer be sustained alongside the guarantee of respect for privacy and family life under Article 8 of the Convention.

In *Goodwin v UK* (2002),[51] on 11 July 2002, the Court stated that the margin of appreciation held by individual states in relation to their national law was not available to reduce the Convention

---

47 [1996] 2 FLR 90.
48 (1997) 24 EHRR 143.
49 For this PR lifeline, see Chapter 12.
50 (1993) 116 EHRR 1.
51 (2002) No 28957/95.

rights 'so as to impair the very essence of the right'. The Court found that the traditional approach, and the claim that a transsexual, after full reassignment surgery, could only marry in their birth gender, was 'artificial', since as they said in relation to Christine Goodwin, 'The applicant lives as a woman, is in a relationship with a man and would only wish to marry a man. She has no possibility of doing so . . . [H]er right to marry has been infringed.'

The Court also criticised the UK government for not progressing further on this issue, and for failing to take action on the Report of the Interdepartmental Working Group on Transsexual People in 2000.

As this was still at the time a constantly developing area in medical and sociological terms, change was inevitable although by no means straightforward where, also in 2002, in *Bellinger v Bellinger*[52] a majority of the Court of Appeal once again adhered to the party line by pointing as ever to the accumulation of existing authority and tradition, even in the light of medical advances and while the status of transsexual was certainly a recognised medical condition.

However, Thorpe LJ gave a powerful dissenting judgment and the President, Butler-Sloss LJ, led unanimous criticism of government inaction for failing to implement the Working Group's recommendations. It was suggested that the simple speedy solution was a 'recognition' certificate, to be kept alongside the birth certificate, noting the sex realignment, although a Bill to effect this limited change of status then failed in Parliament, before the **Gender Recognition Act 2004** finally achieved the necessary result.

This Act came into force in April 2005. Now a person over 18 can, under s 1, obtain the necessary certificate if it can be shown that s/he has taken steps to live fully and permanently in the new gender, and by s 9 this becomes that person's gender for all purposes, including for issue of a new birth certificate. The Gender Recognition Panel can issue only an interim certificate to a married applicant: s 4, but if within six months of issue of that certificate the marriage is ended a full certificate can be obtained: s 5. The Panel must be satisfied that the applicant has gender dysphoria, has lived in the acquired gender for the preceding two years, and intends to continue to do so until death. As far as parenthood goes, by s 12 the person is recognised in the new gender but retains the original legal status as father or mother of any children; this bizarre but clearly necessary result has caused one of the greatest confusions in the arena of the new family forms which have developed following human assisted reproduction[53] and other advances designed to recognise the various newly emerging personal rights[54] which have had judges and others grappling with the vocabulary, for example what are the children to call their parents in these new roles?

Curiously, not all cases of void marriages under this head concern transsexuals, although one would expect that to be the context of any problems generated by the complexities.

❖ CASE EXAMPLE

In *J v ST (Formerly J)* (1997),[55] CA, the marriage was void because the 'husband' was in fact a woman who managed to conceal from the wife during a lengthy marriage where children were adopted that she was in fact female. The deception was found by the court to be sufficiently cruel as to bar the 'husband' from ancillary relief since it must have been obvious that the marriage could not be valid.

---

52 [2002] Fam Law 150; [2002] 2 WLR 411.
53 See Chapter 13.
54 See also Chapters 8 and 9.
55 [1997] FCR 349; [1997] 1 FLR 402.

2.3.4 Where the marriage is not valid because polygamous and either party is domiciled in England and Wales: MCA 1973, s 11(d)

This rule does not always apply, however, if the parties are not necessarily intending to live in England at the time of the marriage.

> ### ❖ CASE EXAMPLE
>
> In *Radwan v Radwan (No 2)* (1972)[56] the husband was Egyptian and already married to an Egyptian woman when he contracted a second marriage to a domiciled English woman at the Egyptian Consulate in Paris, intending to live with her in Egypt. Eventually when they returned to England the marriage was still held to be valid, as it was so by the law of the intended matrimonial domicile at the time of the ceremony.
>
> In *Hussain v Hussain* (1982)[57] there was a similar situation.

Thus, if there is a potentially polygamous marriage which would not in fact ever have the chance of becoming actually polygamous (e.g. because the husband was an English-domiciled man who would not be able while subject to English law to take a second wife), the marriage will not be void.

2.4 The effect of a void marriage

Lack of capacity or defective formalities to the knowledge of the parties will make the marriage incurably void: such a union can never be valid regardless of the parties' wishes, and none of the defences or bars which apply to voidable marriages will have any effect on a void marriage.

2.5 Grounds on which a marriage will be voidable

Where a marriage is voidable it will, on the other hand, be valid until annulled according to the law of nullity which is contained in ss 12 and 13 of the MCA 1973 (see Chapter 3).

2.6 Current debates

Ideas for research on these current discussion questions can be accessed on the companion website updates.

- Does the state benefit from marriage, considering there is often a demonstrable stability in alternative relationships?
- Should marriage cease to have any legal consequences?

---

56 [1972] 3 WLR 939; [1972] 3 All ER 1026.
57 [1982] 3 All ER 369.

- What could be any alternative means of recognising the status of two people in a close 'family' relationship? Could this include siblings such as the Burden sisters, who could obviously not benefit either from marriage (see MCA 1973 s 11(a), above 2.3.1) nor from civil partnership (see Chapter 8) owing to their blood relationship?

2.7 Summary of Chapter 2

Marriage as a status

- Traditionally, English marriage has been regarded as voluntary, for life, heterosexual and monogamous.
- The spouses must have capacity to marry and observe the necessary formalities in the Marriage Act 1949, as amended, including now by the Marriage (Same-Sex Couples) Act 2013.
- Faulty formalities are not necessarily fatal if the parties did not knowingly and wilfully disregard them, but normally marriages must be conducted in compliance with the law in order to be valid and to achieve the status of marriage.
- There is no longer any common law marriage in England and Wales, although it has been possible to establish marriage retrospectively in Scotland – provided the status of marriage has not been expressly rejected – by means of 'cohabitation, habit and repute'.

Void marriages

- A marriage is void if
  - the formalities of the Marriage Act 1949 are knowingly and wilfully not observed; or
  - if the parties are within the prohibited degrees of relationship;
  - under the age of 16 at which marriage may be contracted;
  - already validly married; or
  - if the marriage is polygamous and either party is domiciled in the UK (MCA 1973, s 11 (d)).
- Section 11(c) of the MCA 1973 is now omitted from the 2013 Act (Part II of Schedule 7 of the 2013 Act) and s 1(1) makes same-sex marriages 'lawful'.
- The UK approach to post-operative transsexual marriage long remained unaltered by modern scientific and medical developments in this area.
- From 2002 the European Court of Human Rights no longer continued to respect the margin of appreciation in English law in this matter: *Goodwin v UK* (No 28957/95) (11 July 2002).

Effect of a void/voidable marriage

- A VOID marriage can never be valid regardless of the parties' wishes and third parties can seek such a declaration.
- But VOIDABLE marriages remain valid until avoided and no third party can seek to avoid them.

2.8 Further reading

Auchmuty, R, 'What's so special about marriage? The impact of *Wilkinson v Kitzinger*', [2008] CFLQ 475.

Barker, N, *Not the Marrying Kind: A Feminist Critique of Same-Sex Marriage*, Basingstoke, Palgrave Macmillan, 2013.

Cretney, S, *Same Sex Relationships: from 'Odious Crime' to 'Gay Marriage'*, Oxford, OUP, 2006.

Eekelaar, J, 'Why people marry: the many faces of an institution', (2008) *Family Law Quarterly* 41: 413.

Freeman, M (Michael), 'Understanding Marriage and Other Relationships' in *Understanding Family Law*, London, Sweet & Maxwell, 2007.

Gilmore, S, '*Bellinger v Bellinger* – Not Quite Between the Ears and the Legs – transsexualism and marriage in the Lords', [2003] CFLQ 295.

Chapter 3

Nullity

Chapter Contents

Learning outcomes for this chapter

A sound understanding of the law of nullity, including:

(i) An awareness of the attractions of this remedy for the victims of forced marriage.
(ii) An appreciation of the importance in some sectors of a multicultural society of the legal and psychological impact on personal status of obtaining an annulment rather than a divorce (even where the marriage was not forced).
(iii) An ability to analyse fact patterns to detect the relative suitability of a decree of divorce or nullity in relation to discrete areas of English law relevant to the family context, e.g. settlements and trusts including pensions.
(iv) an awareness of the recent criminalisation of forced marriage and the tensions that this may raise within an ethnic family and the hopes, if any, of a victim for family reunification at some stage.

3.1 Introduction

In the mid-1990s, when the Family Law Act 1996 sought to 'modernise' the grounds for divorce, it was thought that the remedy of nullity was outdated and should be abolished, as divorce was likely to be the preferred method of ending marriages from which one or both parties wished to escape. There was some logic to this, since nullity required a court hearing and could not be dealt with under the then 'special procedure' or, as the public chose to call it, 'quickie divorce', and which was in fact eventually the standard procedure. With so little stigma attaching to either divorce or remarriage, and the gradual erosion of religious objection to divorce, it was thought that no one could seriously prefer the recondite, and more expensive, remedy of annulment. However, this hasty conclusion ignored the essential difference between divorce, which could only dissolve an unwanted marriage and release the parties from its obligations, and nullity, which could declare that a marriage had never existed in the first place. To some, it seemed, that still mattered, because not only did they not wish to be married, but did not wish *ever* to have been married at all.

Distant memories of Henry VIII spring to mind, and of his desire at all costs to pretend that he had *never* been validly married to his first wife so he could (in that superstitious and overtly pious era, when divorce was not socially respectable – though not unknown) marry the younger and prettier mistress of the moment, who was also arguably more likely to produce the urgently required son and heir.

However, there are two significant modern constituencies which have unexpectedly turned out to favour nullity over divorce in the late twentieth and early twenty-first century: (1) victims of the forced marriage syndrome which, during that period, has swept the minority ethnic communities in contemporary Britain to the extent that the Foreign and Commonwealth Office (FCO) has had to set up a discrete Forced Marriage Unit (FMU) with their associated government departments, the Ministry of Justice (MOJ) and Home Office; and (2) parties to some arranged marriages in such communities, which while not 'forced' as such have apparently followed the traditions of their culture, but without success when these arranged matches have foundered. Since such communities disfavour divorce as much as they favour orderly arranged marriages, annulment also suits them better than divorce, since sometimes even carefully arranged marriages go awry and need to be dissolved in such a way that, in that culture, the parties can remarry elsewhere, which is often not the case following divorce which is frequently disapproved of – as divorce was socially unacceptable in purely indigenous English social circles of whichever class of society a few years ago. It has to be remembered that parties from minority ethnic groups contracting civil marriage in England and Wales today often go on to contract a religious marriage within their own communities, and in particular the Jewish and Muslim religions (which are now widely practised in the UK following substantial immigration over the past 80 years) require dissolution both religiously and civilly so that divorce under the **Matrimonial Causes Act (MCA) 1973** may not be suitable for remarriage in those cultures.

Thus, despite the extensive changes in the legal and moral landscape since it was thought nullity was obsolete, the real catalyst for the retention and practical resurgence of a market for annulment has not been a religious revival (at least not in the Christian churches, which have become progressively more tolerant of divorce) but the forced marriage syndrome which escalated so much in the decade since before the turn of the century that the FMU has not only been obliged to provide information as well as practical help and support for potential and actual victims, but also to consider, and eventually at last to legislate for, criminalisation of forced marriage.[1] Nevertheless, ever since such criminalisation was first formally suggested in the consultation in 2012, it has been feared by some that such steps will simply drive the incidence of forced marriages underground[2] because it was clear from the consultation meetings that many charities and others working in the field are not, and have never been, in favour of criminalisation owing to precisely this fear, in respect of which they have made clear that they infinitely preferred that the ordinary criminal law should be left to deal with the matter.

This was, and is, an entirely valid argument, since of course in the commission of any offence there is likely also to be an inevitable breach of some other provision of the general criminal law, such as false imprisonment, some type of assault, and in extreme cases murder, or attempts. Several scholarly articles have appeared in this vein.[3] However, the government has chosen to press on, insisting that this is a major advance in the prevention of forced marriage, while among those who live and work in the areas where victims are congregated in the ethnic minority neighbourhoods in which such practices are likely to be preserved as a part of the traditional 'culture' it is said that 'no one wants this'.[4]

Moreover, as victims of these forced marriages (usually young people of both sexes from the minority ethnic communities) often feel that they have never actually been married (as they gave no true consents) and divorce is frowned upon in their cultures, they have almost exclusively opted for annulments rather than divorces when caught in such forced marriages but eventually having the opportunity to escape. This has led to a significant resurgence of the use of nullity, especially as (although the summary procedure for divorce decrees could not be used, and a court hearing was therefore usually necessary) the courts have been helpful in arranging for the hearing to be as easy as possible for the luckless victims. Evidence has been allowed in some cases by video link and in even more protected circumstances, and petitioners allowed to withhold their addresses from respondents, in case of unwelcome reaction from the respondent or respondent's family.

However by the **Family Procedure Rules (FPR) 2010** (in force from 6 April 2011, replacing the former FPR 1991 which always required a hearing for nullity) undefended nullity petitions can technically now be processed through the replacement for the FPR 1991 'special procedure', now called the summary procedure, although in theory there is a possibility that this might be changed when divorce becomes a purely administrative process, as it appears is intended once the new unified Family Court becomes established and further procedural reform will be likely. At any rate, at the present time

---

1 The Anti-Social Behaviour, Crime and Policing Act 2014, s 121, enacted on 16 June 2014, creates a new offence of coercing any person into a marriage which the perpetrator knows or believes will result in that person's entering such a marriage without free consent, and in addition s 120 inserts a new s 63CA into the Family Law Act 1996 creating an offence of breaching the civil remedy of a Forced Marriage Protection Order (FMPO).

2 See Moore, J, Lexis Nexis, Family Law News and views, www.lexisweb.co.uk, 8 July 2014.

3 Gangoli, G and Chantler, K, 'Protecting Victims of Forced Marriage: Is Age a Protective Factor?', (2009) 17 *Feminist Legal Studies*, p 267; Wilson, A, 'The forced marriage debate and the British state', (2007) 49 *Race and Class*, p 25; Razack, S, 'Imperilled Muslim Women, Dangerous Muslim Men: Legal and Social Responses to Forced Marriages, (2004) 12 *Feminist Legal Studies*, p 129.

4 See n 2.

there is now a summary paper determination available which is the only FPR 2010 process unless, for some reason, a court hearing is required (which for *defended* nullity would clearly be the case).

The retention of nullity has therefore turned out to be a positive step since the victims of forced marriage are not alone in wishing to have their marriages annulled instead of dissolved, so it would be a mistake to write off the remedy of nullity as being only another panacea for violence against (mostly) women. It has a respectable background in the theory of English law and is a genuine alternative for the second of the two contemporary pro-nullity constituencies, i.e. those who, for religious or other reasons, do not wish to have their marriages dissolved by divorce (even if most of those who still oppose divorce may no longer be exclusively the white Anglo-Saxon Christian population for which this remedy in English law was originally developed[5] but again parties from the minority ethnic communities which, for reasons of cultural and community protection and preservation of traditions, practise arranged marriages).

As no significant reason was after all advanced for the abolition of the remedy of nullity (neither when the **Divorce Reform Act (DRA) 1969** was passed, when the special procedure was introduced for divorce under the FPR 1991, nor when the new family litigation Rules were drafted in the form of the FPR 2010) there seem strong reasons for retaining it even if the divorce process shortly becomes purely administrative, since to preclude its selection as the remedy of choice instead of divorce or dissolution in the context of forced or arranged marriages would obviously deprive identifiable constituencies of a remedy which they value, especially as undefended nullity need use no more of the court's time under the FPR 2010 than the alternatives of undefended divorce or judicial separation.

Nor is there a valid reason to phase it out simply because it is thought that comparatively few people use it, and because those who do could use the alternative remedies instead.

To take another minority use analogy, few people use the facility of registered civil partnership provided by the **Civil Partnership Act (CPA) 2004** instead of the same-sex partners merely living together informally[6] and probably such civil partnerships will be even less used now the alternative of full gay marriage is available. However, far from any suggestion that this registered union should be abolished as it caters for so few people, the government has now introduced (from December 2014) the opportunity provided for in s 9 of the **Marriage (Same-Sex Couples) Act 2013** to provide a transition to legal marriage for this small group, so as to advance their status to that of marriage identical to that already accessed by those who were free to do so on 29 March 2014 when the first same-sex marriages were able to be conducted (i.e. for those who were then not hampered by already being in a civil partnership with no transitional legislation yet available unless their existing civil partnership was first dissolved in the usual process – understandably not regarded by existing civil partners as an option).

In the circumstances, there seems even less reason to discontinue nullity just because it is hoped that the numbers of those seeking annulment of forced marriages will eventually be contained and hopefully reduced owing to the impact of the recent criminalisation, as this would still leave those seeking to leave unsuccessful arranged marriages, which might well actually rise in any case, as often the reason for such failures is the impact of Westernised thought on young members of minority ethnic communities who ultimately find that they cannot support the traditions of their culture once their community is transported to Western contexts.[7]

---

5 It is clear from a perusal of some of the cases which come before the religious courts of minority ethnic communities that there is as strong a sense of religious importance in these communities as there used to be in the indigenous English population which used to regard divorce as a social blemish. The Muslim, Sikh and Hindu communities abhor divorce, and although both Muslims and Hindus permit it in appropriate circumstances it is a significant stigma in both cultures, besides which the Sikhs regard marriage as monogamous and in theory do not accept divorce at all.

6 There are about 6,000 civil partnerships a year.

7 See e.g. *Quoreshi v Quoreshi* [1985] FLR 760 where it was agreed that Westernised Muslims would not be married polygamously but when the husband nevertheless took a second wife the marriage broke down.

The use of nullity as a particular remedy in addressing forced marriage is considered further elsewhere, alongside the treatment of other species of domestic violence.[8]

3.2 Annulling voidable marriages

Unlike void marriages, which can never be valid whatever the parties wish,[9] voidable marriages present a practical alternative to divorce: 'annulment' under the law of nullity, pursuant to ss 12 and 13 of the MCA 1973. This remedy had not been much used of late until revived for dissolving the spate of forced marriages, since the categories of indigenous English persons whose religious objections to divorce used to favour nullity had shrunk to near vanishing point in recent decades. Moreover, as nullity was never obtainable via the 1970s special procedure, under which undefended divorces have been granted without a hearing for over 40 years, this was a discouragement to seeking an annulment instead of divorce in practically all cases emanating from the indigenous English population.

However, once the potentially powerful new market for nullity reprieved this alternative decree from obsolescence, owing to the increasing incidence of breakdown of marriages in ethnic communities whether or not they turn out to have been forced, its use seems to have swelled as availability has been combined with the increasing willingness of Westernised women of Asian origin to resist unacceptable pressure from their families to forego a Western-style marriage to a person of their own choice, so that the falling numbers of marriages involving the family's choice of partner within their race and religion has also encouraged their older (formerly less assertive) sisters finally to leave marriages to which they never truly consented.

For such women the remedy of nullity is preferable since they have never regarded themselves as genuinely married, and will almost certainly wish to contract the Western-style marriage that they wished in the first place without the unwelcome 'baggage' of a divorce decree. Since they seek a decree of nullity of a voidable marriage, such a decree enables their children always to be and to remain legitimate while they themselves can start a new life on the basis that they have never been validly married, despite their belief that they were obliged to do what their families wanted at the time of the ceremony. There are no relevant statistics but anecdotally it seems that such women generally still want to marry (rather than to 'remarry') and to prefer marriage to cohabitation, though this is now an identifiable trend in the population outside their own ethnic circles. It is possible that it is only coincidental that neither of the most recent leading cohabitants' property cases to reach the House of Lords or Supreme Court[10] concerns a minority ethnic partnership, but the overwhelming majority of minority ethnic partnership disputes in the reports appear to concern nullity or divorce, not cohabitation.

The FCO has been exploring further ways in which to prevent the continued abuse of imposing forced marriages on young women and girls in the minority ethnic communities. This follows the **Forced Marriage Protection Act (FMPA) 2007** which enables orders to be made preventing such marriages, and imposing sanctions, including custodial sentences, on those who nevertheless engage in such practices, which are perceived as a species of domestic violence[11] and which therefore usually form part of several current initiatives to address violence against women in all its forms.[12]

---

8 See Chapter 11.
9 See Chapter 2 and MCA 1973 s 11 for potential formal defects.
10 *Stack v Dowden* [2007] UKHL 17; *Kernott v Jones* (2011) Times Law Report, 10 October 2011.
11 See Chapter 11.
12 The Centre for Family Law and Practice at London Metropolitan University undertook two funded small-scale studies of pastoral provision for women university students of the age range particularly vulnerable to this syndrome in 2012 and 2013: the Centre is no longer in existence at the university but the reports can still be accessed on the researchers' new website, www.famlawandpractice.com/researchers/research.htm, at their newly established International Centre for Family Law, Policy and Practice.

Obviously the new crime of arranging or assisting such a marriage is now available and thought by the government to be useful, but there are other possible initiatives which might be more likely to assist such as continued raising of awareness, including in the potential target areas in which victims may be found and protected, such as Further Education Colleges and Universities and Higher Education institutions, in respect of which there is likely to be a follow-up funded project to the two existing small-scale studies already undertaken[13] to provide training for FE and HE administrative staff, in turn likely to include awareness of the remedy of nullity for those for whom prevention came too late, although it should be noted that an *arranged* marriage, of which there are many good examples, will not necessarily be *forced*. Meanwhile, some solicitors are already raising awareness of the existence of nullity as an alternative to divorce for those who are finally able to emerge from these unwelcome marriages.

The range of situations which give rise to voidable marriages includes (besides lack of consent and duress) incapacity or wilful refusal to consummate the marriage, mistake, unsoundness of mind and pregnancy by another man at the time of the marriage (see 3.3 below).

A voidable marriage can thus be annulled pursuant to ss 12 and 13 of the MCA 1973 with little more delay or difficulty than obtaining a decree of divorce, albeit that there may have to be a hearing, and as with divorce an undefended case will be easier to conclude than one that is defended.

3.3 Nullity: MCA 1973 ss 11–13

The historical background to nullity is in ecclesiastical law before divorce was developed.[14]

3.3.1 Two categories of null marriages: void and voidable

Unlike in the case of void marriages, the validity of which anyone may challenge, annulment of a voidable marriage requires action on the part of one of the parties, as the marriage remains valid for all purposes until annulled.

In *De Reneville v De Reneville* (1948) Lord Greene MR, famously expressed the distinction:

> A void marriage is one that will be regarded by every court in any case in which the existence of the marriage is in issue as never having taken place and can be so treated by both parties to it without the necessity of any decree annulling it; a voidable marriage is one that will be regarded by every court as a valid subsisting marriage until a decree annulling it has been pronounced by a court of competent jurisdiction.

3.3.2 Void and voidable marriages compared

Voidable marriages require a decree which may only be obtained by the parties and during the lifetime of both of them; however, any third party can challenge the validity of a void marriage, for example, a trustee of a marriage settlement. Void marriages do not require a decree, though this may be required for financial provision.[15] The financial and property orders which the court may make following a decree of divorce or judicial separation[16] also extend to nullity or dissolution of civil partnership.[17]

---

13 See n 12.
14 See Chapter 4.
15 See Chapter 7.
16 See Chapter 5.
17 See Chapter 8.

Children of voidable marriages are legitimate, as are the children of void marriages, provided both or either parents believed the marriage was valid at the time of conception, artificial insemination or marriage, whichever was the later, and the father was domiciled in England and Wales at the date of the birth, or if he died beforehand at the date of his death: **Legitimacy Act 1976**, s 1 as amended by the **Family Law Reform Act 1987**.

In the case of void marriages, it is presumed that one of the parties reasonably believed the marriage was valid unless the contrary is shown.

3.3.3 Effect of a nullity decree on a voidable marriage

The marriage is valid until the decree is granted: MCA 1973 s 16. This is not always very convenient to the parties; the practical importance is shown by two cases.

❖ CASE EXAMPLES

In *Re Roberts (Decd)* (1978),[18] a husband made a will giving property to a woman, whom he then married, in apparent ignorance of the fact that the marriage revoked the gift to her in the will. The husband then died and the wife wanted to argue that the marriage was voidable because of the husband's insanity within the meaning of s 12(c) of the MCA 1973 so that she could still receive the property left to her. Unfortunately for her, the court held that this was irrelevant as even if she were correct about the insanity, by s 16 of the same Act the marriage remained valid for all purposes until a decree absolute was obtained so that the gift had been revoked by the marriage and remained revoked.

Ward v Secretary of State for Social Services (1990)[19] was a similar case, where the wife married a Royal Naval officer who died, so that she obtained a Navy pension which ceased if she remarried. Some years later she did remarry, but then discovered that her new husband was a manic depressive. As the marriage was never consummated and had only lasted a week, she was able to obtain a s 12(a) decree and attempted to retain her Navy pension on the ground that her second marriage had been annulled. However, again the court held that by s 16 the marriage was valid until decree, so the regulation depriving her of the pension had come into effect during that period and operated to end the right to the pension.

It should be noted that there are possible defences under s 13 of the MCA 1973 to a petition for a decree annulling a voidable marriage (see 3.5 below). A petition to obtain a nullity decree is the same as for divorce and the two decrees can be petitioned for in the alternative. The same financial provision is obtainable after nullity as after divorce.

3.4 Grounds on which a marriage will be voidable

Broadly, these strike at the concept of the marriage relationship, as a consensual contract creating the relationship of husband and wife, so that the marriage should be freely entered into by persons

---

18 [1978] 3 All ER 225.
19 [1990] Fam Law 58.

with the mental capacity to appreciate its obligations and should be consummated. There are several distinct situations to consider here.

3.4.1 If the marriage is not consummated owing to incapacity of either party to consummate it: MCA 1973 s 12(a)

A party can petition on his or her own incapacity (but see *Harthan v Harthan* (1948),[20] where the husband actually tried to petition both on his own incapacity and on his wife's wilful refusal to consummate, which the court not surprisingly found mutually exclusive grounds).

There are several definitions the exact meaning of which need to be considered in relation to non-consummation.

Incapacity

This has a precise meaning:

- the defect must be incurable;
- it must be incapable of remedy, or only so with danger or little chance of success; or
- the respondent must refuse treatment.

Incapacity must be in existence at the date of the marriage and there must be no practical possibility of consummation at the date of the hearing.

❖ CASE EXAMPLE

In *Napier v Napier* (1915)[21] it was necessary to seek an adjournment because the wife had undergone an operation six days before the hearing, and the petition was eventually dismissed as the incapacity was curable.

Medical inspection may be required in defended cases, but note that by Part 3 of Schedule 4 of the **Marriage (Same-Sex Couples) Act 2013** this provision does not apply to same-sex marriages: because no consummation is required as in opposite-sex marriage, s 12(a) cannot be relied on for dissolution of the marriage.

3.4.2 If the marriage is not consummated owing to wilful refusal of the respondent: MCA 1973 s 12(b)

A party cannot petition on that party's own refusal under this section. The meaning of consummation is important. It must be:

- after marriage, not before; and
- ordinary complete intercourse.

---

20 [1948] 2 All ER 639.
21 [1915] P 184.

The following should be noted:

(a)   sterility or inability to ejaculate is irrelevant;
(b)   lack of satisfaction is irrelevant;
(c)   the birth of a child by fertilisation outside the body owing to incomplete or attempted inter-
          course is not consummation;
(d)   contraceptives do not prevent consummation and neither does incomplete intercourse.

Note that by Part 3 of Schedule 4 of the Marriage (Same-Sex Couples) Act 2013 this sub-section
does not apply to same-sex couples since no consummation is required of their marriage.

❖ **CASE EXAMPLE**

Baxter v Baxter (1947)[22] although an old decision is still the leading case on non-
consummation. The decision suggests that tact and persuasion must be employed to
attempt to reverse a refusal or the petition on this ground might fail.

Wilful refusal
The meaning of 'wilful refusal' is that there is a 'settled and definite decision come to without just
excuse': per Lord Jowitt in *Horton v Horton* (1947).[23] A failure to undergo medical treatment to cure
an incapacity to consummate, where that treatment is not 'dangerous', may be 'wilful refusal'. An
examination of some of the leading cases shows what this means and how it works in practice.

❖ **CASE EXAMPLES**

In *Jodla v Jodla* (1960)[24] it was established that a just excuse may include religious reasons.
In that case, two Roman Catholics married in a Register Office but it was expressly understood that they would not live together until there had been a religious ceremony. The
husband refused to go through with the religious service and this was held to amount to
refusal to consummate.

In *Kaur v Singh* (1972)[25] there was a similar decision, where the parties were Sikhs. It was
intended according to the religious and social custom of their people that a religious ceremony would have to follow their marriage, but the husband, who had the obligation of
arranging that ceremony, refused to do so and this too was held to amount to refusal to
consummate.

In *Morgan v Morgan* (1959)[26] and *Scott v Scott* (1959)[27] it was established that just excuse
may include an agreement that the marriage is for companionship only and that there

---

22 [1947] 2 All ER 197.
23 [1947] 2 All ER 871.
24 [1960] 1 All ER 625.
25 [1972] 1 All ER 292.
26 [1959] 2 WLR 487; [1959] 1 All ER 53.
27 [1959] 2 WLR 447; [1959] 1 All ER 531.

would therefore not be intercourse. In the case of *Morgan* the parties were respectively aged 72 and 59, and the agreement was therefore held to be reasonable having regard to their ages, but in the case of *Scott* there was initially some doubt since the parties were only 43 and 40. Nevertheless, it was held that the parties had accepted the condition because the wife found intercourse distasteful and the husband was not allowed to petition so as to remarry when he met another woman without the same aversion. Nevertheless, this fact pattern might today be a sufficient basis for divorce, as opposed to nullity, especially where the parties were of the ages of the Scotts, if the agreement was less than clear and if the lack of sexual intercourse had adverse medical effects since the behaviour fact has both subjective and objective elements.

In *Potter v Potter* (1975)[28] it was held that mere loss of sexual ardour is not sufficient. The husband tried to consummate the marriage immediately after the wife had had an operation to cure a physical defect, but failed, after which he refused to try again. However, the wife did not succeed with her petition because his failure on the sole occasion on which he had attempted consummation had been natural and not a deliberate refusal.

In *Ford v Ford* (1987)[29] the court clarified a common misconception that a pre-marriage relationship including intercourse obviates the necessity for specific consummation after the celebration of the marriage. In that case, the husband was in prison for five years and the marriage actually took place in prison, where there was no opportunity for consummation. When he was eventually released on a visit prior to the end of his sentence he did not go home but stayed with a former girlfriend. When the wife eventually petitioned, it was held that he had not refused consummation in prison as there were no facilities, but he *had* done so as soon as he had the opportunity on a visit out of prison prior on his release, so that his conduct then had demonstrated wilful refusal to consummate the marriage either at that time or in the future.

In *A v J (Nullity)* (1989)[30] it was held that there may be *indirect* refusal to consummate. In that case there appear to have been tantrums on both sides: the marriage was an arranged one between two Indians and there was to be a civil ceremony followed by a religious one some four months later. Between the two ceremonies the husband was abroad on business, which the wife seemed to seize on as an excuse not to go ahead with the religious ceremony, as she said he had been offhand with her in going abroad. She declined the husband's apologies, and the court held that *she* was the one who was wilfully refusing to consummate the marriage owing to her adamant refusal to go ahead with the religious ceremony which was essential for them to cohabit.

3.4.3 If the marriage is not valid owing to lack of proper consent due to mistake, unsoundness of mind, duress or otherwise: MCA 1973 s 12(c)

These grounds all strike at the essential concept of *consent* to the marriage.

---

28 [1975] 5 Fam Law 161.
29 [1987] Fam Law 232.
30 [1989] Fam Law 63.

Mistake

This must be as to the identity of the other party or as to the *nature* of the ceremony, not as to the quality or fortune of the potential spouse, or other mistake of fact, such as pregnancy by another man. The scope of mistake in this context is best illustrated by the cases since it is a situation in which the *species* of the mistake and its *consequences or effect* are often misunderstood.

❖ CASE EXAMPLES

Nature of the ceremony

In *Mehta v Mehta* (1945)[31] there was a sufficient mistake as to the nature of the ceremony to annul the marriage where the ceremony was thought to be one of conversion to the Hindu religion – clearly a fundamentally different matter from marriage.

In *Valier v Valier* (1925)[32] there was a similar mistake where an Italian who did not speak English thought a Register Office wedding was merely one of many formalities preceding marriage (as is common in Italy) rather than the ceremony itself – clearly also a different situation from the binding ceremony of marriage.

Consequences or effect of the mistake

In *Kassim v Kassim* (1962)[33] it was clear that mistakes as to the *effect* of the ceremony, rather than its *nature*, are in a different category. This was a case where the mistake was insufficient to avoid the marriage, since it was to the effect that the marriage was polygamous instead of monogamous (an obvious example of a mistake only as to the *effect* of the ceremony rather than the nature of it).

In *Way v Way* (1949)[34] the husband thought that the Russian wife would be allowed to leave Russia to live with him in England – another mistake only as to the *effect* of the ceremony, and therefore of course insufficient, however important her departure with him might have been to that husband.

In *Vervaeke v Smith* (1982)[35] there was a similar mistake about the effect of the ceremony, in this instance an inaccurate belief in a resulting protection from deportation, again with the same result.

In *Puttick v Attorney General* (1979)[36] (see 2.3.1 above), where the wife gave a false name, this was insufficient to avoid the marriage, because any mistake on the part of the other spouse was only as to the *quality* of the party giving the false name, since the intention is usually to marry the person actually present for the ceremony.

---

31 [1945] 2 All ER 690.
32 (1925) 133 LT 830.
33 [1962] 3 WLR 865; [1962] 3 All ER 426.
34 [1949] 2 All ER 959.
35 [1982] 2 All ER 144.
36 [1979] 3 WLR 542; [1979] 3 All ER 463.

Unsoundness of mind

It might be thought that unsoundness of mind would be an absolute prohibition on a valid marriage. However, the cases do not support this generalisation unless there is an established mental illness which effectively prevents the meeting of minds. See below at 3.4.4.

❖ CASE EXAMPLES

In the case of *In re Estate of Park* (1953)[37] it was established that no high degree of understanding is required for capacity to enter into a marriage. The test is whether the party in question was capable of understanding the nature of the marriage contract and the duties and obligations that it involves. There is a presumption of valid consent when a marriage is contracted.

Re Roberts (see 3.3.3, above) is a more recent case on similar facts.

Duress

This means a fear so great that there is no reality of consent. However, the party claiming duress must not himself be responsible for being put in fear. It is now established that the fear in question need not literally be of life, limb or liberty.

❖ CASE EXAMPLES

In *Szechter v Szechter* (1971),[38] which is the leading case in modern times, it was said that the 'will of one of the parties must be so overborne by genuine and reasonably held fear that the constraint destroys the reality of consent'. The case was one of a Polish woman in prison in Poland following arrest by the security forces, who married so that she could leave both prison and Poland itself. It was accepted that she was in poor health and that her life was in danger if she remained, and this was accepted as sufficient duress for a decree to be granted.

In *Parojcic v Parojcic* (1958)[39] a similar decision was reached in the case of a refugee from Yugoslavia who was forced by her father to marry a man on her arrival in England on pain of being sent back to Yugoslavia.

In *Hussein v Hussein* (1938)[40] the marriage was entered into under threat of being killed by the husband, again sufficient for a decree.

In *Singh v Singh* (1971),[41] on the other hand, the only duress compelling the marriage was the young Sikh bride's respect for her parents, which was held to be insufficient.

---

37 [1953] 3 WLR 1012; [1953] 2 All ER 1411.
38 [1971] 2 WLR 170; [1970] 3 All ER 905.
39 [1958] 1 WLR 1280; [1959] 1 All ER 1.
40 [1938] 2 All ER 344.
41 [1971] 2 WLR 963; [1971] 2 All ER 828.

But compare this with *Hirani v Hirani* (1982),[42] where again there was no physical duress but the Hindu parents threatened to withdraw all support from their 19-year-old daughter and eject her from the family home if she did not comply with their wishes for her marriage. The judge said that threat to actual life, limb or liberty is not essential to establish duress, provided that what is done is extreme enough that it 'overbears the will of the individual'. This sort of duress is at the root of many marriages now being annulled in the wake of the initiatives against forced marriages.

In *Buckland v Buckland* (1967)[43] there were false accusations of crime and threats of unjustified exposure for such untrue offences, which were held to be sufficient, provided the accusations were unjust as otherwise the situation would not meet the requirement that the party coerced should not himself be responsible for the duress applied to him. There is some doubt over whether the test of fear should be objective or subjective. What is established is that there must be some fear or coercion, not merely an ulterior motive imposed by the party alleging he is coerced.

In *Silver v Silver* (1955)[44] there was just such a distinction to be made, where the only coercion was the German petitioner's own desire to come to England to live with an Englishman (other than the one whom she married in order to gain entry to the UK).

3.4.4 If the marriage is not valid owing to mental disorder, etc.: MCA 1973 s 12(d)

The marriage may not be valid because at the time of the marriage either party, though capable of giving a valid consent, was suffering (whether continuously or intermittently) from mental disorder within the meaning of the **Mental Health Act 1983** of such a kind or to such an extent as to be unfitted for marriage. However, this does need to be a certifiable medical condition.

> ❖ **CASE EXAMPLE**
>
> In *Bennett v Bennett* (1969)[45] the wife was not clinically ill, but suffered from a temporary hysterical neurosis resulting in a tendency to be periodically difficult, but this was insufficient to invalidate the marriage.

3.4.5 If the marriage is not valid due to venereal disease: MCA 1973 s 12(e)

The marriage may not be valid if a party to the marriage is suffering at the time of the ceremony from venereal disease in a communicable form.

---

42 (1982) 4 FLR 232.
43 [1967] 2 WLR 1506; [1967] 2 All ER 300.
44 [1955] 2 All ER 614.
45 [1969] 1 WLR 430; [1969] 1 All ER 539.

3.4.6 If the marriage is not valid owing to pregnancy *per alium*: MCA 1973 s 12(f)

This means pregnancy of the respondent at the date of the ceremony by someone other than the petitioner. This ground is now entirely statutory as, owing to the decision in *Moss v Moss* (1897),[46] when it was held that pregnancy *per alium* (which means 'by another man') at the time of the ceremony and concealed from the petitioner was not sufficient to nullify consent to the marriage, legislation was required to provide a remedy for the situation in an appropriate case.

3.5 Bars to a nullity decree

These only apply in the case of a voidable marriage. There are two only:

- approbation: MCA 1973 s 13(1); and
- other statutory bars after three years from the ceremony: MCA 1973 s 13(2) and (3).

3.5.1 The bar of approbation: MCA 1973 s 13(1)

The section has enacted the pre-existing bar of approbation, so that a decree of nullity will not be granted if the petitioner, with knowledge that it was open to him or her to have the marriage annulled, so conducted him- or herself in relation to the respondent as to lead the respondent reasonably to believe that s/he would not seek to do so, and it would be unjust to the respondent to grant the decree.

For this bar to operate, the court must be satisfied on three points:

(1)   That there is evidence of the petitioner's actual knowledge that s/he had a legal right to a decree of nullity.

(2)   That there is evidence that despite this knowledge s/he behaved towards the respondent in such a way as to lead the respondent to believe that s/he would not seek a decree. What this means is best illustrated through the cases.

❖ CASE EXAMPLES

In *Aldridge v Aldridge* (1988)[47] it was established that an express agreement between the parties not to have the marriage annulled is an absolute bar.

In *W v W* (1952)[48] it was established that institution of other proceedings in some way relating to the marriage (in this case adoption of a child) suggests that the petitioner has treated it as valid and might be a bar to a nullity decree.

In *Tindall v Tindall* (1953)[49] (where the proceedings were for maintenance) the court reached a different conclusion on similar facts to *W v W*. This might be because maintenance would still be a possibility even if the marriage were annulled.

---

46   [1897] P 263.
47   (1988) 13 PD 210.
48   [1952] 1 All ER 858.
49   [1953] 2 WLR 158; [1953] 1 All ER 139.

(3)   That there is evidence that it would be unjust to the respondent to grant the decree.

> ### ❖ CASE EXAMPLE
>
> In *Pettit v Pettit* (1962)[50] the husband had always been impotent, but the wife had had their child by artificial insemination and had been a particularly loyal wife, including taking responsibility for the outgoings of the matrimonial home during World War II by paying bills and the mortgage. When after 20 years the husband wanted a decree of nullity so as to marry another woman, the court was not minded to give him one on the grounds that it would be unjust to the wife.

It is therefore essential (especially in the context of the sudden resurgence of marital agreements following *Radmacher v Granatino* (2010)[51]) that care should be taken with the wording of any alleged agreement putting the respondent on notice that the petitioner reserves the right to petition notwithstanding, for example, an adoption or artificial insemination. If consent to either of these courses is given and the petitioner makes it clear that s/he would still petition if the marriage is never consummated, then s/he will obviously not be debarred from doing so, perhaps with catastrophic emotional consequences for the respondent to such a petition. Similarly, since approbation or lack of it clearly depends on knowledge and, where appropriate, notice, there will be no approbation if an adoption or artificial insemination takes place in ignorance of one of the parties' rights to have the marriage avoided for non-consummation, as happened in *Slater v Slater* (1953).[52]

3.5.2 Other statutory bars after three years from the ceremony: MCA 1973 s 13(2) and s 13(3)

These sections provide respectively:

(1)   a bar against a nullity decree on any of the statutory grounds in s 12(c), (d), (e) or (f) (i.e. all s 12 grounds but non-consummation) unless proceedings are begun within three years of the date of the ceremony: s 13(2). There is an exception where leave for later institution of proceedings is granted under s 13(4) (which allows an extension of time if the petitioner has at some time been suffering from mental disorder within the meaning of the Mental Health Act 1983, and it would be just to grant leave for such an extension);

(2)   a bar against a nullity decree on any of the statutory grounds in s 12(c) (d) (e) and (f) unless the court is satisfied on the basis of the facts alleged that the petitioner was ignorant of the true situation at the time of the marriage.

3.6 Relationship between nullity and divorce

There may be overlap in the following areas.

---

50   [1962] 3 WLR 919; [1962] 3 All ER 37.
51   [2010] 2 FLR 1900, SC.
52   [1953] 2 WLR 170; [1953] 1 All ER 246.

- Pregnancy *per alium* or venereal disease in a communicable form at the time of the marriage (nullity) may be an alternative to establishing a case of adultery if the pregnancy arose or the venereal disease was contracted after the ceremony (when divorce would be appropriate) provided of course the marriage has been consummated: if it has not, nullity may be an alternative available *instead* of divorce.
- Mental disorder at the time of the marriage (nullity) may be an alternative to establishing a case of behaviour under Fact B sufficient for divorce[53] where the mental and/or physical illness may not qualify under that head.
- Invalidity of marriage sufficient to make it voidable (nullity) may be an alternative where there is only a weak basis for divorce or where the first year is not up.[54]

Nevertheless, the reformers periodically return to the old arguments about abolishing nullity because there are 'only' a few hundred nullity petitions a year, about the same number as the forced marriage cases that are dealt with by the FMU. The academic lobby also sometimes alleges that this relatively small number of petitions a year does not justify keeping the complex law of nullity, despite the Law Commission's support[55] for its retention on the very grounds that the victims of forced marriage argue that it is important to keep the remedy for those who require annulment not divorce. Other academics have urged leaving nullity for the religious bodies, given that most nullity petitions are brought for religious reasons, by the minority ethnic women married under duress who want annulments, not divorce, and who could use the courts of their own religions. This seems inappropriately discriminating if they must still obtain a civil decree.

At present it provides a choice and an important pathway which is appreciated by the minority ethnic young people (young men as well as women) who are the traditional victims of the forced marriage syndrome *and* sometimes of failed *arranged* marriages. It is difficult to see why they should be deprived of this remedy when it is presented by the FMU as one of the means by which, if the worst happens and no one succeeds in deterring the young people's elder relatives from forcing a British teenager into a marriage, the government can help to restore the victim's freedom of association and marriage where s/he wills – as in the case of any other young person of marriageable age in the West.

The recognition that nullity suits are still sufficiently numerous and significant to warrant the provision of new procedural rules in the FPR 2010 (and at last from 2011 obviating the need for a hearing in undefended nullity petitions) suggests that the court takes the need for continued nullity petitions sufficiently seriously for the Rules Committee's making this change and that it is premature to consider the remedy redundant.

3.7 Current debates

Ideas for research on these current discussion questions can be accessed on the companion website updates.

- Should forced marriage have been made the subject of a new criminal offence of forcing someone to marry?
- Is there a sufficient case for preserving the nullity jurisdiction?

---

53 For which see Chapter 5.
54 See Chapter 5 for these situations.
55 Law Commission Report 33 (1970).

3.8 Summary of Chapter 3
Nullity (MCA 1973 ss 11–13)

- Nullity has its origins in ecclesiastical law and approaches the marriage on the basis that it is an imperfect union and should therefore be annulled rather than dissolved.
- Voidable marriages are ended by a decree under the law of nullity: ss 11–13 of the MCA 1973.
- Nullity may be used either to secure a freestanding nullity decree or in the alternative in a divorce petition in cases of factual overlap.
- Voidable marriages (which are valid until annulled) must be distinguished from void marriages, which are void from the start and need no decree, though one may be desirable for various reasons.
- A voidable marriage will always need a decree to annul it.

Grounds for a nullity decree

- A marriage may be voidable for incapacity or wilful refusal to consummate, for lack of consent due to mistake, unsoundness of mind, duress, or other vitiating factor, and also on the statutory grounds of mental disorder, venereal disease or pregnancy by another man at the time of the ceremony.
- There are, however, bars to the grant of a decree: approbation (where it would be unfair for a decree to be granted), or where proceedings on one of the statutory grounds have not been instituted within three years, although there might be an extension of time if the petitioner was suffering from mental disorder within the meaning of the Mental Health Act 1983.
- There may also be formality defects pursuant to s 11 of the MCA 1973 (see Chapter 2).

Overlap with divorce

- There is some overlap with adultery and behaviour in the law of divorce.
- Undefended nullity is now available (after 6 April 2011) via the abbreviated paper procedure for obtaining divorces and a hearing is therefore no longer always necessary.
- Nullity may still appeal to persons with religious objections to divorce, and those who wish to leave forced marriages to which they considered they never validly consented.

3.9 Further reading

Gill, A and Anitha, S, 'The illusion of protection? An analysis of forced marriage protection and policy in the UK' (2009), *Journal of Social Welfare and Family Law* 31: 257.

Gaffney-Rhys, R, '*M v B, A and S (By the Official Solicitor)* – protecting vulnerable adults from being forced into marriage', [2006] CFLQ 295.

Proudman, C, 'The criminalisation of forced marriage', [2012] Fam Law 42: 460.

Robert, R. 'When we are married. Void, non-existent and presumed marriages', (2002) *Legal Studies* 22: 398.

Vallance-Webb, G, 'Forced Marriage: a yielding of the lips not the mind', [2008] Fam Law 565.

Forced Marriage: A Wrong not a Right (2005), Home Office and Foreign and Commonwealth Office.

Forced Marriage Unit, Foreign and Commonwealth Office, https://www.gov.uk/government/organisations/foreign-commonwealth-office

Chapter 4

Divorce: The Theoretical Background

Chapter contents

Learning outcomes for this chapter

A sound understanding of the background to modern divorce law and contemporary attempts at reform including:

(i) An awareness of the key concepts
(ii) An ability to analyse and debate the issues raised by the present divorce law which practically every commentator agrees is flawed, but of which there appears no immediate prospect of replacement other than by procedural change from a judicial to an administrative system process in the new unified Family Court.
(iii) An appreciation of the contribution of the practitioner in making the present 1970s legislation work through the professional philosophy of reducing confrontation between separating parties in relationship breakdown.

4.1 Introduction

This chapter takes an overview of English divorce law, and attempts to uncover the underlying theory of divorce in English law through its long history and development, leading to the contemporary attempts to reform it in line with whatever was current thought at the particular stages when contemporary opinion has progressed towards no-fault systems. Published views are both academic and practitioner generated (and through such research as we have, to some extent customer led).

There is hardly anyone, lawyer or layperson, who does not have a view as to what is required of a modern law of divorce. Contributors to this debate have included the leading family law academics (virtually unanimously finding fault with the proposed 1996 reforms) and a number of leading practitioners whose reports of the views of their clients provide much useful anecdotal evidence of public perception. Unfortunately it is unlikely that there will be any fundamental change in the statute for some time to come, as neither the policy makers, nor the government resources which would have to support such a fundamental change, appear to have either the will or, in present straitened times, the financial capacity to undertake such a task.

However, the one thing that is clear is that religion, and observant religious objection, is not the reason for long-standing failure to reform English divorce law so as to facilitate the consensual divorce that is explicitly available in other jurisdictions, since even an outline trace of the historical background shows no such influence.

Marriages have been dissolved as and when it was convenient since the Romans occupied Britain, with little attempt to conceal that the rationale for such an approach was the demands of contemporary culture: the Church merely found the way to do it, and that was not because of any religious reason but because the clerics were also the first English lawyers. It is thus another of the myths associated with marriage that the Church has been responsible for a restrictive approach to divorce; quite the opposite, the Church facilitated divorce for social reasons from earliest times, initiated research in the 1960s before the Law Commission and cooperated in their later work. It was the ill-informed tabloid press and public that ruined the chances of success of Part II of the **Family Law Act 1996**, albeit that it was a deeply flawed and impractical piece of legislation in any case, as pointed out (*inter alia* and most graphically by Cretney) at the time.

4.2 Origins of English divorce law and its impact on the underlying theory

Contrary to popular belief, English divorce law did not entirely originate in the ecclesiastical courts and, in relation to the original background of English law in this respect, religion as such does not appear to be the reason for the failure to update the current legislation, the **Matrimonial Causes Act (MCA) 1973**, which consolidated the fundamental reforms of 1969 and 1970. Rather it appears that social stability has been a key driver in decisions in modern times not to facilitate dissolution of marriages.

This was not always the case in the past. In the early Middle Ages – an age of superstition and extensive religious observance – divorce and remarriage was in fact *not* uncommon, since among the landed classes marriage was undertaken both for the purpose of obtaining, consolidating and protecting property and for providing heirs to it, and in particular for the personal protection of women in a violent society. A landed widow was thus seldom left unmarried for long and her marriage was often in the gift of the king, who could much favour one of his supporters by facilitating such a union, since all property in a marriage at that time belonged to the husband. Indeed this was the cause of the **Clandestine Marriages Act 1753**, requiring publicity for proposed marriages, since women were frequently forced into marriage by men who coveted their property, so there was a policy decision involved in requiring public formalities to attest to the consent of the bride.

In early times therefore, both Church and State recognised that marriages *could* be dissolved by what was known as divorce *a vinculo matrimonii* (literally 'from the chains of marriage'), permitting remarriage without undue fuss, and without any social or doctrinal disapproval. This medieval approach is the closest to the contemporary attitude of State and Church, i.e. that divorce is regrettable but, being a fact of life, not socially unacceptable and, even in the eyes of the more liberal clergy not now a total bar to remarriage in church.[1] That medieval attitude was probably a relic of the influence of the Roman Empire in which serial marriages and divorces were common and politically acceptable; suitable political and property alliances were regarded as essential to preserve both wealth – mostly in income-producing land and military resources at that time – and personal relationships.

It was only after the Church of Rome, basing its view of marriage on the Gospels, adopted the concept of the indissolubility of the marriage bond that the English ecclesiastical courts, in order to preserve something of their established dissolution facility, began to distinguish between validly contracted marriages and those which had had an impediment at formation upon which a fully dissolving decree could be based. Senior clerics were well suited to making these intellectual distinctions as in the early Middle Ages churchmen were essentially interdisciplinary, combining the work of the Church, the law and politics.

Thus when the stage was reached that marriage was regarded as indissoluble if correctly contracted, the only way of dissolving a valid marriage which the Church considered it could logically employ was by means of a decree of dissolution *a mensa et thoro* – literally translated as severing the physical links 'from the common table and home' shared by the spouses, and relieving them of a duty to live together, but *not* breaking the spiritual marriage tie, a result similar to a modern decree of judicial separation.

However, the concept of the invalid marriage still offered the opportunity of continuing the complete annulment which society was reluctant to discontinue, and the Church proceeded to exploit this, basically granting annulments (no doubt for valuable consideration according to the applicant's ability to pay) whenever pressed to do so in order to facilitate a new marriage, such as to permit the birth of a legitimate heir for an important landowner, or indeed the king himself. This was relatively easy at the time since in the Middle Ages the tables of kindred and affinity (relation-

---

1 For example the Scottish kirk at Crathie, near Balmoral, remarried the Princess Royal to her present husband, although this liberality is practised only by some individual clergy in the Church of England, where the practice is generally of a blessing following a civil remarriage (as in the case of her brother, the Prince of Wales) although there are some clergy who will actually marry a couple, one or both of whom are divorced.

ships by blood and marriage which prohibited intermarriage) were in any case much stricter than today and even included cousins up to the 'fourth degree'. There was a reason for that when the population was relatively tiny compared to today, with the result that genes did not get replenished and inbreeding occurred unless new bloodlines were introduced, although the Church could usually get round this cousin situation with a dispensation, especially if valuable property or political necessity was involved and the resources to engage their cooperation were available.

For example, on the cusp of the twelfth and thirteenth centuries an annulment was promptly effected without the slightest fuss for King John (the sovereign who in 1215 was forced by his Barons to grant Magna Carta, the 'Great Charter' of liberties of the people of England which is the origin of some of the most important principles of the common law, and of which the 800th anniversary falls in 2015). This annulment of his first marriage permitted John to marry again in the lifetime of his first (childless but wealthy) wife, who happened to be a first cousin to whom he had been married in his youth, since despite the fact that in the Middle Ages this was considered far too close a relationship in the table of kindred and affinity for validity, her wealth was more important at the time, when being the youngest of a large family he was so short of lands that had been shared out amongst his older siblings that he was known for years as 'John Lackland'.

An annulment in the changed circumstances in that particular case also avoided a second civil war within living memory (such as had already occurred on the previous occasion some seventy years before when there had been no direct legitimate heir to his great-grandfather, King Henry I, who had left only a single surviving legitimate daughter, a lady who was not only not particularly popular but also an unsuitable sovereign in those lawless times, which required a strong man who could lead an army and inspire his subjects to join it to fight their king's quarrels, always much more important in fact than any religious principles).

In the circumstances of his own annulment so as to remarry and acquire a male heir once he was king, John was thus instantly able to rely on the technical defect in his first marriage which had been contracted when he was an unimportant youngest son, whom no one had ever thought of as likely to be needed as King of England, owing to his having at that time three healthy elder brothers – obviously all dead and childless by the time he succeeded the last surviving brother in 1199, a situation the exigencies of which the Church of the time understood perfectly.

Thus until the Reformation the law of divorce and nullity was flexibly applied in a manner not unlike the way it is today, since the lawyers of that time (then mostly clerics, since they were the only people who could read and write, and were therefore adept at manipulating religious as well as legal concepts to suit the social context) quite openly interpreted the law to suit the circumstances when the social context demanded.

Similarly, in our own time the same practicality is revealed by a cursory examination of the case law which very soon after it was enacted promptly built up over the application of the MCA 1973 s 1(2) (a) and (b) in relation to the use of 'mild' behaviour or adultery to deliver the consensual divorce which was not articulated in the Act,[2] indicating precisely the same approach on the part of our contemporary legal profession when the divorce explosion of the 1970s and early 1980s gathered momentum[3] so that the profession had to make use of the law with which they had to work to deliver the results that their clients wanted.

There thus appears no ground for any claim that the law of divorce cannot be reformed owing either to religious reasons or because tradition is not compatible with the no-fault divorce which is available in other jurisdictions, since fault appears to have little to do with contemporary (unreformed) divorce in English law as it is applied at present or with its similar history in the past.

---

2 See Chapter 5.
3 For which see Chapter 5.

4.2.1 Sixteenth-century restrictive developments

However, while divorce and nullity in the Middle Ages worked extremely well until the Reformation, there then began several hundred years of complications which, while some progress was made in the ninteenth century with the enactment of the first MCA 1857, continued in one way or another up to the 1969 reform – regarded at the time as a great watershed, but which more than forty years on has still left us with a divorce law which has been plagued, whenever reform looked promising, by unnecessary references to the indissoluble nature of marriage, despite the tacit acknowledgement that few in the indigenous English population are in fact particularly religious. Traditional they may be, and interested in preserving the culture of the married family with children which is thought by some to be the essential building block of society, but falling numbers in attendance at the broad spectrum of Christian churches and rising cohabitation indicate that what the indigenous inhabitants of England and Wales are not is overtly religious; any notable religious observance appears to be the noted characteristic of the immigrant minority ethnic communities which have settled in the UK.

The fact that England and Wales has lagged behind other Western jurisdictions in reforming its divorce law into twenty-first-century mould is probably down to the consequences of a sharp reverse of a culture of dissolving marriages when socially necessary following the scandal of King Henry VIII's abortive, and severely bungled, attempts over several years from the 1520s to 1533 at undoing his marriage to his first wife, Catherine of Aragon, during which he tried both nullity and divorce, and in both attempts ultimately failed abysmally, both doctrinally and in practice, thus obliging him to take the extreme step of seceding from the Catholic Church, with the result that he could then require his ministers to grant his own religious and civil divorce.

However, especially as this coincided with an upheaval in religious thought arriving with extreme Protestantism from the continent, it was probably Henry's messy matrimonial history which was responsible for creating the cultural reverse which basically lasted until the mid-nineteenth century, and which in turn has slowed down the development of divorce law ever since, so that in the early twenty-first century there are muddled issues which are still not properly resolved.

Whether or not this was because the subsequent attacks by the King and his ministers on the Church for its corrupt practices (thus enabling Henry and his ministers to justify the dissolution of the monasteries and repression of the Church for its vices, which no doubt included their liberal attitude to dissolution of inconvenient marriages, especially where that service contributed to its riches) this was a pity since at the time that that particular divorce saga began in the 1520s the resulting muddle over the King's divorce was really unnecessary.

This was because the English Church (although up to the 1530s still the Church of Rome in England as elsewhere in Christendom) was not even in the habit of referring its systematic annulments to Rome, but of quietly proceeding to grant them itself, and it had duly developed for the purpose the clever concept and separate remedy of nullity, which was the sure solution for any marriages which could be said either not to have been validly contracted, and/or not consummated – consummation being a condition of validity which has survived into the MCA 1973, as it was initially perceived that a Christian marriage must be consummated, since this was important in an era when legitimate heirs were a priority in order to ensure the reliable transmission of property from generation to generation, and thus a childless union might be a far-reaching disaster. This system was working perfectly for most people in the higher echelons of society, where it mattered because of the dynastic and property considerations, as such convenient annulments therefore enabled unsatisfactory marriages to be declared void from the start, thus permitting the parties to remarry from a single (not divorced) state, since they had technically never been married before.

From this practical origin was developed the English law of nullity which is still available today, and which has enjoyed a recent renaissance owing to the requirements, in a multicultural society poised between old and new worlds, of a modern class of applicants whose philosophies and needs dictate that if a traditional arranged marriage fixed up by their elders does not work out they would vastly prefer that no marriage had been contracted, rather than that an existing one should be dissolved by divorce; the only difference being that today the usual reason is not failure to consummate (indeed in same-sex marriage no consummation is required) but lack of appropriate consent.[4]

Based on this doctrinal approach, annulment is thus now relatively easy again nowadays and does no violence to the underlying theory of marriage in English law, as was precisely the case in the Middle Ages, though for different reasons, since the widespread influence of the medieval Church meant that apparently strict religious doctrines could, and should, be put to practical use in rearranging unwanted matrimonial relationships on social grounds.

4.2.2 From liberal annulments to problematic divorce

The usual method of finding marriages invalid up to the early sixteenth century was progressively to narrow the table of kindred and affinity so that only those less closely related than third cousins could marry. Any closer relationship was an impediment, as were even spiritual relationships of religious rather than matrimonial affinity: thus standing as godparent to a child or children would place the godparent in a close family relationship with the child's parents. In appropriate cases a dispensation could nevertheless be provided in any case of such affinity, whether either actual or spiritual, but if no prior dispensation had materialised (or been requested – and sometimes dispensations even when granted were deliberately not immediately followed up in case the marriage might need to be abandoned if it became politically inconvenient) this facilitated the instant invalidity which could found the decree to free the parties who wished to leave a marriage, and to marry again as single persons. As marriage was essentially a contract even an engagement to marry could prove an impediment to a subsequent marriage, thus providing another fertile ground for annulment of a subsequent union. Accordingly King Henry VIII had the most unfortunate bad luck both in his lawyers and in the political issues of the time, which were complicated by religious factions but were in fact about power in Europe, which at the time was in effect the world.

Like King John 200 years before, Henry (or rather his Cardinal Archbishop Thomas Wolsey and Secretary of State Thomas Cromwell, on his behalf) at first went confidently for a decree on the usual ground of consanguinity, as Queen Catherine was in any event a cousin 'within the fourth degree' since, although she was Spanish, both he and she were directly descended through six generations from a son of the English King Edward III, and this too close relationship was compounded by the fact that they were also brother- and sister-in-law (as she had been first married to his deceased elder brother). A dispensation had in fact been sought from the Pope for their marriage although there was some anecdotal evidence that they had not waited for the document to arrive before hastily marrying in 1509 in her favourite church in London when he succeeded to the throne on the death of his father.

However, this was where the formerly cooperative and liberal stance of the English Church failed the King and embarked English law on a long period of restrictive divorce only eventually ended in the twentieth century. The reason for this change was probably partly the impact of the more extreme Protestant ideas from Europe, which were causing their own upheaval, but also because Henry, instead of sticking to a simple annulment on the routine ground of consanguinity, then unwisely embroidered his case with further religious arguments, which seem to have been what involved Rome. This was a pity as it seems to have been Henry's inept mismanagement of this

---

4 See Chapter 3 for the contemporary nullity syndrome.

uncoupling from Catherine which was responsible for the following 300 years of problems in developing a suitable law of divorce to replace the liberal medieval practice. It also seems to have been the root of other subsequent problems too, which was unfortunate especially as Henry, like King John before him, actually needed a new wife to provide a male heir, since while by his existing marriage he had had several children only a daughter had survived; so that another civil war beckoned if a new and fertile marriage could not be achieved, a possibility which was of course regarded as catastrophic because the entire previous century had been spent by rival kings and their factions fighting through several decades in the Wars of the Roses, decimating the nobility and causing chaos in the country.

If the King's case had stopped where it started with consanguinity and continued into a quiet annulment by the English Church without involving the Pope (and other powerful European Catholic factions) all might have been well. Unfortunately, the obstacle which the two royal advisers overlooked when setting out to annul that King's marriage was that in King Henry's case he had introduced a major dispute of fact, which led to a long-running theological problem (known at the time as 'the King's Great Matter') and ultimately resulting in the English Church's break with the Pope in Rome, so that Henry could install himself as Head of the Church in England and grant himself his own decree, since the Pope declined to do so.

The dispute of fact concerned the additional claim by the King and his ministers that his wife, Queen Catherine, having previously been legally married to the King's deceased elder brother, Arthur, Prince of Wales, and the marriage having been consummated, was not only a cousin within the prohibited degrees of kindred and affinity, but also too closely related to contract a valid marriage with King Henry, particularly since he also relied on Biblical texts in the Book of Leviticus forbidding such a marriage.

This, however, gave the Queen the opportunity to ridicule this claim and also to insist that it was not true, because she and her first husband had in fact *not* consummated the marriage (so that *that* marriage could in fact have been annulled had the Prince not died), a version from which she was immoveable. Moreover she did not recognise the relevance of the Biblical authority on which the King relied – a proposition with which the Pope agreed, as did the Queen's nephew, the King of Spain and Holy Roman Emperor, who enforced his belief with an army surrounding the Papal States. Worse, in this case the Papal Bull of dispensation for their marriage was in fact still in existence, and although it had not been delivered at the time of the marriage it permitted, had not been lost and is in fact still available to researchers today. Further, with the army of the Queen's nephew (the most powerful sovereign in Europe) besieging the Papal dominions in Italy the Pope was not likely to change his mind whatever the King of England chose to do in his own territory. Thus there was a messy incident of the sort that today would have been on the front pages of the tabloid press for weeks.

In modern terms this might be said to have been very poor crisis management leading to long-term ill effects, which had it been better handled might have been avoided: if the English Church had simply quietly annulled the marriage as was their custom at that time, without involving the Pope, thereupon allowing the King to marry as a single man, when (owing to the law and practice of primogeniture) any son of a subsequent marriage would clearly have taken preference in succeeding his father over an elder sister, as indeed eventually occurred in the order in which King Henry's children succeeded to the throne – but as things were done, after much bloodshed and upheaval.

Thus this early high-profile defended nullity case inaugurated a period of several hundred years during which divorce, and even nullity, from having been fairly freely available, immediately became extremely difficult, even for the nobility who were in a position to make the Church's cooperation financially worth their while, and also expensive, since following the scandals of King Henry's reign which eventually involved six marriages, three more divorces and two wives executed for adultery, divorce was often not readily available even for the great landowners, who were obliged to rely on annulment or remain married, since despite the increased absorption of Protestant doctrines from the Reformation on the continent, the Church of England was not only not minded to extend divorce, but rather also to restrict access to the former ecclesiastical remedy of nullity.

4.2.3 Seventeenth- and eighteenth-century stalemates

In the seventeenth and early eighteenth centuries, therefore, a parliamentary method of divorce *a vinculo matrimonii* by private Act of Parliament was developed which enabled the aristocracy, which needed heirs to their estates, to end marriages which were infertile or otherwise inconvenient. In practice, at least at first, this was available only to men. For example, the Duke of Norfolk obtained such a divorce, petitioning the House of Lords for a Bill of divorce in 1701 on the grounds of his wife's adultery, and his lack of an heir. Later Parliament allowed wealthy business and professional men (including clergymen) to avail themselves of this remedy for their domestic problems.

The method (which was expensive, involving an Act of Parliament and having to rely on adultery which had to be provable, unlike today when the parties often agree who shall admit it in the routine court documents) was to obtain a divorce *a mensa et thoro* from the ecclesiastical courts, then to sue the wife's co-adulterer for 'criminal conversation', prior to petitioning and attending the House for cross-examination over whether the petitioner had connived at or colluded with the adultery, or partially or wholly caused it by living apart from his wife. It was hardly a popular service: only 317 divorces were thus obtained between 1714 and 1857. From this came the hugely complex pre-1969 law of divorce which was only ended with the **Divorce Reform Act 1969**, much of which must be laid at the door of restrictive Victorian morality and social practices (although hardly religion, as Victorian society was traditional not pious).

Nevertheless, reform was needed even for men, as was shown by the case of R v Hall (1845),[5] in which Mr Hall, a poor working man, was indicted for bigamy, which it was perfectly true he had committed since he could not afford to obtain a divorce prior to remarrying. His original wife had both committed adultery and deserted him, after having made their married life a misery with her drunkenness and dissipation – mitigation which the judge dismissed as 'irrational excuses', adding that the fact that Hall was a poor working man who could not afford the parliamentary procedure was 'not the fault of the law', which was 'impartial', making 'no difference between rich and poor'! Happily, the sentence was no more than Hall had already passed in jail, so he was released immediately. None of this background indicated a religious origin for any theory of indissolubility of marriage which should indicate any difficulty in dissolving marriages by consent today.

4.3 The Matrimonial Causes Act 1857: divorce and judicial separation

The nineteenth- and early twentieth-century pattern of divorce does not disclose any particular adherence to religious principles which need inhibit reform at the present time; rather the Victorians made a moral issue of dissolution of marriage, on social grounds, since their legislation shows the inferior position of women in marriage as in all other respects in that century, not that there was any particular aversion to divorce for religious reasons. Following Lord Campbell's Royal Commission of 1850, the **Matrimonial Causes Act (MCA) 1857** transferred the existing divorce

5 (1845) 1 Cox 231.

and matrimonial jurisdictions from Parliament and the ecclesiastical courts to a new court, the Court for Divorce and Matrimonial Causes, which assumed responsibility for all decrees of divorce and nullity and renamed the decree *a mensa et thoro* as 'judicial separation' (JS), a decree which is also still available today[6] in much the same form, although this decree is now the one which is dying the natural death that was previously expected for nullity.

The grounds were not much changed: a husband could still present a petition on the basis of adultery only, whereas a wife also required some aggravating factor, such as incestuous adultery, cruelty, sodomy, bestiality or desertion for two years. Gladstone, who as a liberal reformer agreed in principle with the Act, was strongly against this gender distinction.

The Act made the process more accessible but did not vastly increase petitions compared to the previous processes (1857–61 saw 781 divorce petitions and 248 for JS). However, the magistrates entertained increasingly numerous applications for matrimonial maintenance and separation orders by poorer people (87,000 between 1897 and 1906). To this day the magistrates still do brisk business maintenance orders, which are obtainable without decree of divorce, nullity, JS or dissolution of civil partnership under the **Domestic Proceedings and Magistrates Courts Act 1978**, although they now do so in the unified Family Court as the former FPC has been subsumed into that court.[7] Although they have no power to grant separation orders as such their financial orders only operate if the parties are in fact not living together.

4.4 Early twentieth-century reform

In 1909 there was another Royal Commission, chaired by Lord Gorell, which recommended that the sexes should be placed on the same footing (implemented in **Lord Buckmaster's Act** in 1923). Decentralisation of divorce was also recommended so that local registries could provide cheaper access to justice for people of small means (implemented in 1946) and extending the grounds to include cruelty, habitual drunkenness and incurable insanity (implemented in the MCA 1937).

The watershed in divorce reform appears to have been World War II. Wives left behind at home to stand on their own feet became unwilling to remain in marriages where they were undervalued, but it was not until legal aid became available in 1949 that divorce was a serious alternative, since most women had no independent money: most matrimonial homes and investments were in the husband's name in the culture of the time. A Private Member's Bill in 1951 first proposed divorce after a period of separation (seven years was then suggested) instead of reliance on allegations of a matrimonial offence. This was a radical change which, especially when viewed in conjunction with the new legal aid, scared the government sufficiently for them to withdraw the Bill and to promise another Royal Commission.

This was the 1956 Morton Commission which, although the final report was not unanimous, recommended against change, largely ignoring the perjury that was frequently occasioned by the existing law, and the concerns about illicit unions and illegitimate children. This was backed up by the Church, which said that the doctrine of the matrimonial offence was in accordance with the New Testament and that any change would threaten society and the stability and structure of the family. Happily their stance is now much changed on this point so that it is difficult to see how any religious objection, which historically appears to have arrived very late on the scene, should now stand in the way of a no-fault divorce system, especially as even in the 1960s the Church was quick to reconsider, setting up a working group which reported in 1966.

---

6 See Chapter 5.
7 See Chapter 10.

The Archbishop of Canterbury's research group report, entitled *Putting Asunder — A Divorce Law for Contemporary Society*,[8] drew three main conclusions:

(1)   that the Church should cooperate with the State in recognising a secular divorce law, subject to protection of the weak and strengthening the law to support Christian marriage;
(2)   that the existing mix of fault-based and non-fault-based grounds (such as insanity) was inept; and
(3)   that the courts should inquire thoroughly into whether a marriage had broken down and, if so, dissolve it.

They also recommended that the basic ground for divorce should be irretrievable breakdown.

4.5 The Divorce Reform Act (DRA) 1969

Following the Archbishop's Group Report, the Law Commission undertook a thorough inquiry into divorce law. Its report was entitled *Reform of the Grounds of Divorce — The Field of Choice*[9] with a twin goal: to support marriages which had a chance of survival and to bury with decency and expedition those which were already dead 'with the minimum of embarrassment, humiliation and bitterness'. They were against the inquest into the marriage suggested by the Archbishop's Group, but accepted the concept of divorce after separation, two years with consent of the other party, and five or seven years, subject to safeguards, without.

The report was backed up by some assumptions about public opinion which have never been scientifically substantiated. They were apparently the results of contemporary research, and appear to have some foundation in contemporary experience of divorce, for example the lack of connection between the matrimonial fault relied on for the divorce and the actual breakdown of the marriage, such as in the treatment of adultery as a symptom rather than a cause of divorce, which may confidently be said to have generated Sir Roger Ormrod's approach to civilised divorce about which he wrote in the jointly authored text *Divorce Matters* (1987).[10]

The resulting cocktail of reforms — one sole ground for divorce of irretrievable breakdown evidenced by one of five facts, three fault-based and two based on simple separation, which was for the first time to be a basis of divorce — was enacted in the DRA 1969. This was subsequently consolidated with the **Matrimonial Proceedings and Property Act (MPPA) 1970** into the MCA 1973 which, as amended, still comprises the English law of divorce.

The subsequent **Family Law Act (FLA) 1996**, Part II of which was radically to reform the law again by removing virtually the entire 1973 system, was only ever implemented in respect of Parts I, III and IV, leaving the scheme of Part II to languish on the statute book without either repeal, amendment or practical introduction. The Lord Chancellor eventually confirmed that Part II had been abandoned and that (when a suitable opportunity arose) would be repealed, which has in fact only just been effected by the **Children and Families Act (CAFA) 2014**.

It was at the time anticipated that in due course some other reforms would be brought forward but there are at present no signs of any legislative progress in this direction, and it would seem that reform of the law of financial provision is much more urgent.[11]

---

8 Society for the Promotion of Christian Knowledge, 1966.
9 Cmnd 3123, 1966.
10 See further Chapter 5.
11 See further Chapter 7.

However, reform has been put back on the agenda by the Law Society and Resolution (still often known as the SFLA), the Parliamentary All Party Group (which, before recent discontinuance, was considering various issues in Family Law) and Baroness Ruth Deech's 2009 Gresham Lectures in the winter of 2009–10.

Nevertheless, the present position is that in England and Wales divorce law depends on the legislation and culture of over 40 years ago, albeit that professional pragmatism has made the system work so that in effect there is *already* a species of divorce by consent in force, notwithstanding that that analysis is incorrect in law, and is achieved by practical use of the statutory provision which bears no little resemblance to the legal fictions by which other areas of law were developed in the Middle Ages to create the law of contract and tort.[12]

This leads commentators to claim that the present law is hypocritical as (unless the parties want to wait for two or five years from the breakdown of the marriage) one party must take proceedings against the other on one of the fault bases in order to achieve the divorce by 'consent'; that as a divorce law it is inappropriate as it perpetuates the need for the parties to blame one another and for the respondent to desist from defending in order to achieve the decree; and that it is inaccurate as members of the lay public regularly incorrectly state – and obviously believe – that they have obtained a 'divorce by consent' when this process has only been achieved by the respondent taking the advice of his/her lawyers or other advisers not to defend, which is doctrinally a substantially different situation, but nevertheless achieves the same result – the end of the marriage.

4.6 Current initiatives

Resolution has a vested interest in promoting reform of divorce law, since the entire rationale of this organisation of around 6,000 Family Law solicitors is to promote less confrontation in family justice and more holistic agreement for the benefit of the family as a whole, including in divorce or other relationship dissolution. Thus reform of divorce law is central to their ongoing campaigns, details of which can be found on their website.[13] In principle, the Law Society Family Committee supports this view, and has long recommended that all solicitors, whether members of Resolution or not, should adopt their non-confrontational code, which is publically available on the Resolution website.

The thrust of Resolution's interest in reform of divorce law is that the present system is inevitably confrontational because it is part of the adversarial system of litigation embedded in the MCA 1973, itself (while a reform of earlier statutory bases) much influenced by the previous restrictive history of the nineteenth and early twentieth centuries, and thus inevitably requiring divorcing couples to base their applications for a decree on one of the three fault-based 'Facts' by which irretrievable breakdown can be proved, i.e. adultery, behaviour or desertion; only two of the five Facts depend on separation, either for two years with the consent of the respondent or five years without any need for such consent.

Other solicitors counter that, although the framework of the statute is adversarial, in practice divorce is on demand as the way in which the statute works is that the parties decide they want a divorce, they agree which Fact they will use and which spouse will be the petitioner (i.e. which will apply for the divorce), the details of the marital complaint relied on will be agreed by them or their respective solicitors and the court (which does not even require a hearing) will issue a decree in almost all cases on the basis of what the petition contains.

---

12 See Maitland, F, *Forms of Action at Common Law*, Cambridge, CUP, 1969.

13 www.resolution.org.uk

The parties will then contain any further arguments in the arenas of money and property (formerly known as 'ancillary relief' but re-designated 'financial provision' in the FPR 2010) and which is decided separately after the initial decree has been granted, and similarly in relation to disputes about childcare and contact issues. Others claim that while this may be so – i.e. because the profession has learned to live with an outdated statute – it is still hypocritical, and also unnecessarily expensive (as the fee for filing a divorce petition, even if no solicitor is used, has for some time been £340 and it is proposed to put it up to over £700 in order to make some money to fund other aspects of the family justice system).

A more radical view is that the fee should perhaps be reduced, to reflect that the divorce is in effect by consent, which is in reality the system in use except for the tiny minority of well under 1 per cent of all the actual applications for divorces which are ultimately defended, because all the costly arguments and bitterness are focused on the money and property and children disputes.

4.6.1 The Deech perspectives

Baroness Deech, a well-known Family Law academic, in her Gresham lectures in 2009–10 took a slightly different view. She deplored the divorce statistics (the highest in Europe) and rehearsed the adverse consequences[14] in terms of impact on health, education and families, the link between public and private morality and the conflicting demands on mothers which she clearly blamed for some or all of these adverse consequences. She pointed to the drop in the numbers of those getting married (231,000 in 2007, the lowest for 112 years) and the fact that 40 per cent of marriages are now ending in divorce (as opposed to only 60,000 at the end of World War II, 119,000 at the time of the enactment of the Divorce Reform Act in 1969 and 165,000 in 1993). She blamed this escalation on various contributory social factors – housing shortages, the age at which marriages take place, the numbers of more fragile remarriages – but also on the fact that divorce law is easier. For this she blames the 'quickie divorce', introduced in the 1970s by the special procedure, which still delivers decrees through the paper-based process, which means that obtaining the actual divorce decree is no more difficult than applying for any other bureaucratic document – and indeed easier than many.

Her focus on easier divorce law seems to support the view of those solicitors who routinely say that while the framework of the MCA 1973 is adversarial, the process in practice is that there is agreed divorce on demand with little disagreement or acrimony except in relation to the money, property and child-based disputes which follow.[15] This is despite the fact that around 85 per cent of all divorces are granted on the two fault-based facts of adultery and behaviour, which suggests that the contentions of those supporting earlier reforms were correct in their assessments (i.e. that adultery was seen as a symptom and not a cause of marriage breakdown, and no longer attracting social disapproval) that the 'mild behaviour' petition was the most civilised basis for divorce.[16]

Deech goes on to assess the cost of this scale of divorce at £20–40 billion in legal aid, welfare, extra housing, family courts, judges, lawyers, accountants, conciliators, illness from stress, children taken into care – and the failure of the child support schemes.[17] In relation to children alone she adds to the list of consequential catastrophes poorer educational attainment and employment

---

14 *Divorce – A Disaster?* September 2009, Gresham College; [2009] Fam Law 1048.
15 See the *Law Society Gazette* online correspondence, which may be accessed via the Law Society's website, www.lawsociety.org.uk.
16 The view of the late Lord Justice Ormrod, in Burgoyne, J, Ormrod, R and Richards, M, *Divorce Matters*, Harmondsworth, Penguin, 1987.
17 See Chapter 21.

outcome, drink, drugs, psychological harm, relationship breakdown and physical harm. She takes the view that there is no need to change the law in any complex or sophisticated way, as this would only push the divorce statistics up again, but does suggest that there should be a waiting period of twelve months from start to finish of the divorce process with a three-month cooling-off period after filing of the petition, as mediation and conciliation do not save marriages.

This does to some extent resonate with the extensive anecdotal evidence from those involved in divorce that although the marriage might have been unsatisfactory, the divorce process was worse. Deech takes this up with suggestions that legal aid in family matters should be preserved,[18] that education should be included at school about the impact of divorce on relationships, costs and parenting, there should be more help for women to be self-supporting through childcare and career advice, and a change of public and political attitudes is required.

Not long after this lecture Baroness Deech became Deputy Chair of the All Party Parliamentary Group on Family Law, which had been taking evidence on a number of current issues. Clearly one of their recommendations, if they had reported prior to discontinuance of their work, was likely to be whether or not there should be a fault-based system of divorce, what lessons are to be learned from the failure of the reforms in the 1996 Act and how reform might succeed in the future.

In the meantime, although it seems that all academics, practitioners and judges and a fair section of the public agree that the system needs change, we still retain the system devised in the late 1960s and consolidated in 1973.

4.6.2 Impact of the Family Justice Review

Into this unsatisfactory situation then came the Final Report of the Family Justice Review (FJR), published in November 2011.[19] At 4.16 the Report proposes that divorce (and the equivalent dissolution of civil partnership) should become an administrative, not judicial, process unless a case is defended, and that the new procedure be based on a Family Justice Service 'hub' with application made online and information obtained from the same single source which should also carry all necessary documentation for the new administrative process.

It is stated that respondents (e.g. the Citizens Advice Bureau) to the consultation 'generally supported these proposals'. It was also proposed in the Interim Report that the present two-stage process of an initial provisional decree ('decree nisi') followed shortly afterwards by the final decree permitting remarriage ('decree absolute')[20] should be abolished and only one such decree pronounced. This is not to be proceeded with, however. While it is unlikely that anyone would disagree with saving judicial time by transferring the present procedural framework before the District Judges (DJs) to an administrative process, there are actually sound juridical reasons for opposing a change in the two-stage dissolution process, because of the consequential impact of the change of status which a final divorce decree has (now in any case called a divorce 'order' in the new FPR 2010), because there are many instances in which the status of 'spouse' remains important until all future arrangements are finite, for example in relation to pensions[21] and also where a religious divorce is also required e.g. a *get* in the case of Jewish parties: see MCA 1973 s 10A. This proposal has therefore been dropped as a result of consultation responses from Resolution and the Board of Deputies of British Jews.

---

18 Recently, and since 2009, the government has proposed increasingly severe cuts in this field, and is in fact now relying on using more ADR: see the 2010 Green paper, *Support for All*, Norwich, The Stationery Office, 2010.

19 Published on behalf of the Review Panel by the Ministry of Justice, Department for Education and the Welsh Government. Available at https://www.gov.uk/government/uploads/system/uploads/attachment_data/file/217343/family-justice-review-final-report.pdf.

20 See below at 4.9.

21 See Chapter 7.

However, the Report recites that the Law Society makes clear that they are principally unhappy that 'the adversarial grounds [sic][22] for divorce' are not dealt with by the Report, and the Centre for Social Justice is similarly concerned because the review would fall 'short of the magnitude of change desired and required', but the Report records that these 'are important matters but outside our remit'.

4.7 Overview of the current law: the Matrimonial Causes Act 1973

While since the great watershed of 1969, and the consolidation of the 1969 and 1970 Acts in the **Matrimonial Causes Act (MCA) 1973**, there have been ongoing initiatives to continue the reform of contemporary divorce law, the last culminating in Part II of the FLA 1996,[23] most of which were never brought into force, the law of divorce in England and Wales remains in its time warp, albeit applied by the practising profession in a manner which serves the purposes of the divorcing public. This 'making do' is very much in the historical tradition of English law, which developed this method in the Middle Ages, when the rigid formulaic approach of the writs by which actions were started in those early times was simply circumvented by draughtsmen's adaptations, quickly known as 'legal fictions', to make them fit whatever legal process was required. In a sense, therefore, since this 'make do and mend' approach is in the long tradition of English law, the tardy executive and legislature which has not found time or resources to reform the law should be grateful for the ingenuity of the family practitioners who have made the existing adversarial law work to the advantage of the parties within the non-adversarial process proposed by Resolution. However, it does seem unfortunate that when a Family Justice Review was initially proposed a holistic approach was not taken so that contemporary divorce law could have been thoroughly updated.

4.8 The MCA 1973 in practice

Both the existing law and attempts to reform it are now firmly based on an acceptance by academics and practitioners alike that the legal resolution of marital problems is not conveniently achieved by a predominantly litigious approach, and this continues to lead to increasing reliance on dispute resolution, or N-CDR as now renamed by the President in his regular modernisation.

Even where a firm of solicitors consulted about or already involved in a divorce has no specialist family department, and the work is probably therefore undertaken by a non-specialist litigator, the Law Society's recommendation that all solicitors should observe the spirit of the Resolution Code of Practice (whether they are themselves personally members or not) should secure, for the conduct of the divorce and its ancillary issues, the contemporary non-litigious approach.

In the contemporary climate of mediation (which also influences funding for divorce and now virtually entirely replaces funding for obtaining the actual decree) it is curious to reflect that it is in fact only 30 years since the SFLA was founded for the precise purpose of encouraging a conscious change of gear from the usual approach of the civil litigator. Many family law practitioners do now join Resolution automatically upon commencing a family practice and some become further recognised as specialists under the Association's Specialist Accreditation Scheme. Moreover, it is impossible not to recognise the SFLA's contribution to the tailoring of the provisions

---

22 The term 'grounds' is incorrect. There is only one ground for divorce, irretrievable breakdown of marriage. The Report means to refer to the five Facts, one of which must be proved in order to establish irretrievable breakdown. See Chapter 6.

23 Now repealed by the Children and Families Act 2014, s 18.

of the MCA 1973 to the need for cooperation in shared parenting generated by the **Children Act (CA) 1989**, which has been a major catalyst in promoting the current trend towards greater cooperation between the parties to the actual divorce.

The Association was established with the aims of taking family matters as far as possible out of the atmosphere of contentious litigation and of achieving agreed solutions which, while not substantially different from what the court would order if the matter were acrimoniously contested, might with cooperation be achieved at less cost, emotionally as well as financially.

The CA 1989 gloss came later, since in the earlier 1980s that codification of Child Law was still only a gleam in the eye of the then Family Law Commissioner, now Baroness Hale of the Supreme Court.[24] Indeed, the research that generated the legislation which, in families with children, would permit the continued parenting role envisaged by the CA 1989 concept of parental responsibility (PR) was only beginning. This infrastructure was also built upon in reforms to divorce procedure, such as the Ancillary Relief Pilot Scheme, which was adopted nationally in June 2000 and is now the standard financial dispute resolution (DR) mechanism of the Family Court, but originally sought to end the previously very long-drawn-out and costly ancillary proceedings for financial relief which sometimes followed and much soured a relatively quick and easy divorce decree. The scheme also aimed to preclude the inevitable tactical moves resorted to in the past, by setting down a clear, precise system, under the control of the court, and making it difficult for the parties to manipulate it.

Nevertheless, even with a new name of 'financial provision' in the FPR 2010, these 'rogue' ancillary relief proceedings have remained stubbornly expensive, caused delays in obtaining a hearing date, and have other defects, such as constant changes of judge on adjourned hearings, so that other initiatives, such as collaborative law and the Chartered Institute of Arbitrators' Family Arbitrators' scheme, which became operational in February 2012, have stepped in, attempting to reduce costs more significantly and also to replace the stress of such court proceedings, since these schemes form a halfway house between the extremes of negotiated settlements and contested court proceedings.

While it is true that collaborative law has drawbacks[25] and an arbitrator also makes a determination (rather than facilitating a settlement, as solicitors and mediators do) the parties can at least choose their arbitrator, and participate in determining the arbitrator's terms of reference, besides much speeding up the process, which is capable of being completed in half the time the parties will otherwise often wait for a hearing date. However, further modernisation of the court and out-of-court processes is intended by the President, who has set up a working group to produce a new Money Arrangements Programme (MAP) similar to the new Child Arrangements Programme which has had to be designed following the enactment of the **Children and Families Act 2014** and the inauguration of the unified Family Court.

In theory these more cooperative initiatives should have been further assisted by the enactment of s 1 of the FLA 1996, which helpfully sets out in statutory form the objectives of contemporary divorce law; commentators might be forgiven for wondering whether there is in fact any connection at all, considering the defects in family justice in the years since 1996, but it is perhaps worth reproducing that section since it was meant to influence how divorce law developed:

---

24 Then Professor Brenda Hoggett.
25 See Chapter 6.

Part I

Principles of Parts II and III

The general principles underlying Parts II and III

The court and any person, in exercising functions under or in consequence of Parts II and III, shall have regard to the following general principles –

(a) that the institution of marriage is to be supported;

(b) that the parties to a marriage which may have broken down are to be encouraged to take all practicable steps, whether by marriage counselling or otherwise, to save the marriage;

(c) that a marriage which has irretrievably broken down and is being brought to an end should be brought to an end –

  (i) with minimum distress to the parties and to the children affected;

  (ii) with questions dealt with in a manner designed to promote as good a continuing relationship between the parties and any children affected as is possible in the circumstances; and

  (iii) without costs being unreasonably incurred in connection with the procedures to be followed in bringing the marriage to an end; and

(d) that any risk to one of the parties to a marriage, and to any children, of violence from the other party should, so far as reasonably practicable, be removed or diminished.

There is no new philosophy in this section, but its inclusion in a statute for the first time in 1996 was an innovation (since no such provision was included in the MCA 1973, although that Act was informed by much the same principles).

Thus the current divorce law is still based in the MCA 1973, as amended, although the practice which facilitates its contemporary application depends on the initiative of practitioners who have 'made do' with the existing law by interpreting the Act's provisions literally to serve the demands of contemporary society, as a comparison of current case law with its earlier equivalents will show. The academic student will sometimes make the point that this must be an abuse of the system; however, as procedure and practice is as valid an element of the law as the legislation which it administers, the better view is that the experienced practitioners who have made the MCA 1973 serve the purposes of the late twentieth and early twenty-first century have followed faithfully in the tradition of English legal history in using an existing remedy, with a useful twist here and there where necessary, rather than addressing deaf ears about a new one.

4.9 Terminology in divorce suits

To emphasise the difference between the law of divorce and the course of ordinary litigation, it should be noted that the procedural terminology is still distinct, despite some modernising when drafting the FPR 2010 (replacing much older terminology from 1969 and the former FPR 1991). This is partly due to the origins of divorce in ecclesiastical law, although the FLA 1996 would have changed the familiar vocabulary on the grounds that in modern times it is inappropriate and sends the wrong messages, possibly another mistake that added to that Act's unpopularity. Under the MCA 1973:

(a)   the parties have always been known as the petitioner and the respondent (not plaintiff and defendant, nor – following the reform of civil justice in the CPR – claimant and defendant);

(b)   the parties proceed by petition (not statement of claim, particulars of claim or even simply claim as under the CPR) but under the FPR 2010 a divorce is now applied for by an 'application' – although the form of application remains a petition, now in a form updated to contain more precisely the information required;[26] and

(c)   a party defending files an 'answer' and, where appropriate, cross-petition (not a defence and counterclaim).

The marriage is then ended by a divorce order which is still the old-fashioned 'decree', which comes in two parts: first 'decree nisi' (which decides in effect that the petitioner is entitled to the decree) and then (from six weeks after decree nisi) 'decree absolute', which finally ends the status of marriage. The courts having jurisdiction in divorce are also quite distinct. All divorces used to commence in a Divorce County Court (i.e. a county court designated to deal with such work, which not all county courts were) and were then tried there unless transferred to the High Court (**Matrimonial and Family Proceedings Act 1984**, ss 33 and 39). Now all applications are to the unified Family Court, which then decides, when applications are received, where within the Court they shall be allocated. At present petitions go to DJs and when there is a change to administrative divorce for undefended petitions this will presumably be to some other personnel in order to free up the DJs for genuine judicial work.

The primary source of the law of divorce is (and is likely to remain) the MCA 1973, as amended, and the main procedural source from 2011 the FPR 2010, as amended.

There are other primary sources – in particular those dealing with other aspects of family and divorce practice and procedure, and with special topics such as jurisdiction, occupation of the home, financial provision without dissolution of the marriage and child matters – but the basic working knowledge of divorce law and procedure which both the academic and vocational student require in order to understand how the substantive law works may be obtained from the MCA 1973 and the FPR 2010. The relevant parts of the Act are conveniently reproduced in the standard family law statute books and in the leading practitioner text, *Rayden and Jackson* (a large loose-leaf work often simply referred to as 'Rayden') and *The Family Court Practice* (known as the 'Red Book'). In *Rayden* or the Red Book will be found all the statutory material referred to (including the various rules of court) which is needed to understand how the divorce process has been adapted to accommodate both contemporary drivers towards agreed divorce and the black letter law.

4.10 Jurisdiction

Jurisdiction in divorce in England and Wales is governed by s 5 of the **Domicile and Matrimonial Proceedings Act (DMPA) 1973**, subject from 2003 to 'Brussels II bis', Council Regulation (EC) No 2201/2003, which amended Brussels II (i.e. the EU requirements of the **Brussels Convention of 1998 on Jurisdiction and the Recognition and Enforcement of Judgments in Matrimonial Matters** (No 1347/2000): Art 3 of the Council Regulation is designed to harmonise Member States' courts' jurisdiction for divorce, regulation of forum proceedings and international child arrangements across the EU States). It must be read in conjunction with the FPR 2010.

---

26 More fundamental change was made impossible at the FPR 2010 stage by the limitations of the current IT systems. Hence the 'application' still being a 'petition'. This might be a possible area for further reform as part of the switch to administrative undefended divorce.

This means that for divorce, judicial separation, and presumption of death and dissolution of the marriage, the court has jurisdiction under the Act if either of the parties is domiciled in England and Wales on the date when the proceedings are begun, or was habitually resident in England and Wales throughout the period of one year ending with that date, or at least the applicant is a national who has been resident for at least six months before the application for the decree was made. Thus s 8(2) of the DMPA 1973 was amended, giving the English or Welsh court jurisdiction if the court has jurisdiction under the Regulation and no other EU state has jurisdiction. But if another EU State is involved, at least six months' residence in England and Wales is now required and, if proceedings are also started in another State, the first in date will establish the forum for the suit. This may be of some importance since the approach to financial provision is markedly different in the various States of the EU, both from that in England and Wales and also often from one another. In general terms, most States use the approach of 'community of property', which is unknown to English law. Thus the selection of a sympathetic jurisdiction will be uppermost in the minds of any couples with cross-border affiliations.

In practice there has in the past rarely been any difficulty if a petitioner wished to obtain a divorce in England and Wales, and we may perhaps expect to see much more forum shopping in the future as England, with its discretionary jurisdiction in financial provision,[27] is an attractive location for divorce – as was demonstrated to achieve advantage to the husband in *Dart v Dart* (1996)[28] where he expressly moved the family to England to establish sufficient residence, in order to evade the 'wife-friendly' community property jurisdiction of the US State of Michigan.

The basic concept of the DMPA 1973 is that jurisdiction should be based on domicile (of origin, choice or dependence). A detailed study of domicile is beyond the scope of this book, but the basic concept, which must be grasped in order to understand the alternative roles of domicile and habitual residence, is that to establish domicile requires the existence of a physical presence in a country together with a degree of settlement and without looking forward to any alternative permanent home: *Plummer v IRC* (1988)[29] – although once this is established the country in question may be left for visits elsewhere provided there is an intention to return. Residence, on the other hand, which also requires a physical presence (although visits elsewhere may still be made), only requires a more limited settled purpose, e.g. for education (*Kapur v Kapur* (1985))[30], although the House of Lords has confirmed that for residence to become 'habitual' it must last for an appreciable period[31] (and in the case of the MCA 1973 that is expressly stated to be for one year). 'Habitually resident' normally means the same as 'ordinarily resident'.

Domicile must be distinguished from nationality, which is irrelevant to divorce law. If domicile is relied on for jurisdiction, that may be domicile of origin, domicile of choice or domicile of dependence. Domicile of origin means that the party to the divorce was born to a parent or parents having domicile in England and Wales and has not changed that domicile since attaining majority; it should be noted that the *place* of birth is irrelevant if a person was born to such parents with domicile in England and Wales. Domicile of choice may be acquired by an adult deciding to change a domicile of origin by leaving that jurisdiction and taking up a domicile elsewhere. Domicile of dependence means that the party is a person under the age of majority who will automatically have the same domicile as the parent or parents on whom dependence is presumed until the age of majority. Thus, if the father of a legitimate child or the mother of a child born outside wedlock

---

27 See Chapter 7.
28 [1996] 2 FLR 286, CA.
29 [1988] 1 All ER 27.
30 [1985] 15 Fam Law 22.
31 See *Mark v Mark* [2004] 1 FLR 1069, [2008] UKHL 42 where the petitioner was an 'overstayer' in immigration terms but both the CA and HL confirmed that she could still be domiciled and resident for the purposes of the Article and for Art 6 of the EU Convention on Human Rights.

changes his or her domicile of origin, and acquires a domicile of choice, that domicile of choice will at the same time change the domicile of the dependent child. At majority the child will take the domicile of dependence as a domicile of choice until he or she changes it again by moving elsewhere.

4.11 The first year of marriage: the absolute ban on divorce

4.11.1 First year of marriage and the ban on petitioning during that period: MCA 1973 s 3

It is not possible to *petition for divorce* during the first year after the celebration of the marriage: MCA 1973, s 3(1), inserted by the **Matrimonial and Family Proceedings Act (MFPA) 1984**, s 1. The purpose of this is, of course, the policy of supporting marriage by discouraging any early decision to divorce before the marriage has had a chance to settle down. It seems unlikely that this would be changed if any amendments are made to the Act as a result of the transfer to administrative undefended divorce.

This one-year bar on starting divorce proceedings is now an absolute bar to which there are no exceptions, although when the Act was passed in 1973 there was originally an absolute bar of one year and a further discretionary bar of three years which could be displaced on the facts by suitable circumstances. The remaining absolute bar still applies even where early presentation of the petition is inadvertent.

> ❖ **CASE EXAMPLE**
>
> In *Butler v Butler* (1990)[32] the contravention of the s 3 rule occurred where the petition was originally presented (quite properly within the first year of marriage) for JS (which required no one-year wait to petition), not divorce (to which s 3 applied), and only later *amended* for divorce. This proved fatal, since the date of *presentation* of the amended petition was technically that of the original petition for judicial separation, and there was no remedy but to present a new one. The absolute bar during the first year is intended to encourage the newly married who regret the step to give the marriage a chance before seeking dissolution.

4.11.2 Absence of practical impact of s 3

This ban has never had any practical importance: see 4.12.8 below.

4.12 Alternatives during the first year

There are, however, a number of other options open to the petitioner who dislikes s 3, although with the exception of obtaining a nullity decree none will permit remarriage, which realistically is what the would-be petitioner probably wants when considering divorce, even though there may be

---

32 [1990] Fam Law 21.

no potential new spouse yet in view. Often, though, a potential petitioner merely wants a finite dissolution of the existing marriage so that new attachments may be formed with a clear conscience and with the bad experience firmly in the past. In these circumstances the law provides various possibilities that can utilise what scope there is for putting the reluctant spouse's affairs in order in a sensible manner while waiting to petition for divorce.

Because it would probably be foolish for most spouses with one failed marriage behind them to be in a position to contract another before the first anniversary has been reached, the year's wait is not in practice much of a drawback. Practitioners therefore tend to concentrate on pointing out to their clients the various alternatives available, some of which may apply in a particular case, and on either taking emergency or temporary action where appropriate or else in disposing in the intervening year of the 'baggage' which it will be undesirable to take into any new relationship (particularly as statistics show that many second and subsequent marriages fail because of unfinished business of one sort or another left over from the previous one). If, however, some legal step, rather than a temporary practical solution, is insisted upon by the disappointed spouse, the law can assist in the ways set out at 4.12.1 to 4.12.8, below.

4.12.1 Alternative decrees: judicial separation or nullity

It often comes as a surprise to non-lawyers to learn that divorce is not the only decree available, and that the alternatives of JS (MCA 1973, s 17) or nullity (MCA 1973, ss 11 and 12[33] may be applicable. Either of these decrees may be applied for if appropriate within days of the marriage ceremony, and in the case of nullity a lengthy delay in presenting a petition can even be fatal.

A detailed knowledge of these alternative decrees is often outside the scope of the average family law undergraduate syllabus, but all students should be aware of their usefulness for those who oppose divorce on religious grounds,[34] or for whom it is important to achieve a formal break with a spouse where dissolution of the marriage by divorce is temporarily either:

- not possible (owing to s 3); or
- not advisable even when the initial year is up;

for example owing to an unresolved property dispute affected by the termination of the status of marriage, such as where steps must be taken to retain the spouse's rights under a pension scheme.

A student should therefore be aware of the existence and basic principles of the law of nullity and JS so as to be able to judge whether either of these alternative decrees might be suitable in an appropriate situation. Recent concern about the continued practice of forced (as opposed to consensual arranged) marriages in some ethnic communities has expressly highlighted the contemporary relevance of nullity, which had recently suffered a drop in popularity owing to the decline of religious objection to divorce and ease of obtaining a divorce decree under the MCA 1973.

4.12.2 Judicial separation

A decree of *judicial separation* (JS) can be obtained on the same facts as divorce save that it is not necessary to prove irretrievable breakdown of the marriage.[35]

---

33 For which see Chapter 3.

34 Common in ethnic minority communities since, for example, some Indian religions thoroughly disapprove of divorce. There is a diaspora of five million Indians resident in England and Wales.

35 See Chapter 5.

This may in particular satisfy the new spouse who wants to achieve a formal break in a situation where the marriage has obviously ended for all practical purposes but divorce is not yet possible. A further advantage is that such a decree records the separation, which can later be used for a divorce when the year is up (i.e. it preserves the evidence). However, JS is not to be recommended where the real objective is remarriage since it will inevitably cost the same as a divorce to obtain and by the time it is obtained it is likely to be time to petition for divorce.

Judicial separation used to be popular in cases where it was desired to preserve the status of marriage while permitting the parties officially to abandon the state of consortium which usually defines the 'normal' marriage. This might be, for example, where it was not possible fairly to compensate for the loss of pension rights by 'earmarking' under the **Pensions Act 1995**, or by variation of settlement on the lines of that adopted in *Brooks v Brooks* (1996),[36] and no other form of compensation (e.g. a lump sum or increased share of the matrimonial home) was possible. However, now that pensions can be shared by pension attachment under the **Welfare Reform and Pensions Act 1999**, also known as 'splitting', this use of JS is likely to decline, and it may be that it will die a natural death as nullity was once predicted to do.

4.12.3 Nullity

A decree of *nullity* can be obtained where the marriage is either *void* or *voidable*.[37] A decree of nullity in respect of a *void* marriage can always be obtained on proof of the relevant fact on the basis of:

- defective formalities;
- one of the parties already being married; or
- its polygamous nature, provided one of the parties is domiciled in England and Wales.

Following enactment of the **Marriage (Same-Sex Couples) Act 2013** the couple may be either male and female or two parties of the same sex. Transsexuals who have a gender recognition certificate can also marry in their new gender following the **Gender Recognition Act 2004**, so there is now no scope for gender mismatch making a marriage void.

There is no time limit for petitioning on any of these grounds since the marriage is void anyway, and strictly no declaration to that effect is actually necessary for it to be regarded as void. A void marriage can *never* be valid *whatever* the parties wish. Sometimes, however, an actual declaration is required, for example, by trustees of a settlement, who may wish to know whether to treat a marriage as void or voidable. Therefore, if any of the grounds apply which make a marriage void, the sooner a petition is presented the better, so that the true status of the marriage may be formally recognised.

Where the marriage is *voidable*, a petition sometimes needs to be presented within three years of the marriage, and even if that time limit does not apply, a delay in petitioning might give rise to the defence of approbation of the marriage – that is, that the petitioner acted as though he or she were willing to honour the marriage regardless of the fact that it could be annulled.

Where a marriage is voidable it is too late to dissolve it after the death of one of the parties. The marriage will have subsisted as a valid marriage until death and will therefore at that stage have been dissolved by death, upon which the surviving partner will have the status of a widow or widower in the normal way.

---

36 [1996] AC 375; [1995] 3 All ER 257, HL.
37 See Chapter 3.

4.12.4 Separation agreements

Some non-lawyers are surprised to discover that a decree is not essential to effect a formal separation and that a separation agreement can deal formally with all matters over which a court has jurisdiction without the necessity of going to court, save only for ultimately dissolving the marriage when the parties are finally ready and able to seek a divorce.

Separation agreements have the added advantage over court proceedings that it is possible with very few limits to insert into them virtually any provisions which the parties desire, although care needs to be taken to remember that financial arrangements may have a subsequent influence on provision which the court may order on dissolution of marriage.[38]

It is of course open to the parties merely to separate, by informal mutual agreement or by the unilateral decision of one of them, without either decree or formal separation agreement, save only that if one leaves the other without just cause they will technically be in desertion and might ultimately be divorced for it.[39] However, if any amendments are to be made to the MCA 1973 in association with the transfer to administrative undefended divorce, the Fact of desertion might be a candidate either for deletion or significant amendment, since it is little used owing to its complexity.

4.12.5 Sources of funds

If the real reason behind consideration of a divorce is because the breakdown of the marriage has caused financial problems, there are three possible sources of funds without the need to petition for any decree whatsoever (four if the parties have children):

- DPMCA 1978 ss 2, 6 and 7;[40]
- MCA 1973 s 27;[41]
- welfare benefit advice;[42] and, if the parties have children,
- the Child Maintenance Service (CMS).[43]

Alternatively, it might be possible to negotiate voluntary payments from the other spouse. Much will depend on the reason for the marital breakdown and on whether the separation was consensual.

4.12.6 CA 1989 proceedings

Very often the catalyst bringing a prospective petitioner to a consideration of divorce is a problem about the children. In this case a freestanding application is now brought exclusively under the CA 1989, without taking any proceedings in relation to the *marriage* as such. The whole concept of the Act was to take child matters out of divorce, and to treat the children of married and unmarried parents in substantially the same way; however, to underline the separation between the CA 1989 (dealing with children) and the MCA 1973 (dealing with divorce) with a view to preserving the concept of PR for all parents regardless of their marital status, the MCA 1973 s 41 has been repealed by CAFA 2014, as a result of which no post-divorce arrangements for the children will now be

---

38 See Chapter 6.
39 See Chapter 5.
40 See Chapter 10.
41 See Chapter 10.
42 See Chapter 10.
43 See Chapter 21.

considered with a petition; CAFA 2014 also abolished the former residence and contact orders, replacing them with a new-style Child Arrangements Order (CAO). Depending on the nature of the issue, possibly other orders under s 8 CA 1989 may be appropriate.[44]

4.12.7 Injunction orders and declarations

Similarly an act of violence or a dispute over occupation may be the immediate reason a prospective petitioner has thought of divorce.

The law in this area has now long been consolidated in the FLA 1996 Part IV, which provides for a simple regime of non-molestation and occupation orders to replace the formerly variegated terminology and substance of the preceding law.[45] The courts (both High Court and county courts) also have inherent powers to grant injunction orders ancillary to any suit before them so that such orders can be granted ancillary to divorce, wardship or CA 1989 proceedings, and if such proceedings are already on foot it might be expected that any injunction would be ancillary to the proceedings in question. However, if the case falls within Part IV this is normally the preferred route in which to seek such protection.

4.12.8 The nil practical impact of the MCA 1973 s 3

As the absolute bar imposed by s 3 only affects presentation of a divorce petition for the relatively short period of one year from the celebration of the marriage, it is generally considered that it is more cost-effective to prepare such a petition to file as soon as possible rather than to waste time and money obtaining a temporary decree of JS which will ultimately need to be superseded by one for divorce in order to leave the petitioner free to remarry. This is different from the position in some other jurisdictions, including in Europe, in some of which it is essential to be officially separated first before a divorce can be commenced. The suggestion in England and Wales therefore tends to be:

● making use of any of the remedies described at 4.12.1 to 4.12.7 above which suit their client's circumstances; and to concentrate on such practical matters as:

    ○ money to live on;
    ○ somewhere suitable to live; and
    ○ absence of any harassment, interference or violence from the other spouse.

It should be noted that a petition for divorce on the basis of either adultery or behaviour[46] can be presented one year and a day after the ceremony, regardless of how early in the marriage the matters relied upon occurred, as the statute places the ban on *petitioning*, not on reliance on the actual conduct which needs to be shown in order to obtain a decree, which is in no way limited by s 1(2). Moreover, the statute makes it explicit that the ban is on actually petitioning during the first year of marriage, and that any matters occurring during that year may still be relied on as the substance of the petition: see MCA 1973 s 3(2).

---

44 For all of which see Chapter 16.
45 See Chapter 11.
46 See Chapter 5.

4.13 The relationship between divorce, financial and child proceedings

It will be clear from the above overview of the modern law of divorce that in the past 40 years the post-DRA 1969 regime has been developed to provide a framework of divorce and related law which can dissolve or annul marriages, or issue decrees of JS as appropriate, and also decide or formalise all consequent financial matters completely independently of the issues concerning children and other domestic disruption not necessarily requiring divorce.

The related statutes – the CA 1989 and the the FLA 1996 Pt IV – can deal on an entirely free-standing basis with matters concerning the children of a marriage and/or with domestic violence and occupational rights in the home. It is important that students understand at an early stage that these jurisdictions are separate, and that although there are special provisions within both the 1989 and the 1996 Acts relating to the married as distinguished from the unmarried, these two latter statutes are designed to cater overall for both the married and the unmarried in a comprehensive framework.

Now that s 41 MCA 1973 has been repealed by the CAFA 2014 s 17, there are no restrictions on dissolution of either a marriage or a civil partnership which have any connection with the children of the family. This was presumably enacted in preparation for administrative undefended divorce since it completely effects the separation of divorce and dissolution from the child matters to which the DJ considering whether to certify a case for issue of a divorce or dissolution order before April 2014 would have had to give consideration, but which would have been an unsuitable task for administrative staff not of judicial rank.

Thus, family law seems to be moving consciously away from the concept of the married family as the core unit of society. In effect, there is now a corpus of divorce law (for the married), a law of children (with parents of either status) and a domestic violence law (applying not only to the married and the unmarried but to a much wider class of 'associated persons' whose original connection with one another is through a concept of extended family of the most informal type).

The next chapters in this section, Chapters 5 to 8, examine the law of divorce and registered civil partnership as such and the financial provision on divorce or dissolution of civil partnership or where divorce or dissolution has not yet been initiated; cohabitation, domestic violence and child law topics are covered separately in later discrete chapters since these topics also relate to the extended family rather than the couples' relationships, although both same-sex cohabitants who have no formal civil partnership and opposite-sex cohabitants who have remained outside the married and civil partnership regimes are still generating much discussion amongst both academics and practitioners as to whether there should be some formal, perhaps default or opt-out, regime for their relationships as well.

4.14 Current debates

Ideas for research on these current discussion questions can be accessed on the companion website updates:

- Is it appropriate for all issues concerning children of a marriage to be dealt with in a separate jurisdiction from divorce? Are children not relevant to the question of whether a marriage should be dissolved at all?
- Is divorce really the watershed of all the ills identified by Ruth Deech in her Gresham Lecture?
- Should divorce be made more difficult or should it be simplified, both in relation to the underlying theory (should it be a no-fault scheme?) and practice (easier and quicker?)?

4.15 Summary of Chapter 4
Origins of English divorce law

- Early English divorces were not uncommon, probably a relic of the Roman Law influence where divorce and remarriage was a normality; demand continued to be driven in the Middle Ages by the requirement for noble landowners, sometimes including the King, for dissolutions which permitted remarriage to a fertile wife if their marriages were not producing heirs.
- Subsequently, the ecclesiastical courts, believing in the indissolubility of Christian marriage, would only grant the equivalent of JS, or an annulment where the marriage could be categorised as having an initial impediment so that it was an invalid marriage.
- After the Reformation, when Henry VIII seceded from the Church of Rome in order to obtain a divorce himself which that Church would not grant, and the English Church came under criticism for its liberal approach to facilitating divorces and annulments for the wealthy, the position paradoxically became more restrictive rather than easier, as the new Protestant influence from Europe reacted against the English Church's extensive grounds for annulments, and a parliamentary method of divorce by private Act eventually had to be developed for the nobility and moneyed classes.
- This lasted until 1857, by which time only about 300 divorces had been granted to upper-class people, including only four women.
- The sole ground on which men could obtain a divorce in this way was simple adultery, which enabled them to obtain an ecclesiastical decree, the equivalent of JS.
- They were then obliged to sue the alleged co-adulterer in the courts for 'criminal conversation', only finally petitioning Parliament for a private divorce Bill.
- Women were obliged to allege some aggravating factor, such as cruelty or incest, and had no equivalent right to their husbands to divorce. Lord Cranworth justified this on the basis that women's adultery could foist a bastard onto an unsuspecting husband, whereas wives were not subject to this risk.

MCA 1857

- This statute created a new divorce court which had jurisdiction in matrimonial cases previously enjoyed by Parliament or the ecclesiastical courts.
- The basis for divorce was gradually widened in the recommendations of Royal Commissions until, by World War II, much of the present law of divorce was recognisable in successive Matrimonial Causes Acts.
- Men and women received equal access to remedies from 1923.
- The real watershed in this respect was the creation of legal aid in 1949, which enabled women to afford to bring petitions.

DRA 1969

- This followed a Royal Commission, the Archbishop of Canterbury's Group Report in 1966, and a report by the Law Commission.
- It was subsequently consolidated with the Matrimonial Proceedings and Property Act 1970 to become the Matrimonial Causes Act 1973, the source of contemporary divorce law.

Contemporary reform initiatives

- The FLA 1996 Part II (which was never implemented) was repealed by the CAFA 2014, but no further formal reform initiatives have so far been proposed.
- However, the Law Society, Resolution and others have proposed a reassessment of no-fault divorce.
- Ruth Deech has reviewed the adverse results of divorce in her 2009–10 Gresham Lectures, following which she became Deputy Chair of the All Party Parliamentary Group on Family Law which began to consider contemporary issues in Family Law before ceasing work.
- The 2011 Final Report of the FJR proposes a change from judicial to administrative divorce in undefended cases, but no changes to the ground and Facts in the MCA 1973 on which entitlement to a divorce is established, as these issues were outside the Review's remit; however, it is likely that there might be some amendments to facilitate such a transfer since the Act is overly complex and contains some obsolete and obsolescent provisions.

MCA 1973 and FPR 2010

These are the basic resources of modern divorce law and practice.

MCA 1973 in practice

- The Act is in practice interpreted in a non-litigious manner, largely owing to the influence of Resolution.
- A cooperative approach to the resolution of all aspects of contemporary divorce cases is reinforced by the philosophy of the CA 1989, by procedural reforms such as the FPR 2010, and by the enactment of this cooperative spirit in the FLA 1996 s 1.

Terminology in divorce suits

- Terminology differs from that of civil litigation as a whole. Family courts have also always been distinct and are now unified in the single Family Court incorporating all previous levels.
- The MCA 1973 and FPR 2010 are reproduced in the leading practitioners' work, *Rayden and Jackson* ('*Rayden*') and in *The Family Court Practice*, known as the 'Red Book'.

Jurisdiction

This is governed by the Domicile and Matrimonial Proceedings Act 1973 and the EU Regulation Brussels II *bis* (2003) though it is rarely a problem in practice (see e.g. *Dart v Dart* (CA)).

First year of marriage: the absolute bar on divorce

- There is an absolute bar on *petitioning* during the first year after the celebration of the marriage (MCA 1973 s 3(1)).
- The bar is absolute even when contravention is inadvertent (*Butler v Butler* (1990)).

Alternatives during the first year

● There are several alternative options, which are probably beneficial to the proposed petitioner, although none permit remarriage.

● These are judicial separation or nullity, a separation agreement, sources of funds if early divorce is financially motivated, and injunctions and declarations to address domestic violence and disputed occupation of the home.

The relationship between divorce, financial and child proceedings

● Divorce (or nullity or judicial separation, 'JS') and dissolution of civil partnerships, together with related financial matters ('ancillary relief') are obtained under the MCA 1973 or the Civil Partnership Act 2004 respectively, but the divorce/nullity/JS/dissolution suit and the consequential financial provision are completely separate sets of proceedings.

● Any proceedings in relation to children are similarly separate from the divorce or other decree and are dealt with under the Children Act 1989.

● Proceedings in relation to domestic violence or occupation of the home are separate again, and are governed by Part IV of the FLA 1996.

● These two latter Acts provide remedies whether the adult parties are married or unmarried, again emphasising their discrete existence and operation independently of any divorce.

● This separation of functions of the different statutes underlines the contemporary withdrawal from the concept of the family as the core unit of society.

4.16 Further reading

Facing the Future: A Discussion Paper on the Ground for Divorce. Law Com 170 (1988).
Family Law: the Ground for Divorce. Law Com 190 (1990).
Looking to the Future: Mediation and the Ground for Divorce: Cm 2424 (1993).
Looking to the Future: Mediation and the Ground for Divorce: the Government's Proposals: Cm 2799 (1995).
Bird, R and Cretney, S, *Divorce: The New Law*, Bristol, Jordan, 1996.
Clout, I, *The Matrimonial Lawyer: A Survival Guide*, Bristol, Jordan, 2001.
Day Sclater, S and Piper, C, *Undercurrents of Divorce*, Aldershot, Ashgate, 1999.
Eekelaar, J, *Regulating Divorce*, Oxford, Clarendon Press, 1991.
Gold, J (ed.), *Divorce as a Developmental Process*, Washington DC, American Psychiatric Press, 1988.
Haskey, 'Divorce Trends in England and Wales', [2008] Fam Law 1133.
Parker, D, Sax, R, Ray, P and Franklin J (eds), *Know How for Family Lawyers*, London, Sweet & Maxwell, 1993.
Reece, H, *Divorcing Responsibly*, Oxford, Hart, 2003.
Shepherd, N, 'Ending the blame game; getting no fault divorce back on the agenda', [2009] Fam Law 122.

Chapter 5

Divorce: The Contemporary Process

Chapter Contents

Learning outcomes for this chapter

A comprehensive overview of the present divorce system including:

(i)   An appreciation of the manner in which practitioners (and the judiciary) have made the MCA 1973 work for contemporary users, not necessarily in a way in which it was originally meant to operate.
(ii) An ability to analyse and appraise its provisions.
(iii) An awareness of the intellectual and practical arguments for potential reforms.

5.1 Introduction

While there have been many initiatives for reform, because of the criticisms on various grounds of the provisions of the MCA 1973, fundamental reform is unlikely in the foreseeable future. This is especially so owing to lack of immediate resources for any reform project. The current statutory basis of divorce law is therefore still to be found in the 1973 Act as amended (consolidating the reforms originally promulgated in the earlier DRA 1969 and the MPPA 1970) and in the FPR 2010. This basis is likely to continue unless perhaps the Law Commission includes reform of the ground for divorce in their next law reform programme, as has been pressed for by some, or perhaps a decision is taken to simplify the Act to facilitate the transfer from judicial consideration of undefended divorce petitions to a purely administrative system.

5.2 The ground for divorce and 'the five Facts'

Theoretically, there is only one ground for divorce – irretrievable breakdown of the marriage: MCA 1973 s 1(1). As this is the sole ground, it is technically incorrect to speak of 'the grounds' for divorce. However, in order to prove the ground in s 1(1) it is necessary to prove one (or more) of the five 'Facts' which evidence that irretrievable breakdown. These are specified in s 1(2)(a)–(e). Thus, while academics usually appreciate the distinction, both practitioners and public often speak of 'the grounds for divorce', by which they mean the s 1(1) 'ground' of irretrievable breakdown *and* the Fact or Facts by which the technical ground will be proved. It should be noted that 'Fact' or 'Facts' in this sense is often written with a capital F to distinguish the use in this sense from the factual matrix of the case, and are referred to as Facts A to E to correspond with the five sub-sections detailed in s 1(2)(a)–(e).

The Facts are:

- Fact A: adultery;
- Fact B: behaviour;
- Fact C: desertion;
- Fact D: two years' separation with consent of the respondent; and
- Fact E: five years' separation.

All statutory references in this chapter are to the MCA 1973 unless otherwise stated.

Adultery and behaviour are the two most commonly used Facts, accounting for over 85 per cent of cases. They are probably the most popular as they are the only two for which separation prior to the presentation of a petition is strictly unnecessary, and which facilitate the consensual 'divorce on demand' which is in practice available under English law. The other three Facts, for which separation is an essential prerequisite, are probably less used because of the complications which can be attached to each of them; for example, the *apparent* consensual Fact, Fact D, enables a respondent to demand virtually unlimited conditions in return for agreement to divorce by consent under that Fact. Thus Facts A and B are the real consensual Facts and Fact D is the 'false friend'!

5.3 Proof of the ground in s 1(1)

Sub-sections (1) and (2) are separate requirements which must be individually satisfied; one without the other will be insufficient.

❖ CASE EXAMPLES

In both *Buffery v Buffery* (1980)[1] and *Richards v Richards* (1972)[2] there was irretrievable breakdown but no Fact was proved. The court held that both elements were required by the statute.

In *Biggs v Biggs* (1977)[3] there was a suitable Fact but no irretrievable breakdown.

In *Stevens v Stevens* (1979)[4] it was held that while both elements were required for a decree to be pronounced, no link was, however, necessary between the two requirements.

Consideration of a common practical example may help to show how this works when the law is applied. Inability to satisfy both sub-sections (1) and (2) occurs more often than might at first be thought. It is common for marriages made in haste to be repented fairly quickly also, but undoing the status of marriage is more difficult. If a couple separate early in the marriage, for example out of boredom with each other, and when neither has committed adultery, nor could either be said to be guilty of sufficient 'behaviour' for a successful Fact B petition, they will need to wait for two years before being able to use Fact D for a successful separation petition. Although both may be quite sure that the marriage has irretrievably broken down, and even if evidence could be provided of that situation as in the first two cases mentioned above, it will not be possible to prove any Fact, so no decree can be obtained until such proof is provided.

If tactful enquiries do not reveal the slightest chance of a case of behaviour that the other spouse would not defend, and the parties are unwilling to wait, the practitioner's advice may be that one or other of the spouses should commit adultery as soon as possible, since the court's inquiry into this fact is now cursory at best and it is likely to be less still once undefended divorce moves to the proposed administrative basis. This is because it is no longer even necessary to name a co-respondent, as was the case during the first few years following the enactment of the MCA 1973, i.e. until it was seen that that adultery was genuinely more a symptom than a cause of marriage breakdown, and that it was not only unnecessary to involve the third party's name in the divorce, but often actually detrimental to future relationships, especially if the co-adulterer were later married by one of the spouses and thus became a step-parent of the children of the family.

---

1 [1980] 2 FLR 365.
2 [1972] 1 WLR 1073; [1972] 3 All ER 695.
3 [1977] 1 All ER 20.
4 [1979] 1 WLR 885.

Moreover, as it is immaterial which party petitions since, where both parties want a divorce, no tactical advantages are to be gained by petitioning or being petitioned against, it is also extremely common for the parties and/or their lawyers to discuss who files the petition and which Fact should be relied on. This sort of discussion is no doubt the source of the lay comment frequently encountered that 'a quickie divorce' has been obtained 'by consent' – whereas the words of the statute indicate no such possibility except in the case of two years' separation and consent of the respondent under s 1(2)(d). It is also, of course, the origin of commentators' remarks that the present divorce law is hypocritical and misleading.

The academic student may be surprised by this situation, although research relied on when the **Family Law Act (FLA) 1996** was going through Parliament indicated that the practical application of the law in this respect was little understood by the general public. It was clear from the Hansard reports of the debates in both Houses that ordinary people still appeared to believe that divorce under the MCA 1973 was genuinely fault based and firmly rooted in traditional ideas of morality, so that divorce should not be possible unless an 'innocent' party divorced a 'guilty' one. The reality, as explained in earlier chapters, is that the Act is more often than not manipulated by both parties to a marriage and their advisers to obtain the result which they personally want, and the strict interpretation of the statute permits this result without any abuse of the law.

This, of course, is the difference between the lawyer's interpretation of the letter as well as the spirit of the law and that of the untutored layperson, not used to the interpretation of statutes (a common and widely understood illustration of this would be the famous court scene in Shakespeare's *Merchant of Venice*, where Shylock's mistake in assuming that he could with impunity cut off a pound of Antonio's flesh is revealed – his loan agreement with Antonio did not permit him also to take the *blood* which would inevitably accompany the severance of the flesh to which he was entitled).

Despite this now well-established manipulation of contemporary divorce law, of which everyone in the case, including the judge, is well aware, the court still theoretically has a duty to enquire, as far as it reasonably can, into the facts alleged by the petition. This, however, is balanced by a philosophy of avoiding pointless enquiries into conduct and fault which post-1969 divorce law is designed to escape, a comment that was made as long ago as the case of *Grenfell v Grenfell* (1977).[5]

Therefore, if the court is satisfied that one of the Facts has been proved, it has a duty under s 1(4), subject to the restrictions of the s 5 defence to divorce after five years' separation[6] to grant the decree of divorce[7] unless it is satisfied on all the evidence that the marriage has *not* broken down irretrievably. In other words, proving a Fact leads to a presumption of irretrievable breakdown. With the introduction of the administrative divorce and civil partnership dissolution process proposed by the FJR[8] for cases not disputed by the respondent(s) such consideration is bound to comprise a somewhat perfunctory system in which non-lawyers can be successfully trained to recognise precisely what is adequate to establish a Fact and heavy reliance is likely to be placed on the petitioner's assertion that the marriage has broken down irretrievably. However, this is unlikely to cause injustice since it is accepted that there is, in effect, already divorce by consent, unless the court is alerted to obvious deceit.

Thus has English divorce law travelled far from the pre-1969 concepts of 'Collaboration' and 'Collusion',[9] which in those days was sufficient for outright refusal of a decree.

---

5 [1977] 3 WLR 738; [1978] 1 All ER 561.
6 See below at 5.10.
7 Section 1(4).
8 See Chapter 4.
9 Hangovers from the cumbersome eighteenth- and nineteenth-century jurisprudence which persisted until 1969.

5.4 Adultery: Fact A

STATUTORY EXTRACT

The requirement to establish this Fact is that

'the respondent has committed adultery and the petitioner finds it intolerable to live with the respondent': s 1(2)(a).

Note that there are two separate elements to this Fact:

- the act of adultery; and
- that the petitioner also finds it intolerable to live with the respondent, *not necessarily because of the adultery.*

This is another example of the necessity to read the statute closely, without importing into it any vernacular gloss derived from the layperson's belief in what the law ought to be according to traditional morality. The elements of adultery must be examined in detail.

5.4.1 The act of adultery

'Adultery' means voluntary sexual intercourse between a married person and a person of the opposite sex, whether married or not, who is not that married person's spouse. It is necessary to consider the meaning of the individual words of the section in this definition.

'Voluntary'

As the act must be voluntary, a wife who has been raped does not commit adultery: *S v S* (1962);[10] neither does a child who cannot consent voluntarily to intercourse, but this will not stop the adult party being guilty of adultery: *Barnett v Barnett and Brown* (1970).[11] However, once intercourse is established it is for the respondent to show that it was not voluntary: *Redpath v Redpath* (1950).[12] Being intoxicated is generally not an excuse for adultery: *Goshawk v Goshawk* (1965).[13]

'Sexual intercourse'

There must be some penetration although a complete act of intercourse is not required.

❖ CASE EXAMPLE

In *Dennis v Dennis* (1955)[14] an impotent respondent spent a night in bed with a woman, giving rise to an inference of adultery, which was nevertheless rebutted because he could prove he was incapable of penetration.

---

10 [1962] 2 All ER 816.
11 [1970] 2 All ER 33.
12 [1950] 1 All ER 600.
13 (1965) 109 SJ 290.
14 [1955] 2 WLR 187; [1955] 2 All ER 51.

Sexual familiarities short of intercourse, such as might have applied in the last case, are not enough: *Saps-Ford v Saps-Ford* (1954).[15] However, such an association might be a basis for a Fact B behaviour petition because this might amount to an intimate relationship from which the petitioner justifiably felt excluded, and thus be 'behaviour', such that 'the petitioner cannot reasonably be expected to live with the respondent'.[16]

It should be noted that traditionally in England and Wales adultery used not to be possible with a person who has changed sex, because in English law a person's biological sex was regarded as established at birth by chromosomes which cannot be artificially changed by a later sex-change operation. A different view has long pertained in some American jurisdictions: see *Corbett v Corbett* (1970).[17] However, following the ECtHR ruling in *Goodwin v UK* No 28957/95 (11 July 2002),[18] and the GRA 2004 there may now be room for academic debate about whether adultery does result from intercourse with a transsexual who has undergone full gender reassignment surgery (there are viable arguments both ways for the reasons given above, although consequential amendments have been made to English law, and s 9 of the GRA 2004 states that 'where a full gender recognition certificate is issued to a person, the person's gender becomes for all purposes the acquired gender').

It should also be noted that while following the enactment of the **Marriage (Same-Sex Couples) Act 2013**, same-sex partners are now able to marry in the same way as opposite-sex partners, pursuant to s 3(2) of Part 3 of Schedule 4, they are partially excluded from the use of adultery as a Fact on which to base a petition for divorce, since this section amends s 1 of the MCA 1973 to add a new s 1(6) which states: 'Only conduct between the respondent and a person of the opposite sex may constitute adultery for the purposes of this section.' Thus sexual infidelity with another person of the same sex as the respondent in a same-sex marriage dissolution is not 'adultery' in the same way as it would be when a heterosexual respondent has heterosexual intercourse with another person, although that same same-sex infidelity can qualify as 'behaviour' on which a same-sex petitioner could rely.

This might be an example of a part of the Act which could benefit from some simplification (possibly removing the term 'adultery' altogether for both opposite-sex and same-sex marriages) as any physical infidelity is likely to offend a same-sex partner as much as adultery may still offend in an opposite-sex marriage, and this provision is one of the differences between same-sex and opposite-sex marriages about which anecdotally it appears that gay couples are already complaining.

5.4.2 Proof of the act of adultery

Proof of adultery may be something of a mechanical exercise in contemporary divorce suits since it is unusual for divorces to be defended: fewer than 1 per cent even commence as defended. The most common way of proving adultery is therefore by the respondent's admission, for which provision is made on the Acknowledgment of Service form sent out to the respondent by the court with the petition; see below.

However, should the facts of a case indicate that it would be necessary to prove adultery, in the absence of clear evidence it would be necessary to consider whether there is any other Fact which could be relied upon instead. This is because the standard of proof required (which would certainly

---

15 [1954] 2 All ER 373.
16 See 5.5 below.
17 [1970] 2 All ER 33. This case appears in the volume of *Landmark Cases in Family Law* by Gilmore, S, Herring, J and Probert, R (eds), Oxford, Hart, 2011, p 47, '*Corbett v Corbett*: Once a Man, Always a Man?' by Stephen Gilmore, providing both interesting background and detailed discussion of this case, the decision in which remained valid in English law until 2002.
18 Mentioned at 2.3.3 above.

apply in a contested case) is (in theory) not the general civil standard of proof but a higher (not precisely specified) standard based on the lingering historical background which has always regarded adultery as a serious accusation which used to be, at best, a grave offence and, at worst, a crime. This is curious as adultery is now generally regarded as a *symptom* rather than a *cause* of marriage breakdown, although in the past the standard of proof was agonised over (for example, in Blyth v Blyth (1966),[19] where the House of Lords was divided in its opinion, much of which was in any case *obiter*, i.e. not central to the rationale of the decision). It is also odd as in child sex abuse cases, which were regarded as a similarly serious allegation,[20] the Supreme Court has more recently confirmed that there is only one standard of proof, the ordinary civil standard, so perhaps this may now apply to adultery too. Nevertheless, it means that, where adultery may not be admitted, it is neither sufficient nor wise merely to allege it without some seriously credible evidence: see *Bastable v Bastable* (1968).[21]

❖ CASE EXAMPLE

In *Bastable v Bastable* the husband petitioned on the basis of a mere suspicion of adultery, owing to the wife's persistent association with another man. His petition was dismissed.

5.4.3 **Methods of proof of adultery**

Possible methods of proof are as follows:

(1)   Circumstantial evidence – in other words inclination and opportunity to gratify it: *Farnham v Farnham* (1925)[22] A rebuttable presumption will be raised by the parties spending the night in the same room: *Woolf v Woolf* (1931),[23] but this may be rebutted by evidence such as in *Dennis*, above.

(2)   Confession statement – a method once much used, and still useful if adultery is not admitted on the Acknowledgment of Service form (as, conveniently for the contemporary 'quickie' process, it can be).

  In the sort of case where strong suspicions of adultery need to be confirmed, for example by a private detective sent to watch the parties because the adultery is not admitted, the detective may also invite the parties to volunteer a formal written confession. Respondents will often give a confession statement when they realise that if they do not the private detective will give acceptable evidence anyway, and this is especially so if by giving the confession the respondent is able to keep the name of the third party involved out of the suit, as is now the norm: see below.

(3)   Birth of a child as a result of the adultery, which may be proved by entry on the birth register if the third party has signed the Register of Births in place of the father (*Jackson v Jackson and Pavan* (1961)[24] or even by the absence of an entry in the space for the father's name: *Mayo v Mayo*

---

19 [1966] 1 All ER 524.
20 E.g. *Re S-B (Children)* [2009] UKSC 17, per Baroness Hale.
21 [1968] 3 All ER 701.
22 (1925) 153 LT 320.
23 [1931] P 134.
24 [1961] 2 WLR 58; [1960] 3 All ER 621.

(1948).[25] This is now much more common since it has become much more usual than previously for couples to live together before they marry and, as noted by the Law Commission in its 2006–7 reports on cohabitation, often to have one or two children before marrying.

(4) *Living with another partner* – one of the easiest methods since, whether or not the new partner is named in the petition,[26] if the court sees that the respondent has set up house away from the petitioner with a new partner, adultery will be presumed, especially if a child has also been born.

(5) *Findings in other proceedings*, e.g. where the respondent is named as co-respondent or is cited as a party in other divorce proceedings and adultery is proved, or where there are successful proceedings against the respondent spouse under the CA 1989 Schedule 1 for property transfer or a lump sum for the child of an adulterous association,[27] or a conviction of rape against a respondent husband, or where adultery has already been used to obtain a decree of judicial separation, which by s 4(2) enables the judicial separation decree to be treated as proof of adultery.

(6) *DNA or blood tests* (usually now the near 100 per cent accurate DNA testing is used, for obvious reasons). Both types of test have always been possible if directed by the court. However, the court's power was until a little over a decade ago limited to giving a *direction* rather than *ordering* a test against the will of the parties to be tested, since in the absence of some authority this would have amounted to an assault. A person with care of a child must usually consent on behalf of the child whose blood or genetic sample is required: FLRA 1969, s 20(1), although ways round this have been found, e.g. in one case the solution of Hale LJ (as she then was) was for the Official Solicitor to consent on behalf of the child to whom he was made guardian *ad litem*, though this was criticised as inappropriate. Also, the court can consent for a child who is a ward of court.

However, the **Child Support, Pensions and Social Security Act 2000** ultimately addressed the former problems: tucked away in s 82(3) appeared an amendment to FLRA 1969 s 20, enabling the court to consent if it 'considers that it would be in [the child's] best interests' for the samples to be taken. This resolves the court's previous lack of jurisdiction to compel a mother who has sole care and control of a child to consent to samples being taken: see *Re O and J (Children)* (2000).[28] Late in 2001, Bodey J granted one of the first applications for testing under the new provisions, overturning the adverse decision of the FPC.

But neither of these tests may still be directed to *establish* adultery: *Hodgkiss v Hodgkiss* (1985),[29] but only to discover true parentage where that is in the interests of the child, which it usually is: *S v S* (1972).[30] In *S v S*, Lord Hodson said this was rarely not the case in modern times, as there is some psychiatric evidence that children need to know their true origins. If, however, a test is directed to establish parentage and it shows adultery must have been committed, then the results may be used to *prove* that adultery. Tests may be directed on the application of any party or on the court's own motion, but if the application is contested the direction may only be given by the judge.

Inferences may be drawn if a test is not taken: FLRA 1969 s 23(1). In particular, an applicant for financial relief is likely to have the application dismissed if a test is refused: FLRA 1969, s 23(2). In *McVeigh v Beattie* (1988),[31] a man's refusal to take a test was held

---

25 [1948] 2 All ER 869.
26 See below at 5.6.
27 See Chapter 21.
28 [2000] 2 All ER 29.
29 [1985] Fam Law 87.
30 [1972] AC 24; [1970] 3 All ER 107, HL.
31 [1988] 2 All ER 500.

to amount to the necessary corroboration of the woman's assertion that the child was his, so as to obtain an affiliation order. However, sometimes there are good grounds for refusing a test.

❖ CASE EXAMPLE

In *B v B and E* (1969)[32] the mother did not raise the question of the child's parentage until he was three years old. The father established in court that it was reasonable for him to rely on the presumption of legitimacy after such a long period of believing the child was his.

Unfortunately, only the DNA fingerprinting test is virtually 100 per cent reliable; blood tests can only exclude (and not identify) any party as a parent of the child so until the use of DNA testing became common paternity was often difficult to establish through blood testing. Generally, the result of the latter test, unless a rare blood group is involved, will only indicate whether a person could or could not be a parent of the child, and indicate within what percentage of the population such a person falls as a potential parent.

There is, however, a *strong presumption of legitimacy* and, in the absence of proof of adultery, a child born in wedlock or within nine months of the last possible date for married intercourse is still presumed legitimate, although this might always be rebutted by proof of non-access. Rebuttal of the presumption is on a balance of probabilities: FLRA 1969, s 26, but the standard of proof in such a case has always been a heavy one: *Serio v Serio* (1983).[33] Legitimacy issues in some of these older cases were generated by the 'swinging sixties' syndrome of 'wife-swapping', when DNA testing was not yet developed, and easily accessible blood tests were not conclusive and it might be quite difficult to ascertain paternity at all reliably. Nevertheless, following Lord Hodson's decision in *S v S* in 1972 it is now nearly always accepted that it is better for a child to know who his father is than to adhere to the presumption of legitimacy, although sometimes where an older child resists testing the court will not insist on tests being carried out: see Chapter 13.

However, in divorce this presumption of legitimacy will not always operate in favour of a respondent accused of adultery and against whom adultery cannot be *proved* in one of the usual ways.

❖ CASE EXAMPLE

In *Preston-Jones v Preston-Jones* (1951)[34] – still the classic case on non-access – the wife was of a serious and sober disposition and there was no evidence of any associations or loose behaviour on her part. Adultery was still established, however, as her husband had been abroad between six and 12 months before the birth. Thus the period of gestation was entirely incredible and adultery was held to be established.

---

32 [1969] 3 All ER 1106.
33 (1983) 4 FLR 756.
34 [1951] AC 391; [1951] 1 All ER 124.

If adultery cannot be proved, because there has apparently been no sexual intercourse, the non-adulterous association of some intimacy might be sufficient for a behaviour petition presented on the basis of Fact B.[35] This is because it has been accepted by the Court of Appeal that such a relationship may be more destructive of marriage than an act of adultery, since adultery is now seen as a symptom rather than a cause of marital breakdown: *Wachtel v Wachtel* (1973).[36]

5.4.4 Proof of the intolerability element of Fact A

The petitioner must also find it intolerable to live with the respondent. The actual act of adultery and the fact that the petitioner finds it intolerable to live with the respondent are construed independently, although it is doubtful if this is what Parliament intended when the DRA 1969 was passed. The matter was raised in *Goodrich v Goodrich* (1971),[37] where it was held that the two requirements were independent of each other, and also that whether it was intolerable for the petitioner to be obliged to continue to live with the respondent was a subjective test for that particular petitioner. As a result, if the actual adultery alleged is proved and the petitioner states that further cohabitation with the respondent is intolerable, the court has no option but to grant the decree.

The independence of these two elements of Fact A has since been confirmed in *Cleary v Cleary* (1974)[38] and *Carr v Carr* (1974),[39] which together ably illustrate how unrelated the two essential elements of the fact can be.

> ### ❖ CASE EXAMPLES
>
> In *Cleary* the intolerability sprang from the wife's going out, leaving the husband to baby-sit, and by corresponding with another man, although neither of these actions was linked to the adultery.
>
> In *Carr* the intolerable aspect was the wife's treatment of the children, which similarly had no connection with the adultery.

5.4.5 Time within which adultery petitions must be presented

An act of adultery only remains a valid basis on which to petition for divorce for six months after it is discovered by the potential petitioner. Thus, if the parties continue to cohabit after *discovery* of an act or acts of adultery, then after a *total period of six months* of such continued cohabitation after the last act relied on, a petition will not be possible on the basis of *that* adultery – some renewal of the adulterous association, or some fresh act of adultery with another person, will be required (s 2(1)). This is designed as a reconciliation provision, so that the parties may attempt to overlook such

---

35 See below at 5.5.
36 [1973] 2 WLR 366; [1973] 1 All ER 829, CA. This case also appears in *Landmark Cases* referred to above at n 17. See p 135, 'Bringing an End to the Matrimonial Post Mortem: *Wachtel v Wachtel* and its Enduring Significance for Ancillary Relief' by Gillian Douglas. The case established that conduct, unless inequitable to disregard, and above all the Fact on which the divorce was based, was irrelevant to financial relief, and did much to establish adultery as a mechanical means of ending a marriage rather than a subject for any moral blame.
37 [1971] 1 WLR 1142; [1971] 2 All ER 1340.
38 [1974] 1 WLR 73; [1974] 1 All ER 498, CA.
39 [1974] 1 WLR 1534; [1974] 1 All ER 1193, CA.

incidents of adultery, even possibly separating and then resuming cohabitation, following the initial discovery that adultery has been committed. It is clear that many couples do this because they are not sure if the marriage is really over.

This ambivalence is *completely irrelevant* – it does not matter how many times they separate and then change their minds until there has been six months' *actual* cohabitation since the adultery in question was discovered. Periods of *separation* are not counted in the total six months which finally bar a petition under s 2(1).

It should be remembered that it is the date of *discovery* of the adultery, not the date of its commission, which is relevant to the continued ability to petition, so it is still possible to petition on the basis of an act of adultery which took place many years before, provided discovery was more recent so the s 2(1) bar does not apply.

5.5 Behaviour: Fact B

STATUTORY EXTRACT

The requirement to establish this Fact is that

> 'the respondent has behaved in such a way that the petitioner cannot reasonably be expected to live with the respondent': s 1(2)(b).

There is no finite list of conduct which does or does not constitute sufficient 'behaviour' for this Fact, so that it is less straightforward to use than adultery. On the other hand, like adultery, behaviour does provide an opportunity for an immediate divorce on the basis of the petitioner's complaints against the respondent.

Indeed, given that the marriage will have broken down for some reason or reasons which have given the petitioner (and possibly the respondent also) cause for dissatisfaction, and given that there is such a low incidence of defended divorces, it is well known that a practice has developed whereby it is possible to obtain a divorce on the basis of quite slight behaviour, provided the allegations are not too (objectively) trivial for the court to allow, provided it is stated that they have been (subjectively) unacceptable to the petitioner and provided the respondent does not defend. It is not therefore surprising that behaviour and adultery usually between them account for the largest number of decrees.

If it is suspected that a petition might be defended, greater care would obviously in practice need to be taken in advising a spouse to petition on Fact B than if the suit was likely to go undefended, but the fact remains that the law as set out in the statute permits interpretation of the provisions to be used in this way. In such a case the drafting of the particulars of behaviour will be crucial, but the law permits a divorce to be granted and it is nevertheless very rare that an undefended petition will fail: see below.

The academic student will need to acquire a good grasp of what is and what is not behaviour within the meaning of s 1(2)(b), so as to gain a working knowledge of the main such groupings where case law has established that such behaviour qualifies, and also to appreciate the role of intention in this context as it is now established, through ponderous case law in arriving at this conclusion, that behaviour for Fact B does not have to be either deliberate or positive. In practice, it is very unlikely that cases coming before the court will be on all fours with those which have appeared in the law reports, and much the same may be said of those appearing in tutorial and examination problems. It is therefore essential to be able to distinguish between what is worth skill and effort in the drafting of a petition and what is really too feeble an allegation to succeed, especially if the petition were to be defended. While drafting is not usually within the academic law syllabus, although some law schools have adopted such practical methods of teaching, it is in fact very difficult to understand whether any given behaviour might be sufficient for a Fact B petition without appreciating that drafting skills may tip the balance in a borderline case (so as to make the most of such material as is available for the petition). Provided the suit is undefended, good drafting can obtain a decree on the basis of initially quite unpromising material, as consultation of a good collection of precedents will indicate!

A classic case was that of *Richards v Richards* (1972).[40]

❖ CASE EXAMPLE

In *Richards*, the husband was a depressive, but his depression was not 'clinical', essential for medical recognition as an illness at the time, although it was still causing a great deal of discomfort to his wife and family; and it was crystal clear that because of his behaviour the marriage had broken down irretrievably. However, in 1972 unless depression was clinical it was not sufficiently serious to clear the 'trivial' hurdle, which the court considered a bar to a divorce where conduct was thought not sufficiently serious to constitute a matrimonial offence. Recognition of the nature of the varieties and variations of the depressive condition, and medical treatment of it, was rudimentary at that time compared to today's specialist knowledge of these illnesses.

In any case depressive behaviour was recognised to be involuntary, which confused the courts which had not yet grappled with the fact that even an involuntary illness could be sufficient to meet the statutory requirement if it was too much for the respondent to be expected to live with.

The circumstances of this case, which would certainly be sufficient to obtain a decree today, indicate that in 1972 neither practitioners nor the judiciary had really grasped the theory behind the potential of the new Fact of behaviour so as to use it successfully in cases where the old matrimonial offence of cruelty would not have been made out. Nor had practitioners' drafting of the particulars of a Fact relied on in the petition been developed to the heights of sophistication which later emerged.

5.5.1 The test for behaviour

The test by which the court will decide whether any conduct is or is not behaviour is a hybrid one, partly subjective and partly objective. It should always be remembered that the Fact is not one of 'unreasonable behaviour' – and it is incorrect to speak of Fact B in this way – because, as the Court of Appeal stated in *Bannister v Bannister* (1980),[41] the behaviour contemplated by the working of the section is significantly different from 'behaving unreasonably' (i.e. eight years after the *Richards* case they had thought through the potential of the statute, although some judges had arrived at the contemporary position rather earlier). In *Carew-Hunt v Carew-Hunt* (1972),[42] Ormrod J confirmed this

---

40 See above at 5.3.
41 [1980] 10 Fam Law 240, CA.
42 (1972) *The Times*, 28 June.

view and added that it was not up to the court to pass moral judgements and to say whether a person's behaviour was 'right or wrong, good or bad'.

The correct test for this Fact is generally regarded as that stated in *Buffery v Buffery* (1980),[43] namely (to paraphrase the judgment):

> Can this petitioner (looking at the petitioner's own behaviour) be expected to live with this respondent (looking at the respondent's behaviour), taking into account the kind of people they are and also whether there has been any provocation, deliberate or otherwise, for example through anti-social conduct or even illness?

This test builds on the much earlier judgment of Bagnall J in *Ash v Ash* (1972),[44] a case of violence and alcoholism, where the judge suggested that like can always be expected to live with like – for example the violent/alcoholic/sport-addicted petitioner with the like respondent – so the situation where each party is as bad as the other might logically result in neither being able to obtain a divorce as, equally logically, there ought to be some disparity in the parties' conduct.

However, although this might have been the case in 1972 when the wording of the statute was new to everyone, and judges and practitioners alike were used to the old 'cruelty' ground, which was very different from the concept of 'behaviour', in practice this situation no longer arises very often. This is because most petitions are not defended and go through to decree nisi without a hearing; thus the court will not know that the petitioner's behaviour is just as bad as that complained of in the respondent. The exception would be where the case was defended when it was common for a defending respondent also to cross-petition in the same document, in which case if each spouse appeared to the judge to be as bad as the other the court might grant cross decrees. Otherwise if the allegations are objectively of the type that a petitioner might reasonably complain of, a decree will be granted especially if the case is undefended, as it usually is.

This is therefore a classic example of the impact of procedure on substantive law in divorce, a most important pointer to the academic student's understanding of the subject, and to a grasp of the fact that contemporary divorce is in effect already available on demand, is often consensual and has become so because practitioners have made the best use of a statute which was almost certainly not intended to work in the way that it now does.

Dunn J put this practical approach in a nutshell in *Livingstone-Stallard v Livingstone-Stallard* (1974),[45] when he suggested a 'jury approach', as in 'what would the right-thinking man conclude' about the behaviour complained of. The case also established that, although the behaviour relied on should not be absolutely trivial overall, a weight of trivia taken together may be sufficient.

❖ CASE EXAMPLE

> In *Livingstone-Stallard*, the husband, a much older man, had basically nagged, bullied, criticised and irritated his younger, rather nervous, wife to the point where she lacked all confidence and could no longer stand living with him; her petition succeeded. This case is therefore a useful precedent where, as in the majority of contemporary marriages, the conduct complained of is not far off what in other jurisdictions would simply be called 'incompatibility', which is not, however, a basis for divorce in English law, although it may be in those other jurisdictions.

---

43 See above at 5.3.
44 [1972] 2 WLR 347; [1972] 1 All ER 582.
45 [1974] 3 WLR 302; [1974] 2 All ER 776.

The case of *O'Neill v O'Neill* (1975)[46] (as to which see further below) affirmed this approach and also stressed that no other extraneous concepts should be imported into the test, such as that the behaviour should be 'grave and weighty' (as it used to be required to be under the pre-1969 law, which involved the completely different concept of cruelty).

The modern approach, therefore, is primarily concerned with assessing any conduct which is not utterly trivial and in looking at that conduct objectively in the light of its effects on the particular petitioner (thereby importing the subjective element of the hybrid test). A good example of this approach, more recent than the 1970s and 1980s when the court was still working out what the statute meant, is *Birch v Birch* (1992),[47] where the petitioner insisted that the behaviour complained of affected her particularly badly and her assertion was accepted.

5.5.2 The role of intention

From these developments it can be seen that intention has progressively assumed a more minor role than either in the early days of the post-1969 reformed divorce law or under the old pre-1969 concept of cruelty. In the early 1970s there was a discernible backward-looking tendency in decisions which adhered to the philosophy of the former, entirely fault-based, law and which seemed to insist that intention must play a major part in any 'behaviour' which was seen as an active, rather than a passive instance of conduct. However, when *Katz v Katz* (1972)[48] and *Thurlow v Thurlow* (1975)[49] (both cases of physical and mental deterioration) came before the court, the approach changed significantly. Previously, it seemed that the court had always been influenced by the concept of marriage being 'for better for worse, for richer for poorer, [and particularly] in sickness and in health', so that obtaining a decree based on the respondent's involuntary behaviour due to mental and/or physical illness was in logic problematic.

Thus, *Katz* established that mental illness of even a relatively minor sort could be sufficient to obtain a decree if, after making full allowances for the respondent's disabilities, the temperament of both parties and the obligations of marriage, the type and seriousness of the behaviour was such that the petitioner should not really be called upon to endure it; curiously a case in the same year as *Richards*, but too late for Mrs Richards' original petition.

Thurlow, however, three years later, was really the watershed in establishing acceptance as 'behaviour' of a sufficient degree of mental or physical illness combined. In that case, a depressing degree of deterioration was regarded as 'behaviour' within the terms of Fact B. In particular, *Thurlow* established that such 'behaviour' was nevertheless acceptable for Fact B, despite its being involuntary, and despite the ordinary connotation of the word 'behaviour' suggesting something positive and active, rather than unavoidable and passive. The judge decided that it was for the court to say in each case whether despite the obligations of marriage the petitioner could be called upon to withstand the stress imposed by the respondent's condition, considering in particular the length of time the condition had existed and the effect on the petitioner's health.

5.5.3 Some types of Fact B behaviour

Each case turns on its own facts, but it is helpful to look at cases where sufficient behaviour has been found to establish the Fact. For example:

---

46 [1975] 1 WLR 118; [1975] 3 All ER 289.
47 [1992] 1 FLR 564.
48 [1972] 1 WLR 955; [1972] 3 All ER 219.
49 [1975] 3 WLR 161; [1975] 3 All ER 979.

- violence (physical and verbal), including false accusations (especially if combined with alcoholism);
- insensitivity;
- lack of communication;
- excessive unsociability;
- general neglect;
- bullying;
- constant criticism;
- financial irresponsibility;
- excessive financial restrictions; and
- obsessive DIY.

Examples of all the above classes of generally unpleasant behaviour appear in the cases below, and may be expected to recur with some regularity; so if a potential petitioner's complaints do not seem to disclose enough material to petition (since practitioners report that clients are sometimes extraordinarily reticent in providing detail, though others will give a blow-by-blow account), practitioners find that it is always worth considering whether any of the less obvious ones apply. Thus has the law developed over time since 1969 to provide the easy divorce which is criticised by commentators, but which in effect already delivers, albeit in a roundabout manner, the consensual divorce which it is claimed should be explicitly provided by English law.

Approaching the statute in this way, the following effects on the petitioner are unlikely to qualify, unless they can be shown to be caused by the respondent's behaviour (though because of the subjective element of the test to be applied they might be sufficient if *injury to health* results and if the incidents relied on are carefully pleaded to link them to some identifiable fault on the respondent's part):

- emotional dissatisfaction (but is there *neglect, insensitivity* or *selfishness?*);
- sexual dissatisfaction (but is this neglect or caused by the *respondent's serious illness?*);
- desertion (but is it *neglect* or the respondent *not appreciating the commitment of marriage?*); and
- boredom or growing apart (but is it *insensitivity, inability to communicate* or *general neglect?*).

It is essential in these latter cases to be able to show that the respondent has breached some marital obligation, even if that is only the mutual enjoyment of each other's company socially, and the affection and moral support which one spouse is entitled to expect from the other. It is possible that when (and if) divorce becomes an administrative rather than a judicial matter as recommended by the FJR, and now supported by the President, these grey areas will create problems for the administrative staff, who will then be obliged to decide whether a petitioner has made out the Fact of behaviour or not, and that not as much time may therefore be saved by this supposed reform, whereas a DJ who had been reading divorce petitions for years would probably be able to decide this point in a few seconds of reading the particulars of the behaviour complained of.

5.5.4 Violence

Where there is actual physical violence it is obviously best if the petitioner has reported the matter to a doctor or the police. Not doing so will not necessarily lead to the conclusion that such violence has been tolerated, but evidential problems clearly might arise. Although the petitioner can always give such evidence without corroboration, and may be believed if the suit is not defended, some independent evidence is obviously helpful. Lack of this might lead to a hearing under the present procedural system, whereas with a doctor's letter the matter would have gone through on the papers in the usual way. Any psychological violence, such as what used to be referred to as mental cruelty, should obviously also, if possible, be substantiated by medical or psychiatric evidence for the same reason. It is uncertain how this type of case might be dealt with under the proposed administrative divorce: perhaps it will be necessary to file such medical evidence with the form of application.

5.5.5 Insensitivity, lack of communication, excessive unsociability or general neglect

If any one of these is alleged, it is essential that some conduct can be imported to the respondent and tied to incidents which can be given as examples. In *Buffery* (see above), this did not succeed as the parties had really each gone their own ways and neither was more to blame than the other. However, in *Bannister* (see also above), the petition was successful because it could be said that the husband never took the wife out and never told her where he was when he went out himself, sometimes at night, and indeed never spoke to her if he could avoid it! A practitioner would tackle this problem by obtaining some detail when interviewing the client and relying on careful drafting to present a picture of unacceptable behaviour. The academic student will need to develop similar imagination in order to identify circumstances in which what may appear a thin case could succeed in practice.

5.5.6 Bullying or constant criticism

Bullying or constant criticism which fall short of violence, or strong verbal abuse which might otherwise appear to be trivial, also needs in practice to be carefully particularised to show an overall picture which is unacceptable as these elements of behaviour are naturally a matter of fact and degree. In *Livingstone-Stallard*, for example (see above), the incidents individually were insufficient, but together presented such a horrible picture of life in the *Livingstone-Stallard* household that the court had no difficulty in drawing the necessary conclusion.

5.5.7 Financial irresponsibility or excessive financial restriction

This is established Fact B behaviour, especially where it adversely affects the family and causes stress as in *Carter-Fea v Carter-Fea* (1987),[50] and this may also be 'conduct' within the meaning of s 25(2)(g) of the Act which would reduce the respondent's entitlement in subsequent financial provision proceedings (see Chapter 7), especially if it has had the effect of dissipating the family assets.

Similarly, excessive financial restriction will usually be behaviour but has always needed to be carefully pleaded with some concrete examples, since a wife's cry of 'not enough money' is often seen as a classic 'sitcom' joke. Moreover, if a wife has managed to live frugally despite the husband's parsimony, this may have repercussions in establishing what she needs for the purposes of ancillary relief, although this will now only be relevant where there are insufficient resources to follow the current trend to treat marriage as a partnership and to split them more or less equally.[51]

5.5.8 Obsessive DIY

The classic case on obsessive DIY is *O'Neill v O'Neill* (1975), mentioned above.

---

50 [1987] Fam Law 131.
51 See Chapters 6 and 7 on splitting the assets on divorce.

❖ **CASE EXAMPLE**

In *O'Neill v O'Neill* the court at first hesitated to decide that two years of 'home improvement' was not something that the wife and daughter should have been called upon to endure – although this was a particularly bad instance of living in discomfort for the sake of financial gain, since it included mixing cement on the living room floor and leaving the lavatory door off for eight months (which particularly embarrassed the teenage daughter). At first instance, the petition was unsuccessful as the incidents complained of were said to be no more than the ordinary wear and tear of married life and the underlying DIY work undertaken for the benefit of the family as a whole, but the Court of Appeal eventually accepted that the situation went beyond such a mundane description and that marriage ought not to require such stoic endurance! However, it may be that what really tipped the balance was that, in addition to making life so physically uncomfortable, the husband also cast doubt on the paternity of the children of the family. (In the absence of some evidence this has never been regarded as good matrimonial conduct and would also qualify as bullying or verbal abuse.)

5.5.9 Emotional dissatisfaction

This has not been conspicuously successful in Fact B case law, the leading case being *Pheasant v Pheasant* (1972),[52] but this was probably because the wife in that case had done absolutely nothing wrong in matrimonial terms, and the husband was, to say the least, a little strange, as he claimed that he needed an excessive amount of demonstrative affection owing to his particular nature and personality, and that his wife had failed to provide it. Moreover, this was an early case, after the 1969 Act but before the 1969 and 1970 Acts were consolidated into the MCA 1973. It is hard to see how this fact pattern could not be sufficient to obtain a decree nowadays. This is because it can now probably be safely said that in the ordinary case, if a petitioner were able to show emotional dissatisfaction linked to some aspect of the respondent's conduct which could be said to breach a matrimonial obligation, while the petitioner remained a committed (if perhaps less than sparkling) spouse, then there is no reason why emotional dissatisfaction should not be a basis for a successful petition, especially as this is the usual reason for a marriage to break up. However, such emotional dissatisfaction should probably at least in theory be *evidenced* by the normal 'distress' which every well-drafted behaviour petition alleges the petitioner suffers as a result of the respondent's unacceptable behaviour. In cases of emotional dissatisfaction, it is essential to look for instances of insensitivity, selfishness and general lack of the mutual consideration which in any civilised relationship one spouse is entitled to expect from the other.

5.5.10 Sexual dissatisfaction

Although not found sufficient in *Dowden v Dowden* (1977),[53] sexual dissatisfaction is probably in a similar category to emotional dissatisfaction. In *Dowden*, the wife's petition was unsuccessful, despite her claims of frustration and tension because of the husband's lack of interest in sex. However, like *Pheasant*, this was an early decision on the new DRA 1969 law, only consolidated in the MCA 1973

---

52 [1972] 2 WLR 353; [1972] 1 All ER 587.
53 [1977] 8 Fam Law 106.

the following year, before either the court or the practising profession had firmly grasped the potential of the new provisions. Moreover, in view of the later *Katz* and *Thurlow* decisions (above), had the petition alleged some disorder on the part of the husband, causing the conduct complained of, as well as emphasising the effect on the petitioner, it is difficult to see how, in the light of the now established test for Fact B behaviour, the petition could have failed. The same might be said of the case of *Mason v Mason* (1980),[54] where the Court of Appeal held that sexual incompatibility leading to a wife's refusal of intercourse more often than once a week was incapable of being behaviour, whereas now it would surely qualify. While these decisions must be viewed in the light of their date it is useful to compare the much earlier, pre-DRA1969 case of *Sheldon v Sheldon* (1966),[55] where the wife's petition for lack of sexual intercourse on the basis of the then ground of cruelty was unsuccessful at first instance but allowed by the Court of Appeal.

5.5.11 Desertion is not 'behaviour' but can become so

It goes without saying that ordinary cases of desertion are not behaviour and should therefore be categorised as Fact C and not Fact B: see *Stringfellow v Stringfellow* (1976).[56]

❖ CASE EXAMPLE

In *Stringfellow* the parties' falling out and going their separate ways were said to be only the steps preparatory to separation and not what is normally understood by the word 'behaviour', which suggests some actual positive conduct.

Again this decision might be a little harsh in the light of the now accepted test for behaviour, since if the parties grow apart from each other, go their separate ways and in the process one is *inconsiderate, insensitive, neglectful* and *boorish* there is logically no distinction between that happening immediately prior to separation and its happening years before. Parties in this situation want a divorce, and provided the petition is properly pleaded and not defended, in logic it should succeed and is entitled to.

This is therefore a classic example of circumstances in which, with the passage of time, and established good drafting practice in the practising profession, a skilled practitioner now salvages what will otherwise be insufficient in law to found a decree of desertion if the separation has not lasted the requisite time, by turning it into a petition for behaviour. To do this the actual finite incident of leaving is generally well advised not to be drafted to include the fatal words 'desertion' or 'deserted' as an instance of behaviour. If previous instances are pleaded as 'being constantly away from home' (e.g. 'staying out late', 'not telling the petitioner of the respondent's whereabouts', 'apparent lack of appreciation of the nature of marriage and commitment to it', etc.), there should be no problem in obtaining a decree, either within the theory or practice of the spirit as well as the letter of the statute, since the DJ who considers the papers has every right to grant one on the basis of such allegations.

This is also a classic case of a situation in which appreciation by the student of divorce procedure, as well as of the black letter law on which divorces are granted, is essential in order to

---

54 [1980] 11 Fam Law 144.
55 [1966] 2 All ER 257.
56 [1976] 1 WLR 645; [1976] 2 All ER 539.

make a correct assessment of whether a particular petitioner may be entitled to a decree. It is also another example of the fact that divorce is in effect already available on demand under the present system, and consensually: if the parties either expressly agree, or are advised, not to defend, and adhere to that decision, a successful decree is assured.

5.5.12 Boredom and growing apart

Where these are relied upon, meticulous care will again be needed to avoid confusion with simple desertion. The petition needs to detail enough incidents prior to the actual departure to make it clear that the petitioner has some actual behaviour to object to (irrespective of desertion), which, in cases where behaviour is the selected basis of the divorce, will usually not yet have qualified for Fact C by not having lasted for two years.

Such a case where the drafting was probably to blame was *Morgan v Morgan* (1973).[57] Here the marriage simply 'petered out' when the parties were in their sixties. This was at a time when they sold their matrimonial home and began to live separately, which allowed their case to be dismissed as one of simple desertion, whereas had the reasons for their separating been examined, there might well have been enough 'behaviour' that properly pleaded would have justified a Fact B decree.

5.5.13 Potential bars to a behaviour decree

It should be noted that the same reconciliation provisions apply to adultery and behaviour, save that by s 2(3) if the parties live together for more than six months after the last incident of behaviour relied upon it will not automatically constitute a bar to obtaining a decree based on that behaviour, but the period of cohabitation will be taken into account by the court in deciding whether or not it is reasonable for the petitioner to be obliged to live with the respondent, given that the behaviour in question will have been tolerated for at least the last six months. In any case, any cohabitation will be disregarded if the petitioner has nowhere else to go, as in *Bradley v Bradley* (1973),[58] where the wife could not be re-housed until after decree.

The cohabitation bar applies even after decree nisi and the decree will not usually be made absolute if the parties are still living together when it is applied for. If the parties have cohabited briefly and then separated again between the two decrees, this will not usually affect decree absolute. Very often, the cohabitation is irrelevant anyway, since much 'behaviour', such as selfishness, insensitivity, verbal abuse, financial irresponsibility, etc., is of a continuing nature (so that there is no last incident of behaviour).

However, care may need to be taken as it seems that there are some limits to the apparent informality of divorce under the MCA 1973 because in *Savage v Savage* (1982)[59] the court refused to make the decree absolute because the parties resumed cohabitation three months after decree nisi and were still living together three-and-a-half years later! However in *Court v Court* (1982)[60] the court took the view, probably more correct intellectually, that it had already been held by the court at decree nisi stage that it was unreasonable for the petitioner to have to live with the respondent, so the fact that the parties had resumed cohabitation and then separated again if anything underlined this finding; thus, the subsequent delay and cohabitation did not change the situation.

---

57 (1973) 117 SJ 223.
58 [1973] 1 WLR 1291; [1973] 3 All ER 750.
59 [1982] 3 WLR 418; [1982] 3 All ER 49.
60 [1982] 3 WLR 199; [1982] 2 All ER 531.

5.6 The importance of drafting in an effective petition

It is obvious from the above account that skilled drafting is essential for the success of a behaviour petition under the contemporary law. This is the more so because of the nature of the process by which entitlement to the decree is decided. While this used to be called the 'special procedure', introduced in the 1970s to dispense with hearings in undefended divorces, it rapidly became 'standard' and practitioners knew they had to make their case on paper in such terms that the DJ would not call a hearing for further explanation.

Contrary to the suggestion in the name, all but a tiny percentage of divorces have since been processed without problems in this way (that is to say entirely on paper without an oral hearing of any kind) and in the new FPR 2010 the word 'special' was simply replaced, so the 'summary procedure' now routinely processes all undefended divorce on paper only.

Thus, only if the particulars of behaviour pleaded in the petition gave the court any cause for wondering whether the ground and the Fact were made out, did queries arise and delay set in. Where this has happened, practice has shown that it is nearly always possible to get the suit back on track, either by amending or by supplying further evidence, but this means that additional costs are inevitably incurred. Conversely, if the petition is well drafted (i.e. explicitly to reflect the literal as well as the spirit of the meaning of MCA 1973 s 1(2)(b)), what appear to be unpromising facts to start with may well result in a decree being granted. Obviously, there will also be a difference between those cases where the suit is undefended (so only the minimum standard of behaviour to satisfy s 1(2)(b) must be clear on the face of the documentation before the DJ) and those which are defended (so that the case will be thoroughly tested by an oral hearing with the usual cross-examination of witnesses) and in the latter case a borderline situation might result in a decree not being granted.

Nevertheless, much may still be achieved by positive drafting of the particulars of behaviour relied on. What may happen when divorce is an administrative matter may not be so sure (unless the law is also meanwhile changed to allow a simple declaration that the marriage has broken down irretrievably and an application made for divorce).

The trick in establishing 'behaviour' for this purpose at present is to remember that the key word is 'behaved': this is on the face of it an active word, not a passive one. What needs to be shown is that the respondent has done something to which the petitioner may take exception and done it to the extent that the petitioner cannot, in the words of the statute, be expected to live with the respondent. While this 'doing' element can be achieved by 'being' (as the cases of *Katz* and *Thurlow* have demonstrated), and without the necessity to show intention on the part of the respondent, it is nevertheless still essential to show, as a minimum, a state of affairs that can realistically amount to 'behaviour' such that the respondent cannot be expected to tolerate it in a normal matrimonial relationship. Thus, if illness or a passive physical condition is relied upon, and that results in involuntary behaviour, the resulting state of affairs must amount to something that the petitioner could not realistically be called upon to endure. For a situation that potentially falls into this problematic category, careful drafting can still make the difference between failure and success.

Post-1969, it is no longer the case that the petition should set out to disclose conduct which is outrageous in quality or quantity. Showing that the petitioner is entitled to a decree is a factual exercise, not a moral one, so the court requires a succinct, unemotional, impersonal, precise statement of the facts relied upon to bring the petitioner within s 1(2)(b). This is not the purple prose of the indignant old-fashioned advocate.

This is, in fact, the spirit of the Resolution approach adopted by the best contemporary practitioners, but the style and format of such drafting in behaviour petitions has an earlier origin. In the opinion of the late and distinguished family judge Sir Roger Ormrod, if neither party had committed adultery (the easiest Fact to use for an immediate divorce desired by both parties), what he called 'the mild behaviour petition' was the next best choice. What he meant by this was that the petition should both show the minimum safe level for the grant of a decree under Fact B (in other words it had to meet what is now the *Buffery* test) and at the same time not be unnecessarily offensive to the respondent. In making this suggestion, Ormrod, who was an early champion of civilised divorce suits, thought first of the desirability of not making it impossible for the parties ever to speak to each other again (as was often the case under the pre-1969 law and an obvious consideration where the presence of children meant there must be ongoing parenting), and only second of the benefit to divorce procedure if behaviour particulars are kept within a sensible framework.

The original Ormrod suggestion was that behaviour particulars should ideally be limited to about three incidents. These he categorised as 'the first, the worst and the last'. The phrase has subsequently often been expanded by practitioners to the 'first, worst, last and witnessed' and it is generally accepted that the most extensive particulars should not detail more than about six incidents or the court may think that the petitioner's case must be weak if so many incidents are relied on. In any event, dates, times, places and any other details should in theory be as specific as possible although the lack of defence in most cases means more generalisation is in practice acceptable. Thus, a good précis may be necessary in some cases, particularly where the marriage has been long and the parties have apparently soldiered on against the odds for some time.

While every academic student is unlikely actually to be tested in drafting (although there are some undergraduate courses which do teach the subject in this practical context) a working knowledge of the above best practice is essential in understanding what conduct is, or is not, likely to result in a decree of divorce being obtainable. Moreover, this is highly relevant to the current debate as to whether (or not) the MCA 1973 system is hypocritical, outdated and needs changing to a no-fault regime based on the parties' consensual approach to dissolution of their marriage. In this respect there are viable arguments on both sides: on the one hand it is said that we already have a consensual system of divorce on demand, and on the other that it is humiliating and out of step with social change to retain a system which is only adapted from earlier fault regimes. Deech claims that it is not a good idea to change the law at all, since that will only promote an increase in the numbers of divorces, which she sees as widely destructive.

5.7 Desertion and constructive desertion: Fact C

This Fact, in its present form, is a prime candidate for abolition in any reform of the law of divorce. The present scheme, under s 2(1)(c) of the MCA 1973, is so highly technical that it has fallen out of use for all but any case in which there is no other hope of securing a decree. It really belongs to another era, where there was no possibility of divorce by separation with consent of the respondent (or after long separation even without such consent), no 'behaviour' (pre-1969 cruelty was hard to prove), and using adultery meant that the respondent's co-adulterer had to be named in the petition as Co-Respondent or Party Cited, sometimes with catastrophic results for future relationships with the children. None of these problems still exist, and, as may be seen by the decision in *Stringfellow* above, what was seen by the court in the past as technically desertion can today easily be recycled as 'behaviour'.

5.7.1 What is desertion?

STATUTORY EXTRACT

The requirement to establish this Fact is

'that the respondent has deserted the petitioner for a continuous period of at least two years immediately preceding the presentation of the petition': s 1(2)(c).

Academic courses still sometimes study this Fact with the others in s 1(2), and it remains available as the basis for proving that a marriage has irretrievably broken down despite the now lengthy obsolescence which is evidenced by a far greater lack of current s 1(2)(d) case law than in the case of adultery and behaviour, which also have little reported, though in their case this is because their application is so well understood.

However, unless the case is extremely clear-cut and definitely will not be defended, desertion is so rarely used in practice because of its technical requirements. Moreover, a respondent who has deserted a petitioner for two years as required for Fact C is unlikely either to defend or to resist a request to consent to a divorce on the basis of Fact D (i.e. the same two years' separation plus the respondent's consent to the decree).

In theory, 'desertion' under Fact C can take two forms: either simple desertion, where the petitioner is left by the respondent without just cause and without the petitioner's consent, or 'constructive desertion', where it is actually the petitioner who leaves the respondent, but there is just cause for his or her departure.

Nevertheless, 'constructive desertion' is even more rarely used in practice as a basis for divorce than actual desertion itself, which is why there have been virtually no reported cases since the early 1970s. This is because any petitioner who can show constructive desertion can also show behaviour under Fact B and much more easily; apart from being able to present such a petition immediately without waiting for two years to accrue, the test for behaviour is actually much easier to satisfy than that for constructive desertion. This is because for constructive desertion the standard of conduct must be 'grave and weighty' (a real relic from past perceptions following the replacement of cruelty with behaviour) but which, as was expressly stated in *O'Neill v O'Neill* (see above), is not necessary for a successful behaviour petition. The reason for this is precisely because desertion increasingly fell out of use following the introduction of Facts B and D in the DRA 1969 and thus, unlike behaviour (which also at first used to be interpreted as needing to be 'grave and weighty' but was quickly modernised as the new statutes settled into regular use), desertion has missed being updated by developing case law.

5.7.2 The four elements of desertion

The following must be separately established:

- actual separation;
- intention to desert by the respondent;
- lack of consent to the separation by the petitioner; and
- that the separation is without just cause.

5.7.3 Actual separation

This is often clear because one party has left the other and gone to live elsewhere. Sometimes it is less clear because there is coming and going, or the parties consider they are separated but live at the same address.

Establishing that actual separation has occurred is important not only for desertion but also for Facts D and E, especially where the parties are still living in the same house, so this needs examining now. The principles are the same for Facts C, D and E, i.e. that it is essential that the parties, even if living at the same address, are living in separate 'households' (i.e. more in the style of flat sharers living independent lives than in a cohabiting sense as husband and wife). A distinction is drawn between one 'unhappy' household, where there may be little contact, and two separate households where the parties usually only still occupy the same premises because there is no alternative. Thus, desertion (and separation) may be available in situations where at first sight it appears unlikely.

> ❖ **CASE EXAMPLE**
>
> In *Naylor v Naylor* (1961)[61] the wife removed her wedding ring and decided never to perform any domestic services for the husband again, while he in turn gave her no housekeeping money. They shared no family or communal life, and the wife was held to be in desertion.

Naylor is the basic situation which will suffice for separation to be established where the parties are still living under one roof. This might happen frequently in present circumstances, where spouses may decide to separate but neither has any alternative accommodation. Other cases fall one side or the other of the 'shared life' marker and accordingly either amount to sufficient or insufficient separation.

Basically, the fatal flaws to check for in an alleged separation under the same roof are:

(1)   Mending, washing or cooking done by the wife specifically for the husband.

> ❖ **CASE EXAMPLE**
>
> In *Le Brocq v Le Brocq* (1964),[62] the parties had separate bedrooms, sexual intercourse had ceased as the wife bolted the husband out of her bedroom, they did not even speak to each other and they communicated by note only when essential. However, the wife *did* carry on cooking her husband's meals – which proved fatal to her claim of having separated from him.

It should be noted that a wife who returns to domestic tasks which she has abandoned will bring her separation to an end even if she refuses to resume sexual intercourse: *Bull v Bull* (1953).[63] However, this might not be held today if there were children involved and the meals were only provided for the husband when the shared parenting encouraged by the CA 1989 required such meals to be taken as a family. This is especially so when in *Bradley*, above, the court accepted that Mrs Bradley had nowhere else to go but that remaining in the matrimonial home in these circumstances did not prevent a behaviour decree being granted.

(2)   Shared cleaning or other housework.

---

61 [1961] 2 WLR 751; [1961] 2 All ER 129.
62 [1964] 2 All ER 464.
63 [1953] 2 All ER 601.

> ### ❖ CASE EXAMPLE
>
> In *Mouncer v Mouncer* (1972)[64] the parties were held not to be separated because they shared the general housework despite the fact that the wife did no laundry for the husband, the parties were on bad terms and they had separate bedrooms.

(3)   Communal life, especially eating meals with the family. This needs to be distinguished from the 'shared parenting' situation which is a contemporary phenomenon.

> ### ❖ CASE EXAMPLE
>
> In *Hopes v Hopes* (1948),[65] no domestic services complicated the issue (as in *Le Brocq* above), and there was no shared bedroom or sexual intercourse, but there was a certain amount of communal life, including eating meals with the family in the dining room and sharing the remainder of the house. The separation was held to be insufficient, as Lord Denning said, because there were not two separate households but one unhappy one in which there was chronic discord and gross neglect.

One aspect of the shared (albeit inharmonious) life which convinced the court that the parties were not separated in *Mouncer v Mouncer* was that, while the husband had no desire to remain in the house, he in fact did so in order to help look after the children. This case was, of course, decided long before the CA 1989 put into statutory form an expectation that separated parents would remain good parents in the interests of the children. As there clearly was on the facts of that case only one unhappy household and not two separate ones, it is unlikely that the same situation would be decided any differently merely because of the more recent concept of PR. However, it may be that if the parents are otherwise living discernibly separate lives under the same roof, helping to look after the children would not be fatal to establishing separation, especially if the parties have nowhere else for the children to spend time with the parent in respect of whom a separate life is claimed.

This must be especially so in view of the fact that in some cases separation has been recognised where the petitioner had nowhere else to go.

> ### ❖ CASE EXAMPLE
>
> In *Bartram v Bartram* (1949)[66] the parties had separated, but were forced to resume living under the same roof, even sleeping in the same bed and eating at the same table, without sharing any common household tasks (although it is fair to say that Mrs Bartram made her feelings clear by treating her husband like a lodger whom she cordially disliked). Obviously in this sort of situation great care is needed in showing separation under the same roof, save, in the case of a shared parenting context, for occasions for the *specific* benefit of contact of the other parent with the children.

---

64 [1972] 1 All ER 289.
65 [1948] 2 All ER 920.
66 [1949] 2 All ER 270.

Bona fide residence in the home as a lodger will always qualify as separation, although Mrs Bartram's situation was certainly unusual. There have been more 'normal' lodging scenarios.

> ❖ **CASE EXAMPLE**
>
> In *Fuller v Fuller* (1973)[67] the parties separated in the normal way, the wife leaving the husband for another man and taking the children with her. When subsequently the husband went to live with them as a lodger (he had been told that he had a terminal illness and only a year to live during which he should not be alone), the separation was held to have continued, even though he shared the entire life of the household, having all his meals with them and his laundry done by the wife, as this was in his capacity as a lodger, not husband. (In the event, he turned out not to be terminally ill after all – which was presumably why the decree was ultimately necessary.)

5.7.4 Other elements required for desertion to exist

Apart from separation, for desertion it will also be necessary to show the intention to desert permanently which is called the *animus deserendi*; also lack of consent to the separation by the petitioner, of which there are two elements: (1) no agreement to the respondent's leaving; and (2) no refusal of a reasonable offer from the deserting spouse to return; finally, also, (3) the separation must be without cause.

Only the last of these – separation without cause – is interesting in the contemporary context because it was where desertion was *with cause to leave the other spouse* that the former case for 'constructive desertion' arose, i.e. a state of affairs which qualified for a petition to be brought on 'constructive' rather than simple desertion because the other spouse had driven the apparently deserting spouse out of the marriage by conduct which would today qualify as 'behaviour' under s 2(1)(b). If this was conduct such that the petitioner could not be expected to live with the respondent there is now no point under the MCA 1973 in alleging 'constructive' desertion when that Act also provides the much simpler, less technical, Fact of 'behaviour'. Thus any such behaviour can be – and frequently is – used for a behaviour petition today, without any need to show the 'grave and weighty' conduct which had to be evidenced in the days when constructive desertion petitions were the only alternative to cruelty, which was itself the only alternative before the DRA 1969 provided the new Fact of behaviour. Some of the pre-1969 cases on which constructive desertion was based were quite colourful:

- keeping 30 dirty cats so that the house is uninhabitable: *Winans v Winans* (1948);[68]
- being overbearing, dictatorial and violent: *Timmins v Timmins* (1953);[69]
- being lazy and slovenly to the extent of driving out a moderately civilised spouse: *Gollins v Gollins* (1963);[70]

all of which could easily qualify now as 'behaviour' under s 2(1)(b). One of the (very few) modern cases which would easily have qualified as 'behaviour' is that of *Quoreshi* below, and in the light of the contemporary ease of obtaining a decree on the basis of behaviour or adultery, it seems strange

---

67 [1973] 2 All ER 650.
68 [1948] 2 All ER 862.
69 [1953] 2 All ER 187.
70 [1963] 2 All ER 966.

that such a petition should have been brought in 1985 on the much more roundabout basis of constructive desertion.

> ### ❖ CASE EXAMPLE
>
> In *Quoreshi v Quoreshi* (1985)[71] the parties were Muslims but lived in a Westernised manner, the wife expecting the husband to be willing to marry monogamously; when nevertheless he contracted a second polygamous marriage, although the first wife had expressly requested that he should not take a second wife this was held to amount to constructive desertion, although it could clearly have qualified as behaviour then and would certainly be Fact B behaviour in such circumstances today.

All the above cases were fought hard at the time they were decided, as it was by no means a foregone conclusion that the circumstances would be sufficiently 'grave and weighty' to justify the wife in leaving, although, in defending at all, it must have appeared to Mr Gollins, and probably Mr Timmins too, that there was nothing at all 'grave and weighty' about staying in bed, not washing, 'telling the wife off' and 'knocking her about a bit'. Fact B behaviour is now available for far less serious behaviour. The time warp is emphasised by another case from before s 2(1)(b) came into existence.

> ### ❖ CASE EXAMPLE
>
> In *Bulcher v Bulcher* (1947)[72] the wife left her husband because he had formed a strange relationship with one of his farm hands. As this fell short of homosexuality, it was held that she did not have just cause for leaving (and therefore was in desertion), although she was upset by it, embarrassed by local gossip, and felt 'left out' and starved of affection, all of which would have been treated quite differently today under s 2(1)(b), the decision in *Wachtel* having now established that non-adulterous relationships qualify as behaviour in such circumstances as they can be more hurtful than adultery itself.

Other relevance of old constructive desertion decisions is that there is still some intellectual dispute over whether on the old authorities refusal of sexual intercourse is just cause for leaving and therefore for petitioning under Fact B, although in the light of contemporary expectations this could probably be addressed, as other grey areas are, with careful drafting.

> ### ❖ CASE EXAMPLES
>
> In *Weatherly v Weatherly* (1947)[73] the wife was held not to be in desertion for such refusal, but in *Hutchinson v Hutchinson* (1963)[74] it was held that a wife could actually leave a

---

71 [1985] FLR 760.
72 [1947] 1 All ER 319.
73 [1947] 1 All ER 563.
74 [1963] 1 All ER 1.

husband who refused to have sexual intercourse. Despite the decision in the behaviour case of *Dowden* (see above) it is probably correct to say that refusal of sexual intercourse, if coupled with other insensitive and non-communicative behaviour, must now be sufficient for Fact B (a further reason, if refusal of sexual intercourse must be relied upon, for avoiding desertion and choosing behaviour).

5.7.5 Timing for presentation of petition in desertion (and separation) cases

The two-year period relied on for Fact C must immediately precede the presentation of the petition and this is the same in the case of Facts D and C (two and five years' separation). There are also similar reconciliation provisions in desertion and the separation cases under Facts D and C to those in connection with Fact A, in that the parties may live together for a period or periods totalling less than six months and no account will be taken of any periods of cohabitation in calculating the necessary two-year period to found desertion under this Fact (or the periods of desertion in relation to the Facts D and E cases). However, desertion must in total last two years immediately preceding the presentation of the petition, so if periods of cohabitation less than six months in total are to be disregarded, clearly the original desertion or separation will have taken place up to two-and-a-half years prior to the presentation of the petition, or longer in a Fact E case (see below).

5.8 The separation decrees: Facts D and E

These decrees were introduced in 1969, initially to an ambivalent reception from lawyer and layperson alike, not unlike that which greeted the introduction of the Bill which became the FLA 1996. The reasoning behind this initial opposition to the introduction of the two separation decrees was simple: Fact D brought divorce by consent into English law for the first time since the easy annulments of the Middle Ages, and since of course no one remembered the earlier history – and the common recall was of hundreds of years of discouragement of divorce on social grounds – this was seen as a mixed blessing, while (even worse in some people's perception) Fact E enabled an 'innocent' respondent to be divorced against his or, more usually, her will. Public opinion did secure protection for 'innocent' respondents on the basis that, as they did not themselves seek divorce, and indeed generally opposed it, it was right that adequate financial protection should be provided. This was thought to balance the mutually exclusive aims of recognising the sanctity of marriage, and giving due weight to one of the key principles of the divorce reform movement (i.e. that those marriages identified as dead should be given decent, timely and dignified burials).

5.9 Two years' separation with the respondent's consent: Fact D

STATUTORY EXTRACT

The requirement to establish Fact D is that

'the parties have lived apart for a continuous period of at least two years immediately preceding the presentation of the petition and the respondent consents to a decree being granted': s 1(2)(d).

5.9.1 Living apart

The principles used in desertion cases to decide whether the parties when living at one address are living in one household or two (see above) also apply to cases under Fact D, save that the Act actually provides that the parties are to be treated as living apart unless they are living with each other in the same household: s 2(6).

In addition to actual separation, a successful petition under Fact D requires recognition that the marriage is at an end, and when the parties are already living apart at the time that that decision is taken, some evidence of the changed status of the marriage will also be needed.

> ❖ **CASE EXAMPLE**
>
> In *Santos v Santos* (1972),[75] the husband lived in Spain and the wife in England, although they visited each other. For their divorce to be granted, it was held that a mental element was required to indicate the changed circumstances of the separation, and that the two years could only start when one party recognised that the marriage was over, but that once that had been done there was no need actually to communicate the decision to the other or to anyone else.

However, it will be necessary, where the decision is unilateral, for the petitioner to pinpoint the moment when he or she decided the marriage was over and for there to be some evidence of that. In practice, this means no more than that the petitioner is able to identify in the statement in support of the petition both when the decision was made and when the separation began if, as is usually the case, that was at a different time.

Sometimes there is actual evidence of a positive step (e.g. one party writing a letter) or at least a change in the pattern of behaviour (e.g. discontinuing visiting a spouse who is in prison or in hospital or elsewhere away from home, a cessation of communication with a spouse working overseas, or setting up home with a third party).

5.9.2 Consent of the respondent to the decree

Positive consent is required and not mere failure to object.

> ❖ **CASE EXAMPLE**
>
> In *McGill v Robson* (1972)[76] the husband was living in South Africa and the wife's solicitors, in serving the papers, somehow failed to send him a form of acknowledgment of service (usually included with the petition and upon which a willing respondent normally consents to the decree). He nevertheless acknowledged service and wrote saying that he wanted the proceedings completed as soon as possible – but in the absence of a specific written consent no decree could be granted.

---

75 [1972] 2 All ER 246.
76 [1972] 1 All ER 362.

One drawback of using Fact D is that consent must be positive – and the suit simply cannot proceed under Fact D without it – *and* the respondent can exact conditions in return for the essential consent. The common condition is that the respondent will pay no costs, as in *Beales v Beales* (1972),[77] but as it is now usual in Fact D cases for each party to pay their own costs this is not of far-reaching importance.

A more tedious condition can be that the respondent wants to exact a sharp deal on financial provision but, in general, if both parties want a divorce and the respondent sees that one will not be obtainable without some sort of suitable financial relief package, consent will usually be forthcoming. If the marriage has broken up anyway, the alternative might be to risk a petition being served on a fault-based Fact, such as behaviour. As allegations need not be profoundly shocking for such a petition, it would usually not be possible or desirable to defend such a petition successfully, so this is sometimes the remedy where an expected consent turns out to be lacking. Moreover, costs, unlike in Fact D cases, might legitimately be asked for in such a case, especially if the respondent has refused to consent to a Fact D decree.

In these circumstances, the usual course adopted by practitioners is to suggest that all outstanding matters are agreed before a Fact D petition is filed and then the agreed financial provision package can go ahead by consent. However, a further hazard of Fact D is that there is power to withdraw consent at any time before decree nisi and also power to apply for rescission of the decree nisi where the respondent has been misled in relation to any matter taken into account in deciding whether to give consent: s 10(1). Consequently the existence of this ability to exact a price for consent remains a problem for reformers in devising an alternative 'consensual divorce' provision that does not include this element of undue pressure. Moreover, under s 10(2) a respondent to a Fact D petition can apply to the court to have the final decree ending the marriage held up until his/her financial position after the dissolution has been considered by the court, so this can be a real hazard for the petitioner.

It should be noted that a respondent must have capacity to consent to a Fact D decree: see *Mason v Mason* (1972),[78] where it was established that the test for capacity is usually the same as for contracting marriage. This test, laid down in *In re the Estate of Park* (1953),[79] is basically: 'Is the respondent capable of understanding the nature of the contract into which he is entering?' In case of any doubt it will be up to the petitioner to establish that the respondent had capacity.

5.9.3 Timing in Fact D

Where a period of separation of at least two years is required prior to the presentation of the petition this must be observed exactly and the day of separation cannot be included in the calculation.

❖ **CASE EXAMPLE**

In *Warr v Warr* (1975)[80] it was held that this period is crucial – the day of separation was included in the calculation of the two years and a new petition had to be served.

---

77 [1972] 2 WLR 972; [1972] 2 All ER 667.
78 [1972] 3 All ER 315.
79 [1953] 2 All ER 1411.
80 [1975] 1 All ER 85.

No account will be taken in calculating the two years of any periods which do not qualify because the parties were cohabiting: s 2(5).

5.10 Five years' separation: Fact E

This Fact is substantially the same as Fact D save that the period of separation must be five years and no consent is required from the respondent. The respondent may be divorced without giving any consent unless able to use the special defence of 'grave financial or other hardship' provided by s 5(1) to preclude the grant of a decree in certain cases (see below).

5.10.1 Grave financial or other hardship: the s 5 defence to Fact E petitions

This special defence applies only to Fact E cases (and not to those brought under Fact D) and only where no other Fact is alleged in the petition. It is of limited application because the number of cases where grave financial or other hardship can successfully be shown is very limited, especially now when it is usually possible to obtain a satisfactory pension sharing order or some alternative compensation.

It should be noted that 'grave financial hardship' within the meaning of s 5 is now virtually entirely limited to loss of pension rights cases, and only where the petitioner cannot make alternative provision to compensate for pension rights which will terminate for the defending spouse with the status of marriage. The importance of this defence was further reduced pursuant to the **Welfare Reform and Pensions Act 1999** from 1 December 2000 when it became possible to share a pension by asking in the prayer of the petition for a pension order.[81]

The defence is also limited because where such marriages have broken down more than five years previously and the respondent has been obstructive in refusing consent to a Fact D decree, the petitioner often ultimately feels inclined, even if this was ruled out before, to petition on the basis of a fault-based Fact which the respondent will at least be put to some trouble to defend. Moreover, the respondent will then be precluded both from defending the petition on the fault-based Fact and from cross-petitioning, as once the five-year separation period is admitted there is no room for the respondent to obtain a decree because the petitioner is already entitled to one: *Parsons v Parsons* (1975).[82]

In order to invoke the defence, the respondent must file an answer, thus making the suit defended and, unlike most divorce proceedings, potentially eligible for public funding, although in the current context of deep cuts in public funding in family cases this is likely to be one where public funding is hard to get if still available at all, and it will probably be similarly difficult, now

---

81 See Chapter 7.
82 [1975] 1 WLR 1272; [1975] 3 All ER 344.

legal costs are no longer routinely provided for as part of maintenance pending suit, to obtain an order under MCA 1973 s 22ZA for funds to be made available to the respondent by the petitioner for the costs of proceedings, because very few such orders have been granted recently since it is necessary to show that there is no other means of funding the litigation.

In order to mount a successful s 5 defence it must be shown that it would be wrong in all the circumstances to dissolve the marriage, which, of course, will not be possible if the petitioner can also rely on Fact A, B or C, and which is why the defence is exclusively reserved for petitions brought under Fact E alone. The rationale for this is that when the law was fundamentally changed in 1969 to introduce Fact E, it was realised that special arrangements would have to be made to avoid injustice either to petitioner or respondent. Fact E and s 5 were therefore combined to achieve two independent but linked results:

(a) to enable spouses who were previously unable to obtain decrees to petition. Previously, such spouses were technically the 'guilty' party (usually having left to form other relationships but not having divorced their spouses) and had no possibility of petitioning under the law, which provided no separation decrees; and

(b) to protect the elderly, and especially financially dependent, spouses (usually wives), who could now be divorced against their will, from being cast off without at least proper financial provision being made for them.

The reason for combining the new Fact E with the s 5 defence was because Fact E was at the time regarded as a 'Casanovas' charter', enabling, as it did, those husbands who had traded in faithful, if now boring, middle-aged wives for a newer model to obtain divorces against their wives' will. Husbands who availed themselves of Fact E therefore benefited from the new law in being able at last to make an honest woman of a sometimes long-standing cohabitant when they could at last bestow a marriage certificate (and the future status of widow entitled to their pensions) on the 'bimbo' whose existence their wives had always refused to recognise (by declining to take the divorce proceedings only they, the deserted wives, had grounds for). It was thus thought right that these husbands be obliged to make effective financial provision for the discarded wife in order to obtain the decree.

A further class of spouses whom s 5(1) was intended to protect were those for whom religious objections to decrees were a serious consideration, especially in relation to foreign ethnic communities where divorce was said to be a social disgrace. These cases have, however, never really had much success, and have only infrequently been brought since the 1970s.

Furthermore, Fact E is now largely irrelevant as the stockpile of old cases where it benefited the errant husbands and the second families they had set up were all worked through in the 1970s. Section 5(1) defences are, therefore, usually now only employed as a bargaining tactic where divorce is likely to be inevitable and the only question is whether better financial terms can be exacted in return for truncating the delay and expense which a s 5(1) defence will cause. Generally, as good if not better terms can be secured at the earlier stage of consenting to a Fact D decree (see below).

If reform of the ground for divorce is eventually tackled again – especially if a drastically recast statute is introduced as has been suggested should now be done to bring the MCA 1973 up to date – the replacement for the now repealed Part II of the FLA 1996 might considerably strengthen the position of a respondent claiming hardship, including on religious grounds, as this seemed to be one of the few components of the discarded Part II of the 1996 Act which found favour with a section of the public. However, considering the eventually much reduced opposition to the **Marriage (Same-Sex Couples) Act 2013** when it was finally enacted, it may be that the religious issues with dissolution of marriages have also diminished in the 18 years since the FLA was in Parliament.

5.11 How the statute works in practice

An academic study of the present divorce legislation often gives readers the wrong impression of the law. As most divorces are undefended, it is as well to remember that most Facts can be proved without difficulty as long as the suit *remains undefended*. Esoteric points of law are usually only going to arise if the respondent disagrees so strongly with the Fact on which the decree is sought that an irresistible desire to *defend* arises which cannot be discouraged either by the respondent's own good sense or second thoughts or the combined advice of lawyers and friends. These cases therefore come to court for a contested oral hearing.

Another area of confusion is if there are multiple Facts on which a petition could proceed. In those circumstances it is not usually advisable to proceed on the basis of more than one Fact even if the situation qualifies, as this merely makes the petitioner's case look weak. If the case is weak, using more than one Fact will usually make it look weaker, except in the case of combining a fault-based Fact with Fact D in the hope that the respondent will consent to the Fact D decree and the other Fact need not be proceeded with. Thus, capable practitioners usually select the strongest Fact and only fall back on the suggested alternative in rare cases, since if there is a fault-based Fact available, a draft petition shown to the respondent or respondent's solicitors before service may result in an agreement that consent will be forthcoming to a Fact D decree. This is in any case recommended by Resolution in the interests of promoting their non-confrontational policy. If, however, a respondent is actually felt to be untrustworthy and likely to use the s 10 provisions to hold up the final decree,[83] then it may be better to plead the two Facts in the alternative, and if the desired consent is then given and maintained, the petition can be amended to delete the second Fact and its particulars. This is preferable to having to change Facts after filing, as that always looks foolish. Amending the petition to delete one Fact may be done without the leave of the court unless an answer has been filed in the suit.

Thus, although Fact D is supposed to be the 'consent' Fact, in practice, because of the hazards of a respondent imposing conditions, behaviour and adultery tend to be the 'consent' Facts instead. However, strictly there is no such thing known to English law as a divorce by consent on the basis of either adultery or behaviour. This does not stop laypersons stating that they have obtained a 'divorce by consent on the grounds of adultery or unreasonable behaviour', a statement which contains more inaccuracies than that no respondent can 'consent' as such to a divorce on either ground.

If it is *agreed* that there shall be a divorce and the basis selected is either adultery or behaviour, the divorce decree is achieved not by either party's *consenting* to the divorce but by the respondent *not defending* a petition brought by the petitioner — a significant difference. Nevertheless, whether or not the parties are in agreement, it will still be necessary for the petition and supporting documents to show a sufficient case of adultery or behaviour to enable the court to pronounce that the petitioner is entitled to the decree. This is so because, in view of the paper-based nature of the routine divorce process, there will be no other evidence on which the DJ deciding the case can rely to form the view that a decree is justified.

In these circumstances the bureaucratic nature of the present system is perhaps a valid criticism although the financial protection under s 10 is theoretically a positive factor, as the reluctant respondent should perhaps receive something in return for an uncomplicated consent to divorce, without necessarily being able to extract the conditions which can be demanded in return for that consent (which can often lead to an undesirable imbalance of power between the parties). Usually, such a respondent can extort a high price for Fact D consent (as otherwise the petitioner will have

---

83 See below at 5.12.1.

to wait three more years and still face a costly financial provision package to secure a decree). There is, however, some balance for a respondent to remember in relation to Fact D consent, in that it is rare that any respondent gets a better deal after having kept the petitioner waiting five years: it is therefore better for a respondent to threaten the three-year delay and stand out for a good financial package in return for consent at Fact D stage, than to be on the defensive after five years (when the respondent has nothing left to bargain with).

This is another example of why divorce is not a field of law which can usefully be studied academically in isolation from an appreciation of practice, since other provisions of the Act, and also practice and procedure, significantly limit the impact of the purely substantive provisions of ss 1 and 2.

There are others. For example, a weak petition on the basis of behaviour under s 1(2)(b) will appear in the academic view, and in the absence of experience of practice, to lack sufficient behaviour to establish Fact B, since in such a case there is always room for intellectual argument as to whether the test in *Buffery* (see above) is met.

The student who looks through the eyes of the practitioner, however, knows that the petition will almost certainly succeed, provided the particulars of behaviour are carefully drafted so that it appears on the face of the petition that the petitioner could be entitled to a decree, and the respondent also wants a divorce and does not mind being divorced on the basis of that particular Fact, so that the petition remains undefended. Moreover, it is entirely proper, despite the weakness of such allegations, for the practitioner to present such a petition since the law permits a decree to be granted provided a minimum level of evidence ensures that a case is made out which complies with the wording of the statute. This may be felt to be an abuse of the system, but English law has always made the best of whatever provisions the law offered, pending or in place of reform, a habit of the profession developed around the rigid common law writs before the rise of equity. There are also good reasons for choosing Fact B even when the qualifying facts are weak, despite the possibility that the respondent might have been coaxed into consenting to a decree under Fact D. If Fact D had been chosen instead, the respondent could have attached unwelcome conditions which cannot be used in a Fact B suit – so that the necessary consent for a Fact D decree might have become unduly expensive.

5.12 Financial protection for reluctant respondents to Fact D and E petitions

Every divorce will usually provide some fair financial provision for both parties on decree of divorce. This is built in under the ordinary law of financial provision, where the court (which is usually not in any way influenced by the Fact on which the decree was obtained) will seek to divide the assets as cleanly and fairly as possible, irrespective of which party technically 'owned' them while the parties were married.[84]

However, the two 'separation' Facts – Facts D and E – have their own enhanced protection: this is expressly because prior to their inclusion in the present divorce law, decrees were possible only on proof of fault. It was thought, therefore, that such a radical change as a separation decree – either on the sole basis of a short separation and consent, or a lengthy separation and against the respondent's will – should only be granted if the respondent could be sure that the post-decree financial position was definitely going to be satisfactory. This is achieved in different ways for Facts D and E.

---

84 See Chapter 7.

5.12.1 MCA 1973 s 10

It is not always appreciated how powerful s 10 may be in holding up a final decree where a difficult respondent is minded to do so. The provision of s 10(1) permitting withdrawal of consent to the divorce may or may not have any connection with financial protection, but is an extremely powerful bargaining chip where the petitioner wants a divorce badly and has no other Fact to rely on. Therefore, it may well be used in a financial context. The consent can be withdrawn, for any reason, at any time up to pronouncement of the decree *nisi* which conditionally dissolves the marriage.

It should be noted that decree *nisi* is the first of *two decrees* required fully to dissolve a marriage, and must be distinguished from the second (decree absolute), after the issue of which the parties are both free to remarry. They are not, in any jurisdiction in the world, allowed to remarry between decree *nisi* and decree absolute, although this has sometimes not stopped people claiming they believed themselves to be free to marry again at this stage and doing so bigamously. There is normally a *minimum* period of six weeks between the two decrees, largely for the court's administrative purposes, although it can in practice be much longer at the will of the parties if there are good reasons (e.g. hard bargaining in the financial provision context, especially where there is no satisfactory compensation for pension rights which depend on the continued status of marriage).

In financial terms, this limbo period can be used to good tactical effect by both petitioners and respondents. For all these reasons the profession (successfully) resisted the proposal in the Interim Report of the FJR that the two-decree system should be abolished and that there should only be one decree. In practice there are simply too many problems associated with such a change and the Final Report conceded that the idea was not a good one.

First, if it transpires in a Fact D divorce that the respondent has actually been *misled* in any way, in relation to any matter which was taken into account when consent was given, s 10(1) permits the consent to be withdrawn after pronouncement of decree *nisi*, provided action is taken before the decree becomes final at the decree absolute stage. The section even permits such a respondent to apply to have the decree *nisi* rescinded (so that if the petitioner still wants a decree another Fact will have to be used, or a new deal negotiated with the respondent).

This is obviously a powerful weapon in the hands of the respondent and in theory can apply to *any* condition which might be imposed, no matter how ridiculous, although there are no reported cases on the degree of absurdity to which this might be taken. Abolishing the two separate decrees would have led to numerous complications and inevitably extra work for the judiciary, rather than saving any time or imparting other benefits.

Second, by s 10(2), Fact D respondents who cannot claim to have been misled in any way, and also Fact E respondents unable to defend the Fact E petition[85] can still hold up the final decree dissolving the marriage by applying to have their financial position specially considered by the court, and this too can be a powerful weapon if the petitioner is in a hurry to remarry. Indeed such a petitioner who has to rely on Fact D is giving hostages to fortune, and obviously only uses Fact D if there is no fault-based Fact available. The Interim Report proposal would have done away with this safeguard.

Third, by s 10(3), the court will consider the s 10(2) application and will not allow the decree *nisi* granted on the basis of the respondent's consent to be made absolute until they are satisfied that either:

(a) the petitioner does not need to make any such financial provision for the respondent; or
(b) the financial provision made for the respondent is reasonable or fair or the best that can be made in the circumstances. The Interim Report proposal would have similarly destroyed this protection.

---

85 See below at 5.12.2.

Finally, by s 10(4) the petitioner can rescue the position – which may be desperate if, for example, he has promised early marriage to a pregnant new partner who insists on being married at the birth, or where the respondent or the new partner has a terminal illness – by applying to the court to relax the provisions of s 10(3), in that:

(a) there are circumstances which make it desirable to make the decree absolute without delay; and

(b) he will make such financial provision for the respondent as the court may approve, *and give an undertaking to the court to that effect.*

These provisions can be exploited by both parties even though any undertaking must be sufficiently precise to be useful.

❖ CASE EXAMPLES

Two cases have refined the court's s 10(4) requirement where they are minded to accede to a s 10(4) application:

In *Grigson v Grigson* (1974)[86] it was established that the general formula 'such provision as the court may approve' is inadequate and that precise proposals are required if the applicant is to be granted an expedited decree absolute.

In *Parkes v Parkes* (1971)[87] the reason for this precision on a s 10(4) application was demonstrated and showed how important it was for the respondent that the s 10(3) power existed, since the agreed provision in that case was not sufficiently clearly defined to prevent the petitioner from exploiting ambiguities in (and in effect depriving the respondent of the fruits of) the agreement. Had there been no s 10(3) power enabling the respondent to insist on the petitioner keeping the spirit as well as the letter of the agreement, the respondent would have lost out significantly.

Two more cases show where the court will not entertain s 10(4) applications where they are inappropriate:

In *Lombardi v Lombardi* (1973)[88] it was demonstrated that some applications are entirely unnecessary as in that case no more was awarded than the approximate offer in accordance with the then 'going rate' already made by the husband, so a s 10(4) application was not successful.

In *Krystman v Krystman* (1972)[89] the circumstances were even more absurd, where the Fact E wife respondent was better off than the husband and the parties had cohabited for only two weeks out of a 26-year marriage. Not surprisingly, the court decided that this hasty and long-abandoned wartime marriage should be dissolved without further provision and declined to entertain a s 10(4) application.

---

86 [1974] 1 All ER 478.
87 [1971] 3 All ER 670.
88 [1973] 3 All ER 625.
89 [1972] 3 All ER 247.

By s 10(3), this consideration of the respondent's financial position is a thorough stocktaking of the position as it will be after decree absolute and if the petitioner should die first, taking into account for example the age, state of health, conduct, earning capacity, financial resources and financial obligations, exactly as falls to be considered under s 25 of the MCA 1973 in relation to financial provision. Indeed, a s 10(2) application and the usual comprehensive claim for financial relief are usually heard together, supported for convenience by one statement in support.

A s 10(2) application is therefore a useful delaying tactic which tends to secure better financial terms in many cases. Even where it may not actually work at the substantive hearing, it will still have a nuisance value in that the final decree will be held up at least until that hearing, whereas otherwise the marriage might have been dissolved on the petitioner's application for the final decree earlier than the financial hearing could be arranged. This is because a court date for such a hearing will not be fixed until the parties' advisers have worked through all the stages of the financial provision procedure and it is clear how much court time will be required for the hearing. From this point the state of court lists generally means the wait for a hearing could still be some months.

However, s 10(2) can only be used where Fact D or E is the sole basis of the petition, so in practice it is not available where a fault-based Fact can be used, and a petitioner who fears a s 10(2) application from the respondent therefore usually petitions on a fault-based Fact if at all possible.

5.12.2 MCA 1973 s 5

Instead of being merely a useful delaying tactic, s 5 provides an actual defence which if successful will stop a decree being granted at all. This section applies in Fact E cases only – it is not available to Fact D respondents. Fact E respondents who cannot use s 5 can still obtain some tactical advantage by using s 10 (above) to delay a final decree which they know they cannot ultimately prevent in due course.

The section provides that the respondent may oppose the grant of a decree under s 1(2)(e), despite proof of five years' separation, if it can be shown that the dissolution of the marriage will result in grave financial or other hardship to the respondent and that it would be wrong in all the circumstances to dissolve the marriage (MCA 1973 s 5(1)). If the respondent is successful the court will have to dismiss the Fact E petition.

Obviously it is only worth using the defence if the petitioner cannot rely on any other Fact, as if the Fact E petition is dismissed the petitioner is only likely to present another one, this time on Facts A, B or C.

In order to use s 5, the respondent must file a formal defence to the petition, called an 'answer'. For technical reasons it is never possible to cross-petition on a s 5 defence, so unlike in cases under s 1(2)(a)–(d) the defence will be a simple answer not incorporating a cross-petition based on any other Fact, even if one exists. This is because, as shown by *Parsons v Parsons*,[90] once the five-year separation period is admitted, which is essential in order to invoke the s 5 defence at all, there is no opportunity for the respondent to petition since the petitioner is already entitled to a decree. The whole purpose of s 5 is to ask the court to formally not grant the decree to which the petitioner has shown entitlement (by proving the five years' separation – the period of separation being the sole requirement of s 1(2)(e)) because of the special circumstances afforded by s 5 (i.e. if the respondent can prove that those special circumstances apply in the particular case).

It should be noted that where a five-year separation already exists and one party petitions not on Fact E but on a fault-based Fact (e.g. Fact B), the respondent can defend the Fact B petition and cross-petition on Fact E, but in that situation, as is shown by *Grenfell v Grenfell*,[91] the original petitioner will not

---

90 See above at 5.10.1.
91 See above at 5.3.

be able to use the s 5 defence against the Fact E cross-petition. This is because the petitioner cannot then say that s/he does not want a divorce nor that it would be wrong in all the circumstances to dissolve the marriage when, as in the case of Mrs Grenfell, a petitioner has him- or herself already petitioned for divorce! Mrs Grenfell's s 5 defence was struck out as an abuse of the spirit of the defence.

Section 5 defences rarely succeed, except in cases where the respondent can show that the dissolution of the marriage will have adverse financial effects which cannot be compensated for (e.g. in the past where lucrative pension rights would have been lost). The scope of this defence is now severely limited because of the court's power, pursuant to the **Welfare Reform and Pension Act 1999**, to share pensions in the case of all petitions presented after 1 December 2000. It is usually impossible to show 'other hardship' in the sense of some social disadvantage, even in the lives of ethnic minorities where divorce is a disgrace which impacts on children's marriage prospects. Such a cultural stigma does not usually apply in a Westernised context and in most overseas communities divorce is either now tolerated, or separation (not the actual dissolution of the marriage) has already done the damage complained of. The court usually looks to terminating such empty marriage ties, so that it is not worth looking at the previous case law since no respondent has succeeded on this point for many years.

Wives' pension cases might still sometimes succeed, since the complex rules of pension schemes may still preclude the wife from genuinely sharing in the husband's pension rights where they cannot conveniently be shared and the scheme for some reason does not agree to pay his benefits to her. In these circumstances a decree of divorce may be undesirable because it ends the status of marriage (and therefore her pension entitlement). However, if there is nothing in the pension scheme to preclude the wife from receiving the widow's pension on the husband's death regardless of whether they live together, judicial separation will mean that the wife will still be provided for if the marriage is not actually dissolved. For post-December 2000 petitions, this is likely to be a very remote possibility (e.g. where there is a non-UK-based pension scheme).

However, usually the husband is able to provide for the wife in another way so as to compensate for the lost pension rights and in this case the s 5 defence will fail.

❖ CASE EXAMPLES

In *Dorrell v Dorrell* (1972)[92] the parties were both over 60 and the wife was living on welfare benefits. Although the husband claimed she could quite well manage on this without the widow's rights from his small local government pension, the defence was upheld as the court said that the amount – tiny as it was – was a significant part of her small income and, as there was apparently no way of compensating her, the marriage should not be ended.

Julian v Julian (1972)[93] was a case of a police pension where the husband could not close the gap between what was lost and what was required to compensate, and the result was the same as in *Dorrell*.

In *Le Marchant v Le Marchant* (1977),[94] however, where there was a Post Office pension, only at the last minute was the husband able to take out an insurance policy to compensate the wife, though the court would not make the decree absolute until he had actually done so.

92 [1972] 1 WLR 1087; [1972] 3 All ER 343.
93 (1972) 116 SJ 763.
94 [1977] 1 WLR 559; [1977] 3 All ER 610.

Nevertheless, the court can only act within its powers as set out in MCA 1973 ss 22–24. It can hold up a decree absolute while the husband volunteers a solution to enable a decree to be made absolute, but it has no power actually to order the husband to take out an insurance policy or to compensate the wife in other ways, except within its ordinary powers to order lump sum payments or property transfer from one spouse to another under s 22 or 23. Sometimes the availability of welfare benefits can be sufficient to persuade the court that sufficient provision is available without the husband making more.

The s 5 defence will not, however, work where the wife is young and/or the marriage has been short. Nor will the defence succeed where the respondent cannot establish that it would be wrong in all the circumstances to dissolve the marriage (i.e. where the respondent has to shoulder some blame for the breakdown of the marriage, although the decree is sought under Fact E).

❖ CASE EXAMPLE

In *Brickell v Brickell* (1973),[95] the wife had no difficulty establishing financial hardship on the loss of a Ministry of Defence pension, but her behaviour during the marriage was fatal, since she had had an obsessive belief that the husband had committed adultery with someone who worked in their business which had so adversely affected the business that it had had to be closed down, so that it was not wrong in all the circumstances to dissolve the marriage.

It should be noted that despite initiatives to achieve a fair division of the husband's pension rights on divorce, this problem of compensating the divorced wife for lost pension rights still subsists, despite the fact that sharing will now be possible, because in practice the cash equivalent transfer value (CETV) of the lost rights is not fully compensating, since it ignores the future payments that would have been made up to retirement age. Some pensions can still be shared more effectively in other ways outside the statutory scheme, as in *Brooks v Brooks* (1996),[96] where Lord Nicholls of Birkenhead accepted that some such pensions (set up by the spouses themselves as part of a private company scheme) could be varied under s 24(1)(c) of the MCA 1973 as a post-nuptial settlement.

The wife's solicitors have a duty to obtain an actuarial valuation of the pension rights and to seek a substantial sum in compensation, or run the risk of a suit for negligence. Above all, whether or not s 5 is invoked, case law has shown that a final decree dissolving the marriage should never be sought except on express instructions of the party concerned where pension rights may be lost as a result, since while application may be made for all available forms of financial provision, leverage will have been lost if the marriage is already dissolved and the pension rights have actually gone by the time the hearing is reached, not least because the pension is usually under the control of the trustees of the pension scheme and not of the parties or the court.

Cases of financial hardship other than on the basis of pensions are not common, but in *Lee v Lee* (1973)[97] a divorce was refused owing to inability to provide a satisfactory financial provision package outside a pension context. In that case the problem was the financial and other demands

---

95 [1973] 3 All ER 508.
96 [1996] AC 375.
97 (1973) 117 SJ 616.

made on the wife by a seriously ill son and, since the husband could not give the wife enough money for her to address this commitment, the court declined to dissolve the marriage.

It should be noted that such successful defences could undoubtedly increase if and when there is a replacement for FLA 1996 Pt II, as the new divorce and procedural provisions in that Act would have multiplied the opportunities for objecting to a decree on the basis of hardship other than for financial reasons, and it may be that these provisions, which were not at the heart of the objections to the 1996 Act, might be replicated. On the other hand, the opportunity to object to divorce under that Act or under the MCA 1973 on the basis of loss of pension rights is likely to be reduced now legislation is in force to enable all pension rights to be shared, that is unless the pension arrangements can still be shown to be unsatisfactory in the particular case.

Where they are still unsatisfactory, however, no doubt the court will continue to entertain such applications in an appropriate case, as it appears possible even to rescind an existing divorce decree nisi if the parties agree that better ones can be arranged under the post-2000 pension-sharing orders: see S v S (*Recission of Decree Nisi: Pension Sharing Provision*) (2002),[98] where Singer J did this at the request of both parties as they both wanted to be subject to the new pension order regime.

It may be that there is a case for *not* reforming the present law of divorce, not least in the present straitened economic circumstances in which resources for a complex redesign are not likely to be available, and the present system does seem to have been made to work, although it is generally agreed that the MCA 1973 framework is unsatisfactory. Cretney has commented: 'English divorce law is in a state of confusion. The theory remains that divorce . . . is only allowed if the marriage can be demonstrated to have irretrievably broken down. But the practical reality is very different, divorce is readily and quickly available if both parties agree . . .'

5.13 Other decrees: judicial separation and presumption of death and dissolution of the marriage: MCA 1973 ss 17 and 19

Judicial separation (JS) is available under s 17(1) of the Act on the basis of the same five Facts in s 2(1) as for divorce, save that the court does not need to consider the issue of whether the marriage has broken down irretrievably as the marriage is not to be ended but only a separation decree pronounced, which ends the obligation of the parties to live together. Presumption of death and dissolution of the marriage may also be decreed by the court under s 19(1) and (3) where the missing spouse has been absent for seven years or more. Financial provision is available after any of these decrees.[99]

5.14 Current debates

Ideas for research on these current discussion questions can be accessed on the companion website updates.

- Reform of the ground of divorce.
- Proposals by Resolution for a consensual system of divorce with no requirement for the parties to separate pending decree.

---

98 [2002] 2 FLR 457.
99 See Chapter 7.

- Why if the MCA 1973 is so unsatisfactory did the CPA 2004 mirror it in practically every provision?
- Should divorce or dissolution be fault based?

5.15 Summary of Chapter 5
The ground for divorce and the five Facts

- There is a distinction between the sole ground for divorce (irretrievable breakdown of marriage) and the five Facts (adultery, behaviour, desertion, separation for two years with consent of the respondent or separation for five years), one of which must be shown in order to prove the sole ground.

Proof of the ground

- Both the ground and one of the five Facts must be proved separately; one without the other is insufficient.
- But proof of a Fact raises a presumption of proof of the ground unless the court has reason to believe otherwise.

Adultery

- Adultery is defined in MCA 1973 s 1(2)(a) as follows: 'That the respondent has committed adultery and the petitioner finds it intolerable to live with the respondent.' There need be no connection between the two limbs of the sub-section.
- Adultery must be voluntary, between persons of the opposite sex, one of whom is married (but not to the other) and must involve an ordinary act of heterosexual intercourse: indecent familiarities are not enough.
- Adultery if not admitted must be proved (e.g. by blood tests, confession, birth of a child of whom the petitioner is not the father (though there is a strong presumption of legitimacy), circumstantial evidence or findings in other proceedings). Proof of the intolerability element is subjective. A petition must be brought within six months of discovering an act of adultery to be relied on.

Behaviour

- The requirements of the 'behaviour' Fact are defined by MCA 1973 s 1(2)(b) as follows: 'That the respondent has behaved in such a way that the petitioner cannot reasonably be expected to live with the respondent.'
- The test of behaviour within this sub-section is a hybrid one, part objective and part subjective.
- Behaviour can be involuntary: the role of intention is a minor one and intention can be completely absent in an appropriate case, such as where the respondent is ill.
- There is no finite list of qualifying behaviour; any gratuitously anti-social conduct is likely to be sufficient if it derogates from matrimonial obligations.
- Behaviour must be distinguished from desertion. Careful drafting of the particulars of behaviour in the petition to bring them squarely within the meaning of s 1(2)(b) may make the difference between success and failure to obtain a decree.

- The distinguished family judge, the late Sir Roger Ormrod, considered the 'mild behaviour petition' (alleging the minimum safe level of behaviour to secure the grant of a decree) the most civilised method of obtaining a divorce if neither party had committed adultery.

Desertion and constructive desertion: Fact C

- This fact is no longer much used as the law is highly technical and has in effect been abandoned since the 1970s: desertion cases can often proceed as separation with consent under Fact D and constructive desertion as behaviour cases under Fact B.

The four elements of desertion

- Desertion is defined in MCA 1973 s 1(2)(c) as follows: 'That the respondent has deserted the petitioner for a continuous period of at least two years immediately preceding the presentation of the petition.'
- This requires the four separate elements of actual separation, intention to desert by the respondent, lack of consent to the separation by the petitioner and absence of just cause for the respondent's leaving.
- Actual separation means that the parties must be living apart or, if still under the same roof, in separate households, rather than in one unhappy household.
- Lack of the petitioner's consent means that there must be no agreement to the respondent's leaving, nor refusal of a reasonable offer to return.
- Timing: the parties must not be living together at the time of the presentation of the petition but the two years are not fatally interrupted by periods of cohabitation, so long as these do not exceed six months in all.

The separation decrees: Facts D and E

- These decrees were introduced in 1969 to provide divorces after periods of separation respectively of two and five years, without any matrimonial fault having to be shown.
- A Fact D decree requires the positive consent of the respondent who may exact conditions for that consent.
- A Fact E decree is available without the consent of the respondent, but there is a special defence under MCA 1973 s 5. This is provided to Fact E respondents only, and solely where they can show grave financial or other hardship if a decree were granted, and where no other Fact besides Fact E is relied upon by the petitioner.
- The s 5 defence requires an answer to be filed to the petition, and if it is successful the petition will be dismissed and no decree will be granted at all.

Protection for reluctant respondents

- The Act provides mechanisms for respondents to both Fact D and Fact E petitions to ask for special consideration of their financial positions following dissolution of the marriage.
- These are contained in s 10 and include both delay of the final decree (decree absolute), where financial arrangements are not yet satisfactory, and rescission of the first decree (decree nisi), where the respondent has been misled.

- The s 5 defence is most successful where a respondent can show that there will be severe financial hardship in relation to loss of pension rights which the petitioner cannot compensate in some other way.
- Claims of hardship on religious or social grounds have never been very successful, since such hardship or disadvantage has usually already arisen following the separation, and is not generally made any worse by the grant of a decree formally ending the status of marriage.

Other decrees available

- Judicial separation, same Facts as divorce, but no need to prove irretrievable breakdown: s 17.
- Presumption of death and dissolution of the marriage after seven years' absence by the other spouse: s 19.

5.16 Further reading

Bainham, A, 'Men and Women Behaving Badly: Is Fault Dead in English Family Law?' (2001) *Oxford Journal of Legal Studies* 21: 219.

Cretney, S, 'Marriage, divorce and the courts' [2009] Fam Law 900.

Cretney, S, *Family Law in the 20th Century*, London, Sweet & Maxell, 2003.

Deech, R, 'Divorce – a disaster?' [2009] Fam Law 1048.

Eekelaar, J, *Family Life and Personal Life*, Oxford, OUP, 2006.

Hood, H, 'The Role of Conduct in Divorce Suits and Claims for Ancillary Relief' (2009) Fam Law 39: 948

Matrimonial Causes Procedure Committee (the Booth Committee), *Family Law – The Ground for Divorce*, Law Commission Report 192 (1990).

Mears, M, 'Getting it Wrong Again' [1991] Fam Law 21: 231.

Rowthorn, R, 'Marriage and Trust' (1991) *Cambridge Journal of Economics* 23: 661.

Scott, E, 'Marriage Commitment and the Legal Regulation of Divorce' in Dnes, A and Rowthorn, R (eds) *The Law and Economics of Marriage and Divorce*, Cambridge, CUP, 2003.

Chapter 6

Divorce: Non-Court Dispute Resolution

Chapter contents

Learning outcomes for this chapter

An understanding of the four currently available alternatives to litigation for settlement of family disputes, including

(i)   An overview of the development of Non-Court Dispute Resolution.
(ii) A sound knowledge of the role of marital agreements in family financial proceedings.
(iii) An appreciation of the potential of the growing influence of collaborative law.
(iv) An awareness of the now statutory status of MIAMs and the mediation process as the gate-keeper (with some exceptions) for access to litigation in privately funded as well as public funding cases.
(v)   An understanding of the potential for family arbitration in the settlement of financial provision on divorce and other family financial disputes.

6.1 Introduction: 'N-CDR', marital agreements, collaborative law, mediation, family arbitration

Repeated attempts have been made in recent years to reduce the financial and emotional cost of Family Law litigation, particularly at the financial provision and child dispute stages of divorce. In both of these contexts the parties often expend escalating amounts of money, energy and emotional capital in bitter litigation which the new President of the Family Division of the High Court, Sir James Munby, has indicated he is determined, as a key part of the ongoing modernisation of family justice, to tackle through alternative means, to which he has given the new name of 'N-CDR': 'Non-Court Dispute Resolution'. His immediate predecessor as President, Sir Nicholas Wall, famously commented on the damage to children, clogging of courts and waste of public resources caused by such attritious litigation, when both energies and resources could be better used elsewhere.

In the current economically straitened circumstances in which family justice is under great pressure, further cuts in resources, including public funding, are inevitable; and not only in legal aid, which from April 2013 was largely removed by LASPO 2012 from private family law, save for a few exceptions, such as where domestic violence is involved or a children case is urgent (where delay is prejudicial). Thus a Mediation Information and Assessment Meeting (MIAM), culminating in the issue of a mediator's certificate that the case is unsuitable for mediation, is a precondition to commencing private law property, finance and child dispute proceedings, regardless of whether legal aid is sought or whether the parties are paying their lawyers privately or acting for themselves as self-represented LIPs. The main reason for this is because adversarial litigation is not considered the best forum in which to resolve family disputes, although there was also an economy driver since the costs of maintaining the courts is now also an issue.

The mediation precondition to proceedings originally appeared in paragraph 3A of the **Family Procedure Rules (FPR) 2010** (in force from 6 April 2011), which contains a mediation protocol requiring a MIAM to take place before proceedings can be issued, other than in a few exceptions, but has now achieved statutory force in the **Children and Families Act (CAFA) 2014** s 10. This was initially criticised by Resolution and others on the grounds that there were not enough qualified mediators, and that because there would therefore be a resource problem, a new delay would be added to resolving disputes – the queue for a mediator. Happily there have been the few exceptions where the requirement for the applicant's case to be assessed for mediation first did not apply, but the main problem since April 2013 has been that, owing to the widespread removal of legal aid, many disputants did not know about mediation or MIAMs, and the take-up of MIAM appointments or indeed of access to mediators fell dramatically, since the parties knew about neither MIAMs nor the availability of mediation, or that it still attracted public funding where the parties qualified financially, despite the removal of funding for litigation.

Nevertheless, the pan-professional stakeholders are more deeply concerned than ever before, and in October 2011, following a meeting to consider the implications of the proposed changes, they issued a Manifesto for Family Justice. This was led by the Bar Council and FLBA and included Resolution and other organisations of a more general nature such as Gingerbread, the National Federation of Women's Institutes and the Children's Commissioner. Together these ten organisations presented to the government a formal statement of their concerns about the long-term, and apparently unnoticed, impact of the cuts proposed in the then LASPO Bill intended to effect these economies, but seen by all involved in family justice as of doubtful ultimate value. The Manifesto[1] called on the government to

- protect vulnerable women and children;
- listen to the experienced practitioners working in family justice, who understand that mediation, while beneficial in many cases, will not resolve many others; and
- consider with care whether the decision to remove legal aid from private family law cases will save the government money or, in fact, cost more and lead to poor outcomes.

However, MIAMs and mediation are only one initiative on which the government has pinned its hopes for cutting the cost of family justice. Heightened interest in marital agreements, fed by the Supreme Court case of *Radmacher v Granatino* (2010)[2] and the recommendations of the recent Law Commission report[3] is expected potentially to be an even more important initiative for success in cutting down on contentious litigation following divorce or dissolution of marriage or civil partnership, particularly in financial and property matters. Certainly there is anecdotal support for an increase in client requests for such agreements after the positive result in *Radmacher*, in which the court has confirmed that such agreements can be upheld in England and Wales, assuming that adequate regard is had to the usual basic requirements of prior disclosure, fairness, the parties' prior access to legal advice, arrangements for addressing changes of circumstances, and especially adequate provision for any children, all conditions which the Law Commission has included in its report.

It is therefore hoped that more couples will embrace this opportunity, entering into valid agreements that can be upheld so as to avoid lengthy, expensive litigation over the division of a couple's assets on separation and/or divorce.

The Law Commission's work has now fed into this movement for some significant private ordering. This started with a consultation on its paper on pre-nuptial agreements, in which it sought comment on its proposals on the basis that such agreements should be binding if there is full and frank disclosure, the agreements are in writing, the parties have taken legal advice and the agreement entered into is 'fair'. The Commission began work on the project in 2009 with a small-scale pre-project research study, and after the consultation closed in April 2011 the work was expanded to include a study of the reality and meaning of 'needs' in s 25 of the MCA 1973, and the concept of potentially ring-fenced marital property. The final report, with a recommendation for some guidance to be drafted by the Family Justice Council to clarify the 'needs' element, and a draft Bill was eventually issued in February 2014.

This may in fact prove to be a watershed for some progress towards not only a culture of some private ordering, but a normative approach to a couple's assets. A previous private member's Bill in 2007 was not taken forward. Obviously marital agreements entered into as a result of the surge of interest following the Supreme Court decision would not, and have not, helped the

---

1 Available at www.barcouncil.org.uk.
2 [2010] UKSC 42; [2010] 2 FLR 900.
3 *Matrimonial Property, Needs and Agreements.* Law Com 343, 27 February 2014.

existing divorce caseload which is still causing great delay in obtaining a hearing where the parties consider they need one, since those parties currently involved will not have had the benefit of encouragement to enter into such an agreement. However, as an additional plank in the modernisation of family justice, marital agreements may be of some assistance in the future, if and when those who enter into such agreements now themselves in turn come to divorce. In a sense this is a gloomy prospect in that it seems that the trend for serial marriages and divorces is now officially anticipated. However the only good news in this connection is that recent divorce statistics show that the current numbers of divorces are the lowest since 1977 (just under 114,000 in 2009). The latest figures released in 2012 show a very slight – and statistically insignificant – increase in numbers in the last year to be published, but figures still hover around the low of 1977.

The third strand which may assist the economy drive is collaborative law, of which the level of public knowledge, and even knowledge within the profession and academe, is as low as was that of mediation a dozen years ago, i.e. some people (barristers, solicitors, clients and judges) have heard of it, many people know no more, and many more have not heard of it at all, having no idea of its existence or characteristics.

Like mediation, collaborative law was developed in North America in the 1990s and later introduced into the UK. There is now a little research (conducted by Resolution) which shows how their schemes are working, and it has been enthusiastically adopted by Resolution, which offers training courses for its members.

The system is a species of DR in which the parties and their lawyers agree not to go to court to litigate but to attempt to resolve their differences in round-table discussions, either 'four-way' with the parties and their lawyers, or in a larger group including multidisciplinary advisers providing a 'one-stop' brainstorming facility to move forward the practical side of the divorce and the consequent new arrangements required for settlement. The difference from standard negotiation through the parties' solicitors is that if someone breaks the agreement and opts for litigation, a change of legal advisers is required, since the original participants have all agreed not to resort to court, thus placing some pressure on everyone to make the system work.

The fourth strand is the relatively newly developed scheme of Family Arbitration, announced by the Minister in his keynote speech at the annual Resolution DR Conference at Cambridge in September 2011 and formally launched in February 2012. The scheme, which was developed by the pan-professional stakeholders including Resolution and the FLBA, in collaboration with the Chartered Institute of Arbitrators (CIArb), applies only to financial matters, and cannot at present include any children issues. The first 100 plus qualified Family Arbitrators are available around the regions (and not only in London) to take cases under the MCA 1973 and a number of other statutes making provision for financial and property disputes, including **TOLATA (Trusts of Land and Appointment of Trustees Act 1996)**. It has received enthusiastic support from the President: see 6.5 below.

The inclusion of TOLATA is surprising; this is not a family law statute at all, and proceedings under it are not subject to the FPR 2010 but come under the CPR. Further, such cases are heard in the Chancery Division of the High Court and county courts, not in the Family Court. However, the logic of including TOLATA (which *inter alia* governs most cohabitants' claims disputes) is inescapable, since opposite-sex cohabitants, same-sex partners not registered under the CPA 2004 and other family members sharing property rights (or without explicit rights) now comprise the only form of couple partnership which is not subject to its own discrete regime: married couples have the **MCA 1973**, civil partners the **CPA 2004** (or owing to the **Marriage (Same-Sex Couples) Act 2013** same-sex partners can since 29 March 2014 now marry). The recent Supreme Court case *Kernott v Jones* (2011)[4] has again highlighted the gap in the law which does not provide for long-

---

4 (2011) Times Law Report, 10 November 2011.

standing opposite-sex cohabitants with or without children, a gap which has noticeably existed for some decades, and with a visibility which is constantly growing as more and more couples elect to cohabit rather than to marry or enter civil partnership.

Each of these four tools in the DR portfolio bears closer examination. The one most favoured, as it would (if successful) preclude any litigation at all, is an increase in the use of marital agreements, and would come closest to a default regime if most couples could be persuaded to adopt one before marrying, and to update it regularly when circumstances changed, for instance when children were born, when one party gave up work to care for the home and family, or when one shouldered a greater financial burden – perhaps when the other undertook further training or education in pursuance of greater career advancement for the benefit of the family as a whole.

6.2 Marital agreements

Married couples have been able to enter into agreements about what is to happen to their property for a long time, the only embargo being on some separation agreements which were traditionally regarded as contrary to public policy if providing simply for future separation, which was considered likely to prejudice marriage – a result, of course, contrary to public policy. However MCA 1973 ss 34–36 contain provisions for agreements between the spouses and it has always been perfectly in order to enter into an agreement containing terms for *immediate separation* or for resumption of cohabitation if the parties are already separated.

These agreements can contain, *inter alia*, provisions in respect of property and finance (and other matters) which will be effective if the parties should separate again, one of their advantages being that they can be customised to include any provisions which the particular couple wish to include, which is a distinct advantage over a court order, which will contain only those provisions which the court is in a position to order. Where there is an agreement in respect of what is to happen on divorce, the court has power under s 35(2) to insert further terms if the agreement does not adequately cover financial provision for any child, or for change of circumstances, although by s 34(1) such an agreement cannot oust the jurisdiction of the court, as the state has an interest in regulating the marriage status of its citizens.

However, since the 2008 Privy Council decision in *Macleod v Macleod*[5] it has been realised (not least by the judgment in that case) that there is no longer an enforceable duty on a married couple to live together, since that was abolished by the **Matrimonial Proceedings and Property Act (MPPA) 1970**, thus there is now no rule that agreements between spouses for future separation are contrary to public policy. Consequently marital agreements, whether pre- or post-nuptial, are perfectly valid, and, contrary to the Privy Council's view in *Macleod*, the Supreme Court has decided that there is no distinction between pre- and post-nuptial agreements in enforcement terms.

The Privy Council also took the opportunity to approve the case of *Edgar v Edgar* (1980),[6] which, however, also indicates that such agreements can have serious consequences in locking the weaker spouse financially out of the jurisdiction of the court, as agreements will be enforced unless the court finds that that spouse had been exploited unfairly, that there was misrepresentation or that there were other vitiating factors, such as no independent legal advice, no provision for change of circumstances or some sort of unsuitable pressure. Nevertheless these agreements do have the advantage of certainty, finality and of saving the costs, both financial and non-financial, of litigation.

---

5 [2008] UKPC 64; [2008] 1 FLR 641.
6 [1980] 1 WLR 410; [1980] 2 FLR 19.

Another problem of such agreements is that each case is considered individually by the court, and a determination made on its own facts, if one party attempts to disown the agreement, so it is difficult to know whether an agreement will be upheld or not, although it has been emphasised more than once that the fact that the court would have made different orders if the case had come before it under the s 25 criteria is irrelevant, and that the court will not lightly allow a party to disregard the agreement (as in 1980 the court would not allow Mrs Edgar to do). Instead, if the agreement is potentially valid, the court applies the s 25 criteria thoroughly and fairly to come to a just conclusion as to whether any agreement was enforceable. Some examples of previous outcomes illustrate how such agreements may be viewed by the court.

❖ CASE EXAMPLES

In *G v G (Financial Provision: Separation Agreement)* (2004)[7] an agreement was upheld which had been made between spouses who had each been married before and were used to regulating their affairs contractually. This was despite the fact that it had been concluded at an emotional time, and without legal advice. A warning indeed that such agreements can have serious consequences, although it is fair to say that this was recognised as a highly unusual case.

In *X v X (Y and Z Intervening)* (2002)[8] Munby J would not let the wife repudiate the agreement, where she had had legal advice and entered into it willingly.

In *Crossley v Crossley* (2007),[9] a watershed case establishing a practical new short procedure for use in this type of marital agreement's challenge, the court required Mrs Crossley to 'show cause' why she should not be held to the agreement which she had signed with her husband of 14 months, during which period they had mostly lived apart, and the marriage was not only short but childless. The parties were each independently wealthy and the agreement had provided that each should leave the marriage if they separated with what each had come into it with, and make no claims on each other. Thorpe LJ said that this was a paradigm case for upholding the agreement, which was of 'magnetic importance' and justified the new short procedure, requiring just cause to be shown why the agreement should not be upheld, which had been created for this type of case.

In *S v S (Ancillary Relief)* (2008)[10] Mrs Justice Eleanor King again used the new short procedure in another case where the agreement was also identified as of 'magnetic importance'.

This would appear to be the way forward in this type of case, should frequency of such applications to set aside develop into a marital agreement's challenge syndrome, which would defeat the object of aiming for certainty if the court ended up having to decide numerous such challenges in any case.

---

7 [2004] 1 FLR 1011.
8 [2002] 1 FLR 508.
9 [2007] EWCA Civ 1491; [2008] 1 FLR 1467.
10 [2008] EWHC 2038 (Fam); [2009] 1 FLR 254.

There has been a sustained campaign (from practitioners including judges and academics) for marital agreements to be made binding, and for 'due respect for adult autonomy', *inter alia* on the grounds that any suggestion that such contracts are or should be void 'reflects the laws and morals of earlier generations'. Speaking in the judgment in *Radmacher v Granatino* in the Court of Appeal, Thorpe LJ went on: 'As a society we should be seeking to reduce and not to maintain rules of law that divide us from the majority of the member states of Europe. Europe apart, we are in danger of isolation in the wider common law world if we do not give greater force and effect to ante-nuptial contracts.' This is the real issue about reform: cross-border marriages and much mobility around the world complicate matters, so that if such agreements are enforceable in one jurisdiction and not in another much expensive misery will ensue.

In *Charman v Charman (No 4)* (2007)[11] Sir Mark Potter, then President of the Family Division, had the same thought: the difficulty of harmonising the law in England and Wales with the law in other Member States in the EU where such agreements were upheld could lead to more, not less, litigation. The *Radmacher* case was just such a situation where the parties came from jurisdictions (France and Germany) where such agreements *were* normal, so that the decision of the Supreme Court that such agreements are potentially recognisable under English law, subject to fairness and there being no vitiating factors, is helpful. However, since such agreements are not usual in England and Wales, further detail and the legislation proposed by the Law Commission in their February 2014 Report would be even more helpful, especially as the courts have now started asking applicants seeking to set aside pre-marital agreements to show cause why their agreement should not be valid.

In support of such a reform it has been said that to include specific recognition of pre-marital agreements might encourage more people to get married, as there is certainly anecdotal evidence of a reluctance to marry and to risk the sort of litigation we have seen, particularly amongst the more moneyed sections of society, and particularly where a second or subsequent marriage is concerned.

However, there are all sorts of arguments against making such agreements binding, as is made clear by practitioners who say that crafting such an agreement takes considerable time, also requires an intimate knowledge of the law of every jurisdiction where the parties might live, that there is the risk in professional indemnity insurance of dissatisfied clients' suing their lawyers if the agreement 'goes wrong' in whatever way, and also the fact these agreements are in essence 'lock out agreements' which do not usually provide benefits in return for the weaker party's being willing to accept less than would be awarded under the contemporary law of the jurisdictions where s/he (it is usually she) is to live and might contemplate going to the court for financial provision on divorce if the marriage broke down.

This does not seem to many members of Resolution, a significant number of whom are also members of the International Academy of Matrimonial Lawyers (IAML), a very happy situation for them to be in. Frequently practising across borders, and as advisers to (usually) young women who are keen to enter into the marriage which has inspired the potential husband's desire for an agreement, they obviously feel uncomfortable where it is not easy to see any alternative for their young female client to entering into the proposed agreement if she wishes the marriage to take place.

Nevertheless, the Law Commission has recommended that such agreements should be upheld provided they comply with a menu of conditions which are set out in their report,[12] these conditions being very similar to the outline suggested in the Supreme Court's *Radmacher* judgment. In summary, they recommend that agreements having the potential status of a 'Qualifying Nuptial Agreement' ('QNP') should be established by amendments to the MCA 1973 and CPA 2004, conditions for recognition of which they set out in their accompanying Draft Nuptial Agreements Bill

---

11 [2007] EWCA Civ 503; [2007] 1 FLR 1246.
12 *Matrimonial Property, Needs and Agreements*, Law Com 343, 27 February 2014.

(which is an appendix to the Report); and that these QNPs should be contractually enforceable save that it would not be possible to contract out of an obligation under existing legislation in those Acts to address the financial *needs* of either party.[13]

The conditions for recognition of an agreement as a QNP are

- contractual validity under the law of England and Wales wherever the QNP is made;[14]
- no undue influence[15] (but they recommend some reform to the law of undue influence, in relation to QNPs only, so that undue influence shall not be presumed in this context);[16]
- made by deed,[17] and containing a separate declaration that the deed is recognised to be a QNP and the limiting effect of its content is understood, including that it does not exclude provision for needs;[18]
- made at least 28 days before the marriage or civil partnership;[19]
- full disclosure of each party's financial situation made at the time of making the agreement,[20] which cannot be waived;[21]
- legal advice to both parties at the time the QNP is made;[22] this to articulate the effect of the QNP in preventing the court from making the statutory orders which would otherwise have been available, save for in relation to needs, and that there should be a separate statement signed by the parties and the legal adviser(s) confirming compliance with the legal advice requirement[23] – and that this requirement cannot be satisfied by using one joint legal adviser;[24]
- variation and/or updating permitted, but must comply with all the same conditions as for initial agreements;[25] revocation permitted but only with signed agreement of both parties.[26]

A response is thus now awaited from the government about whether the draft Bill will be taken forward. In the meantime it seems there is at least a presumption that if an agreement is of the sort envisaged in the *Radmacher* judgment as potentially enforceable, the court to which an application is made to set it aside is likely to ask the applicant to show cause why it should not be applied.

6.3 Collaborative law

If there must be a dispute perhaps the second option of choice would be collaborative law, which aims to resolve outstanding matters without recourse to litigation at all.

Collaborative law is a process aimed at:

- maximising informed client decision-making;
- producing fair outcomes at reasonable cost;
- producing outcomes outside court;

---

13 Ibid., paras 5.84–5.86.
14 Ibid., para 6.12.
15 Ibid., para 6.16.
16 Ibid., para 6.29.
17 Ibid., para 6.36.
18 Ibid., para 6.40.
19 Ibid., para 6.67.
20 Ibid., para 6.91.
21 Ibid., para 6.103.
22 Ibid., para 6.125.
23 Ibid., para 6.145.
24 Ibid., para 6.159.
25 Ibid., para 6.186.
26 Ibid., para 6.190.

- producing outcomes paced according to the participants' needs and respecting their priorities.[27]

The definition of the IACP[28] Board continues:

Clients are each represented by their own collaborative professional who is engaged to resolve a matter under a written collaborative agreement. The collaborative participation agreement requires disqualification by all professionals who sign the participation agreement from participation or continued involvement in a contested intervention of a court or other body which renders a binding decision after presentation of evidence or legal argument.

As collaborative law is so new as a dispute resolution practice in the UK, there is no established senior collaborative law community (which contrasts with mediation, where there are practitioners who have been working in this field since the 1980s). However, Resolution has created a group with representation on its DR Committee which forms a focus for training of members, practice and information sharing in the collaborative law field.

Collaborative law is much less developed in the UK than in other countries such as the USA, Canada, Australia and Europe, and has been promoted by Resolution because, in comparison with other jurisdictions in which the members practice in international family law, England and Wales is lagging behind the rest of the world in this particular DR methodology. Other jurisdictions, such as Australia, hold collaborative law conferences.[29]

Collaborative lawyers believe that raising awareness of dispute resolution is the key to helping couples to identify the most appropriate method of resolving their disputed issues and avoiding court proceedings where possible. They believe that information about alternatives to court should be made available to all separating and divorcing couples and those in disputes about children. Resolution is spreading this information through booklets and leaflets which they provide to their members, who can then inform their clients of the options available.

However, there is a concern that currently there is no public funding for collaborative law so that it cannot be as accessible to family law clients as mediation is. Moreover, the Resolution research in 2009 has revealed that there were clients who would, if they had the choice, choose collaborative law over mediation (for which there has been public funding since the 1990s when it was formalised following the FLA 1996). The reason given for this preference was that such clients feel more confident having their own lawyer with them throughout the collaborative law meetings, which is not always the case in family mediation. As a result many solicitors are unable to act for clients as a collaborative lawyer since there is no public funding available, although the collaborative process would provide legally aided clients with another alternative to the court process if they do not feel comfortable with mediation. Resolution contends that collaborative law is at least as effective in encouraging shared parenting as mediation and may be more effective in some cases, so that they feel that publicly funded clients should not be denied this form of DR as an alternative to court.

Of course not all clients are suited to collaborative law, which is not passive but requires a participative engagement, the ability to see others' points of view and to act in a dignified non-aggressive manner, not to be revenge-seeking or to be backward rather than forward looking. Clients therefore need to be assessed for this process before it is decided to try it.

---

27 Edwards, J, Pirrie, J and Hogg, W, 'Collaborative Law Protocols – Vehicles to Share Practice, or Potentially Barbed Straitjackets?', *The Review*, Resolution, September 2009. The same article also appeared in *New Law Journal*, 31 July 2009.
28 International Academy of Collaborative Professionals, formed 2000, with 3,500 international members around the world.
29 E.g. *Collaborating Down Under*, Sydney, NSW, March 2009, where speakers included the Chief Justice of the Family Court of Australia and the Attorney-General of Australia. At the Cork Collaborative Law Conference, May 2008, Mary McAleese, President of Ireland, was a speaker. The European IACP Collaborative conference was hosted by Germany on 11 and 12 June 2010 in Munich.

Resolution argues that collaborative law is the best DR method for

- support and reassurance following a stressful separation of a couple with children, especially if those children are pre-teens or teenagers;
- addressing the children's interests and ensuring that their wishes and feelings are taken into account from the start;
- clarifying and prioritising aspirations;
- enabling all the parties to understand one another's priorities and developing recognition of others' claims to resources;
- generating options;
- clarifying figures and agreeing the principles by which participants will carry out their bargaining;
- managing the bargaining process and closing the deal;
- recording the agreement and making sure it is reliable.

The process includes leaflets such as Resolution's 'Living Apart Together' factsheets, obtaining places for clients on the association's 'Parenting After Parting' workshops, and introduction to the Resolution website, www.resolution.org.uk, which contains much useful information which is freely available to members of the public.

The meetings, which after the initial preparation appointment are usually 'four-way' to start with – i.e. with both spouses and their solicitors – are then interdisciplinary, including accountants and financial planners, so as to develop budgets (probably much smaller than the clients have been used to) and to work out how two viable households can be created from the resources available.

Resolution practitioners contend that this sort of work is most safely carried out under a collaborative contract, where even the financial planner is a neutral who is used to working with collaborative lawyers. They say that a couple addressing the usual issues arising on separation and divorce are more prepared to try interim budgets on a trial basis if they go into them through the collaborative process. This process also allows the lawyers to engage with their clients' value systems and to find flexible solutions where assets cannot be disposed of in an adverse economic climate. They also consider that the multi-professional approach offers lower-cost and speedier solutions than court proceedings or other DR alternatives, and is more effective than other DR methods because the clients are more confident with the process.

There is, however, a drawback: if collaborative law fails to achieve a settlement there will be a duplication of legal costs as all the lawyers must be changed on both sides, since this is required by the initial collaborative law agreement because all of them will have agreed, when signing the participation agreement, not to involve the court in that particular case. Moreover, while it may suit those who want to keep a relationship with the other (ex-) spouse, there are some practical drawbacks, for example that it may not be possible to obtain as full a disclosure of assets and financial circumstances as could be obtained in court proceedings, if necessary by court order, and there may not be much that can be done about that if the other spouse will not cooperate.

6.4 Mediation

If collaborative law is unsuccessful and the parties have to resort to other means of resolving their disputes mediation is probably the next most likely process to use, although sometimes parties will go straight there first without even trying collaborative law. Moreover, if they are considering litigation, whether without considering collaborative law first or following its failure, they will need to engage with the FPR 2010 and CAFA 2014 requirement for the MIAM process before they can commence litigation. Only if mediation is not an option for some reason, which is certified by the mediator conducting the MIAM, or no MIAM is required in certain exceptional cases, can this stage be omitted.

Unlike collaborative law, family mediation has been well established in England and Wales since the 1990s, and mediators who have qualified as family mediators (with the Family Mediators Association (FMA)), or cross trained to become family mediators, are recognised by the Family Mediation Council (FMC). Family mediators who conduct publicly funded mediation are recognised by the Legal Aid Agency (LAA) for the purpose, and have to comply with the Mediation Quality Mark. The Law Society of England and Wales also accredits mediators for membership of its Family Mediation Panel.

Mediation is a voluntary process, and there are four principles. These are:

- the process is voluntary;
- the mediator is impartial;
- the sessions are confidential;
- the process is flexible.

The process requires a mediator, the parties, any lawyers or other supporters they wish to bring with them and three rooms: one for plenary sessions, and one each for the opposing parties (or more if there are more than two parties).

Mediation has also been settled within the litigation process in England and Wales since the 1990s, when representatives of the main large providers shared the establishment of mediation services at a number of county court Civil Trial Centres where short mediations were held in three hours after the end of the court day. Research projects by Professor Hazel Genn QC have evaluated these schemes and the Ministry of Justice (MOJ) has now set up court mediation schemes at many courts with resident mediators in place so that cases can be referred appropriately. Following the introduction of the CPR[30] some 15 years ago, the Civil Justice Council (CJC) has promoted mediation through its DR sub-committee and the FJC has done the same in respect of family mediation – which was not welcomed by the public in 1996 when it was proposed as a part of the no-fault divorce regime to be enacted under the FLA 1996 Part II, as contemporary research showed.

However, since that time a slow awareness and acceptance seems to have spread. In the last ten years the MOJ has set up and supported a National Mediation Helpline and a National Family Mediation Helpline, which have been serviced in turn by the larger mediation providers; but while numbers of mediations, whether successful or not, have climbed slowly, there has hardly been a rush to engage in this form of dispute resolution.

In short, mediation in general and family mediation in particular have had a longer and more formally established history within the litigation process in England and Wales than collaborative law, with access to public funding and the support of the government, which has encouraged the use of this DR method both in disputes in its own departments and between those departments and any commercial or other outside organisation with which they may have relationships.

The latest developments have seen much greater reliance being placed on mediations so as to discourage litigation, and to reduce the numbers of cases going to court, and in particular from April 2013 this is an indication of the firm establishment of mediation within the legal culture. This inclusive status should confirm mediation as an integral part of the litigation process, rather than as previously in the eyes of some as a 'bolt on', and enhance its value as a settlement tool.

Nevertheless, it has not apparently established itself as well in the perception of the public, as is demonstrated by the fall in the numbers of mediations since LASPO 2012 came into force in 2013, removing legal aid from most family law cases – and indicating that perhaps solicitors were

---

30 As part of the Woolf reforms of civil justice.

a more positive marketing ally than some mediators thought. The government has pledged to provide better support to mediation in view of the fact that it was their decision to remove legal aid from much of family justice which has resulted in the army of LIPs which is currently clogging the courts, since the LIPs, now having no solicitors to advise, frequently do not find out about mediation in time to head off their contested proceedings.

Mediation is suitable for the resolution of all family law disputes unless there has been domestic violence within the family. In that case there has never been a requirement for any potential litigant to be assessed for mediation since it is accepted that the history will be likely to impede any significant confidence between the parties, so that achieving a settlement is unlikely or at best likely to suffer from considerable handicaps.

Unlike in collaborative law, mediation can involve just the parties to the dispute or the parties and their lawyers. Sometimes lawyers are not present but available at a distance, such as on the telephone, and instead the parties may be supported by 'Mediation Friends' (others with knowledge of mediation who attend with the parties to help and support them through the process: a number of specialist charities perform this function, including the pro bono departments of law schools, who train vocational students in this work).

The method is usually an 'intake' session for each party, in which screening for domestic violence should be carried out before the parties are together in any appointment, and then for the mediator to hold a plenary session, where s/he explains the process, sets down ground rules, and then invites each party briefly to outline his/her perception of the dispute. Following this introduction the mediator will often shuttle – 'caucus' – between each party's individual retiring room, holding discussions with each and where appropriate asking questions and suggesting options, until a deal is brokered, when it will then be recorded in a settlement agreement – usually heads of agreement, identifying any clauses which may need further work by lawyers, such as a consent order to submit to court.

However, some family mediators do not do this, preferring to see both parties together all the time. Each party must have confirmed on arrival that s/he has come to the mediation with authority to settle the case that day as if anyone else is involved who should be consulted before agreement is reached this can derail the agreement.

Mediation is usually 'facilitative' – the mediator assists the parties, in his/her capacity as a trained third-party neutral, to consider options for resolving the dispute. The mediator does not advise, on the law or any other matter, although, if asked, may give an indication as to the likely outcome if the dispute ended up in court. The mediator does not impose a solution. Sometimes there are co-mediators, such as a lawyer and social worker or psychologist, or indeed a second mediator whose discipline is not connected with family law at all.

It is unusual that a mediator offers formal suggestions to the parties as to how the dispute might be settled (rather any such creative ideas are usually offered in the form of questions such as 'What if . . .' and 'Have you considered . . .') but if asked to do so a mediator will usually be willing to give the parties an idea of what the court might do if the mediation was unsuccessful and the parties were obliged to go to court after all. Moreover, although the original draft of the CPR following the Woolf Reforms in civil justice omitted the opportunity to make mediation a constituent part of litigation rather than a 'bolt on', redrafts and case law have affirmed its position as an integral part of the process, in that any refusal to consider mediation may ultimately lead to costs orders, despite the fact that as few costs orders are made in family justice this may not be much of a deterrent in a family case, although litigation bad behaviour is one such possibility for costs orders to be made. Moreover, the rules both require judges to consider the use of mediation at the case management stage and permit them to adjourn cases at any time while a settlement is sought through mediation or other DR means. The FPR 2010 were thus culturally well placed to embody the MIAM process into the new rules governing family law cases in rule 3A and the Protocol thereto.

Advantages of mediation are that it is less expensive than court proceedings and can usually be accessed more quickly. It remains to be seen how this requirement is going to work in the long term if and when there is better publicity about the availability of mediation as an out-of-court alternative to settle family disputes. The pan-professional organisations' Manifesto to the government on the subject of the legal aid cuts draws their attention expressly to the fact that it is considered that, while mediation is often useful, it is not appropriate in every case.

6.5 Family arbitration

It is intended that the new CIArb pathway of Family Law Arbitration will now formally be regarded as another tool in the box of dispute resolution methodology. There has been approval of the concept by Family Division judges, such as Baker J in *AI v MT* (2013),[31] since when there has been further solid support from the President of the Family Division, in particular in his endorsement in the judgment in the case of *S v S* (2014),[32] in which he said:

> Where the parties had bound themselves to accept an arbitral award of the kind provided for by the Institute of Family Law Arbitrators' Scheme, that generated a 'single magnetic factor' of determinative importance, and in the absence of a countervailing factor or factors, the arbitral award should be determinative of the order the court made.

While a change in primary legislation would be needed to facilitate *automatically binding* arbitration in family cases, the status of an IFLA Family Arbitration award is no weaker in that regard than any agreed order by consent submitted to the court under MCA 1973 s 33A,[33] and a good deal stronger than some. This is nothing to do with the **Arbitration Act (AA) 1996**, under which arbitrations of all sorts are conducted, but because of the well-known discretionary nature of family justice. The fact that IFLA awards will not be *automatically binding* on the court is because of the ultimate discretion of the court to approve compromises in financial proceedings, which is currently expressly preserved by the MCA 1973 and will probably apply under other relevant statutes. However, Sir James Munby's comment above says it all: in the absence of any vitiating factor – an error of law or natural justice or other manifest irregularity – the court will endorse the award and a formula will shortly be forthcoming amongst the new forms which are being crafted for the Family Court to expedite any consent order that may be required to enforce an award elsewhere, for example a pension order, in exactly the same way as a mediation or collaborative law agreement which settles a case. The difference is that the Family Arbitrator will actually have made a determination within the terms of the AA 1996 and the IFLA Rules.

Moreover, since the parties will have jointly elected to submit their disputes to an accredited Family Arbitrator, this will be strong evidence that in all the circumstances of the case there is a valid agreement which, if entered into appropriately, would be considered by the court to be binding in any case, unless there is some vitiating factor – i.e. identical to the s 33A consent orders which the court routinely accepts where the parties have reached a compromise, unless perhaps there is some reason why such an order did not provide appropriately for any party or a child.

Thus the most effective way of making progress to provide this alternative to expensive, stressful and time-consuming contested litigation in court was to create a system whereby trained and accredited arbitrators would make awards in such a way that they would be regarded by the

---

31 (2013) EWHC 100.
32 [2014] EWHC 7 (Fam); 1 WLR (D) 1, www.bailii.org/ew/cases/EWHC/2014/7.html, http://www.familylawweek.co.uk/site.aspx?i=ed126784, 21 January 2014.
33 See Chapter 7.

court as *Edgar v Edgar* type agreements,[34] such as the court is already in the way of approving. In such circumstances and in the event that either party sought to disregard the award the courts would therefore be likely to be very reluctant to set such an award aside, thereby making such awards as 'enforceable' as possible within the present constraints of the governing statutes, for which there appears at present to be no political will or resources to amend so as to provide expressly binding force.

The background to this project was as follows. The CIArb offers arbitration in all fields and, several years ago, they and Resolution experimented in creating a scheme for Family Arbitration, which was then not taken forward. More recently, a pan-professional committee of stakeholders formed a collaborative project with the Institute. During the past few years a small committee, including members from each organisation, worked towards the formulation of a training scheme to qualify experienced family lawyers to the level where they could be accredited to arbitrate (in Family Law alone) through membership of the Institute. The committee included members of the FLBA, Resolution, the Bar Council and the Centre for Child and Family Law Reform, a small research group sponsored by City University, and became collectively known as the Institute of Family Law Arbitrators (IFLA), of which the Chairman is Lord Falconer of Thoroton, QC, a former Labour Lord Chancellor and active member of the House of Lords.

It was proposed that the scheme should cover financial applications only in the early stages, but might be extended to children issues later, as it was thought that to do this from the start would overcomplicate the initial launch of the service, since the court has a more proactive role in matters concerning children and the paramountcy of their welfare. The only applicable law is that of England and Wales, but provided English and Welsh law applies the actual arbitration can take place anywhere in the world. The benefits are that the scheme puts the parties in control of the timing, the cost and the choice of arbitrator and there is privacy, which is not the case in financial provision litigation in court. The scheme could result in saving much court time and therefore making some savings for HMCTS.

Resolution currently administers the arbitration scheme. A critical mass of arbitrators has been trained, who form a panel for the administrator to which to refer requests received from solicitors on their client's behalf or requests received directly from the parties to a financial dispute. Specific arbitration rules have been drafted, upon which the Institute-approved training scheme has been based. Senior judiciary and the FJC have participated in the discussions around the establishment of this new Institute pathway and the scheme was formally launched in February 2012, since when arbitrations have taken place in the regions as well as London, and in which disputes in relation to assets of high, medium and low value have been dealt with.

The potential is striking for the interface of mediation to decide child law issues between the parties and for family arbitration to determine the money and property disputes (and in a less costly, less delayed and less stressful manner than waiting many months for a court hearing).

6.6 The way forward in family dispute resolution

For some time it has been evident that an understanding of practice and procedure in family law is vital to the academic student's appreciation of the heavily discretionary nature of family law, since without a knowledge of how the law works in practice such a student is unable to follow the manner in which practitioners have taken the 'black letter' substantive law and adapted its application to the requirements of contemporary family life.

---

34 See Chapter 7.

How the law works in practice often has a profound effect on the statutory content, since there is little reliance on precedent owing to the existence and application of the discretions. Now it seems that even this is not enough and that the new academic field of DR also impacts significantly on the practice of family law. In view of the status given to it by the FPR 2010 and the CAFA 2014, and the impact of budgetary restrictions on the manner in which family disputes are now encouraged to avoid court proceedings where possible, mediation is obviously now set to play an increasing role in the resolution of those disputes, especially pending any adoption of the Law Commission's draft Bill on QNPs.

There was also at one stage a move[35] to rename ADR as 'Appropriate Dispute Resolution', on the basis that it is no longer 'alternative', having now been embodied in the FPR 2010, and this position re-enforced by the LASPO 2012 provision. It was thus envisaged that the MIAMs now in force would appropriately be similarly renamed 'ADRIAMs'.

However, since the government decided to go for 'Dispute Resolution' and 'DR' as the new name and acronym, and the President of the Family Division chose his own label of 'Non-Court Dispute Resolution' ('N-CDR'), both the full term and the acronym ADR now appear to have dropped out of the picture, along with the potential for ADRIAMs, since MIAMs appear firmly ensconced in the legislation, the CAFA 2014, which makes them a compulsory stage before most family proceedings can be commenced.

Consequently, it seems that mediation is still ahead as the main general N-CDR tool, with Family Arbitration a close second for financial provision, since the Family Arbitrators comprise a very experienced specialist financial and property panel which many family mediators will not be able to match in financial provision. The potential for the interface between these two appears even more promising, especially as some solicitors have already arranged to work with mediators and arbitrators to provide a 'one-stop shop', both locally in the regions and in London.

Whether the same growth and achievement of status will be seen in respect of collaborative law is another matter entirely – comparatively this is a tiny movement worldwide in the context of the spread of national and international mediation over the past 15 years. However, the process has received the support of the recently retired High Court Family Division Judge, Coleridge J, in the case of S v P (*Settlement by Collaborative Process*) (2008),[36] when it was held that collaboratively negotiated agreements which required a s 33A consent order could be fast-tracked to court on one day's notice.

If these DR options were really to catch the imagination of the public clearly a great deal of time and stress, and the attendant costs for both parties and HM Court Service, could be saved.

Whether marital agreements will also progress to a more significant role in Family Law is also difficult to predict. Much will depend on the outcome of the government's consideration of the Law Commission's report and draft Bill, and the timing is certainly not unduly propitious, with an election in 2015, to further that Bill. In the meantime there is a growing literature in the fields of both mediation in particular and DR generally, including on Family Arbitration. It may be this new initiative that emerges as the one likely to be more cost effective than litigation through the courts where other DR methods fail, and, having the support of the key personnel in the family justice system, besides chiming with the current economic goals of reducing cost without compromising quality, could prove a most useful addition to the portfolio of dispute resolution methods.

One great advantage of Family Arbitration, besides the benefit of the parties' being able to participate in framing their own points of dispute to be resolved by the arbitrator, is that much delay in waiting for court hearings can be avoided, since an arbitrator could be appointed

---

35 Raised at the annual Resolution ADR Conference at Cambridge, 22–23 September 2011.
36 [2008] 2 FLR 2040.

immediately (thus no wait for a court date months or over a year ahead) and the parties will be able to choose their arbitrator – whereas they cannot choose their judge, which will always depend on the ordinary listing procedures of the court. In his speech announcing the project in 2011, the Minister commented that, while costs should be saved, the government did not see Family Arbitration as a method of delivering cheap justice; the other side of the coin is that unless the assets involved are very valuable, it does not need to be an expensive option *and* can be completed in half the time it currently requires just to obtain a court hearing date.

Nor is there any concern about enforceability, despite the fact that there are currently no plans to amend s 25 of the MCA 1973 to make Family Arbitration formally binding. This is because it is desired to retain the ultimate discretion of the court to approve all agreements made between the parties subject to that statute (and others which relate to financial disputes which could be litigated in court). This is largely because this is the essence of family justice in England and Wales, since it depends on the very discretionary nature of English family law which separates our jurisdiction from those civil justice systems on the Continent and elsewhere where the system is based on a civil code. Nevertheless, there is no reason to suppose that agreements made between the parties to be subject to the decision of a properly qualified Family Arbitrator will not be enforced if there is any subsequent disagreement between the parties, just as any other agreement by consent is enforced under MCA 1973 s 33A if not contrary to the principles on which the Family Law judiciary exercise their ultimate discretion.

6.7 Current debates

Ideas for research on these current discussion questions can be accessed on the companion website updates.

- Should marital agreements be formally binding?
- Should collaborative law be available on public funding?
- Will the public accept the status once again accorded to mediation by inclusion within the CAFA 2014, given their rejection of this process in connection with the FLA 1996?

6.8 Summary of Chapter 6

Marital agreements

- Marital agreements, both pre- and post-nuptial, may now be enforced in England and Wales, subject to certain safeguards: *Radmacher v Granatino* (2010).
- Practitioners report certain drawbacks in advising on these agreements although there is pressure for harmonisation with other countries both in Europe and worldwide in the common law jurisdictions so as to avoid British isolation in this respect.
- The Law Commission has delivered its February 2014 Report incorporating a draft Bill, creating a legislative system with conditions for recognition of QNAs which now awaits government adoption.

Collaborative law

- This is a new species of DR, with a tiny membership worldwide, principally in Europe and North America.

- It offers a multidisciplinary service to facilitate settlement of family disputes without going to court.
- In England and Wales the prime mover in this field is Resolution, which organises training and other facilities for its members.
- There is no public funding at present for collaborative law.

Mediation

- Mediation is longer established in English legal culture than collaborative law or other DR methods over at least 15 years.
- Mediation has been supported by the MOJ and its predecessor government departments since at least 2000.
- Assessment for mediation is now compulsory under rule 3A of the FPR 2010, and the CAFA 2014 s 10.
- This rule will apply to applications to start court proceedings by privately paying clients as well as those few who can still receive public funding in family cases.

Family arbitration

- A new DR tool in Family Law, created by the CIArb with the approval and participation of the pan-professional stakeholders.
- Launch to the public February 2012.
- Awards enforceable by the Family Division of the High Court pursuant to its discretion as in the case of any other agreement by consent.
- The President's special support for IFLA awards: *S v S* (2014).

 ## 6.9 Further reading

Boulle, L and Nestic, M, *Mediator Skills and Techniques: Triangle of Influence*, Haywards Heath, Bloomsbury Professional, 2010.
Brown, H and Marriott, A, *ADR Principles and Practice*, London, Sweet & Maxwell, 3rd edition, 2012.
Davis, G, *Monitoring Publicly Funded Family Mediation*, London, Legal Services Commission, 2000.
Family Mediation Council, www.familymediationcouncil.org.uk.
Harris, I, *Marital Agreements*, London, Sweet & Maxwell, 2nd edition, 2011.
Irvine, C, 'Mediation and Social Norms', (2009) Fam Law 39: 51.
Resolution, *Collaborative Law in England and Wales: Early Findings*, Orpington, 2009.
Roberts, M, *Mediation in Family Disputes*, Aldershot, Ashgate, 2014.
Stone, M, *Representing Clients in Mediation*, London, Butterworths, 1998.
Thorpe, LJ, 'Statutory arbitration in ancillary relief', [2008] Fam Law 27.

Chapter 7

Financial Provision on Divorce or Dissolution

Chapter Contents

Learning outcomes for this chapter

A sound understanding of the theory and practice of the discretionary jurisdiction of the English court in making financial and property orders on financial provision following divorce or dissolution including:

(i) An overview of the development of the law and practice in financial provision: ss 22–25.
(ii) An ability to synthesise and apply the principles which emerge from the decision in *White v White* (2000) and succeeding cases.
(iii) An appreciation of the issues in the debate on proposals for reform of financial provision on divorce or other decree.
(iv) An understanding of the impact that marital agreements may have on financial provision applications: these may still not always be upheld.

7.1 Introduction

Writing his 2003 survey of the major divorce reform of 30 years before, Cretney commented that 'English divorce law is in a state of confusion.'[1] He was actually referring to the ground for divorce in the MCA 1973, which has certainly caused enough largely fruitless debate,[2] but he might as well have meant financial provision on divorce, which at the time used to be called ancillary relief, and is arguably in a far greater state of confusion than the ground for divorce, since the provisions for grant of decrees do actually work, even if that is because the practising profession and the judiciary have made them work over a long period since 1973.[3]

Nor was the subtle adaptation of the divorce provisions in the MCA 1973 the first time in a thousand years of English law in which the legal profession has taken something intended to be used entirely differently and made it serve another purpose because resources for replacement were lacking. Such successful adaptations were common in the Middle Ages when the existing Latin writs had to be made to serve the purpose of every action coming to the King's courts.

However, whether under its old name of ancillary relief – i.e. separate proceedings from those for grant of the decree, this time for financial remedies 'ancillary' to a divorce or other dissolution – or its new FPR 2010 label, 'financial provision', this area of law is not apt for such treatment and has long required the fundamental rationalisation not so far possible, although since everyone working in family law realises this there is a chance that the topic might figure in the Law Commission's next programme of work alongside, or instead of, the ground for divorce.

The seminal *Radmacher v Granatino* (2010)[4] Supreme Court case has once again turned the collective academic and professional mind to the principles of English law on matrimonial property and finance. But it may be wrong to continue to insist that financial provision is as hopelessly disordered as comments suggest. There is in fact a pattern of sorts which can be discerned in the latest decisions of the courts on splitting marital assets on divorce. The judiciary appears to have devised a working model under the MCA 1973: there is a theme which (with careful reading) does emerge from the reports.

On the contrary, the really burning issue now appears instead to be the severely disordered state of the law relating to cohabitants' property disputes, since these continue to be decided under legislation never intended for their purposes, and moreover under the CPR in the Chancery Division of the High Court (or the Chancery Lists of the county courts) not the FPR 2010 in the new Family Court.

---

1 *Family Law in the Twentieth Century*, London, Sweet & Maxwell, 2003.
2 See Chapters 4 and 5.
3 See Chapter 5.
4 [2010] 2 FLR 1900, SC.

The only small advantage of this (as there are certainly no other advantages for the parties in this inappropriate allocation of jurisdiction) is that rule 3A, the associated Protocol under the FPR 2010 and the CAFA 2014 s 10, which now gives the Rules provision statutory force, do not apply to such disputes (since they are outside the Family Court and the FPR). Thus the parties are not obliged to go to a MIAM before they can issue proceedings where the dispute goes to litigation, whereas for financial provision the Final Report of the FJR merely recommends that there should be a further separate specialist review of the law and practice of financial provision on divorce,[5] meanwhile recommending that such disputes should where possible be resolved by 'all issues' mediation[6] and should be subject to the currently planned cuts in legal aid in private Family Law cases, with all the attendant escalation of LIPs attempting to do this work on their own without legal advice and representation even after they have been to a MIAM.

7.1.1 The impact of the Family Justice Review (FJR)

Nevertheless, the Report does state[7] that it is appreciated that this should not hold up resolution of disputes about children where resolution of all issues cannot be achieved at once, and that it is recognised[8] that family practitioners make a significant contribution to support the parties through such difficult times, sometimes obviating the need for proceedings at all, at the same time indicating that the FJC's response to the FJR consultation also recognised this positive factor.

However, the Review also records that in the USA many more parties go to court without legal representation, that there is dedicated support for this from information hubs, (specifically referring to a report produced in California),[9] and that HMCTS in England and Wales was producing a similar guide for parties without a solicitor. It is fair to say that some of these guides have now begun to appear, although after around a year and a half of disorientated LIPs one could add 'better late than never', as their timely production, to coincide with the legal aid cuts of April 2013, would have not only saved a good deal of disorganisation through the sudden swell of LIPs but also much time, and therefore costs, of disproportionately lengthened hearings as judges attempted to cope with the lack of lawyers and the LIPs' confusion.

The Final Report of the FJR had also added[10] that the committee hoped that their recommendations (i.e. for more DR) would effect an improvement in England and Wales by 'helping more people to stay out of court' although they also recommended that the Ministry of Justice (MOJ) and the Legal Services Commission (LSC)[11] should carefully monitor the impact of the proposed reforms.

7.1.2 Other current trends

This chapter thus considers the present trends in financial provision on divorce under the current law in the light of these changes. One of these trends is towards pre-marital agreements which

---

5 Para 4.162. The President of the Family Division is now tackling this in his twelfth and thirteenth 'Views from the President's Chambers', having set up a working group led by Cobb J to provide a brand new MAP (Money Arrangements Programme) on the same radical lines as Cobb J and his CAP (Child Arrangements Programme) has already done for child orders. The MAP working group is obviously going to be a longer running project than can be covered in the text of this book although the first report has already emerged in August 2014 suggesting a new streamlined process, potentially more radical than the 2001 Ancillary Relief Scheme, but full updates will be an ongoing topic for the book's accompanying website.

6 Para 4.170.

7 Para 4.172.

8 Para 4.177.

9 *Statewide Action Plan for Serving Self-Represented Litigants*, Judicial Council of California, 2004.

10 Para 4.182.

11 Now the Legal Aid Agency, the replacement of the LSC being another of the many reforms of the 'modernisation' of family justice.

could assist in addressing the current anxiety to reduce the costs to the courts of financial provision disputes. Practitioners report a much increased workload in this respect in that following the *Radmacher v Granatino*[12] Supreme Court decision there is a surge in demand from clients.

This may or may not be a positive development since this is only one case in which the Supreme Court has simply determined that such agreements *could* be enforceable subject to certain safeguards, i.e. no vitiating factors, but it should be remembered that this decision does not open the door to wholesale enforcement of such agreements, and while the Law Commission has reported on its recent work on Marital Agreements, Needs and Matrimonial Property and included a draft Bill to enact their recommendations, these have not yet been accepted by the government, and even if they are it will take time to legislate.

First, the parties were foreigners, one French and one German, and in their home jurisdictions such agreements tend to be widely, indeed virtually uniformly, enforceable. That is not so in England and Wales. Second, in the foreign jurisdictions where such agreements are the norm unless there is already a matrimonial regime in force by default or agreement, both the culture and the legal systems are different. Third, those jurisdictions do not recognise the principles of the discretionary jurisdiction of the English court in family law cases (or, if they do, they variously categorise them as quaint or hypocritical since the English court can redistribute assets on divorce whoever owned them in the first place, an outcome which civil law jurisdictions do not understand).

The impact of *Radmacher* is thus quite possibly that it is likely still to be considered alongside existing principles such as that in *Edgar v Edgar* (1980)[13] (where such an agreement was enforced) but that in the case of English parties' agreements there is just as likely to be a refusal to uphold an agreement, especially if it is seen as unfair, if circumstances have changed and if it makes no proper provision for the carer parent of a child. This could therefore open the floodgates to extra litigation, rather than reduce it as dissatisfied parties attempt to get the agreements they regret set aside on one ground or another.

It may be strongly suspected that the last has not been heard of this issue, in particular where such an agreement does nothing but restrict the weaker party's ability to make application to the court and confers no actual benefits – which pre-marital agreements in most continental systems in fact do, thus making the agreement a much fairer contract.

7.2 Orders which the court may make

Financial provision is available not only following decrees of divorce, but also of nullity, JS and presumption of death and dissolution of the marriage. The range of the court's powers, contained in MCA 1973 ss 23 and 24, arises in the case of orders for spouses 'on granting a decree', and is subject to the court's consideration of the matters contained in s 25 of the Act, which details the matters which the court must take into account when exercising its powers under ss 23 and 24.

Orders made in favour of spouses to take effect before decree absolute are called 'interim orders', but become 'final' on decree absolute. The various types of order are not mutually exclusive – a package of financial provisions may contain all the various orders or only those most appropriate to the case.

Orders for children are always called interim orders, because technically no order can ever be final in relation to a child, whose maintenance may always come back before the court whenever appropriate. These orders can be made at any time if agreed between the spouses. Alternatively, if

---

12 [2010] UKSC 42.
13 [1980] 2 FLR 19.

the children are 'children of the family' who are not fully catered for within the jurisdiction of the Child Support Agency (CSA) or new CMS (Child Maintenance Service)[14] an application can be made to the court by the parent with care even if the other spouse does not agree. If the child's parents save the CSA or CMS the task of assessment by agreeing maintenance for the child between themselves informally, the intervention of the Department for Work and Pensions (DWP) at that time can be avoided as the agreement may still be embodied in an order of the court which is made by consent. The DWP must, however, assess the child's maintenance and enforce payment against the absent parent if the child and/or the child's custodial parent are on welfare benefits or a court order is transferred to the DWP.[15]

There is also in s 22 a power to order maintenance pending suit (MPS), prior to the financial stage and for the period between filing of the petition and decree absolute, although this is likely to be on a subsistence standard, since its essence is that the court will not yet have all the information required to make a long-term order. However, although MPS was wide enough to cater for an applicant's legal fees, this being part of necessary subsistence,[16] this is no longer the case and separate application must now be made for an order for such fees to be provided by the respondent to the applicant.[17]

7.3 The court's discretionary jurisdiction

Subject to the constraints of the MCA 1973 ss 23–25, the court has a complete discretion as to how its powers to make financial orders should be exercised (including whether they should be exercised at all), since there is no regime of matrimonial property under the law of England and Wales.

This is criticised by some jurists overseas who are constrained by an inflexible code of automatic matrimonial joint ownership. They claim that the English law of financial provision is defective in that it is inappropriate to the modern concept of matrimony as a partnership, since it is 'a law of separation of assets'; and that it is illogical in a marriage partnership in which in theory there should be 'community of property' unless there are special reasons for contracting out of such a position.

Pre-nuptial contracts make no difference to the discretionary nature of financial provision in English law, although the Radmacher decision has confirmed that they may now be taken into account as part of 'all the circumstances of the case'. This does not really change anything, as such agreements always could be taken into account under that duty and power of the court under s 25, nor does it mean that they will be regarded as automatically valid now; however, if they are not unfair they may be upheld. Previous cases, which have been before the English court periodically, were never this clear, although wherever there was an arguable case for taking such an agreement into account the court has reasoned its way through any decision it has taken on such an agreement. The results have been variable, depending on whether the agreements were taken into account or not.

---

14 See Chapter 21, which explains how the CMS is taking over from the CSA and that both are run by the DWP.
15 See Chapter 21 for how this operates.
16 See per Holman J in A v A (Maintenance Pending Suit: Provision for Legal Fees) [2001] 1 FLR 377, Fam Div, where this was established, as the wife in that case, who was wholly dependent on her wealthy Muslim Arab husband, was without capital or income and already owed legal fees of £40,000, since her legal aid certificate had been withdrawn when an earlier MPS order had been made. Accordingly, legal fees in divorce were a recognised item in an MPS budget but this then fell foul of the principle that in the ordinary course of events no costs orders were made in financial provision cases.
17 See MCA 1973 s 22ZA.

❖ CASE EXAMPLES

In *F v F (Ancillary Relief: Substantial Assets)* (1995)[18] Thorpe LJ took the view that such contracts have limited significance in English law.

In *N v N (Foreign Divorce)* (1997)[19] Cazalet J considered that they may be relevant.

In *S v S (Staying Proceedings)* (1997)[20] Wilson J, as he then was, now Lord Wilson of Culworth since his elevation to the Supreme Court, considered that the day of such contracts would come, probably in serial monogamy cases where the enforceability of such a contract was crucial to a marriage taking place at all; a shrewd thought from a wise and experienced Family Law judge, now the second family lawyer in the Supreme Court, where this issue is likely to be considered further, since unless and until the Law Commission's recent recommendations are actioned by the government[21] we are not yet at the end of this debate.

The Law Commission's recent report[22] was not the first formal work on marital agreements. Nearly two decades ago the government's 1998 consultation paper, *Supporting Families*,[23] suggested that pre-nuptial contracts should be enforceable subject to specific conditions (but it was never implemented although it had support from various sources, including the Law Society and Resolution which publishes pre-marriage precedents, and is broadly in favour of introducing some sort of financial agreement on marriage).

The Family Division judges responded to the consultation paper in the March 1999 issue of the journal *Family Law* and distinguished these agreements from the only similar pact then commonly taken into account by the court, namely the *Edgar v Edgar* (1980)[24] maintenance agreement.

Edgar was quite similar to *Radmacher*, apart from the gender reversal, in that the husband was a multi-millionaire who agreed to pay Mrs Edgar £100,000 but she was not to seek any further provision. Unlike Mr Granatino she had taken legal advice and her solicitor advised her not to sign because she could get better provision from court. On divorce she received a lump sum of £760,000 but, on appeal by the husband to the Court of Appeal, lost it, as they found that she had not been exploited and should be bound by the agreement.

Sitting on that case was another wise and experienced Family Law judge, Ormrod LJ,[25] who observed that 'formal agreements, properly and faithfully arrived at with competent legal advice' should not be disturbed save on 'good and substantial grounds' that an injustice had been done by holding a party to the agreement. He added that such grounds included pressure from one side, exploitation of a dominant position, no or bad legal advice, inadequate knowledge or unforeseen

---

18 [1995] 2 FLR 47.
19 [1997] 1 FLR 900.
20 [1997] 2 FLR 669.
21 See Chapter 6.
22 Law Com No 343.
23 Home Office, 1998.
24 [1980] 1 WLR 1410.
25 The originator of the 'mild behaviour petition' as the ultimate basis of the contemporary practice of consensual (almost 'no-fault') divorce, see Chapter 5.

circumstances and that 'the existence of a freely negotiated bargain entered into at the instance of one of the parties and affording him or her everything he or she has stipulated must be a most important element of conduct which cannot lightly be ignored'. He went on to say that there often was disparity of bargaining power but that where (as is often the case) that was in the hands of the husband the crucial question was 'whether he exploited it in a way that was unfair to the wife, so as to induce her to act to her disadvantage'.

This is interesting as it was the only case before *Radmacher* where, over 30 years ago, the decision cut firmly across the established discretion of the English court, and the rejection in principle of agreements that ousted that discretion.

7.3.1 'England: the divorce capital of the world'

The distinct discretionary approach of English law in financial provision is often the reason for international multi-millionaire divorces being conducted in England rather than in the default community property jurisdictions which exist in much of the rest of the world.

The reason for the selection of an English forum for divorce in these cases is that these community property jurisdictions are unfriendly to the rich husband, since the law of those states usually considers that the spouses already actually or notionally own the matrimonial assets jointly, whatever the spouses themselves desire or declare, whereas English law has more usually proceeded on the basis of what provision was actually reasonably needed for the financially weaker spouse (who was generally the wife) rather than that the spouse should receive any particular proportion of the assets available for distribution.

When this approach was criticised and departed from in contexts such as the seminal case of *White v White* (2000),[26] and also in *Lambert v Lambert* (2002),[27] the English court still preserved an element of discretion in deciding which assets should be 'ring-fenced' rather than included in the matrimonial 'pot' for distribution and periodically gave credit for 'stellar contribution' by one spouse (usually the husband).

This rejection of the purely 'arithmetical approach' was foreshadowed by the Court of Appeal in *Dart v Dart* (1996),[28] where from assets of around £400 million the wife received under £10 million. The husband had carefully planned the family's 'habitual residence' in London so as to avoid the US jurisdiction of Michigan.

The English scheme is thus one where the *actual ownership* in law of any asset which the court considers is available as a resource at its disposal is mostly still *irrelevant*: by s 24, and subject only to s 25, the court has the power to rearrange ownership of the spouses' assets on divorce as they see fit, although since the *White* decision they do appear in the end to be looking at a 50 per cent split as a starting point (although this is denied in some judgments which say there is no such presumption), at least where there are assets surplus to needs – subject of course to the ring-fencing potential. The result of this is that it is impossible to be sure what the result will be on any financial provision application.

Moreover, since the s 24 jurisdiction is a discretionary one, the court is not officially bound by precedent, a point stressed in the *Dart* decision, and not changed by the House of Lords in *White v White*. In *White*, Lord Nicholls of Birkenhead said that a judge should always check his award against the notional yardstick of equality, but a careful examination of his speech makes it clear that he thinks that, in the search for fairness between the parties, closer adherence to the s 25 factors is the route which English law should follow rather than attempting any specifically equal division; and

---

26 [2000] 2 FLR 981.
27 [2002] EWCA Civ 1685.
28 [1996] 2 FLR 286, CA.

that, *inter alia*, this is because express equal division may not be fair, whether in average or big money cases such as *White*.

This permits the distinctly English approach to the wife's reasonable needs to be interpreted in accordance with the particular circumstances, including age, length of marriage and former life-style of the parties, without any confusion over whether 'needs' is the same as 'reasonable require-ments' where assets exceed the ordinary meaning of 'needs', even generously interpreted. Indeed in the big money case of *Lambert v Lambert* (above) the Court of Appeal did comment that the award in the lower court did not take sufficient account of the wife's 'needs'.

This confusion over the precise meaning of 'needs' has currently resulted in the Law Commission's recent report,[29] which, besides considering marital agreements, was also concerned with ring-fencing and needs, referring the specific articulation of 'needs' to guidance from the FJC, which has allocated the work to its 2014–15 Business Plan.

Conversely, as shown by Hale J (as she then was)[30] in B v B (1997),[31] closely following the s 25 factors may *incidentally* produce a substantially equal division, about which Mr Burgess complained, on the basis that the judge must have misdirected herself in ignoring his allegedly superior needs, as the result of her order was equality of division; however, Waite LJ on appeal found no fault with her meticulous application of the factors to produce what appeared to be a fair result. Nevertheless Lord Nicholls in *White* emphasised that there was no principle of equal division in English law as that would be an impermissible gloss on s 25 so that such an introduction was a matter for Parliament and not for the courts. He also said there would be less confusion as to whether 'needs' was the same as 'reasonable requirements' if judges adhered to the precise wording of MCA 1973 s 25(2)(b), which actually uses the word 'needs'.

7.3.2 Developing the principles in *White v White*

Following Lord Nicholls' leading speech in this watershed case, a number of other cases developed the move away from 'needs' to polish the fairness approach and in doing so laid down some new principles to help in interpreting what was meant by the yardstick of equality without necessarily dividing the assets on a 50:50 basis. Academics and leading practitioners were not sure what this meant[32] and their views ranged from expecting more pre-marital agreements to be entered into (because of the uncertainty involved in deciding what the law was) to fewer marriages because of that uncertainty, and mentioning in passing that the case had not really given any steer towards future decisions and was so confusing that it was likely to cause much expense and emotional distress – also because of the uncertainty.

Some clarification came from the commercial background of the then President of the Family Division, Sir Mark Potter, in *Charman v Charman* (No 4) (2007),[33] who said in his judgment, in effect collating and summarising the post-*White* case law, that *White* had not resolved 'the problems faced by practitioners in advising clients or by the client in deciding upon what terms to compromise'.

Criticisms nevertheless continued to include that there was nothing in the statute about a 'yard-stick of equality' (though this might have come from Mrs White's strong contention in the case that she was a business partner in the parties' farming enterprise, as well as a wife in a marriage which was also a partnership); further that the House of Lords had emphasised sticking to the statute while introducing this extraneous factor, at the same time elevating one of the s 25 factors

---

29 Law Com 343, 3.1–3.151.
30 Formerly Professor Brenda Hoggett, Professor of English Law at King's College London, and Law Commissioner at the time of the work on the Children Act 1989, and academic of distinction before the Bench, now Deputy President of the Supreme Court.
31 Reported in the Court of Appeal *sub nom Burgess v Burgess* [1997] 1 FCR 89; [1996] Fam Law 465; [1996] 2 FLR 34.
32 See the Further Reading for their contributions.
33 [2007] EWCA Civ 503; [2007] 1 FLR 1246. See further below in the case examples for the impact of this case.

(s 25(2)(f), which required consideration of each party's contribution to the welfare of the family during and after the marriage), and had introduced into that further glosses of equality principles of fairness and discrimination.

The refinements added by later cases have developed Lord Nicholls' initial thoughts as case followed case, so that in fact we do now have an outline of what the court is likely to do, although (owing to the overriding discretion) not much idea of how the end result will look, not least because of the number of variables in each factual scenario. Some examples will illustrate what this means in percentages of the assets awarded in practice.

❖ CASE EXAMPLES

In *Cowan v Cowan* (2001)[34] came the husband's 'special contribution' to the wealth of the family which justified a departure from the yardstick of equality. Mrs Cowan received 38 per cent of the couple's wealth.

This 'special contribution' was to some extent checked in *H-J v H-J (Provision: Equality)* (2002),[35] where Coleridge J awarded the wife 50 per cent on the basis that there was nothing special in her husband's contribution and to recognise such a thing would be to disown the adherence to s 25 emphasised in *White*.

In *G v G (Financial Provision: Equal Division)* (2002)[36] the same judge expressed concern about the routine argument by counsel of husbands' special contributions, because he said it was not conducive to settlement.

In *Lambert v Lambert* (2002),[37] where the first instance judge had awarded the wife 37.5 per cent of the assets on the grounds that the husband's contribution was 'really special' the Court of Appeal had given the wife 50 per cent, on the grounds that the judge had fallen into the gender trap, and had also given insufficient consideration to her *needs* (although she had argued her major contribution as a homemaker and parent while her husband was accumulating the assets). Lord Justice Thorpe added that 'there must be an end to the sterile assertion that the breadwinner's contribution weighs heavier than the homemaker's', though he also emphasised that there was no principle that equality meant a 50:50 division, but that the court could award unequal amounts, even when the parties' contributions had been equal, because of the impact of other s 25 factors.

Following these cases there was a variety of approaches and awards ranging from 54 per cent given to a wife who scored in both the home and the business, to 37 per cent given to another where her husband persuaded the court of his special contribution (and where this was now routinely being called a 'stellar contribution'). There then followed another spate of cases which further refined the approach.

---

34 [2001] EWCA Civ 679; [2001] 2 FLR 192.
35 [2002] 1 FLR 415.
36 [2002] EWHC 1339 Fam; [2002] 2 FLR 1143.
37 [2002] EWCA Civ 1685.

❖ CASE EXAMPLES

The four key cases are *Miller, McFarlane, Charman* and (less famously) *B v B*.

In *Miller v Miller* and *McFarlane v McFarlane* (2006),[38] heard together by the House of Lords, there was an opportunity to consider the underlying principles which had developed in the six years since *White*. Mrs Miller was arguing that her youthful age (36) and short childless marriage (three years) to a very successful businessman (aged 41) should not disentitle her to a significant award, especially as the breakdown of the marriage was the husband's fault for leaving it for another woman whom he subsequently married. Further, his wealth had rocketed during the time that they had been married. The House dismissed his appeal, on the basis that she had had a legitimate expectation of leaving the marriage with better than she had entered it, especially as she had given up work (when earning £85,000 p.a.) to furnish the couple's two houses and he had been responsible for the breakdown of the marriage. The husband was ordered to transfer to her the matrimonial home worth £2.3 million and to pay her a lump sum of £2.7 million. Three principles were then laid down for determining the distribution of resources on ancillary relief orders:

- the needs (generously interpreted) generated by the relationship between the parties;
- compensation for relationship generated disadvantage; and
- sharing of the fruits of the matrimonial partnership.

It should be noted that all three strands are not always engaged. In *McCartney v Mills McCartney* (2008)[39] neither compensation nor sharing were present, as it was held that the wife had exaggerated her case for compensation for loss of career opportunity (having had only a modest modelling and public-speaking career before the marriage) and sharing was irrelevant as most of the husband's wealth had been accumulated long before they married.

In relation to Mrs McFarlane, the House considered whether the *White* principles applied to periodical payments as well as capital and property. It was said that hers was a 'paradigm' case for compensation as she had given up a lucrative career to devote herself to the family.

Apparently, Mr Miller considered his case should go to the ECtHR on the grounds that English law is so uncertain on this matter that it infringed his human rights.[40] This seems a harsh criticism since there clearly has been a basic pattern emerging, especially after the House of Lords articulated the three salient 'needs, compensation and sharing' points to be considered in relation to any case.

In *Charman v Charman (No 4)* (2007)[41] the wife originally conceded that the husband had made a stellar contribution, although she had given up work to look after the children

---

38 [2006] UKHL 24; [2006] 1 FLR 1186.
39 [2008] EWHC 401 (Fam); [2008] 1 FLR 1508.
40 See Deech, R [2009] Fam Law 1140.
41 [2007] EWCA Civ 503; [2007] 1 FLR 1246.

(adults by the time of the case), sought 45 per cent of the matrimonial assets and received 36.5 per cent (£48m). The husband appealed, arguing that the judge below (Coleridge J) had not made a sufficient allowance for his stellar contribution and had calculated the award incorrectly, by starting from a position of equal division and then deducting for his contribution instead of starting with the s 25 factors and then considering applying the discount for his contribution. He also complained that offshore trusts (of which his own was worth £68m and his children's at least £30m) should not have been treated as his financial resources as they were for the benefit of future generations. The Court of Appeal (led by the President of the Family Division, Sir Mark Potter) dismissed the appeal, refused permission to appeal to the House of Lords, and held:

- that 'special contribution' was still a live factor, but that the bar was set very high and that there could be non-financial special contribution, though this tended not to happen in practice;
- that the s 25 criteria were vital to the determination and that the three needs, compensation and sharing principles were derived from s 25;
- that the 'yardstick of equality' had morphed into the 'equal sharing principle' or 'sharing entitlement';
- that the three 'needs, compensation and sharing' principles must be applied to all resources though there might be a good reason to ring-fence some 'non-matrimonial' property;
- that needs required consideration of financial needs, obligations and responsibilities, standard of living, age and any disabilities of each party;
- that compensation relates to financial disadvantage as a result of decisions taken for the benefit of the family as a whole, e.g. giving up a career or loss of pension rights on ending a marriage;
- that sharing relates to contributions by each party to the welfare of the family, and can include taking account of conduct;
- that where a conflict exists in relation to any of these principles this must be resolved by what is fair.

In *B v B (Ancillary Relief)*(2008)[42] the concept of potentially ring-fencing[43] inherited or other 'non-matrimonial property' was confirmed, provided of course it is not required for the 'needs' of one of the parties, about which a further word must now be added below; although it is clear how it operates in relation to 'needs' because 'needs' are a s 25 consideration, this is certainly capable of becoming an elastic variable depending on how 'needs' are interpreted pending the FJC work on the recommended guidance. In this case the wife had purchased the home and a business from her inheritance and it was held on appeal that an equal division was not 'fair' in the particular circumstances. It was held also that equality was not the starting point: the starting point was the parties' financial positions and the s 25 criteria, and the equality yardstick was the *final* check.

In these differing results it at first appears that all the cases have really done in the last analysis is to confuse the picture further and regenerate the calls for reform of the law! However, this does seem

---

42 [2008] EWCA Civ 284; [2008] 2 FLR 1627.
43 See below at 7.3.3.

not to give credit for the principles now clearly being applied since inevitably there will be percentage differences depending on whether or not any pre-acquired or separately received property (such as inheritance) is ring-fenced or not. Meanwhile the court's discretion is as wide as ever it was, the only fetter being the s 25 criteria which again may introduce variables which impact on the arithmetical calculations.[44] Thus in that particular respect it may be that there is not much change since 1973.

It is a pity that the principles for calculating the quantum of orders give the appearance of being so confused, as otherwise the financial provision system that has been honed since the MCA 1973 is in fact fairly orderly, has been the subject of a variety of sensible judicial contributions over the years which are not challenged, and has been further polished by the contemporary financial provision procedural system introduced nationally after adoption of the 2000 pilot scheme.

It is also especially easy to follow some of these principles where there is no excess of assets over 'needs' (and it should be remembered that this is a key word in s 25). Thus the big money cases have little practical relevance because of the 'needs', and the value of retaining the discretion is evident. Accordingly, despite the confusion it should not be forgotten that there is a good deal of the financial provision process which works very well and in which settled principles have been established over time.

7.3.3 'Ring-fencing'

The Law Commission devoted Chapter 8 of their Report to the topic of 'non-matrimonial property', but after much discussion of consultees' responses concluded that the way forward was that any property which the parties wished to ring-fence as such should be dealt with in their pre-nuptial agreement or, at any rate, at some stage by agreement, as the Commission had struggled with, and abandoned, any attempt to find a non-matrimonial property definition which could be excluded from the marital 'pot' for sharing. It would therefore seem that if needs can be met without touching property which might meet this description – inherited, pre-acquired or in some way separately treated by the parties – such property will continue to be ring-fenced at the judge's discretion (as in the case of Mrs White, whose needs could be met without invading the property which had been given by her parents-in-law). Where it is needed to meet 'needs' (for the precise articulation of which we await the FJC guidance) then non-matrimonial property must presumably continue to yield to the demands of 'needs' as set out in s 25.

7.4 Applying for financial provision

All initial claims for any species of financial provision order must be made by a petitioner in the prayer of the petition, or by a respondent in the answer if one is filed.[45] These claims should always be made at the outset of the suit, or if this has not been done, the petition must be amended. The financial provision application is then activated and pursued within the relevant FPR constraints and this may be done at any time after decree nisi has been obtained, prior to which the long-term money and property aspects of the case cannot be progressed, though temporary orders can be obtained.[46] This is because the power of the court in the statute to make orders for spouses arises 'on granting a decree . . . or at any time thereafter'.

---

44 See further below. A grasp of all the principles involved in working out quantum is essential before the questions 'how much' and 'by which orders' can be answered, and repeated cases have shown that this decision is based squarely within the s 25 criteria.

45 Alternatively, there is provision in the rules for respondents to make such applications without filing an answer.

46 See Chapter 10. However, some ongoing changing can be expected in relation to financial provision applications, now the MAP working group led by Cobb J is considering this from scratch; see the accompanying website.

Thus all the MCA 1973 ss 23 and 24 long-term orders are restricted to taking effect only upon decree absolute, and the application for them made in the prayer of the petition may not be activated until decree nisi has been pronounced. Although the power of the court arises 'on making a decree of divorce', or at any time thereafter, it is not unknown for applications to be made many years later for which leave would be required. This would only be granted if there is some reason for the delay and such delayed application would not cause injustice.

Accordingly, many cases are settled by negotiation to avoid the likely wait for a full hearing if the initial procedure before the DJ is not successful in resolving the matter – this involves a First Appointment to take stock and case manage, followed by a Financial Dispute Resolution appointment (FDR) to explore options and attempt to reach a settlement, before the case is then set down for final hearing. At this early stage the lack of clarity in the law is as much a drawback as the futility of trying to guess what the final outcome might be depending on the way the judge views the factors in the case, the principles that have come out of the decided cases and even which judge the parties are listed before, and many spouses go to mediation, negotiate through their solicitors or find other ways of settling the outcome between themselves, for example abandoning the court and going to a Family Arbitrator under the IFLA Rules.[47] If any of these is successful a fast-track consent order to record the deal struck can be approved by the court under s 33A of the Act, otherwise the case must go to final hearing.

7.4.1 Income orders: MCA 1973 ss 22 and 23

Basic maintenance in most cases – weekly, monthly or annually – will be provided by *periodical payments*, either for the spouse or the children or both – and will be awarded in the long term under MCA 1973 s 23(1)(a) for spouses and s 23(1)(d) for children. The duration of such orders will depend on what the court orders as suitable for the particular case. For short-term maintenance, MPS (under s 22) also provides periodical payments, but usually more at the rate of a subsistence allowance than to match the quantum of likely longer-term orders, where more of the relevant facts will be known about the payee's needs and the payer's ability to pay than at the initial stages of a financial application. Income orders or 'maintenance' are usually the core of such a package unless there is to be a clean break with which they are incompatible. Sometimes it is found more convenient to apply for temporary maintenance pending fuller consideration of the parties' financial positions after decree nisi.

Periodical payments

For a spouse, periodical payments (unless they are secured, as to which see below) usually last during joint lives of the payer and payee or until remarriage: MCA 1973 s 28, or for a limited period if intended to be part of a clean break arrangement: MCA 1973 s 25A. If no duration is specified at all, payments continue until further order of the court, which usually means until the payer or the payee applies to vary them under s 31 of the MCA 1973.[48]

Obviously a payer is likely to apply to vary the order downwards (e.g. because of job loss so that the payments are no longer affordable, or an increase in the payee's resources, so that they are no longer necessary) and a payee is likely to apply to vary it upwards, perhaps because the payments are no longer enough. This might be owing to a combination of a rise in the cost of living generally and also an extension of the items of routine expenditure which the payee is called upon to fund. Variation commonly occurs where children grow up and become more expensive and their requirements for more space at home increases the regular outgoings, such as the ordinary utility bills (e.g. when children are simply at home more, such as during the common occurrence of home study before A level or other public examinations, whereas they might previously have been at school at

---

47 See Chapter 6.
48 See below at 7.10.

least five days a week). Any of these situations would produce a further order of the court whether that order reduced, increased or entirely discharged the original order.

Secured periodical payments

Where periodical payments are secured in favour of a spouse pursuant to s 23(1)(b), they can be made to last beyond the death of the payer. Secured periodical payments are not usual, since they require to be secured on assets, which are not generally available in sufficient quantity to fund such security. Moreover, such an order would not be made without good reason, such as that the payer had a bad payment track record, or might leave the country to work elsewhere, taking assets out of the jurisdiction at the same time. Secured periodical payments are therefore only likely to be applicable where the payer is particularly rich or particularly impecunious and it is necessary to protect the position of the payee by making a secured order.

❖ CASE EXAMPLE

In *Aggett v Aggett* (1962)[49] the husband was so irresponsible that, in case he left the jurisdiction (as anticipated), payments were secured on his house.

In *Parker v Parker* (1972),[50] in a similar situation where he was not trusted to pay, a second mortgage was taken out on the husband's house to secure an annuity.

Secured periodical payments for a child, which are possible pursuant to s 23(1)(e), are extremely uncommon, although there are sometimes good reasons, for instance to secure continued payment out of a payer's estate after his death without the necessity of taking further proceedings. For the court to make such an order, a payer, usually the father, would generally have to be a persistently unreliable; also, since the court only retains jurisdiction in cases where the CSA/CMS would not assess contested orders, secured periodical payments for children will be restricted to consent orders where the payer agrees to the security or to cases where the payment is sought in contested proceedings for children of the family who are not within the DWP's remit (i.e. stepchildren whose absent natural parent the CSA/CMS cannot trace, either because of the parent's death or disappearance or in some cases where the father of a stepchild is not actually known).

Children's periodical payments

The normal form of routine maintenance for a child who is within the court's jurisdiction will therefore be:

- unsecured periodical payments, and by the MCA 1973 s 29(2) these will last in the first instance until the child's 17th birthday; or
- by the MCA 1973 s 29(3) until the child finishes full-time education or training.

The same section permits a child who is over 18 to continue to receive periodical payments if his or her welfare requires it (e.g. if he or she is handicapped).

---

49 [1962] 1 WLR 183; [1962] 1 All ER 190.
50 [1972] 2 WLR 21; [1972] 1 All ER 410.

All child orders terminate on the death of the payer in the same way as those for spouses: s 29(4), unless secured. Prior to the grant of the decree nisi no order may be made under s 23 for a spouse (though this restriction obviously does not apply to periodical payments for children for whom an interim order may be made at any time). This restriction to post-first decree orders is required because the court's power to make orders has not yet arisen since the statute states that the power arises on making a decree, so if periodical payments are desired at this stage, it will be necessary to apply for MPS as soon as the petition is filed. These payments can be backdated to the date of the presentation of the petition and will automatically terminate at the end of the suit on grant of decree absolute. The amount of MPS will not be generous since it is regarded as a subsistence allowance and is granted *separately* from the main application for long-term periodical payments, and at a more basic rate, precisely because it will not be possible until the financial provision proceedings are further advanced to determine the terms and quantum of the final order.

7.4.2 Capital payment orders: s 23

Instead of or in addition to the basic maintenance of periodical payments, in some but not all cases a cash lump sum order may be made, either for a spouse or for a child or children, or for all of them, and this also may be done under s 23(1)(c) for spouses and s 23(1)(f) for children.

The reasons for lump sums are many and various, although it was early established in *Wachtel v Wachtel* (1973)[51] that no particular purpose or justification is required for such an order to be made. A lump sum order may in fact be particularly appropriate in a variety of cases (e.g. where the payee is likely to remarry, so that periodical payments would cease under s 28). An applicant may always prefer to seek a lump sum payment, since any lump sum will be outright, and will not therefore be affected by remarriage. However, in some cases, where the degree of bitterness is such that periodical payments would be undesirable, a lump sum can be a tactful way of ending the war between the spouses. The modern approach focuses on the needs of the parties: see *Dew v Dew* (1986),[52] where it was established that this approach was untrammelled, at least in the first instance, by ideas of proportionate division of assets, though the post-*White* concept of checking the order against a notional yardstick of equality may have some influence now.

However, in cases where remarriage is not ruled out, care must be taken that the lump sum order is not *specifically* made as a form of capitalised maintenance, as it could then be attacked and set aside if there had been any deliberate misrepresentation over whether the payee was planning to remarry. This was the case in *Livesey v Jenkins* (1985),[53] where the wife omitted to mention that she was already engaged to be married shortly after the order was made.

Established cases particularly suitable for a lump sum include:

(a)   where there is available capital of which the wife should have a share, as in *Trippas v Trippas* (1973),[54] where the wife had been promised a share of the proceeds of the business because of her moral support in setting up and establishing it;

(b)   setting up a business, as in *Nicholas v Nicholas* (1984)[55] and *Gojkovic v Gojkovic* (1990),[56] in which money was needed to set up respectively a guest house and a hotel, through which the payee spouse would be able to become self-supporting;

(c)   reducing or replacing periodical payments, as in *Gojkovic* above, where the degree of bitterness and the capability of the payee spouse both made this desirable, and in *Duxbury v Duxbury*

---

51 [1973] 2 WLR 366; [1973] 1 All ER 829; [1973] Fam 72.
52 [1986] 2 FLR 341.
53 [1985] AC 424; [1985] 2 WLR 47; [1985] 1 All ER 105.
54 [1973] 2 WLR 585; [1973] 2 All ER 1.
55 [1984] FLR 285.
56 [1990] Fam Law 100.

(1987),[57] in which the now famous *Duxbury* calculation was first used to identify a sum which could be invested in a planned and cost-effective manner to provide a particular applicant with lifelong maintenance, living at times off the income and the capital and at others a combination of the two;

(d)   achieving a clean break as in *Duxbury*;

(e)   compensating for loss of a matrimonial home, as in *P v P (Financial Provision: Lump Sum)* (1978);[58]

(f)   replacing maintenance where enforcement is likely to be difficult or as a punishment for concealing assets as in *Martin v Martin* (1976)[59] and *Nicholas*, above, where the husbands were both potential bad payers and/or had tried to conceal their wealth, so that a clean break was a better alternative to periodical payments.

Where a lump sum payment is made to a spouse, only one such lump sum may be ordered, though the lump sum may be paid in instalments and expressed in the order to be so payable: s 23(3)(c), and such payment secured to the satisfaction of the court. It is a drawback of instalments that they may always be varied, or extinguished altogether, although Balcombe LJ said that this power should be exercised with caution: see *Penrose v Penrose* (1994).[60]

Where a lump sum order is made in favour of a child, this 'once only' restriction does not apply, so successive lump sum orders may be made.

In both cases, interest can be ordered if payment is deferred: s 23(6), assuming such provision is made in the order. If so, then the interest will be payable from whatever date the order specifies: see per Ewbank J in *L v L (Lump Sum: Interest)* (1994).[61] This is obviously a useful provision from the payee's point of view in case of payer default.

It used to be thought that lump sums were only appropriate where the parties were wealthy and there was substantial capital, but it is now established that the exercise of this power is not restricted to such cases, provided the payer can reasonably raise the sum required: *Davis v Davis* (1967).[62] A more recent instance of this is to be found in *P v P* (above and in the case example), which is clear authority for the proposition that no more than is really needed by the payee, and no more than can realistically be raised, will be ordered where it must come from a business, or home and business, which is needed for the family's support.

❖ CASE EXAMPLE

In *P v P* the wife owned the family home and business property, a farm where she and the three children of the family lived and where the parties had worked. It was accepted that the husband owned £8,000 of the stock and contents of the farm (the total value of which was £102,000). He appealed against an order of £15,000 payable in three instalments over a year, having asked for a lump sum and also a transfer of property order. It was held that the wife could not realistically pay more, since in order to maintain herself and the children (and having accepted only a nominal periodical payments order for the children and nothing for herself) she would need the property to remain unencumbered by more than the £15,000 that would suffice for a home for the husband.

---

57 [1987] FLR 7, CA.
58 [1978] 1 WLR 483; [1978] 3 All ER 70.
59 [1976] 2 WLR 901; [1976] 3 All ER 625.
60 [1994] 2 FLR 621.
61 [1994] 2 FLR 324.
62 [1967] 1 All ER 123; [1966] 3 WLR 1157.

Restriction on the grant of lump sums

The court will not cripple a spouse's earning power, nor a business off which the family must live, nor put a home at risk, as was shown in *Martin v Martin* (see above), and this principle is still very much alive: see *Dharamshi v Dharamshi* (2001),[63] where it was made clear that an order would not be made if it would 'bring down or cripple the whole family's financial edifice'. This is best illustrated by some actual cases.

❖ CASE EXAMPLES

In *Martin* an order was reduced from £5,000 to £2,000 to avoid a husband's having to sell his hotel and thus lose his home as well as his business.

In *Smith v Smith* (1983)[64] the lump sum of £40,000 awarded was cancelled altogether because to raise it the husband would have to sell shares in his company which was his only income-producing asset, which would have benefited nobody.

In *Kiely v Kiely* (1988)[65] the order was cancelled since to raise a £4,000 lump sum each for the children of the family meant selling the former matrimonial home, which was not guaranteed to raise enough, but would leave the husband in contempt of court through no fault of his own *and* unable to pay the order.

Otherwise if there are assets available, the court will not hesitate to make use of them to create a suitable package, and the judge does not mind where the assets originated if they are required to do justice and can reasonably be raised without violating the principles stated above.

It should, however, be noted that where a business is not to be sold, because it supports the family, it is pointless to spend money on valuations. These are sometimes obsessively indulged in by spouses keen to get compensation for the value of an asset which cannot be sold, but of which they reckon they are entitled to a share, and are determined that this shall be achieved by sale of some other asset. Again, an actual case aptly illustrates this principle.

❖ CASE EXAMPLE

In *P v P* (1989)[66] a wife in these circumstances was criticised by the court, where the argument was about the value of shares in a haulage company which on any view could not be sold. It was held that it was pointless to spend money on a precise valuation since the court only wanted a broad view of the value of matrimonial assets which were not being sold, and as there was another source of a lump sum for her – the proceeds of the matrimonial home, which was to be sold anyway – they could take the approximate value of the shares into account when making orders from those liquid funds. As a result, Mrs P received

---

63 [2001] 1 FLR 736, CA.
64 [1983] 4 FLR 154.
65 [1988] 18 Fam Law 51; [1988] 1 FLR 248.
66 [1989] 2 FLR 248.

£240,000 out of the £260,000 sale proceeds of the home and Mr P kept the shares; it would have been reckless to put the business at risk by raising money from his fixed assets.

Adjournment until funds become available

Sometimes lump sum orders cannot be made because there are not, when the case is before the court, sufficient assets from which to order a lump sum, though it is anticipated that there will be in the foreseeable future. The solution here is to adjourn the case, which may be done for up to about five years — a period suggested in *Roberts v Roberts* (1986)[67] — if this is the only means of achieving justice between the parties. In the same year, in *Davies v Davies* (1986)[68] the court considered the general desirability of this type of adjournment, holding that ideally the matter should be dealt with as soon as possible, but if there was a possibility of capital becoming available in the foreseeable future, adjournment was permissible to achieve justice. This is still the approach.

Adjournment, rather than making some compromise order, is more appropriate where the future quantum of the anticipated asset is uncertain. Practical solutions in actual cases most aptly illustrate the court's thinking in this context.

> ### ❖ CASE EXAMPLE
>
> In *Morris v Morris* (1977)[69] the prospective sum was the likely amount of the husband's gratuity when he left the Army. He was a warrant officer and it was uncertain how much longer he would serve in the Army, which was directly relevant to the amount of gratuity. He was ordered to notify the wife of the receipt of the money so as to revive the application at that date.
>
> In *MT v MT (Financial Provision: Lump Sum* (1992)[70] the principles applying to such adjournments were reviewed in a case dealing with the husband's prospects of inheriting from his 83-year-old father on the latter's death, which was said to be reasonably foreseeable. It was held that the court has a discretion to adjourn in any case where it would be suitable to do so because of the foreseeable prospect of capital becoming available.
>
> In *CR v CR* (2007)[71] Bodey J said that now that it is essential, post-*Miller*, to identify matrimonial property, a broad view approach should be taken, avoiding too constricting and formulaic an approach, as financial provision valuation was an art and not a science or accounting exercise. This does not appear to restrict the principle that adjournment is still possible where appropriate to do justice.

7.4.3 Property transfer orders: s 24(1)(a)

The court may transfer freeholds, leaseholds, protected and statutory tenancies within the meaning of the **Rent Act 1977**, secure tenancies within the meaning of the **Housing Act 1985**, and council houses

---

67 [1986] 2 FLR 152.
68 [1986] 1 FLR 497.
69 [1977] 7 Fam Law 244.
70 [1992] 1 FLR 362.
71 [2007] EWHC 3206; [2007] 1 FLR 323.

and flats. The consent of the local authority is not required, but they have a right to be heard. The consent of a building society or bank may not be required, but they should be given a chance to be heard: *Practice Direction, 1971*.[72] This 'chance' may not make much difference as is shown by decided cases.

❖ **CASE EXAMPLES**

In *Lee v Lee* (1984)[73] the authority opposed the transfer because it disrupted its housing policy, but the court did not consider that merited the hardship that the wife would suffer and ordered the transfer.

In *Buckingham v Buckingham* (1979)[74] the court was similarly rather hard on a private landlord when a transfer was ordered despite his objections, although a landlord's objection to a particular tenant is regarded as of significant importance in landlord and tenant law because of the close proprietorial relationship which the parties in this context must have (called in some historical texts on land law the 'sacred relationship' because of its origins in the feudal system, the modern equivalent being the close relationship that tenancy creates which suggests that a landlord should have a choice of a quality tenant who will observe the obligations of a lease, hence the references required).

In *Tebbut v Haynes* (1981)[75] it was held appropriate to hear the concerns of third parties who live in the home (in this case the husband's mother and aunt) so that such third parties will be considered if the order would turn them out.

The most common use of the transfer of property power is to transfer the matrimonial home, especially if it is to effect a clean break.[76] However, it may also be used to transfer ownership of chattels such as cars, furniture, works of art and indeed anything which needs to be transferred to achieve the necessary reorganisation of the parties' financial affairs.

7.4.4 Settlement of property: s 24(1)(b)

This section enables the court to set up settlement orders in relation to the matrimonial home, such as the *Mesher*, *Martin*, *Harvey* and similar occupation orders which enable a spouse to remain in the home with the children until the latter are grown up, or even in some cases for longer. It can also be used to enable a spouse to establish a settlement of capital to provide for the other spouse and children, usually with reversion to the settling spouse or possibly ultimate remainder to the children.

7.4.5 Variation of settlements: s 24(1)(c) and (d)

This is the power which allows variation of an ante- or post-nuptial settlement in favour of the parties or their children, including any settlement made by will or codicil. This provision, which permits the

---

72 [1971] 1 All ER 896.
73 [1984] FLR 243.
74 (1979) 129 NLJ 52.
75 [1981] 2 All ER 239.
76 See below at 7.5.

interest of a spouse to be reduced or extinguished, also sometimes permits variation of pension funds as in *Brooks v Brooks* (1995),[77] although there are very few cases where this possibility applies.

❖ **CASE EXAMPLE**

In *Brooks* it was possible to vary the provisions applicable to the pension fund so as to give the wife an immediate annuity and a deferred index-linked pension payable from the date of the husband's death. The court went on to direct that these two pensions for the wife were to be provided in priority to the pension for the husband, so that if necessary he would take less. However, this could only be done as the pension scheme was the parties' own small company scheme, whereas most pensions which would ideally be split on divorce were subject to the discretion of the trustees of the pension schemes in question, which were not subject to the orders of the court.

This pension-sharing problem has now been widely addressed by earmarking or sharing orders in respect of pensions: the **Pensions Act 1995** s 166 added new provisions in MCA 1973 ss 25B–25D for 'earmarking' of pensions, effected by an 'attachment' order, and the **Welfare Reform and Pensions Act 1999** inserted further provisions in MCA 1973 ss 21A and 24B for pension sharing in the case of all petitions filed after 1 December 2000. These provisions directly affect the resources taken into account by the court under s 25(2)(a) and enable pension fund trustees, whether of an occupational or personal pension scheme, to be ordered to pay part of the pension or lump sum available to one spouse to the other according to the court's direction.

However, it may still be more beneficial in some cases to obtain compensation by another route rather than actually to go through the process of valuing and dividing the share to be transferred, which usually tends, owing to the 'blunt instrument' method of CETV (cash equivalent transfer value) used, to result in the recipient receiving a less valuable asset than the appropriate fraction would suggest. The *Brooks* method may still therefore be preferable in some cases.

7.4.6 Order for sale: s 24A

Whenever the court makes any of the above orders other than one which is simply for unsecured periodical payments, it may also order a sale of any property in which either of the parties has a legal beneficial interest. This power, not originally included in the MCA 1973, was introduced to permit the court not only to order a sale so as to facilitate payment of its orders – an obviously useful consequential benefit for the payee – but to make facilitating arrangements, such as that the court's order be paid out of the proceeds of sale: s 24A(2)(a), that the property be offered for sale to specified persons or classes of persons: s 24A(2)(b), and to add any other condition of a practical nature that it thinks fit (e.g. which party's solicitor should have the conduct of the sale). This can be very important since clearly the applicant's solicitors would ideally prefer to be in control of such a transaction, rather than having to deal with the respondents to ascertain or encourage progress, whereas some respondents would (sometimes rightly) be anxious about not being in control of the disposal of major assets.

Like other orders, those under s 24A cannot take effect until decree absolute.

---

77 [1995] 3 WLR 1292; [1995] 2 FLR 13; [1995] 3 All ER 257, HL.

7.5 The s 25 factors, s 25A and the ideal of spousal self-sufficiency

A detailed consideration of s 25 is undertaken by the court in order to compose a suitable financial package in each individual case. A similar approach is taken by practitioners negotiating a package intended to be in the ballpark area of what the court is likely to order after a contested hearing, so as to avoid the costs and uncertainties of litigation. Thus s 25 – recourse to which is repeatedly mentioned in the key judgments which have followed *White* – is an extremely important central plank of the applicable law.

The method is to look at the orders available under ss 23 and 24,[78] then to apply the s 25 considerations[79] systematically to the facts and finally to propose the combination of orders which most suits the family's circumstances, and is fairest in relation to the relevant criteria. Obviously any such scheme will give priority to the particular applicant's interests where possible, but will also take into account what suits the family as a *whole*, which is also likely to be in that applicant's interests, and facilitate life after divorce – especially important where there are children and an ongoing relationship is likely to be essential.

An inexperienced practitioner, or one whose regular work is outside family law, and most students, will need explicitly to work through the range of orders and the s 25 factors on the checklist principle, in order to build up a suitable package. However, such a structured approach is not usually necessary once some experience of the orders and factors is acquired, when the one or two points which are particularly relevant will be spotted, which tends to be the method used by judges and is apparent in their judgments. The academic student may find that, to start with, the structured approach is required, but in relying on this should take comfort from the identical approach in *Burgess v Burgess* (1996)[80] of Hale J as she then was.[81] This approach was upheld by the Court of Appeal in *Burgess*. Her consideration of the s 25 factors in that case is pure textbook application. It is this closer relation to the provisions of s 25 which Lord Nicholls was advocating in the House of Lords' consideration of *White v White*, to which detailed further reference must inevitably be made in relation to the overall impact of the s 25 factors, and to which judges in succeeding cases have constantly referred as essential to the assessment of appropriate orders.

The considerations themselves are contained in the sub-paragraphs of s 25, which is conveniently broken into two sub-sections:

- s 25(1) sets out the court's 'general duty' in applying the whole of the section; and
- s 25(2) itself may rationally be broken into two sub-parts:

  ○ s 25(2)(a) deals with the resources out of which the court will make its orders; and
  ○ s 25(2)(b)–(h) sets out the checklist through which the court will work in deciding whether and to what extent it should make orders.

Additionally, s 25A has since 1984 given the court the power to *order* a 'clean break', if necessary, regardless of the parties' wishes, a power which in the absence of the *agreement* of the parties no court had prior to the 1984 amendment. The clean break is in accordance with the policy of spousal self-sufficiency (relatively innovative in 1984, a decade after the 1973 consolidating reform) by which, if a clean break is not possible immediately, the court at least considers whether even formerly dependent and untrained wives could work towards independence; if necessary taking

---

78 For which see above at 7.4.
79 In this section, 7.5 and in 7.6.
80 [1996] 2 FLR 34, CA.
81 Now Baroness Hale, see n 30 above.

part-time work, acquiring a skill or, if older and out of the workplace for many years, perhaps retraining.

7.5.1 Welfare of any child of the family: s 25(1) and 'the general duty' of the court

Section 25(1), while requiring the court to have regard to all the circumstances of the case, makes the welfare of the children the first consideration in every case where there are children of the family. It is important to understand the interaction of this principle with that of the clean break. The existence of children does not necessarily make a clean break impossible between their parents (though of course impossible between either of their parents and them), though it may make it inappropriate, or inappropriate for the time being.

❖ CASE EXAMPLE

In *Suter v Suter and Jones* (1987),[82] a long-standing classic case in this context, the wife with young children received nominal periodical payments as the future was insufficiently clear to impose a clean break immediately, despite the fact that she was cohabiting with a lover who could make a substantial contribution to the household as long as he remained with her.

The children's welfare in the context of s 25(1) is usually interpreted as meaning that during their minority they must have a secure home and a sufficient income for them and their primary carer to live on.

❖ CASE EXAMPLE

In *Harman v Glencross* (1986),[83] the occupation of the former matrimonial home had to be given to the wife, with whom the children lived, otherwise they would have had no adequate home.

This principle, articulated in *Harman* but established much earlier, was the watershed from which sprang the now well-established line of *Mesher* order variants, so called because their origin was *Mesher v Mesher* (1980).[84] Children in the context of s 25(1) means 'children of the family' within the meaning of s 52 (i.e. a child of both parties, or a child of one party treated by the other as a child of the family). Step-parents can therefore successfully evade liability for their partners' children, but this would need to be done expressly as the court is slow to recognise any such situation, as is illustrated by the example below.

---

82 [1987] 2 FLR 232.
83 [1986] 2 FLR 241.
84 [1980] 1 All ER 126, but decided some five years earlier than the report, so an early case under MCA 1973.

> ❖ **CASE EXAMPLE**
>
> In *Day v Day* (1988)[85] the actual marriage lasted only six weeks, as Mr Day quickly decided that he preferred the bachelor life, although there had been lengthy pre-marital cohabitation. When he sought to avoid paying maintenance for the wife's two children, neither of whom apparently had a father available for their support, the court decided that he had fully understood his commitment and obligations towards the children for whom he had accepted responsibility so he must therefore pay maintenance for them both despite the brevity of the actual marriage.

It should be noted that a secondary but also well-established principle in connection with the court's general duty is the desire of judges to end financial dispute between the parties, a goal which will always remind the court of its duty to consider a clean break pursuant to s 25A in those cases where drawing such a line is possible. This is often possible if there are sufficient assets for a lump sum so that ongoing maintenance is not paid.

7.5.2 The checklist: s 25(2)(a)–(h)

The first paragraph of the sub-section, s 25(2)(a), looks at the assets out of which provision may be made. The remaining paragraphs, s 25(2)(b)–(h), look at the considerations which must be weighed in dividing those assets.

7.5.3 Evidence of the parties' means: s 25(2)(a)

This paragraph of the sub-section requires that all the parties' means are taken into account to establish the nature and extent of the resources out of which the court will make its orders. Clearly the size of the 'pot' is the first relevant point before it can be divided, and the items included will be vital to establishing both the precise make-up of the resources and the size of the percentages available.

The reality of the situation is that the court must consider more than the surface of the parties' respective financial positions. In order to do this, whether the case is to be contested or the subject of a negotiated settlement in the region of what the court might *order*, it is usual for both parties to make full disclosure.

If it is certain that the case will be contested, or at least that it must be started on that basis, then both parties formally and concurrently file a statement of means, now no longer in the affidavits formerly used, but in the much more precise and uniform 'Form E' devised for use with the original reformed Ancillary Relief Scheme in 1999–2000 (which was tried and tested in both the Principal Registry of the High Court, which then acted as the divorce county court for central London, and in a number of designated divorce county courts around the country before in June 2000 being applied nationally). Disclosure is sometimes an issue here, since the recent case of *Tchenguiz v Imerman* (2010)[86] has placed some limitations on use of documents which can be classified as 'confidential' to a party, thus inhibiting an applicant's self-help in securing copies of documents not voluntarily disclosed if they are kept in an area of the home confidential to him or in any private location such as a briefcase or laptop.

---

85 [1988] 1 FLR 278.
86 [2010] EWCA Civ 908.

Where a negotiated settlement is the initial aim, it is common to make disclosure in some other convenient manner; for example, the parties may choose to exchange Form E informally in draft, or to provide each other with information by letter or in person at a meeting, supported by such bundles of documents as are necessary for verification. Where such negotiations are successful, the court may simply be invited to make an order by consent upon lodgement (without a hearing) of a draft consent order under s 33A, making a considerable saving in both time and costs.

Section 25(2)(a) requires the court to take into account:

> . . . the income, earning capacity, property and other financial resources which each of the parties to the marriage has or is likely to have in the foreseeable future, including in the case of earning capacity any increase in that capacity which it would in the opinion of the court be reasonable to expect a party to the marriage to take steps to acquire.

Looking below the surface, the court will need to be alert not merely to what the parties have but to what they might have, for example:

(1) Both parties' future earning capacity as well as present earnings, including any potential improvement in earning capacity which might be acquired by retraining or other reorganisation of a party's lifestyle.

(2) Family money, e.g. from wealthy parents or a private company on which the family habitually draws. This is very important as it often makes a life-changing difference in the resources that may be available to the parties and their children.

❖ CASE EXAMPLES

In *Thomas v Thomas* (1995),[87] still the leading case in this context, a husband's appeal against some fairly onerous orders (including for school fees) which he said exceeded his income, was dismissed because the judge said the husband had no real complaint, provided his wealthy family came to his aid to pay some school fees as had been understood would happen before the divorce. Waite LJ drew attention to the court's almost limitless powers in redistributing assets and to the necessity in modern times 'where the forms of wealth holding are diverse and often sophisticated, to penetrate outer forms and get to the heart of ownership'.

In *White v White* (1988)[88] this principle was rearticulated in the now well-known context of the husband and wife farming partnership where the wife objected to receiving only what the court took to be her reasonable needs when her commercial partnership rights indicated that she was entitled to more. The husband did in fact finally receive slightly more of the family assets than the wife because his family had contributed more to start with.

In *Prest v Petrodel* (2013)[89] the Supreme Court unanimously held that the husband beneficially owned properties apparently in the ownership of his companies on a resulting trust as he had paid for their purchase (thus it was not necessary to pierce the corporate veil, which the CA below had declined to do).

---

87 [1995] 2 FLR 668.
88 [1998] 2 FLR 310, CA, for the report of the Court of Appeal hearing in this case, which was then appealed to the House of Lords, for which see [2000] 2 FLR 981.
89 [2013] UKSC 34.

(3)   The principle of financial independence in so far as is consistent with the welfare of the children.

Besides family money, the variety of sources to be taken into account for this purpose will often include damages or compensation, anticipated interests under a will or settlement, the earnings of a new spouse or cohabitant, and property acquired since the separation and/or divorce, besides the spouse's true income or earning capacity where that is different from what is being claimed in disclosure. Welfare benefits are not a routine resource for ancillary relief purposes (see further below).

Damages or compensation

The general rule is that damages for pain and suffering and loss of amenity are not taken into account.

❖ CASE EXAMPLES

In *Jones v Jones* (1975)[90] any alternative to the rule would have been particularly unsuitable, since the damages in question were an award of only £1,800 for injuries following a knife attack actually perpetrated on the wife by the husband, which had severed the tendons in her hands and made it impossible for her to continue to earn her own living as a nurse.

In *Daubney v Daubney* (1976),[91] however, it was held that general damages are normally regarded as a resource, which was particularly appropriate in the context of the particular case where the wife had used the general damages in question to buy a flat, which necessarily counted as a resource of hers in the ancillary relief proceedings.

In *Jones v Jones* (1983)[92] the husband did not have to bring into account damages of £167,000 to provide care for the rest of his life after a motorcycle accident, as is usual where damages have been calculated to provide care for a projected lifespan, so these are not counted as a resource of that spouse.

In *C v C (Financial Provision)* (1995)[93] the wife and child were on state benefits but a settlement was refused because all the damages were needed to provide for the husband's needs.

Wagstaff v Wagstaff (1992)[94] is in contrast to *C v C* as the sum actually received exceeded the recipient's needs and some of the excess was required to do justice between the parties by correcting the disparity which would otherwise exist between the parties' respective financial positions. The husband had received £418,000, after a motorcycle accident, of which £32,000 was awarded to the wife, who had no particular need for the

---

90 [1975] 2 WLR 606; [1975] 2 All ER 12.
91 [1976] 2 WLR 959; [1976] 2 All ER 453.
92 [1983] 1 WLR 901; [1983] 2 All ER 1039.
93 [1995] 2 FLR 171.
94 [1992] 1 All ER 275; [1992] 1 FLR 333.

money except as an emergency fund, on the basis that she had contributed to a 12-year marriage, had a child to support, and the husband did not need all the damages. In *Wagstaff*, the court specifically took the opportunity to differentiate between smaller awards of damages specifically for pain and suffering (or any awards where the disabled spouse's needs used up all the money awarded) and those cases, like *Wagstaff*, where the amount of the damages, even if some of them were for pain and suffering, clearly indicated that they should be considered a resource.

Interests under a will or settlement

Here policy varies, and the proximity of the availability of the money, together with the likelihood of its actually being received in due course, will influence the decision as to whether the money will be considered a resource for s 25(2)(a): *Michael v Michael* (1986).[95]

The alternative, especially if justice cannot otherwise be done, is to adjourn a decision on the ancillary relief application until the money becomes available, which may be done for four or five years as in *Roberts v Roberts* mentioned above, or the court may make the order on the basis that the money will eventually come in, if that is fairly certain, but that payment pursuant to the order should not be made until the funds have actually been received, as in *Calder v Calder* (1975).[96]

However, the eventual availability of the assets must be reasonably certain: it is not possible to subpoena aged and ailing parents to state their testamentary intentions, as was discovered in *Morgan v Morgan* (1977).[97] Cases do arise where, while it is by no means certain whether or when such an inheritance will be received, some account nevertheless has to be taken of the expectations so that the wealth, degree of relationship, age and health of the testator or testatrix will all be relevant – how relevant will depend on the circumstances of each case.

❖ CASE EXAMPLES

In *B v B (Real Property: Assessment of Interests)* (1988)[98] there was a quantifiable interest under the will of a wealthy mother which the court held it could not ignore.

In (a different case of the same name) *B v B* (1990),[99] the advanced age of the testatrix enabled the court to take account of an expected inheritance without adjournment: the mother from whom one of the parties was to inherit was in that case aged 84 and the inheritance was held not to be too remote.

In *K v K* (1990),[100] however, the testatrix was only aged 79 and in good health and the court ignored the inheritance as a resource as being too remote.

In *MT v MT (Financial Provision: Lump Sum)* (1992) mentioned above, the wife's application was adjourned pending the death of her 83-year-old German father-in-law, because under German law the husband would definitely inherit one-eighth of the estate. Following

---

95 [1986] 2 FLR 389.
96 [1975] 6 Fam Law 242.
97 [1977] Fam 122.
98 [1988] 2 FLR 490.
99 [1990] 1 FLR 20.
100 [1990] 2 FLR 225.

this case respondents with firm expectations in some foreign jurisdictions may expect the court to be more likely to take those expectations into account so as either to adjourn the case until the inheritance was received or determine the quantum and direct that the payment not to be paid until the funds were actually received.

In *Browne v Browne* (1989),[101] the wife was eventually committed for contempt for not paying under an order which had been quantified on the basis that she had access at will to two offshore trusts where the trustees (who had previously handed over whatever money she asked for) refused to meet her request for funds for the purposes of the order. Interests under offshore trusts are thus not safe from being counted as a s 25(2)(a) resource.

Where a spouse is a beneficiary under a settlement this can of course be varied pursuant to s 24(1)(c) or (d) if applicable, but it is also common for the court to treat the spouse's beneficial interest as one of settled assets and to make an order on the basis that the paying spouse can borrow against his or her expectations: see B v B (1982).[102]

While the court knows that no order is directly enforceable against offshore trusts outside the jurisdiction, judges do not hesitate to make orders taking into account offshore assets if they are satisfied that the money is normally at the disposal of the beneficiary.

Thus trustees cannot in fact help such a beneficiary by suddenly refusing to carry out requests to pay over money if they have been in the habit of doing so in the past (as is usually the case where offshore trusts are of the type designed to be of financial benefit to the beneficiaries who obtain fiscal advantages by the money technically being owned by the trustees offshore).

Resources of a new spouse or cohabitant

This is always a problematic area. No order can be made which actually has to be paid out of the new spouse or cohabitant's pocket.

❖ CASE EXAMPLE

In *B v B (Periodical Payments: Transitional Provisions)* (1995)[103] an order was held to be wrongly made against a father with a significant overdraft, which in effect meant that his partner had to pay the order, although it was right to take into account the fact that he was being supported by her having been out of work for two months.

There are, however, two ways in which the new spouse or cohabitant can indirectly make money or assets available to the first family:

(a)   by making over capital or property to the spouse; or
(b)   by paying some or all of the spouse's living expenses, thus releasing more of the spouse's income for the maintenance of the first family. Some actual decisions show how this works.

---

101   [1989] 1 FLR 291, CA.
102   [1982] 12 Fam Law 92.
103   [1995] 1 FLR 459.

❖ **CASE EXAMPLES**

In *Ibbetson v Ibbetson* (1984)[104] the former wife's cohabitant placed their new house into joint names, thus giving her a half share which had to be counted as an asset of hers in the ancillary relief settlement.

In *Re L (Minors) (Financial Provision)* (1979)[105] the payee spouse had a new partner, so his income was relevant, as in the case of *Suter v Suter and Jones* already mentioned.

In *Wynne v Wynne* (1981),[106] however, the former husband was supported in great style in a luxurious flat in Knightsbridge, but being a 'kept man' could pay no order himself, nor could the new partner be asked to pay that particular expense for him had an order been made against him – despite her willingness to pay for anything else he might desire. Consequently, if such a former spouse simply gives up work and elects to be kept by the new spouse or cohabitant, no order will be able to be made at all against either the former spouse or the new partner.

It is impossible to compel a new partner to make any disclosure, even to establish what the ex-spouse might reasonably have access to financially. The only way to obtain such detail is to compel the respondent to the financial provision application (i.e. the ex-spouse personally) to give such detail as he or she knows of the new partner's means in the respondent's own disclosure (or in response to a questionnaire; these are still allowed under the current financial provision regime). Even a production appointment ordered by the DJ will not help unless the information is forthcoming through the respondent since this only enables an order to be made to compel a person who could have been compelled to produce a document in the course of the proceedings to do so at an earlier stage than the actual hearing: *Frary v Frary* (1993).[107] Nevertheless, disclosure ordered in the jurisdiction of England and Wales is so superior to that obtainable in most other jurisdictions that this is another reason for the choice of England and Wales as (in the words of Lord Justice Thorpe) 'the divorce capital of the world'.

Assets acquired after separation or divorce or pre-acquired

These are not excluded as a resource, especially if needed to do justice between the parties, nor are necessarily those assets which are pre-acquired or inherited, and the recent Law Commission work has not changed this.

However, they may be ring-fenced in certain circumstances, especially if not required to meet needs. There have been at least two recent cases in which this issue has been raised: *Robson v Robson* (2010)[108] and *Jones v Jones* (2011).[109]

---

104 [1984] FLR 545.
105 [1979] 1 FLR 39.
106 [1981] 1 WLR 69; [1980] 3 All ER 659.
107 [1993] 2 FLR 696.
108 [2010] EWCA 1171.
109 [2011] EWCA Civ 41.

❖ CASE EXAMPLES

In *Schuller v Schuller* (1990),[110] where the wife inherited a valuable flat from a wealthy friend after the marriage had ended, this had to be brought into the pot for ancillary relief. This was the trend at the time of this decision, especially if the asset was required to do justice between the parties.

In *Jones v Jones* (2011) the principal issue was how the husband's company should be treated. He had owned it for ten years before the marriage, which had then lasted ten years, and had then sold it soon after the parties separated, for £25 million. The wife wanted £10 million, which was 40 per cent of the total assets. The husband wanted the value of the company at the date of separation (£12m) to be taken as the value for the purpose of the asset split, although he had sold it the following year for over double, as he did not want her to share in the post-separation increase. The Court of Appeal adopted the husband's approach, assigning values to the company as at the date of the marriage and applying a figure for the increase in value from that date to the date of the sale. They then deducted this sum from the total assets at the date of the sale in order to identify the matrimonial assets. The resultant figure of £16 million was divided in half on the sharing principle, which was 32 per cent of the matrimonial assets and fair to both parties. This methodology was subsequently approved by Mostyn J in *N v F* (2011).[111]

Robson v Robson (2010), a big money case where the assets were inherited by the husband, was the subject of guidance by Ward LJ on the treatment of inherited assets. The marriage was a long one but the inherited assets had been developed by the husband's father and not particularly well preserved by the husband during the marriage, when the parties had lived off capital in order to support a high standard of living. Thus neither party had done anything to increase the value of the assets during the marriage.

The first instance judge had overestimated the wife's housing needs and awarded her £5 million, and capitalised her income needs at £3 million, but she had bought a house for £4 million and the husband applied to introduce new evidence in order to revise the award downwards and to apply for a clean break, which application was dismissed.

On appeal the wife's income needs were reduced by 10 per cent and she ultimately received £7 million rather than the £8 million first awarded. Ward LJ commented that such cases should be treated strictly in accordance with s 25 of the Act, in particular the matters listed in s 25(2), using the concepts of needs, compensation and sharing in the search for fairness – taking inherited wealth into account in accordance with s 25(2)(a) but not 'invading' the inherited wealth unnecessarily, since it is different from the 'marital acquest' acquired by joint efforts. He emphasised that the object must be to reach a just result.

The spouse's true earning capacity

The court has never been deceived by disclosure alleging a tiny income where the lifestyle does not match.

---

110 [1990] 2 FLR 193.
111 [2011] EWHC 586 (Fam).

❖ CASE EXAMPLE

In *J v J* (1955)[112] the husband was a property developer living far beyond his apparent means, but actually declared a tiny taxable income. The order was based on his lifestyle and not on his apparent income.

In *Newton v Newton* (1990)[113] the court eventually decided that nothing the millionaire husband said could be relied on and based their order on his lifestyle. He had made his case worse by suggesting that his 53-year-old agoraphobic wife should 'pull herself together and get a job'; thus it may be deduced that the court is not slow to take action where they realise that they are being deliberately deceived.

In the well-known case of *Wachtel v Wachtel* (1973),[114] however, the respondent went too far, and the court must have felt their intelligence was being insulted where the husband's income was supposed to be £4,000 p.a., but he actually spent £5,000 and was in fact accumulating savings. He came from a wealthy family and the court took the obvious step in the circumstances of treating his income as at least £6,000.

Where the respondent is from a wealthy family, it is not necessary for there to be actual deceit of this kind before the court will take the view that family money is likely to be available and that the respondent could reasonably expect to tap into those funds even to make a lump sum payment to his wife, as happened in the 1995 case of *Thomas*, already mentioned, where the court took note of his wealthy family's support so as to require the respondent to pay school fees.

The court adopts the same sceptical approach when measuring actual earnings, even if the level of those earnings is demonstrably true, but where the spouse in question could and should be earning more. The case law shows that it is no good such a spouse taking a low-paid or unpaid job with a charity or working from choice for a friend at subsistence level if a more suitable level of earnings is genuinely realisable.

❖ CASE EXAMPLES

In *Hardy v Hardy* (1981)[115] the husband went to work for his father, a wealthy racehorse trainer, on a stable hand's wage of £70 per week – the court had no hesitation in making an order of £50 in favour of his wife and children on the basis of what he could really earn.

In *McEwan v McEwan* (1972)[116] the husband was actually already retired at the age of 59 on a police pension of £6 per week, but the court still made an order of that amount on the basis that he could still earn something as well.

---

112 [1955] 3 WLR 72; [1955] P 215.
113 [1990] 1 FLR 33.
114 [1973] 2 WLR 366; [1973] 1 All ER 829.
115 [1981] 11 Fam Law 153.
116 [1972] 1 WLR 1217; [1972] 2 All ER 708.

This attitude is not confined to immediate decisions on current earnings.

> ### ❖ CASE EXAMPLES
>
> In *Mitchell v Mitchell* (1984),[117] the court also took the view that the mother of a 13-year-old daughter could return to work and raise a small mortgage when the girl left school so as to give the husband a bigger share of the matrimonial home when the house was sold on completion of the daughter's education.
>
> In *Williams v Williams* (1974),[118] however, the court recognised that where a spouse has genuine difficulty finding work and is obviously not simply workshy, an order should *not* be made on the basis of earning capacity: in this case the husband was made redundant and while the judge at first instance took the view that he must be wilfully on welfare benefits and so made a maintenance order based on what he should have been earning, this was reversed on appeal when the court was satisfied of the true position.
>
> In *M v M (Financial Provision)* (1987)[119] the chances of a middle-aged woman's returning to the employment market after several years' absence were recognised as problematic.

Pensions

The amendments to the 1973 Act now require the court to examine the parties' pension position for the purposes of s 25(2). (These were s 25B, inserted by the **Pensions Act 1995** s 166, and the **Welfare Reform and Pensions Act** 1999 ss 21A and 24B.)

Resources now include both existing and likely future pension benefits, so as to enable the court to consider whether an order should be made pursuant to the MCA 1973 to require payment of part of the pension to the applicant spouse, either by 'attachment' or by sharing. The court takes into account all the possibilities, including attaching death benefits and nominations which could be deployed in favour of the applicant. This is a most logical inclusion in the calculation of what the applicant should receive since the pension is often the most valuable of a couple's assets, sometimes more valuable than the former matrimonial home, and it is clearly fair to include such an asset, which will have probably been built up during the marriage while the applicant wife has been looking after the home and the children – since *Lambert* recognised to be as valuable as the bread-winner's financial contribution to the marriage.

However, applicants often choose to take another asset in compensation for loss of the share of the pension since valuations are seldom as high as the pension's actual ultimate worth since the CETV obtained omits the contributions yet to be made unless the respondent is actually about to retire.

---

117 [1984] FLR 387, CA.
118 [1974] 3 WLR 379; [1974] 3 All ER 377.
119 [1987] 2 FLR 1.

7.6 The court's considerations in exercising its discretion: s 25(2)(b)–(h)

Once the s 25(2)(a) resources are identified, and the parties know on what figures their negotiations will be based, suitable orders will be worked out in accordance with the remaining
s 25 considerations. This means looking at s 25(2)(b) as qualified by ss 25(2)(c)–(h).

7.6.1 The parties' needs, obligations and responsibilities: s 25(2)(b)

Under this head, the court looks at the parties' needs and obligations – all the basic categories such as
food, clothes, housing and expenses in connection with the upbringing of the children, whose welfare
will be the first consideration. Obviously common sense is helpful here – some regard will have to be
had to a suitable lifestyle for each of the parties, and some sort of budget in keeping with that, in order
to assess what 'needs' actually means in each case. In deciding what the needs are, the court usually has
two (sometimes inconsistent) aims in view, namely both to maintain a residence for the custodial
spouse and children and to divide the family assets fairly (especially the matrimonial home, which is
usually the largest asset). 'Needs' can be seen to have figured highly in the considerations of the court
in the various post-*White* decisions in which closer recourse to the s 25 criteria has been emphasised.

The prime need will usually be for a home for each party, but while the court does operate on
a rule of thumb of 'homes for all', because of the contact with the non-resident parent that s 25(1)
will require, the roof will obviously be especially important for the party who has care of the children. *Mesher v Mesher*, already mentioned above, was the first case in which the need of the wife and
children to be housed, which precluded the sale which might otherwise have been ordered, led to
a settlement of the matrimonial home to enable them to occupy it for as long as necessary and then
for the proceeds to be divided later on the deferred sale.

This case, the origin of the term 'Mesher order' as a generic description for occupational settlement orders in relation to the matrimonial home, has led to many variations on the theme, such as
the *Harvey* order (where instead of leaving at the end of the occupation period, the spouse in occupation pays to the other an occupational rent, assessed at a fair market rate), and the *Martin* order (where
the spouse in occupation, usually the wife, controls the date at which the home is ultimately sold
since the trigger event is that of her remarriage, cohabitation, voluntary removal or even death).

Husbands can benefit from the court's policy of requiring that each party should, if possible,
have a home. This can best be illustrated by some actual cases.

❖ CASE EXAMPLES

In *Calderbank v Calderbank* (1975)[120] it was held that the husband needed a house in
keeping with the lifestyle he had enjoyed during the marriage to a wealthy woman, in
which to receive access visits by the children.

In *Browne v Pritchard* (1975)[121] the husband and children remained in the matrimonial
home since the wife had a council house and the unemployed husband could not afford to
buy out her share of the former home.

---

120 [1975] 3 WLR 586; [1975] 3 All ER 721.
121 [1975] 1 WLR 1366.

In *R v R (Financial Provision: Reasonable Needs)* (1994)[122] it was reasonable for a wife to remain in a 'superb Queen Anne style house' worth £1.3 million, especially as the husband had moved with his mistress to one costing £2.7 million.

These occupational orders have therefore established a principle that ownership of the matrimonial home is relatively unimportant; what matters is where everyone is going to live. The reasonable needs of affluent parties may include a luxurious standard of living. Obligations to a second family must be fully taken into account, though extravagant expenditure when resources are limited will be ignored: *Slater v Slater* (1982)[123] (see below).

Special situations

The court will also have to take into account any factors which increase needs or reduce ability to pay because of other obligations: the two most obvious and frequently occurring of these are *special needs* and *second families*. The reasonable needs of affluent parties may cover a luxurious standard of living (e.g. Mrs Dart in *Dart v Dart*, who was nevertheless discontented to receive only £10 million as she had wanted at least £200 million; also Mrs Gojkovic in *Gojkovic v Gojkovic* (1991), who needed £1 million to set up her own business; Mrs R in *R v R (Financial Provision: Reasonable Needs)* (1994),[124] whose award of £1.9 million was for a short time the largest reported in the mid–1990s when millionaire awards became commonplace (though it was said that there were many higher unreported, and this was soon overtaken by Mrs F in *F v F (Ancillary Relief: Substantial Assets)* (1995),[125] whose needs were £9 million comprising a house in London, a mansion in the country, a villa in Switzerland and £5 million in cash). The *Duxbury* calculation, devised in *Duxbury v Duxbury* (1987),[126] can detail the precise sum required to produce any desired level of annual income for this type of applicant.

Special needs

Needs will obviously take account of *special needs* in a health or education sense, especially where this affects the children.

❖ CASE EXAMPLES

In *Smith v Smith* (1975)[127] the court took account of Mrs Smith's need to do part-time work as she looked after a daughter with a kidney complaint. As a result she had no job security and clearly would not be able to re-house herself if the matrimonial home were sold and the proceeds divided, even if the daughter were to leave home. In the circumstances, the court transferred the home to her absolutely.

Second families

However, it is now established that the needs of second families are just as valid as those of the first family – there is no 'pecking order' as such: *Barnes v Barnes* (1972).[128] *Barnes* was the seminal case

---

122 [1994] 2 FLR 1044.
123 [1982] 3 FLR 364.
124 For these three cases already mentioned in other contexts see above.
125 [1995] 2 FLR 45.
126 [1987] FLR 7, CA.
127 [1975] 2 All ER 19.
128 [1972] 1 WLR 1381; [1972] 3 All ER 872.

which established that no one is entitled to throw the burden of maintaining a spouse and family onto the state; they are expected to be supported by the other spouse's employment if at all possible. This is sometimes called 'the rule in *Barnes v Barnes*'. The case also settled the principle that the obligation to a second wife and family does not rank second after that to a first wife and family, so that the subsequent obligations must be given the same weight as any other responsibilities. *Stockford v Stockford* (1982)[129] and *Furniss v Furniss* (1982)[130] were both decided on the basis of this principle and resulted in the first wife coming off worse in her claim for what money there was since she, being alone and without a waged partner, could rely on welfare benefits if unable to work, while the new wife, having both a partner in work and younger children, was unable either to fall back on social security or to work herself.

These decisions have been followed in the later leading case of *Delaney v Delaney* (1990),[131] where the judge, in justifying a similar decision, expressly invoked the principle that it is now recognised that 'there is life after divorce', although extravagant expenditure may be ignored: *Slater v Slater* (1982),[132] where the court disapproved of a husband who had chosen to live in a country house with consequently high maintenance and transport costs.

7.6.2 The standard of living prior to the marriage breakdown: s 25(2)(c)

This requires the court to consider how the parties lived during the marriage and is responsible for some of the apparently very generous orders in high-value divorces.

Obviously, wealthier families may suffer no drop as in *Calderbank v Calderbank* (above), where the husband was able to maintain his previous lifestyle on the basis that the children would expect it when they visited him, and *Foley v Foley* (1981),[133] where the wife had to be financed to maintain her lifestyle on a par with that to which she had become accustomed, including buying a house with a piece of land, so as not to lower her usual standard of living.

The very wealthy husband used to benefit from this principle by invoking it in the form usually known as the 'millionaire's defence', in which it was claimed that a detailed account of such a husband's assets was not required to be sworn in an affidavit of means because the husband in question was so wealthy that he could easily meet any order the court might reasonably make, based on the parties' marital lifestyle. This happened in *Thyssen-Bornemisza v Thyssen Bornemisza (No 2)* (1985),[134] where the wife's request for full details of her husband's assets (so she could be sure she was getting a large enough settlement) was refused by the court since the standard of living criteria in s 25(2)(c) meant that they only had to provide for her needs in preserving her usual lifestyle, for which it was not necessary to put the husband to more expense in preparing financial detail than was actually required to satisfy the court that he had the means to pay the order made.

It is questionable whether post-*White* the millionaire's defence is still available as the court must now check their s 25 based award against the fair outcome; this used to be against 'the yardstick of equality', although this has since been recast as 'fairness', which means that equality might not be 'fair'. Moreover, Moylan J in H v H (2008)[135] has placed it on record that detailed accounting is not required, but only a broad analysis so that 'fairness' can be assessed.

---

129 [1982] 3 FLR 52.
130 [1982] 3 FLR 46.
131 [1990] 2 FLR 457.
132 [1982] 3 FLR 364.
133 [1981] 3 WLR 284; [1981] 2 All ER 857.
134 [1985] FLR 1069.
135 [2008] EWHC 935 Fam; [2008] 2 FLR 2092.

It would appear that a greater forensic search than is really required in relation to wealth and contribution has been occurring, as this was first noted following the *Cowan* decision in 2001, when judges expressed concern about the volume of costly evidence being presented, also increasing the length of hearings. While the new CPR which govern the remainder of civil litigation in the post-Woolf reforms era do not apply to family law, their philosophy of 'the overriding objective' (of dealing with cases swiftly and avoiding disproportionate expense and delay) has been specifically reflected in the financial provision procedure for some years, including more recently in the new FPR 2010, while family law case management is now, post the FJR, inevitably likely to take an even stricter approach to excessive expense in this respect.

However, it may be that s 25(2)(c) will not even be relevant where the marriage has been short and childless. In *Attar v Attar (No 2)* (1985)[136] an air hostess who had been married to a wealthy Saudi Arabian with disclosed assets of £2 million received only a lump sum equivalent to two years' pay at the rate of her former salary to enable her to readjust to the end of her marriage and dependence on the husband. It must be asked where this decision now sits with *Miller*, although the case can perhaps be distinguished by the fact that the air hostess was not earning £85,000 before the marriage, and her husband's behaviour had not ended the marriage. Nevertheless the expectations of enhanced lifestyle must be fairly similar since the husband's fortune in 1985 terms was substantial although perhaps not as great as Mr Miller's.

Low- and middle-income families tend, however, to have difficulty in sustaining the former lifestyle, although the court tries to leave the parties on similar standards of living so the drop is shared equally as in *Scott v Scott* (1982).[137]

Where there is a dispute about the appropriate standard of living as in *Preston v Preston* (1981)[138] the standard of living during the marriage may not be replicated in applying s 25(2)(c). The principle is aptly illustrated by this case.

❖ CASE EXAMPLE

In *Preston* (1981) the wife had managed on a very small amount of money while the husband was building up the business on which they lived. However, it was held that the payee spouse is not restricted to that minimum level but can insist on a less frugal amount reflecting how the parties lived once their life had become more prosperous.

Nevertheless, sight should not be lost of the post-1984 goal of making the parties self-sufficient where possible.

7.6.3 Age of the parties and duration of the marriage: s 25(2)(d)

There is a clear recognition of the relevance of a spouse's non-financial contributions as well as of the realities of life in this section. For example, a wife's age will clearly be relevant to her earning capacity (and therefore also to the clean break potential) and a husband's to his retirement and ability to pay an order, whereas the duration of the marriage (which normally used to exclude any

---

136 [1985] FLR 653.
137 [1982] 1 WLR 723; [1978] 3 All ER 65.
138 [1981] 3 WLR 619; [1982] 1 All ER 41.

period of prior cohabitation, although this now tends to be taken into account as part of the true length of the relationship) will be some guide to the contribution which the parties have both made to the relationship – which should be recognised in distributing the assets. It will thus be seen that the ages of the parties and the duration of the marriage in relation to the financial package has nothing to do with the merits of the case and everything with the capability of the financially weaker spouse (usually the wife) to work and be self-sufficient following the divorce and where relevant to the husband's ability to pay.

❖ CASE EXAMPLE

In *A v A (Elderly Applicant: Lump Sum)* (1999)[139] there was a 79-year-old husband and a 76-year-old wife, and a marriage of 43 years, with two adult children. Both parties had worked during the marriage; the wife had £1.034 million including £750,000 in the bank, and the husband £61,000. A *Duxbury* calculation to produce an adequate income for his life expectancy would have given him a lesser lump sum than the length of the marriage and his contributions over the years appeared to warrant.

Singer J both rejected the wife's claim that a *Duxbury* fund of £87,000 would be sufficient and reduced the award at first instance of £389,000 to £350,000 so as to provide for his reasonable needs, while reflecting the husband's contribution over 43 years. This case shows how important the court's discretion is in cases of long marriage and older parties.

An older wife who married in the tradition of non working wives and mothers is less likely to be expected to work (or to retrain if her skills are outdated or she has never had commercial skills or an employment history) than a younger one who has grown up used to the culture of working wives and mothers. Moreover, a younger wife who can work can raise a mortgage, whereas an older one with less earning capacity may not be able to.

Cohabitation before marriage was not normally relevant in calculating the length of a marriage until very recently, although in an exceptional case it might be. This reluctance to include the cohabitation years was because of the difference recognised between formal commitment to marriage and the more flexible state of cohabitation, a difference emphasised in *Campbell v Campbell* (1976),[140] where it was expressly noted that the obligations of marriage begin only after the ceremony, despite the fact that the marriage in that case was of only two years' duration, while it followed cohabitation of three-and-a-half years.

However, cohabitation pre-ceremony now seems to be accepted as all part of the circumstances of the case, as the court takes note of the period alongside the length of the marriage. Whether they then notionally add the cohabitation years to those of the marriage in calculating the length of the marriage for s 25(2)(c) or only do so in considering the length of the personal relationship which has included the marriage (which is not always clear from the decisions) it is clear that the court is noting the fact where pre-marriage cohabitation has taken place. In the past it was a rare case when the court was even interested in anything but the length of the marriage as such.

---

139 [1999] 2 FLR 969.
140 [1976] 3 WLR 572; [1977] 1 All ER 1.

> ❖ **CASE EXAMPLE**
>
> In *Kokosinski v Kokosinski* (1980)[141] the marriage was extremely short but the period of cohabitation was 22 years, and the wife, unable to marry the husband throughout almost the entire 22-year period because he was not free to do so, changed her name by deed poll, helped the husband in his business, bore him a son and, as the court specifically noted, gave him the best years of her life. Exceptionally, she received a large lump sum to enable her to buy a flat near her work.

More recently there was for a period a detectable tendency at least to look carefully at any period of cohabitation before deciding not to take it into account, although in B v B (1995)[142] Thorpe J specifically recognised the reality of the increase in pre-marriage cohabitation as a relevant factor. Since then the cohabiting years seem to have crept in, in order to expand the length of the relationship.

Care should obviously be taken to obtain compensation, whatever the length of the marriage, where a spouse has given up a lot to marry in the first place and has lost out as a result (e.g. a good job, a business opportunity or a residential tenancy as in L v L, above). In the case of a short marriage this might not be a large sum in relation to the payer's assets, as in *Attar v Attar (No 2)*; see above. This proportionate approach is likely to be wrong, however, if there is a child, as the burden of the child's dependence is likely to cancel out the shortness of the marriage, and once more require an assessment of needs: *C v C (Financial Relief: Short Marriage)* (1997).[143]

7.6.4 Physical or mental disability of either party: s 25(2)(e)

This is clearly relevant to earning capacity and capabilities generally. Such considerations will usually immediately identify themselves as in *Jones v Jones*, the case already considered in another context of the wife injured by the husband's knife attack who could not continue to work as a nurse.

> ❖ **CASE EXAMPLES**
>
> In *B v B* (1982)[144] the wife needed, and obtained, extra money for her expenses since she had multiple sclerosis.
>
> In *Newton v Newton* (1990)[145] the wife had serious physical and psychological difficulties which required a regular companion and help with transport, which she obtained.
>
> In *Sakkass v Sakkass* (1987)[146] the husband had multiple sclerosis, and the court felt that there had to be a *Mesher* order to enable the wife and children to remain in the home. In this case, however, the court could not decide on the eventual shares of the proceeds on sale until there was up-to-date information on the husband's condition because his future

---

141 [1980] 3 WLR 55; [1980] 1 All ER 1106.
142 [1995] 1 FLR 9.
143 [1997] 2 FLR 26, CA.
144 [1982] 12 Fam Law 92.
145 [1990] 1 FLR 33.
146 [1987] 2 FLR 398.

needs could not be properly determined at the time the house fell to be sold. This type of case may require an adjournment while the true position is ascertained.

7.6.5 The past, present and future contributions (financial and other) made or to be made to the welfare of the family by each of the parties: s 25(2)(f)

Contributions to be considered here may be either positive or negative, and this paragraph has been the most significant of any provision in securing adequate recognition of the contribution of unwaged spouses who remain at home to care for the household and family. This sort of contribution has been immortalised in such cases as *Vicary v Vicary* (1992)[147] in judicial comments such as 'the wife had supplied the infrastructure and support in the context of which the husband was able to prosper and accumulate wealth'.

Wachtel v Wachtel (1973)[148] is still good law on the value of the wife's unpaid work in homemaking and childcare as being every bit as deserving of recognition in money terms as the husband's in going out to work to earn a living for the family as a whole.

As Lord Denning said in that case, the wife contributes in kind to enable the husband to acquire assets for both parties, and the value of the wife's work in this area is clearly demonstrated merely by costing the price of hiring help to do the domestic work which she undertakes for the benefit of both spouses and the children. In *Lambert* (2002), already mentioned, this recognition of the equal value of the wife as homemaker was formalised in the judgment of Lord Justice Thorpe, who rejected the idea that the wife's contribution was less weighty than the husband's as breadwinner.

The value of this contribution, as an item in itself which earns the right to compensation, is in logic similar to a golden handshake on termination of employment after a lengthy period of service, and is quite independent of the need to maintain the spouse who has made that contribution.

❖ CASE EXAMPLES

In *Smith v Smith (Smith Intervening)* (1991)[149] this quantifiable value is demonstrated, where the wife committed suicide six months after an order was made giving her a substantial capital sum, and (although the court rescinded the part of the order which represented capitalised maintenance payments, for which being dead she no longer had either a need or a right) it did not disturb that part which represented recognition of her contribution over a 30-year marriage, which sum survived for her estate.

B v B (1982),[150] already considered above, shows that a husband is of course equal before the court in this respect. The wife came from a wealthy family but the husband had worked hard to achieve success independently, had kept the family together despite the demands of his work, and on divorce obtained custody of one of the children. It was held that he was in the same position as a wife in similar circumstances who did not legally own the bulk of the family assets.

---

147 [1992] Fam Law 429.
148 [1973] 2 WLR 366; [1973] 1 All ER 829.
149 [1991] 2 All ER 306; [1991] 2 FLR 432.
150 [1982] 12 Fam Law 92.

Contributions to the success of a business also count under this head, such as in *Gojkovic v Gojkovic*, already discussed above in other contexts, and this is especially so where a business in which the wife's hard work and willingness to turn her hand to everything has paid off so as to generate profits only at the time that the divorce occurred.

Both the above cases involved hotels where initially the wives had given unfailing support, undertaking long hours of menial work to get the business off to a good start. There will usually be a similar approach where the spouses have endured some financial hardship in order to help initially struggling businesses, as in *Kokosinski* and *Preston*. Moreover, *Trippas v Trippas* (1973), mentioned above, shows that in appropriate circumstances mere moral support without actual work will be enough to establish a spouse's right to a share in the proceeds if there has been a promise to that effect that the court can oblige the other spouse to honour, or a clear contribution, albeit perhaps not much more than moral support, but if more contribution is recognised that can significantly raise an award. Some actual cases illustrate this aptly.

❖ CASE EXAMPLE

In *Conran v Conran* (1997),[151] the high-profile journalist wife's reasonable needs were supplemented by an extra award for her outstanding contributions over 30 years to the development of the Conran furniture and restaurant businesses.

In *West v West* (1977),[152] the negative side of contribution is also aptly illustrated, where the wife would not even set up house with the husband. Instead she insisted on remaining with her parents, where she stayed with the children, for which lack of ordinary marital commitment she received a reduced maintenance order. This type of negative contribution can be a way of recording due debit for less than supportive behaviour which does not amount to conduct under s 25(2)(g).[153]

In *E v E* (1990),[154] however, the wife somehow escaped her just deserts by successfully claiming that any such reduction would not be in the interests of the children, whose welfare is required by s 25(1) to be given first consideration. Her extravagance and adultery, neglect of the children and walking out on the husband not only amazingly did not amount to conduct within the meaning of s 25(2)(g) but also failed to attract any reduction in maintenance despite the negative contribution this portfolio of shortcomings undoubtedly constituted. The court, while entirely agreeing about the negative aspect of such behaviour, concluded that leaving her in financial difficulties or even in severely reduced circumstances would not be in the children's interests, so she received a large lump sum on a clean break.

In *Piglowska v Piglowski* (1999)[155] the parties actually spent their entire assets of £128,000 on the financial provision litigation, only to have the House of Lords uphold the assessment of the DJ at first instance who had concluded that the wife's contribution was such that she should have the lion's share of the limited assets, especially as the husband had left her to live in Poland with another woman before returning to claim a share of their matrimonial assets in order to buy a house in England.

151 [1997] 2 FLR 615.
152 [1977] 2 WLR 933; [1977] 2 All ER 705.
153 For which see below at 7.6.6.
154 [1990] 2 FLR 233.
155 [1999] 1 WLR 1360; [1999] 2 FLR 763.

However, the House of Lords unfortunately did not take the opportunity of the *Piglowska* appeal to examine the relationship between contribution and conduct. This is clearly relevant to assessment of the balance between the various s 25 criteria, since contribution and conduct appear to be opposite sides of the same coin; but the impact of s 25(2)(g)[156] is that conduct as such is not relevant except in very exceptional circumstances. Lord Hoffmann merely referred to 'value judgments' that had to be made in such cases 'on which reasonable people might differ', but like Lord Nicholls in *White* appeared to be sticking firmly to the remainder of s 25 without offering any illuminating guidance on this point. The subsequent cases of *Cowan v Cowan* and *L v L* have, however, refined and debated the issue of contributions; see above.

Contributions should usually be made over at least an average-length marriage, in other words one that has lasted at least the four-and-a-half to five years envisaged by Balcombe LJ in *Leadbeater v Leadbeater* (1985);[157] but *Cumbers v Cumbers* (1975)[158] makes clear that such contributions if sufficiently significant will still be counted even in a short marriage, as it is the quality of the contribution itself which is relevant, and in relation to this concept the appropriateness of a substantial award even after a short marriage has certainly been taken up and found worth adopting in *Miller*.

7.6.6 Conduct: s 25(2)(g)

The wording of s 25(2)(g) requires the court to take into account any conduct of either of the parties which in their opinion it would be 'inequitable to disregard'. This means exactly what it says and no other extraneous descriptions or terminology need to be imported into the definition. Moreover, the trend in modern divorce law is to *disregard* conduct *unless* it is shown that it is or may be inequitable (i.e. unfair overall) not to take it into account because, as was stated in *Duxbury v Duxbury*,[159] the application of s 25 is a financial and not a moral exercise.[160] Consideration of 'conduct' is another opportunity to look at the extraordinary case of *Leadbeater v Leadbeater* (see above), where there was the most spectacular bad conduct on both sides, so much so that the judge, Balcombe J, as he then was, could not avoid concluding that they were as bad as each other, so that he might as well disregard conduct altogether.

In any case, as was expressly recognised in *Vasey v Vasey* (1985),[161] it is very difficult to discern what goes on in other people's marriages, an approach which has led to the essentially non-judgemental approach that is now felt appropriate, a distinct shift in both the general emphasis and the burden of proof in the matter, which should be noted. This can initially be traced back to the decision in *Wachtel*, which may be regarded as the watershed case for the contemporary approach to conduct unless firmly established in the s 25(2)(g) context, further to be refined in subsequent cases.[162]

The overall result is that if conduct is going to be relevant at all it will have no relation to any ordinary considerations of morality, so one should abandon all 'normal' preconceptions in this regard, since in practice the conduct in question will need to be so appalling that it simply cannot be ignored. The following are (non-exhaustive) possibilities which may be helpful in assessing whether there is relevant 'conduct' or not.

---

156 See below at 7.6.6.
157 [1985] FLR 789.
158 [1975] 1 All ER 1; [1974] 1 WLR 1331.
159 This case is already mentioned above in other contexts.
160 See also the other frequently mentioned case *Wachtel v Wachtel* (1973), an early example of the general non-relevance of conduct unless breathtakingly bad.
161 [1985] FLR 596.
162 This case is analysed in Chapter 8, 'Bringing an End to the Matrimonial Post Mortem and its Enduring Significant for Family Law' in Gilmore, Herring and Probert's (eds) *Landmark Cases in Family Law*, Oxford, Hart, 2011.

❖ CASE EXAMPLES

(1) *Murder and conspiracy to murder* will always qualify.

In *Evans v Evans* (1989)[163] the husband, having regularly paid maintenance for 32 years, was the victim of a plot by his wife and another to kill him – her maintenance order was discharged.

Encouragement of suicide is in the same category.

In *Kyte v Kyte* (1987)[164] the wife deceitfully planned to rid herself of the husband to set up house with another man, divorcing him for his behaviour as an unpredictable suicidal manic depressive, and obtaining an injunction to get him out of the house. In the process she lied to the court about her other relationship and did everything possible to facilitate the husband's demise to benefit from his estate; not even by taking his own conduct into account could the court possibly consider hers anything but inequitable to disregard.

(2) *Significant violence* will be sufficient, depending on the frequency, nature and/or degree, especially if a weapon is used and if such conduct has financial consequences.

In *Armstrong v Armstrong* (1974)[165] the wife fired a gun at the husband.

In *Jones v Jones*, already mentioned above, the knife injuries to the wife put an end to her nursing career and the husband was sent to prison for three years.

In *Bateman v Bateman* (1979)[166] the wife stabbed the husband twice.

(3) *Financial irresponsibility* will generally be sufficient because it is directly relevant to financial order, especially where assets have been dissipated.

In *Martin v Martin* (1976)[167] the entire £33,000 lost by the husband in a string of unsuccessful business ventures set up with his mistress was counted as his share of the assets, which convinced the court that the remainder should be allocated to his wife, subject only to paying off his mortgage and giving him a small lump sum.

In *Day v Day* (1988),[168] already mentioned above, the husband had encouraged the wife to build up rent arrears so that money could be spent on other things, and this was held to qualify as conduct.

In *Suter v Suter and Jones* (1987)[169] the court looked askance on the young wife inviting her lover to live in her home without asking him to contribute to the household budget since they considered that this was capable of amounting to conduct within the meaning of the section.

---

163 [1989] 1 FLR 351.
164 [1987] 3 All ER 1041.
165 (1974) 118 SJ 579.
166 [1979] 2 WLR 377.
167 [1976] 2 WLR 901; [1976] 3 All ER 625.
168 [1988] 1 FLR 278.
169 [1987] 2 FLR 232, another case already mentioned earlier in other contexts.

(4) *Misleading the court in financial matters* will be conduct especially if done deliberately, as in *Kyte*, as well as separately qualifying as contempt of court.

(5) *Alcoholism and laziness if severe* will in theory be conduct, again because of the direct effect on financial matters, but as in *Martin*, see above, tends not to deprive the culprit entirely of financial relief for the simple reason that a home will still have to be provided.

In *K v K* (1990)[170] the husband behaved very badly after being made redundant, as a result of which the matrimonial home had to be sold, his behaviour contrasting sharply with the wife's energy and industry, which had resulted in her obtaining a well-paid job and a flat of her own. However, the court had to award him 60 per cent of the proceeds of the home when it was sold as this was the minimum he needed to re-house himself. The court did, however, turn down his impertinent claim for maintenance from the wife.

(6) *Leaving the blameless spouse/being the sole cause of the breakdown* may be conduct, but will still tend to be reflected in the court's making an order at the lower end of a scale rather than in distinctly down-rating the award, and/or in the court's taking some care to try to see that the blameless spouse whose life has been disrupted is left as comfortable as possible. Nevertheless, in the relatively recent cases where the respondent wives could give no explanation for their actions their orders were reduced.

(7) *Deliberately committing bigamy or contracting an invalid marriage* is not only conduct, but will sometimes even preclude financial provision because the marriage could not possibly have been thought to be valid.

In *Whiston v Whiston* (1995)[171] the respondent was barred from ancillary relief as the conduct in deceiving the petitioner was regarded as so bad.

In *J v S-T (Formerly J)* (1996)[172] knowingly contracting an invalid marriage as a transsexual was held to be in the same category as bigamy.

(8) *Blatant marital, financial and litigation misconduct* is conduct and will be reflected in quantum.

In *Clarke v Clarke* (1999)[173] the wife, in her forties and in debt, ill-treated her eighty-year-old husband over a marriage of six years, but never consummated the marriage, during which she lived with her lover in the matrimonial home while making her husband live in a caravan in the garden. The wife nevertheless extracted large sums from the husband, who had assets in excess of £3 million, lost money in speculative ventures after he paid off her debts, transferred his share portfolio to herself and bought herself several properties. On appeal, her first instance award of £552,500 was reduced to £125,000 and she was allowed to keep assets of £50,000.

---

170 [1990] Fam Law 19; [1990] 2 FLR 225.
171 [1995] 3 WLR 405; [1995] 2 FLR 268, CA.
172 (1996) The Times, 25 November, CA.
173 [1999] 2 FLR 498.

(9) *Really repugnant sexual behaviour* will be conduct: the facts speak for themselves in a couple of cases.

In *Bailey v Tolliday* (1983)[174] the wife had an affair with her father-in-law.

In *Dixon v Dixon* (1974)[175] the husband committed adultery with his daughter-in-law in the matrimonial home.

(10) *Adultery* is only sufficient if coupled with some other generally gratuitous and antisocial behaviour.

In *Cuzner v Underdown* (1974)[176] the wife conducted an adulterous affair during the marriage, said nothing about it when the husband generously transferred their home (to which she had contributed nothing) into joint names, and then applied for an order for sale so as to raise money to set up house with her lover, of which the court took a poor view.

It should be noted that adultery and cohabitation after separation are definitely not 'conduct' within the meaning of s 25(2)(g). This covers all cases of simple adultery, or what used to be called 'living in sin' – cohabitation with a new partner after separation from the spouse. None of this is conduct within the meaning of s 25(2)(g) even if, as in the *Duxbury* case, both parties had had affairs during the marriage as well. The following leading case may surprise but has been held to be good law despite challenge.

❖ CASE EXAMPLE

In *Atkinson v Atkinson* (1987)[177] such cohabitation following a decree absolute, but without remarriage, was found to be financially motivated, but the most effect which such cohabitation will have in financial terms is that the live-in lover will be expected to contribute to the ex-spouse's budget if s/he can afford to do so.

In the case of Mrs Atkinson the court was not even able to make an order on the basis that some contribution should be made, because Mrs Atkinson's new man was so financially ineffectual that according to the court she needed her continuing maintenance even more because she was cohabiting.

It is possible the court was influenced by the fact that the husband was a millionaire and could afford to continue to support his ex-wife while the court could opine, correctly, that cohabitation did not connote the same obligations as matrimony, so that it would be wrong to reduce or cancel her right to support from her ex-husband which had been duly ordered following her divorce.

---

174 [1983] 4 FLR 542.
175 (1974) 6 Fam Law 58.
176 [1974] 1 WLR 641; [1974] 2 All ER 357.
177 [1987] 3 All ER 849.

Good conduct is naturally as relevant under s 25(2)(g) as bad conduct, as *Kokosinski*, see above, amply shows.

Where there are allegations of conduct, transfer for hearing by a High Court judge may be ordered: *Practice Direction* [1992] 3 All ER 151.

7.6.7 The value of any benefit lost on the dissolution of the marriage: s 25(2)(h)

This paragraph requires the court to consider the value of any such benefit lost – in the past this was usually, but not exclusively, pension rights – and to award compensation. If such compensation was impossible there might have been a successful s 5 defence[178] or the applicant (if a respondent to a Fact D petition) may have been able to use s 10 to hold up decree absolute until financial provision was satisfactory.

The wording of s 25(2)(h) can still cover any benefit which is lost on dissolution of the marriage, although pension rights, which can now also be dealt with pursuant to the specific amendments to s 25, have always been the most likely losses for consideration under this head. However, despite the 'earmarking' provisions of the **Pensions Act 1995**, still preserved after the **Welfare Reform and Pensions Act 1999**'s sharing provisions as an attachment order, there may still be financial benefits lost if the husband retires early or dies.

> ### ❖ CASE EXAMPLE
>
> In *Milne v Milne* (1981),[179] where there was such an anticipated pension loss, the husband had to pay the wife the anticipated sum involved immediately. Except in the few cases where pension rights could already be split under other provisions, for instance in the case of company schemes (as in *Brooks v Brooks*) which can be varied under MCA 1973 s 24, any solicitor acting in financial provision must obtain an actuarial valuation of the pension and seek a lump sum in compensation if attachment or splitting pursuant to the new provisions is not suitable, since it may still be possible to achieve some compensation under this section.

In any event the value of the pension rights must be considered and the best recompense obtained for their value as well as for any other loss quantifiable under s 25(2)(h), such as in *Trippas*, where the court compelled the husband to pay the wife the share of the profits of the business in which she had been supportive, simply because he had promised she would receive such a share.

7.7 The clean break: MCA 1973 s 25A

Making use of the range of orders available under MCA 1973 ss 23 and 24 must always be subject to the provisions of s 25A, only formally inserted into the MCA 1973 by the **Matrimonial and Family Proceedings Act (MFPA) 1984**, but prior to that already common practice in ordering financial provision.

---

178 See Chapter 5.
179 [1981] 2 FLR 286.

The practical result is that the court must assess whether there should be no periodical payments in the financial package (i.e. a clean break) or substantive or nominal periodical payments (i.e. continuing spousal financial interdependence), or whether any periodical payments that must be ordered should be for a limited term, providing a deferred clean break (e.g. because a solely capital package is impossible at the time). The only difference made by the MFPA 1984 was that prior to the insertion of s 25A the court could not actually *impose* a clean break unless the parties themselves agreed; now, whenever the court makes s 23 or s 24 orders, it can and does, such power being given by s 25A(1), (2) and (3) in the following manner.

7.7.1 The court's clean break duty: s 25A(1)

STATUTORY EXTRACT

By s 25A(1), when exercising its powers under ss 23 or 24:

'. . . it shall be the duty of the court to consider whether it would be appropriate so to exercise those powers that the financial obligations of each party towards the other should be terminated as soon after the grant of the decree as the court considers just and reasonable.'

This is the general duty of the court to consider a clean break in every case, but not to impose one regardless unless that is suitable.

The importance of this point was emphasised in *Clutton v Clutton* (1991),[180] which is a helpful example.

❖ CASE EXAMPLE

In *Clutton v Clutton* a wife's clean break order was cancelled on appeal because it transferred the matrimonial home absolutely to her in return for cancelling her maintenance order, which the court thought unnecessary for the following reasons.

First, it unjustly deprived the husband of his share of the matrimonial home acquired by their joint efforts, and that was not even necessary, since all that was required was an occupation order for the wife and the one child remaining at home, until she remarried, cohabited or died.

Second, the court stated that if it was desired to achieve a clean break that could still be done, and much more fairly, by a *Martin* order, which would enable the house to be sold and the proceeds divided in the proportion of one third to the husband and two thirds to the wife, with the sale postponed until one of the triggering events occurred. As Lloyd LJ added, this solution, providing in effect 'a charge which does not take effect until death or remarriage which could only be said to offend against the principle of the clean break in the most extended sense of the term', is often acceptable and practical where a clean break is possible.

---

180 [1991] 1 All ER 340, CA.

Following *White v White*, and subsequent cases developing the fairness principles established in that case, this approach is likely to be adopted *in lieu* of other types of clean breaks, in order to do justice to the husband where there are insufficient assets to finance a clean break fairly in any other way.

7.7.2 Adjusting without undue hardship: s 25A(2)

STATUTORY EXTRACT

By s 25A(2), when making any periodical payments orders under s 23:

'. . . the court shall in particular consider whether it would be appropriate to require those payments to be made or secured only for such term as would in the opinion of the court be sufficient to enable the party in whose favour the order is made to adjust without undue hardship to the termination of his or her financial dependence on the other party.'

This is the section which requires the court to consider *limited term periodical payments*, though again to impose them only if appropriate, as part of an ancillary relief package.

7.7.3 Termination of obligations: s 25A(3)

STATUTORY EXTRACT

By s 25A(3), again when hearing any application for a periodical payments order under s 23:

'. . . if the court considers that no continuing obligation should be imposed on either party to make or secure periodical payments in favour of the other, the court may dismiss the application with a direction that the applicant shall not be entitled to make any further application in relation to that marriage for an order under s 23(1)(a) or (b).'

This is the section which empowers the court not only either to dismiss an application for periodical payments outright instead of setting a limit on the period for which they should be paid under s 25A(2), but also to direct that no further application should be made, either at all or to extend a limited term imposed under s 25A(2), and also to exclude future applications under the **Inheritance (Provision for Families and Dependants) Act 1975**.

7.7.4 Orders that can be made under ss 23 and 25A

Thus the three sub-sections of s 25A give the court wide and flexible powers either to approve what the parties have agreed themselves or to impose suitable terms if the parties cannot agree. Circumstances will dictate whether s 25A will be applicable at all and if so which precise type of order it will be most suitable to make. Orders may be made in the following forms.

Open-ended periodical payments order: s 23

This is the simplest order, under s 23, i.e. an order for the amount of maintenance required by the payee, payable by periodical payments, where they continue indefinitely at the rate originally ordered, unless or until the payee or payer applies to vary them because of a change of circumstances. This is sometimes called a 'substantive' order, as opposed to a 'nominal' order (as to which see below). There is obviously no application of s 25A here.

Nominal periodical payments order: s 23

This is an open-ended order, similar to that above, but for a *nominal* amount of maintenance, usually 5p or £1 p.a., which is meant only to indicate the payee's *continuing right* to maintenance, providing a long stop in case of future need for a substantive order; for example to protect the children if their mother loses her job, rather than the maintenance actually being needed as financial support at the time the order is made. It will continue in the same way as an ordinary open-ended order unless terminated by the court.

Nominal periodical payments must be distinguished from 'small' periodical payments, which used to have a technical meaning, being paid (when maintenance was not tax free in the hands of the recipient) gross and without deduction of tax. Nowadays if anyone mentions 'small' periodical payments (although they will manifestly be for a small amount, probably for the good reason that the payee is cash restricted for the time being, but it is thought right to collect some contribution on principle), such orders will be for something other than 'nominal' amounts – i.e. perhaps £10 p.w. but not 5p p.a. However 'small', these periodical payments are only a sub-species of open-ended periodical payments if not specifically expressed in the accepted nominal format.

However, neither open-ended nor nominal periodical payments are compatible with a clean break because they continue the dependent financial link between the parties.

Fixed term periodical payments with power to extend the fixed term: s 25A(1) and (2)

This is the order contemplated by the philosophy of spousal self-sufficiency introduced in 1984 and is the only type of periodical payments order which can co-exist with a clean break, because it only preserves the dependent financial links between the parties for a strictly limited period. This will remain the case even if that period is subsequently extended by the court, since if limited term periodical payments were thought suitable in the first place such extension will not be granted lightly. Where limited term periodical payments are used there will be a 'deferred clean break'.

It will depend on all the circumstances of the case whether there should be open-ended or nominal periodical payments (i.e. no clean break) or a clean break (i.e. no periodical payments at all to a spouse, since periodical payments may still of course be paid to the *children* without affecting a clean break between the *parties*). However, the important point to appreciate is which orders are *compatible* with a clean break and which are not, and then to decide whether or not a clean break is even feasible, which in turn will depend on whether the spouse who is financially weaker is capable of an independent financial existence without receiving regular maintenance from the other. Such independence may be achieved in a variety of ways.

The payee must apply to the court for variation under s 31 to extend the period of payment *before* expiry, unless there has been a direction that this is not permitted, otherwise the payments end at the end of the fixed term originally ordered.

Outright dismissal: s 25A(3)

This is the 'sudden death' tool for ending all claims by one spouse against the other, in life and in death, and is only appropriate as a complete clean break.

Lump sum order: s 23

Under s 23, a lump sum order can be made freely whether or not there is to be a clean break, since this is a once-and-for-all payment, the only restriction being that only *one* lump sum order can be made per spouse. Thus, if lump sums are required for various different purposes, they must all be totted up and one global figure inserted into the order.

7.8 Clean break options

As may be seen in *Suter v Suter and Jones*, above, the existence of children does not necessarily preclude a clean break between the spouses, though a nominal order may be more suitable if periodical payments are not really necessary at the time of the financial provision proceedings. Generally there probably will be no clean break where there are children and the wife is unable or otherwise ill equipped to work, unless there is capital which could provide an alternative method of effecting a clean break, as in cases such as *Duxbury* where a sufficient sum of capital can be invested to provide an annual income that would otherwise have to be provided by the periodical payments which would preclude the desired clean break. There may be the same problem with older couples, where the wife's health and job prospects may be uncertain, as in *Scallon v Scallon* (1990).[181]

The clean break is therefore likely to be more suitable for short, childless marriage cases or those where there is sufficient money to provide the wife with capital.

If, however, there is to be a clean break, what is the most suitable way of dealing with a spouse's periodical payments orders? The two possibilities are:

- fixed or limited term periodical payments; or
- outright dismissal.

7.8.1 Fixed term periodical payments

Periodical payments on a temporary basis, but for a fixed term rather than an indefinite period, will be suitable where a spouse has or will have a recognisable earning capacity, and although unable to realise it immediately (e.g. because of domestic responsibilities) can reasonably certainly be expected to do so within the foreseeable future.

The type of case where this might apply would include that of the wife in *Mitchell v Mitchell* (see above) (where the trained secretary could be expected to earn a good salary once her daughter, who was 13 at the time of the divorce, had left school), and also for any wife able to go back to work as soon as she has found a job using existing training and/or experience, such as the air hostess in *Attar v Attar* (although in her particular case, as she had no children, she received her two years' maintenance all at once in the capitalised form of a lump sum, which will always be preferable to limited term maintenance if there are no children).

Fixed term periodical payments would also suit any wife who embarks on a retraining course, or could be re-employed if she did (as in the case of Mrs Leadbeater (above), who although 47 and out of touch with modern methods had been a secretary before the marriage). The court can see reasonably reliable prospects in all such retraining cases as in most secretarial and other office fields there is usually a chance of obtaining a job without difficulty either at the end of the course or within a reasonable period afterwards.

---

181 [1990] 1 FLR 193.

Sometimes the court expects the limited term to end as soon as children are at boarding school, as in *Evans v Evans* (1990),[182] where the wife was already a trained secretary, and *CB v CB* (1988),[183] where the wife had capital of her own but no income and the court awarded limited term periodical payments only until the youngest child was 18 while she arranged some other source of income. In both cases the order was clearly influenced by the acrimony and bitterness of that divorce, obviously making a clean break desirable as soon as possible. Sometimes the limited term will be staged as in *C v C* (1989),[184] where there was an order for £10,000 for two years, then £5,000 for two years, ending with dismissal of the payee spouse's claim.

The key to the use of limited term periodical payments is therefore *reasonable certainty* about the payee's future plans and prospects of employment. Limited term periodical payments are thus not suitable for older wives who cannot be reliably employed or re-employed, and who cannot therefore be expected to adjust to the absence of maintenance even after a generous term to allow for gradual change, e.g. those in *Morris v Morris* (1985),[185] where the wife was already 56, and *M v M* (1987),[186] where the 47-year-old wife had only worked part-time during the marriage and having lost her husband's pension rights on divorce would have been too much at risk at the end of the limited term, while the husband remained secure on his pension; it was accepted therefore that no s 25A(2) order could be made.

Other cases where limited term maintenance under s 25A(2) will be no more suitable than an immediate clean break under s 25A(1) are where there are young children, e.g. *Suter v Suter and Jones*, or where there are children, an older wife *and* uncertainty about job prospects, which all came together in *Barrett v Barrett* (1988),[187] a helpful example of how these principles work.

❖ CASE EXAMPLE

In *Barrett v Barrett* the wife was aged 44, without work experience and therefore also without a pension, and there were three children, including one still at home, after a 20-year marriage. In such cases it was established that the right approach is that the husband should pay ordinary open-ended periodical payments (and apply later to vary them if and when the wife gets work) or if she is willing to try earning her own living that there should be a nominal order (which can then either be dismissed if she becomes independent or varied upwards to a substantive order if her attempts at financial independence fail).

The court is cautious about limiting the right to apply for an extension of a limited term maintenance order and does not like to do so if there is any chance that an extension will be needed, as is shown by *Waterman v Waterman* (1989),[188] another telling example.

---

182 [1990] 2 All ER 147.
183 [1988] Fam Law 471.
184 [1989] 1 FLR 11.
185 [1985] FLR 1176.
186 [1987] 2 FLR 1.
187 [1988] 2 FLR 516.
188 [1989] 1 FLR 380.

❖ CASE EXAMPLE

In *Waterman v Waterman* a wife with one young child appealed both against a five-year limited term order following a short marriage of one year and against the restriction on applying to extend the five-year term in appropriate circumstances. The appeal court did in fact confirm the five-year limited term, but said there was no justification to exclude the wife's application to extend the limited term after the initial five years, as she might need to extend it if circumstances changed. Thus it will only be in the clearest of cases that such a final cut-off as excluding the right to apply to extend the limited term would be ordered, and if an application is made to extend before the end of the term the court can grant a further term, though they will take into account the reasons for the original limiting order: *Richardson v Richardson (No 2)*.[189]

7.8.2 Outright dismissal

This will only be suitable if the weaker spouse has a sufficient alternative source of income and does not need the transitional assistance of limited term maintenance. It will thus be suitable for wives who are going to remarry within a short period, wives who already earn a good income, and wives who are to receive a capital settlement in lieu of any orders, e.g. Mrs Duxbury, and will be especially suitable where there is plenty of capital, as in *Gojkovic*.

Alternatively, outright dismissal may be suitable where the parties are on welfare benefits and nothing is to be gained by trying to assess (and regularly vary) what sums should be paid by one to the other when neither could really afford any lifestyle outside social security, as for example in *Ashley v Blackman* (1988)[190] (also known as *A v B*). This was a courageous decision of Waite J who said that outright dismissal was the only solution:

> to prevent a couple of acutely limited means from remaining manacled together indefinitely by the necessity of returning to court at regular intervals to thresh out at public expense the precise figure one should pay to the other, not for the benefit of either, but solely for the benefit of the tax paying section of the community to which neither of them had sufficient means to belong.

The wife was mentally ill and living entirely off welfare benefits and the husband had remarried and had a wife and child to support. He earned so little his income even fell below the lowest tax threshold. The only reason for the application was to see if the DSS[191] could recover some of the money they paid to the wife when her maintenance order was unpaid; thus, this decision can only be classed as a victory for common sense over bureaucracy.

Such orders will also be suitable in any case where the court is dividing the assets fully and finally on divorce and is at the same time minded to make an order under s 25A(3), e.g. *Seaton v Seaton* (1986),[192] where the quality of life of the severely disabled husband meant that there was no point in preserving his right to apply for maintenance from the wife because nothing she could pay him could improve it or his existing financial security for his tiny needs, which were already provided for by his living with his parents on a disability pension.

---

189 [1994] 2 FLR 1051.
190 [1988] 3 WLR 562.
191 The former government benefits arm, the Department of Social Security (the current equivalent is the DWP).
192 [1986] 2 FLR 398.

For the sake of completeness, where a full clean break is effected all possible applications for financial provision in all its forms should be made or be deemed to be made and be formally dismissed, including where appropriate an order made under s 25A(3) prohibiting a future application by either party against the estate of the other under the **Inheritance (Provision for Family and Dependants) Act 1975**, thus meeting the aim of s 25A.

7.8.3 When is a clean break likely?

Traditionally clean breaks are for short childless marriages and for older couples where the family has left home and there are sufficient resources to provide each party with a home and divide everything else without leaving the wife on social security in retirement.

They are also for big money cases such as *White* and its big money successors which are obvious candidates for a clean break. The result in that situation should usually be a split of assets, based on 'fairness', and probably approaching equality, owing to the House of Lords' *White* requirement, approved in later cases, of checking the judge's tentative award based on the s 25 factors against 'the yardstick of equality' at the last stage, or since the *Miller* principles against 'fairness'.

However, the post-*White* cases, e.g. *Cowan v Cowan* (2001)[193] make it clear (as the FLBA's Summer 2001 Newsletter wittily commented when *Cowan* was decided) that fairness, like beauty, is in the eye of the beholder: Mrs Cowan (like Mrs White) did not get 50 per cent, and despite appealing her original 27 per cent (£3.2m out of £11.5m) to the Court of Appeal, only obtained 38 per cent of the assets on the basis that it was Mr Cowan's 'Midas touch' which had accumulated the fortune in the first place, so she should not get as much as he merely owing to helping to set up the business and then keeping the home fires burning during a long marriage.

Nevertheless, a clean break must now be *considered* on every divorce, although not necessarily *imposed* regardless if the circumstances are not suitable. Nonetheless, in every case the court likes the parties working towards a clean break even if that must be deferred. Wives of whatever social class, and of all ages except those nearing ordinary retirement age, are therefore expected in principle either to work or, if they come from a wealthy background where they have never been expected to work, that there will be a clean break provided by the available capital. The policy is now *spousal self-sufficiency* and not the 'meal ticket for life'.

7.8.4 Welfare hazards of the clean break

There is a little-known hazard of clean breaks, following the well-disguised amendment to the social security legislation by the **Social Security Act (SSA) 1990** s 8, which amended the SSA 1986 to make a spouse liable for the support of an ex-spouse even after decree absolute if the ex-spouse is in receipt of welfare benefits. This is obviously only likely to apply in a small minority of small money cases but could be disastrous in certain circumstances.

The effect of this amendment to the SSA 1986 is that if a clean break is achieved by an order for outright transfer of the matrimonial home to the wife in return for surrender of her right to periodical payments under whichever limb of s 25A, then there will be nothing to stop any government agency attempting to recover any benefits paid to the ex-spouse if that ex-spouse gets into financial difficulties and is has to claim them.

This is a direct reversal of the previous position, where spouses could be advised to make such transfers as, if the other spouse got into financial difficulties without periodical payments, an application could always be made for benefits. Now it will be unwise to achieve clean breaks by

---

193 [2001] EWCA Civ 679; [2001] 2 FLR 192.

capital payment or property transfer unless the payee spouse is thought to be responsible and likely to be able to achieve financial independence without difficulties which might involve an application for benefits.

This is subject, of course, to the qualification that at no time will any benefits agency of the time that this occurs (currently the DWP) be able to recover any money from a spouse who has none! Thus, if such a husband were himself on benefits, or of very limited means, the DWP when trying to recover money its predecessors have paid out will be unlucky.

The liability to pay maintenance to children under the CSA 1991–1995 as amended must also be remembered, since whatever the parties agree between themselves, this ongoing liability will remain if the case returns to CSA/CMS jurisdiction. Also, if a wife applies to the CSA/CMS after a private agreement involving capital the husband will have to pay again subject to small relief introduced for capital payments in 1995.

As clean breaks are possible only between spouses, not between parent and child, even if a lump sum is paid to the custodial parent on the understanding that that is in consideration of the payee parent assuming responsibility for maintenance of a child (Crozier v Crozier (1994))[194] each parent's liability to maintain children remains intact. While rules were made permitting capital settlements to be taken into consideration by the CSA/CMS in computing the non-custodial parent's obligation to pay child maintenance, they were never generous, and the only effective way of achieving the former situation, where a custodial parent obtained the lion's share of the assets in return for assuming full responsibility for the children, would be by the creation of a trust.

7.9 Quantum of orders – calculating spouse maintenance

Quantum is always the most difficult part of financial provision: the basic law is straightforward and logical enough, and most grey areas have been clarified during the four decades since the MCA 1973 has been in use, but assembling any financial package, whether in a capital or income context, challenges many an academic and student, practitioner and judge alike. The underlying problem for the student is lack of practical experience, very often both of financial matters generally and in particular of how household budgets and financing a family work in practice, and also of how to fit together the various provisions of the MCA 1973 ss 22–31. It is first important to grasp that maintenance for the spouse and maintenance for the children are two completely different and separate assessments[195] and the calculations must be made independently of each other. However, they will naturally have a knock-on effect on each other, except in cases where the parties' means are not limited. This is exactly the same whether the family whose package is to be put together exists in a seminar or in reality. For spousal support and capital provision the post-White case law (which continues to provide new case reports all the time, mostly only illustrating or making minor adjustments in some way to those of the previous cases) simply underlines the comment made by Sachs LJ in the 1969 case of Porter v Porter[196] and apparently approved by Lord Nicholls in White: 'The law is a living thing moving with the times and not a creature of dead or moribund thought.' The constant stream of cases do not therefore necessarily all need to be read as they are mostly at the present time of the illustrative and minor adjustment type, while the profession waits for further legislative and FJC guidance on the recent Law Commission report.

---

194 [1994] 1 FLR 126.
195 For child maintenance see Chapter 21.
196 [1969] 3 All ER 640.

7.9.1 The arithmetic

It has been suggested that spouses from middle- and low-income families will need to have their maintenance measured against the yardstick of one of the long-accepted guidelines, namely the net effect calculation or the one-third rule.

However, the latter is really out of date as it belongs to the pre-1988 era of maintenance paid in a different tax system from that now in place, where it was thought that one-third of the joint incomes was appropriate for the wife, although the net effect calculation may be of some use, as it will at least check the feasibility of a proposed order (important for low-income families). The net effect calculation is achieved by taking either an existing order or a hypothetical offer by either party, establishing the *net effect* of the proposal by calculating the parties' *respective spendable incomes* net of tax, national insurance, pension contributions and work expenses (e.g. travel); reasonable mortgage rent and council tax; and proposed maintenance, which will give the parties' net resources, and then calculating each party's actual needs, that is reasonable expenses for: food, clothing, etc; and gas, electricity, telephone, TV, etc. This will show whether the proposed maintenance is the correct figure, and if it fails to meet either of the party's actual needs then it must be adjusted accordingly until it produces a fair result. These methods were pioneered as long ago as 1982 on the basis that the net effect calculation suited low-income families better because it enabled the court to see precisely what each side would have to spend.

The court has a subsistence level approach to orders in low-income families. It will obviously not make an order which depresses the payer below subsistence level as this would be pointless, although the relevant level, which may be that which the DWP permits before requiring a contribution from a liable relative, is in fact slightly more generous than actual subsistence since it preserves 15 per cent of the liable relative's earnings above income support and allied benefit rates before contribution is required.

7.10 Variation

Variation of financial provision orders is governed by MCA 1973 s 31 and the general principles will be found in this section. Not all orders can be varied, however, and it is important to understand precisely what can be done under s 31 on an application for *variation*, and what requires some other approach. In some cases where *variation* as such is technically not possible because of the provisions of s 31, there may be another way of achieving what is wanted; this is clearly important to the assessment of financial provision on divorce, which must look ahead to all eventualities, including those normally expected, for example the children growing up and/or the carer or non-resident parent remarrying.

7.10.1 Routine variation

This is likely to happen some years from the initial order, simply for expected and unexpected life changes. Similarly, it may be important to preclude variation, in order to achieve certainty, at the point of initial assessment of quantum and type of orders. Thus it is impossible to assess appropriate quantum without taking into account the potential for variation, or lack of it. Generally, only continuing money orders may be varied, in other words periodical payments (whether secured or unsecured) including maintenance pending suit and interim maintenance orders, and instalments of lump sums (s 31(2)). There is no power to vary:

(a)   fixed term periodical payments where a prohibition on extension of the fixed term has been attached pursuant to the MCA 1973 s 28(1A);

(b)   the amount of a lump sum order (although if it is directed to be paid in instalments, the instalments may be varied) nor the time within which the lump sum is to be paid unless the order itself provides for that, by expressly giving 'liberty to apply for extension of the time for payment' in an appropriate case;

(c)   a property adjustment order under s 24(1)(a); and

(d)   a settlement of property order under s 24(1)(b) or a variation of settlement order under s 24(1)(c) or (d) unless the order was made after a decree of judicial separation.

Prohibitions (c) and (d) are often unexpectedly found very inconvenient, such as in *Carson v Carson* (1983),[197] where the wife wanted her property adjustment order varied to give her the husband's share of the matrimonial home in return for her giving up her periodical payments, a reasonable exchange often incorporated into clean break orders following divorce. The object of her proposal was so that she had enough money to buy a new home on the sale at the end of the *Mesher* period to which her existing home was subject, but the court could not help because of the prohibition on varying property adjustment orders. The moral is that it is essential to consider at the time the original order is made whether the wife might ultimately need to make such a swap, because it can be done at that stage (such an arrangement commonly being called a '*Hanlon* order'), but not later on variation.

There is a strange exception to this non-variation of property orders rule: an order for sale under s 24A, which certainly does not logically fall into the category of continuing money orders, may be varied by changing the date of the sale (s 31(2)(f)). It may therefore rightly be asked why the date of sale in a *Mesher* or similar order cannot similarly be changed – but unless the order has been specially drawn to cover that eventuality, in fact it cannot. Nor can the words 'liberty to apply' (usually added to consent orders to facilitate enforcement of the order) be interpreted so liberally as to permit this – they apply only to implementation of the order, so as to clarify the terms and to facilitate payment under it without there being unnecessary enforcement problems; such words do not permit actual changes in the order which, once the order is made, is a variation governed by s 31.

Moreover, until the amendment of MCA 1973 s 31 by the FLA 1996, when any of the continuing money orders were varied, this could originally only be done by increasing or decreasing the amounts to be paid, or discharging them completely. It was not possible to vary such orders by discharging them and substituting a different type of order: for example, a periodical payments order could not be varied by making a lump sum order on the variation application, even though the applicant had received no lump sum in the original order which the application sought to vary, and even though it would have been convenient to order a lump sum as capitalised maintenance and this could have been done when the order was originally made. Now that the FLA 1996 has amended s 31 by inserting new sub-sections 7A and 7B, periodical payments orders may sensibly be varied by capitalising the payments into a lump sum order.

Notwithstanding the old s 31(5), it has always been possible to vary a child's periodical payments by ordering a lump sum. This is because it was always recognised that it might be convenient to give a child a lump sum (e.g. for an older child who needs the money for higher education), and the approach to child orders has always been somewhat more flexible (e.g. there has never been any need to wait for decree nisi to make orders for children, and unlike spouses they can also have more than one lump sum).

The most common occasions of variation applications are when there is a change of circumstances in the lives of either the payer or the payee. In the case of the payer it will usually be because he or she has:

---

197 [1983] 1 WLR 285; [1983] 1 All ER 478.

- been promoted, dismissed or made redundant or has lost opportunities for overtime (and therefore can afford more or less than the original order), constituting a change in the s 25(2)(a) considerations; or
- remarried, started to cohabit or acquired a new family (and therefore has new obligations), constituting a change in the s 25(2)(b) considerations.

In the case of the payee it will usually be because of:

- inflation; or
- the children being older and more expensive (in both of which cases an increase is likely to be sought by the payee), or because of:
- cohabitation or receipt of financial support from a third party, but where there is no remarriage; or
- children leaving home, thus increasing the payee's earning capacity

(in any of which cases a decrease is likely to be sought by the payer).

When the court does vary orders in any of these circumstances it may increase, reduce, discharge, suspend or revive such orders (s 31(1)). The court also has the power to remit arrears, completely or only in part: s 31(2A).

7.10.2 What the court considers when deciding whether to vary an order

On variation, the court is still expressly locked in by s 31 to the same s 25 considerations which had to be checked off before making the decision when the *original* order was granted, but this time it will focus on any *change* in those matters, in accordance with s 25(1), *still* observing the general duty to consider all the circumstances of the case, *first consideration* being given to the welfare while a minor of any child in accordance with s 31(7).

Sometimes, changes will be *non-monetary* such as in *Evans v Evans* (1989),[198] already mentioned in connection with conduct, where the husband had paid maintenance regularly and uncomplainingly for 32 years, for which he was rewarded by the wife entering into a conspiracy to murder him. The court took the view that this was a sufficient change of circumstances to justify discharging the order.

7.10.3 The impact of the s 25A clean break principle on variation

Even if there has been no clean break at the time of the original order, by s 31(7) any court dealing with an application for variation must consider whether the order should be varied so as to impose a fixed limited term for periodical payments, after which the payee should have been able to adjust without undue hardship to their terminating altogether; a statute book is helpful when considering such variations owing to the s 31 amendments and all the other provisions that may impact. However, marked reluctance has been displayed to make use of this section, and a payer is often left indefinitely vulnerable to a nominal order as the payee's 'longstop'.

As in other instances, the working (or absence) of the clean break in this situation is best illustrated by consideration of some hard cases. The leading cases are actually all somewhat graphic in their facts and results.

---

198 [1989] 1 FLR 351.

❖ CASE EXAMPLES

Atkinson v Atkinson (1987)[199]

The case of Mrs Atkinson (already mentioned above in connection with cohabitation as conduct) was one where one might have thought the court would take the s 31(7) duty to consider a clean break on a variation application somewhat seriously. Mrs Atkinson was cohabiting with a man who had no intention of their marrying as he did not want to support her. Her husband, however, did not want to go on supporting her either, despite his wealth, which made this extremely easy for him to do, because he thought her boyfriend should do so. But instead of the reasonably expected abatement or extinguishment of her periodical payments order, this case produced the rather curious result that (while expressly finding that Mrs Atkinson's reason for cohabiting rather than remarrying was financially motivated) the court nevertheless would not end her maintenance order, because (as they commented) a wife who cohabits might need the money more than one who was not cohabiting; this was because cohabitation is a relationship which by definition is even less permanent and committed a relationship than marriage, and in particular had none of the financial obligations which attend the dissolution of a marriage by divorce.

The case was also complicated by the fact that the cohabitant was not even in a position to contribute to Mrs Atkinson's support, let alone to assume responsibility for it instead of the husband, since he had carefully chosen a low-paid part-time job.

Hepburn v Hepburn (1989)[200]

Was Mrs Atkinson's an exceptional case, then? It was not.

Much the same happened in the case of Mrs Hepburn, another cohabitation scenario where the wife went to live with another man, after dissolution of a ten-year marriage, and then entered into business ventures with him which the husband claimed were financially irresponsible. When he was aged 45 and she 40, the husband succeeded in getting her order reduced to a nominal one, but not in getting it discharged altogether; the court again talked of the backstop safety factor, saying that cohabitation is not the same as marriage and that unlike cohabitants, husbands did have obligations and should discharge them. It probably did not help Mr Hepburn that, like Mr Atkinson, he was himself wealthy and could afford to do so.

Whiting v Whiting (1988)[201]

Sometimes, however, one does find a dissenting judgment in this type of case, such as that of Balcombe LJ in the case of Mrs Whiting, where only he seems to have grasped what the legislation meant to do. In that case, in his famously forthright and well-judged way, the late Balcombe LJ stated that it was absurd to keep a nominal maintenance order alive for purely safety net purposes, as it was clearly contrary to the clean break legislation, which had been passed for good reasons of policy and should not be flouted unnecessarily.

---

199 [1987] 3 All ER 849.
200 [1989] 3 All ER 786.
201 [1988] 1 WLR 565; [1988] 2 FLR 189.

In the case of the Whitings it is hard to fault his view, and curious that this is such a rela-tively lone one. Mrs Whiting, who had admittedly had to give up work in the early part of a 14-year marriage when the children were young, was by the time they were older a full-time teacher with a good salary, whereas the husband, who had remarried, had been made redundant and forced to take a new job at a much lower salary than previously. He spent all his income on his second family and had therefore (not illogically) applied to end his first wife's nominal maintenance order once she was established in full-time employ-ment. The court of first instance refused to do this since they took the view that he was the wife's only longstop against ill health or redundancy and that she could not be assumed to be independent of him indefinitely since she had limited capital resources. However, if there is not to be a clean break on variation in this type of case, it is difficult to see when that *would* be right.

Fisher v Fisher (1989)[202]

It is Mrs Fisher who perhaps presents the most astonishing case and makes it clear that it is not just the relative impermanence of cohabitation and commitment of marriage that prevents the court from imposing a clean break on variation applications where they otherwise might reasonably do so. *Fisher* shows that even where the parties' children have grown up, and the wife (having been maintained while they were young) might rea-sonably be expected to go out to work, this may not be possible – meaning the husband's obligations continue, through no fault of his own, even though he may have been awaiting the day he could gain a certain financial freedom on the termination of a long period of obligation to an ex-wife with care of children.

In *Fisher*, the wife had care of a child who was 15 and applied for an upward variation of periodical payments owing to inflation, which inspired the husband to cross-apply for discharge of her order altogether – their child was 15 and the wife should have been able to go out to work. Not so: meanwhile she had had another *much younger* child in an affair with another man, and claimed she could not work owing to her obligations to this younger child.

The court agreed with her, holding that she had a limited earning capacity, but that because of her obligations to the younger child she was prevented from working and that it made no difference that the younger child who was the reason for this was not the husband's. They examined the meaning and purpose of ss 25A and 31(7) and restated the principle that while their combined effect was to discharge the so-called 'meal ticket for life', this did not extend to bringing about a clean break regardless in appropriate cases. They had regard to the meaning of the words 'undue hardship' in both sections and reiterated their wide discretion to do what was appropriate. They considered that it was much too soon because of the existence of the younger child to think about a limited term order (logical reasoning as far as it went, and in accordance with other principles of family law, but not surprisingly the press, as well as Mr Fisher, were incredulous).

---

202 [1989] 1 FLR 423.

Ashley v Blackman (1988)[203]

To some extent this account of the curious interpretation of s 25A does eventually begin to acquire some practicality, though another word might be 'compassionate' in relation to the only other well-known clean break case under s 25A, *Ashley v Blackman* (already mentioned above). This was an exceptional case where the judge (this time Waite J, like Balcombe LJ another luminary of the Chancery Bar who served both the Family Division and the Court of Appeal well in the incisiveness of such decisions) did courageously terminate the order.

This decision was obviously correct, despite the so-called principle in *Barnes v Barnes*, which apparently did not permit the husband to give up paying maintenance to throw his burden onto the state, since fortunately the judge realised that it was absurd that anything the husband paid would be surpassed by the benefits otherwise payable to his former wife. Nevertheless, the exceptional facts appear to have precluded wider use of this approach in the subsequent cases in this section, above.

7.10.4 Variation after a clean break consent order: MCA 1973 ss 25A and 33A

Potential for variation after a clean break will necessarily be limited, since the entire philosophy of the s 25A clean break is supposed to be in full and final settlement. However, that does not necessarily mean that a *consent order* is not variable: it is but the scope for variation is likely to be limited since clean breaks and consent orders are supposed to deal with the matter once and for all, which is the whole point of clean breaks.

Therefore, if a consent order is to be variable, that should be made clear when it is made, as otherwise the parties may be stuck with the terms of it without possibility of alteration as in *Dinch v Dinch* (1987).[204] In that case, where the Court of Appeal had thought it could vary a property adjustment order but the husband was able to have the purported variation set aside, Lord Oliver of Aylmerton, in declining to confirm the variation to help the wife in unforeseen difficulties under the original order, had some hard things to say about practitioners who do not check the terms of orders sufficiently, to the detriment in such a case of their clients when there are new circumstances and nothing can be done to the consent order scheme to meet them.

7.11 Appeals out of time

The alternative where there is a problem with varying a consent order may be to appeal out of time, for which leave will be given in limited circumstances, on the principles set out in *Barder v Barder* (1987).[205] That case had bizarre and tragic facts involving the death of both the wife and the two children of the family for whom provision had been made, when the wife killed both children and then herself. Four conditions need to be satisfied. These are that:

(a) a new event (or events) has invalidated the basis of the order *and* that the appeal is likely to succeed (this includes fresh evidence which could not have been known at the time the order was made, but *not* any new or more correct interpretation of what was then known all along);

---

203 [1988] 2 FLR 278.
204 [1987] 1 All ER 818.
205 [1987] 2 WLR 1350, HL; [1987] 2 All ER 440.

(b) the new event has occurred within a few months of the order;

(c) the application for leave is made reasonably promptly; and

(d) no prejudice will occur to third parties who have acted in good faith and for valuable consideration on the basis of the order.

Similarly tragic situations arose in *Smith v Smith (Smith Intervening)* (1991)[206] and *Barber v Barber* (1992).[207] In the former an appeal out of time was granted, but in the latter, where the wife died three months after the order, recognition was given to the contribution a wife makes to the marriage and the building up of assets by distinguishing between the part of a capital order made by way of 'golden handshake' at the end of a marriage, and the part made to provide for a wife and children after divorce (e.g. by buying a home or providing a lump sum to do so). In the latter case the court felt that the wife's share of the home should pass to the children of the marriage when they were grown up and did not accede to the husband's request that the order be rescinded on the basis that its whole purpose was nullified.

The court will not vary orders where the alleged basis is not really new but relies on facts which could have been ascertained at the time the order was made, as in *Barber v Barber* (1980).[208] In that case, the wife knew about the husband's pension rights at the time of the order so no variation was allowed. Thus in similar cases it is no good saying that tax calculations have been erroneous and that overseas legal proceedings have turned out differently from what was expected, nor that the payer's wealth has dramatically increased because of land values depending on planning permission if that could have been foreseen. The courts do not like granting such leave, although they have done so in really exceptional cases.

7.12 Varying *Mesher* orders

This is no longer a problem following the amendment of s 31(7), which is as well since, post-*White*, such orders have become popular again, since they permit the family to be housed pending the end of the children's dependency, but also preserve the possibility of being 'fair' to the husband. *Mesher* orders often were not so fair in the past: the wife usually obtained more than half the proceeds of sale at the end of the trust.

7.13 Preventing evasion of liability, and enforcing orders obtained

Some respondents never intend that financial provision orders will be made against them or, even if they are, that such orders will never be successfully enforced. However, the powers of the court would be empty if respondents to financial applications could get away with such schemes. If a party entitled to financial provision suspects such a situation to exist or that it might arise, urgent steps can be taken to prevent assets being moved out of the jurisdiction (or in any way put beyond the applicant's reach, for example, by their being transferred into the names of third parties).

Especially in cases where there is an international element, this matter is routinely considered at the first opportunity, when it is usual in any event to establish at the outset of a divorce case whether any action needs to be taken to register a party's matrimonial home rights (i.e. right of occupation, regardless of ownership) under FLA 1996 s 30.

---

206 [1991] 2 FLR 432, CA.
207 [1992] Fam Law 436.
208 [1980] Fam Law 125.

If protection is also required for other assets not within the FLA 1996, there is special provision in MCA 1973 s 37 which will usually meet the applicant's needs. However, in an appropriate case a freezing order[209] or a search order[210] is also available just as in other types of civil litigation, although owing to the expense and strict requirements for such orders the use of MCA 1973 s 37, which does not have such disadvantages, will generally be sufficient, unless the respondent is very rich and the assets very widely spread around the world. All or any of these remedies may be used individually or together.

7.13.1 Preserving the assets against which orders are made

In view of the ongoing harmonisation of European family law pursuant to the EU divorce jurisdiction rules, this particular provision may increase the attraction of commencing divorces with an international flavour in England and Wales, since other European jurisdictions, which are generally significantly behind England and Wales in practical procedural and evidential matters, do not have legislation as effective. In matrimonial property cases, this is probably because most European jurisdictions operate a system of community of property and compulsory testamentary obligations, so that there is less opportunity and therefore incentive to indulge in the concealment or dispersal tricks possible under the English system where there is no regime of matrimonial property as such, although in general terms litigation in Europe is a much less advanced science overall.

Conversely, the past background of English matrimonial law in property – including the concept of the wife as the husband's chattel whose quality was damaged by the criminal conversation of adultery, and the single legal personality of husband and wife – possibly explains the strong restitutionary element in the contemporary law. It is after all incredibly still only just over 40 years since the abolition of the action for breach of promise of marriage.

As with other procedural aspects, an understanding of prevention of evasion, and ultimate enforcement of orders available under the substantive law, is important for the academic student to analyse the effectiveness of the law.

7.13.2 Asset protection: s 37

This section can achieve two distinct results:

- *preventing a suspected disposal*: s 37(2)(a);
- *setting aside a disposal* which has already taken place: s 37(2)(b) and (2)(c).

By s 37(1)(b), a disposition made before the court that has had time to make a financial order may be set aside, and by s 37(1)(c) a disposition made *after* the court's financial order, and with the intention of preventing enforcement, will be similarly caught.

In all cases the actual or intended disposition must be for the purposes of *defeating the applicant's claim*, that is to say:

(a) *preventing financial relief* being granted at all, either to the applicant or any child of the family; or
(b) *reducing the amount* which might be granted; or
(c) *frustrating or impeding enforcement* of an actual or anticipated order (s 37(1)).

---

209 Formerly called a *Mareva* injunction.
210 Formerly an *Anton Pillar* order.

Thus, if the respondent is wealthy and wishes to transfer property which is not in practice needed to meet any order that the court might make, the section cannot be used to prevent this, or commercial paralysis would follow.

7.13.3 Activating the protection of s 37

In order to use any of these provisions the applicant will need to have started proceedings against the respondent for financial provision. That means that:

- in divorce a petition must have been filed claiming ancillary relief in the usual way;
- if the applicant is not the petitioner a Form A[211] must have been filed;
- in a variation case an application must have been made under s 31 (or s 35);
- in s 27 proceedings[212] an application must have been made for provision.

Once whichever of these steps is appropriate has been taken, an application can be made under s 37 immediately, sometimes with quite dramatic results, as in *Hamlin v Hamlin* (1985),[213] where the husband was stopped from selling a house in Spain, which happened to be the only matrimonial asset.

There is a *presumption* that the disposition was in fact *designed to defeat the claim* if made within the past three years and if it would in fact defeat the claim if not set aside (s 37(5)). Such a disposal is called a 'reviewable disposition', and by s 37(4) includes *any disposition* made otherwise than for valuable consideration, other than marriage, to a person who at the time of the disposition acted in good faith and without notice of any intention on the part of the respondent to defeat the applicant's claim for financial provision.

By s 37(6) a 'disposition' includes a conveyance, assurance or gift of property of any description, by instrument or otherwise, except any provision contained in a will or codicil, for example mortgaging a house, giving away assets or even dissipating money (although in the latter case some assistance might be required from the law of trusts under the doctrines of knowing receipt and dealing).

7.14 The matrimonial home: the policy of homes for all

The fate of the matrimonial home will usually be the linchpin of any financial provision package for the simple reason that every family needs somewhere to live; whether it is to be sold, transferred outright to one party or made the subject of a deferred settlement the fate of the home will have a profound effect on the remainder of the provision ordered, especially in the context of a middle- or low-income family.

It is therefore usual in our contemporary home-owning times for the court to view the resolution of the various competing claims to what may loosely be termed the 'matrimonial assets' (although in English law there is technically no such thing) by making one order dealing with all aspects of the parties' financial provision applications, and unless there is (as rarely) no former joint home involved, to build their order holistically around the disposal of the home. This highly discretionary duty of the court to make appropriate orders in relation to the home has developed naturally as a consequence of the post-war expansion in home ownership generally, and also from the

---

211 Applying for financial provision.
212 See Chapter 10.
213 [1985] 2 All ER 1037.

development over the past 30 or more years of the trend towards regarding marriage as an equal partnership, the routine joint tenancy of the matrimonial home and of the normality of the wife's working in order to help fund the mortgage payments and the expenses of bringing up a family, which appears no longer to be possible out of one salary.

Within the spirit of these social trends, and the letter of s 25 of the MCA 1973, the outcome of the dilemma surrounding the destination of the home may well be decided at the outset by the court's duty under s 25(1) to give first consideration to the welfare of the minor children of the family. Alternatively, there may be considerable choice as to the precise manner in which the parties' assets should be distributed. Whichever is the case it will usually be easier to put the overall package together if a practical decision is reached first about the home. This is especially so as, with the possible exception of the husband's pension rights, which have only recently received anything like the same attention from either the law or the parties as the importance of the disposal of the home, the home will usually be the parties' most valuable asset.

The home is therefore almost always the most important ingredient of whatever financial mix is to be proposed, since it will usually be not only the most valuable asset but also potentially either a roof for one of the parties or the source of two new post-divorce homes. Only rarely is there so much money available that the destination of the home is completely irrelevant.

Quite apart from its duty to the children under s 25(1), the court operates (where resources permit) a policy of 'homes for all': M v B (*Ancillary Proceedings: Lump Sum*) (1998),[214] where this aim was articulated, although the principle is much older, expressly surfacing in *Calderbank v Calderbank* (1975) already mentioned above. This was one of the early post-1973 cases where a wealthy wife had to provide a home for the husband to receive access visits from their children in suitable surroundings; thus any order will be driven by the principle that each party must if possible have a home, so that an order that leaves one of the parties potentially homeless is, in the absence of special circumstances, unacceptable.

However, it should be noted that while the court frequently restates the principle of 'homes for all', which appears to be a laudable basic goal, it is sometimes inappropriate in the particular circumstances of a case. For example, in the case of *Piglowska v Piglowski* (1999),[215] the House of Lords stressed that, especially where resources are limited, there is no right for a party to receive a home – especially the freehold ownership of a home – as a part of the financial package. In that case the Court of Appeal does seem to have been unduly influenced by the husband's claim for a home in this country, although he appeared still to have one in Poland.

Nevertheless, the requirement of s 25(1) that, while giving first priority to the welfare of the children, the court must consider 'all the circumstances of the case' does often create a potentially insoluble problem for the court, in that it is usually trying to achieve at least three (often inconsistent and mutually exclusive) aims, namely to:

- maintain a residence for the minor children and the carer parent;
- provide a home for each party; and
- divide the family assets fairly, especially the matrimonial home, which apart from its use as a home is likely to be the most valuable asset apart, perhaps, from the husband's pension.

7.14.1 Potential solutions

Thus, in addition to looking for guidance in the detail of the various s 25 factors, in order to obtain a general picture of each party's overall claims on what resources there are, recourse must also be

---

214 [1998] 1 FLR 53.
215 [1999] 2 FLR 763.

had to the various well-tried home disposal packages which have been put together in cases which have come before the court in the past.

These packages tend to go by the name of the case in which that particular method of dealing with the matter was first used, such as the well-known *Mesher* and *Martin* orders. This sometimes confuses the inexperienced, who are bewildered by the range of what appear to be mere drafting solutions, and unsure which precise variety to select – until they remember that these precedents are meant to be a useful tool and not a shackle; none of the orders necessarily has to be adopted in total and unchanged, since most cases which arise in practice are not precisely the same as that of the Mesher or Martin family.

It follows that whatever order is ultimately crafted by the court (or in negotiation for settlement) will only be *genetically* a *Mesher* etc. order, but will in fact be *individually created* for the case in question. Thus if the name of the family in the case is Smith, and some practitioner's ingenuity produces a useful variant of a *Mesher* order, that particular precedent may be filed away, at least in the firm's library, as a precedent for a *Smith* order (and if it is ingenious enough may also become more widely known in the profession under that tag).

Practitioners and judges are not therefore afraid to innovate where nothing suitable has yet been used for a particular situation, providing the components of the order proposed are not mutually exclusive (e.g. no draft will be using any form of ongoing periodical payments for a spouse where a clean break is desired, since in that case limited term periodical payments will be required in order to sever the former financial interdependence as envisaged by MCA 1973 s 25A). In working out the best destination for the former matrimonial home, it is safe to assume that good drafting will be likely to be able to effect any sensible package which negotiation and settlement is likely to propose. We are likely to see more of such creative work, especially in the low- and middle-income case, in view of the current pressure to keep disputes out of court.

The potential offered by the comprehensive financial provision order is a fascinating development, in the full tradition of the complex layers of legal and beneficial ownership created by trusts, and of the deployment of the ownership and occupation of land for the use and benefit of different members of the former single family unit. This enables the law of financial provision to adapt in a super flexible manner to the changing needs of the family members, even the challenge of the latest twist in trends, the post-*White* era.

7.14.2 Order of priorities and alternatives

Because of the welfare of the minor children which by s 25(1) must be given first consideration, the first priority, whether of practitioner or court, will be to:

(a)   look to the *purpose* for which a home is required (i.e. *residential occupation*); then
(b)   see how the children and the parent with care of them can best be housed; then
(c)   see how the other parent can be housed; and only then
(d)   check on the fairest way to divide actual *ownership* of such assets as there are.

Thus, the first step will be to seek to arrange matters on an *occupational* basis, for the moment disregarding questions of *ownership*. The second will be to consider ownership and property rights entirely separately.

By s 24, whatever changes of ownership need to be made can be effected by the court at will, so who owns the various assets (including the matrimonial home) is of less importance than what the court wants to do with that asset. Unlike in strict property law, the approach here is not 'whose is this?' but 'to whom should this be given?'

Priorities are therefore likely to be approached in the same order as the court's competing aims, namely:

- Where are the children and the spouse with care of the children going to live?
- Where is the other spouse going to live?
- What is to be done about *ownership* of the home?

This leaves three possible alternative fates for the matrimonial home:

- immediate sale and division of the proceeds;
- outright transfer to one party; or
- a trust for sale.

Each needs to be looked at in more detail.

Immediate sale and division of net proceeds (often, but not necessarily, in equal proportions: s 24A

Obviously, the parties can always agree to sell the house, but sometimes the court will order sale even if the parties are not agreed. This is suitable for three typical situations, where there is.

- sufficient equity in the home;
- enough equity to make a sale worthwhile but one party already has alternative accommodation; or
- no significant equity in the home and neither party, nor even really both of them together, can afford the home at all.

Outright transfer to one party: s 24

This is suitable as part of a clean break or where one spouse must receive a transfer as the only means of security which the court can award.

> **❖ CASE EXAMPLE**
>
> In *Bryant v Bryant* (1976)[216] the husband was a disaster: he had paid neither maintenance nor the mortgage on time, had assaulted the wife and been found guilty of persistent cruelty, and had three times been to prison for contempt for disobeying court orders. The court said they could never see him supporting the wife and children and the only way to protect them was to give the wife his half share of the house.

An outright transfer can be effected in three ways:

(1) On immediate payment of a cash sum by the transferee to compensate the other spouse for losing that spouse's interest in the home, or in other words a 'buy out' as in *Wachtel*, the well-known case already mentioned in other contexts (although the trend for dubbing the various orders with the names of the cases in which they were first noted has not for some reason extended to this being habitually known as a *Wachtel* order).

---

216 [1976] 6 Fam Law 108; (1976) 120 SJ 165.

(2)   In return for a charge over the home either for a fixed sum or for a percentage of the sale proceeds either at a fixed date or upon a certain event or when the transferee chooses to sell (and since in the latter case this choice may *never* be made it may mean that the charge is not enforceable until the transferee's death).

(3)   With *no* cash payment and *no* charge, but in return for some other benefit which will accrue to the spouse losing their interest in the property, such as the transferee foregoing periodical payments (this is called a *Hanlon* order).

Any *Hanlon* order must be effected *at the time that the order is first made*, since property adjustment orders under s 24 *cannot be varied* later under s 31. This caused a problem in *Carson v Carson* (1983) as already mentioned above where the wife had a *Mesher* order incorporating periodical payments for herself, but had run into financial difficulties and wanted the order changed to an outright transfer of the husband's share of the home in return for surrender of her periodical payments. Of course the court could not accede to her request, although an ingenious way has since been found round the difficulty: following amendment of MCA 1973 s 31(7), the periodical payments order can now be varied by ordering a lump sum to be paid to capitalise them, and the wife can then use that money to compensate the husband (if he is willing, as he usually will be if he has to find the capital sum anyway) for his share of the home.[217] However, the principle is equally applicable to property adjustment orders, which still cannot be varied, in that providing the parties arrange the matter themselves rather than the court illegally varying a property adjustment order, the *Mesher* order can be unlocked to their mutual satisfaction.

7.14.3 A trust of land: s 24

This is the method of effecting a *Mesher* order and also all the variants, including the *Martin* and *Harvey* orders. A *Harvey* order may sometimes also be referred to as a *Brown* order after *Brown v Brown* (1982),[218] in which a somewhat similar order was made.

Where any of these settlement orders are made, the order may also provide for the payment of the outgoings, whether of the mortgage only or also of others such as repairs, insurance, utilities, etc. precisely as it seems fair to the parties, their advisers or in the last resort the judge, that these should be paid by one party or the other or both equally or unequally. In a small money or middle-income case the court will work through all these points in detail, while also attempting to apply the principles of needs, compensation and sharing in pursuit of a 'fair' result. As a task this is obviously significantly more difficult and disproportionately time-consuming, where there are usually not enough assets to go round, than dealing with the multi-millions of the big money cases, where the decisions to be taken are in relation to the same principles of needs, compensation and sharing in pursuit of the 'fair' result, but are likely to be more intellectually demanding (in relation to what is, or is not, matrimonial property) than practically challenging in making ends meet.

Mesher orders

The *Mesher* order is suitable where children and the custodial parent need to be housed until the children are independent: the order vests the matrimonial home in both spouses on trust for sale, giving a right of occupation to the custodial parent *either* until the children reach independence (which will in some cases be when the youngest child is 17 *or* where appropriate when the youngest finishes full-time education or training), upon which event the house is to be sold and

---

217 See the string of cases *S v S* [1987] 1 FLR 71; *Boylan v Boylan* [1988] 1 FLR 282; and *Peacock v Peacock* [1991] 1 FLR 324 in which this variation method has been adopted.
218 [1982] 3 FLR 161.

the proceeds divided in an appropriate ratio, such division of the proceeds being decided by the court at the time the order for settlement is made.

The parties may already be trustees of the matrimonial home, as joint tenants in law and in equity (since joint ownership of their home is now the norm rather than the exception in the case of most couples), so it will only be necessary for the order to vest the home in the parties as trustees if one was formerly the sole legal owner. However, even if the parties are already trustees, so the order will then direct that the home *remain vested* in the joint names of the parties, it will still be necessary to go on to declare new trusts (because the standard trusts under the former joint ownership would usually merely have been that the parties should hold the property on trust for themselves beneficially, which is obviously no longer appropriate once a *Mesher* order is to be imposed giving sole occupation to one spouse for a period, and then declaring the ultimate interests in the proceeds of sale).

However, the order is only suitable where the proceeds of sale will be sufficient to re-house the occupying spouse on sale and the spouse out of occupation has somewhere else to live.

A *Mesher* order is final and cannot be varied (e.g. to postpone the date of sale). For this reason the circumstances always need to be thought through carefully by the parties, their advisers and, in the last resort, the judge. While the order was first greeted with great enthusiasm as a solution to the problem of otherwise having to sell the house and disrupt the children's lives, it was quickly realised that it only stored up trouble for the future in a number of cases. This was because in the late 1970s and early 1980s house prices were unstable and many victims of the *Mesher* order found that when they came to sell there was not enough money to re-house the occupying spouse; and yet the order could not be varied, so other methods had to be found to deal with the situation.

Further, following the introduction of s 25A in 1984, the then latest fashion was for the clean break, with which the *Mesher* order is incompatible. However, following the property market collapse at the end of the 1980s, *Mesher* orders came back into fashion more or less by default since houses which were not actually repossessed for negative equity were often actually *unsaleable* so that a *Mesher* order was the only solution. At the present time *Mesher* orders are favoured again because of the necessity, post-*White v White*, to consider the concept of fairness and, ultimately, the yardstick of equality – so that an outright transfer to the wife may not be appropriate – coupled with the need in families of limited means to house the family until the children are grown up. These practical considerations are of course at the very heart of a family lawyer's work, and the court's decisions, on property division following marriage breakdown, as a result of which both practitioners and the court, and academic students therefore, need to be fully abreast of current economic affairs as they will affect the ordinary family. This may prove to be a new lease of life for *Mesher* orders in an increased trend towards orders supported by periodical payments so as to give a fairer division of capital assets to husbands and income to wives.

Martin orders

A *Martin* order differs from a *Mesher* in that while the settlement is the same, the period of occupation is not linked to the children in any way; indeed there may be a *Martin* order where there are no children, as in the original case, provided the only other essential requirement (that the other spouse has secure alternative accommodation) is met. In the original *Martin* case, Mr Martin had a council flat, and although the Martins had no children, Mrs Martin needed somewhere to live; there had been a 15-year marriage and the court was of the opinion that but for the divorce the house would not have been sold for another 20 years. Thus instead of the children reaching adulthood, the triggering event in a *Martin* order case will be either the occupying spouse's death, or earlier remarriage, sometimes cohabitation or becoming dependent on another partner, or voluntary removal.

Obviously this order is less attractive to the spouse out of occupation than a *Mesher* order, since the non-occupying spouse might never see the proceeds of sale, which may ultimately only accrue to that spouse's estate many years later, but it does preserve the capital of the spouse out of occupation, rather than giving it up completely as would be the result if there were an outright transfer for no value. This was the entire rationale of *Clutton v Clutton* (1991),[219] and since the sale is postponed for so long and is under the occupying spouse's control (and the order is therefore in effect virtually indistinguishable from an outright transfer with a deferred charge) it does not fall foul of the clean break rules as was confirmed in *Clutton*. Nevertheless an outright transfer with a deferred charge payable on any of the usual *Martin* triggering events will usually be preferred by the occupying spouse and really makes no significant difference to the spouse out of occupation.

Harvey order

This order, sometimes also called a *Brown* order, is a variant of the *Martin* order where the occupying spouse still has the right to remain indefinitely in the property but, upon the children becoming independent or the mortgage being paid off (usually whichever is the later), is then required to pay a market rent to the spouse out of occupation for that spouse's share of the property, so as to provide some return for that spouse on the capital tied up in the house. Such rent is usually to be determined by the DJ in accordance with market rates at the date at which the triggering event occurs.

Another feature of the *Harvey* order is that it may specify a greater share of the ultimate sale proceeds for the occupying spouse who is paying the mortgage and the outgoings, in recognition of the fact that whoever is in occupation will probably end up paying more of the mortgage than the spouse who is out of occupation. However, this provision may always be written into any order drafted, since as explained at the outset it should always be remembered that the order being drafted is a *customised order* for *the case in hand* and all clauses of all these well-known orders may be swapped about to produce something totally original, provided the resulting package does not put incompatible clauses together.

When deciding upon a suitable order, it should of course be remembered that there are hazards in any form of outright transfer, unless in 'buy out' form, in relation to potential future claims for welfare benefits by the transferee and also the very limited account taken of such capital transfers by the CSA/CMS.[220] Thus a *Hanlon* order would pose potential risks for the husband on both these points.

7.15 Current debates

Ideas for research on these current discussion questions can be accessed on the companion website updates.

- Should there be a presumption of actual equality of result in distribution of assets on divorce or other decree?
- Could this fit with the principle of primacy of the interests of children in divorce?
- Should conduct be relevant in assessing financial provision?
- Should inherited property be ring-fenced?

---

219 [1991] 1 All ER 340, CA.
220 See Chapter 21.

7.16 Summary of Chapter 7
Financial provision – orders the court can grant

- The orders which the court can grant following a decree of divorce, nullity or JS are contained in MCA 1973 ss 22–24, and comprise money orders (periodical payments, secured and unsecured, and lump sums) and property orders (transfer or settlement of property, variation of settlements and pension orders) in favour of both spouses and children of the family, in the latter case only for children whose maintenance is not assessed by the CSA/CMS. MCA 1973 is the main statute for financial provision.
- The court's jurisdiction is discretionary, and there is no regime of matrimonial property dividing property of the spouses on marriage breakdown either equally or in any other proportion.
- Pre-nuptial contracts were unenforceable in England and Wales, though they may be taken into account, but may now be enforceable following *Radmacher v Granatino* (2011) in the Supreme Court, and if the recommendations of the Law Commission are enacted by the government.
- Following *White v White* (2000) and succeeding cases the court has worked out a new approach to dividing assets; it is not equally as such but in relation to considerations of 'needs', compensation and sharing, in pursuit of a goal of 'fairness', checked against 'the yardstick of equality'.
- Final orders take effect on decree absolute, save in the case of children, whose orders always remain 'interim', since they can come back before the court at any time.

Applying for financial provision

- Application is made in the prayer of the petition and activated following the grant of decree nisi.
- Interim orders can be made for both spouses and children.

Income orders

- Income orders or 'maintenance' are usually the core of a financial provision package, unless there is to be a clean break with which they are incompatible. Their duration varies.

Capital orders

- There is no special reason required for a lump sum order, although there are some specific situations for which lump sums are appropriate (e.g. to start a business, compensate for loss of a share of the former matrimonial home, or to capitalise maintenance).

Property orders

- These generally concern the home but enable the court to transfer any property from one spouse to another, or to vary settlements, and also to order sale and make consequential orders in respect of the proceeds.

The s 25 factors and the court's discretion

- The general duty of the court is to take into account all the circumstances of the case, giving first consideration to the welfare of the minor children of the family. In practical terms this means to see that they have a roof over their heads and adequate funds to live on.
- The court then works through the s 25 factors and applies them to the facts of the case.

The assets over which the court has jurisdiction: 25(2)(a)

- The court requires that full and frank disclosure is made of all assets of both parties and is at liberty to use any or all of them in redistributing ownership to arrive at a fair resolution of the couple's financial disputes on the dissolution of their marriage.
- Assets commonly include capital and income, earning capacity, damages, future inheritances, pensions and any other resource (actual or potential), including assets acquired after separation or divorce.
- If actual earnings declared are suspect, the court will assess resources based on lifestyle.
- The resources of a new spouse or cohabitant are taken into account if they release funds which, but for reliance on the new partner's assistance, would otherwise have had to be expended by a divorcing spouse in his or her own support. Earning capacity is regarded as important and any unrealised capacity in this respect is expected to be accessed, if necessary by retraining. This is because of the philosophy of spousal self-sufficiency, which has generated the concept of the clean break.

Matters the court takes into consideration: s 25(2)(b)–(h)

- These include the ages of the parties and length of marriage, all their contributions, financial and non-financial, to the marriage (including that of the housewife and mother who does not work outside the home and including future contributions, e.g. by bringing up the children or maintaining the family), the parties' lifestyle during the marriage, the health of the parties including any disability, any other special factors, and any loss that has been or will be occasioned by the dissolution of the marriage (e.g. loss of pension benefits).
- Conduct is not taken into account unless inequitable to disregard, although positive or negative contribution may affect the quantum of any award by placing it at the upper or lower end of a scale of generosity.

The clean break: s 25A

- The court has no obligation to order a clean break, but only to consider one: *Clutton v Clutton* (1991).
- Appropriate cases for clean breaks include young childless spouses, and older spouses whose children have grown up.
- A clean break is not incompatible with a young family but less likely to be practical unless the carer is also able to work full-time and/or there is sufficient capital.
- Options for a clean break include limited term periodical payments, leading to a deferred clean break, or sufficient capital provision for an immediate one, so that periodical payments can be dismissed outright, or some combination of the two.

Quantum – calculating spouse maintenance

- The net effect calculation is now most used, the one-third rule (always more a guide than a rule) having fallen largely into disuse, being now outdated and mostly as inappropriate to the rich as to the poor. Some judges still find it useful in middle income cases, however. Nevertheless, this must be of questionable value following *White v White* (2000).
- The CSA/CMS calculation will usually need to be done first if the CSA/CMS is to be involved, in order to discover what is left for the spouse.
- Even if the overall package is to be agreed and the children's maintenance is to be incorporated into their parents' consent order and the CSA/CMS not directly involved, children's maintenance will need to be allowed for within the ballpark area of what the CSA/CMS would assess.

Variation: s 31

- Most orders can routinely be varied, including consent orders.
- Periodical payment orders can now be varied by making lump sum orders (see MCA 1973, s 31(7A) and 31(7B).
- Consent orders tend to be more difficult to vary, unless provision has been made for variation, because they are intended to be in full and final settlement.
- Late application, variation on the basis of the welfare of the child, appeals out of time varying *Mesher* orders can be used to attempt to vary orders which appear otherwise unvariable.

Preventing evasion of liability, and enforcing orders obtained: s 37

- There is statutory provision in s 37 to obtain orders protecting assets required for financial provision orders. Other injunction orders can also be obtained.

Preserving the assets against which orders are made

- There is specific statutory provision in s 37 to enable assets required for the fair disposal of financial provision claims to be frozen pending resolution of those claims. The section is equally effective either to prevent or to set aside dispositions caught by the legislation.
- To invoke the section, proceedings must have been commenced, in divorce a claim has been made in the petition or a Form A filed by a respondent, and in claims under MCA 1973 s 27 or s 31 or DPMCA 1978, an application must actually have been filed.
- Ordinary freezing or search orders may also be used as in any civil suit, but the customised s 37 has advantages in not requiring the same quality of undertakings as the other orders.
- Matrimonial home rights pursuant to FLA 1996 s 30 may also be registered, and all or any of these precautionary remedies may be used individually or in concert.
- Not all assets may be frozen: those not required for satisfaction of the quantum of the financial provision claim or validly charged in priority may be beyond reach, e.g. where a mortgage is given to a bank which a wife is unable to claim to set aside for undue influence.

The matrimonial home – homes for all

- The court attempts to provide a home for both parties from the assets to be divided, although regardless of FLA 1996 s 30 their first priority pursuant to MCA s 25(1) will be the welfare of the children of the family, which means a secure roof over their heads and sufficient income to live on during their minority.
- Sometimes a home for the non-custodial spouse cannot be provided.

Possible disposals of the home

- Sale and division of the proceeds is appropriate where there is sufficient equity for two homes, or where one spouse has other accommodation, or where there is insufficient equity and sale is the best option to provide some liquid capital for both, both parties then going into rented accommodation.
- Outright transfer to one spouse is appropriate where one spouse can compensate the other, where one spouse will take a deferred charge, or where there is a trade-off of the home for some other benefit given up (e.g. where the wife takes the home and no periodical payments).
- Trust of land is appropriate where there needs to be a home provided for the children and custodial spouse, resulting in a deferred sale at the triggering event (e.g. when the children are grown up, or the wife remarries, cohabits or elects to move). There are many variants of this (e.g. *Mesher, Martin, Harvey/Brown, Browne v Pritchard* etc. orders).

 7.17 Further reading

Bailey-Harris, R, '*Lambert v Lambert* – towards the recognition of marriage as a partnership of equals', [2003] CFLQ 417.

Barlow, A and Smithson, J, 'Is modern marriage a bargain? Exploring perceptions of pre-nuptial agreements in England and Wales', [2012] CFLQ 304.

Barton, C, '*White v White* and co: the not-so-well-off and a "balance of needs"', [2012] Fam Law 963.

Bird, R, '*Miller v Miller*. Guidance or confusion?', [2005] Fam Law 874.

Chandler, A, ' "The law is now reasonably clear": the court's approach to non-matrimonial assets', [2012] Fam Law 163.

Cooke, E, '*White v White* – a new yardstick for the marriage partnership', [2001] CFLQ 81.

Cooke, E, '*Miller/McFarlane:* law in search of a definition', [2007] CFLQ 98.

Cretney, S, 'Community of property imposed by judicial decision', [2003] LQR 349.

Deech, R, 'What is a woman worth?', [2009] Fam Law 1140.

Eekelaar, J, 'Property and financial settlement on divorce – sharing and compensation', [2006] Fam Law 754.

Greensmith, A, 'Let's play ancillary relief', [2007] Fam Law 203.

George, R, Harris, P and Herring, J, 'Pre-nuptial agreements, for better or worse?', [2009] Fam Law 934.

Harris, P, 'The *Miller* paradoxes', [2008] Fam Law 1096.

Hodson, D, 'Financial provision: a formula will do nicely sir', [2007] Fam Law 57.

Miles, J, '*Charman v Charman (No 4)*: making sense of need, compensation and equal sharing after *Miller/McFarlane*', [2008] CFLQ 378.

Miles, J, 'Analyse this: *Radmacher v Granatino*: Upping the ante-nuptial agreement', [2009] CFLQ 513.

Miles, J and Probert, R (eds), *Sharing Lives, Dividing Assets*, Oxford, Hart, 2009.

Resolution (ongoing information for members and the public), www.resolution.org.uk

Thorpe, LJ, 'London, the divorce capital of the world', [2009] Fam Law 21.

Chapter 8

Civil Partnership

Chapter Contents

Learning outcomes for this chapter

A sound understanding of the effect of the Civil Partnership Act 2004 including:

(i) An overview of the legal and social consequences, academic criticisms and positive and negative factors associated with the formalising of same-sex relationships in English law.
(ii) An awareness of the background to the introduction of the Act, the long-standing legal theory and social and moral philosophy and the debates behind civil partnership status, and the concept of gay marriage.
(iii) An ability to compare the legal status of civil partnership with marriage and informal cohabitation.

8.1 Introduction and background theory

The **Civil Partnership Act (CPA) 2004** came into force on 5 December 2005 and enables same-sex couples to form legally recognised civil partnerships. This followed earlier informal arrangements, e.g. the London Partnership Register, which did not address the previous practical problems of such partnerships – e.g. whether a partner was next of kin for various essential purposes – all of which have now been provided for by the Act. Nevertheless, full gay marriage is now possible and the relevant parts of the MCA 1973 which formerly prevented same-sex couples from marrying have been amended accordingly. The **Marriage (Same-Sex Couples) Act 2013** now permits full marriage for gays and lesbians, stating in its first section that such a marriage is 'lawful', although it is the **Marriage Act 1949** and the **MCA 1973** as amended which bring gays and lesbians within the fold of marriage.

The CPA 2004 nevertheless still stands apart, permitting a registered civil partnership which is *not* available to any but same-sex couples, despite a certain lobby suggesting that such a secular partnership should be available to opposite-sex couples as well (as it is in France in the PACS system, the Pacte Civile de Solidarité).

These 'partnerships' under the 2004 Act must therefore still be distinguished from marriage if those gays and lesbians who want to adhere to that format of intimate relationship continue to do so, even though the rights and responsibilities thereby assumed are mostly identical to those of married couples, and distinguished from informal cohabitation between same-sex partners, and indeed opposite-sex cohabitants; only registered civil partnership *alters the status* of same-sex partners in a relationship by elevating it to a legally recognised entity. In this respect both same- and opposite-sex cohabitants are now distinguished by having no legal status as a couple, and thus remain in law as two single persons, in comparison with both married couples and civil partners. However, there is some anecdotal evidence that some same-sex couples do not, and did not, want marriage and wish to remain in their civil partnerships, so it seems this status is going to continue alongside marriage for any couples who want it, although the statistics seem to suggest that the normative couple relationship is now the unmarried cohabiting opposite-sex partners and that marriage is dwindling away, although there for those who want that.

The consequential amendments to every statute affecting family law bring the provisions of those statutes into line with the CPA 2004 by adding the words 'civil partner(s)' to every provision affecting the rights and obligations of married couples, so that a civil partner can, for example, obtain parental responsibility for a child of the other or inherit property, and there are some special arrangements for parentage of a partner's child when IVF is used.[1]

---

1 See Chapter 13.

As a result the CPA is very lengthy: 264 sections and 30 schedules. A cursory examination of key statutes indicates how complete this consequential amendment is: see the **Adoption and Children Act (ACA) 2002** (civil partners' parental responsibility); the **Family Law Act (FLA) 1996** (civil partners' non-molestation orders); the **Sex Discrimination Act 1975** (discrimination); the many statutes governing wills, inheritance, family provision on death, tax, social security and child support – all have received copious amendments to add civil partners to their provisions.

A careful reading of the text of these and other statutes indicates the detail that went into the consequential amendments when the CPA 2004 was passed. Civil partners are also now in the same position as married couples in relation to giving evidence in criminal cases, and Cretney points out that the detail in the consequential amendments includes Acts as esoteric as the Explosive Substances Act 1883![2] Baroness Hale commented that civil partnerships have 'virtually identical legal consequences to marriage'.[3]

One dissonant note, however, has been commentary on the legal and social status of a civil partner's relationship with the wider family of the other which does not, apparently, replicate that enjoyed by married couples.[4] There are also, of course, articulated religious, spiritual and policy objections to the concept of the existence of a status of civil partnership at all, but these have to be balanced against the alternative of the identifiable practical and emotional problems that existed previously. There are many non-religious arguments against same-sex marriage but legal theorists argue that creating civil partnerships short of marriage, but genuinely equal to the traditional concept of that relationship, still sends a homophobic message.

It is perhaps principally for this reason, among several others, that the government announced after quite a short interval from the CPA 2004's coming into force in 2005 that it was intended to legislate to provide the alternative of actual marriage for gay relationships, and then did so in the winter of 2012–13, also bringing the **Marriage (Same-Sex Couples) Act 2013** into force as early as March 2014; a speedy result despite statistics showing that there have been on average only around 6,000 CPA 2004 registrations annually. Thus in practice a much smaller number is affected by this status than the escalating increase in the numbers of opposite-sex cohabiting partners, which are projected to reach 30 per cent of the population by 2031.

Most significant of all, the provisions for dissolution in the CPA 2004 almost exactly mirror those of the MCA 1973, despite the critical comments of academics and others that, if the MCA is as defective as practitioners claim, we should be considering legislative reform of that Act, rather than using it as a template for civil partners! However, the government always firmly adhered to the line that the CPA 2004 did not create gay marriage, although this was possible in some other jurisdictions worldwide, and then underlined this by promoting the statute providing for actual marriage for same-sex partners as a government Bill.

So far there have been over 26,000 civil partnerships formed, initially mostly of male relationships, and already a number of dissolutions, but very little case law. In 2007 (the first possible year for dissolutions) there were already 42 dissolution orders, and 189 in 2008, mostly to female partnerships, indicating that the Act was not after all a panacea. Annual registrations hover at around 6,000 to 7,000 but it is too early to compare this with marriage figures.

8.1.1 The impact of the Marriage (Same-Sex Couples) Act 2014

It is suggested, therefore, that the government's change of heart in conceding legislation to create gay married status was generated by the perception that to refuse gay marriage is incompatible with

2 In which it is not particularly clear as to the relevance to civil partners!
3 [2006] 1 FCR 497.
4 Manthorpe, J and Price, E, 'Lesbian Carers: Personal Issues and Policy Responses', [2005] *Social Policy and Society*, 5:15.

commitment to equality, especially in view of the recent overhaul of equality and diversity legislation in the **Equality Act 2010**. The lack of recognition of gay marriage can also create problems for individuals whose married status is recognised in their home jurisdiction, but not when they come to England and Wales, so that the cross-border impact was possibly also a driver.

The anecdotal indications that there are some civil partners who do not want marriage, and never did, is therefore confusing, although there is no particular reason why they cannot logically retain civil partnership status if they wish. Possibly they are not religious (although some civil partners who want to marry in their local churches clearly are), and those not interested in gay marriage perhaps want a secular non-married relationship; this would resonate with some feminist writers such as Rosemary Auchmuty, who is well known for her work on feminist perspectives on marriage which are not specifically incompatible with those of a civil partner.

But what of the religious aspects of same-sex marriage, where concerns mainly centre on objections that marriage is a religious and/or a biological concept, since those constituencies both make the point that the core rationale of marriage is that men and women are complementary?[5] What about the long-standing definition of marriage in *Hyde v Hyde* (1866)?[6] While it is true that the other characteristics identified in that judgment – the commitment and the voluntary nature of the union – subsist, the divorce statistics already indicate that the 'for life' element is seldom taken seriously even at the point of contracting the marriage. Now the 'heterosexual' element will also have to be foregone, and while civil partnerships seem to have been widely acceptable it may be that 'gay and lesbian marriage . . . may still be controversial and antagonistic to some'[7] although there was less antagonism than was expected when the 2013 Act was going through Parliament, whereas some people expected it to be thrown out.

Parliament's changing the definition of marriage in *Hyde v Hyde* does not appear to be a problem, since of course Parliament can change the law whenever it votes to do so and even if what it enacts is impossible. Indeed Parliament can pass an Act that says that the UK is in the southern hemisphere of the world if it wishes to do so, and no one can stop it even though we know this not to be the truth (unless the world were to change its axis quite fundamentally). So same-sex marriage can be made lawful, and it has been.

With regard to the religious aspect, this may be a little more complicated, because same-sex marriage is contrary to the beliefs of several world-class religions (indeed it appears that there is *no* religion which expressly permits it) and it is also contrary to Christian belief as well as to various texts in the Bible (the Old Testament of which is shared with the Jewish religion, which shares much Christian culture having originated in the same part of the world). It is also so much contrary to the long-standing cultural beliefs of indigenous English and Welsh people that the ECtHR long recognised (until 2002) the special margin of appreciation that should be accorded to the UK in respect of our refusal to recognise transsexuals in their new gender (an indulgence which must also have included the Presbyterian Scots, although for the purposes of the law they have their own jurisdiction and legal system and are not concerned with the 2013 Act).

Nevertheless, it may be that (as suggested by Herring[8]) it is now time to uncouple the Church and State in family law (since although these two entities have mostly managed to co-exist very comfortably for over a thousand years that was mostly because an accommodation could be found for any apparently conflicting tenets, which may no longer be the case; since modern life, in seeking to recognise everyone's freedoms, has generated many conflicting rights and duties which may not be capable of fitting together with some unmodernised beliefs which originate from earlier civilisations).

---

5 Herring cites a good deal of literature to this effect: Herring, J, *Family Law*, 6th edition, Harlow, Longman Law Series, 2013, p 85.
6 See Chapter 2.
7 See Herring, op. cit., p 81 et seq.
8 See Herring, op. cit., p 83.

Indeed much of English law was developed by wise churchmen in the early Middle Ages – at that time important figures in government of the realm, when the Church was a significant influence in an age of superstition, were usually exactly the same people who headed the Church[9] – but times have now demonstrably moved on and different moralities apply, jostling with one another for supremacy in the intellectual, spiritual and emotional order. Moreover, psychologists now populate family justice, changing our attitudes to the treatment of those who might be damaged by discrimination, which is not a concept which modern socio-legal studies permits to impact.

With regard to gay and lesbian relationships, it appears that the government has decided that equality is more important in a modern society (which knows from science that lack of gender equality is very damaging to those who will otherwise consider they are discriminated against, and in fact be so) than being overly considerate to the feelings of what must now be recognised as a minority religious interest. This also calls for recognising that many people are not religious, and that some do not adhere to any religion at all, so that a statute which does not interfere with the religious continuing to practise their religion, but also independently grants equality to others, does appear to do no harm and probably some good.

Such an approach would be more logical if the Church of England were not the established Church, whereas in Wales (where there are still significant numbers of religious people attending chapels) the Church is not established as the national religion. It should also be remembered that there are significant numbers of people living in England now who are not Christian, but belong to other religions.

One must then reflect that both the UK as a whole and England and Wales (and Scotland now that secession is apparently not to happen) are somewhat behind other European states in formally secularising intimate relationships as well as granting the persons involved equality of freedom in entering formally into those relationships.

France was first, in 1789, since secular marriage was the first demand of the women of the Revolution. Spain was rather later, when in 1978 they tactfully drafted their new post-Franco constitution (so as both to secularise their state and at the same to require respect to be shown to the historic religious past, thus enabling all their citizens to feel comfortable with the equality which was the linchpin of the new state which succeeded Franco's long rule, during which adultery had been a crime[10]). This was a bold step for Spain, formerly a deeply religious Catholic country which only 40 years before had fought a gruesome civil war, inter alia over religion, and it is notable that such equality steps could be taken in both France and Spain, which were historically both such deeply religious countries that their Catholic Kings were formally designated by the Pope respectively as their Most Christian and Most Catholic Majesties. Spain, however, has had same-sex marriage for some years, and France had a pre-PACS concubinage system recognising cohabitation for social security purposes long before the welfare state even treated cohabitants as a couple.

Further, all over Europe there are same-sex partnership and marriage systems, as well as in other continents such as North America. There therefore appear to be good reasons both for the retention of civil partnership if some people want it and for gay marriage, especially as surveys seem to show that for every protest there are others perfectly happy with same-sex relationships.

The National Centre for Legal Research found in 2010 that only 36 per cent of religious people thought that same-sex sexual relations was 'almost always wrong', whereas in 1983 it had been 62 per cent, from which Herring deduces that opposition is mostly from older people. Nevertheless

---

9 See Chapter 4 for the role of the Church in facilitating medieval divorce and nullity when politically and socially necessary.
10 Which it still is in some parts of Africa, and also a capital crime.

the reaction from those who support the traditional English view of marriage, whether they are genuinely or only culturally and traditionally religious, is not specifically known at this stage as it appears that no research has been done on whether gay *marriage* makes any difference to attitudes, though Herring[11] seems to think that marriage will be the last straw for some objectors.

Anecdotally there are reports that some gays and lesbians are outspoken in their opposition to the concept of gay marriage as such (which they say they did not want, preferring the civil partnership mode they already had), while on the other hand some civil partners were outraged that the government had delayed providing the mechanisms legislated for under s 9 of the 2013 Act for transferring from civil partnership to full marriage,

Thus at least one couple who had planned to marry on 29 March 2014 when the Act came into force were unable to do so because they could not without applying for dissolution of their partnership, which clearly they did not want as they would have to have alleged the fault-based Fact of behaviour in order to achieve an order since there was no time to accrue sufficient separation to use one of the separation Facts. The government appears to have attempted to defuse this irritation by promising that no civil partner would have to pay any new fee to transfer to full marriage from civil partnership, and that the framework for this transfer would be settled during the year 2014, which has now in fact occurred: from 10 December 2014 civil partners may register their transfer to marriage without further fee.

Whatever their perceived urgency to get the 2013 Act through Parliament (which was probably, as they said, because it was an equality issue) it has helped cross-border same-sex marriages, as shown in the case example below.

❖ CASE EXAMPLE

In *Wilkinson v Kitzinger* (2006)[12] two female same-sex partners who had been married in British Columbia, Canada (where same-sex marriage is recognised), sought a declaration that their marriage should be recognised in English law, as this relationship was only recognised as a civil partnership in the UK. The High Court refused such recognition on the grounds that the ECtHR had recognised the concept of marriage in English law as between opposite-sex partners only and had interpreted Art 12 of the Convention accordingly, although the petitioner contended that the English law stance was a breach of Arts 8, 12 and 14. The court, however, insisted that the English law interpretation which treated same-sex and opposite-sex couples differently, requiring them to be of opposite sexes for marriage,[13] was reasonable and proportionate, although Sir Mark Potter, P, indicated that civil partnership accorded to same-sex couples all the same advantages as civil marriage does for opposite-sex couples, except in the name.

The government's change of heart about legislating to introduce gay marriage suggests that further consideration had been given to the reasons for the introduction of registered civil partnership in the first place. Providing the same protection that legal marriage gives to opposite-sex couples cannot be the reason as the CPA 2004 addresses the gay community's former objections to informal

---

11 Op. cit.
12 [2006] EWHC 2022 (Fam).
13 MCA 1973 s 11(c), for which see Chapter 3.

partnerships (including their dissatisfaction with lesser supporting mechanisms such as the London Partnership Register introduced in 2001), namely that these former arrangements had no legal significance because they conferred no status, since the CPA 2004 (as explained above) does a very thorough job of creating such a status.

It can no longer be said, for example, that endless practical and legal difficulties are created (which was Stonewall's argument in advancing the case for the statutory certainty of the CPA 2004). What probably can be said, therefore, is that gay partners were still not afforded full equality if they could not marry as such. This was the theme behind the introduction of the CPA 2004 in the first place, as seen in the initial June 2003 consultation paper[14] which was issued by the Women and Equality Unit of the Department of Trade and Industry and was said to be 'an important equality measure'. At the time, however, the government was keen to emphasise that the proposals did not import gay marriage, and were clearly anxious not to offend religious groups or to give grounds to those who might say that the measure undermined traditional marriage.

Baroness Scotland emphasised that the Act was a *secular* vehicle for recognising same-sex couples' partnership because they '*cannot* marry', so that the government would 'continue to support marriage and recognise that it is the surest foundation for opposite sex couples raising children'. (How this sits with their alternative support for families headed by a cohabiting couple in other statements at other times can best be left for Chapter 9, which will consider those separate problems.)

8.2 Formation of civil partnerships

Civil partners must be of the same sex and the civil partnership is formed only when the partnership is registered, not when vows are taken as in civil marriage of opposite-sex couples, as is made clear by the legislative provision: s 1.

STATUTORY EXTRACT

'1. Civil partnership

(1) A civil partnership is a relationship between two people of the same sex ("civil partners")
 (a) which is formed when they register as civil partners of each other –
 (i) in England and Wales . . .'

Unregistered relationships which would otherwise qualify are not 'civil partnerships' since registration is essential to create this status. Like marriage under the MCA 1973 the registered relationship lasts until death, annulment or dissolution: CPA 2004 ss 1(3) and 37. As in the case of civil marriage, notice must be given to the registrar of the local authority where the partners wish to register, which cannot take place in any other venue, especially in a religious building as it is a civil ceremony[15] though it is now possible for same-sex marriages to be religious and as with marriage there is a residence requirement of seven days,[16] a notice requirement and a civil, non-religious,

---

14 Civil Partnerships: A Framework for the Legal Recognition of Same Sex Couples.
15 CPA 2004 s 6(1).
16 CPA 2004 s 8(1).

ceremony during which the civil partners sign a document in the presence of two witnesses:[17] it is this registration document by which the partnership is formed since there are no 'vows'.

Prior to registration, the parties can enter into a civil partnership agreement if they choose, which can either be regarded as the equivalent of an engagement to marry[18] or as a pre-nuptial agreement, since, like cohabitation contracts in the case of opposite-sex couples, such contracts can be valid if there are no vitiating circumstances, since the CPA[19] provides for largely the same rights on dissolution of the civil partnership as on decree of divorce under the MCA 1973.

There is no equivalent of the banns procedure as the ceremony cannot take place on any religious premises, though it is usually possible to have a religious blessing in the partners' local church.[20] However, the parties have to wait for 15 days from the time they give notice in case there are any objections following the notice,[21] though this can be reduced in case of illness or military posting[22] and both parties must make a declaration that there is no impediment to the registration of the civil partnership and that the residence requirement is satisfied.[23]

The same minimum age (16, with consent of parents if either of the partners is under 18[24]) is required and, as with a marriage, the parties must not be married to someone else or within the prohibited degrees of relationship;[25] for this reason there was some publicity when two sisters, who wished to form a civil partnership to protect family property for inheritance tax reasons, were unable to do so.

Deech has criticised this limitation[26] since the relationship created by civil partnership is not marriage and no sexual relationship is required to enter a civil partnership (unlike traditional marriage, which requires consummation without which a marriage can be annulled, unless there has been approbation[27]). Cretney is concerned by this situation for another reason: he thinks that such an extension of civil partnership would be abused for such financial reasons since no consummation is required.[28] However, this is hard to see as an objection; marriage was initially the vehicle of choice for protection of property in the lawless Middle Ages[29] and later remained so for cultural reasons until well after women were able to own property personally and, following the end of World War II, assumed more independent lifestyles. Why should the role of marriage as a financial shelter be so different today?

There is in fact a good deal of literature on the theory behind both civil partnership and gay marriage which may be found in the 'Further reading' list below and is recommended, as by no means all the underlying theory in this area is settled since both concepts are relatively new, although the dates of some pieces indicate that the debates have been active for some time.

---

17 CPA 2004 s 2(1).
18 In which case it will have the same non-contractual effect as an engagement, and the same rules about property rights will apply as in the case of termination of an engagement of opposite-sex couples: CPA 2004 ss 73–74.
19 CPA 2004 s 72 and Schedule 5.
20 Some churches have said they will marry same-sex partners, but the legislation provides that no church has to do so.
21 CPA 2004 ss 10–13.
22 CPA 2004 s 20.
23 CPA 2004 s 8(4).
24 CPA 2004 s 4(1).
25 CPA 2004 s 3(2) and Part I of Schedule 1.
26 See the Gresham lectures 2009, 'Sisters, sisters', available at www.gresham.ac.uk.
27 See Chapter 3.
28 Cretney, S, *Same Sex Relationships*, Oxford, OUP, 2006, p 50.
29 Indeed it was the very reason in the Middle Ages for the usually hasty remarriage of widows of property so that a new husband could physically protect their assets; e.g. Adelicia of Louvain, the second wife of Henry I, who was widowed young, was fairly promptly remarried (to one of his Norman barons, an ancestor of the Dukes of Norfolk, prominent and powerful landowners) at the start of the civil war of succession between Henry's nephew Stephen and daughter Matilda, and it was obvious that this was one of the more necessary of such marriages as the country quickly descended from the post-Norman Conquest order into lawlessness. Otherwise she would have had to go for safety into one of a number of royal abbeys or nunneries and lost her dower property to the Church.

❖ **CASE EXAMPLE**

In *Burden v UK* (2008)[30] two elderly sisters had lived together for many years and complained to the ECtHR that they were denied the inheritance tax benefits of married couples and civil partners as they did not have the right to form a civil partnership. The reasoning of the court was that the sibling relationship was 'qualitatively of a different nature from that of married couples and [civil partners] . . . the very essence of the connection between siblings is consanguinity, whereas one of the defining characters of Civil Partnership Act union is that it is denied to close family members'.

8.3 Dissolution of civil partnerships

A civil partnership can be annulled on any of the grounds which apply to nullity of marriage as set out in the MCA 1973 except for non-consummation and venereal disease, and dissolved on any of the grounds set out for divorce in the case of a marriage in the same Act save for adultery, which is not included in the CPA 2004. Professor Michael Freeman sees no reason why any infidelity in a civil partnership should not be treated as behaviour for dissolution purposes, although it could never be behaviour in a marriage, where it must be duly pleaded as adultery under the MCA 1973 which provides such a Fact.[31] However, he also comments that in simply mirroring the MCA 1975 when drafting the CPA 2004 'opportunities to rethink have been lost'.[32]

There is the same bar against application for dissolution during the first year following the ceremony of civil partnership as in the case of petitioning for divorce; CPA 2004 s 41.

By s 49 a civil partnership is void if the registration document is void or not duly issued, due notice had not been given or the registrar was not present, the place of registration is not the one in the notice, or if the parties are not eligible to register a civil partnership. The bars to an annulment order are the same as for the bars to annulment of a marriage.

The relationship is ended by a dissolution order, first a 'conditional' one and secondly a 'final' order, six weeks after the first, rather than by the decrees used in divorce.

8.4 Distinction between marriage and civil partnership

Apart from the differences between the provisions of the MCA 1973 for spouses and those of the CPA 2004 the key difference between marriage and civil partnership is that, in England and Wales, civil partnership is not marriage as same-sex marriage is provided for in the **Marriage Act 1949** as amended and the **MCA 1973**. In some other jurisdictions civil partnership is a marriage, including Belgium, the Netherlands and Spain, some states of the United States of

---

30 [2008] 2 FLR 787.
31 See Chapter 5.
32 Freeman, M, *Understanding Family Law*, London, Sweet & Maxwell, 2007.

America and some provinces of Canada. However, now the promised legislation has been introduced couples such as those in the case of *Wilkinson v Kitzinger* will be able to have their overseas marriages recognised in English law. The court already has the power under the CPA 2004 to recognise overseas civil partnerships, dissolutions, annulments and separations[33] which is equivalent to recognition of overseas marriages and divorces, but as seen in the Canadians' case provision had to be made in the new legislation to recognise overseas gay marriage.

This was presumably the case that was a factor in persuading the government that there had to be legislation to create gay marriage as well as the civil partnership already on the statute book. The petitioner argued that the requirement pursuant to the MCA 1973 s 11(c) that the parties must be male and female in order to contract a valid marriage was a breach of Arts 8, 12 and 14 (the right to family life, the right to marry and the right not to be discriminated against in respect of any such right) of the European Convention on Human Rights (ECHR). As a result it is unlikely to be coincidental that those drafting the Marriage (Same Sex Couples) Act 2013 have simply provided that s11(c) be removed from the Matrimonial Causes Act 1973 and s1(i) of the 2013 Act merely provides that 'marriage of same sex couples is lawful' thus opening the way to recognition of foreign civil partnerships by marriage as appropriate.

Professor Michael Freeman considers that the fact that overseas civil partnership was initially not recognised as a marriage is discriminatory, and that it would have been easy for the new relationship to be recognised as a marriage but that the government did not want 'gay marriage', so no provision to recognise other jurisdictions was obviously the solution of the time. He says that the fact that the Department of Trade and Industry Women and Equality Unit described the 2004 Act as 'an important equality measure for same sex equality'[35] is manifestly untrue since the fact that same-sex partners were not allowed to marry was no true equality because the 'separate' provision of civil partnership is 'not equality' but discrimination, and that to establish that true equality opposite-sex partners should be allowed to have civil partnerships (as in effect they are permitted to do under the French system of PACS where opposite-sex partners are also allowed to register).

Analytical comparisons between registered civil partnership, marriage[36] and informal cohabitation[37] between partners of either sex can now be made in respect of a number of incidences of their respective relationships, but the only legally recognised units are those of married and registered partnerships. Critics comment that this leaves opposite-sex cohabitants – in a relationship as long-standing as marriage – without any definable relationship or property regime; and that this is illogical and improvident when more couples are now cohabiting than marrying, and there are many more such relationships than civil partnerships.

In the circumstances it must be asked whether when legislating for gay marriage the government could not have done anything to bring *unregistered* civil partnerships into the new statutory arrangements, perhaps through a default regime; since it seems this was *not* even discussed, it is hard to see why these unregistered partnerships, as in the case of opposite-sex cohabitants, have been left to remain without any specific status, and with all the same problems as beset opposite-sex cohabiting couples.[38]

---

33 CPA 2004 ss 233–238.
34 [2006] EWHC 2022 (Fam).
35 *Civil partnership: A framework for the recognition for same sex couples* (2003).
36 See Chapter 2.
37 See Chapter 9.
38 See Chapter 9.

8.5 Current debates

Ideas for research on these current discussion questions can be accessed on the companion website updates.

- Should the law treat marriage, civil partnership and informal cohabitation (by either same-sex or opposite-sex couples) in the same way where they perform broadly the same function as a family unit?
- Is there an argument for a civil partnership for other family members such as siblings or other family members related by blood, such as the Burden sisters?
- Were civil partnerships a positive innovation and is there a rationale for keeping them now same-sex marriage is possible?

8.6 Summary of Chapter 8

- The CPA 2004 created a legal status of civil partnership which is virtually in all but name same-sex marriage with very few distinctions.
- It is not same-sex marriage, and apparently initially policy was the reason for this.
- Formation and dissolution closely follow the provisions for civil marriage and divorce under the MCA 1973 with minor exceptions.
- English law formerly recognised foreign jurisdictions' gay marriages as equivalent to civil partnership in England and Wales. These are now recognised as full marriage.
- Sibling relationships cannot qualify as civil partnership in England and Wales though they could in France under the PACS regime.
- There is already a substantial literature of legal theory and philosophy on the policy and theoretical infrastructure of the concept of civil partnership and same sex close relationships.

 ## 8.7 Further reading

Auchmuty, R, 'What's so special about marriage? The impact of *Wilkinson v Kitzinger*', [2008] CFLQ 475.

Bamforth, N, ' "The benefits of marriage in all but name?" Same sex couples and the Civil Partnership Act 2004', [2007] CFLQ 133.

Bamforth, N, 'The role of philosophical and constitutional arguments in the same sex marriage debate, a response to John Murphy', [2005] CFLQ 165.

Cretney, S, *Same Sex Relationships: From 'Odious Crime' to 'Gay Marriage'*, Oxford, OUP, 2006.

Diduck, A and Kaganas, F, *Family Law, Gender and the State*, Oxford, Hart, 2006.

Eskridge, W, *The Case for Same Sex Marriage*, New York, Free Press, 1996.

Finnis, J, 'Law, Morality and Sexual Orientation', (1994) *Notre Dame Law Review*, 69: 1049.

Freeman, M (Michael), *Understanding Family Law*, 'Understanding Marriage and Other Relationships', London, Sweet & Maxwell, 2007.

Kirby, R, 'Equal treatment of same sex couples in English Family law?', [2007] Fam Law 413.

Kurdek, L, 'Relationship Outcomes and their Predictors: Longitudinal Evidence from Heterosexual Married, Gay Cohabiting and Lesbian Cohabiting Couples', (1998) *Journal of Marriage and the Family*, 60: 53.

Posner, R, *Sex and Reason*, Cambridge, Massachusetts, Harvard University Press, 1992.

Murphy, J, 'Same sex marriage in England: a role for human rights', [2004] CFLQ 245.

Probert, R, '*Hyde v Hyde*: defining or defending marriage?' [2007] CFLQ 322.

Probert, R, *The Changing Regulation of Cohabitation: From Fornicators to Family*, Cambridge, CUP, 2012.

Probert, R and Barlow, A, 'Displacing marriage – diversification and harmonisation within Europe', [2000] CFLQ 153.

Sullivan, A, *Same-Sex Marriage Pro and Con*, New York, Vintage Books, 1997.

Tatchell, P, 'Civil Partnerships Are Divorced From Reality', *Guardian*, 19 December 2005.

Chapter 9

Cohabitation

Chapter Contents

Learning outcomes for this chapter

A sound understanding of the law in relation to cohabitants including:

(i)   An awareness of how little discrete or coherent legal provision there is in English law specific-ally relating to cohabitants.
(ii) An overview of the suggested reforms.
(iii) An ability to analyse and synthesise the law in relation to cohabitants, civil partners and married couples and to appreciate the context of the proposed reforms.

9.1 Introduction

As has been made clear in other chapters, the prevalence of cohabitation, of births outside marriage or civil partnership, and through Human Assisted Reproduction (HAR) has led to the necessity to reconsider what precisely is now understood by 'the family'. The Rowntree Foundation has long been engaged in research on the contemporary concept of the family, which has in recent times experi-enced such changes that inevitably practitioners now encounter significant numbers of unmarried clients and need to be aware of their separate problems, which require a distinct approach.

Academics, the Law Commission, the Law Society and Resolution have all contributed signifi-cantly to the debate. Thus the unmarried family has also become a routine study in the academic context and attracts its share of the attention of law reformers. Already some steps have been taken to minimise the effect for children of the fact that often their parents are not married, for instance in the application of the **Child Support Acts (CSA) 1991–1995**, which apply to both married and unmar-ried non-resident parents in exactly the same way, regardless of their marital status, if they are not maintaining their children. Gradually the position has been reached that there are as many similarities as differences between the married/civil partnered family and the unmarried/informally cohabiting family; and many more differences than similarities between those two broad types of the contem-porary family and the traditional 'nuclear; family of husband, wife and 2.4 children' of not so long ago.

Problems arise because the law still largely caters for that now much rarer nuclear family and from the fact that there is still a widespread belief amongst non-lawyers that there is a legal entity called 'common law marriage', applying to cohabiting couples after a certain period (variously believed to be two or five years). People are then shocked to discover that this is a myth and that there is little or no remedy available to either party, particularly if one is more disadvantaged than the other on breakdown of the relationship. Until there is a discrete regime for cohabitants, their property problems have to be (very unsuitably) decided according to the ordinary law of trusts, which if there is no formal document recording the parties' intentions will mean litigation to attempt to establish what the parties meant to do.

9.2 Current initiatives

Both the academic and the vocational student will be familiar, through study of the core subjects, with the range of property problems which arise where cohabitants buy and occupy property together. Other chapters of this book deal with the existence of remedies available to cohabitants for domestic violence, the operation of the former CSA and new CMS in obtaining maintenance for children from their non-resident parents, and the provision under the CA 1989 for unmarried fathers to obtain both PR and other orders in respect of their children.[1] Unfortunately, there is very

---

1 For which see further Chapters 12, 16 and 17.

little else apart from this small portfolio of remedies which is available to unmarried parties when a relationship breaks down. However, two other useful possibilities should be stressed:

- a CA 1989 capital order (i.e. for transfer of property), which may be obtained to enable an unmarried carer parent to secure the occupation of the former cohabitants' home for that parent and the child or children (although this is normally only until the youngest child attains majority: see *T v S* (1994)),[2] thus normally leaving the carer parent without a home in middle age; and
- the **Law Reform (Succession) Act 1995**, which has improved the rights of cohabitants on the death of their partners.

Nevertheless, the law reform society JUSTICE had little success when in recent years it initiated a campaign to inform cohabitants of the pitfalls of unmarried cohabitation without taking some steps to protect themselves in the event of relationship breakdown. In this respect it is especially women who appear to suffer most from informal arrangements about property, particularly in relation to jointly acquired homes, and who appear blissfully unaware of the possibility of entering into cohabitation contracts or at least of securing recognition of the respective property rights of the parties at the initial conveyancing stage. The sad fact is that this can quite easily be done, by either having both parties' names on the TR1 form or (if only one is to be the transferee) by making their own declarations of trust to be kept with the copy transfer, recording at that point their intentions in respect of their shares of the property (usually the family home), rather than leaving this for a dispute later when the parties are separating. But cases repeatedly coming to court indicate that this is simply not done, however much it is encouraged.

The importance of such an information initiative as JUSTICE attempted, and which was followed up by the government's (equally failed) Living Together information campaign, cannot be sufficiently stressed, since there is no statutory provision similar to that which is available to wives under MCA 1973 s 24 on marriage breakdown and to civil partners under the CPA 2004 s 72 and Schedule 5 on dissolution of their partnership.

Thus to facilitate division of the cohabiting couple's assets on relationship breakdown, since they cannot access either of these statutory regimes, requires either privately negotiated agreement, mediation or litigation in the Chancery Division of the High Court (or the Chancery List of a county court with a Chancery List) and is therefore not for the faint hearted, both as to cost, unfamiliarity and delay, and stress over the necessary period during which the dispute will endure, so that at the least some sort of cohabitation agreement is realistically required, although even this needs some care. While cohabitation contracts are not necessarily void as such, if they simply govern the relationship between cohabiting adults with relation to their property – since this is not contrary to public policy even if a sexual relationship is intended – such contracts may be void on other grounds, such as undue influence, misrepresentation or lack of intention to create legal relations, as in the case of *Sutton v Mishcon De Reya and Gawor & Co* (2004),[3] where such a contract led to a negligence suit although when it came to court this did afford an opportunity for the judge to confirm both (i) that such contracts are not necessarily invalid but also (ii) that the validity and effect of the terms will be a matter for the court's determination.

It may be that this obvious gap in the law, now affecting a substantial constituency of cohabiting families, will be addressed before long; although following the Law Commission's work on

---

2 [1994] 2 FLR 883. And see Chapter 21.
3 [2004] 1 FLR 837. This case was actually about the resulting negligence suit in which the defendants had drafted an agreement for the parties from which one of the parties backed out before it was executed and the matter had been settled by negotiation. However Hart J had confirmed the essential validity of cohabitation contracts, though he indicated that the courts scrutinise them extremely carefully.

cohabitants' property rights on which they reported in 2007[4] and the government has taken no action, there is now a new Cohabitants' Rights Bill[5] going through Parliament which aims substantially to effect the proposed reforms.

Despite the contemporaneous comments of Stuart Bridge, the Law Commissioner in charge of the project, to the effect that the scheme proposed in the 2007 report 'struck the right balance between protecting the vulnerable and respecting freedom of choice', unfortunately at present the Coalition Government is clearly not inclined to progress their recommendations in the present resource-restricted climate. The previous (Labour) government in any case announced in 2008 that they were waiting to see how the relatively new Scottish system under the **Family Law (Scotland) Act 2006** worked out before taking any steps. This system, however, has been relatively successful in operation, although there has been some academic comment on early evaluation; see below. There is a similar statute in force in Australia which has equally attracted mixed academic comment, another in New Zealand which seems successful, and some provision, on a regional basis, in Spain, which had a new constitution in 1981 which provides equality for cohabitants, although precise provision has been left to the regional provinces, all of which have now legislated, including the Canary Islands.

9.3 Property disputes

Where cohabitants or former cohabitants cannot agree on property rights, a declaration of ownership can always be sought whether of real or personal property. This will of course not be under the **Married Women's Property Act (MWPA) 1882**, except in the case of formerly engaged couples, as the parties are by definition not married, but is still obtainable under the strict rules of property rights applied under the ordinary law of property.

Similarly, a cohabitant may also seek an order for sale under the **Trusts of Land and Appointment of Trustees Act (TOLATA) 1996** ss 14 and 15, which have replaced s 30 of the **Law of Property Act (LPA) 1925** for this purpose. If these remedies are adopted, the law is basically the same for married or unmarried couples (see below for resulting and constructive trusts). Unfortunately many cohabitants remain unaware of them, and when they do know about the role of trusts in such practical ownership of cohabitants' property they frequently do nothing about it and/or cling stubbornly to the erroneous belief that after two years' cohabitation they will achieve the mythical status of 'common law marriage' which gives them quasi-marital rights[6] (which it does not, as the supposed status does not exist).

9.3.1 Declarations of ownership

To assess the rights of a cohabitant to a declaration of ownership it will therefore be necessary (as in the case of married parties):

- to check the deeds for any express legal or equitable title; and
- if the cohabitant was ever engaged to be married to the other party, to apply for a declaration of ownership under the MWPA 1882 s 17, together with a consequential order for sale, exactly

---

4 *The Financial Consequences of Relationship Breakdown*, Law Com 307. [2007] Fam Law 785, where the Commissioner in charge of the project comments on the scheme proposed in that paper.

5 A private member's Bill launched by Lord Marks of Henley-on-Thames (Jonathan Marks QC), although it is likely, unless the government were to support it, that this will share the fate of previous Bills introduced by Lord Lester which did not progress beyond a second reading; however, should this Bill succeed after this book has gone to print, see the associated website for full update.

6 See Probert, R, 'Why couples still believe in common law marriage', [2007] Fam Law 403.

as in the case of a married person, except that in the case of a former fiancé(e) it is necessary to make the application within three years of the termination of the engagement.

It should be noted that if a formerly engaged cohabitant has made any substantial improvements to the property, this may provide a share or an increased share under the MPPA 1970 s 37, which former fiancé(e)s – but not other cohabitants – may use pursuant to the right given to them by the **Law Reform (Miscellaneous Provisions) Act 1970** s 2(1) and (2). If the cohabitant was not ever engaged to be married then it is only possible to apply to the court for a declaration under the LPA 1925 s 53(2).

9.3.2 TOLATA 1996, ss 14 and 15

TOLATA 1996 ss 14 and 15 is the normal jurisdiction for an order for sale where land is held on trust for the parties jointly, and cohabitants may use this where the position is clear that the land is held jointly, as in that case it is automatically held on trust of land, or where a declaration has been successfully sought. The court will then have the same discretion over whether to order a sale as in the case of spouses, and the decision will depend on whether the terms of trust of land have or have not in fact come to an end.

9.3.3 Occupation to the exclusion of the other

The cohabitant has no rights similar to those of a spouse under the former Matrimonial Homes Acts, which have been replicated by the FLA 1996 ss 30 and 31, although there are other provisions in that Act which now apply to cohabitants. There are, however, four ways of achieving sole occupation of the home for a cohabitant, either:

(a) under the domestic violence rules, currently Part IV of the FLA 1996, which now applies specifically to cohabitants, which section depending on whether they or their partners are entitled or not,[7] or by establishing the new statutory tort of *harassment* under the **Protection from Harassment Act (PHA) 1997**, which enables an injunction to be granted ancillary to those proceedings in tort (i.e. under the inherent jurisdiction of the court);[8] or

(b) by establishing a licence to occupy, either as a *contractual licence* or under the rules of *proprietary estoppel* (see below); or

(c) by establishing an interest in the proceeds of sale which carries with it a right to occupy: Bull v Bull (1955);[9] or

(d) by obtaining a Transfer of Property Order under CA 1989 Schedule 1 whereby the property is held for the benefit of the minor child of the relationship.

It should be noted that it may also be possible to obtain a domestic violence injunction, for a short period only, ancillary to an order under the CA 1989,[10] as the old pre-1996 route to injunctions outside the FLA 1996, i.e. under the inherent jurisdiction of the High Court ancillary to other proceedings, was not closed by the enactment of Part IV of that Act.

Otherwise neither party can occupy the property to the exclusion of the other; thus, if it would be essential to obtain an occupation order under the inherent jurisdiction, such an application must be in support of some recognised legal or equitable right.

---

7 See Chapter 11.
8 See Chapter 11.
9 [1955] 1 QB 234.
10 See Chapter 16.

> ❖ **CASE EXAMPLE**
>
> In *Ainsbury v Millington* (1986)[11] the order could not be made ancillary to an order for custody, care and control of children since the joint owner mother seeking it could not assert a superior title to that of the co-owner father.

For this reason most cohabitants will now rely on Part IV of the FLA 1996, pending a longer-term resolution of the property problem, by transfer of ownership or of tenancy.[12] The provisions cover transfer by one cohabitant joint tenant of his or her interest to the other.[13] The Schedule 7 criteria generally favour the financially weaker party, with a child or children, who will find it difficult to find alternative accommodation.

9.3.4 Trusts

All the usual rules of resulting and constructive trusts apply in determining cohabitants' interests. There will usually be a rebuttable presumption of a resulting trust where money has changed hands, as in any joint purchase, but cases may sometimes be complicated where a cohabitant is also involved with other members of the family – the precise status of payments made must be determined, and the payee often claims that the payments in question were not made with an intention or agreement to share in the property but were pursuant to some other transaction; rent, loan or gift are the most common claims.

> ❖ **CASE EXAMPLES**
>
> In *Sekhon v Alissa* (1989),[14] one of the wider family cases which may provide arguments by analogy, there was a complex mother-and-daughter investment in a property, which the daughter (unsuccessfully) tried to pass off as a gift. Examination of the fact pattern, into which the mother had originally entered in order to gain a tax benefit, established that it was no such thing.
>
> In *Passee v Passee* (1988)[15] there was an even more complex extended family arrangement of a man, his aunt and her daughter, where he (unsuccessfully) claimed the payments made towards the mortgage were either loans or rent.

9.3.5 Hazards

In each case the fact pattern needs to be examined carefully and the facts applied to ordinary trust principles. The cohabitant often has to contend with specious arguments intended to rebut what is

---

11 [1986] 1 All ER 73.
12 See Chapter 11 for transfer of tenancies under s 53 and Schedule 7 to the FLA 1996.
13 See Bridge, S, 'Transferring tenancies of the family home' [1998] Fam Law 26; and Woelke, A, 'Transfer of tenancies' [1999] Fam Law 72.
14 [1989] 2 FLR 94.
15 [1988] 2 FLR 263.

otherwise a fairly obvious case of a resulting trust; for example, a claim is made that money spent was a 'loan'. This is very unsatisfactory as unless the specious claim can be settled by showing that it is a 'try on' it will be necessary for the applicant ex-cohabitant to initiate legal proceedings, which is expensive, and contrary to present pressures not to do so but to settle out of court. Fortunately as no discrete regime has been created for cohabitants despite the Law Commission's work in this area, such proceedings are not caught by rule 3A and the associated protocol of the FPR 2010 because such proceedings are not 'family proceedings' under the FPR, since they are trust proceedings under the CPR and heard not in the Family Division but in the Chancery Division or the Chancery List of the county court. This means that no MIAM is required before proceedings can be commenced, but the 'benefit' is illusory as the legal proceedings will be complex and expensive. Only the speed at which Chancery Division business has been effected in recent years is of some assistance, since the Chancery Division has transformed itself into a modern arena for the conduct of heavy commercial litigation where clever judges and efficient disposal of business avoid the delay that might otherwise ensue in other overloaded courts. Small comfort for the involuntary litigants, however, as the stress will certainly remain.

❖ CASE EXAMPLES

In *Risch v McFee* (1991)[16] there was a loan, but as it had been interest free and was never repaid this was one of the happier outcomes as it was treated as a part payment towards the purchase.

In *Stokes v Anderson* (1980)[17] two unmarried people lived together, the woman gave the man money to buy out his ex-wife's share and when they fell out the man claimed – again unsuccessfully – that this had been a loan. A happy outcome for the woman, but litigation was required to achieve it which should not be necessary if there were a discrete regime delivering a default result.

The cohabitant's situation will often share similarities in this situation as with the cases of other family members whose financial affairs have become entangled.

❖ CASE EXAMPLE

In *Re Sharpe* (1980)[18] the loan was in fact from an aunt to a nephew. She had lent him the money towards the purchase of a house on the understanding that she could live with him for the rest of her life. When he went bankrupt she claimed an interest in the house. Although she succeeded on other grounds her claim that this was a resulting trust so that she should have the money back was rejected, and the court distinguished a similar case[19] where there had been a loan to a son-in-law for an extension to a house on

---

16 [1991] 1 FLR 105.
17 [1980] Fam Law 310; [1991] 1 FLR 391.
18 [1980] 1 WLR 219; [1980] 1 All ER 198.
19 Hussey v Palmer [1972] 1 WLR 1286.

the grounds that it would be unjust for him to keep the money and deny that his mother-in-law had an interest in the house.

Such extended 'family' cases are often of assistance in arguing for recognition of financial contributions to a home which were not intended to be made by way of non-proprietorial payments such as loans, rent, etc. but it is clear that this is far too complicated for the purpose of establishing such a routine matter as cohabitants' proprietary interests in the home. It is easy to see how unsuitable it is for cohabiting couples to have to litigate in relation to trusts in this way when all the outside appearances of their relationship are more similar to those of married couples and registered civil partners, especially as the Law Commission has also done extensive work in investigating the circumstances of other family members sharing homes[20] without producing effective results in that context either.

❖ CASE EXAMPLES

Kernott v Jones and *Stack v Dowden*

The judgments in the most recent cohabitant case of *Kernott v Jones* (2011)[21] to reach the Supreme Court have heavily criticised the continuing lack of an effective regime for cohabitants, since this followed an earlier case of *Stack v Dowden* (2007),[22] in which the same issues had arisen, namely the parties' shares on sale of the joint family homes.

In both cases the parties had lived together, had children and separated, having contributed unequal amounts to the purchase of the home, held the property in joint names but had had no declaration of trust. Mr Stack and Ms Dowden had also complicated their situation by subsequently selling and reinvesting, and keeping their respective finances separate for investing elsewhere as well as in their house, while they both contributed to the mortgage, Mr Stack paid the endowment policy premiums supporting it and Ms Dowden paid the household bills. In both cases Baroness Hale restated the principle that the equitable interest normally followed the legal title and that it was for the applicant who wished to disturb that principle to establish the contrary outcome that that beneficial interest is different from the legal ownership.

In *Stack v Dowden* the judge at first instance opted for 50/50 shares. The Court of Appeal did some calculations based on what each had paid and awarded 65 per cent to Ms Dowden and 35 per cent to Mr Stack. The House of Lords followed the Court of Appeal's reasoning and upheld their figures.

In *Kernott v Jones* the judgment of the Supreme Court (initially of Lord Walker and Lady Hale) welcomed the opportunity to revisit *Stack v Dowden* 'for some clarification', commenting on the 'almost unqualified disapprobation' by academics[23] of the earlier

---

20 See below at 9.9.
21 (2011) Times Law Reports, 9 November.
22 [2007] UKHL 17.
23 Gray, K and Gray, S, *Land Law*, 6th edition ('qualified enthusiasm'); Dixon, M, 'The Never Ending Story – Co-Ownership After *Stack v Dowden*', [2007], Conv 456; and Swadling, W, 'The Common Intention Trust in the House of Lords: An Opportunity Missed', (2007) LQR 123: 511 ('almost unqualified disapprobation').

decision, although they added that counsel in the case before them had not argued that the earlier case had been wrongly decided. Their judgment in the *Kernott* case went on to 'make clear' that ('in line with *Stack v Dowden*') in respect of

> a purchase of a house or flat in joint names for joint occupation by a married or unmarried couple, where both are responsible for any mortgage, there is no presumption of a resulting trust arising from their having contributed to the deposit (or indeed the rest of the purchase) in unequal shares. The presumption is that the parties intended a joint tenancy both in law and in equity. But that presumption can of course be rebutted by evidence of a contrary intention, which may more readily be shown where the parties did not share their financial resources.

The judgment refers back to the previous situation, on which Swadling had commented that traditionally unequal contributions had been regarded as leading to equitable tenancy in common in proportion to their contributions, but that that had been the subject of a majority decision of the House of Lords in *Stack v Dowden* when it had been held that this rule no longer applied in the case of 'matrimonial or quasi-matrimonial homes'. Their Lordships added that the decision in *Stack v Dowden* had in fact divided the net proceeds between the parties roughly in accordance with their contributions, the majority inferring a common intention in accordance with constructive trust principles while the dissenting judgment of Lord Neuberger had reached the same result by applying classic resulting trust doctrine.

In considering the *Kernott v Jones* appeal the Supreme Court accepted that the parties had started out as joint tenants in the disputed property in law and equity in 1985, both having contributed to its purchase and the later improvements for which they had taken out a joint loan, but that their intentions had changed when they had separated in 1993, after which Mrs Kernott paid for everything herself, and Mr Jones bought a new property partly with the proceeds of a joint insurance policy which the parties had cashed in and divided between them and which he had used to provide the deposit on his new property. Meanwhile he did not provide any support of his children or for the former family home or take any interest in the former home.

In the proceedings which Mrs Jones started in 2006 for a declaration of their beneficial interests in both houses, she conceded that there might not have been enough evidence in 1993 when they had separated to establish that their respective intentions had changed, but that subsequent events, including the purchase of Mr Kernott's new home, did supply this evidence. At first instance the trial judge accepted this, indicating that Mr Kernott had at least as great a capital appreciation in his own property and divided their interests 10 per cent to Mr Kernott and 90 per cent to Mrs Jones.

On appeal to the Court of Appeal that court upheld his appeal and divided the value 50:50, holding that the parties held as tenants in common in equal shares (Lord Justice Jacob dissenting on the basis that the trial judge had been right in calculating what was fair). The Supreme Court then upheld the trial judge's calculation, on the basis that he had accepted that Mr Kernott's interest had crystallised at the separation in 1993, after which each would have the sole benefit of any capital gain on their respective houses. This approach had produced a result so close to that of the trial judge that the Supreme Court decided that any disturbance of his award would be wrong and no further accounting was necessary.

The principles emerging were therefore

(1) the starting point is that equity follows the law;
(2) but that this can be displaced by evidence of a different common intention at the time of acquisition or later;
(3) their common intention to be imputed as deduced from their conduct;
(4) in any other case where their common intention cannot be deduced, 'each is entitled to the share the court decides is fair';
(5) each case turns on its own facts.

The judgment adds that the approach is different if a property is in one name alone, when it might be the case that the other party was not to have any beneficial interest at all, let alone any presumption of joint ownership.

The appeal was allowed and the order of the judge restored. Lord Collins agreed with Lord Walker and Lady Hale in the result, commenting however that

> the absence of any legislative intervention [which continues despite the Law Commission Report *Cohabitation: the Financial Consequences of Relationship Breakdown*, 2007] made it necessary for the judiciary to respond by adapting old principles to new situations. That has not been an easy task. It is illustrated by the fact that in both *Stack v Dowden* and in this case, the results at the highest appellate level had been unanimous but the reasoning has not. . . . I would hope that this decision will lay to rest the remaining difficulties.

He added that he did not think that the different reasoning of the five judges who had heard the case was a problem as the differences in reasoning were largely terminological, making no difference to the end result, and this was echoed by Lord Kerr. Lord Wilson also agreed with the result and added his own comment on the absence of legislation in this complex area which had resulted in any advance being left to the judiciary and sums up the frustration that has obviously been felt by lawyers at the long period of uncertainty in which litigants had been left without clear resolution:

> In the light of the continued failure of Parliament to confer upon the courts limited redistributive powers in relation to the property of each party on the breakdown of a non-marital relationship, I warmly applaud the development of the law of equity, spearheaded by Lady Hale and Lord Walker in their speeches in *Stack v Dowden*, and reiterated in their judgment in the present appeal, that the common intention which impresses a constructive trust upon the legal ownership of the family home can be *imputed* to the parties to the relationship.

This would appear to be the doctrinal guidance that the legal profession must now follow pending any further indication that a discrete regime for cohabitants may be provided now the promised legislation for gay marriage (potentially benefiting far fewer people) has been enacted – when perhaps there will eventually be political will and resourcing for legislative provision for the constituency comprising the fastest increasing numbers of the population who are without a default regime on relationship breakdown.[24]

---

24 There is significant literature on potential regimes which will be found in the 'Further reading' section of this chapter.

Meanwhile some cases will be simpler than others: the simplest cohabiting situation in which to interpret the parties' behaviour to find common intention is where (as in the case of married couples) a 'joint venture' can be established, which is naturally much easier to establish in the case of spouses than in the case of an unmarried couple since the spouses, being married, have this most basic joint venture to point to, especially as the married relationship is now often looked on as a partnership. However, sometimes cohabitants have an easier task to establish a similar venture even when there has been no marriage, no talk of marriage and not even an engagement which would provide the declaratory relief designed for fiancé(e)s.

❖ CASE EXAMPLES

In *Bernard v Josephs* (1984)[25] both parties contributed and pooled their earnings, but had made unequal contributions to the deposit to buy their home. The court (in a 'broad brush' exercise similar to that adopted later in *Midland Bank v Cooke* (1995))[26] deduced that there had been a joint venture and, on separating, the parties were held to own the house in equal shares. On the other hand, cases can go the other way and it is difficult to tell in advance which way the decision will fall!

In *Walker v Hall* (1984),[27] although this was a similar case to *Bernard v Joseph* no joint venture was discernible and the woman received only a quarter share, no doubt being very disappointed that in her case the outcome had been 50 per cent worse than an apparently similar case.

It should be noted, however, that one of the problems in these unmarried contexts is that the broad brush approach of *Midland Bank v Cooke* is not to be relied on in cohabitants' cases, since in *Midland Bank v Cooke* Waite LJ had the assistance of a long marriage relationship on which to rely in applying the law to the facts, since he was reviewing the entire history of the financial relationship, and it was a married not an unmarried one. Thus he ultimately decided the case on the basis that 'equality is equity', but the court only resorts to such measures if genuinely unable to discern the amount of the respective contributions; in a marriage, the very marriage may be regarded as a joint enterprise, whereas in a cohabitants' relationship the reverse is often the case, with independently maintained bank accounts and financial profiles.

The problem cases in cohabitants' property terms are always those such as *Windeler v Whitehall*, *Burns v Burns* and *Richards v Dove*[28] (respectively 1990, 1984 and 1974), where no trust could be established according to strict property rules and which thus require some evidence of common intention if a constructive trust is to be established. However, in the later Burns-type case of *Hammond v Mitchell* (1991)[29] the woman did manage to gain a half share of the family home on the basis of a long-passed and brief conversation with her former partner which was taken by Waite LJ to evidence the vital common intention to share the property which Mrs Burns could not show. This perhaps indicates that practitioners were becoming more adept at preparing cohabitants' property

---

25 [1984] FLR 126.
26 [1995] 4 All ER 562, CA.
27 [1984] FLR 126.
28 [1990] 2 FLR 505; [1984] Ch 317; [1974] 1 All ER 888.
29 [1991] 1 WLR 1127.

cases by the early 1990s, by requiring their clients to search their memories for the essential evidence of the 'agreement, arrangement or understanding' which Lord Bridge required in *Lloyds Bank v Rosset* (1991),[30] 'however imprecise or imperfectly remembered'. This will establish, if it can be shown, the existence of the necessary common intention, although Waite LJ also said of the parties in *Hammond v Mitchell* that they were both 'prone to exaggeration', yet another indication of the uncertainty of outcome of these cases. Clearly this is an area of the law that needs reform and precision, which is long overdue, not least as the ordinary layperson is so ill informed.

According to the 2008 *British Social Attitudes Report* almost nine out of ten people thought that cohabitants should have financial provision on separation if the relationship was 'long' and had produced children. As long ago as 1984 the Court of Appeal drew attention to the unfairness of the cohabitants' position in the *Burns* case. Since then the Law Society, Resolution, judges, legal practitioners and academics have all pressed for reform and there have been failed Cohabitation Bills in Parliament, including one in 2008–2009, which had followed a consultation paper *Reforming the Law for People Who Live Together* which had proposed two schemes:

- one based on the Law Commission's 2007 economic disadvantage compensatory framework; and
- another similar to the discretion given to the court on divorce of married people under the MCA 1973.

The second was the one chosen, and this became the private member's Bill introduced by Lord Lester of Herne Hill in July 2008, but it went no further after March 2008 following opposition from the House of Lords. There was then another private member's Bill in July 2009, which had its second reading in the House of Lords but then also went no further. Considering the fate of these two Bills, immediately after the apparently positive survey of public attitudes in 2008, the criticisms of the Supreme Court in *Kernott v Jones* are hardly surprising, given the length of time that this unsatisfactory situation has endured.

9.4 Maintenance of the partner in life

There is no direct obligation on a partner to maintain a cohabitant when the parties are not married unless there is some contractual arrangement between them, although indirect support may be obtained if there is a child support assessment where a percentage of the amount paid over is in fact a payment towards the expenses of the child's carer.

Thus the only possible claim for support for a cohabitant is usually to make an ordinary application to the DWP for income support or other benefits, when there will nevertheless be only one claim per household. If the parties are still cohabiting, as is often the case when a relationship is breaking up, and the client is without funds, either the partner who is in work must provide support voluntarily, or if both parties are out of work, one or other of them must make an application for benefits on behalf of both. Once they separate, each partner may make separate applications, and the whole range of benefits will be available.

It should be noted that a female cohabitant with children has always usually had child benefit including the single parent rate, where appropriate, and could make an independent claim for child support in respect of her children. This is strange considering the couple's benefits claim has to be made by one or the other, and they are treated for that purpose in effect as if they were married. Some underlying logic seems to need to be applied to cohabitants, especially as there is significant

---

30 [1991] 1 AC 107.

academic research on the functionality aspect of their relationship which is also usually as much 'like' marriage as it can be without the actual ceremony.

9.5 Maintenance of the partner after death

This is provided for by the **Inheritance (Provision for Families and Dependants) Act (I(PFD)A) 1975** s 1(1)(c) if the cohabitant can show that he or she 'immediately before the death was being maintained, either wholly or partly, by the deceased'.

To use this section, the cohabitant must show that the deceased, 'otherwise than for full valuable consideration, was making a substantial contribution in money or money's worth towards the reasonable needs of that person': I(PFD)A 1975, s 1(3). If these conditions are proved, the court may make an order under s 2.

The court has wide powers to grant periodical payments, lump sums, transfers or settlements of property and even acquisition of property for the benefit of the surviving cohabitant, using assets from the estate to do so.

However, many cohabitants were unable to show the necessary dependence, for example, where the reason that the parties did not marry was because the surviving cohabitant had independent means, such as a pension which would be forfeited on remarriage. However this has now been changed and the **Law Reform (Succession) Act 1995** s 2 now provides for them, amending the I(PFD)A 1975 enabling non-dependent cohabitants to apply, but at the same time requiring the court to have regard to a different set of guidelines from those applying to spouses. In particular, the court must consider:

(a) the applicant's age and the length of time he or she lived as husband and wife with the deceased in the same household; and

(b) the contribution made by the applicant to the welfare of the family, including any contribution made by looking after the home and caring for the family.

The cohabitant applicant can only receive such provision as would be reasonable for maintenance, whereas spouses receive such provision as would be reasonable, whether or not it is required for maintenance.

9.6 Maintenance of children

Children of cohabitants are, however, in a much more advantageous position. They may obtain both maintenance from their natural parent, through the old CSA/CMS,[31] and orders for capital provision. These are of two types:[32]

(1) Lump sums up to £1,000 (formerly from the FPC, now the unified Family Court).

(2) Lump sums of any amount and orders for transfer or settlement of property for their benefit: CA 1989, s 15 and Schedule 1, from the Family Court.

A parent who is not married to the child's other parent and who is able to secure such an order for the benefit of the child is thus able indirectly to obtain financial assistance with the upbringing of

---

31 See Chapter 21.
32 See Chapter 21 for both these.

the child beyond mere maintenance, even including obtaining the right to remain in the family home, which may be transferred for the benefit of the child under the CA 1989 s 15 and Schedule 1.[33]

9.6.1 Establishing paternity for maintenance

If it is necessary to establish paternity in order to invoke the maintenance provisions of the CSA 1991–1995, as amended, or the relief obtainable under the CA 1989, it will be necessary to apply to the court for a declaration to establish relationship to the child: CSA 1991, s 27. The application for declaration of parentage may be made by the carer parent, the Secretary of State (on behalf of the carer parent, who must authorise the Secretary of State to act if the carer is receiving a specified welfare benefit), or the alleged non-resident parent.

There are certain situations, as set out in the CSA 1991, s 26, where parentage will be assumed, and these include:

- where the parents were married at some time in the period between the conception of the child and the child's birth and the child has not subsequently been adopted;
- where the father has been registered as the child's father on the child's birth certificate;
- where the non-resident parent has refused to take a scientific test to prove parentage, or has taken such a test and been proven to be the parent;
- where the non-resident parent has adopted the child;
- where the parent has been declared as such under the provisions of the **Human Fertilisation and Embryology Act (HFEA) 1990 or 2008**;
- where there has been a declaration of parentage in other proceedings, and the child has not subsequently been adopted.

Scientific tests can be provided at a reduced cost under the CSA 1991. If the carer parent (normally the mother) refuses to undergo scientific testing herself, or refuses permission for the child to be so tested, the assumption can be made that the alleged non-resident parent is not in fact the parent. If there is a refusal, and it is deemed to be in the child's best interests to know who his or her parents are, then the court can order tests despite the mother's refusal: FLRA 1969, s 21, as amended.

If, exceptionally, there is some good reason why this information should not be divulged, or scientific tests undertaken, the carer may explain this position to the child support officer, for instance if there is a risk of violence or other undue harm or distress which is likely to be suffered. If this is not accepted by the child support officer then the benefits received by the carer parent may be reduced although the carer parent is no longer obliged to reveal this information.[34]

9.6.2 Establishing paternity for other purposes

For the purposes of Child Arrangements Orders (CAOs) and others under s 8 of the CA 1989, the natural father is treated as a 'parent', and therefore does not require permission to apply for such an order, whether or not he has parental responsibility (PR), which is a separate issue. If, however, the mother steadfastly refuses to recognise that the natural father is the child's father, and there is no proof one way or the other, then the father will probably have to obtain a declaration using scientific tests and an application to the court using the FLRAs 1969 and 1987.

---

33 See Chapter 21.
34 See Chapter 21.

If the parties have lived together, and hence with the child, for at least three years, the father would have the right to apply for an order in relation to the child living with or spending time with him without the permission of the court: CA 1989, s 10(7), although this will not answer the question of paternity. Otherwise s 1 of the FLRA 1987 gives the unmarried father status as a parent in all cases where paternity is accepted or proved, including in all statutes where the word 'parent' would otherwise include him if he were married to the mother.

9.7 Parental responsibility

The default position has always been that the mother of a child has sole parental rights if not married to the father. However, the father could always acquire PR rights in a number of ways provided by of the CA 1989 s 4.[35] For a long time this was not very satisfactory in that it left the child officially fatherless unless some step was taken, despite the Lord Chancellor's declared intention of introducing legislation to give PR to all unmarried fathers who registered the birth with the mother (about 75 per cent of whom had been in the habit of doing so) and which was eventually effected. The situation now is that pursuant to the **Adoption and Children Act (ACA) 2002** from December 2003 birth registration normally includes the unmarried father's name if the parents go together to register the birth unless there is a reason for the mother not wanting this and instead registering the birth on her own. Statistics show that there is a small percentage of births (under 10 per cent) where the mother registers alone.

It has also always been a further discrimination against the unmarried father that parental responsibility could later be removed from unmarried fathers for bad behaviour, whereas nothing a mother or married father does could result in such a penalty. It appears that the ECtHR accepts this on the basis that there are reasons to distinguish the two types of father, as in the following case.

> ❖ **CASE EXAMPLE**
>
> In *Smallwood v UK* (1992)[36] the court even considered that PR should be removed in case the father used it to disrupt the children. This had always been regarded as a strange anomaly, given the disruption caused by some mothers and married fathers.

However, since the ACA 2002 effected the long-awaited voluntary change, the unmarried father has been more closely aligned with the married father in respect of rights and duties towards his children. It was intended by the last Labour Government that in due course all unmarried fathers would register the births of their children with the mother unless there was good reason not to, and in that case there will be automatic PR, although it has been said that this is more for the purpose of making it easier to ensure such fathers contribute to their children's maintenance than to advance the spread of PR amongst unmarried fathers. However, this provision (in the **Welfare Reform Act 2009**) was highly controversial in relation to giving such fathers PR whether they were suitable to have it or not, and the Coalition Government immediately announced repeal.

---

35 See Chapter 13.
36 [1992] EHRLR 221.

9.8 Cohabitation contracts

As a result of the above, there is now a modest growth rate in the provision of cohabitation contracts, which can provide for the parties whatever terms they wish to regulate their relationship, both while they are cohabiting happily and when the relationship breaks down. They have a similar role to play for unmarried couples as separation and maintenance agreements do for married couples who separate, save that cohabitation agreements can sometimes hold the relationship together in the first place, while separation and maintenance agreements[37] usually provide a way forward for those who know that they can no longer live together. In either case, this is an opportunity for imaginative advice and creative drafting, usually on the part of the solicitor of one of the parties, although both parties should have independent legal advice before entering into them. Thus, usually one party or the other will have to take the initiative in producing a working draft. Cohabitation contracts are contracts like any other and are perfectly legal.

Many firms of solicitors now keep precedents on the word processor and suitable forms will also be found in some drafting encyclopaedias, besides which there is at least one specialist collection commercially available. In view of the high incidence of cohabitation and of births in families who do not fit the marital template, yet which are at least semi-permanent (or at least as permanent as some marriages), further formalisation of cohabitation relationships is likely. Meanwhile, practitioners have become increasingly prepared to use such law as is available to assist their unmarried clients by providing such remedies as can be accessed when relationships break down, or better, by attempting to obviate problems by recommending a cohabitation contract and explaining to their clients what will happen if one is not entered into.

9.9 Proposals for reform

A paper on the reform of property law for sharers, within and outside families, was yearly expected from the Law Commission over a long period and was finally issued in late July 2002, but was a great disappointment as it did not address the fundamental cohabitants' property problems. The last Labour Government on coming into power in 1997 promised that it would work across departments to support the family, but although it quickly published a consultation paper, *Supporting Families*,[38] and hovered between supporting marriage and then saying that no particular family unit was better for bringing up children than any other, the White Paper we supposed would follow is still awaited. Resolution has, however, proposed detailed statutory reform. Their Cohabitation Committee published a report entitled *Fairness for Families*, making the following proposals:

(1) Cohabitants' relationships should be defined to recognise that they are different from marriage, but offer commitment, in both heterosexual and same-sex couples.
(2) A new statute should enable cohabitants to apply to the courts for financial relief on relationship breakdown.
(3) A qualifying period for this should be two years unless there are children, when no minimum period should apply.
(4) There should be a discretionary jurisdiction taking account of all the circumstances of the case, as in the case of married persons who separate and divorce.
(5) Similar relief should be available on cohabitation breakdown to that on marriage breakdown, but maintenance should be limited to three years after separation, unless there is severe

---

37 See Chapter 10.
38 Home Office, 1998.

financial hardship. (This is similar to the **Family Law (Scotland) Act 1985** provisions for divorced wives in Scotland.)

(6)   The CA 1989 should be amended so as in an appropriate case to obviate the hardship to women in a *T v S* (1994)[39] situation (where a home transferred to a mother for the benefit of a child of an unmarried relationship normally reverts to the settlor father when the child achieves majority, thus depriving the carer mother of her home).

Resolution also recommends extended use of cohabitation contracts, which should:

● be by deed;
● state that they are intended to be legally binding: see *Layton v Martin* (1986);[40]
● be comprehensive, dealing with all (and only) property and financial issues;
● be made with legal advice; and
● be effected when the parties are already living together or intending to do so shortly.

The Cohabitation Committee has produced a set of precedents.

There is much to be said for these proposals. Occasionally in England and Wales a former cohabitant wins a case which makes it clear that morally the merits in the claim were with that person and that this would have been recognised if the parties had been married.

❖ CASE EXAMPLES

In *Fitzpatrick v Sterling Housing Association Ltd* (2000)[41] it was recognised that same-sex couples are members of the same family and should be entitled to equal rights as are those of married couples under the Rent Acts.

In *Rowe v Prance* (1999)[42] a half share of her lover's yacht was achieved by the claimant owing to his express declaration of trust, even though she had not contributed financially to the purchase.

In *Haywood v Haywood* (2000)[43] there was a similar trust of chattels.

The Law Society has also published proposals with some differences from Resolution's, suggesting for example that there should be no minimum qualifying period, that qualification for benefits should be the same as for the DSS (now DWP), and that public acknowledgment of the relationship as well as stability should be a key ingredient (similar to the former status of common law marriage which ended in 1753 with the passage of **Lord Hardwicke's Clandestine Marriage Act**). Meanwhile, the Scots have now had around seven years' experience of their new statute to replace their courts' existing power to regularise marriages by recognition of cohabitation with 'habit and repute'.

---

39   [1994] 2 FLR 883.
40   [1986] 2 FLR 227.
41   [2000] 1 FLR 271.
42   [1999] 2 FLR 787.
43   (2000) *Lawtel* 2 August 2000.

This statute was introduced owing to proposals from the Scottish Law Commission to improve the position of cohabitants in Scotland by bringing the law applicable to them largely into line with that of spouses under the **Family Law (Scotland) Act 1985**. This regime aims to compensate spouses on divorce by sharing wealth accumulated during the period of marriage and, as mentioned above, therefore to restrict spousal maintenance to three years from separation. The **Family Law (Scotland) Act 2006** introduces a compensation scheme for cohabitants on separation, not identical to the 1985 Act but with some similar infrastructure. The first appeal from this Act has been heard by the Supreme Court.[44] Nevertheless it should be noted that the Scottish courts are still occasionally hearing cases under the old common law principle (which in fact have not been decided particularly consistently, so that Scottish lawyers broadly welcome the new statute).[45]

In France, there is now their PACS which enables opposite- and same-sex couples to enter into a form of civil agreement for a common life. This is regularised by sending the agreement to the local magistrates' court, and the content is up to the parties – similar to an English cohabitation agreement.

In Australia, where New South Wales has had a De Facto Relationships Act since 1985, most states, including the Capital Territory, now have statutory rights for cohabitants, effected by their federal legislation, and New South Wales, the pioneer, has recently amended its Act to cover same-sex couples, thus placing Australia well ahead of England and Wales, and indeed of most other jurisdictions. In New Zealand there is also a more recent Property Relationships Act which has been amended to include cohabitants with the married parties it was originally to cover.

9.10 Other discrimination

While various irritating differences still distinguish married, registered civil partnership and cohabiting status, none is perhaps as irritating as tax treatment, although the results are not quite as adverse in the UK as in France. In the former, there is the lack of the married persons' advantages on death (whereby married couples may plan their estates in a beneficial way so that assets pass between the spouses at nil inheritance tax rate). This is hardly support for the unmarried family if it is recognised as such at all. The only consolation is that in France there has always been an extra penalty for being unmarried, in the form of an expressly much higher inheritance tax rate for a non-spouse beneficiary, which suggests that in that jurisdiction, while the wages of sin are not necessarily death as such, they are certainly payable on death! However, perhaps this extra penalty is not even now noticed in France where all taxes are high.

Basically, the question must be asked as to whether it is still appropriate to set cohabitants apart from both married couples, and (especially now that same-sex partners have obtained gay married status) from civil partners. All three head families, and successive governments have stressed commitment to 'the family' which is, incidentally, also protected by the most recent version of the European Convention to which the UK signed up at Lisbon. The traditional objection to treating marriage and settled cohabitation as even by analogy similar in role has been that the status of marriage in English law is special, and has both religious and cultural significance in England and Wales (even although

---

44 *Gow v Grant* [2012] UKSC 29, in which Baroness Hale considered that the Scottish Act worked and 'English and Welsh cohabitants deserved no less'.
45 An early appraisal of the new system has been included by Professor Elaine Sutherland of Stirling University in the 2011 edition of the *International Survey of Family Law*: see the 'Further reading' section below. There has also been an empirical study in conjunction with a small sample of 97 practitioners with 19 follow-up interviews by F. Wasoff, J. Miles and E. Mordaunt, *Legal Practitioners' Perspectives on the Cohabitation Provisions of the Family Law (Scotland) Act 2006* (Edinburgh: Centre for Research on Families and Relationships, 2010), available at www.crfr.ac.uk/cohabitation.

adult partnership has its own separate characteristics apart from in practice heading families). Moreover there has been a further argument that if opposite-sex cohabitants really want any status other than as the traditionally dubious unmarried state referred to as 'living in sin' they can get married; the same was not true of same-sex couples for whom marriage was not open.

So much change has now occurred to signal retreat from these traditional views that it must be asked why it is that the same comprehensive approach cannot be taken to the concept of the family for all three forms of adult relationship and the law adjusted accordingly to provide the same status to cohabiting heads of families as is now enjoyed by married couples and by civil partners. And moreover that this should be done in a holistic manner rather than relying on piecemeal amendments. This should not be difficult since the difference between married and cohabitant status, if really necessary to preserve, has already been addressed in the FLA 1996 Part IV. To meet the criticism of those who say that cohabiting rather than marrying indicates that the parties expressly chose an alternative to marriage, new legislation, such as that proposed by the experienced family solicitors at Resolution, can quite well address any desirable differences in consequences to reflect the distinct status of the two types of relationship.

9.11 Current debates

Ideas for research on these current questions can be accessed on the companion website updates.

- What is the best way to reform the law for cohabitants? Everyone accepts the desirability, but no one can agree on the best scheme. The Law Commission has rejected codification, Lowe and Douglas have spent considerable thought on this,[46] and the Law Commission of Canada considers that we should go back to the fundamentals of relationships in order to assess whether they really matter.[47]
- Should there be some reform of the law applying to home sharers not able to enter into a civil partnership or marriage (because related within the table of kindred and affinity, such as the Burden sisters[48]) so that they and other family members in a similar home-sharing situation might benefit from the favourable tax treatment accorded to other family relationships in marriage, civil partnership and cohabitation?
- Is it worth attempting some reform of cohabitants' property? The result in the leading case of *Stack v Dowden*[49] that the woman should receive 65 per cent under the ordinary law of trusts as she had paid more in the first place broadly reflected what she had paid, but she had to go to the House of Lords to achieve that result. Is it right that she should have had to do this, as well as Mrs Jones in the later case of *Kernott v Jones*[50] on the same issues, which took her to the Supreme Court in order to obtain a similar assurance, and at a time when the public is being urged to stay out of court and to use DR?
- Is it a concern that even in *Kernott v Jones* there was a dissenting judgment as to reasons by Lord Neuberger of Abbotsbury, although this nevertheless arrived at the same numerical result?

---

46 Lowe, N and Douglas, G, *Bromley's Family Law*, London, Sweet & Maxwell, 2006 at pp 153–69.
47 *Beyond Conjugality: Recognising and Supporting Close Adult Relationships*, 2002. Cossman, B and Ryder, B, 'What is Marriage-Like like? The Irrelevance of Conjugality', *Canadian Journal of Family Law*, 2001, 18: 269.
48 *Burden v UK* [2008] 2 FLR 787.
49 [2007] UKHL 17; [2007] AC 432.
50 [2011] UKSC 53.

9.12 Summary of Chapter 9

Cohabitants' property

- There is no regime of cohabitants' property, which needs therefore to be specifically conveyed to reflect the parties' interests.
- If this is not done they are reliant on the ordinary law of resulting and constructive trusts to unravel and establish their respective interests.
- Orders for sale may be obtained under TOLATA 1996 ss 14 and 15.
- Orders under the CA 1989 may protect the home for the female cohabitant and children. FLA 1996 Part IV can secure occupation of the home for a cohabitant in case of violence by the partner, but not usually long term, although a transfer of tenancy of a rented property may be possible.
- The Law Reform (Succession) Act 1995 gives some recognition to cohabitants' rights in the family home. Cohabitation contracts can address these and other financial and non-financial issues.

Maintenance of cohabitants in life and after death

- There is no right to maintenance for cohabitants, although the children may be maintained either under the CSAs 1991–95, as amended, the CA 1989 or under the I(PFD)A 1975.
- A cohabitant who has been dependent in life may be maintained under that Act after the partner's death.

Parental responsibility (PR)

- Only married fathers have parental responsibility unless the mother gives it to an unmarried father by agreement, registers the birth with the father (from December 2003) or he obtains it from the court.

Reform

- Clearly the situation is unsatisfactory given the numbers of families now involved.
- Resolution and the Law Society have proposed detailed reforms, and a consultation paper from the Law Commission on home sharing was published in 2002.
- Australia (the pioneer since 1985), New Zealand, Scotland, France and Spain are all ahead of England and Wales in recognising de facto relationships, although two Private Members' Bills have sought to introduce greater rights for cohabitants who register their partnerships, and a third is currently before Parliament.

9.13 Further reading

Barlow, A, Burgoyne, C, Clery, E and Smithson, J, 'Cohabitation and the Law: Myths, Money and the Media', *British Social Attitudes 24th Report*, London, Sage, 2008.

Barlow, A, Duncan, S, James, G and Park, A, *Cohabitation, Marriage and the Law: Social Change and Legal Reform in the 21st Century*, Oxford, Hart, 2005.

Barton, C, 'Cohabitants, Contracts and Commissioners', [2007] Fam Law 407.

Bridge, S, 'Money, marriage and cohabitation', [2006] Fam Law 641.

Bridge, S, 'Cohabitation: why legislative reform is necessary', [2007] Fam Law 911.

Cooke, E, 'Cohabitants, Common Intention and Contributions (again)', [2005] *Conveyancer and Property Lawyer*, 555.

Cooke, E and Barlow, A, 'Community of property: a regime for England and Wales?' Paper given at the University of Staffordshire, annual seminar, Centre for the Study of the Family, Law and Social Policy, 2006.

Deech, R, 'The Case Against Legal Recognition of Cohabitation', (1980) *International and Comparative Law Quarterly* 29: 480.

Deech, R, 'Cohabitation', [2010] Fam Law 40: 39.

Douglas, G, Pearce, J and Woodward, H, 'Dealing with property issues on cohabitation breakdown', [2007] Fam Law 36.

Douglas, G, Pearce, J and Woodward, H, *A Failure of Trust: Resolving Property Issues on Cohabitation Breakdown*, Cardiff Research Papers No 1 (July 2007), www.law.cf.ac.uk/researchpapers/papers/1.pdf.

Duncan, S, Barlow, A and James, G, 'Why don't they marry? Cohabitation, commitment and DIY marriage', [2005] CFLQ 383.

Eekelaar, J, 'Why people marry: the many faces of an institution', *Family Law Quarterly* 41: 413.

Hess, E, 'The Rights of Cohabitants: When and how will the law be reformed?', [2009] Fam Law 405.

Hale, B, 'Coupling and Uncoupling in the Modern World', F A Mann Lecture, November 2005.

Herring, J, 'Who decides on human rights?', [2009] LQR 1 (discussing *Re P* [2008] UKHL 38).

Hibbs, M, Barton, C and Beswick, J, 'Why marry? Perceptions of the affianced', [2001] Fam Law 31: 197.

Lewis, J, 'Marriage and Cohabitation and the nature of commitment', [1999] CFLQ 355.

Maclean, M and Eekelaar, J, 'Marriage and the moral bases of personal relationships', (2004) *Journal of Law and Society* 31: 510.

Probert, R, 'The Cohabitation Bill', [2009] Fam Law 150.

Sutherland, E, '"The Easing of Certain Legal Difficulties": Limited Legal Recognition of Cohabitation under Scots Law', in Atkin, B, (ed) *The International Survey of Family Law*, Bristol, Family Law, 2011, www.advicenow.org.uk/go/living-together

Chapter 10

Financial Support Without Decree

Chapter Contents

Learning outcomes for this chapter

A sound understanding of financial support for separated spouses/civil partners/cohabitants and their children without (or before) decree of divorce, nullity or judicial separation including:

(i) An appreciation of the practicalities of orders available under MCA 1973 ss 22 (MPS) and 27 (lump sum and income orders) and DPMCA 1978 ss 1, 2, 6 and 7.
(ii) An awareness of the potential of a cohabitation, separation or maintenance agreement and the pitfalls to avoid in relation to later application for permanent provision.
(iii) An ability to select the optimum remedy for the contemporary atypical family and to research welfare benefits if necessary.

10.1 Introduction: the impact of LASPO

The **Legal Aid, Sentencing and Punishment of Offenders Act (LASPO) 2012**, generated by the impact of ongoing government cuts in public funding in family cases and by the recommendations of the FJR, has now fundamentally changed the way that financial support is sought on relationship breakdown. If anything, the impact is worse when interim emergency support is sought at the time that the family first breaks up than on longer-term financial provision application, when there is more potential for seeking alternative ways of managing without lawyers, as opposed to the need for orders at this initial stage where lack of legal aid can simply throw more people onto welfare benefits – surely not the government's intention.

At the time that the Act was going through Parliament, the Bar Council-led Manifesto for Family Justice[1] immediately made clear to the government the pan-professional concern about these cost-cutting provisions. Indeed, from the moment they were first announced, the Act was immediately identified, by both practitioners and associated professions working in family justice, as much more likely to cause greater delay in the court system than save time and judicial workload, simply because of the impact of the inevitable consequence of the vastly increased numbers of LIPs, unfamiliar with the law and the courts, if there was a significant reduction in legal aid.

While persistence in bringing forward the legislation was therefore surprising in itself, since the 2010 Jackson Report[2] had only recently recommended that civil legal aid should *not* be cut further than it already had been, there was even keener concern about the fate of the women and children who would obviously be those largely worse off owing to these 'economies', since they are the majority of applicants for both mainstream family law remedies and also interim or emergency orders, including for temporary financial support pending divorce or other decree.

David Pannick QC, writing in the legal pages of *The Times* soon after the LASPO cuts were announced,[3] said at that time that the Bill would 'turn access to justice into life's little luxury' unless substantial amendments were made. They were not made, and the predicted results have duly arrived entirely as foreseen, indeed impacting very significantly on applicants for Family Law orders.

He refers in this article to the speech of Sir Hartley Shawcross, the Labour Attorney-General, when introducing the **Legal Aid and Advice Act** in December 1948 (the very Act which first benefited women in permitting them for the first time to consider divorce proceedings). In this Sir Hartley said that, 'just as the Grill Room at the Ritz is open to all', the doors of the courts are in theory open to ordinary people, but that obtaining and acting on legal advice were 'luxuries which were beyond their reach'. Unfortunately this is exactly what has happened.

---

1 See Chapter 6.
2 *Review of Civil Litigation Costs*, by Lord Justice Jackson, published 13 March 2014.
3 *The Times*, 24 November 2011.

However, wider principles are engaged. Lord Pannick made a number of points in this seminal article which suggest that such amendments to the Bill as he considered necessary were important because otherwise rights would be

undermined to the extent that people cannot enforce their legal entitlements through the judicial process. The Law and democracy itself are brought into disrepute. The 1949 Act addressed the problem by creating a legal aid scheme by which the State funds advice and representation for the poor in appropriate cases.

His key points were:

(1) 'The Bill does not recognise that access to justice is an important constitutional principle.' He said that a duty must be imposed on the Lord Chancellor 'to secure, within the resources made available, that individuals have access to legal services that effectively meet their needs'.

(2) 'The Bill removes from the scope of legal advice and assistance family cases except where domestic violence is alleged', including 'welfare benefit cases and many other complex areas where the law is a vital safeguard of basic needs for the most vulnerable sections of society'. He added that the removal of legal aid would 'result in many hopeless claims being pursued by litigants in person and in many proper claims not being brought or being pursued ineffectively by litigants in person. Do-it-yourself litigation will be as effective as do-it-yourself medical operations ... In family law there would be what the Commons Justice Committee described as "a perverse incentive" to make allegations of domestic violence to secure legal aid.'

(3) 'The Bill confers on the Lord Chancellor by subordinate legislation to take further categories of services out of the scope of legal aid. That is inherently objectionable, and all the more so when the Bill confers no power on the Lord Chancellor to add services back into the scope of legal aid, for example if experience shows the lack of wisdom in the exclusion or when the economy improves.'

(4) 'The money that the Government hopes to save by these measures needs to be assessed by reference to the financial costs that will have to be met by the State. Judges will need to deal with many more hearings in which litigants in person waste valuable and expensive court resources. The health and housing agencies of the State will have the burden of dealing with the consequences of vulnerable children and adults being denied the benefits to which the law entitles them.'

He said that it was justifiable criticism that the government had conducted no study of the costs of the provisions contained in the Bill, and as the figures routinely emerge, they have in fact proved him entirely correct in his predictions: it is also clear that the Government did not, and still has not, grasped the costs generated by the cuts, and above all has not reacted to the situation that has been created.

The suspicion was at the time that resources would not permit a turnaround on these points, whatever the consequences; this has unfortunately proved to be the case, and although Lord Pannick's suggestion that there should be provision to add back services when the economy permitted was obviously a good one, of course that has not occurred either.

However, although family lawyers had already made all the points he singled out (and have repeated them whenever later pointing to the realisation of the predicted outcomes) this too has unfortunately been without sympathetic reception by the government. Nevertheless, the picture is perhaps not entirely as bad as it might be since, first, the most expensive financial proceedings, i.e. for financial provision on divorce or other decree, are not available at the initial stage of family breakdown as those financial provision proceedings cannot be started till after the main divorce or dissolution suit has been progressed,[4] and/or such welfare benefits as have not already suffered their own round of cuts are not the only source of financial provision at the crucial initial stage of breakdown where it used to be possible to get legal aid to obtain legal advice and representation to go to the FPC or the county court for a temporary financial order.

10.1.1 Some 'non-court' alternatives

One silver lining to this black cloud of problems is, curiously, the steadily increasing numbers of cohabitants, and projected further increases in those numbers, as cohabitants do not qualify to use any of the court applications open to the married parties and their children who have both the MCA 1973 and the DPMCA for emergency financial support on family breakdown. Thus the absence of legal aid is of no concern to them, and if they are now forming the largest group, then in logic at least numbers of women and children trying to access the MCA and DPMCA for temporary financial orders must be correspondingly reducing.

Cohabitants cannot use these statutes, as the only maintenance obligations between unformalised same-sex or opposite-sex partnerships arise not on separation but on dissolution of their unions – except for the fact, which may now be perceived as welcome, that there is an obligation in social security law for any couple living together to be responsible for each other's financial support, whether married, unmarried, in a registered civil partnership or in an informal union. While spouses and civil partners are expressly included in **Social Security Administration Act 1992** s 105, the practice of the DWP and its predecessors has always been to rely on a variety of statutory provisions[5] to treat cohabiting couples living as though they were husband and wife as one household, and to enforce this strictly even where the parties were not sleeping under the same roof all the time, thus also catching those in the 'living together apart' syndrome.

If welfare benefits are required because no other resources are available, the latest information and discussion of applicability and interaction with other resources is always available from the 'welfare benefits bible', the Child Poverty Action Group (CPAG)'s *Welfare Benefits and Tax Handbook*, of which there is usually at least an annual edition and which is sufficiently straightforward for anyone who would otherwise be an LIP to access. Although benefits are not a primary resource for financial provision on decree or dissolution of marriage or civil partnership[6] they can be in certain circumstances, including at initial family breakdown when emergency funds are required, and it is possible in view of the current economic conditions that this reliance on benefits is going to feature much more strongly in family law, and in particular the law on financial provision in the future.

However, apart from resort to welfare benefits as a regular source of income, or possibly negotiating voluntary payments, the law does provide alternatives for the separated spouse or civil partner who does not wish to petition for one of the principal decrees, and the new unified Family Court is learning to cope with LIPs accessing them.

There are three possibilities for obtaining formal maintenance in such a situation, besides which there is within the welfare benefits system an ongoing right and obligation for each spouse to support, and be supported by, the other spouse, regardless of the abolition by the **Equality Act 2010** of the common law obligation for a husband to maintain his wife and to supply her with the necessities of life.

The welfare benefits system is therefore likely to step temporarily into the financial breach on separation of a couple even if court proceedings then have to be taken to secure ongoing

---

4 See Chapter 7.
5 There are separate Regulations for the various income benefits following the Welfare Benefit and Other Payments Act 2008, the various Tax Credits, Housing Benefit and Council Tax Benefit (now called CT Rebate), and in social security law the Regulations are at least as important as the statute, since these statutory instruments are more easily and more often altered.
6 See Chapter 7.

maintenance. If proceedings are to be taken the former applications to the FPC are now available in the regional Family Court which retains the magistrates within it, the only snag being that whereas the FPC used to be found in every sizeable town and was regularly used to litigants in person, the Family Court now tends to be sited in less widely available court centres, although it still has the same magistrates sitting in it, who will retain this ability to cope with the LIP, thus affording even the LIP a channel through which to obtain maintenance.

On the other hand any same-sex or opposite-sex informal cohabitants without children will have to rely exclusively on welfare benefits (unless in either case there is a voluntary payment agreement in place) while the separated spouse/civil partner has the three options other than welfare benefits before financial provision following decree or dissolution is available, and all three court options can be obtained from the unified Family Court.

The three court options are:

(a) a maintenance order under DPMCA 1978 Part I (i.e. what used to be known as a 'matrimonial order');

(b) a maintenance order under MCA 1973 s 27 (rather similar to the income element of financial provision on divorce or dissolution, without the necessity to obtain a decree first); or

(c) a separation and maintenance agreement (a possibility frequently overlooked, although this does need to be handled carefully with regard to the possible effect on later court orders[7]). These agreements do not start with the court but in private ordering between the parties, but once made, such an agreement can be *varied* by the Family Court. This is also a remedy open to registered civil partners, who would otherwise have to use welfare benefits or go for financial provision on dissolution under the CPA 2004, and such agreements (but in their case *not* including the court's power of variation) could also be a solution for informal cohabitants of the same sex or opposite sexes.

Of these the MCA 1973 s 27 may be slightly more daunting for an LIP than the DPMCA 1978, as it was formerly a county court-level application which has an equivalent level in the Family Court, although circuit judges at this level will now be sufficiently familiar with LIPs as to make s 27 a possible jurisdiction for a party acting in person, as may now have to be all too frequent a case where there is no legal aid. The magistrates, however, were always an inexpensive, brisk venue, used regularly for processing lengthy lists with expedition, and enforcement procedures were also always extremely effective, which is expected to continue in the Family Court. Under former legal aid systems, the FPC was always the cheapest, and therefore the most likely court in which legal aid proceedings would be authorised, as it used less of the state's resources since the lay magistrates are unpaid (although they receive expenses). In the current era of austerity the family justice system is likely to see the public making increased use of the magistrates in the Family Court for the LIP accessibility mentioned.

If an applicant has a dependent resident child or children, there are two other potential sources of income, namely:

(d) the CSA or its successor the CMS as Child Support Maintenance under the **Child Support Acts 1991–95** as amended will include an element for the carer as well as for the child: see Chapter 21.

(e) the **Children Act 1989**, s 15 and Schedule 1 under which there is a power to order maintenance (and also capital and property provision including the purchase or transfer of a home if necessary: see Chapter 21) although the property provisions may not be particularly speedy

---

7 See Chapters 6 and 7.

since they are more akin to those under the MCA 1973. Nevertheless these are powerful protections for the abandoned parent of a child who cannot access any other statute. These are important resources as children will inevitably be the innocent vulnerable sufferers in the immediate aftermath of separation if parents are left to fend for themselves without adequate help and support of some kind. In this respect, court staff will doubtless be an important source of help in completing application forms despite cuts in their numbers as well. Unfortunately the CSA processes are notoriously slow.

It is therefore not entirely true that vulnerable children and women will be without any alternative to instructing lawyers on legal aid, although there may be certain disadvantages. It does suggest, however, that the FJR's recommendation that there should be a root-and-branch review of financial proceedings is well founded, since the alternative scenarios of besieged benefits offices and two levels at the new unified Family Court being clogged with LIPs, besides being an impractical backlash of the legal aid restraints, do not accord well with the government obligation to provide adequate legal processes for family maintenance where private arrangements have broken down.

10.2 Domestic Proceedings and Magistrates' Courts Act (DPMCA) 1978

If welfare benefits are not appropriate (e.g. in a *Barnes v Barnes* (1972)[8] situation where the obligation to maintain the family cannot be thrown onto the state (see Chapter 7)) and there is no potential for negotiation of a temporary voluntary arrangement, so that an order of some sort does need to be sought, a magistrates' maintenance order is probably the quickest and easiest type to obtain: the DPMCA (Domestic Proceedings and Magistrates Court Act) was the magistrates' equivalent of the MCA in the FPC but its jurisdiction was preserved in the Family Court along with magistrates who moved there when the FPC was abolished. Moreover, such an order not only has no adverse impact on later financial provision on decree or dissolution, even if a later petition is contemplated, it can also be much more convenient than MPS and it is not incompatible with petitioning for divorce.

Unless the low £1,000 per applicant ceiling on lump sums is insufficient for the expenses of the interim budget (e.g. where it is contemplated that there will be substantial legal fees to be met in processing the divorce or financial provision, in which it is now established that MPS cannot cater for these in total, so an order must be sought under MCA s 22ZA) there is much to be said for using the DPMCA order as a temporary source of funds in the often financially awkward transitional period up to decree absolute.

While the magistrates have lost to the CSA or the CMS much of their former jurisdiction to make orders for children, they can still make them for spouses and, at the same time and on the same application, include orders for children of the family not within the CSA/CMS jurisdiction. These orders are principally:

- orders for stepchildren;
- child orders outside the CSA's powers (i.e. for lump sums as opposed to periodical payments);
- orders for 'topping up' of periodical payments above the CSA's ceiling (e.g. for school or further or higher education fees); and
- orders for children over 19 who are at that age outside the CSA age limit.

---

8 [1972] 1 WLR 1381; [1972] 3 All ER 872.

The DPMCA 1978 is therefore a species of magistrates' court jurisdiction equivalent to the MCA 1973 for these purposes, for use when a decree is not, or not yet, being sought. Only a spouse can apply, but child orders can always be made at the same time provided, of course, the child in question qualifies in some way: DPMCA 1978, ss 1 and 6(1)).

The magistrates (lay Justices of the Peace ('JP's) who used to be called the 'FPC' when exercising their matrimonial and domestic jurisdiction) are based on a commission area, for which JPs are always appointed. A particular FPC used therefore to have jurisdiction to hear a DPMCA 1978 Part I application if either the applicant or the respondent ordinarily resides within the commission area in which the court is situated: DPMCA 1978, s 30. Domicile is irrelevant, unlike in divorce or one of the other principal decrees.

Three distinct orders are obtainable:

- under s 2, for which grounds set out in s 1 must be established;
- under s 6, which may be made purely on agreement of the parties;
- under s 7, where the parties have resided apart for at least three months and one has been making payments to the other for that party or for a child of the family.

As only spouses can apply under the Act, divorced (i.e. former) spouses cannot use it, nor of course can cohabitants.

A 'child of the family' is defined in DPMCA s 88 and is the same as that of a child of the family in MCA 1973 s 52 (see Chapter 7).

Children who are not children of the family cannot be included in any orders under the DPMCA 1978, but they may be able to claim maintenance under the CA 1989 (see Chapter 21).

10.2.1 The types of orders available

Both periodical payments and lump sums can be awarded but no property orders can be made under this jurisdiction (though they might be able to be made by the same magistrates under the CA 1989, if appropriate).

Periodical payments can be made weekly or monthly, for whatever term the magistrates think fit, including for a limited period, as in the case of *Robinson v Robinson* (1983),[9] where the period was for five years. However, pursuant to s 4:

- no order can *begin* before the date of the application;
- all orders *end* on the *death* of either the payer or payee; and
- an order will end on the remarriage of the payee, although any accrued arrears will remain payable provided they are claimed within one year: as s 95 of the **Magistrates' Courts Act 1980** as inserted by the **Maintenance Enforcement Act (MEA) 1991** gives the magistrates power to remit them in whole or part, and they usually will remit all arrears over a year old and might do so faster in the case of remarriage. Therefore, application for enforcement in this case should be prompt.

Divorce has *no effect* on a DPMCA order. Cohabitation has very little effect. Both s 2 and s 6 orders can still be *made* if the parties are living together, though s 7 orders cannot and a s 7 order will cease *immediately* if the parties resume cohabiting: s 25(3). However, even s 2 and s 6 orders will be *discharged* if the parties cohabit for more than six months at any time: s 25(1).

Orders for *children* are totally unaffected by their parents' cohabitation: s 25(2).

---

9 [1983] 1 All ER 391; [1983] Fam 42.

Children's orders end at 17: s 5(2), unless s 5(3) applies which permits the court to make:

- an order for a child which will last beyond the child's 18th birthday;
- an order for a child already over 18. In either case such an order can be made if:
  - the child is in full time education or training (whether or not also in gainful employment); or
  - there are special circumstances justifying the order.

Such periodical payments will always end on the death of the payer.

Lump sums are subject to a limit of £1,000: s 2(3), though where there are children more than £1,000 may be awarded by giving lump sums to each of them as well as £1,000 to the applicant spouse: *Burridge v Burridge* (1982).[10] Moreover, the £1,000 limit does not apply if the order is made by agreement under s 6.

Lump sums can be made payable by instalments or time can be given for payment: Magistrates' Courts Act 1980, s 75. There is no rule that lump sums cannot be ordered unless the payer has capital, since all that is necessary is that the payer should have capacity to pay, from income or otherwise: *Burridge v Burridge*, above.

Where a lump sum order is payable by instalments, these can subsequently be varied, on application to the court, either as to amounts or numbers of instalments or dates on which they are payable: DPMCA 1978, s 22.

Altogether this presents an extremely useful opportunity to obtain quick, easy and inexpensive provision, the only real drawback being the limit on lump sums (though the limit of £1,000 applying to each applicant, i.e. spouse and any number of qualifying children can assist in that respect) and the lack of a property order jurisdiction.

10.3 Orders under the DPMCA 1978 s 2

Periodical payments and lump sums can be ordered for a party to a marriage or to a child of the family if the other party to the marriage has:

- failed to provide reasonable maintenance for a spouse;
- failed to provide reasonable maintenance for any child of the family;
- behaved in such a way that the applicant cannot reasonably be expected to live with that other party;
- deserted the applicant.

The grounds can be relied on in the alternative. Brief details of any behaviour alleged must be given in the written application for a s 2 order, which must now be made on Form 1 specified under the current rules which are the FPR 2010 as amended.

10.3.1 How 'reasonable maintenance' is determined

There is no formula in the Act or elsewhere. The court simply:

- takes the figure which it would have ordered if making an order from scratch on the basis of the s 3 considerations set out below; and

---

10 [1982] 3 All ER 80.

- compares it with what is being paid; if it is significantly less, the respondent is not making reasonable provision.

There is no need to prove that the respondent's failure is morally reprehensible, indeed the respondent need not even know that maintenance is required, so the ground can even be proved by a wife in desertion, as in the case of *Robinson v Robinson* mentioned above, which would clearly be illogical if any moral element were required in the failure to pay.

The respondent is *probably still failing to provide reasonable maintenance* even if a suitable amount has been hurriedly paid between the application and the hearing. There is no specific decision on the point, although by analogy the case of *Irvin v Irvin* (1968)[11] decided that in the case of *desertion* that must continue up to the date of the hearing, so the same approach would mean that if the track record of failure to maintain had not been sustained there would be no basis for the application. However, it is thought that it is equally logical that one or two payments cannot alter a well-established pattern of *chronic* failure, since it would be ridiculous if a respondent could get out of paying regularly simply by making such trivial and token payments just before coming to court.

10.3.2 Establishing behaviour and desertion

These are the same as under the MCA 1973.

The test for *behaviour* is exactly the same: *Bergin v Bergin* (1983).[12] Cohabitation after the last incident of behaviour is irrelevant, although application must be made to the magistrates within six months of the last incident relied on, unless it is a continuing form of behaviour which is alleged: Magistrates' Courts Act 1980, s 127.

The elements of desertion are also exactly the same as under the MCA 1973, save that it is not necessary for a period of two years to have passed since the desertion – simple desertion with no particular minimum period is all that is required.

10.3.3 Matters to which the court must have regard when making s 2 orders: DPMCA 1978 s 3

This is the magistrates' equivalent of s 25 of the MCA 1973.

By s 3(1) there is the same general duty as under s 25(2) of the MCA 1973, whereby the court must consider all the circumstances of the case, giving first consideration to the welfare while a minor of any child of the family who has not attained the age of 18.

The s 3 factors are virtually the same as those under s 25 of the MCA 1973 except for the following:

(1) Section 3(2)(c) directs the court to have regard to the standard of living enjoyed by the parties to the marriage before the *occurrence of the conduct alleged* (compare MCA s 25, where the standard is that before the breakdown of the marriage).

(2) There is no s 3 equivalent of MCA s 25(2)(h) whereby the court considers the value to each of the parties of any benefit that might be lost by the dissolution of the marriage (e.g. a pension), as the magistrates do not dissolve marriages and thus do not trigger any such loss which might depend on status.

---

11 [1968] 1 WLR 464; [1968] 1 All ER 27.
12 [1983] 1 WLR 274; [1983] 1 All ER 905; [1983] 4 FLR 344.

The clean break provisions also do not apply before the magistrates for the same reason.

The old so-called 'one-third rule'[13] does apply if it is appropriate to the case, but often it is not because of the relatively limited means of those who normally apply to the magistrates. There is, however, no rule that only those of limited means may use the DPMCA, nor is it at all unknown for it to be used as an easier alternative to MPS, however well off the parties might be.

The magistrates now take the same approach to conduct as is the case under the MCA 1973 in the higher jurisdictions. For a time between 1973 and 1978, when the magistrates finally received jurisdiction in their own new 'MCA 1973 equivalent Act' in the DPMCA 1978, there was a difference, since the magistrates were then applying the law as it had universally been before the DRA 1969 changed the approach of the divorce courts, while the county court and High Court was already applying the new regime.

10.4 Agreed orders under the DPMCA 1978 s 6

This is the magistrates' version of a consent order: the only grounds are that the parties have agreed the order: s 6(1). The type(s) of financial provision agreed, and the amount and term of any periodical payments, must be specified in the written application, which must be made on the form specified for the purpose. Either party, payer or payee, may apply for the order to be made. However, it is not a rubber-stamping procedure since there is still a general duty for the court to be satisfied that the provision is broadly right.

By s 6(3) the court has the right to approve financial provision for a child and will not do so unless it considers that the order makes a proper contribution towards the child's financial needs. Otherwise, the court will normally make s 6 orders if:

● it is satisfied that the applicant or the respondent as the case may be has agreed to make the provision; and
● it has no reason to think that it would be contrary to the interests of justice to exercise its powers under s 6.

If it is not so satisfied, the court will refuse to make the order unless the parties agree to make any amendments which the court wishes to see made, including that either party makes any further provision that the court requires: s 6(5).

The *advantages* of having a s 6 order are that:

(a) the parties are more likely to observe an order which they had a hand in putting together, rather than one that is imposed on them from above;
(b) the terms of the parties' agreement are embodied in the order just as on a consent order after divorce; and
(c) neither party can repudiate the order unilaterally.

On the other hand, once made, the order can only be varied by agreement of both parties on returning to court for a variation, which might put some parties off. The court can treat a s 2 application as a s 6 application if the parties agree terms before the s 2 application is heard.

---

13 See Chapter 7.

10.5 Orders under the DPMCA 1978 s 7 to continue voluntary payments made during separation

The advantage of this order is that it can be made where the parties are living apart but where they cannot:

- make out any one of the four grounds required for a s 2 order; or
- come to a sufficient agreement for a s 6 order.

The parties *must* have been living apart for a continuous period of three months, neither being in desertion since that would permit an order under s 2. One of the parties must have been paying maintenance for the benefit of the other or of a child of the family.

The payee party must specify in the application the aggregate amount of payments made by the other to that party and the children of the family in the three months: s 7(1). The respondent cannot be ordered to pay more under the order than the rate of payment during the three months: s 7(3)(a). The court must check that the order is in line with what they would have ordered under s 2 (s 7(3)(b) and (3)(c)), in other words:

- not too much; and
- not to a child of the family who is not the respondent's child unless they would have ordered this.

The court will not make an order under this section if it thinks that it would not provide reasonable maintenance for a child: s 7(4) or for the applicant, and would then treat a s 7 application as one for a s 2 order.

The s 3 considerations apply to s 7 orders, including the standard of living enjoyed by the parties, prior in this case to their separation, rather than prior to the conduct relied on in s 2: s 3(2)(c).

10.6 Procedure

This is very straightforward and it has not for some time been uncommon to find LIPs before the magistrates so that the current economy measures restricting legal aid are not likely either to concern that court unduly or to impact significantly adversely on an applicant who has to conduct a case personally.

Application is on a form. The forms contain a statement of means of the applicant, which must be completed when the application is prepared, a notice of hearing (or directions appointment) which the court completes, and a blank form for the respondent's answer and statement of means (which the respondent will complete in due course). Public funding has for a long time been very limited and although in theory some may be available for financial proceedings where a party qualifies this is subject to a cost–benefit analysis and now to the new restrictions.

The application is lodged at the court with a copy for service on the respondent and the justices' clerk (now called the 'legal or judicial adviser') will fix the date, time and place for the hearing (or directions) and enter these details.

Pursuant to the **Magistrates' Courts Act 1980** s 65 as amended, the hearings are domestic proceedings and are held in private with a restricted attendance, including only court officers, the parties, their legal representatives, witnesses and other persons directly concerned with the case, the press, and, pursuant to s 69(2) of that Act, 'any other person whom the court may in its discretion permit'. By s 67(2), it must be before magistrates from the domestic panel and there should be a man and a woman among them: s 66. The respondent is supposed to attend, and failing such attendance there is likely to be an adjournment, although the court can proceed in his or her absence. A respondent to a s 6 application can send a statement of means and need not attend.

The allegation is put to the respondent, but such is the habit of centuries and the parochial manner of proceeding in the magistrates' court that the evidence is usually still heard anyway – even if the respondent admits everything – though this may not continue in the Family Court.

The applicant opens the case, witnesses are called and examined, cross-examined and re-examined, and then the respondent (or his or her advocate) addresses the court. If there is a question of law, the respondent's advocate (if any) will be given leave to address the court on that and then, if there is a further speech for the respondent, the applicant will have a second speech also.

If either party is an LIP, the court is under a duty to help that party: Magistrates' Courts Act 1980, s 73; in this circumstance, the case may take a long time since such help must be meticulous. This is probably the only drawback of the likely increase in the magistrates' work following the restrictions on legal aid, in that more applicants will lead them to overrun their sitting times, while the duty to help LIPs will make the overload worse. However, the magistrates have been dealing with parochial-style justice in this way since the mid-fourteenth century (when they were actually created to address another national economic crisis – in that case the Black Death, so that the justices were needed to administer the Statute of Labourers) so it is unlikely that they will be completely unable to deal with contemporary pressures although there may be some delay.

The court has power to make interim orders: DPMCA 1978, s 19, although this has been reduced by the CSA jurisdiction. Such orders can be backdated: s 19(3), but will expire when the case is finally determined, or after three months or some other date specified by the court. By s 19(7), only one interim order is supposed to be made, but that can be extended if time is running out, provided it does not last for longer than three months from the first extension, so that an interim order has a maximum life of six months: s 19(6).

10.7 Variation

All orders are variable, revocable or can be suspended. The format is to consider the case *de novo*. Some sort of change of circumstances will be required and the court can give effect to any agreement between the parties so far as it seems just to do so: s 20(1). On variation, the court will be able to specify the method of payment of the new order if it has not already done so in respect of the earlier one: **Maintenance Enforcement Act (MEA) 1991**, s 4, amending the Magistrates' Courts Act 1980, s 60. Suspended provisions of an order can be revived under s 20(6). Curiously, periodical payments orders under ss 2 and 6 can be varied by making lump sum orders, but this power does not apply to those orders made under s 7.

10.8 Enforcement

The magistrates have always been well known for enforcement and this role continues today, including of foreign orders, which have always been able to be registered with a particular FPC; this should continue with the new unified Family Court though it may take time for foreign courts to realise the changes that have taken place to constitute the single unified Family Court.

Since even before the MEA 1991 the clerk provided an excellent service in receiving and paying out maintenance and enforcing any order which was not paid, and for this a legal aid certificate often extended to registration in the magistrates' court of one substantive order obtained elsewhere. Besides this, the 'diversion procedure' developed to ensure payment of welfare benefits by the relevant government department (which would then recover maintenance from an unreliable payer in order to reimburse the public money thus utilised) has always been extremely useful to those applicants who would otherwise be on welfare benefits one week and chasing maintenance payments from their 'exes' the next.

The MEA 1991 was originally an interim measure pending the implementation of the CSA 1991 in April 1993, but it has nevertheless made some useful permanent contributions to enforcement of maintenance payments generally. Pursuant to s 2, an amendment to the Magistrates' Courts Act 1980 s 59 enabled magistrates for the first time to specify how payments should be made, e.g. by standing order or attachment of earnings, previously only possible if the debtor consented or was previously in default on payments, due to wilful refusal or culpable neglect. The court could even for the first time require that a bank account be opened to enable a standing order to be set up.

Now any DPMCA 1978 money orders may be enforced as a magistrates' maintenance order: DPMCA 1978, s 32(1). This is effected by:

- attachment of earnings: Attachment of Earnings Act (AEA) 1971;
- committal to prison: Magistrates' Court Act 1980, s 76;
- distress (also s 76); or
- registration in the High Court under the Maintenance Orders Act 1958: not generally worthwhile except for high sums, e.g. accumulated arrears, but it does permit access to High Court methods of enforcement which may frighten the payer, e.g. sequestration which is notoriously expensive.

Foreign orders are sometimes registered with the magistrates for the area where a respondent resides when the clerk will enforce them in the same way as an English order. There are reciprocal enforcement provisions in respect of a number of foreign jurisdictions, which the trainee may sometimes have to research to enforce English orders overseas and vice versa. See *The Family Court Practice*[14] ('the Red Book') for full particulars of participating jurisdictions.

10.8.1 Committal to prison

There are stringent conditions before this method can be used:

(a)   the court must be of the opinion that the debtor has not paid due to wilful refusal or culpable neglect;

(b)   attachment of earnings or some other method if available must be used first unless the court is of the opinion that that is inappropriate; and

(c)   the debtor must be present when imprisonment is imposed: Magistrates' Courts Act 1980, s 93(6).

The maximum is only six weeks: s 93(7). However, pursuant to s 76 and Schedule 4, a lesser maximum may apply, and payment of the debt will prevent imprisonment, or secure release if it has already been imposed, with reduction in the time to serve *pro rata* for part payment: s 79, and arrears do not accrue, unless the court otherwise directs, while the debtor is in prison: s 94.

It is, however, fairly easy to avoid committal. Any debtor can apply for the order to be reviewed and the warrant of committal cancelled: Maintenance Orders Act 1958, s 18(4), and although the debt is not cancelled by time served, it is not possible to be imprisoned more than once for the same debt: Magistrates' Courts Act 1980.

---

14 Jordans, Bristol, 2014; this new edition has all the latest information following the inauguration of the Family Court in April 2014.

Most usually the court will suspend any committal order if the debtor pays the maintenance in future and also pays something off the arrears each week: Magistrates' Courts Act 1980, s 72(2). The debtor will be warned if he stops paying before the warrant is issued so as to have a chance to show cause why the committal order should not take effect, and only if that opportunity is not successfully seized will committal occur: Maintenance Orders Act 1958, s 18. Sometimes the court will merely adjourn the hearing to see what the debtor does. If no attempts have been made to pay by the time the adjourned hearing resumes, then committal may well follow.

10.8.2 Enforcement procedure

The clerk normally automatically brings proceedings for enforcement if requested in writing to do so by the payee: Magistrates' Courts Act 1980, s 59. This was the major advantage of the clerk's service in the days before the MEA 1991 or the CSA and, as the court kept the record of payment (or non-payment), proof of default was easy. The clerk now has a standing authority to take proceedings if payment is normally made through the court. The Magistrates' Courts Act 1980 was amended by the MEA 1991 to insert new ss 59A and 59B to facilitate this type of enforcement, and s 59B imposes financial sanctions if the debtor fails to make payments by the methods which can now be specified. By s 94A (inserted by the MEA 1991, s 8), interest can now be ordered on all or part of unpaid maintenance.

The debtor will normally receive a summons for proceedings, but if necessary a warrant of arrest will be issued: s 93(5).

10.9 Matrimonial Causes Act (MCA) 1973 s 27

This section allows a freestanding application to the Family Court (i.e. which used to be to the county court) for financial relief without petitioning for any of the principal decrees, though a s 27 order can also be made after a decree of judicial separation.

By s 27(1), either party may apply if the other spouse has failed to:

- provide reasonable maintenance for the applicant; or
- provide or make reasonable contribution towards reasonable maintenance for any child of the family.

An order is available upon proof of the fact; it is apparently no longer necessary that the respondent should actually know of the requirement for maintenance and of course, as in the case of the DPMCA 1978, it is not necessary for the failure to pay to be morally reprehensible.

The possible orders available under this section are those for:

- periodical payments;
- secured periodical payments; and
- unlimited lump sums including by instalments.

Lump sums orders can be made for any purpose, including to defray debts incurred in providing reasonable maintenance for the applicant and/or children prior to the application. No maintenance pending suit is possible since the application is the whole suit, unlike in the case of financial provision following a divorce suit.

Orders are available for both spouse and children irrespective of failure to maintain only one or the other of them.

The s 25 considerations must be taken into account as on financial provision, and the duration of orders is the same as after one of the principal decrees: MCA 1973, ss 28 and 29.

This section has been very little used in the past as it involved county court costs, and normally the applicant has sought funding as for financial provision on divorce with the sole small benefit over the DPMCA 1978 that lump sums ordered are subject to no limit. However, it is very likely to be used more by LIPs now that all applications are to the Family Court, especially regionally, since if access to maintenance orders is required and financial provision cannot be accessed at the time (i.e. if no petition has been issued yet) this is the obvious remedy if the magistrates' jurisdiction is unsuitable.

10.10 Separation and maintenance agreements

It is often forgotten that a separation or maintenance agreement is a seriously viable alternative to a formal order from a court, and that if it is carefully drafted such an agreement can also actually be superior to an order where no proceedings for a principal decree are immediately contemplated. They can also be used by civil partners who need maintenance after separation. They do have certain advantages:

(1)   Within reason an agreement can be designed to incorporate virtually whatever provisions the spouses desire to include, thus importing more flexibility than even the most advantageous consent or agreed order, which can only include either clauses which the court is able to order under MCA 1973 ss 23 and 24 or undertakings which the court is willing to accept. These categories exclude all orders which only a can make under the CA 1989, whereas an agreement is able to incorporate arrangements for the care of the children.

(2)   Agreements are cheaper and less trouble than obtaining an order from the court, which is bound to be an attraction in the present context of both restricted legal aid and MIAM-controlled access to courts.

(3)   Agreements provide evidence of the fact that the parties regarded the marriage as at an end, which is essential for proving separation when that is necessary in divorce and judicial separation, and of the *date* of such separation: *Santos v Santos* (1972).[15] The same would be true of later access to civil partnership remedies.

(4)   An agreement which is observed will rebut any claim on the basis of failure to maintain under either the MCA 1973 or DPMCA 1978.

(5)   Any tax relief available for a court order is similarly available for an agreement.[16]

(6)   Human nature being what it is, the parties are more likely to observe an agreement they have forged themselves with the assistance of their lawyers (and more likely to embark on such observance in a non-confrontational frame of mind conducive to a fresh start which will benefit themselves as well as the children) than if they have just been engaging in adversarial litigation, which often brings out the worst in the parties even if the case settles.

However, there are *disadvantages* in that such agreements can be:

(a)   more difficult to enforce;

(b)   not so final, as the court's ultimate financial provision jurisdiction cannot be ousted;

(c)   not so easily varied unless the parties agree; and

(d)   unless the agreement is within MCA 1973 s 34 (see below), consent of both parties will be needed to effect any variation. Care also needs to be taken with drafting as there are a few points to watch.

---

15 [1972] Fam 247, see Chapter 5.
16 Although tax relief is now largely irrelevant.

An agreement for immediate separation is legal, as is a *resumption of cohabitation* agreement containing provisions for *possible* future separation if the reconciliation does not work out.

❖ CASE EXAMPLE

In *Wilson v Wilson* (1848)[17] it was established that an agreement for future separation is in itself *invalid* as being contrary to public policy because it prejudices the status of marriage and probably would have the same effect in the case of registered civil partnership especially when civil partners have obtained the right[18] to enter into legal marriage, but that such an agreement is *valid* if the parties are *already separated* or on the point of it since it may regulate their life following the *fact* of separation.

In *Re Meyrick's Settlement* (1921),[19] however, it was established that care was still needed in drafting as even such agreements for *resumption of cohabitation* needed such careful drafting so that the overall effect of the agreement is to *promote reconciliation*.

Separation and maintenance agreements can be oral or written but are usually *written*, for obvious reasons, and are usually by deed.

10.10.1 Usual clauses

To live separate and apart
This clause terminates both the duty to cohabit and therefore precludes desertion whether it has begun or might otherwise begin; if such a clause is not included, the agreement is only a *maintenance* agreement so that desertion can still start or continue.

Not to take matrimonial (or presumably civil partnership) proceedings if a CP agreement
This must be expressly included and will not be implied. It is not contrary to public policy as ousting the jurisdiction of the court, because the effect is to forgive past conduct (none of which can then be used in proceedings in the future) rather than to preclude filing a petition.

The clause is sometimes called a '*Rose v Rose* clause' after *Rose v Rose* (1883),[20] which gave it its name.

Non-molestation clause
This is a clause which excludes any act that would annoy a reasonable spouse and excludes any act done with the *authority* of the spouse as well as personally by that spouse. It does not preclude starting divorce proceedings, as was established in *Fearon v Aylesford* (1884).[21]

---

17 (1848) 1 HLC 538.
18 Pursuant to s 9 of the Marriage (Same-Sex Couples) Act 2014, but not yet available to existing civil partners; see Chapter 8.
19 [1921] 1 Ch 311.
20 (1883) 8 PD 98.
21 (1884) 14 QBD 792.

A *dum casta* clause (literally 'whilst chaste')

This must also be *expressly* included. It is still sometimes inserted for the protection of husbands whose liability to maintain a wife who is committing adultery can then be ended. Such a clause probably would not be appropriate in a same-sex partnership separation agreement since there is no adultery Fact included in the CPS 2004 and registered civil partnerships do not require consummation or indeed any sexual relationship. However, since virtually *any* term can be included in a privately negotiated agreement some clause limiting cohabitation with another person of either sex could be appropriate on the basis that this would give rise to an alternative source of maintenance.

Maintenance for either party

This can take the form of periodical payments, secured or unsecured, or lump sums and should again ideally be limited by some phrase such as 'while the parties are married and living apart', which, coupled with a *dum casta* clause, prevents a husband from assuming an open-ended obligation which might otherwise last not only beyond adultery or cohabitation with another man but possibly even after the death of the payer when it could still be enforced against his estate, and as indicated above future cohabitation with another person might be appropriate in a same-sex partnership separation agreement.

The impact of the CSA on such agreements should not be forgotten – if any member of the family is on benefits, the CSA assessment will take priority over anything agreed under such a clause, and such a clause would also not prevent the carer parent from asking the CSA for an assessment which again would take priority over the agreement: CSA 1991, s 9(2) and (3). It would, however, be possible to link any such assessment to a reduced share of the division of any family property (e.g. at the triggering event of a *Mesher* type order, which can be included in the property clause of the agreement; see below).

Great care is required in drafting this clause – there should be no covenant not to claim maintenance from the court (as this is void since it tends to oust the jurisdiction of the court). If such a covenant is included, the remainder of the agreement is valid: MCA 1973, s 34(1), including any other financial arrangements: s 34(1)(b), but this will *not* be the case if the *whole purpose of the agreement* can be interpreted as to oust the jurisdiction of the court, in which case the entire agreement, and *not just the objectionable covenant*, will be *void* and *of no effect*.

An agreement relating to property

This could be, for example, a *Mesher* or similar type trust regulating the occupation of the matrimonial home during the children's minority and providing for eventual sale and division of the proceeds.

Care and maintenance of children

This type of clause is only enforceable if for the benefit of the child or children.

There are two very important points in relation to these agreements:

(1) Stipulations encouraging the end of marriage will always be void.
(2) Both parties should have *separate legal advice* so as to obviate any suggestion of fraud, *mistake* or *undue influence*.

10.10.2 Applying to the court to vary written financial arrangements: MCA 1973 s 34(2)

This only applies to certain written agreements under this Act, and oral agreements cannot be varied under s 34. The reason is that MCA 1973 ss 35 and 36 permit variation of written agreements which meet the definition in s 34(2) by the court if the parties cannot agree this themselves, so it is essential first to know to which agreements this applies, and second, what are the precise terms of the agreement which is to be varied, which is hardly compatible with the variation of oral agreements of which the record, if any, may be disputed.

The agreements which are within the section are:

(a) any agreements containing financial arrangements whether made during the continuance or after the dissolution or annulment of the marriage; and

(b) separation agreements which contain no financial arrangements in a case where no other agreement between the same parties contains such arrangements.

There is a wide interpretation of 'financial arrangements': the term includes periodical payments and any dispositions for both parties and any child, not necessarily a child of the family.

10.10.3 Potential snags

There are a few points which need to be observed.

Observing all the rules

This is very important as case law shows how vital it is to be careful in observing all the rules applying to separation and maintenance agreements if one wants to apply to the court either for variation or enforcement.

❖ CASE EXAMPLE

In *Sutton v Sutton* (1984)[22] the wife entered into an oral agreement which was not formalised as a deed or even put into writing after the parties were divorced. The husband was supposed to transfer the home to the wife and she to pay the mortgage and not to apply for maintenance. He did not make the transfer. The wife could not apply to the court to vary the agreement as it was oral and thus outside s 34. She could not apply to enforce it either as it purported to oust the jurisdiction of the court under ss 23 and 24 and therefore rendered the whole agreement void. She thus had to fall back on applying under s 24 in the normal way for a transfer of property order ancillary to divorce as the only means of getting financial arrangements moving again.

There is certainly potential for much more of this type of muddle in the likely context of more DIY divorce and financial provision following the removal of legal aid in this type of case.

It will be necessary to show that because of a change in circumstances (including a foreseen change) since the arrangements in the agreement were made, there should be an alteration to make different arrangements or that the agreement does not contain proper arrangements for a child of the family.

---

22 [1984] 2 WLR 146; [1984] 1 All ER 168.

The court's discretionary powers on variation

Variation by the court includes revocation or insertion of such arrangements as appear just, having regard to all the circumstances: s 35(2). *Gorman v Gorman* (1964)[23] established that this will be considered from an objective point of view.

Sometimes the court will decide to vary an agreement because of subsequent change of circumstances. Sometimes the circumstances are adjudged not to be sufficiently changed.

> ### ❖ CASE EXAMPLES
>
> In *D v D* (1974),[24] for example, the fact that the parties had taken legal advice when making the agreement made the court decide against variation when the home, which the wife had agreed to transfer for only £1,500, suddenly escalated in value, part of the reasoning being that by the time of the application the husband had remarried and had spent considerable sums on the house so it did not seem fair to change the agreement.
>
> In *Simister v Simister (No 2)* (1987),[25] however, the court did vary the agreement. The husband had agreed to pay one-third of his salary to the wife, and when he received a very substantial increase he tried to argue that it exceeded her needs – clearly a different situation, especially because of the importance of needs in deciding what a wife should receive in accordance with the established rules of quantum.

Agreements are variable after the death of the payer if:

- they provide for payment after death; or
- the deceased died domiciled in England and Wales: MCA 1973 s 36.

An alternative is always available in this case, namely to apply under the **Inheritance (Provision for Family and Dependants) Act 1975**.

10.10.4 Procedure for application to the court for variation

Application could previously be made either to the county court or the FPC and will now be to the Family Court. The county court powers have always been wider and included inserting:

- unlimited lump sums;
- secured and unsecured periodical payments;
- property adjustment orders; and
- variation of periodical payment orders.

The FPC could only:

- vary or terminate periodical payments orders;
- insert unsecured periodical payments: MCA 1973 s 35(3).

---

23 [1964] 3 All ER 739.
24 [1974] 118 SJ 715.
25 [1987] 1 FLR 194.

Transfer to the High Court is possible. Matrimonial and Family Proceedings Act 1984, s 37; Practice Direction [1987] 1 All ER 1087. Now the Family Court is likely to decide the level of court to which an application should be allocated.

10.10.5 The effect on future financial applications of entering into an agreement

The existence of such an agreement will always be considered in subsequent financial provision proceedings as part of all the circumstances of the case: MCA 1973 s 25, because the jurisdiction can never be ousted. Whether the substance of the agreement will influence the court is another matter and will depend on the particular circumstances. Some principles emerge from the case law on the subject.

The basic situation is that no agreement will ever prevent the court from using all its usual powers under MCA 197 ss 23 and 24, because it is simply not possible to oust the jurisdiction of the court. However, the fact that the agreement was entered into, whether freely or not, whether with advice, and the extent to which the agreement has been carried out by both parties, will all be relevant to the general duty under s 25: *Dean v Dean* (1978).[26] Nevertheless, an earlier agreement can act as a 'lock out' for future exercise of that jurisdiction by the court.

❖ CASE EXAMPLES

In *Edgar v Edgar* (1980)[27] Mrs Edgar entered into a maintenance agreement with her husband which included a term that she would not apply to the court for maintenance, although her solicitors told her that the court would give her better terms. When divorce proceedings were later started, she did apply to the court, thus breaking the agreement. However, the court decided in its discretion that it would not go behind the agreement since the view inevitably was that she was bound as she had had legal advice. The moral of this case would appear to be that if a client wants to do this sort of thing, it is better done behind the solicitor's back, since taking advice and ignoring it is fatal and is an awful warning of what happens when advice *is* obtained and is then *ignored*. This may be particularly important now in view of the fact that in *Radmacher v Granatino* (2010)[28] the Supreme Court held Mr Granatino to the pre-marital agreement he had entered into with his wife even though he had *not* had independent legal advice and did not speak the language of the agreement well (as it was not his first language). The evidence was that he had not taken legal advice since he knew what the agreement stated and had decided that he was going to enter into it because, like his fiancée, he came from a wealthy family and at that time did not apparently consider he needed to protect his future income needs.

In *Jessel v Jessel* (1979),[29] however, the court decided to intervene although the wife had clearly agreed not to apply under MCA 1973 s 31 to increase an existing order. It is fair to say that this does sometimes happen, if there is some reason to strike down the

---

26 [1978] 3 WLR 288; [1978] 3 All ER 758.
27 [1980] 1 WLR 1410 already mentioned in Chapter 6.
28 [2010] UKSC 42.
29 [1979] 1 WLR 1148; [1979] 3 All ER 645.

agreement, such as a clear vitiating factor (e.g. lack of independent legal advice). However, if the Supreme Court was not willing to do so in the case of Mr Granatino, who had clearly signed away his needs without any provision in the agreement for the change in his financial circumstances – which in his case *had* occurred by the time of his litigation over the agreement – it is hard to see the logic of how the courts will decide where to interpose their discretion.

As a result of this decision trends in the consideration of pre-nuptial agreements indicate that the weight to be given to the terms of any separation or maintenance agreement on subsequent divorce and application for financial provision is still uncertain unless there is a clear *Edgar* type situation.

It therefore should be stressed that it is more than likely that, following the Supreme Court's decision and the trend towards both autonomy in private ordering and the economy-driven discouragement of litigation, such agreements will be more easily upheld in the future. They should therefore only safely be entered into if this risk is accepted, especially as it is now more than ever clear that any separation and maintenance agreement (particularly in the context of obtaining some temporary financial resources pending taking divorce or other proceedings) needs to be considered very carefully; Mrs Edgar's case makes it clear that it can be a short-term benefit but a longer term false step.[30]

It was hoped that there might be some further light shed on these short-term remedies if there were shortly a Law Commission comprehensive investigation into reform of financial provision as recommended by the FJR[31] since there is a clear distinction between their current work on pre- and post-nuptial marital agreements (on which they have reported) and a separation agreement designed to serve a short-term financial purpose. However, there is at present no sign of further reform of financial provision,[32] although Baroness Deech has introduced a Divorce Financial Provision Bill[33] into the House of Lords as a private member's Bill which has achieved a second reading – but it does not deal with the impact of short-term agreements prior to application for long term financial provision.

10.11 Which remedy?

The choice of short-term financial remedy following separation and without divorce or other decree will obviously depend on the circumstances of the individual applicant, who should weigh up the pros and cons of each possibility and make a decision based on convenience to the case. However, if the rules are *observed* to avoid the hazards which can arise, and the agreement is carefully drafted, there is much to be said in the case of separated spouses for an agreement which can be varied under MCA 1973 ss 34–36, since on balance that combines the best of all

---

30 See Chapter 6 for discussion of pre- and post-marital agreements as a tool for achieving certainty in ancillary relief.
31 See Chapter 7.
32 Other than procedurally, in the forthcoming MAP (Money Arrangements Programme of the new Family Court) mentioned above in fn 34 of Chapter 1. When this programme is finally complete it will be fully detailed on the supporting website.
33 Progress of this Bill too late for inclusion in this book will be followed in the associated website updates.

the remedies and is unlikely to affect subsequent financial provision if it is clearly crafted to serve the short term.

10.12 Current debates

Ideas for research on these current discussion questions can be accessed on the companion website updates.

- Reform of financial provision, including short-term maintenance solutions pending divorce or other decree, as recommended by the FJR.
- Enforceability of marital and other personal partnering agreements, including separation agreements.
- The role of mediation and family arbitration in resolving financial disputes.

10.13 Summary of Chapter 10

Potential sources of financial support without a decree or dissolution order

- There are three to five possible such sources other than voluntary payments or welfare benefits: an order under the DPMCA 1978, an order under MCA 1973 s 27 or a separation/maintenance agreement, plus (where an applicant has children) the CSA/CMS and CA 1989.
- These other resources of benefits and agreements are more often likely to be used now following the legal aid restrictions created by LASPO 2012.
- However, if a court application is essential this is now becoming an established option for LIPs, especially as the former FPC magistrates, who now sit in the new unified Family Court, are used to LIPs, so their jurisdiction has other litigant-friendly advantages, besides which the local county courts judges have also been absorbed into the new Family Court and will have already become used to seeing many LIPs too.
- Possibilities are more limited for civil partners and informally cohabiting persons whether same sex or opposite sex.

DPMCA 1978

- The DPMCA 1978 provides the usual (normally contested) adversarial orders under s 2, agreed orders under s 6 or a formalising order (where there is a regular pattern of payments already established) under s 7. These are likely to be used more for interim maintenance as the magistrates from the former FPC now sit at their own level in the Family Court and are used to LIPs.
- Orders under s 2 are made on the basis of failure to maintain either spouse or child, desertion (no particular period required) or behaviour, which has the same meaning as in the MCA 1973. The magistrates make orders in accordance with its own criteria under DPMCA s 3, which is similar to MCA 1973 s 25, save that the magistrates will not dissolve the marriage so there is no room for an equivalent tomcat s 25(2)(h).
- Only periodical payments and lump sum orders may be made (no property adjustment orders) and lump sums are limited to £1,000 per person involved in the application (i.e. each child may also receive £1,000).

- The CSA/CMS has removed the courts' periodical payments jurisdiction over natural children whose absent parent can be assessed by the CSA under the CSAs 1991–95 as amended.
- Enforcement is particularly efficient in the magistrates' jurisdiction and orders obtained elsewhere, including overseas, may be registered with them for enforcement. Such orders may be varied as well as enforced.
- For an applicant with a resident child or children there is also CA 1989 s 15 and Schedule 1.

MCA 1973 s 27

- MCA 1973 s 27 provides a similar jurisdiction, without restriction on the amount of lump sums.

Separation or maintenance agreements

- While there are common standard clauses, separation or maintenance agreements may contain virtually any provisions the parties wish.
- Provided that any child provisions are for the benefit of the child or children concerned, and the agreement is not void for seeking to oust the jurisdiction of the court or (if read as encouraging future separation) being contrary to public policy because such a provision undermines the status of marriage.
- Such provisions can either make the whole agreement void or, if severable, merely be disregarded.
- There are advantages of agreements as opposed to orders: e.g. such agreements are flexible, cheaper and more likely to be observed if crafted by the parties; and disadvantages in that they are more difficult to enforce and vary unless the parties are in agreement.
- There is, however, statutory provision for the variation of written agreements (and separation and maintenance agreements are usually by deed).
- Such agreements are always taken into account by the court on any future application to them for financial provision, but may or may not influence the subsequent decision.
- Usually if the parties have both had independent legal advice they will be held to their agreement, unless it is manifestly unfair, or disadvantageous to a child.

Which remedy?

- The circumstances of the applicant (and if applicable children) requiring provision will dictate which is the most appropriate source of financial provision in their case.
- It is essential to draft separation and/or maintenance agreements carefully so that they do not preclude application to the court for ancillary relief at a later stage unless they are intended to be a final agreement

10.14 Further reading

Supporting Families, Home Office, 1998.

Child Poverty Action Group, *Welfare Benefits and Tax Credits Handbook*, 16th edition 2014–2015, London, CPAG.

Cretney, S, Masson, J and Bailey-Harris, R, *Principles of Family Law*, London, Sweet & Maxwell, 2002, p 78.

Department for Work and Pensions, public consultation, *Supporting Separated Families: Securing children's futures*, Cm8399, July 2012.

Jackson, J, *Splitting up Precedents,* London, Sweet & Maxwell, 2011.

Law Society, *Financial Provision on Divorce: Clarity and Fairness – Proposals for Reform*, 2003.

Tod, J, 'Schedule 1 and the Need for Reform: *N v D*', [2008] Fam Law 751.

Wikeley, N, 'Financial support for children after parental separation: Parental responsibility and responsible parenting', in Probert, R, Gilmore, S and Herring, J (eds), *Responsible Parents and Parental Responsibility*, Oxford, Hart, 2009.

Williams, D and Blain, S, 'Voices in the Wilderness: hearing children in financial applications', [2008] Fam Law 135.

Chapter 11

Domestic Violence and Forced Marriage

Chapter Contents

Learning outcomes for this chapter

An understanding of the scope of domestic violence protection including:

(i) An overview of the wider protection afforded by FLA 1996, Part IV, as amended, and of the Protection from Harassment Act (PHA) 1997 in cases not covered by FLA 1996.
(ii) An appreciation of the circumstances in which the more draconian orders can be made, including on an *ex parte* (without notice) basis and with power of arrest where necessary to protect the applicant.
(iii) An awareness of the legislation under FLA 1996 Part 4A and the Anti-Social Behaviour, Crime and Policing Act 2014, in force 16 June 2014, ss 120 and 121 to provide protection from forced marriage (now recognised as a prevalent form of violence against both women and men which requires specific protection, especially of vulnerable age groups).

11.1 Introduction

This area of family law is now governed by the **Family Law Act (FLA) 1996** Part IV and Part 4A. Part IV, implemented in the autumn of 1997, repealed the former domestic violence specific law in its entirety. Although injunctions under the inherent jurisdiction of the court ancillary to other proceedings remain a possibility in appropriate cases, this use would be most unusual and likely to be restricted to special facts, since there is now a codified framework of domestic violence law in FLA 1996, specifically to address violence and harassment within the family; thus neither such an ancillary order, nor any of the other statutory provisions designed to prevent and restrain such anti-social activity generally, will usually be appropriate in a family context when the FLA 1996 has specifically provided for the purpose of restraining domestic violence amongst associated persons.

It should be noted that the recent **Anti-Social Behaviour, Crime and Policing Act 2014**, s 120 (which criminalises forced marriage – one of the most prevalent forms of violence in the family) amends the FLA 1996 by inserting a new s 63CA making it an offence to breach a Forced Marriage Protection Order (FMPO). By s 121 it is an offence to use violence, threats or any other form of coercion for the purpose of causing another person to enter a forced marriage.

It is therefore not necessary, even for the academic student, to learn the earlier law in any detail, but such a student will need to have some overview of the pre-1996 repealed legislation in order to understand the beneficial effect of the codification effected by the FLA 1996.

In order, however, to understand fully how the codified law of domestic violence works, and why it operates as it does, it is essential to appreciate how the former piecemeal legislation came about, and why it thus needed codification around settled principles distilled from the sociological and legal developments of a quarter of a century.

The origin of domestic violence protection centred around the concept of a right to peaceful occupation of the home, at a time when increasing numbers of women (married and unmarried) were becoming joint owners with their husbands or cohabitants, but there were still substantial numbers who were not property owners at all. This in turn was linked to the rising rate of divorce and marriage breakdown and the shifting balance between marriage and cohabitation (the former decreasing steadily in popularity and the latter rising, initially as a form of 'trial marriage' and then as an alternative relationship in its own right, although in the 1990s when the FLA 1996 was conceived, drafted and enacted, it was still fashionable to prefer marriage as the higher norm). Initially domestic violence protection was rooted in the concept of protecting the wife, whether she was a house owner or not, from being driven out of the home (often with the children).

This protection was first provided by means of successive Matrimonial Homes Acts ('MHAs'), giving rights of occupation which could be invoked to remove violent husbands or to exclude them and allow the wife back in. Later, personal protection was added, and later still this was extended to cohabitants (at that time illiterately referred to as 'cohabitees', which is the term that will be noted in those old cases which still have relevance to the modern law).

In these circumstances, it was not surprising that the eventual mass of 'bolt on' provisions needed codifying, the language bringing into line with contemporary conditions, and the codified law providing with new procedural uniformity, in tune with the present day approach to marriage and cohabitation as the two viable and virtually equally acceptable alternatives for family life. One change that particularly needed making by the FLA 1996 was to incorporate the former MHA provisions and the domestic violence legislation into a single unified code, and to create separate rights of occupation for cohabitants (linking those to their property rights where such existed) so as to create an alternative which did *not* leave the cohabitant without a property claim and therefore completely homeless, since it was easily identified as wrong that a woman without a marriage certificate should be necessarily worse off when thrown out of her home than she who had a marriage certificate.

It should also be noted at this stage that *only* the three former domestic violence specific statutory jurisdictions (under the **MHA 1983, Domestic Violence and Matrimonial Proceedings Act 1976** and **DPMCA 1978**) were repealed by the 1996 Act. Thus there may be cases where the facts indicate that the inherent jurisdiction of the higher courts to issue injunctive orders under the former **Supreme Court Act (SCA) 1981**[1] remains more appropriate even where the FLA 1996 could be used, so that that court may still attach any protective injunction (now called simply an 'order') to any substantive suit before the High Court or Court of Appeal, or the county courts.

Clearly this inherent jurisdiction, formerly arising under common law, has also been statutory since the SCA 1981, and the county court, itself only a creature of statute, has a similar jurisdiction, originally under the **County Courts Act 1984**, and now pursuant to the **Courts and Legal Services Act 1990** s 3, and both courts will always use these flexibly to provide the best remedy in the particular case.

Such orders may be granted in support of any legal or equitable right, and although the FLA scheme will be likely to serve most needs there may well be cases which do not come squarely within the statutory framework where an order ancillary to other civil proceedings could be necessary or desirable.

There remains, therefore, a choice of jurisdiction: where appropriate the inherent jurisdiction under the SCA 1981 *may* be used to latch an application for an injunction order onto an existing suit, or one begun for the purpose of obtaining the order, but in general terms the FLA 1996 is so comprehensive, especially in view of the large number of associated persons now identified by s 62 of that Act, that it is unusual to need another jurisdiction for obtaining either of the two available orders. Those orders are:

(a) a non-molestation order (which prohibits either particular behaviour or molestation generally, against the applicant or a relevant child): s 42(1) and (6); or

(b) an occupation order (with a variety of possible terms) declaring existing rights in the family home or regulating its occupation and as mentioned above this is for present or previously married or cohabiting applicants alike.

The 1996 Act increased the range of categories of persons who can apply for these remedies, which are based on the concept of persons who are 'associated' with one another through family or

---

1 Now renamed the 'Senior Courts Act 1981' following the creation by the Constitutional Reform Act 2005 of the new 'Supreme Court' to replace the former House of Lords jurisdiction as the final appellate court in the United Kingdom.

domestic connections or by being parties to the same family proceedings. This is a new concept which did not exist before the FLA 1996 and has been the means of creating a coherent framework of persons who can be protected by FLA Part IV non-molestation orders. The categories of associated persons were again enlarged by the **Domestic Violence, Crime and Victims Act 2004**.

Regardless of which level (in the former triple tier of family courts which now comprise the unified Family Court) has actually granted the orders, only the two orders mentioned are used. Each court had, and each level of the new Family Court now has, the full range of identical powers provided by Part IV (with a minor difference in the case of the magistrates who have moved from the FPC into the Family Court as they, being lay justices, cannot decide an issue of title to land where that is relevant – this is not, however, likely to be a routine issue in their jurisdiction so the distinction is not important).

Thus it is no longer necessary to distinguish between the 'non-molestation' and 'personal protection' or 'ouster' and 'exclusion' orders, nor to decide which court to apply to on the basis of that court's powers. Therefore, all these different terms which will be encountered in the old reports of domestic violence cases, the broader principles of which may still be relevant to the present law, can be disregarded; the contemporary portfolio of protection orders is a 'non-molestation order' for personal protection and an 'occupation order' for protection of occupation of property which has been or was intended to be the married or unmarried partners' (or civil partners') homes.

Non-molestation orders are available to the entire class of associated persons mentioned in FLA ss 62 and 63; occupation orders are available to current and former spouses/civil partners and current former cohabitants, whether or not they have pre-existing rights in the property, and to other associated persons who have such pre-existing property rights.

11.2 Rights of occupation of the home of spouses or civil partners

The statutory right of occupation of the matrimonial home has, since 1967, been protected under successive MHAs, and the rights are now incorporated into FLA 1996 ss 30 and 31 and protected under ss 36–38.

For this reason married rights of occupation need to be looked at first before the law of domestic violence can be understood, because it is onto this concept that occupation rights for cohabitants (who by definition do not have matrimonial home rights) were grafted, to create something 'similar' but sufficiently 'not the same' as to be politically correct at a time (in 1996) when there was still an indignant groundswell of public opinion in favour of the claim for a superior status of marriage. A thorough working knowledge of this legislation is therefore required for a successful grasp of domestic violence orders for both married and unmarried parties (including civil partners) since the FLA regime is dependent on distinctions between applicants who either have some interest in a property or have home rights, which amount to much the same thing, and those who have neither a property interest nor such rights.

While the MHA 1983 has been repealed, it has been substantially re-enacted as well as extended by FLA 1996 Part IV. Also, while this Act renames the married or civil partners' right of occupation, now called 'home rights', the protection available continues much as before. Cynics say that only a link to an interest in property (always sacred in English law) could have placed a cohabitant in a similar category to a married person in this context.

11.2.1 Home rights under FLA 1996 ss 30 and 31

Obviously (matrimonial home) rights apply only to spouses and not to cohabitants (the word which has now replaced 'cohabitees' in the legislation) and are basically no different from the former statutory right to occupy the matrimonial home irrespective of which of the spouses (or civil partners) is the legal owner and whether the claimant has an equitable interest or whether the parties own it jointly: FLA 1996, ss 30(1) and (9) and 31(1). These rights may be enforced under s 33 pursuant to the criteria in s 33(6).

Home rights still do not apply to houses other than the matrimonial or civil partnership home (this means the Act does not apply to holiday homes, for example, although they do now affect a property which was *intended* to be a spouse's or civil partner's home under s 33(1)(b)). This latter provision is a distinction from the former law. Nevertheless, where there is more than one possible house which could qualify as a married or partnership home, an applicant may – and must for the purposes of the application – choose only one to be the subject of that application.

The court may *regulate* home rights as before, as follows:

(a)   by enforcing, restricting or terminating those rights;
(b)   by taking certain *criteria* into account: s 33(6).

These criteria are:

●   the conduct of the parties in relation to each other and otherwise;
●   their respective housing needs and the financial resources of the parties;
●   the housing needs of any children;
●   any significant harm likely to be suffered by the parties or any relevant child on the basis of a new balance of harm test: s 33(6) and (7), which in effect makes it mandatory for the court to make the order sought if the criteria for doing so are satisfied unless the respondent can show that the balance of harm test should go in his favour.

This last criterion is a substantially different provision from anything to be found in earlier MHAs of 1967 or 1983. The statutory rights of occupation are now defined in s 30(2):

(a)   if in occupation, the rights entitle the applicant spouse or civil partner not to be evicted or excluded from the dwelling house or any part thereof by the other spouse or partner save with permission of the court given by an order under s 33;
(b)   if not in occupation, the rights entitle the applicant spouse or partner with the permission of the court to enter and occupy the dwelling house (s 30(2)).

The court's power is wide and as before allows excluding the owning spouse.

Home rights are an equitable charge binding on the owning spouse and third parties: s 34, but must, by s 31, be registered in the same manner as before, because registration of the spouse's or partner's rights is actual notice to any potential purchaser: LPA 1925 s 198(1). But the court can still determine the spouse's rights of occupation in relation to anyone else with a claim to occupy: FLA 1996 s 33(3)(e). However, earlier decisions, such as in *Kashmir Kaur v Gill* (1988),[2] might now be decided differently under s 33(6)'s much wider criteria.

---

2   [1988] Fam Law 110; [1988] 2 All ER 288.

In interpreting the pre-s 33 criteria in 1988 in *Kashmir Kaur v Gill*, the court oddly took into account the interests of a blind purchaser of the home from the husband on the basis that he would be prejudiced by the wife's rights. At the time the distinguished former Chancery Judge and Lord Justice of Appeal, Sir Denys Buckley (dissenting) said that he thought the decision wrong and that Parliament could not have meant a third party to take precedence over the spouse whose interests the legislation was intended to protect.

11.2.2 Additional orders on regulation of home rights

It should be stressed that home rights *exist* for spouses and civil partners whether or not any order regulating them is applied for and that an order may be made regulating those rights completely independently of domestic violence, although domestic violence is the common cause of such an application. The fact that the right of occupation is a registrable property right can impact on financial provision proceedings even if no domestic violence order is sought.

The legislation also provides for ancillary orders which may be made if an order is applied for. This results in the applicant obtaining sole occupation of a home for the duration of the injunction order.

The other spouse or civil partner may still be required to pay for outgoings (i.e. the mortgage, insurance, council tax and water rates) and/or repairs to the home: s 40(1)(a). The court can also grant the use of furniture, etc.: s 40(1)(c). Alternatively, the spouse or civil partner in occupation receiving such an order can require a party to take care of such chattels: s 40(1)(d). However, problems have been identified in relation to the enforcement of ancillary orders to pay the mortgage, as in *Nwogbe v Nwogbe* (2000).[3] Basically, the payer cannot, apparently, be committed for contempt for failure to pay the ancillary orders, and as this is the ultimate sanction for breach of the occupation and non-molestation orders, the breach of such an ancillary order may be successfully committed without fear of incarceration.

A spouse or civil partner entitled to occupy the home may also pay the rent or the mortgage direct to the mortgagee or landlord, and the money must be accepted, as under the earlier legislation: s 30(3). Moreover, such a spouse or civil partner must be notified of mortgage enforcement proceedings and may be entitled to be made a party: s 56.

Home rights in favour of a spouse not otherwise entitled to an interest in the property last until divorce or the death of either spouse: s 31(9), unless the court makes use of s 33(5) to order otherwise: s 31(8). This should always be remembered when dealing with the home in the context of financial provision on divorce or dissolution of civil partnership as this will be relevant in every case where a spouse or civil partner is still occupying the home, whether or not there are domestic violence issues.

11.3 Domestic violence injunctions

These are now comprehensively catered for by FLA 1996 Part IV, although (apart from the inherent jurisdiction mentioned above) there is also a collateral statutory jurisdiction under the PHA 1997. This

---

3 [2000] 2 FLR 744.

is basically for cases outside the Act, having been created primarily to deal with 'stalkers', and is not appropriate unless the FLA 1996 is inapplicable, for instance because the parties do not come within any of the s 62 categories of 'associated persons'. There are two types of orders, as mentioned above, the least serious of which is the non-molestation order, which is therefore also the easiest to obtain.

11.3.1 Non-molestation orders: FLA 1996 s 42

Despite the creation of the new class of 'associated persons', non-molestation orders are also the least complicated of the new orders. The reason for extending protection against molestation and violence to the larger class of associated persons (rather than as formerly to spouses and cohabitants only) was the recognition by the Law Commission that harassment and violence can occur in many types of relationship. While there is specific statutory protection against such tortious behaviour in the PHA 1997, which after its enactment was able to deal with most non-residential boyfriend–girlfriend situations not covered by the FLA 1996, it was thought appropriate when reforming the general law of domestic violence to provide injunctive protection for the whole family rather than simply those in a married or unmarried heterosexual relationship, for example elderly people may need to be protected from abuse by members of the family with whom they are living and many women may need protection from violence at the hands of their teenage or adult sons.

Engaged and formerly engaged couples are also included in the broad spectrum of associated persons, as (now) are the less formal relationships that previously had to rely on the PHA 1997 because they were not in a residential relationship. They will now be covered by s 62(3)(ea) as persons who 'have or have had an intimate personal relationship which is or was of a significant duration'.

11.3.2 Associated persons: FLA 1996 s 62

'Associated persons' are defined by s 62(3) and the applicant for a non-molestation order must show that he or she is associated with the respondent, in that:

(1)   they are or have been married to each other, or are or have been civil partners;

(2)   they are cohabitants or former cohabitants;

(3)   they live or have lived in the same household, otherwise than merely by reason of one of them being the other's employee, tenant, lodger or boarder;

(4)   they are relatives;

(5)   they have agreed to marry each other (whether or not that agreement has been terminated) or have entered into a civil partnership agreement, or have or have had an intimate personal relationship of significant duration;

(6)   in relation to any child, they are both persons falling within s 62(4), which provides that a person falls within its scope if he or she:

   (a) is a parent of the child; or

   (b) has or has had parental responsibility for the child; or

(7)   they are parties to the same family proceedings other than proceedings under FLA 1996 Part IV.

'Cohabitants' are defined by s 62(1) as a man and a woman who, although not married to each other, are living together as husband and wife. 'Former cohabitants' is to be read accordingly, but the term does not include cohabitants who have subsequently married each other.

This means they must be of opposite sexes and have lived together as husband and wife, thus excluding homosexual relationships under this head; although civil partners are already in the list along with spouses, this leaves same-sex partners who are neither married nor in a registered civil partnership obliged to rely on some other heading. However, the *Mendoza* (2004)[4] case could mean this will change, because the House of Lords had decided in that case (under the Rent Acts) that same-sex cohabitants were in the same position as spouses, although if that decision were to be confined to its own facts there is already another s 62 category in which same-sex cohabitants could take shelter.

Persons who 'live or have lived in the same household other than by reason of one of them being the other's employee, etc.' comprise a new class of potential applicants, and would include persons living together who are neither spouses nor cohabitants nor related in any other way, thus including homosexual partnerships in this category.

11.3.3 Other essential definitions

A 'relative' is defined by s 63(1) as the father, mother, stepfather, stepmother, son, daughter, stepson, stepdaughter, grandfather, grandmother, grandson or granddaughter of a person or of that person's spouse or former spouse, civil partner or former civil partner, or the brother, sister, uncle, aunt, niece or nephew (whether of the full blood or of the half blood or by affinity) of that person or of that person's spouse or former spouse, civil partner or former civil partner and includes (in relation to a person who is living or has lived with another person as husband or wife) all these relationships which would have existed if the cohabitants in question had been married to each other.

It should be noted that this definition means that cohabitants and former cohabitants are deemed to have the same family relationships as if they had actually been married.

'Persons who have agreed to marry each other' are not specifically defined in s 63, but s 44(1) provides that written evidence must be available of such an engagement unless there has either been a gift of an engagement ring or a ceremony witnessed by one or more persons present for that purpose. Applications by such people must be made within three years of termination of the engagement: s 42(1).

'Parental responsibility' has the same meaning as in the CA 1989.

'Family proceedings' are defined by s 62(3) to include any High Court proceedings in relation to children under its inherent jurisdiction (e.g. wardship) and any proceedings under the MCA 1973, the DPMCA 1978 and the CA 1989.

The term 'relevant child' is comprehensively defined and means any child who is living with or might reasonably be expected to live with either party to the proceedings, any child in relation to whom an order under the CA 1989, or the **Adoption Act (AA) 1976** is in question in the proceedings, and any other child whose interests the court considers relevant.

'Harm' in relation to the balance of harm test (including where harm is applicable in relation to the grant of *ex parte* non-molestation orders under s 45[5]) is defined by s 63(1) to include (for adults) ill treatment or impairment of health or (for those under 18) to include also impairment of development.

11.3.4 Obtaining a non-molestation order

By s 42(2), the court may make a non-molestation order either on the application of any associated person who can show qualification as such, or of its own volition if it considers that such an order should be made for the benefit of any party or any relevant child. Applications may be made either in the course of other proceedings or on a freestanding basis.

A child under 16 may apply for an order with permission of the court: s 42(1), and such leave may be granted where the court is satisfied that the child has sufficient understanding to make such

---

4 *Ghaidan v Ghodin-Mendoza* [2004] UKHL 30; [2004] 2 FLR 600.
5 See below at 11.3.7.

an application: s 42(2). A child may also be separately represented in existing non-molestation proceedings started by others: s 64. Provision is also made by the Act for third parties (e.g. the police or other agencies) to take proceedings on behalf of an associated person who is reluctant to apply for a non-molestation order personally: s 60. Orders may also be obtained *against* 'children' under 18, although there remain problems of enforcement as such a defendant could not be committed to prison for breach.

11.3.5 Scope of molestation

The FLA 1996 does not define 'molestation', which the Law Commission considered was a sufficiently well-known concept long recognised by the courts. It is wider than violence and will usually encompass any form of harassing or pestering. There is a core body of case law which makes clear precisely what may fall within the ambit of 'harassing or pestering'. The following cases impart the general idea.

❖ CASE EXAMPLES

In *Vaughan v Vaughan* (1973)[6] a husband was a 'perfect nuisance', always making unwelcome visits to his wife from whom he was separated.

In *Horner v Horner* (1982)[7] a husband made offensive telephone calls to his wife from whom he was separated.

In *Wooton v Wooton* (1984)[8] the behaviour in question was the result of epileptic fits, which shows that the conduct complained of can be involuntary rather than deliberate.

In *G v G (Occupation Order: Conduct)* (2000)[9] this approach was confirmed where the behaviour in question was induced by drugs.

In *Johnson v Walton* (1990)[10] the behaviour complained of was more esoteric than most; this was a case of unwelcome publicity where embarrassing revelations about one of the parties was disclosed to the newspapers together with photographs, which brought down a plague of journalists on the unfortunate victim.

In *C v C (Non-Molestation Order: Jurisdiction)* (1997)[11] the conduct complained of unusually did not qualify since it was really centred on the issue of protection of privacy; it was made clear that there is no non-molestation order available for the protection of privacy as such, which was what the case was really about, and the *ex parte* (without notice) order granted was discharged. This was done where revelations of conduct during married life were published some time after the marriage had been dissolved on the basis that a 'higher degree of harassment' was required to invoke the protection of the statute.

---

6 [1973] 1 WLR 1159; [1973] 3 All ER 449.
7 [1982] 2 WLR 914; [1982] 2 All ER 495.
8 [1984] FLR 871.
9 [2000] 2 FLR 36.
10 [1990] 1 FLR 350.
11 (1997) *The Independent*, 27 November 1997.

11.3.6 The court's discretion

In deciding whether to exercise its powers to grant a non-molestation order, the court must have regard to all the circumstances including the need to secure the *health, safety and well-being* of the applicant and/or any relevant child or, where the court decides to make the order of its own volition, the health, safety or well-being of the associated person who the court decides should have the benefit of such an order: s 42(5).

By s 63, 'health' is defined as including physical or mental health and would therefore appear to give the court a very wide discretion.

11.3.7 *Ex parte* (without notice) orders: s 45

Such applications are no longer governed by case law (as they were prior to the FLA 1996) but by statutory provision in s 45. The court may now make such orders whenever it is just and convenient to do so: s 45(1), and must determine whether that is the case in accordance with the guidelines set out in s 45(2), in that it must take into account all the circumstances of the case including whether:

(a) there is any risk of significant harm to the applicant or a relevant child attributable to the conduct of the respondent if the order is not made immediately;

(b) it is likely that the applicant will be deterred or prevented from pursuing the application if an order is not made immediately; and

(c) there is reason to believe that the respondent is aware of the proceedings, but is deliberately evading service, provided it is shown that the applicant or a relevant child will be seriously prejudiced by the delay involved:

- where the court is sitting as a magistrates jurisdiction, in effecting service of proceedings; or
- in any other case, in effecting substituted service.

The court must afford the respondent an opportunity to make representations as soon as just and convenient at a full hearing: s 45(3), and any time which elapses between the initial *ex parte* order and the final order will be included in computing the duration of that final order; thus the final order is deemed to have commenced at the time the *ex parte* order was granted. Non-molestation orders are normally made for a specified period unless there are exceptional or unusual circumstances: M v W (Non-Molestation Order: Duration) (2000),[12] but the Court of Appeal has ruled that they can be made for an indefinite period, thus overruling Cazalet J in the above case, who was of the view that a definite period was essential: see Re B-J (Power of Arrest) (2000).[13]

11.3.8 Undertakings: s 46

The court may always accept an undertaking instead of making an order: s 46(1), and this is as enforceable as an order of the court: s 46(2), i.e. by applying for a warrant of arrest: s 47(8). This is likely to remain the common means of settling domestic violence cases, although previously accepting such an undertaking was based on practice and not on statute. However, it will not be possible to accept an undertaking in lieu of making an order where a power of arrest would otherwise be attached: s 46(2), and see below.

---

12 [2000] 1 FLR 107.
13 [2000] 2 FLR 443.

11.3.9 Power of arrest in relation to occupation orders: s 47

There is no longer any need to attach a power of arrest to a non-molestation order (as breach of that order is now an offence under s 42A, which means the offender can be arrested any time the offence is committed). However, by s 47(1), the court has a mandatory duty to attach a power of arrest where it also makes an occupation order unless it is satisfied that in all the circumstances of the case the applicant or any relevant child will be adequately protected without it. This duty arises whenever it appears to the court that the respondent has used or threatened violence against the applicant or a relevant child: s 47(2).

This is a significant departure from the previous practice where attaching a power of arrest was discretionary and only used if absolutely necessary. This upgraded system may be especially harsh as it may now apply whatever the standing of 'associated persons', so might involve a very distantly associated person indeed. However where there has been serious violence and a non-molestation order is needed it is quite likely that extra protection may be needed in relation to the occupation order so that it is wise to add the power of arrest to the occupation order to make sure that such violence can be contained.

Where a power of arrest is attached, the police may arrest the respondent without warrant if they have reasonable grounds for suspicion that the order has been breached: s 47(6). This affords the applicant significantly greater protection than if a warrant of arrest must be applied for before such action can be taken (normally now the procedure replacing the former application to commit the respondent for contempt). Although the Act is silent on this point, it is assumed that the power of arrest will be attached only to those parts of any order dealing with violence and not to those prohibiting harassment or pestering, and that has certainly been the practice.

Another significant change made by the FLA 1996 is that where a power of arrest is not initially attached, later application may be made for this to be done: s 47(8).

Where the respondent is arrested, he or she will be brought before the court and may be remanded: s 47(10), including for medical reports: s 48(1). Where a respondent is remanded in custody, the court has the same powers as the magistrates under the **Magistrates' Courts Act 1980** ss 128 and 129.

As this power is more sweeping than its predecessor under the old law, it is perhaps useful that, when registered at a police station, the power of arrest must be accompanied by a statement on one of the specially designed forms for Part IV proceedings setting out how the order was served or notified to the respondent.

A power of arrest on an order granted at an inter partes hearing should normally last for the same length of time as the order,[14] but can be for a lesser period if this would give the court flexibility to protect the victim while not restricting human rights more than necessary.

There is a discretion as to which parts of an occupation order the power of arrest should be attached to: Hale v Tanner (2000).[15]

Breach of an occupation order in particular is regarded as a very serious matter and a custodial sentence is not unheard of. The Court of Appeal has given explicit guidance on the matter as may be seen in one decided case.

---

14 See M vW (2000) above.
15 [2000] 1 WLR 237.

In *H v O (Contempt of Court: Sentencing)* (2004)[16] the Court of Appeal indicated how seriously they and society took the escalation of domestic violence which required stronger methods than previously.

11.4 Occupation orders

Occupation orders have always been more difficult to obtain because it has always been accepted that it is a draconian act to turn a person out of his or her home. It is therefore usual always to ask for a non-molestation order, and to add an application for an occupation order if that is felt to be justified. It is rare in a case of domestic violence not to secure the former (especially as no actual violence is required; lesser molestation will suffice: see above) but an occupation order always requires more effort since the application of ss 33–38 is meticulously detailed.

The concept of associated persons is also relevant to occupation orders. However, application for an occupation order is slightly more complicated than that for non-molestation orders. This is because relief must be sought under the section of the FLA 1996 which is appropriate to the applicant, and that in turn depends both upon the matrimonial or other status of the parties and on whether or not they have any property rights in relation to the home of which occupation is sought. An occupation order can only be made in respect of a property which is or was an actual or intended home: see ss 33(1)(b), 35(1)(c), 36(1)(c), 37(1)(a) and 38(1)(a), and never in relation to investment property.

There are three types of potential applicants:

- entitled persons;
- non-entitled persons; and
- persons with home rights (who are very similar to entitled persons).

The last of the three are those who used to have 'rights of occupation' under the MHA 1967 or 1983, although the third category now includes civil partners who did not exist under the former statutes. These rights, now called collectively 'home rights' under FLA 1996 Part IV, are protected by ss 30 and 31 (see above) to cover all the categories. Any of the associated persons identified in ss 62 and 63 may be respondents to occupation order applications.

11.4.1 Entitled and non-entitled persons

Entitled persons and *persons with home rights* apply under s 33, while *non-entitled persons* must apply under one of ss 35–38:

- A *former spouse or former civil partner* with no existing right to occupy applies under s 35.
- A *cohabitant* or *former cohabitant* with no existing right to occupy applies under s 36.
- Where neither spouse nor former civil partner is entitled to occupy, application is under s 37.
- Where neither *cohabitant* is entitled to occupy, application is under s 38.

---

16 [2004] EWCA Civ 1691; [2004] 2 FLR 329.

The distinction between the different sections is important, since the wording of the respective sections is not identical, so that different conditions must be satisfied in the various different situations.

It should be noted that an *entitled* person can apply for a s 33 order against the entire wide class of associated persons identified in ss 62 and 63. Further, although normally home rights only endure until decree absolute or final dissolution order, the court has power to order that they shall continue in favour of a former spouse or civil partner beyond that decree or order: s 30(8). Thus some divorced spouses and former civil partners may be able to apply under s 33. If there has been no such order, a former spouse or former civil partner will apply under ss 35 or 37 (see below).

11.4.2 The court's powers under s 33

The court's powers where the parties are entitled (i.e. where the applicant has an estate or interest in land or home rights.) are set out in s 33(3) and include:

(a)   enforcing, restricting or terminating home rights;
(b)   prohibiting, suspending or restricting the exercise by either spouse or civil partner of those rights to occupy the home or part of it;
(c)   requiring either spouse or civil partner to permit the exercise by the other of occupation rights;
(d)   declaring the applicant's rights;
(e)   requiring the respondent to leave the home or part of it; and
(f)   excluding the respondent from a defined area around the home.

The fact that these powers are similar to those giving rights of occupation of a home to *married* people is no accident, since this section caters for: (1) spouses or civil partners who own; (2) owners, married or not; and (3) spouses or civil partners who are not owners but who by virtue of marriage or civil partnership have home rights, which is entirely consistent with the history of this remedy.[17]

11.4.3 The court's discretion under s 33

New criteria to guide the court were introduced by s 33(6). These criteria are:

(a)   the conduct of the parties in relation to each other and otherwise;
(b)   the respective housing needs of the parties and any children and their respective financial resources;
(c)   the likely effect of any order/lack of order on the health, safety or well-being of the parties and any relevant child; and
(d)   all the circumstances of the case.

The court must also consider whether, if the order is not made, any significant harm will be suffered by the applicant or a relevant child attributable to the conduct of the respondent, and in this case they must make an order unless the *balance of harm* test introduced by s 33(7) is in favour of the respondent and not the applicant.

---

17 See 11.1, above.

These criteria are much wider than those in MHA 1983 s 1(3) which they replaced, as s 33(6) includes a new guideline which requires the court to consider the likely effect of any order or of any decision of the court not to exercise its powers on the health, safety and well-being of the parties or of any relevant child. Moreover, this is to be considered on a *balance of harm* test: s 33(7), and if harm attributable to the conduct of the respondent would be likely to be suffered by the applicant or a relevant child if the order is not made, the court should normally make the order unless that would lead to greater significant harm to the respondent or a relevant child. Thus this provision imposes a *mandatory* duty on the court which did not exist before, the effect of which is that, if the relevant conditions are satisfied and the respondent cannot show that the order should not be made, the court *must* make it.

It should be noted that these new criteria replacing MHA 1983 s 1(3) are exclusive to s 33 and are *not* repeated in relation to the other sections dealing with different classes of applicant – a significant departure from the pre-FLA 1996 law which used to use the same test (i.e. that of MHA 1983 s 1(3) regardless of which jurisdiction was used by the various different applicants who at that time had to choose between different pathways to an order). Each section which provides a remedy under ss 35–38 has its own criteria which are repeated in that section. Broadly, the Act gives greater protection to spouses and civil partners than to cohabitants.

With the addition of the balance of harm test, the new criteria clearly have some significant new elements, and it is debatable how much of the old case law on the former may still be helpful. In particular, children's interests are not only relevant but it may be necessary to balance the competing needs of different children (see e.g. B v B (*Occupation Order*) (1999),[18] which makes this position clear.

❖ CASE EXAMPLE

In *B v B (Occupation Order)* when the court came to interpret the criteria the comparison of relative harms meant the violent spouse remained in the home because of the interests of the child whose needs required this.

Recent case law (which has been sparse) suggests that an occupation order is still a draconian one to make: some harm or seriously anticipated harm to the applicant has to be shown before an order will be made at all and the balance of harm test must come out in the applicant's favour. Such case law as there is gives some indication of how this works.

❖ CASE EXAMPLES

In *Chalmers v Johns* (1999)[19] 'considerable harm' was said to be required, as the order was for extreme cases only.

In *Banks v Banks* (1999)[20] an order against the physically and verbally abusive mentally ill wife would have caused greater harm to her than to her husband if made.

---

18 [1999] 1 FLR 715.
19 [1999] 1 FLR 392.
20 [1999] 1 FLR 726.

In *Re Y (Children: Occupation Order)* (2000)[21] the order was said not to be for the ordinary tensions of divorce, which backs up the earlier decision in *Chalmers v Johns* and is further supported by some of the s 33 decisions set out below.

Where children are concerned, schooling will generally be a critical factor in deciding whether they and their carer parent should remain in occupation.

Some general principles derived from the earlier law therefore remain useful. The s 33 criteria need careful consideration.

The parties' conduct

❖ CASE EXAMPLES

In *Elsworth v Elsworth* (1978)[22] it was established that there must be some 'conduct' complained of which is good reason for the spouse wanting the injunction to seek it: here the wife left and refused to return until the husband moved out, but there was no identifiable reason for her objection to doing so and she did not get her injunction.

In *Myers v Myers* (1971)[23] it was established that the parties may be made to share the property if it is large enough to divide on a temporary basis at least, if the house is sufficiently spacious so that the parties might be kept apart (and if they are relatively sensible and civilised and there is no violence). In these circumstances it was made clear that an injunction will not be granted merely because the situation is unpleasant and tense. This was a case of exclusion after only one incident of violence and much verbal abuse, where the order initially obtained was based on the needs of the children and was set aside on the twin bases: (i) that the wife was possibly being unreasonable; and (ii) a reappraisal of the children's needs.

In *Phillips v Phillips* (1973),[24] on the other hand, it was equally clear that this will not be the case if the premises are very small: here there was a council flat and the divorce had already been obtained. The wife said she and the son would become psychiatric invalids if the situation continued and there was medical evidence to this effect. The injunction was therefore granted.

In *Walker v Walker* (1978)[25] there was a clinically depressive illness involved which could be proved and the injunction was again granted.

In *Summers v Summers* (1986)[26] it was established that an order *cannot* be granted where it is not strictly necessary, for example, simply to give the parties a break in the *hope* that this will help towards a reconciliation, since this would not qualify as *necessary*. In this case the judge gave a two-month exclusion order, as the parties were quarrelling loudly

---

21 [2000] 2 FLR 470, CA.
22 [1978] 9 Fam 21.
23 [1971] 1 WLR 404; [1971] 1 All ER 762.
24 [1973] 1 WLR 615; [1973] 2 All ER 423.
25 [1978] 1 WLR 533; [1978] 3 All ER 141.
26 [1986] 1 FLR 343.

and upsetting the children, both being equally to blame, and the husband had to go and sleep on his grandmother's sofa. On appeal this approach was held to be clearly wrong, since the order is draconian and not capable of being adapted as a solution for this sort of situation.

In *Kadeer v Kadeer* (1987)[27] there was a similar situation where the judge thought that two months apart might settle the parties after the wife had an affair and was sleeping on the floor of the study to escape the husband's excessive sexual demands; again on appeal the order was set aside as being wrong where there was no necessity, such as because of violence.

In *Scott v Scott* (1992)[28] it was clear that violence is not in fact essential if the order can be categorised as necessary for some other reason. Here the husband was excluded on the basis that there was a sufficiently serious situation, so that an exclusion order should be made regardless of the absence of violence, but the emphasis was on the seriousness of the circumstances: the divorce was in process and the future of the 15-year-old daughter of the marriage was not yet settled as contested proceedings were pending. The court nevertheless made an order as the husband was continually pestering the wife about a reconciliation, since he did not accept that the marriage was over. However, she was not amenable to his suggestions, and although he was never violent he had already breached a non-molestation order on numerous occasions; clearly something had to be done in practical terms to bring this situation to an end, as the parties could not live in the same house, and his appeal against the order on the grounds that the reasons for it were insubstantial was rejected.

The parties' needs and resources

This is not always easy to assess. Again cases suggest the right approach.

❖ CASE EXAMPLES

In *Thurley v Smith* (1985)[29] it was established that the court will require detailed information as to how easy (or difficult) it is for either party to be re-housed by the local authority.

In *Lee v Lee* (1984)[30] it was demonstrated that the woman may have the edge if she has the children as they will handicap her in finding alternative accommodation, but this does not always work even in wives' favour. This case involved an unmarried couple with two children, a son and a daughter, who made allegations of indecency against the father. While her mother was in hospital the daughter had to live with her grandmother, an arrangement which she did not like. The court gave occupation of the jointly owned council flat to the woman because the man on his own did not require such extensive accommodation, and the wife and children clearly had a higher degree of need for it.

---

27 [1987] CLY 1775.
28 [1992] 1 FLR 529.
29 [1985] Fam Law 31.
30 [1984] FLR 243.

In *Wiseman v Simpson* (1988),[31] still the leading case on the draconian nature of the order, there was no violence but merely an 'atmosphere', so no order was made: the position was that the young couple who were cohabiting had merely fallen out of love with each other and the existence of a baby who needed to be with the mother was not conclusive in obtaining sole occupation for her.

Children's needs

Children's needs can sometimes swing the balance, as some cases demonstrate.

❖ CASE EXAMPLES

In *Bassett v Bassett* (1976)[32] there was quite a strong case on the needs of the children. A couple and their baby lived in a very small (two-roomed) flat and the husband brought his teenage son to live there also. The wife said that the husband drank and was violent. She went to live with her parents (where they were very overcrowded) and applied for an ouster order which she obtained and which was upheld on appeal. Presumably this was because the husband and the teenage son could find alternative accommodation more easily than a woman with a baby, who tends not to be a popular tenant with private land-lords, thus leaving them reliant on the local authority and possibly with no alternative to bed-and-breakfast accommodation.

In *Samson v Samson* (1982)[33] the wife's allegations of conduct were insubstantial, although they did include over-criticism of her and a resultant undermining of her confidence. Surprisingly, however, the court nevertheless gave her an exclusion order as the children needed to be accommodated in the house, and the wife would not return with them unless the husband left because of her extreme aversion to him, owing to the matters alleged in the petition. While the Court of Appeal said they could not look into the adequacy of allegations in divorce petitions to see whether she was justified in leaving, they made the order on the basis of the children's needs.

In *Richards v Richards* (1984)[34] an exclusion order was refused because the wife's allegations were trivial and 'rubbishy' and the interests of the children were not paramount (but see the later case of *B v B (Occupation Order)* (1999),[35] where the wife's allegations were not insubstantial but the child's needs succeeded in keeping the abuser in the home).

In *Anderson v Anderson* (1984)[36] the accommodation was a two-roomed flat from which the wife departed with the two-year-old son owing to the husband's violence; she refused to return until the husband left, was expecting a second child and was staying in a hostel for battered wives. The husband, however, proposed sharing the flat, with

---

31 [1988] 1 All ER 245.
32 [1976] 1 All ER 513.
33 [1982] 1 WLR 252; [1982] 1 All ER 178.
34 [1984] AC 206.
35 [1999] 1 FLR 715.
36 [1984] FLR 566.

one bedroom for her and the children and one for him, and sharing the kitchen, bathroom and living room. Not surprisingly, the court rejected his proposals and made the exclusion order in the interests of the children.

NB it is always possible that children may swing the balance of harm test in cases where other things are equal.

All the circumstances

Such circumstances may be quite varied, as again the cases show.

> ### ❖ CASE EXAMPLES
>
> In *Jones v Jones* (1971)[37] it was established that this may cover situations as varied as the husband installing his mistress in the matrimonial home (where the court made an immediate ouster order) to trying to pre-empt the ultimate property settlement (which has usually not worked as the emphasis on domestic violence protection has always been 'first aid' pending such final decisions).
>
> In *Hadden v Hadden* (1966),[38] in just such a case one spouse was trying to evict the other, for which domestic violence legislation is sometimes seen as a useful tool by a scheming spouse, but the court is aware of such potential (and in any case even if a party is ordered out of the home on an occupation order it will have precisely nil effect on the ultimate property settlement, which is decided on entirely different principles). In present circumstances, however, such an attempt might obtain legal aid for a spouse who can use the FLA 1996 to establish a case of domestic violence.

It should be noted that it seems that in accordance with previous practice the order should be made only for a determinate period: s 33(10), or should be expressed to be until 'further order', although no time limit is actually specified in the FLA 1996. This contrasts with the earlier practice of only making such orders as a 'first aid' remedy for a limited period pending long-term resolution of outstanding property or underlying problems.

11.4.4 Orders under s 35

These orders, in favour of *former spouses or civil partners* without an estate or interest against *entitled* respondents, protect the former spouses from eviction or exclusion from the home, and if necessary permit the former spouse to re-enter, also requiring the other spouse to allow this.

These terms will be *mandatory* if the court decides to make an order at all. Whether such an order is made is within the discretion of the court, since a *former* spouse who needs to use this section will have no matrimonial home rights, as if such existed application could have been made under s 33.

---

37 [1971] 2 All ER 737.
38 [1966] 3 All ER 412.

There are guidelines for the court in exercising its discretion contained in s 35(6) and these are similar to those under s 33, but the court must also have regard to the length of time since the parties' separation and/or since the marriage was dissolved or annulled, and also to the existence of any pending property proceedings (whether under MCA 1973 or otherwise). Finally, the court must apply the balance of harm test, which again imposes a mandatory duty to make the order unless the respondent shows why it should not be made.

Orders under s 35 are not to last in the first instance for longer than six months, though renewals are permitted: s 35(9) and (10).

11.4.5 Orders under s 36

Orders in favour of *cohabitants* without an estate or interest or *former cohabitants* but where the *respondent is entitled* are made under s 36. Protection and guidance to the court are virtually the same as under s 35, save that in the case of cohabitants s 36(6)(e)–(h) requires the court to consider the nature of the parties' relationship, the length of time for which they have cohabited, whether there are any children for whom both parties have parental responsibility and the length of time since they have ceased to live together.

The balance of harm test under s 36(8) is also weaker than in the case of ss 33 and 35 in that there is no obligation on the respondent in a s 36 case to show why the order should not be made. It is clear from this and from s 41, which requires the court to have regard to the fact that the parties have not given each other the commitment of marriage, that Parliament intended to give the strongest protection to those who are or who have been married and thus to distinguish between married and cohabiting couples in favour of those who have assumed the commitment of marriage.

11.4.6 Orders under s 37

Orders in favour of *former spouses or former civil partners* (but where, unlike those under s 35, the *respondent is not entitled*) are made under s 37. Protection given and guidance to the court are the same as under the previous sections but both parties must still be residing in the home for this section to be used and orders are limited to six months plus one possible extension of a further six months.

11.4.7 Orders under s 38

Orders in favour of *former cohabitants* (again where, unlike those under s 36, the *respondent is not entitled*) are made under s 38, for which the requirements are identical to s 37 save that the parties have never been married, and there is similar protection to that of cohabitants under s 36. Again, the order is limited to six months plus one renewal for the same period.

11.4.8 Powers of arrest

These are attachable to occupation orders but not to non-molestation orders (see above) and are not attached to ancillary orders (see above) if such are included.

11.5 Procedure

The procedure under the FLA 1996 involves both new forms and amendments to the rules and has been streamlined.

There are also civil remedies under the PHA 1997, for which compensation can be ordered. This has been invoked in some cases of family violence.

❖ **CASE EXAMPLE**

In *Singh v Bhakar and Bakhar* (2007)[39] a Sikh girl who had suffered from harassment by her mother-in-law obtained compensation for the depression suffered as a result of the mother-in-law's treatment.

11.5.1 *Ex parte* (without notice) orders

If the application is made *ex parte* (without notice) the statement must explain why this is necessary, since the court has power to abridge the time for service, which is normally only two days, making at least informal notice (e.g. a telephone call) possible in virtually all cases. *Ex parte* (without notice) orders are therefore still only likely to be allowed in the most drastic circumstances.

❖ **CASE EXAMPLE**

In *G v G* (1990)[40] the husband obtained an *ex parte* (without notice) occupation order (previously known as an ouster order) against the wife together with a non-molestation order restraining her from assaulting him, which was set aside on the various grounds that:

- she was readily available for service;
- there was a conflict of evidence;
- there was no danger of serious irreparable harm; and
- the order had been granted for seven weeks, which was far too long, since an *ex parte* order should only be for a very short period pending a hearing on notice.

11.5.2 Child applications

A child may make an application, but only with permission of the court: s 43(1), and only if the child has sufficient understanding to make the proposed application: s 43(2), in which case such application is treated in the first instance as an application for leave to make the application. This is clearly a significant extension of the former powers to regulate the occupation of the family home.

11.6 Transfer of tenancies

Tenancies (either local authority or privately owned) can also be transferred under the Act, providing a longer-term solution than a temporary occupation order. This power is pursuant to the FLA 1996 s 53 and Schedule 7. This would enable one married or cohabitant joint owner to obtain the tenancy to the exclusion of the other. Criteria in Schedule 7 include the suitability of the parties as tenants and the circumstances in which they obtained the tenancy.

---

39 [2007] 1 FLR 889.
40 [1990] FLR 395.

For discussions of these provisions, see Bridge, S, 'Transferring tenancies of the family home', [1998] Fam Law 26; and Woelke, A, 'Transfer of tenancies', [1999] Fam Law 72.

11.7 Forced marriage (a relatively new concern in domestic violence)

Part 4A was inserted into the FLA 1996 by the **Forced Marriage (Civil Protection) Act 2007** in order to introduce civil protection orders for victims of forced marriage, a particular form of domestic violence prevalent in some minority ethnic communities where marriage within their culture is valued, and this is sometimes imposed by force. These communities also experience incidents of so-called 'honour killing', which are often connected with resistance to forced marriage by Westernised teenagers and young people who wish to make their own friends and establish their own relationships. The overall problem is regarded as extremely serious and the Mayor of London has noted its existence within his programme to tackle Violence Against Women in London.

The order can protect against forced marriage before it happens by making a prohibitory order against the suspected relatives, and where necessary delivering the ultimate sanction of a custodial sentence if that injunction order is breached. It is sometimes also of use where the forced marriage has taken place and protection from harassment is required. Under s 63B the terms of the order may also extend to conduct outside England and Wales. Orders can be sought on behalf of victims if such victims prefer not to be involved in such proceedings, as is often the case, where the victim would like the duress and other ill treatment to stop but shrinks from involving family members in legal proceedings.

The former Centre for Family Law and Practice at London Metropolitan University[41] undertook a small-scale funded research programme in 2012–13 into the extent of awareness and pastoral care for the vulnerable age groups of students at universities and colleges in England and Wales, who are likely victims of this syndrome in which it seems that both young women and young men are at risk of forced marriages. Early results published in its report[42] indicated that there are gaps in both awareness and pastoral care which could usefully be filled by training which might assist the ongoing efforts of the Ministry of Justice (MOJ) and the joint MOJ, Home Office and Foreign and Commonwealth Office (FCO) sponsored Forced Marriage Unit (FMU) to address the practical problems. In 2009 the government published a paper on the subject, *Handling Cases of Forced Marriage*,[43] and there has now been legislation criminalising incidences of forced marriage.[44]

In 2001 the Centre for Child and Family Law Reform sponsored by City University published a paper *The Problem of Forced Marriages: The Recommendations of the Centre for Child and Family Law Reform*[45] at about the same time that the Government Working Party paper *A Choice by Right*[46] was announced, when it was considered that education rather than sanctions was the way forward, since the Working Group did not favour legislation to create a specific offence of forcing a person to marry. This view was taken because individual criminal acts committed in the course of forcing such a marriage can

---

41 For some of the work of the former Centre, now closed, and its online journal archive, see www.famlawandpractice.com.
42 See the website of CFLP's successor, the International Centre for Family Law, Policy and Practice for this report, www.famlawandpractice.com, since CFLP and its former website are no longer in existence.
43 HM Government, London, The Stationery Office.
44 See above, Introduction.
45 Available from the Secretary to the Centre, Lucy Cheetham, 4 Paper Buildings, Temple EC4Y 7EX. See also Dabezies, C, 'Forced Marriage: A Paper prepared for the Centre for Child and Family Law Reform', (2010) 2 FLP 1: 28.
46 HM Government, HMSO.

in any event be the subject of criminal proceedings and it was felt that criminalisation might make the minority groups concerned feel discriminated against.

These early initiatives were followed up by a report from the FMU entitled *Forced Marriage: A Wrong Not a Right*,[47] containing a summary of responses to their consultation.

A 2010 update to the Centre for Child and Family Law Reform's 2001 report considers that without creating a separate offence of forcing a person to marry, it might still be appropriate to embark, for example, on secondary legislation along the lines of the **Crime and Disorder Act 1998** s 82, which requires the court in any criminal matter which is racially aggravated to treat the motivation as a factor making the crime more serious, thus in effect creating satellite offences, such as common assault with intent to cause or induce another to enter a marriage, and this also would permit a higher sentence to be imposed which could send a stronger message that forced marriage was unacceptable; a draft of the proposed legislation was annexed to the 2010 paper.

The paper indicates that:

> none of the minority communities in the United Kingdom condone the use of criminal acts to bring about a marriage. It is also an important feature of the proposed legislation is that there is no danger that it can be though to apply to arranged marriages, which by their nature are consensual and will not be tainted by any association with the criminal acts to which the draft legislation relates.

The MOJ continued to keep the issue of further statutory action under review and eventually decided that they would bring forward the legislation enacted recently. However, the matter continues to attract academic as well as practitioner attention[48] and the regular incidence of reported cases in the 15 years since *Re KR (Abduction: Forcible Removal by Parents)* (1999)[49] indicates that the established trend has apparently not been halted despite a protocol with the Pakistani judiciary, and the assurance of the principal judge dealing with such cases in Pakistan (when he spoke to the Women's Interest Group at the 2011 International Bar Association annual conference) that he personally had been involved in the judicial rescue of female victims of the syndrome from relatives who had intended to force them to marry.

In England and Wales the wardship jurisdiction is still regularly used to protect victims as in *Re B; R v FB and MA (Forced Marriage: Wardship Jurisdiction)* (2008),[50] although sometimes recourse to the court is too late, as in *B v I (Forced Marriage)* (2010),[51] where a 16-year-old was forced into marriage in Bangladesh but was unable to alert anyone to help her for three years, which was too late for a nullity petition, which must be brought during that time. Nevertheless the court was able to refuse to recognise the marriage on the grounds that it was incapable of recognition in the United Kingdom. Otherwise she would have had to rely on divorce to end it, which would not have been acceptable to her culture, which disapproved of divorce and would thus have preferred nullity if the alternative solution found had not been possible.

---

47 London, Home Office, 2006.
48 Dauvergne, C and Millbank, J, 'Forced Marriage as a Harm in Domestic and International Law', (2010) 73 *Modern Law Review* 57; Diduck, A and Kaganas, F, *Family Law, Gender and the State*, Oxford, Hart, 2006, p 42. In 2010 the Centre for Family Law and Practice at London Metropolitan University considered the matter at their inaugural international conference, *International Child Abduction, Forced Marriage and Relocation*, articles based on the collected papers from which may be found in that Centre's online journal *Family Law and Practice*, the archive of which is on the website of the journal editor, www.frburton.com, since unfortunately the Centre closed in 2013, together with its former website and the paper banks of its successful 2010 and 2013 conferences.
49 [1999] 2 FLR 542, where the court used wardship to protect an abducted 17-year-old.
50 [2008] 2 FLR 1624 where wardship was used to protect a British national abroad.
51 [2010] 1 FLR 1721.

11.8 Current debates

Ideas for research on these current discussion questions can be found on the companion website updates.

- Is it appropriate for domestic violence and forced marriage to have criminal sanctions?
- Should perpetrators of domestic violence be prosecuted whether or not the victim wants this?
- Are criminal sanctions or rehabilitative psychological sentences more appropriate for dealing with domestic violence?

11.9 Summary of Chapter 11

FLA 1996

- FLA 1996 has codified the law of domestic violence by consolidating the law to provide two forms of order – non-molestation and occupation orders – available uniformly in the triple tier of family courts.
- The orders work on the basis of a concept of 'associated persons', a wide class defined in the Act. The Act additionally provides occupation orders for married, formerly married, civil partners and formerly civil partnered persons, cohabiting and formerly cohabiting heterosexual couples, additionally based on a concept of 'entitlement'.
- This concept regulates the specific criteria on which the court will base its decision, the most protective criteria being accorded to cases involving married couples and those who have an interest in the property concerned.
- Financial needs and resources, children's needs, the conduct of the parties and all the circumstances of the case figure in all cases, but the balance of harm test, stronger or weaker depending on the relationship – married or not, existing or former – is a crucial factor.
- Ancillary orders can also be made to finance the occupation, which will be of longer or shorter duration depending on which section of the Act the parties apply under.

Non-molestation orders

- Orders to restrain harassment or pestering as well as violence may be made under FLA 1996 s 42.
- Such orders may be made without notice where pursuant to s 45 the applicant has good reason not to give notice (e.g. fear of the applicant until protected by the court's order, or inability to find and serve the applicant, or urgency), and may be made when it is 'just and convenient'.
- But a hearing on notice should follow as soon as possible. A power of arrest no longer needs to be attached as breach of this order is a criminal offence, leading to immediate arrest.
- Undertakings may be accepted in lieu but not where a power of arrest is indicated. Committal may follow for breach of an order.

Occupation orders

- Such orders may also be made *ex parte* but only for a short period until a hearing can be held on notice.

- Occupation orders are regarded as draconian and will only be made when really necessary to restrain some identifiable harm and only where the balance of harm test in the appropriate criteria for the section under which the applicant's standing requires the application to be made is in favour of the applicant.
- Such orders may have ancillary clauses to finance the occupation through payment by the respondent of the home's outgoings.
- A power of arrest may be attached to all but the ancillary order clauses.
- Committal may also follow for breach of an occupation order.

Transfer of tenancies

- FLA 1996 Schedule 7 permits the longer-term remedy of transfer of either a public or private sector tenancy to one of joint tenants.

Forced marriage

- FLA 1996 Part 4A has introduced a Forced Marriage Protection Order to assist those placed under duress by their families or communities for resisting a forced marriage.
- The order can be applied for by a third party.
- The Anti-Social Behaviour, Crime and Policing Act 2014 has criminalised forcing a person into marriage.

 ## 11.10 Further reading

Burton, M, *Legal Responses to Domestic Violence*, Abingdon, Routledge, 2008.

Burton, M, ' "Scream quietly or the neighbours will hear". Domestic violence, nuisance neighbours and the public/private dichotomy revisited', [2008] CFLQ 95.

Burton, M, 'The civil law remedies for domestic violence: why are applications for non-molestation orders declining?', (2009) *Journal of Social Welfare and Family Law* 31: 109.

Burton, M, *Domestic Violence Literature Review*, London, LSC, 2009.

Choudhry, S and Herring, J, 'Righting Domestic Violence', (2006) *International Journal of Law, Policy and the Family* 20: 95.

Freeman, M and Klein, R, *University responses to forced marriage and violence against women in the UK: Report on a pilot*, (2012) IFL 285. (This report, and its successor, *College and University Responses*, 2013, by the same authors, can be obtained from Professor Freeman by emailing her at freemanmarilyna@aol.com. The reports are not at present available on any website, but will shortly be downloadable from the website of the International Centre for Family Law, Policy and Practice, www.famlawandpractice.com, of which Professor Freeman is a co-director.)

Herring, J, 'Familial Homicide, Failure to Protect and Domestic Violence: Who's the victim?', (2007) *Criminal Law Review*, 923.

Madden Dempsey, M, *Prosecuting Domestic Violence*, Oxford, Hart, 2009.

Platt, HHJ, 'The Domestic Violence, Crimes and Victims Act 2004 Part I: Is it working?', [2008] Fam Law 642.

Reece, H, 'The end of domestic violence?', (2006) *Modern Law Review* 69: 770.

Chapter 12

The Children Act 1989

Chapter Contents

Learning outcomes for this chapter

A sound understanding of the philosophy and general principles of the Children Act (CA) 1989 including:

(i)   The separate functions of 'public' and 'private' law in the Act and their impact on each other.
(ii) The concepts of parental responsibility and children's rights.
(iii) The flexible nature of child law and the judicial response to trends.
(iv) The impact of Human Rights, decisions of the European Court of Human Rights ('ECtHR') and the Conventions.
(v)   The influence of the Family Justice Review ('FJR') on the modernisation of family justice.

12.1 Introduction

The **Children Act (CA) 1989** made major changes in both the public and private law relating to children, which at the time were considered 'radical', but no longer so after 25 years of implementation and in the context of the current modernisation of family justice.

'Public Law' (cases about the duties of the local authority towards children living in their area, and of the rights of children and parents versus the state represented by the local authority) is the usual label for that part of the Act which deals with the orders sought from the courts to intervene within the family, so as to secure essential protection for the child from harm and to promote the child's welfare.

'Private Law' (cases about the respective rights and duties of children and parents within their own personal parent and child relationship) is the corresponding label for orders of the courts made to regulate the interaction of the child's parents with the child and others, where the child's parents cannot agree on issues concerning the child's upbringing without activating such intervention.

Following the marginalisation of the divorce suit, which 50 years ago formed the bulk of 'family law', the law relating to children now forms a major part of the specialist family lawyer's workload (together with financial provision after decree of divorce, nullity or dissolution of a civil partnership), and some practitioners specialise in child law or financial provision alone.

This significant workload is divided more or less equally between private law and public law, but the latter is regarded as such a specialism that practitioners are usually now accredited by the regulatory authorities for such public law work.

The Act was brought into force on 14 October 1991, placing the private and public law under one statutory scheme, and ridding the previous, somewhat piecemeal, law of most of its complications and anomalies. The intention was to provide a comprehensive code and to a great extent this aim has succeeded. Thus, an academic student requires:

(a)   a sound working knowledge of the private and public law aspects of the CA 1989;
(b)   some outline knowledge of how the public law provisions impact on and interrelate with the private law;
(c)   an ability to identify and monitor trends and appreciate the importance of the latest cases (because of the lack of application of the doctrine of precedent in family law, so that decisions are only a guide to how a court might interpret the exercise of its duty within the statutory framework, particularly since child law can be a fast moving field); this is especially important because the impact of *practice* is as important as the black letter law in child and family law, since both are interdisciplinary specialisms where socio-legal factors may significantly change the court's approach, e.g. in relation to the treatment of domestic violence[1]; and

---

1   See e.g. the court's approach to domestic violence and contact in Chapter 11 on 'Domestic Violence and Forced Marriage' and 12.2.3 for the impact of domestic violence (as 'harm') on s 8 orders.

(d)   adequate research skills to check and update the law where necessary in order to decide whether there are human rights implications which impact upon the core established principles of English law.

> ### ❖ CASE EXAMPLE
>
> In considering, in the conjoined cases *Re L, V, M and H (Contact: Domestic Violence)* (2000),[2] whether the apparently firmly established principle that all ongoing contact with non-carer parents was necessarily for the welfare of the children concerned, the court responded to psychological evidence of damage to children who had witnessed domestic violence. This initial judicial awareness (at the time only anecdotally evidence based) that domestic violence might require a changed perspective had inspired a June 1999 consultation paper by the Children Act Sub-Committee of the Advisory Board on Family Law.[3] That paper was in itself a timely response to concerns in women's organisations such as the 1999 Women's Aid report *Unreasonable Fears? Child Contact in the Context of Domestic Violence: A Survey of Mothers' Perception of Harm.* These initiatives were followed by a report to the Lord Chancellor in 2002 recommending articulated guidelines for good practice, and also more research; and ultimately by a formal Practice Direction. These conjoined cases really mark the beginning of the relationship between research and judicial impact in decided cases.

In studying the provisions of the Act, the first step for the student is therefore a thorough working knowledge of the law and practice, so as to identify the *questions* that must be asked in academic study, even if the answers to the more specialised and complicated issues are unknown, since these can be researched. Family law is a field where there has been much recourse to the **European Convention on Human Rights (ECHR)**: the role of human rights continues to play a major role under the **Human Rights Act (HRA) 1998**, which imported the convention into English law, now in force for over a decade.

It is fortunate that in the case of urgent children cases neither the FPR 2010 r 3A and Protocol nor CAFA 2014 s 10 (making MIAMs compulsory before proceedings may be issued) nor the Final Report of the FJR[4] specifically insist on DR where cases involving domestic violence need to come before the court, while still recognising that greater use of DR might reduce the conflict between parents which is damaging to children.

Nevertheless, the Final Report has much to say about changes in child law proceedings under the Act, criticisms which obviously informed both the various organisations supporting the Manifesto for Family Justice in its protests about the LASPO restriction of legal aid in family law, a statute which the wider profession immediately saw as harming children. The President of the Family Division of the High Court (who also leads the Family Court and family justice) has enthusiastically supported such modernisation and also initiated some projects of his own, for example for greater transparency in all family justice decisions.

---

2   [2000] 2 FLR 334, CA.
3   *Contact Between Children and Violent Parents: The Question of Parental Contact in Cases where there is Domestic Violence.*
4   Published November 2011, https://www.gov.uk/government/publications/family-justice-review-final-report.

12.1.1 Background to the CA 1989

The Act's intention was to provide a comprehensive code for child law, in a framework largely regardless of the parents' marital status – hence the practical separation by court procedure of child orders from the substantive decrees defining parental status and the emphasis by the professional regulatory bodies on practitioners' keeping these two distinct areas of law and practice separate.[5] Acquiring an overview of how this once radical system now works is helpful to students who might otherwise be confused by reading reports of old cases, which are often still a useful guideline to the likely interpretation of contemporary principals, but of course contain the old pre-1989 terminology, which was significantly changed by the Act to emphasise the new concepts which it imported.

Part I of the Act confirmed the basic principle that the child's welfare is paramount in both public and private law.[6] The former concept of parental *rights* and duties (rooted since time immemorial in both historical and religious contexts) was replaced with the more modern one of *parental responsibility* (PR). The FJR was keen to build on this concept and 'make it work' (to which substantial report space is devoted).

Part II of the Act completely restructured the private law of children. It abolished the outdated concepts (and unhelpfully emotive wording) of *custody, care and control* and *access*, and replaced them with a power for the court to make individual orders. These were designed to regulate (in a manner perceived as less emotive and more specifically practical) the issues of a child's *residence* (i.e. where and with whom the child should have a *home*) and *contact* (i.e. when and how the child should keep in touch with the non-residential parent or other relatives). This Part then provided *specific issue* and *prohibited step orders* ('SIOs' and 'PSOs'), empowering the court to make individual one-off decisions, allowing or forbidding any decision a parent might wish to take, without necessarily making any other changes in the child's established residential arrangements.

The **Children and Families Act (CAFA) 2014** has changed this terminology again, since the FJR recommended abolishing both the residence and contact labels and those two orders, and, in tandem with 'making parental responsibility work', replacing them with a 'child arrangements order' ('CAO') which specified with whom the child should 'live' and with whom 'spend time', although the SIOs and PSOs remain for any other discrete parental disagreements.

The remainder of the 1989 Act is concerned with the public law relating to children.[7] Parts III–V reorganised the general powers and duties of local authorities in relation to children, also reorganised emergency protection and created specific *emergency protection* and *child assessment orders*.

When the Act came into force these new orders were perceived as invasive. However, they are now seen, both together and separately, to assist the local authority to carry out its duties to protect children in the authority's area, without the state necessarily intervening in family life more than is essential for that core purpose – a key principle of the Act.[8] The FLR's complaint in this context was that child protection proceedings (which include care, supervision and ultimately adoption out of care, if that is the ultimate plan for a child) were not completed quickly enough; the resulting reform has placed a 26-week limit as the norm within which such applications should be determined.

Other parts of the Act are important for fleshing out the detail, for instance s 91 in Part XI, which deals with duration of orders. It should be noted that the Act is so packed with detail (and with frequent amendments to reflect recent dramatic changes, e.g. parental responsibility in respect

---

5 See the Code of Resolution (formerly the Solicitors' Family Law Association, still sometimes called the 'SFLA') which states that *separate* letters should be written to clients on these two separate topics, even if written on the same day. The Law Society Family Committee recommends that all solicitors follow the Code, whether they are members of Resolution or not.

6 'Confirmed' because the concept of the paramountcy of the child's welfare was not new, having first appeared in the Guardianship of Infants Act 1925, although with some exceptions (such as the high-profile case of J v C [1969] AC 668, HL, see below 12.2.2) it never achieved much prominence until the 1989 Act.

7 See Chapters 19 and 20.

8 See below at 12.2.

of children of civil partners) that it is essential that the student has an up-to-date[9] statute book in order to follow the much amended legislation.

12.1.2 The philosophy of Parts I and II

The package of private child law provided by the Act, and the fresh air it has blown into this area of the law over 25 years, has in fact contrasted very favourably with the former position, where in order to make a simple point about a self-contained decision – such as on selection of a school, or on religious observance – a parent had to embark on a full-blown custody application; this was because under the old law the custodial parent had the right to make such major decisions and impose them on the child and the other parent, whose only recourse was to go back to the court to ask for custody to be changed so that *that* parent could then take over major decisions in the child's upbringing. In the contemporary philosophy of shared parenting, whether parents live together or not, it is easy to see how old-fashioned that was.

The menu of post-1991 orders was provided by s 8 of the CA 1989 and these orders were thus usually referred to collectively as 's 8 orders'.[10] Following CAFA 2014, it is now necessary to distinguish between the new CAO and the remaining two, the Prohibited Steps Order (PSO) and the Specific Issue Order (SIO).

The contemporary structure owes much to concepts derived from the wardship jurisdiction of the High Court,[11] for which it was designed to be an easier and cheaper alternative. Fortunately the FJR made no attack on wardship which, far from being outdated by the CA 1989, has experienced increased use since 1989, for instance as it is so useful in connection with the prevalent trend towards international abduction of children in cross-border families, since it is instantly effective when a child goes missing, whereas any CA 1989 order, even sought urgently, would take significantly longer.

Support for the CA 1989 ethos from the new Family Court and the FPR 2010

Procedural support for the Act alongside that for other family law matters has been found for many years in the **Family Proceedings Rules (FPR) 1991**,[12] now replaced by the FPR 2010 for all courts dispensing family law, in force from April 2011, and recently updated for the new Family Court from April 2014; the student referring to the court rules for any purpose (e.g. when reading old cases) will therefore need to distinguish between the two versions: the FPR 1991, designed for the triple tier of separate courts, and the new FPR 2010, especially the amendments from 22 April 2014 (making some significant changes for the introduction of the new unified Family Court created by the **Crime and Courts Act 2013**). The ultimate introduction of this unified court[13] has much simplified family justice and should, perhaps, meet the FJR's goal of also speeding it up with consequent benefits for families and children.

The immediate impact of the implementation of the unified Family Court is therefore as follows:

(1)   All family proceedings now commence in the Family Court, in London or the regions. With some exceptions, there is no longer any need to go to the High Court or, as formerly, to the FPC or a designated county court. This is potentially a vast improvement on the previous

---

9 Students should be beware of using only online resources outside legal databases, since these often show only the text of the statute as enacted, without subsequent amendments. There is usually a warning to this effect on sites located by general search engines.
10 Covered in detail in Chapter 16.
11 See Chapter 19.
12 1991 SI 1991/1247 as amended for the High Court and county court, and Family Proceedings Courts (Children Act 1989) Rules 1991 SI 1991/1395 as amended for the magistrates in the FPC.
13 First proposed by the High Court judge, Sir Morris Finer, in his Finer Report around 45 years ago.

system where many child cases began in the FPC and were transferred according to various rules if necessary. Save in exceptional circumstances where the High Court is designated *all* private and public law child matters, like any other family case, may now start in the Family Court where the appropriate level will be determined by the court. Thus there is no longer any need to distinguish between county courts designated as 'family hearing centres' or county courts which are 'care centres'. Therefore the existence of child law issues arising in divorce, nullity or civil partnership suits will no longer cause the practitioner to commence the adult decree or order proceedings in a county court also designated as a family hearing centre or a care centre, so as to avoid child proceedings having to be transferred (often causing delay and adverse impact, contrary to the general principles of the Act[14]).

(2) The long-standing separate magistrates' domestic court, in recent years called the FPC, is now abolished and the overall result is that the magistrates (with judges of all levels, save for the Court of Appeal and Supreme Court) will be found sitting in the Family Court.

This potential improvement also accords with some of the key recommendations of the FJR, namely a general improvement in the efficiency and speed of family justice, as although the jurisdiction of the former triple tier of family courts – High Court, county courts and FPC – was said to be 'concurrent' throughout the three tiers, it did not really work in that way. Apart from the delay and lack of consistency in transferring cases between courts and judges (even when this could cut delay in awaiting a substantive hearing where the case was begun) there were always cases where business is formally assigned to one court or another; for example a child's application for leave to be a party in a s 8 application for a residence order to live with someone other than the child's parents was mandatorily heard in the High Court which would not be in the same building and often not in the same town,[15] whereas now High Court judges will be available in the Family Court wherever it is sitting. This unified court system is important to the practical impact of the law in ensuring as far as possible consistency, speed of resolution (important in the timescale of childhood) and every effort being made proactively to promote the welfare of the child.

The overall effect of the unified Family Court is designed to achieve a completely new approach to child disputes which was begun in the CA 1989, in which the rights of the child and the duties of parents and the local authority are emphasised, together with the non-interventionist policy of the law and the court, and the principle that in child cases there should be *no delay* in the resolution of the problem which has invited the court's involvement.

The concept of a child having rights rather than duties, and that of the parent having duties instead of rights, was not new in 1989, but rather traces its history back to the 1959 United Nations Declaration and 1989 Convention on the Rights of the Child to which the UK is a signatory. Earlier signs of such an approach in English law may be seen in the report of the working party of the law reform society JUSTICE in the early 1970s. This caused a stir at the time of its publication, when contemporary thought was not yet on the cusp of substituting the concept of children's rights and parental duties for the historic obverse of these principles; accordingly this new approach took a long time to work its way through to our participation in the International Year of the Child, the establishment of a Children's Legal Centre and the 1980s work of the Law Commission which led to statutory 'parental responsibility' in the CA 1989; see 12.2 below.

Building on the CA 1989's philosophies from 2014

However, despite the FJR criticisms, it is clear that even in the generation since the implementation of the CA 1989, the new approach has been largely successful despite the procedural delays which

---

14 See below at 12.2.
15 See below at 12.3.3 'Children "divorcing" their parents'.

have become notable, and which may now be avoided in the new single building and multi-level Family Court. While it may still take more than legislation to confer on some feckless, damaged or inadequate parents the parental responsibility envisaged by the 1989 Act and now encouraged by CAFA 2014, the 1989 system itself has clearly encouraged *some* potential for improved relations between parents; for instance, taking the context of the 1989 Act at its lowest, when the legislation came into force in 1991 it was immediately no longer necessary in divorce for either parent to insist on having custody (or indeed any order at all) simply so that either parent could get his or her own way in a relatively self-contained area of the child's life (which in bitterly contested pre-1990s cases often meant merely obtaining legal possession of the children at all costs, usually for all the wrong reasons). Progressive amendments of MCA 1973 s 41 (which had originally required a formal order for future custody, care and control of the children of the family) have since completely separated the process of divorce and child matters, so that although a form of 'Statement of Arrangements' for the children of the family continued to be filed with a petition, it was given such cursory judicial attention in the paper process of the 1970s special procedure and the FPR 2010 summary procedure, that unless there were glaring irregularities which alerted the DJ perusing the file, it was ultimately possible to obtain a decree without any significant consideration of the future of the children, let alone orders about where they should live or with whom they should have contact, although a DJ could still in theory make an order under s 41 that a decree was not to be pronounced without the court having an opportunity to consider the children's future arrangements.

This has now been superseded in the amendments to the FPR 2010 to provide for new procedures on the April 2014 implementation of the new Family Court, and in CAFA 2014 s 17 by which s 41 is entirely repealed, so that divorce and child issues are now completely separate, and any child issues will be decided within CA 1989 proceedings.

This progressive weakening of s 41 culminating in its complete repeal has not been without criticism, and the no-fault divorce created by the failed **Family Law Act (FLA) 1996** Part II (also since repealed by CAFA 2014 s 18) would have made it impossible to obtain a final dissolution of a marriage without complete resolution of all outstanding matters, including future child arrangements. However, the contemporary philosophy, 18 years on from the FLA 1996, appears to be to respect adult autonomy in personal relationships by recognising that spouses can already obtain a divorce on demand under the current law,[16] and perhaps should not be prevented from doing so, not least as this may not be in the child's best interest, because of the evidence[17] that witnessing conflict, particularly in domestic violence, harms them.

While the recently retired previous president of the Family Division, Sir Nicholas Wall, complained throughout his term of office that parents (particularly middle-class parents) were harming their children through extended fights over every detail of their post-divorce lives, it is possible that there will now be some improvement in parental cooperation, since (owing to the withdrawal of most family justice legal aid) if such parents wish to continue confrontation they will have either to pay for legal advice and representation in CA 1989 proceedings themselves or go to court as LIPs. Compulsory MIAMs before proceedings may be started, and the encouragement to parents of the new Child Arrangements Programme ('CAP')[18] to rely on parenting programmes and private ordering rather than obtaining actual orders of the court, may also assist in reducing such litigation; although naturally there will be hard cases, since it is naive to suppose that parents who

---

16 See Chapter 5.
17 See n 1 above.
18 Instituted with the inauguration of the Family Court on 22 April 2014 to deliver the new child arrangement orders required by the Children and Families Act 2014. The working group which produced this new scheme was chaired by Cobb, J, who is now chairing the 'MAP' (Money Arrangements Programme) with which the President plans to follow up the child law procedural reforms. See Chapter 7.

divorced (as they could not get on with each other) will *all* suddenly be able to cooperate, even assisted by mediation (which remains funded for those who qualify financially). It seems clear they may instead decide to join the new army of LIPs in going to court themselves without advice or representation, although it is to be hoped that some may seek at least to obtain basic advice from some of the new low fixed fee opportunities being offered by the profession or from such charitable or *pro bono* resources as remain.

Shared parental responsibility and shared parenting in practice post-2014

Until very recently joint or 'shared' residence orders were still not necessarily encouraged, unless that pattern of a family's life was already established – although there has been a discernible trend to be noted in many judgments of the last few years towards at least treating shared residence as a starting point when considering s 8 orders generally; the former rationale was always justified on the basis that a child should generally have one home and not two unless it was already an established fact that that child divided its time entirely amicably between the parents – for instance where there was parental shift employment for which child care arrangements were working well.

However, the reason for that approach was that the provision of the system of pre-2014 residence, contact and specific issue or prohibited steps orders meant that the child could in practice often share time fairly between its two parents, thus enabling *both* to continue to influence a child who was living with one parent and having generous contact with the other, whatever the legal position was called; as sometimes it was labelled 'shared residence' (obviously with no formal contact order) and sometimes 'residence' and 'contact' respectively. This situation has also been supported by the formal initiatives developed in the courts and social welfare services, and amongst practitioners, towards 'shared *parenting*', for example the 'Parenting Plan' stationery and diary tools developed by Resolution.

The most recent judicial approach, evidenced in many reported judgments, does seem to be to have to regard the shared residence order as the starting point, although the debate in England and Wales (inter *alia* fuelled by adverse reports of shared residence in Australia) had not yet concluded on whether this ought to be reflected in amended legislation, when the FJR stepped in, recommending no such presumption, but a root and branch overhaul centred on shared *parental responsibility*, in which parents would work together to achieve the best practical outcomes for their children on parental separation. The government's acceptance of this recommendation has resulted in the CAOs replacing residence and contact orders, pursuant to CAFA 2014 s 12. However, this is not the whole story since the trend to private ordering encouraged by the FJR and CAFA 2014 includes parents agreeing everything between themselves, perhaps in mediation, *without going to court at all* even for a consent order unless that is considered necessary; thus now there *may be no order at all*. It must be asked, is this the triumph of hope over experience? Or an invitation to a greater, and more expensive cataclysm for the Family Court budget, when it all falls apart?

The FJR proposals included Parent Information Programmes, starting with a short leaflet when a child's birth is registered and culminating in instructions about what to do on an internet information hub if, and when, the parents decide to separate; in theory encouraging parental agreement and relying heavily on education designed for parents to 'grasp their roles and responsibilities so that they can cooperate in their shared parenting'.[19]

The prognosis for this system is clearly uncertain. In the absence of the old 'custody' battles, and even if there was a residence or contact dispute, under the 1989 Act the court *has* always been able to separate out any subsidiary arguments by deciding on any specific (educational or other) issue, *without* a pitched battle necessarily having to break out. This has obviated the previous need to

---

19 FJR para 4.9.

disrupt every aspect of the child's lifestyle with a change of physical custody simply because one parent or the other had strong views on some point and wished to enforce them if possible, and this will obviously continue when proceedings are inevitably started in respect of such issues.

It is the inadvisability of dissolving marriages without *any* consideration of the future of the children that is a concern. While it is true that it was rare that a final divorce decree was occasionally held up because the Statement of Arrangements was manifestly unsatisfactory, and that the DJ's consideration of the children's future was extremely superficial, at least it was *read* and any anomalies, however rare, could be addressed.

Now it seems that the FJR envisages throwing everything back into the hands of the parents, and relying on parents' better nature to put their children first, and thus, with information and support, to agree a holistic programme for post-separation parenting. While this is a laudable ideal, it does seem a high-risk strategy as if the parents do not agree despite all encouragement, it seems that the court will have to make orders, which means someone must start proceedings, even if it is only the local authority when the children's situation has deteriorated.

An obvious early exception to this approach is clearly where a change of residence might have to be ordered by the court where the currently residential parent (after the other has probably moved out of the former joint home) is proving uncooperative about contact. The FJR apparently envisaged 'helping them to understand what to do and what to expect where an application to court is necessary'.

Judges are now fairly robust about this last resort if nothing else will work to ensure contact (after a number of years in which rhetoric did not match reality, largely because the judiciary drew back from the obvious custodial sanction for contempt of the court's order, since it was readily seen that this would hardly assist the child's relationship with either parent if its mother was jailed in support of the father's enforcement of contact). There were, however, three salutary change of residence orders from mother to father made in the first couple of years after the contact enforcement provisions of the **Children and Adoption Act 2006** came into force in 2007 although their absence to begin with raised doubts as to whether the court would finally take this draconian step.[20] Consequently where the shared parenting which is apparently expected does not occur perhaps judges will resort to this sort of order again – or perhaps wait for the local authority to intervene.

For those parents who can agree everything without recourse to the court, the FJR vision may, of course, work and actual *orders* may therefore still never be necessary at all, as before. However, for those who do not cooperate, and for whom losing custody pre-CA 1989 would have meant *losing face*, it seems that the combination of generous *contact*, plus the right to seek a *specific issue order* if necessary, and in return for ceding residence to the other parent, may no longer be able to be articulated in the new CAO, as the new order speaks of a child 'living with' one (or presumably more than one) individual and 'having contact with' another (or others). However, the professionals already report that the CAFA 2014 s 11 amendment to the CA 1989 s 1, which provides that 'involvement of some kind, either direct or indirect' of the parent who is not the primary carer is normally to be regarded as for the child's welfare, has already created a fixed concept in the mind of the more militant non-resident parent a belief that that means that the child's time shall be shared equally! This seems a pity as the former 'residence + generous contact' formula has worked well in many cases to neutralise such potential confrontation.

Although the court has said that this secondary face-saving function is *not* what the interface of these orders was for, such a resolution of fiercely competing parental interests may well have been in the child's interests in generating parenting harmony out of previous strife.[21] Reported cases

---

20 See Silver, S, 'Enforcement of Contact', *Family Law and Practice*, (2010) 1 FLP 54. This journal is no longer published but the archive may be found at www.frburton.com.
21 See Harris, O, 'Shared Residence', *Family Law and Practice*, (2010) 1 FLP 48; no longer published, see archive at www.frburton.com.

show this was often so, even where the other parent obtained a residence order which was not initially acceptable until the full potential of 'generous contact' was appreciated by the parent who had lost the residence order application. It may be a retrograde step to give back to parents the opportunity for more strife in an open-ended CAO, where the precise arrangements must be written in, rather than to continue with the tools that seem to have worked except with the most recalcitrant.

All these innovative FJR concepts obviously need to be examined in practical detail when they have bedded down in the public perception. To back up this contemporary approach there do also remain in the CA 1989 certain general principles which apply to both private and public law proceedings, and which are conveniently grouped together in s 1 as a reminder of the statute's broad philosophy, which was developed from previous adverse judicial experience of the old law which had undoubtedly not been fit for contemporary purpose. They are likely to continue to be useful in developing the post-FJR and CAFA 2014 schemes.

12.2 The general principles: CA 1989 s 1

These principles are contained in four sub-sections of s 1:

- s 1(1) (welfare of the child is paramount);
- s 1(2) (the no delay principle);
- s 1(3) (the welfare checklist); and
- s 1(5) (the no order principle).

When these four general principles apply is specified in s 1(4), i.e. the Court must pay particular regard to applying s 1(3) (welfare checklist) in contested s 8 order cases and in all contested applications relating to local authority orders for care and supervision of children, except where those orders are of an emergency nature (when there would not be time to do so).[22] It is specified in s 1(1) that the paramountcy principle in that sub-section applies in any decision affecting the child's upbringing or administration of its property, a wide field.

In theory there is nothing to prevent the court from applying s 1(1) and s 1(3) in other proceedings, but it is only mandatory in the two categories mentioned.

12.2.1 The welfare of the child is paramount: s 1(1)

STATUTORY EXTRACT

The sub-section states that

'When a court determines any question with respect to –

(a) the upbringing of a child; or
(b) the administration of a child's property or the application of any income arising from it,

the child's welfare shall be the court's paramount consideration.'

---

22 See Chapter 20 for this detail.

This does not mean 'first and paramount' as under the **Guardianship of Minors Act 1971**, but that it should be the 'first' consideration,[23] coming before any other in deciding whether to make an order: the word 'welfare' is not defined except in terms of the provisions of s 1(3), the welfare checklist. However, there is no guidance where more than one child is involved if their interests conflict. A 'child' is defined for this purpose as a person under 18,[24] but it is rare that an order is made once a child is 16, i.e. the school leaving age when a child can legally leave home, and even marry with the consent of a parent or guardian.

The child's welfare is usually ascertained through a welfare report under s 7(1), provided by the Child and Family Court Reporter, normally a social worker from Cafcass (Children and Family Court Advice and Support Service). The report is required to be thorough and comprehensive when it is ordered,[25] although this is not done in all cases not least because of resources, which presently often mean a report is not ready by the time the hearing comes on, sometimes 16 or even 20 or more weeks later. In these circumstances, since it is possible for the judge to interview the child directly, this is often perforce the current solution, pending a scheduled overhaul of Cafcass.[26]

The decision on whether a report is required is in any case for the court and not for the welfare officer, but in some cases the importance of a *comprehensive* report to enable the court to be fully informed is obvious, particularly where the report is the only channel between a child who will not be at court and the judge making the decision. Thus a welfare report will usually be essential in contested s 8 order cases, particularly in any case slightly out of the ordinary. Some examples will show how this works.

❖ CASE EXAMPLES

In *Re V (Residence: Review)* (1995)[27] the father had suffered traumatic psychological stress after seeing one of his children drown. He suffered severe head injuries and his condition was so bad that he lost his job. The Court considered that the interests of his son indicated that he should live with his mother rather than his father although this was against the wishes of the child and the recommendations of the welfare report.

In *Re P (A Minor) (Inadequate Report)* (1996)[28] the case was remitted to the Family Proceedings Court for reconsideration when the mother appealed on the ground of the manifest inadequacy of the report: the welfare officer had held one meeting only at her office with all parties present and did not assess the quality of the relationships of the parties and the children.

---

23 Hansard Vol 3 Col 1167.
24 Section 105.
25 *Scott v Scott* (1986) 2 FLR 320, CA, a domestic violence case.
26 Cafcass is now part of the MOJ – another recommendation of the FJR – and this habitual delay in reporting will now also be caught by the other key FJR recommendation, that child cases shall be completed within the new target period of 26 weeks: CAFA 2014 s 14, amending CA 1989 s 11.
27 [1995] 2 FLR 1010.
28 [1996] 2 FCR 285.

12.2.2 The no delay principle: s 1(2)

> **STATUTORY EXTRACT**
>
> The sub-section states that
>
> > 'In any proceedings in which any question with respect to the upbringing of a child arises, the court shall have regard to the general principle that any delay in determining the question is likely to prejudice the welfare of the child.'

The background to this was a history of gross delay in child cases in the decade preceding the CA 1989, when there were some notorious cases of delay so prejudicial as to restrict the court's options.

> ❖ **CASE EXAMPLE**
>
> In *J v C* (1969)[29] delay in deciding the future of a young Spanish boy brought up by middle-class foster parents in an English green belt area resulted in his being unable to return to the working-class background of his natural parents in a poor urban quarter of Madrid, as it had taken nearly ten years to reach a final hearing; having lived all that time in England he did not speak Spanish and would have been unable to relate to vastly different surroundings from those of his first ten years.

As a result of such past delays the court was required by the CA 1989 to draw up a timetable for the progress of private law s 8 orders,[30] and in public law care and supervision orders.[31] The court did take this seriously, expecting the timetable to be adhered to and sometimes, for example, proceeding in the absence of reports if the consequent delay to wait for them outweighed the disadvantage of delay. This obviously posed a dilemma in many cases as in some areas there was a very long wait for a welfare report to be prepared by Cafcass, resulting in Cafcass being under review since the system was said to be in 'meltdown' – hence the FJR recommendations and their adoption by the government.

12.2.3 The welfare checklist: s 1(3)

This statutory checklist is intended to impose a structured approach to judicial decision-making which is highly discretionary in the application of the welfare principle. The content of the checklist was never 'new' as it may be distilled from many previous cases in the decades leading up to 1989, but it did, for the first time, articulate in statutory form the general principles that emerge from case law. It also provided a convenient reminder, as the name suggests, to assist judges in

---

29 [1969] AC 668, HL.
30 Section 11.
31 Section 32.

checking that no relevant consideration was omitted in their deliberations on the facts of cases before them.

STATUTORY EXTRACT

The sub-section states that

'. . . a court shall have regard in particular to –

(a) the ascertainable wishes and feelings of the child concerned (considered in the light of his age and understanding);

(b) his physical, emotional and educational needs;

(c) the likely effect on him of any change in his circumstances;

(d) his age, sex and background and any characteristics of his which the court considers relevant;

(e) any harm which he has suffered or is at risk of suffering;

(f) how capable each of his parents, and any other person in relation to whom the court considers the question to be relevant, is of meeting his needs;

(g) the range of powers available to the court under this Act in the proceedings in question.'

As with s 1(1) there are specific private and public law proceedings in which, pursuant to s 1(4), use of the checklist is mandatory, i.e. whenever deciding to make, vary or discharge a contested s 8 order: s 1(4)(a), and whenever deciding to make, vary or discharge a special guardianship, care or supervision order: s 1(4)(b). The checklist does not have to be applied in emergency protection proceedings, as that would hinder emergency protection. It should be noted that the checklist is not exhaustive, and there is no particular 'pecking order' in the listed headings.

This statutory checklist of welfare points to be taken into account in reaching decisions has now assumed crucial importance in making all s 8 orders, and was specifically referred to in order indirectly to define welfare in a 1995 case in the Court of Appeal by a judge skilfully emerging from a particularly complex (but at the time fairly typical) case involving the denial of contact for a mother against the wishes of her children.

❖ CASE EXAMPLES

In *Re M (Contact: Welfare Test)* (1995)[32] it was held that contact was not a fundamental right as such of the child but that there was a strong presumption in favour of contact. The specific question, therefore, was whether the fundamental emotional need of the child to have an enduring relationship with both his parents – s 1(3)(b) of the checklist – was outweighed by the harm that the child in question would be at risk of suffering – s 1(3)(e) of the checklist – *inter alia* owing to his wishes and feelings – s 1(3)(a) of the checklist – if a contact order was made against the child's will.

---

32 [1995] 1 FLR 274, CA.

This case was approved in *Re L (A Child) (Contact: Domestic Violence)* (2000)[33] where Thorpe, LJ and Butler-Sloss, P, considered it was inappropriate to speak of a right to contact; they preferred an assumption of the benefit of contact as 'the base of knowledge and experience from which the court embarks on its application of the welfare principle' (although it appears more recently to be generally accepted that there is in practice a presumption of contact). The point, however, is that the welfare principle applies to s 8 orders, of which the new CAO is one, welfare is nowhere defined in the Act and *Re M* was a significant early case to pose the question of how a child's welfare was to be ascertained other than through the application of the checklist.

Although contact orders as such no longer exist outside the CAO, clearly this welfare approach to s 8 orders, including the CAOs, will remain.

12.2.4 The no order principle: s 1(5)

This is sometimes called the presumption of no order (although this has been held to be wrong)[34] or the non-intervention principle.

STATUTORY EXTRACT

The sub-section states that

'Where a court is considering whether or not to make one or more orders under this Act with respect to a child, it shall not make the order or any of the orders unless It considers that doing so would be better for the child than making no order at all.'

❖ CASE EXAMPLES

In *Re G (Children: Residence Order: No Order Principle)* (2005)[35] Lord Justice Ward said there was no presumption either way, and that the court must *ask* the question before making any order, 'Will it be better for the child to make the order than to make no order at all?' The Court overturned the DJ's decision in that case as he had considered that there was actually a legal presumption in favour of contact, which was wrong. The idea of s 1(5) was to place primary responsibility for taking decisions about children firmly on the shoulders of parents, who were considered (at least in theory) to be best placed to decide what is right for their children, and this supposition is a fundamental philosophy of the Act. The other motive was to discourage the making of unnecessary applications and the court from making unnecessary (and perhaps positively harmful) orders, which might, for example, exacerbate ill feeling between parents.

---

33 [2000] 2 FCR 404 at p 437.
34 See below *Re* G.
35 [2005] All ER 399; [2006] 1 FLR 771, CA.

In *Dawson v Wearmouth* (1999),[36] a case about change of the child's surname, Lord Mackay, LC, said that a Court should make an order only if there was some evidence that it would be for the benefit of the child's welfare.[37]

In *Re K (Supervision Order)* (1999)[38] Lord Justice Wall (a former President of the Family Division) said that, in a case where it seemed an order was necessary, and the choices were between a care or a supervision order, the court should start with the less interventionist approach.

There is some doubt as to what this 'no order principle' really means. In practice if a case has come before the court and it cannot be settled by conciliation or mediation, there will be an issue which requires determination, in which case it has been held that the court should not abdicate responsibility, taking refuge in the no order principle[39] so it is difficult to see how the sub-section can be respected unless an order is actually made, as judges who make no order purely on the basis of s 1(5) appear now definitely to be seen as wrong.

❖ CASE EXAMPLE

In *Re S (Contact: Grandparents)* (1996)[40] the judge did not make a contact order in favour of grandparents where there was a history of antagonism because by the time the case came to court he was persuaded that the mother would permit it, so he relied on s 1(5). On appeal the Court of Appeal held that since the judge had formed the view that such contact would be for the welfare of the child he should have made the order, not least because this would avoid further difficulties and a possible return to court, because there was a patent risk that the arrangements would break down.

In fact there is no large number of 'no order' decisions in the reports. There is a certain amount of academic literature on this point,[41] but the strongest judicial indication is Lord Justice Ward's view in *Re G* above that there is no presumption either way and that the judge must just ask the s 1(5) question: will it be better for the child to make the order or not?

This is a principle generated by the belief that parents are (or should be) the right people to decide what is best for their children. The court should therefore start with the less interventionist approach. In theory, following the recommendations of the FJR and the philosophy of the CAFA 2014, this principle of prime parental responsibility should be strengthened, if anything: so is there any change in respect of the interpretation of s 1(5)?

Technically, it has *never* been possible to make any s 8 orders by consent (although the old custody, care and control and access orders sometimes were consent orders, especially in relation to

---

36 [1999] 2 AC 308, HL.
37 See Chapter 16 for the impact of orders on change of the child's surname or removal of the child from the jurisdiction while such an order is in force.
38 [1999] Fam Law 376.
39 See *Re P (Parental Dispute: Determination)* [2003] 1 FLR 286, CA, where the court stressed this point.
40 [1996] 1 FLR 158.
41 Bailey-Harris, R, Barron, J and Pearce, J, *Monitoring Private Law Applications Under the Children Act: A Research Report to the Nuffield Foundation*, Bristol: University of Bristol, 1999; Pearce, J, Davis, G and Barron, J, 'Love in a Cold Climate', (1999) Fam Law 22; Phillimore, S and Drane, A, 'No More of the No Order Principle', (1999) Fam Law 40.

joint custody where the parents were agreed that that was the best outcome in their particular circumstances and the court approved). However, that practice depended on an earlier regime and did not fit with the provisions of CA 1989. The way that the court has been giving effect to agreements ultimately made at the door of the court *was* therefore to make no order, which would have been what had happened if the parents had been able to agree in the first place. This is because in accordance with the theory of s 1(5) the court preferred the parties to observe the spirit of the 1989 Act in negotiating and observing a proper parenting relationship.

Sometimes, however, the court did override the united wishes of the parents if there was a child welfare issue involving a third party. It would seem that the Final Report of the FJR and the new CAP do, however, envisage their CAOs sometimes being made by consent, obviously fine if parents agree, but where they do not, presumably the judge will still have to look at ss 1(1), 1(2), 1(3) and 1(5), make up his mind what is best for the child and make the CAO accordingly.

> ### ❖ CASE EXAMPLE
>
> In *Re C (A Child) (HIV Testing)* (2000)[42] the presumption that the best interests of the child coincided with the joint wishes of the parents was actually rebutted. In this instance the local authority wanted to test the child for HIV and the parents opposed that, so the issue had to go to court. In other words, where the local authority is involved as a third party in a public law case, the united wishes of the parents cannot override the child's welfare, which is paramount, and the court decides as between the opposing parties what that is.
>
> In such a case presumably the post-FJR and CAFA 2014 judge decides what is best for the child when approving a CAO that has been agreed and if s/he does not agree substitutes that judge's own view?

Is this really in the child's interests? Prior to April 2014 the court only went on to make an order in such circumstances (i.e. after the parents have agreed to settle their differences) when for some reason everyone thought a formal order would actually help. Although the court in such circumstances would put into the terms of the order whatever the parents have agreed, *technically* it is *not* a consent order as such but an order made by the court for the purpose of providing certainty. This may be splitting very fine hairs, but there is good reason for it in that any order is regarded as, if not precisely a failure on someone's part, at least *undesirable* if it can be *avoided* as it is incompatible with the philosophy of both the 1989 and 2014 Acts, and so strictly reserved for when it serves some *useful purpose*. However, what the FJR seems to have envisaged is a situation in which every child is the subject of a Parental Agreement ('PA')[43] or CAO where the judge might not in fact agree with the parents.

Sometimes orders were made, despite the no order principle, where it was necessary to give practical status (e.g. a residence order in favour of a non-parent). It is by no means clear what is to happen to this facility under the new system but in theory if the CAO contains a 'live with' provision the effect should be the same.

Mediation services have long been widely used to attempt to avoid having to make orders, and there has been a procedure for a meeting before a district judge with a welfare officer present

---

42 [2000] 2 WLR 270.
43 The 'PA's' that the Final Report specifically refers to.

which is the subject of procedural guidance.[44] It would certainly be a pity if this facility were no longer available[45] as to have the input of the judge into the PA for the future CAO seems sensible in practical terms in view of what could otherwise happen.

12.3 Parental responsibility

The concept of parental responsibility (generally abbreviated to 'PR') is found in CA 1989 s 3.

STATUTORY EXTRACT

Parental responsibility is

'all the rights, duties, powers, responsibilities and authority which by law a parent of a child has in relation to the child and his property': CA 1989 s 3(1).

It is central to the concept that a person with PR may not *surrender or transfer* any part of that responsibility: s 2(9); PR may, however, be wholly or partly *delegated* (e.g. to a child's school or to the local authority), or *qualified* or *curtailed* (e.g. as between the parents of the child either informally or by order of the court, i.e. by a s 8 order) and one parent can in routine matters act independently, but not, obviously, in relation to important, irreversible decisions: see CA 1989 s 2(7).

❖ CASE EXAMPLE

In *Re J (Specific Issue Order: Circumcision) (Muslim Upbringing)* (1999)[46] the Muslim father of the child wished to have him circumcised in accordance with his religion and the mother resisted this as she was not of the same faith. Wall, J, as he then was, decided that the mother had the right to prefer that the child was not circumcised, which was an irreversible step, and rejected the argument that as a Muslim boy the child should be circumcised in accordance with that religion, since he held that the child was not yet old enough to decide to belong to any religion, therefore it was necessary for the Court to make an order to resolve the dispute.

When PR is delegated, the parents remain responsible for the omissions of the person with delegated PR. Parental responsibilty is not simply a philosophical concept but actually requires the parent to assume various responsibilities towards the child. 'Parental responsibility' is not defined in the Act but its meaning may be abstracted from case law and statute. Bromley[47] has summarised an agreed minimum of the duties as follows:

---

44 Practice Direction [1992] 1 FLR 228.
45 Which is likely to depend on local resources under the control of each area Family Court's Designated Family Judge (the 'DFJ' who is responsible for organising family justice in his area); see the definition in the new CAP, reproduced in [2014] Fam Law 44.
46 [1999] 2 FLR 678.
47 10th edition, p 377. (Professor Bromley's original version of the list may still be found in the 9th edition (1998) of *Bromley's Family Law*, now edited by Nigel Lowe and Gillian Douglas, at p 350.)

(1) To provide a home for and care for and control the child (or have contact with the child) including disciplining him or her until he or she is 18, marries, enters the armed forces or is adopted, to which consent must be given or dispensed with. With regard to 'control', it is long established and confirmed by the ECHR that *moderate and reasonable punishment* is allowed, but any excess is assault: *R v Smith* (1985).[48]

However, as all parents know, this duty of control of a child is reduced to giving advice as the child grows older and (hopefully) matures, as is shown by the famous *Gillick* case which was the origin of the concept of *Gillick* competence of a child under the age of 16 who is not otherwise formally empowered by the **Family Law Reform Act (FLRA) 1969** s 8(3) to give consent to medical treatment.

❖ **CASE EXAMPLE**

Gillick v Wisbech Area Health Authority (1985)[49] was a case in which a Catholic mother took exception to a government circular which would have had the effect of allowing the family GP to give contraception to her teenage daughters below the age of 16 of whom, and of whose morals, she was protective. The issue was fought up to the House of Lords, where this concept of the *Gillick* competence of a mature child was duly established. An impressive five-judge court, comprising Lords Fraser of Tullybelton, Scarman, Bridge, Brandon of Oakridge and Templeman, decided there was nothing wrong with contraceptive advice regardless of the mother's opinion, if the girl in question had sufficient understanding to consult the doctor for proper and necessary medical treatment without informing the mother. A child with this level of understanding is now formally regarded as *Gillick* competent.

As a result the age at which children are now recognised to be likely to decide such matters – formerly the task of the parent with PR – has descended lower and lower, so that judges now often interview children as young as seven and are likely to be criticised if they do not seek the views of teenagers and sub-teenagers, and sometimes even younger children if those children are of a suitably mature disposition. Clearly, parent–child relationships have come a long way since the onset of sustained family law reform in the 1960s, and social change has advanced them even further in the period since the implementation of the CA 1989.

(2) To consent to the child's marriage.
(3) To consent to medical treatment for under 16s who are not *Gillick* competent, although doctors can always give emergency treatment without parents' consent.
(4) To maintain the child financially, which is enforced by various statutes including MCA 1973 ss 23 and 24; CA 1989 Schedule 1; DPMCA1978; Social Security Act 1992 s 106; and CSA 1991 s 1(1).
(5) To protect the child from physical and moral harm, and determine the child's religion.

---

48 [1985] Crim LR 42.
49 [1985] 3 All ER 402.

This 'protection' head means not doing anything to cause such harm to the child either *carelessly* (which if it caused the death of the child would be manslaughter, which is a crime) nor *deliberately* as in cruelty to children (which is also an offence where a person over 16 having charge of a child assaults, neglects, ill treats or abandons a child or exposes him or her to harm so as to cause unnecessary suffering or injury within the meaning of the **Children and Young Persons Act (CYPA) 1933** s 1). As far as *moral* harm goes, the parent should be aware of the **Sexual Offences Act 1956**, ss 10 and 11 (incest), ss 14 and 15 (indecent assault) and ss 25, 26 and 28 (permitting the use of premises by young girls for intercourse or encouraging them in prostitution, etc.).

❖ CASE EXAMPLE

In *R v Lowe* (1973)[50] a very young father of low intelligence failed to appreciate that his nine-week-old baby was seriously ill and neglected to call a doctor, so that the baby died of dehydration and malnutrition, engaging CYPA 1933 s 1. This was therefore a case of simple medical neglect which under the CA 1989 would now be likely to trigger the local authority's duty, imposed on it by the CA 1989 Part III, to investigate, assist and provide services and support to the family, in the course of which it might have discovered the inadequacies of care; and if voluntary arrangements did not work to have fallen back on the child protection provisions of Parts IV and V. However, at the time this sort of situation was not covered by any such legislation.

(6) To ensure that the child receives education. This is enforceable under the **Education Act 1996** s 437 by a school attendance order, or under s 443 for failing to comply with a school attendance order, or by using other sanctions such as the local authority threatening a care order if the child is suffering 'significant harm' within the meaning of CA 1989 s 31.

(7) To consent to or veto the issue of a passport, or emigration.

(8) To represent the child in legal proceedings.

(9) To agree to the change of the child's surname.

(10) To bury or cremate a deceased child.

(11) To appoint a guardian for the child.

Some have argued that these duties should be made more specific by an amendment of the CA 1989 as they are supposed to reflect the everyday reality of being a parent and to emphasise that this is an actual responsibility. The Law Commission has considered the meaning of PR[51] and the former Lord Chancellor, Lord Mackay, has said that the concept of PR

emphasises that the days when a child could be regarded as a possession of his parent – indeed when in the past they had a right to his services and to sue on their loss – are now buried forever. The overwhelming purpose of parenthood is the responsibility for caring for and raising the child to be a properly developed adult both physically and morally.

The contrast may be seen in the nineteenth-century censuses now available online where children as young as twelve were, for example, performing agricultural services for parents, such as in the capacity of 'dairymaid'.

---

50 [1973] 1 All ER 805.
51 Law Com No 172 para 2.6.

The leading classic article on PR remains that of Professor Nigel Lowe in 1997, 'The meaning and allocation of parental responsibility – a common lawyer's perspective'.[52]

The CA 1989 permits the court to make a 'prohibited steps order' (PSO) to stop a parent taking any undesirable step in carrying out PR in one of these ways,[53] or where appropriate the High Court may also make a wardship order, taking over from the child's parents the task of making decisions in these matters.[54] The 1990s high-profile case involving a 13-year-old schoolgirl allowed by her parents to contract a marriage with a Turkish waiter is an example of just such an appropriate scenario for a wardship order, although wardship is rarely used now save in emergency, since the PSOs and specific issue orders (SIOs) were expressly created so as to obviate the need to incur the expense of High Court wardship except in cases where there is insufficient time to obtain a CA 1989 order in the particular emergency, for example suspected imminent child abduction.

12.3.1 Persons with parental responsibility

There is an extensive list of those who have PR as of right; in principle a rule of thumb is anyone who might be likely to have it does (except some unmarried fathers unless and until they obtain PR in the ways designed for them) and there is a long statutory trail in the CA 1989 supported by some other statutes. Where the provision is not under the CA 1989 any other statute is identified:

(a) **Both mothers and fathers who were married at the time of the child's birth, or who have married since**, and pursuant to the FLRA 1987 s 1 have by the marriage legitimated their child, will have joint parental responsibility: s 2(1) and (3). Pursuant to the **Legitimacy Act 1976** ss 2 and 3, the child is treated as legitimate from the date of the marriage provided the father is domiciled in England and Wales; this will be so even if the father is living in a country where legitimation by subsequent marriage is not recognised, provided the child is in England or Wales.

(b) **Mothers** whether the parents are married or not; this includes a woman in a civil partnership at the time of treatment: s 2(1A), and where a woman is not in a civil partnership but has had treatment and agreed that a second woman is to be a parent: s 2(2A), s 4ZA.[55]

(c) **Fathers** whether married or not who since December 2003 have registered the birth of their children with the mother: s 4(1)(a)/4ZA(1)(a), or who have obtained a residence order: ss 4 and 12(1) and (2).[56]

(d) **Commissioning parents** with a parental order under HFEA 2008 s 54.[57]

(e) **Guardians** where a child has no parent with PR or a parent or guardian with an old residence order or CAO with a 'live with' provision has died during the subsistence of the order: s 5.[58]

(f) **Special guardians** for the duration of the order, 'to the exclusion of any other person with PR': s 14C(1).[59]

(g) **Local authorities** with a care order: s 33(3), although the parents do not lose their PR when this occurs, or with a placement order under the **Adoption and Children Act (ACA) 2002** s 25.[60]

(h) **Adoptive parents**, when the birth parents will lose their PR as the child will become a member of the new adoptive family.[61]

---

52 (1997) 11 *International Journal of Law, Policy and the Family* 192.
53 See Chapter 16.
54 See Chapter 19.
55 See Chapter 13.
56 For human assisted reproduction cases see Chapter 13. The new post-HFEA 2008 rules are highly complex and require separate explanation of the parentage and PR thus created which will be found in that chapter.
57 See Chapter 13.
58 See Chapter 20.
59 Ibid.
60 Ibid.
61 See Chapter 22.

Also

(i) **Any person** with residence order or CAO with a 'live with' provision, or with an emergency protection order so long as the order is in force: s 44(4)(c), although this will only last as long as the order, so will end when the child is 16 unless the residence etc. order is exceptionally extended beyond 16.

This was for some time the normal way of giving PR to step-parents (including those who are civil partners), rather than by adoption, although they can now also obtain PR by agreement with those who already have it (using the same formal procedure for any PR agreement) or leave of the court: s 4A(1)(b), though this can also be terminated by the court on application of anyone with PR: s 4A(3), even the child: s 4A(4) if the child has sufficient understanding.

Step-parents remain the poor relations of the extended family, with no specific duties (unless asked for periodical payments under the MCA 1973) and few rights.[62]

It should be noted that all residence orders in force as at 22 April 2014 were automatically converted into CAOs when the CAFA 2014 came into force on that date.

Fathers *not* married to the mother (often called 'unmarried fathers') do not automatically have PR unless they have registered the birth with the mother, and this has been considered potentially a breach of ECHR although the decided cases have recognised that this is not *necessarily* so, depending on the facts of any particular case.

❖ CASE EXAMPLE

In *McMichael v UK* (1995)[63] the position of the unmarried father was compared with that of married fathers. When examined in the judgment the distinction appeared to be between the varying levels of commitment shown by such fathers because unmarried fathers might not even have knowledge of their children's existence. The court therefore held that those fathers who had established a family life with their children could generally claim equal rights of contact and custody as married fathers. Accordingly the English position, which is that such fathers can apply for PR but do not automatically have it unless they register the birth with the mother, is not necessarily a breach of the Convention.

However, the unmarried father who does not fall into any category above could always obtain PR in one of five ways through CA 1989 s 4:

STATUTORY EXTRACT

(a) making a PR agreement with the mother: s 4(1)(b) in the prescribed form;[64]
(b) applying to the court for a PR order: s 4(1)(a);
(c) applying to the court for a residence order (now CAO);[65]
(d) being appointed the child's guardian by the court; or
(e) being appointed the child's guardian by the mother or by another guardian (s 5).

---

62 See Chapters 6 and 21.
63 [1991] Fam 151; [1995] 20 EHRR 205.
64 Regulated by the Parental Responsibility Agreement Regulations 1991 SI 1991/1478.
65 In which case if the order is granted the court will automatically also make a PR order under s 4(1)(a).

Or, of course, by marrying the mother and thus legitimating the child under the FLRA 1987 s 1, as mentioned above; this will result in the marriage's technically dating back for legitimation purposes to the time of the child's birth, and giving the father PR in the process, provided the parents were legally able to marry at the time the child was born.

It is not uncommon for fathers to apply for PR, and the court will consider whether it is in the child's best interests for the father to have it. Naturally it will be necessary for the father to satisfy the court that he is the father, and this will be on the ordinary civil standard, i.e. on a balance of probabilities.

Case law has now established that the court will need to see evidence of commitment to the child[66] so that it is important for a father seeking an order to be able to show in some way the **degree of commitment**, and the two other factors laid down by Balcombe J in Re H (Minors)(Adoption: Putative Father's Rights) (No 3) (1991),[67] namely the **degree of attachment** between the father and the child and the **reasons for his applying** for the order.

However, the child's welfare will be paramount, and Hedley J has made clear[68] that the award of PR is not 'a prize for good behaviour'. He suggests in his article that the application should be scrutinised for any indication of an improper or wrong reason for applying, and if this is absent the court should make the order unless there is something special in the case which means that the child's welfare requires that the order not be made.

❖ CASE EXAMPLES

In *M v M (Parental Responsibility)* (1999)[69] the father was violent owing to having received head injuries in a road accident and the order was refused.

In *R v P* (1998)[70] the very elderly father was suspected of being a paedophile and of potentially using PR to undermine the much younger mother's care of the child.

Neither lack of actual contact between the father and the child as in Re H (A Minor) (Parental Responsibility) (1993)[71] nor friction between the parents as in Re P (A Minor) (Parental Responsibility Order) (1994)[72] is in itself a reason for refusing a PR order if the three-point test in Re H above is satisfied.

Similarly, the fact that a father does not obtain a contact order for any reason does not preclude his having PR (e.g. because he is convicted of possessing obscene literature as in Re P (Parental Responsibility) (1998)[73] as PR is about duties and responsibilities and does not entitle the father to interfere in the child's day-to-day life: Re S (Parental Responsibility) (1995).[74] Sir Stephen Brown, P reiterated this important point in Re D (A Minor) (1994),[75] where the FPC had refused a PR order on the basis of parental hostility and lack of mutual respect, which were irrelevant to the Re H criteria.

---

66 Re P (A Minor) (Parental Responsibility Order) [1994] 1 FLR 578 and Re H (Illegitimate Children: Father: Parental Rights) (No 2) [1991] 1 FLR 214, CA.
67 (1991) Fam 151.
68 (1994) Fam Law 517.
69 [1999] Fam Law 538.
70 [1998] 2 FLR 855.
71 [1993] 1 FLR 484, CA.
72 [1994] 1 FLR 578.
73 [1998] 2 FLR 96.
74 [1995] 2 FLR 648, CA.
75 Unreported 24 May 1994.

Parental responsibility can always be terminated, even though it cannot be otherwise transferred or lost, if the father does anything which is obviously harmful to the child (e.g. assaulting the child: *Re P (Terminating Parental Responsibility)* (1995).[76] However, cases have occurred where the degree of commitment and attachment has been found insufficient and it has been held that it is for the father to *demonstrate* that there is a sufficient degree of both. In *Re J (Parental Responsibility)* (1999)[77] the father of a 12-year-old had never lived with the child, with whom he had enjoyed only annual contact, and PR was refused although the child's mother was in prison for drug abuse.

❖ CASE EXAMPLE

In *Re H (Parental Responsibility Order: Maintenance)* (1996)[78] it was established that commitment does *not* have to be linked to maintaining the child, when a father successfully appealed against a judge's adjournment for him to demonstrate commitment by paying maintenance, although it is clear that some judges consider that that is an important factor since even a father on benefits can make a minor contribution to 'show willing'.

Re G (A Minor) (Parental Responsibility Order) (1994)[79] and *Re H* (1996), above, have confirmed that the usual PR criteria of commitment, attachment and reasons for application, as set out in the early cases, are not exhaustive but indicative, although *Re G* has established that if these criteria are present they do raise a *prima facie* right to PR. Nevertheless, many family lawyers consider with those judges who have voiced the view that payment of maintenance should be required for grant of PR, as PR includes a right and duty to support the child financially, and there should therefore be some link between PR orders (and indeed contact) and some financial commitment.

It should be noted that although the original triple criteria apply to all PR *orders*, there are no suitability controls if the mother chooses to enter into a PR agreement with the father, even if the child is in care; see per Wilson J in *Re X (Parental Responsibility Agreement: Children in Care)* (2000).[80] Such an agreement must be on a prescribed form available from HM Court Service, which must be signed, witnessed and registered at the Principal Registry of the Family Division: see CA 1989 s 4(2) and the Parental Responsibility Agreement Regulations 1991.

It should also be noted that, while it was at one time repeatedly held by the ECtHR that difference in treatment between married and unmarried fathers in relation to PR does not *necessarily* infringe Art 8 of the European Convention, the Convention is now incorporated into the HRA 1998, which has been in force since 2000, and the point has been continually raised in English PR cases, though to begin with adopting the ECtHR view: see for example B v K (2000),[81] which adopted the argument in *McMichael v UK*, above. However, as in *Marckx v Belgium* (1979),[82] the ECtHR had held that the Article 8 right of respect for family life applied to illegitimate as well as legitimate relationships, and included wider relationships such as with grandparents, so there are now some grounds for criticism of the *McMichael* approach on the basis that there is a similarly wide variety of

---

76 [1995] 1 FLR 1048.
77 [1999] 1 FLR 784.
78 [1996] 1 FLR 867.
79 [1994] 1 FLR 504.
80 [2000] Fam Law 24.
81 [2000] 1 FLR 1.
82 (1979) 2 EHRR 330. See also Stephenson, S, 'Parental responsibility: is there anything more to say?', [1999] Fam Law 296.

relationships between married fathers and their children, and because the *McMichael* decision obviously conflicts with *Marckx*.

However, the one-time syndrome of large numbers of unmarried fathers without PR seems likely to fade naturally to vanishing point in a relatively short time: CA 1989 4(1)(a) and 4(1A) already provide PR status if the father registers the birth with the mother under s 10(1)(a) to (c) of the **Births and Deaths Registration Act 1953** (in force since December 2003). Although the Labour Government provision in the **Welfare Reform Act 2009** s 56 and Schedule 6 was scheduled to demand *compulsory* registration by both parents unless the registrar considered that impossible, impractical or unreasonable[83] it seems that rising numbers of unmarried parents have been registering voluntarily so that the present Coalition Government's decision *not* to bring this into force does not seem likely to reverse this trend to record unmarried births.

Given the increasing legal and social recognition of atypical families (some much more atypical than those merely with unmarried fathers[84]) this is not a surprising step, consistent with the benefit long emphasised of a child's ongoing relationship with both parents.

If either parent misuses PR, the other can always apply for a PSO to stop this,[85] and s 2(8) in any case prevents a parent with PR from acting in any way incompatibly with another order (e.g. a s 8 CAO).

It should be noted that step-parents do not acquire PR on marriage to the child's biological parent, although a step-parent caring for a child and treating that child as a child of the family will create the usual obligations towards such a child of the family, such as in respect of financial provision claims if the marriage founders,[86] irrespective of whether the step-parent has PR: s 3(4)(a). A step-parent without PR may do whatever is reasonable to safeguard or promote the child's welfare irrespective of having PR or not: s 3(5), as may any person who has *de facto* care of a child.

12.3.2 The termination of parental responsibility

Parental responsibility acquired by an order of the court or by agreement ends when the child is 18, as of course it would do automatically in the case of any child reaching majority: s 91. Otherwise it cannot be transferred or lost except by death or adoption: s 2(9) and 2(11), although it could be taken away for good cause by the court where a person did not have it at the child's birth.

❖ CASE EXAMPLE

In *B v A, C and D (Acting by her Guardian)* (2006),[87] where PR was granted on conditions and those were breached, the court was invited to reconsider the whole question of PR, and was able to do so, because the CA 1989 creates a single code for court orders about the welfare of children; thus the full range of orders can be made where a case is 'family proceedings' so that different matters can be consolidated and any order in the family proceedings portfolio may be made of the court's own motion.

However, there is no way of removing PR from a parent who has always had PR, regardless of how badly such a parent behaves, although a care order will restrict such a parent's exercise of PR.[88]

---

83 See the White Paper *Joint Birth Registration: Recording Responsibility*, Cm 7293, 2008 for the background to this provision.
84 See Chapter 13.
85 See Chapter 16.
86 See Chapters 6 and 21.
87 [2006] EWHC 2 Fam.
88 See Chapter 20.

Parental responsibility is thus somewhat like a smile – it can be given out generously to all and sundry without necessarily diminishing the original supply, despite delegation and even increase in the numbers of persons who technically have it.

Where more than one person has PR, each has power to act alone: s 2(7), unless some specific requirement necessitates the consent of more than one (e.g. to adoption, change of surname or removal from the jurisdiction where the parties cannot agree and a residence order or CAO 'live with' order is in force).[89]

12.3.3 Children 'divorcing' their parents

This early to mid-1990s syndrome was not (as thought by some) a transient headline generated by freak journalism, such as periodically occurs when the media misunderstands some aspect of family law (as unfortunately all too frequently still occurs). To the surprise of many family lawyers of the time, it was apparently in all seriousness a class reaction by some children in the early days following the implementation of the Act in 1991 to the publicity in the media emphasising the role of the voice of the child in ensuring the paramountcy of welfare in decisions relating to children, together with the development of the concept of the *Gillick* competent child in making or contributing to any decisions about that child's life and future – especially when this relatively new freedom corresponded with the perceived diminution in traditional parental rights generated by the *Gillick* case.

In particular this perception of potential new 'child power' appeared to fasten on the innovative possibility under the Act of autonomous child applications for change of residence (although no doubt the media was responsible for the 'catchy' headlines as these cases were reported in the tabloids).

Owing to the enduring concept of PR, such 'divorces' as were suggested to be possible through such change of residence applications by children were only a reality in the minds of the children concerned, even where an order was made for the child to live with other relations or the families of friends. See for example *Re AD (A Minor)* (1993),[90] an early case in a long line of decisions by which the court began to be troubled in the early and mid-1990s where children were determined to move house, if necessary against their parents' wishes.

Bainham looked at this phenomenon in his article 'See you in court, Mum: children as litigants'.[91] The basic approach taken by the court in any such cases, where usually the persons with whom the child desired to live would have had to seek leave to apply for a residence order under s 10, was to look at the criteria in s 10(9). These criteria included the nature of the proposed application, the applicant's connection with the child, any risk of harm or disruption to the child's life through the application and, where the child was in local authority accommodation, the authority's and the parents' wishes and plans for the child. Where the child was applying personally, by s 10(8) the court had to be satisfied that the child had sufficient understanding to do so, but the s 10(9) criteria did not apply. This same s 10(8) criterion would apply to the decision of any solicitor willing to represent the child, who would need to be represented in such proceedings since a child cannot apply as a litigant in person.

Resolution, in its code and guidelines, developed guidance to solicitors representing children, and these and the court, in a number of decisions, have suggested that, while the views of competent children should be taken seriously, both the solicitor and the court should be slow to accept children in litigation. One reason for this is that there is every likelihood that children as parties, who are entitled to see all documents in the case, and are liable to be cross-examined, possibly by

---

89 See Chapter 16.
90 [1993] 1 FCR 573.
91 (1996) 6 JCL 127.

parents, would be exposed to adult themes which are not appropriate for them. Some children have established that their wishes are so strong that they must put them forward themselves and not through the court welfare officer: see e.g. *Re C (Residence: Child's Application for Leave)* (1995).[92]

The welfare principle does not apply to applications for leave (or the child might have been denied the right to raise the issue of the s 8 order sought at all), but there is a *Practice Direction (Family Proceedings Orders: Applications by Children)*[93] which requires all such applications to be made in the High Court. This can presumably continue in the Family Court where High Court judges will be available and in theory such orders can still be made in the new context of the CAOs.

12.4 Current debates

Ideas for research on these current discussion questions can be found on the companion website updates.

- What does the no order principle in s 1(5) really mean in practical terms? Is it compatible with the new CAO?
- Should the welfare of the child be further defined in the Act? Or is the s 1(3) checklist sufficient indication?
- Is it logical and fair to treat unmarried fathers differently from those married to the mothers at their children's birth?

12.5 Summary of Chapter 12

The Children Act 1989

The CA 1989 made the following fundamental changes:

- Abolished pre-1989 concepts of custody, care and control, and access in private law cases.
- Replaced them with those of residence, contact, specific issue and prohibited steps orders but the FJR Final Report recommended, and the CAFA 2014 legislated for replacing these with a CAO, although policy prefers that such arrangements are made on the basis of PAs without the necessity of a formal order.
- Created new concepts of PR and children's rights which have endured, resulting in a new approach to child disputes culminating in the policy of strengthening of PR enshrined in the CAFA 2014.

Parental responsibility (PR)

- Almost all parents will now have this at birth of a child or be able to get it, very few exceptions.
- No specific definition but it includes all elements of traditional protection and support.
- Difficult to lose PR, cannot be lost by those who had it at child's birth, even when shared with other parties.
- Therefore children cannot 'divorce' parents.
- Unmarried fathers who do not have PR can be viewed differently by the law without breaching the ECHR.

---

92 [1995] 1 FLR 927.
93 [1993] 1 All ER 820.

- The FJR recommended 'making parental responsibility really work'.
- This has resulted in legislation in the CAFA 2014 abolishing residence and contact orders and substituting the CAO or alternatively private ordering through similar PAs brokered between parents outside court.

General principles of the 1989 Act

- Welfare of child paramount.
- Welfare not defined but can be deduced from checklist which must be applied in contested cases about the child's future or in connection with the child's property.
- No delay to be permitted in deciding cases.
- No order to be made unless better for the child than making no order.

 12.6 Further reading

Bainham, A et al, *Children and Their Families*, Oxford, Hart, 2003.

Barlow, A, 'Out of court family dispute resolution: the lessons of experience', [2014] Fam Law 44: 620.

Blacklaws, C, 'The impact of the LASPO changes to date in private family law and mediation', [2014] Fam Law 44: 626.

Boele-Woelki, K et al, *Principles of European Family Law Regarding Parental Responsiblities*, Antwerp, Intersentia, 2007.

Diduck, A, 'Justice by ADR in private family matters: is it fair and is it possible?', [2014] Fam Law 44: 616.

Freeman, M (Michael), 'The Next Children's Act', [1998] Fam Law 341.

Gilmore, S, 'Contact, Shared Residence and Child Well Being: research evidence and its implications for legal decision making', (2006) *International Journal of Law, Policy and the Family* 34.

Henricson, C, *Government and Parenting*, York, Joseph Rowntree Foundation, 2003.

Hunter, R, 'Access to justice after LASPO', [2014] Fam Law 44: 640.

Hunter, R, 'Exploring the LASPO gap', [2014] Fam Law 44: 660.

Maclean, M (ed), *Parenting After Partnering*, Oxford, Hart, 2007.

Probert, R, Gilmore, S and Herring, J (eds), *Responsible Parents and Parental Responsibility*, Oxford, Hart 2009.

Reece, H, 'Parental Responsibility as Therapy', (2009) Fam Law 39: 1167.

Wallbank, J, '"Bodies in the shadows": joint birth registration, parental responsibility and social class', [2009] CFLQ 267.

Chapter 13

Parentage, Parental Responsibility and Human Assisted Reproduction

Chapter Contents

Learning outcomes for this chapter

An understanding of the impact of innovative medical techniques and social change on traditional family relationships including:

(i) An overview of the partnership of science and law in creating atypical family connections, most recently through the provisions of the Human Fertilisation and Embryology Act (HFEA) 2008.

(ii) An awareness of the radical change in legal philosophy and in underlying social attitudes as a result of such scientific advances in human assisted reproduction (HAR).

(iii) An appreciation of the far-reaching consequences for previous concepts of parentage, social parenting and PR of the legal provisions responding to these techniques.

(iv) An ability to pose, discuss and answer questions about wider implications impacting on other areas of family law – including same-sex marriage pursuant to the Marriage (Same-Sex Couples) Act 2013.

13.1 Introduction

The impact of scientific advance in HAR has for some years been generating significant changes in the study of parentage, social parenting and parental responsibility (PR). However, the most radical change in this area of family law has followed the implementation on 6 April 2009 of the **HFEA 2008**, to which must now be added the additional layer of the impact of the **Marriage (Same-Sex Couples) Act 2013**, meaning that (with rare exceptions) all the provisions applying to opposite-sex married couples now also apply to same-sex couples, provided they are *married*.

In the last few years the entire concept of the family has in any case evolved from that of the traditional nuclear family, so that at the same time 'Family Law' has inevitably moved on from the exclusive study of that type of family. With the benefit of hindsight one can see that the fundamental change from the centuries-old norm of a family unit of opposite-sex parents (whether married or not) together with their children (whether those were the biological children of one or both of those parents or were adopted) began to impact on the study of family relationships sometime in the early 1990s; around the time when the CA 1989 was implemented and probably owing to the new philosophies introduced in that Act.

To begin with there was a barely perceptible shift from the then accepted focus of family law (which was on the parents and their relationships as the core of the family unit, in which the child was only an appendage, although an increasingly empowered one) to the slightly different perspective, which presented an alternative view of the family through the child's relationship with its parents (or at least with its mother, and sometimes with its father, if present in the new family framework). As a result, the independently developing area of child law then expanded to become an entity entirely separate from the law applying to adult relationships, in which it was clear from the first that the new discipline of child law applied to all children, whether their parents were married or not – indeed it was soon said that for most purposes there were no longer any illegitimate children in the old-fashioned sense, only illegitimate parents.

As a result both society and the law also became used to the concept of the different 'family' groupings of single mothers with children, or of same-sex partners with or without children, natural or adopted, as well as with the diminishing numbers of 'nuclear' families, including the corresponding decrease in married partnerships, and an increase alongside that trend of unmarried cohabitants.

However, whereas in the past such alternative families grew up by 'happenstance' – such as where a single mother, often pregnant from an extra-marital relationship which did not endure with her partner, decided to keep her child rather than to give it up for adoption (which was a very unusual course 50 years ago when the concept of the 'illegitimate' child still existed and was a social taboo). An alternative example sometimes arose where gay partners of either sex set up house together, often without existing children, but sometimes adopting them.

Nevertheless, through advances in HAR it is now possible to *create* such an atypical family as a matter of preference, without the former stigma of 'illegitimacy' of any child whom the partners wish to add to their atypical family, and to do this without social disapproval. Moreover, not only may same-sex, as well as opposite-sex, partners be involved in the assisted conception of children with whom they will then have a genetic connection, but it seems that transsexuals, who are now fully recognised in their new gender pursuant to the **Gender Recognition Act (GRA) 2004**, can also participate in the new parenting regime of the 2008 Act.

The enabling legislation in the HFEA 2008 is, moreover, drafted in such a way that even more unusual family relationships may be developed in the future, of which we have so far seen no actual cases in either the law reports, the arts or the popular press: such cases may arise, for example, from the provisions in HFEA 2008 ss 36–38, which permit a man, entirely unconnected with the mother or the child, to be 'treated' as the social and legal father of the child if he is invited to assume this role by the mother, and provided he accepts the agreed fatherhood conditions in HFEA 2008 s 37 This suggests a return to the Victorian model of social parentage whereby a single woman with a child (in those days generally a widow, since single motherhood was not only not usual but condemned) would seek out a husband able to assume the parental role in relation to her child or children. However the 2008 Act equivalent is distinct, in that in this instance the mother appears to be able to invite *any* man who is willing, even, it appears, one married to another woman or indeed in another same-sex relationship, to assume the role of father. The only restriction appears to be that the woman who is the child's mother must not have also invited any other *woman* to be the child's other parent, under the provisions of s 44.

The use of the different terms in ss 37 and 44 – 'other parent' in the case of a woman who might have been invited by the mother to be her child's second parent under s 44 and yet the old-fashioned word 'father' in relation to the man to whom she extends such an invitation under s 37 – is the more confusing; particularly so in the context of the studied avoidance in the Act of any requirement for the child of HAR to have a father at all.

However, the equality and diversity specialists have been pleased to note that both s 37 and s 44 require the same agreed parenthood conditions to be met regardless of the gender of the second parent: essentially the potential 'father' and the potential other 'female parent' must respectively give to the responsible person at the licensed clinic a notice stating that s/he consents to being treated as the father/other parent of any child resulting from the treatment; then the mother must in each case give the responsible person at the clinic a notice that she agrees that either the man or the other parent shall assume this role. Finally, the notices must be in writing and signed by the person giving them, the notices must not have been withdrawn, and the mother must not have asked anyone else to assume the role in question.

13.1.1 Parentage through HAR

Arguably this area of family law provides the most fundamental change in approach to both adult relationships and children's rights since the arrival of family law as a subject of study within the academy. That watershed is generally traced to the second half of the 1940s when the late Lord Shawcross[1] thought family law was a 'very simple branch of the law' requiring 'no study or thought at all'. That this could be said of family law in the newly emancipated post-World War II society where, because of the **Legal Aid Act 1949**, women were for the first time about to be able to afford

---

1 Attorney General in the post-1945 Labour Government.

to divorce uncongenial husbands, was because family law at that time basically consisted mainly of Divorce[2] (despite successive child-focused statutes such as the Guardianship of Infants Act 1925 and Children and Young Persons Act 1933). Child law, and the relationship of children with their parents, was then still realistically only a 'bolt on', whereas HAR existed only in the imagination of science fiction writers. Lord Shawcross, were he still alive today, could be in shock at the extent of the developments in the shape of the contemporary family, regardless of the lack of simplicity of the remainder of family law and the extent of the study and thought that would have to go into nearly 70 years of updating of even the main core of the formerly 'simple' subject.

For example, the implementation of the HFEA 2008 has, in the amendments to the **Births and Deaths Registration Act 1953**, effected the most startling reform of the law which could be imagined, more startling than any other controversial issue of its time at any stage from the 1940s to the present day. Not only can a child now have two *female* parents but they may be formally *registered* as the child's *only* parents, and no *man's* name will appear on the register with those of the two female parents in that case. While it is true that male civil partners can achieve the same result, so that the child can have two *male* parents, and no *woman's* name will appear on the register with those of the two male parents in such a case, what is so startling about this formal recognition of same-sex parentage is that, such was the key role of the *father* in a child's parentage and parenting that the previous case law, such as *Re C* (1991),[3] was for a long period completely hostile to the concept of a child even *living* with two lesbian women unless some appropriate male paternal influence could be discerned in the family scenario under judicial consideration.

At that time the idea of judges accepting the contemporary concept of the absolute absence of formal or informal male influence, which they specifically looked for in another case, B v B (also 1991),[4] was pie in the sky. Such conservatism was the common approach in the 1990s, when the tenor of judgments showed that the court was obviously concerned about problems arising for the child at school because of the 'different' family background that such a child would manifestly have, and which might then escalate and impact on friendships as the child grew up. As a result judges appeared always to be frantically seeking a balance of male influence in the case, and if that could not be found, resolving the matter with the excuse of some other adverse factor which negated approval of the child's residence in a lesbian household. A classic example is the case of B v B in the early 90s where it was clear that a child was only allowed to live in a lesbian household owing to the role the father with contact would play in the child's upbringing.

❖ CASE EXAMPLES

In *Re C* (1991) the court was obviously more than unhappy with allowing a child to live in a same-sex household if that could possibly be avoided, and was equally uncomfortable about articulating this objection, despite the general change in attitudes of the public. Instead they pegged their decision to remove the child on the fact that the wife's female cohabitant had a criminal record.

In *B v B* (1991), however, the youngest child of the family *was* left with his mother, with whom it was obviously preferable that he should live owing to his age, but this was because the consultant psychiatrist in the case felt that the influence of the father, who himself was living with a woman whom he hoped to marry, would be sufficient to

---

2 See Chapter 1.
3 [1991] Fam Law 175.
4 B v B (Minors) (Custody, Care and Control) [1991] 1 FLR 402; [1991] Fam Law 174.

counteract any adverse effects of the mother's lesbian household. Besides this factor the mother was considered not to be a militant lesbian and was able to provide continuous care (which was a positive factor in her favour in terms of the welfare checklist),[5] while the father would have had to use a childminder, a point obviously not in his favour when the court was considering the stability of ongoing care.

The comparison of these two 1991 cases illustrates how uncomfortable the court was both in sanctioning deviation from the nuclear family norm, even in permitting children to reside with a parent in a same-sex relationship, and even more in articulating what were obviously their real reasons. In these circumstances it is difficult to understand how easily the HFEA 2008 apparently reached the statute book, permitting as it does not only actual genetic parentage of children born into a same-sex relationship to be achieved but also formal registration of that fact to be added by amendment of the **Births and Deaths Registration Act of 1953**, when less than 20 years before the implementation of the 2008 Act the court was unhappy about even permitting residence in such a household, and indeed only seven years before, when Christine Goodwin won her case in the ECtHR,[6] they were still refusing either to recognise transsexuals in their new gender for all purposes or to allow re-registration in that new gender so that essential new documentation could be issued – on the grounds that the registers could not be altered. Baroness Deech[7] remains opposed to the re-registration on the grounds that the certificate is then false, commenting: 'What I object to is the falsification of the birth certificate. It is supposed to be a true record of genetic origins of the birth.'

The apparently sudden *volte face* of the legislative changes is easy enough to explain: once the Goodwin case had forced a change of English law in the enactment of the GRA 2004, the writing was presumably on the wall. In 2006, there was a review of the HFEA 1990, revolutionary in its time but which was then beginning to look outdated, and it was accepted that changes were necessary, so as better to recognise the wider range of people who by then sought and received HAR technology in order to have children, although previously this had still been largely taken up by infertile opposite-sex couples.[8] Hansard records that there were some queries about the precise provisions of the Act as the draft Bill went through Parliament, but nothing approaching the uproar over the proposals in the Family Law Bill 1996 that married and unmarried couples who were cohabiting should benefit on remotely equal terms from the consolidation then proposed of the reformed law of domestic violence, and of the corresponding reform of rights in the family home.

However, it is fair to say that despite the smooth passage through Parliament, *after* the 2008 Act was passed there was then some criticism of the 'other parent' provisions when the Act came to be implemented, such as the *Sunday Times* article 'Who's the IVF Daddy? Anyone you care to name?'[9] – an article which discusses the position of single women undergoing fertility treatment who (under the terms of s 37) are able to name almost any other adult (except the usual close blood relations within the traditional prohibited degrees) as their child's second parent on the birth certificate, with no need for biological relationship to the child, or even any close relationship with the mother. Provided (i) the second parent agrees to take on the legal rights and responsibilities and to accept

---

5 See Chapter 15.
6 *Goodwin v UK* [2002] 2 FCR 577, ECtHR.
7 Formerly Chair of the Human Fertilisation and Embryology Authority. Sometime Gresham Professor of Family Law, former Law Fellow and Principal of St Anne's College, Oxford; see her 2009–10 Gresham Lectures, www.gresham.ac.uk, and Deech, R and Smajdor, A, *IVF to Immortality: Controversy in an Era of Reproductive Technology*, Oxford, OUP, 2007.
8 See paragraph 2.67 of the Report of the Review.
9 *Sunday Times*, 1 March 2009, www.timesonline.co.uk.

the agreed fatherhood conditions in s 37, (ii) the man's sperm has not been used, and (iii) the mother has asked no other person to be the child's 'other parent', that person can be named on the birth certificate.

13.1.2 Social attitudes

There is little evidence of adverse social attitudes to HAR parentage in the case of same-sex relationships; in particular neither such a surrogate birth of a child of the singer Elton John and his partner, in which both claimed to have contributed to the conception of the child, which was carried by a surrogate mother in the USA, nor the later birth of a second child to the couple by the same means, appears to have attracted the slightest adverse reaction.

The author Jeanette Winterson has also traced the public acceptance of lesbian parenting through drama on television and in films[10] in which she reviewed 'the surprise hit film of the year' in 2010, The Kids Are All Right, of which she wrote that it was 'about gay mums . . . the kids charmingly call them "the mumses" ', where 'the family is well off middle class, with a detached house and a Volvo'. She asked in this article: 'Have we finally arrived at a time in history when lesbians are no longer weird and a gay "marriage" is a good marriage?'

The Winterson article deduces that 'film and TV representations of lesbians tell us a lot about prevailing views . . . that movies cannot afford to lose buckets of cash and that TV channels need ratings' so that 'that makes visual media conservative'. She identifies earlier gay male and female productions which were 'tricky': her own Oranges Are Not the Only Fruit (1990, winning two BAFTAS, Best Drama and Best Actress for the National Theatre star Geraldine McEwan, and the Prix d'Argent at Cannes) but which nevertheless had to be shown on television after 9pm. Also Russell T. Davies' 'brilliant' Queer As Folk, which as late as 1999 had to be dropped by Channel 4. In 2004–5 The L Word, despite its television success, was shelved as a film. The article further notes the mid-1990s token lesbian themes in the soap operas Brookside and Emmerdale, although also that when Emmerdale tried a second attempt at a lesbian storyline in 2006 the ratings fell and the character Sonia, who had been in a lesbian relationship, 'rushed back to heteroland'.

In view of the timeline thus traced, both by the Winterson analysis and by the apparent lack of adverse reaction to the 2008 Act in those sections of the media where a repeat of the Daily Mail campaign against the FLA 1996 might have been expected, it would appear that the earlier experimental dramas in the 1990s were not entirely acceptable to the wider public in England and Wales, but that sometime between 2006 and 2008–9 this must have changed. It is fair to say that this conclusion is in no way at variance with that of Sir Henry Maine in Ancient Law[11] that social change occurs first, and change in the law follows, rather than vice versa.

Cobb J (then Stephen Cobb, Chairman of the FLBA) also mapped out a very helpful timeline within the establishment, in a review of case law demonstrating the importance of appropriate recognition of 'good' same-sex parenting. His article[12] identifies the cases of Re G (Children) (2006)[13] in the House of Lords and Re D (Contact and PR: Lesbian mothers and known father) (2006)[14] in the High Court Family Division as the key turning point.

In each case the court had to grapple with the most complex facts and concepts, as well as with the inadequacy of the English language and traditional culture to cope with the terminology that a child now needs to understand its family relationships if it has two mothers and a

---

10 'If gay is the new normal where does that leave straight?', The Times Saturday Review, 11 September 2010.
11 Maine, H, Ancient Law, 1861, London, Murray, 1906.
12 Cobb J, 'English courts' treatment of the children of same-sex couples', (2010) Family Court Review 48:3, at p 482, Wiley-Blackwell online.
13 [2006] UKHL 43.
14 [2006] EWHC 2 (Fam).

biological father: in this case the child called the two mothers respectively 'Ma' and 'Mummy' and the judge considered that the term 'the sperm donor' for the father was unhelpful and 'minimised' the father's standing in the child's life. Clearly there is still some cosmetic work to be done in this respect if such family units are not to give rise to some social discomfort, particularly for the child.

❖ CASE EXAMPLES

In *Re G* (2006) the issue was the rival claims of the biological mother CG and her former lesbian partner, the non-biological mother, CW, for primary care of the two children, of whom CG was the natural mother. CW had been given a shared residence order, and the case went back to court when CG relocated with her new partner (without notice to CW) from the Midlands to Cornwall. The children were parties and were represented by a guardian who did not support CW's claim to primary residence but had recommended stricter enforcement of contact.

Residence was nevertheless awarded to CW in the High Court, as the judge, Bracewell J, did not trust CG to facilitate contact. CG then lost again in the Court of Appeal, but recovered residence in the House of Lords, where both Baroness Hale and Lord Nicholls of Birkenhead emphasised the importance of the children's biological link with the mother, but at the same time of the importance of acknowledging the fact of good-quality same-sex parenting. It was in this case that Baroness Hale also articulated and emphasised that there were other forms of valuable parenting, besides that of the biological parent, namely that provided by the social or alternatively psychological parent, so that despite the importance of the biological link this did not mean that there was necessarily no alternative to the biological parent when such a parent was claiming residence.

In *Re D* the court was faced with a child with three parents, two lesbian mothers in a same-sex relationship and the known father, a married man who had answered an advertisement for a sperm donor and had later applied for PR, which the two lesbian mothers opposed, fearing that he would destabilise their relationship and family unit. The court (Black J), however, eventually gave him PR, despite the opposition of the distinguished psychiatrist assisting the court (Dr Claire Sturge) but with conditions that he did not contact the child's school or any health professional without their consent.

The impact of this change of philosophy, policy and practice makes the uproar over other changes, thought dramatic in their time, seem like the proverbial 'walk in the park'.

13.1.3 Parental responsibility in HAR

Parental responsibility would appear to follow acknowledged parentage as in the case of natural reproduction, including in the case of same-sex marriage, provided the same-sex spouse who is not the mother is aware of and agrees to the child's mother's treatment, except of course that (a) a male spouse cannot give birth to a child (at least not yet although it must be supposed that this cannot be ruled out for all time) and (b) a female same-sex spouse who elects to go for treatment to give birth to a child so as to become a mother could not be divorced for adultery if her spouse did not consent to the treatment, although this could in theory be sufficient behaviour for a decree.[15]

Thus PR may now be obtained under HFEA 2008 by two women (and no man) in relation to a child

(i)   by both women in a civil partnership at the time of regulated treatment: s 42(1); or

(ii)   where a woman not in a civil partnership agrees that a second woman shall be a parent: s 43.

This is because where a woman who is undergoing fertility treatment is in a civil partnership,[16] the other party in the civil partnership is to be treated as the 'parent' of the resulting child: s 42, and a female cohabitant[17] who satisfies 'agreed female parenthood conditions' in s 44 (which are identical to those which a male cohabitant must fulfil) will be treated in law as a parent of the child: s 43.

This brave new world requires some explanation, both to understand how HFEA 2008 achieves this innovative situation and to relate the concepts to other established family law principles. It should also be mentioned that following this Act a child even need not have a second parent of either sex; see below at 13.5. This too is a fairly startling development in the law applicable to parentage as it has always been understood in relation to English law. There has been some mildly concerned academic comment.[18]

13.2 Essential terminology

Human assisted reproduction (HAR) is a relatively new area of law, since the underlying techniques are also relatively new. The term covers artificial insemination by a donor (AID) or by the mother's husband (AIH), also in vitro fertilisation (IVF), gamete intra-fallopian transfer (GIFT), egg and embryo donation and surrogacy.

Surrogacy, whereby a woman carries a foetus for commissioning parents to whom she means to hand the baby when born, may be full (i.e. involving both egg and sperm donation by the commissioning parents and IVF) or partial surrogacy (more common) where the surrogate is fertilised with the commissioning father's sperm.

This inevitably led to questions of legal parentage when the practice became established. The legal issues were given detailed consideration by the Warnock Committee on Human Fertilisation and Embryology's report,[19] in which the government accepted the Warnock recommendations but provided that, where a married couple commissioned a baby with egg/embryo donation, the baby would be 'theirs' for succession purposes except in cases involving hereditary titles: HFEA 1990, s 29(4).

The existing law on HAR is not designed as an exhaustive investigation into the medical possibilities of achieving birth.

The topic is not yet by any means regularly included in the academic syllabus, but an awareness of this area of law is extremely important to the family law student, not only because of its necessary inclusion in any account of parentage and PR, but because of its impact on other developing

---

15 See Chapter 2 (Marriage) and Chapter 5 (Divorce).
16 See Chapter 8.
17 See Chapter 9.
18 Deech, R and Smajdor, A, From IVF to Immortality, Oxford, OUP, 2007. Anna Smajdor also gave a paper at the 2011 Summer School at the Centre for Family Law and Practice at London Metropolitan University in which she queried whether some of the more esoteric conceptions now possible should take place at all.
19 Report of the Committee of Inquiry Into Human Fertilisation and Embryology, 1984, Cmnd 9314, London, HMSO. See the White Paper Human Fertilisation and Embryology: A Framework for Legislation, 1987, Cm 259.

areas of family law, such as cohabitation, adoption and social parenting of children through residence orders and the new format of the CAO, introduced by the CAFA 2014. Whereas despite the fact that both same-sex and opposite-sex partners can, as always adopt, surrogacy has a separate appeal, since Elton John demonstrated its facility for enabling same-sex as well as opposite-sex couples to parent children who have some genetic relationship to either or both of them.[20]

In view of the limited relevance of this area of law to many university undergraduate syllabuses, this chapter only offers an outline of the various issues involved, which must be supplemented by those who are interested in gaining greater depth and detail by further reading.[21]

13.3 The Human Fertilisation and Embryology Act (HFEA) 2008

The 1990 Act has been extensively amended by the 2008 Act but the main features of the existing model of regulation are retained.

The 2008 Act is in three parts: Part 1 comprises amendments to the 1990 Act to take account of scientific developments and to reflect changes in social attitudes. Part 2 defines the persons who are to be treated as a parent of a child who is born (*after* the Act is in force, as its reforming provisions are *not* retrospective) as a result of assisted reproduction treatment, and introduces the new concept of parenthood (in certain circumstances) for the mother's female partner, if her partner is not a man. This makes provision precisely equivalent for same-sex and opposite-sex couples. It also tightens up the previous provision in the 1990 Act so that both 'parents' (i.e. the mother and the 'second parent', depending on whether the woman's partner is male or female) must consent in writing to what is intended. Part 3 makes miscellaneous and general provision including amending the **Surrogacy Arrangements Act 1985** (see below).

13.4 Who is the mother?

The answer to this may be found per Lord Simon in *The Ampthill Peerage Case* (1977):[22] 'Motherhood, although also a legal relationship, is based on a fact, being provided demonstrably by parturition.' Historically this has always been so, for example, the witnessing of births of heirs to sovereigns so as to prevent substitution, such as after the suspicious birth of the son of James II and his second wife, Mary of Modena, and the Roman practice of examining women who claimed to be pregnant as recorded by Justinian.

Surrogate parents, who have commissioned a woman (who by the above definition will be the mother) to bear a child for them, can now obtain a parental order in order to become legal as well as social parents, but when the practice first became common (with the birth of Baby Cotton in the mid-1980s: see *Re C (A Minor) (Ward: Surrogacy)* (1985)[23]) problems arose unless the husband's sperm had been used. This was so because the **Adoption Act 1976** made private

---

20 See, for example, Professor Chris Barton's article 'One dad good, two dads better?', (1999) *The Times*, 9 November.

21 See Further Reading section at the end of this chapter. A useful practical text is Birks, D , *Human Fertilisation and Embryology, The New Law*, Jordan's Family Law New Law Series, Bristol, Jordan Publishing, 2009, which also contains a full copy of the Act which, in view of the novelty of the Act's provisions, is absolutely essential in order to follow and comprehend the legislation. Most other texts are now out of date, although the latest Human Fertilisation and Embryology Authority's Code of Practice (HFEA, London) and Bainham, A, et al's text *What is a Parent? A Socio-Legal Analysis*, Oxford, Hart, 2000 are still worth reading. The HFE Authority was unfortunately included on the Coalition Government's list of those institutions whose separate existence was to be axed for economy reasons, with its functions transferred elsewhere.

22 [1977] AC 547.

23 [1985] FLR 846.

placements with non-relatives illegal. The parental order regime had, therefore, to be hurriedly created by the HFEA 1990, and this enabled such commissioning parents to become legal parents. This is the point made by Re W (Minors) (Surrogacy) (1991),[24] in which it was realised that without parental orders the commissioning parents could only become parents by adoption, and of course upon complying with the law in that respect.

The Warnock Committee on Human Fertilisation recommended that the birth mother, and not the commissioning mother, should be the legal mother, since surrogacy was not recognised in the UK or USA (save in California, which gave the legal rights to the commissioning mother, since she had given her tissue and intended to be a parent), although in England and Wales the **Family Law Reform Act (FLRA) 1987** around the same time recognised genetic parentage by testing.

By the HFEA 1990 s 27(1), 'the woman who is carrying or has carried a child as a result of the placing in her of an embryo or of sperm and eggs, and no other woman' was to be treated as the mother of the child, and was the mother for all purposes; this is repeated in the later statute: HFEA 2008 s 33.

Thus by both the 1990 and the 2008 Acts (if the treatment is carried out at a licensed clinic) a surrogate mother will be the mother in all cases. This, of course, was always contrary to the intention of the original arrangement so that (subject to various conditions) parentage may be transferred by a parental order: HFEA 2008 s 54.

If for any reason a parental order is not available parentage can then be transferred by adoption as then the child will be the child of the adopters.[25] (However, it should be noted that simple egg donation is not sufficient for the woman to be treated as the mother: HFEA 2008 s 47.)

The HFEA 2008 now regulates all treatment and research, and the code of practice is issued to all licensed clinics.

13.5 Who is the father?

This point was considered by the Law Commission in its Working Paper on Illegitimacy in 1979 because of the long-standing position in the common law which, owing to the presumption of legitimacy, has always made the child of a married woman the legitimate child of her husband (unless and until he formally rejected it – and in that case would then usually divorce her for adultery). The child of an unmarried woman was always the illegitimate child of the mother, with no legal father since the child was officially filius nullius ('no one's son') although Affiliation Acts were able to fix paternity, but not formal parentage, on a biological father if known, for financial support reasons.

With the institution of HAR, and social trends, all this was disturbed. The FLRA 1987 made the donor in AID (artificial insemination by a donor) the father provided he consented (unless, of course, the donor was anonymous). The common law rule was that the father is the one who provides the sperm, but this is now displaced by statute in certain cases:

(1)   Where AID or IVF is provided to a married woman as a result of which she is implanted with an embryo or she is artificially inseminated, unless the husband did not consent: HFEA 2008 s 35(1).

(2)   Where agreed fatherhood conditions are satisfied: HFEA 2008 ss 36 and 37.

(3)   Where a man donates sperm for the purposes of treatment services: HFEA 2008 s 41(1).

These three cases need to be considered separately.

---

24 [1991] 1 FLR 385.
25 See Chapter 22.

Case 1: In any case where the husband's sperm is not used, he the husband, and no other person, is treated as the father of the child unless it is proved that he did not consent to his wife's treatment

❖ CASE EXAMPLES

Two cases illustrate the meaning of consent: *Leeds Teaching Hospital and NHS Trust v A* (2003),[26] which relates to a similarly worded provision under HFEA 1990 s 28(2), and *Evans v Amicus Healthcare Limited; Hadley v Midland Fertility Services Limited* (2003).[27]

In these two cases the women had undergone fertility treatment with their partners but after the relationships broke down the men in each case withdrew their consent to use of the fertility treatment and storage of the embryos. The women wanted an injunction to restore the men's consent on the grounds that their human rights were prejudiced and that the provisions in the HFEA were incompatible with the ECHR. Wall J (as he then was) declined, as the court had no power to override the men's statutory right to consent or to vary or withdraw consent because if consent had been given to treatment with a named partner that was ineffective once the relationship had ceased. He said it did not breach the women's human rights, under Art 8 (right to family life), Art 12 (right to marry and found a family), Art 14 (right not to be discriminated against in relation to a Convention right) nor even Art 2 (right to life for the embryo, as an embryo was not a person). Mrs Evans appealed to the Court of Appeal (which upheld the lower decision and refused leave to appeal to the House of Lords) and ECtHR, Application No 6339/05, which upheld all decisions by a majority of 13:4.

Lord Justice Sedley, who was one of the judges in the *Evans* case in the Court of Appeal, has more recently revisited that decision in the Summer 2011 issue of the Newsletter of the Association of Women Barristers,[28] when he reviewed Professors Hunter, McGlynn and Rackley's account of their feminist judgment project, *Feminist Judgments From Theory to Practice*,[29] in which Professor Sally Sheldon comments upon *Evans v Amicus Healthcare* and Professor Sonia Harris-Short imagines how the judgment might have gone if a female judge had delivered the speech on an appeal to the House of Lords – and which instead of being refused had been permitted and, the female judge, adopting a different perspective, *had* found that refusal to allow the use of the frozen embryos was a disproportionate interference with Natalie Evans' Art 8(1) rights.

The thesis the book sets out to prove is that a woman judge's different perspective might have changed some decisions, particularly in areas such as the HFEAs and other contexts in which the woman judge's perspective might justifiably have seen the issues in a different light. This is probably as fertile an area for development of the law as the change of judicial hearts after the early 1990s decisions about residence of children in lesbian households.

26 [2003] EWHC 259.
27 [2003] EWHC 2161 Fam; [2004] 1 FLR 67; [2004] EWCA Civ 727, CA; *Evans v UK*, Application No 6339/05.
28 See the AWB website, www.womenbarristers.co.uk.
29 Oxford, Hart, 2010.

Notwithstanding such AID or IVF, this is still of course subject to the common law principle which has always upheld the presumption of legitimacy. This means that even if the husband has not consented to his wife's treatment, neither Act will treat the actual sperm donor as the father of the child where this common law rule means that the child is otherwise legitimate; in other words, the marriage is subsisting, so the child is born to a woman in wedlock, and her husband accepts the child as his. Presumably this presumption of legitimacy also applies, *mutatis mutandis*, in the case of a same-sex marriage where the 'husband' is female (whether or not s/he always was, provided in the case of a transsexual the gender change is recognised for all purposes) or the **Marriage (Same-Sex Couples) Act 2013**, presented as an equality statute, is wanting in the equality provision it was meant to promote.

In these days when many couples are not formally married, a man is logically also to be treated as the father of an *unmarried* woman's child if she and he receive treatment together – which pursuant to HFEA 1990 s 28 made them the parents for the purposes of any will or deed, except for titles and entailed estates. See *Re CH (Contact) Parentage* (1996).[30] Under the HFEA 2008 s 36 the unmarried father in this case must satisfy agreed parenthood conditions set out in s 37.

❖ CASE EXAMPLE

In *Re CH* (1996) the husband of the mother could not genetically be the child's father as he had had a vasectomy. Later, when the marriage broke down, the mother tried to prevent contact on the grounds that he was not the child's biological father, but the judge held that HFEA 1990 s 28 made him so.

On the other hand, pursuant to HFEA 2000 if a woman is unmarried and receives donated sperm under a licensed clinic arrangement, there need be no father, as the 2008 Act provides no requirements that a child should have a second parent of either sex, so it is perfectly possible for a child to have a mother but no father, and the same was true under the 1990 Act. See *Re Q (Parental Order)* (1996).[31] Consequently the HFEA 1990 s 13(5) has been amended by the 2008 Act to provide only that account must be taken of the welfare of any child who may be born as a result of the treatment ('including the need of that child for supportive parenting'). No word about a father. This too is a fairly startling change in the law and social practices of only a quarter of a century ago, but inevitably logical where the concepts of registered civil partnership, informal same-sex cohabitation and adoption by gay partnerships is accepted as a social norm and reflected in contemporary family law.

❖ CASE EXAMPLE

Re Q (1996) was a case where consent was required for a parental order but in law the child had no father. In such a case Johnson J held there was no person other than the mother whose consent was required for a parental order under the HFEA 1990 s 30. However, under the 2008 Act there is no requirement that a child should have a second parent of either sex.

---

30 [1996] 1 FLR 569.
31 [1996] 1 FLR 369.

Case 2: Where agreed fatherhood conditions are satisfied: HFEA 2008 ss 36 and 37

This is designed for the *unmarried* father mentioned above, since of course by no means all couples who go for treatment together are married, yet the contemporary approach to settled cohabitation is that in many ways it equates to marriage as a foundation for a family: the post-2000 Labour Government was at pains to stress that marriage was not necessarily the superior institution in which to bring up children. Both the unmarried male cohabitant and the female cohabitant must therefore both give their consent to his being treated as the father (and must not withdraw it before artificial insemination or placing of the embryo in the female cohabitant) and after this has taken place neither party can withdraw consent, unless the treatment fails and a new cycle begins. The agreed fatherhood conditions are set out in HFEA 2008 s 37 and in order to make sure consent is properly documented the treatment must take place in a UK licensed clinic.

Case 3: Where a man donates sperm for the purposes of 'treatment services': HFEA 2008 s 41(1)

Provided this is at a UK licensed centre and the prescribed procedure in HFEA 2008 Schedule 3 (including consent) is followed the donor man will not be the father of the child. However, if the treatment is outside a UK licensed clinic the old common law rules apply so that the donor genetic father will in law be the father.[32] This can be a problem: see the two contrasting cases of *B v A, C and D* (2006) and *Re B* (2007).

❖ CASE EXAMPLES

Two separate situations in three cases must be contrasted here.

B v A, C and D (Acting by Her Guardian) (2006).[33] In this case a lesbian couple, Mrs A and Mrs C, advertised for a man to father a child. B responded. The child, D, was born, following sexual intercourse between B and Mrs A, i.e. no IVF in a licensed clinic. After the birth of the child B wanted to be involved in the child's life, a contact order was made, and the issue of PR was deferred but subsequently granted conditionally on the basis that B would not visit the child's school or contact any health professional without the consent of Mrs A or Mrs C.

But compare *Re B (Role of Biological Father)* (2007),[34] where PR was not granted in similar circumstances to those of Mrs A and Mrs C as the court held that it was either undesirable or unnecessary as the man would either have to exercise it in such a limited fashion that it would not be worthwhile or he would exercise it fully and undermine the role of the lesbian parents.

Also *Re R (IVF: Paternity of Child)* (2005)[35] was a similar case where the House of Lords held that in conferring the relationship of parent and child on persons who were connected neither by blood nor marriage the rules must be applied very strictly. If as in this case the 'joint enterprise' of fertility treatment had ended by the time the successful treatment had begun the man was *not* the legal father of the resulting child and contact should not be ordered. Although this was a 1990 Act case a decision under the 2008 Act would be likely to be the same.

---

32 See also Heenan and McKinley, 'Consent to IVF treatment', [2004] *Family Law* 674.
33 [2006] EWHC 2 Fam.
34 [2007] EWHC 1952 Fam.
35 [2005] UKHL 33.

13.6 Posthumous parents

By HFEA 1990 s 28(6), some children were fatherless in law even though everybody knew precisely who the biological father was, because if he died before the child's conception and had not consented to the use of his sperm, he could not be treated as the child's father. This was the situation in the case of Diane Blood, who used her husband's sperm to give birth to two posthumous children, but he had not been able to give written consent to the fertilisation procedure as he was already unconscious when at her request the sperm used had been taken and stored. This remained so despite the fact that the couple had been trying to conceive a child so that his consent might in reality have been implied.[36]

As a result the 1990 Act was amended by the **HFEA (Deceased Fathers) 2003** which inserted new provisions into HFEA 1990 by adding s 28 (5A) to (5I) so that a man can now be registered on the child's birth certificate as the father of a child conceived after his death, either using his sperm or an embryo created with his sperm before his death.

These provisions also apply to unmarried and cohabiting fathers, and by HFEA 2008 s 46 a deceased lesbian partner has the same right to registration, whether or not the parties were in a registered civil partnership. The father has to have given his written consent before his death both to the treatment continuing after his death and to the registration, and problems continue if the man dies without having these written consents in place.

13.7 Destroying embryos and foetuses

The ECtHR has confirmed that an embryo is not a person and so has no protection from destruction if the rules for written consents are not observed in relation to stored gametes.

With regard to foetuses, for the sake of completeness in the field of managed reproduction, lawful abortion should be noted, although the criminal law of abortion is outside the scope of this book. Nevertheless since a foetus, like an embryo, also has no separate existence, a father has no right to prevent an abortion if the mother changes her mind about being pregnant: he has to wait for the child to be born before he can obtain parental responsibility (and that depending on whether he is married to or living with the mother or not).

Thus, curiously, although consent is at the core of the law of assisted reproduction, in that treatment cannot be administered at all without it, if the consent is withdrawn a frozen embryo capable of development as a normal child must be destroyed as in the *Evans* case (see above).

A foetus is in the same position, and has no protection other than the ordinary law of abortion which must be complied with as neither an embryo nor a foetus has any rights until birth: see *Paton v BPAS* (1978)[37] (discussed in the next chapter), which confirms that only the mother and not the father has standing to decide whether there should be a termination of her pregnancy, and *Re F (In Utero)* (1988)[38] in which an attempt was made to ward an unborn child to prevent the mother aborting it. This case has been followed up by the further decision in *St George's Healthcare NHS Trust v S* (1998)[39] where it was held that the foetus has no human rights to protect under the ECHR either. That, however, does not mean that once a woman is pregnant and carrying a child termination of a pregnancy can be done outside strict rules of law in accordance with the **Abortion Act 1967**.

---

36 See *R v Human Fertilisation and Embryology Authority ex p Blood* [1996] Fam Law 785; [1997] 2 FLR 742, CA.
37 (1978) 2 All ER 987.
38 [1988] 2 WLR 1297; [1988] Fam 112. See Chapter 19 for the wardship jurisdiction.
39 [1998] AC 245.

The legal background to abortion prior to the 1967 Act lies in the criminal law, including the **Offences Against the Person Act (OAPA) 1861** ss 58 and 59 and in the common law crime of murder, for which Coke's definition is that:

> murder is when a man of sound memory, and of the age of discretion, unlawfully killeth within any county of the realm any reasonable creature *in rerum natura* under the king's peace, with malice aforethought, either expressed by the party or implied by law, so as the party wounded, or hurt etc. die of the wound or hurt, etc. . . . .

Abortion is not, of course, murder, or any kind of unlawful killing if the 1967 Act is complied with; otherwise such an act will be either murder or an offence under OAPA 1861 s 58 or s 59.

Nor is it murder to kill a child in the womb or in the process of being born. It used to be a misdemeanour to kill a child in the womb after quickening (i.e. when the foetus became animated, in that the mother perceived foetal movement), but the present law in all respects is now statutory. On the other hand, the unborn foetus is part of the mother, so acting with an intention to kill or seriously injure the mother will be murder if it causes her death or the death of the child, if the child dies after having a separate existence – this is because of the doctrine of transferred malice. If the mother or child is killed by someone with a lesser intent than death or serious injury, the killer will be guilty of manslaughter.

The Abortion Act 1967 modified OAPA 1861 ss 58 and 59. By the Abortion Act 1967 s 1, as amended by the HFEA 1990, a pregnancy of less than 24 weeks may be terminated on social grounds if to continue with it would endanger the physical or mental health of the mother or her other children.

Termination is still possible after 24 weeks if the child would be likely to be born seriously abnormal or handicapped. These terminations are lawful provided that two registered medical practitioners agree that the conditions are met, and the abortion is undertaken by a registered medical practitioner, who need not be the same as either of the previous two and can be a nurse, not a doctor: see *Royal College of Nursing v DHSS* (1981).[40] By s 2 of the 1967 Act, it is permitted to take account of the woman's actual or foreseeable environment in taking these decisions. By s 3, multiple pregnancies can be reduced.

The good faith of the medical practitioners involved must be certified, but good faith is essentially a question for the jury if challenged. Normally a medical practitioner is acting in good faith if he or she believes that to be the case, and any finding of bad faith would be likely to be appealable unless there was supporting professional opinion.

The question therefore arises as to whether there may still be a defence of necessity where a termination is procured outside the provisions of the Abortion Act 1967, as to procure a miscarriage otherwise than in accordance with the Act is unlawful. In *R v Bourne* (1939)[41] a leading Harley Street practitioner terminated a pregnancy for good medical reasons (so as to preserve the mother's life). Lord Macnaghten took the view that there was not only a right for Bourne to act as he did, but also a duty to save life, so that where a doctor refuses to operate he or she could be considered no better than someone who failed to call a doctor to his or her sick child.

Lord Macnaghten presumably regarded such an omission resulting in the death of the patient as manslaughter, although he did not address the situation of the patient suffering only injury. Note, however, that the Abortion Act 1967 s 4 recognises that a doctor may conscientiously object to performing such an operation, and by s 5(2) that

---

40 [1981] AC 800; [1981] 1 All ER 545, HL.
41 [1939] 1 KB 687.

> 'for the purposes of the law relating to abortion, anything done with intent to procure a woman's miscarriage . . . is unlawfully done unless authorised by section 1 of this Act . . .'

Does this mean that the law as stated in *Bourne* is now superseded and there is no longer a defence of necessity?

There have been numerous criticisms of the Act by academic writers, in particular in relation to the euthanasia debate.[42] However, this statute, and medical practice under it, has been established for a long period.

There is also, of course, the offence of child destruction under the **Infant Life Preservation Act 1929** s 1, which prohibits any action with intent to destroy the life of any child capable of being born alive before it has an existence independent of its mother, unless of course the act causing such death was done in good faith for the purpose of preserving the life of the mother. A child is considered capable of being born alive if of 28 weeks' gestation or more, and proof of this period is *prima facie* proof of the child's ability to be born alive.

13.8 Surrogacy

Surrogacy is the practice whereby one woman (the surrogate mother) becomes pregnant, carries and gives birth to a child for another woman (usually for a commissioning couple, though there are regular examples in the media of family members performing this service for other relatives). The arrangement is usually as the result of a quasi-commercial agreement prior to conception that the child should be handed over to that person or persons after the birth. Payment is prohibited in English law except for reasonable expenses although this is often different in other jurisdictions. The woman who carries and gives birth to the child is the surrogate mother or 'surrogate'.

Depending on the particular circumstances she may be the genetic mother by 'partial surrogacy', i.e. using her own egg with sperm from the commissioning father (or one of them if the surrogacy is commissioned by a same-sex male couple) or she may have an embryo – which may be provided by the commissioning opposite-sex couple, implanted into her womb using *in vitro* fertilisation (IVF) techniques ('host' or 'full surrogacy'). The commissioning couple are 'the people who wish to bring up the child . . . They may both be the genetic parents or one of them, or neither, may be genetically related to the child.'[43] In whichever circumstances the practice is governed by the **Surrogacy Arrangements Act (SAA) 1985**.

By SAA 1985 s 1(2), 'surrogate mother' is defined as a woman who carries a child in pursuance of an arrangement made:

(a)   before she began to carry the child; and
(b)   with a view to any child carried in pursuance of it being handed over to, and parental responsibility being met (so far as practicable) by, another person or other persons.

Treatment in a licensed clinic is highly desirable because then the clinic can ensure that any man who goes for treatment with the woman, but does not contribute sperm, can be the father pursuant to the HFEA 2008 ss 36 and 38(3).

---

42   Tunkel, V, 'How Early, How Late and How Legal?', *British Medical Journal*, 1979; Gardner, R F R, *Journal of Medical Ethics*, 1975; Herring, J, *Medical Law and Ethics*, Oxford, OUP, 2008.

43   Cmnd 4068, 1998. See also Mason and Laurie, *Law and Medical Ethics*, 8th edition, London, Butterworths, 2008.

By SAA 1985 s 2(1), it is an offence to negotiate surrogacy arrangements on a commercial basis. However, by s 2(2), it is not an offence for a woman, with a view to becoming a surrogate mother herself, to do any act mentioned in s 2(1), and similarly it is not an offence for any man, with a view to a surrogate mother carrying a child for him, to do such an act.

Advertising is not permitted in the news media in the UK (including on television or radio): s 3, and no surrogacy arrangement is enforceable either by or against either party: s 1A, even if not illegal. However, the courts may decide that it is in the interests of the child to live with the commissioning parents: *Re P (Surrogacy: Residence)* (2008).[44]

❖ CASE EXAMPLE

In *Re P* (2003) a mother registered with a surrogacy agency and became pregnant as a result of artificial insemination. She then falsely informed the biological father that she had miscarried and brought up the child herself. She later re-registered with the agency and again falsely informed the biological father that she had miscarried. The second father learned the truth and applied for residence, which the court ordered, notwithstanding that the child had lived with the surrogate mother and her husband for 18 months.

These essentially practical provisions were generated by the experience of the 'Baby Cotton' case (1985),[45] where the local authority had obtained a place of safety order (under the pre-CA 1989 law this was similar to the contemporary emergency protection order under the CA 1989) and made the child a ward of court when the commissioning parents wanted to take the child over, although they were subsequently allowed to take the baby to the USA.

Surrogacy has expanded significantly in the three decades since the Baby Cotton case and is now a worldwide practice, in some poorer countries practically an 'industry', which has called for some international regulation. India is so far the only country to attempt this by legalising commercial surrogacy subject to strict controls, although not through direct legislation (which was apparently too long delayed for the 'boom' experienced), but through immigration rules, so that a special visa is now required for foreigners to enter India with a view to making an agreement with an Indian surrogate mother: they can no longer do so on a tourist visa, and will not be able to remove the child from India except to a country where in the opinion of the Indian authorities the welfare of the child will be guaranteed.[46] Inevitably, further developments in other countries are likely to follow; for example Thailand has announced such an intention.

13.9 Parental orders

By HFEA 2008 s 54, a parental order will be made in favour of the applicant commissioning parents, whether married, cohabitants or civil partners, provided that they are both over 18, they

---

44 [2008] 1 FLR 177 (upheld by the CA, [2008] 1 FLR 198).
45 *Re C (A Minor) (Wardship: Surrogacy)* [1985] FLR 846. For a detailed account of surrogacy see Mason and Laurie, *Law and Medical Ethics*, 8th edition, London, Butterworths, 2010, 'Surrogate Motherhood', and the report of the Warnock Committee, 1984.
46 See Malhotra, A, 'Note from Our India Correspondent', (2012) 3 FLP 2: 47. This online journal *Family Law and Practice* is no longer published but the complete archive may be found at www.frburton.com, and its successor International Family Law, Policy and Practice, at www.famlawandpractice.com.

apply within six months of the birth, one of them at least is domiciled in the UK, the gametes of at least one of them has been used: HFEA 2008 s 54(1)(b), and the court is satisfied that no money or other benefit (other than expenses reasonably incurred) has been given or received by the commissioning parents or passed in consideration of handing over the child or of making arrangements for or in consideration of the making of the order or the giving of consent unless such arrangements have been authorised by the court: HFEA 2008 s 54(8), which may be retrospective.

The court can approve higher payments in appropriate cases: see *Re X and Y (Foreign Surrogacy)* (2008).[47] The genetic parents, i.e. the surrogate mother and the legal father, must understand and agree to the parental order: HFEA 2008 s 54(6). The surrogate mother cannot agree until six weeks after the birth. The Court does not have power to dispense with these consents: see *Re X and Y (Foreign Surrogacy)* per Hedley J:

> The court has no power to dispense with a required consent, however unreasonable the withholding of that consent may be or however much the welfare of the child is prejudiced by that refusal . . . the persons whose consent is required have an absolute veto.[48]

If a parental order is not available because the conditions cannot be complied with, the alternative is adoption.

❖ CASE EXAMPLE

In *Re X and Y (Foreign Surrogacy)* (2008) a surrogacy agreement was entered into in Ukraine and provided the surrogate with enough money to purchase a flat. Three questions had to be asked to determine whether the court's consent should be given to this manifestly higher payment than usual: (i) was the sum disproportionate to reasonable expenses? (The answer to which was 'Not so disproportionate as to be an affront to public policy'); (ii) Were the applicants acting in good faith in dealing with the surrogate? (The answer to which was 'Yes'); (iii) Were the applicants a party to any attempt to defraud the authorities? (The answer to which was 'No'). In this case the children were settled with the commissioning parents and their welfare was decisive.

No agreement was required under the 1990 Act, however, where such persons could not be found or were incapable of giving agreement, but nevertheless where communication was possible, such as in the case of a married surrogate separated from her husband, consent of some sort probably remains essential although it might not need to be in writing (i.e. signing the form at the clinic).

McFarlane J skated over this condition in the case of *Re G (Surrogacy: Foreign Domicile)* (2007)[49] by suggesting that all reasonable inquiries should be made before the treatment began as to whether the husband consented.

---

47 [2008] EWHC 3030 Fam. This was a leading case relating to Ukraine, *inter alia*, about allowing higher payments than usual. It must be remembered that Ukraine is an Eastern European state where different values apply so provision of a flat there was obviously not thought disproportionate.

48 Ibid at paragraph 13.

49 [2007] EWHC 2814 Fam; [2008] 1 FLR 1047.

Alternatively, if all the parental order conditions cannot be complied with, formerly a s 8 residence order (now a CAO) could always have been made, or an adoption order, as in the above case of where McFarlane J resolved another issue by making an order under the **Adoption and Children Act 2002** s 84 because neither the Turkish commissioning parents nor the surrogacy agency COTS (Childlessness Overcome Through Surrogacy) had realised that they needed to be domiciled in the UK for a parental order to be granted, nor that they could not take the child abroad for adoption. This s 84 order then conferred parental responsibility on the commissioning parents as prospective adopters.

13.10 Discovering a child's parentage: DNA testing

The advance of medical science in HAR has been accompanied by virtually 100 per cent accurate DNA testing, which has simultaneously changed the approach of the courts to discovering a child's true parentage. This is because of the long-standing concept that it is very important to a child's identity to know its true origins: see per Lord Hodson in S v S (1972),[50] which established that it is rarely, in modern times, not in the child's best interests to know its actual parentage. This is because there is now substantial psychiatric evidence that children do need to know their true origins, so that this principle usually outweighs any submissions that embarrassment may be caused if the true parentage is known.

This is especially so now that adultery no longer carries the potentially onerous disadvantages for an unfaithful wife, as was the case before the MCA 1973, nor is there the same disapproval of single parenthood as was the situation before attitudes changed in the two or three decades immediately after World War II. A typical judicial approach is evident per Lord Justice Ward in Re H (Paternity: Blood Tests) (2001),[51] where, referring to Article 7(1) of the **United Nations Convention on the Rights of the Child**, he expressly stated that 'every child has a right to know the truth unless his welfare clearly justifies the cover-up'.

Bodey J also emphasised this in Re T (Paternity: Ordering Blood Tests) (2001),[52] where he balanced the Art 8 rights to family life of the child and those of the adults in the case, and decided that those of the child came first, so that any embarrassment or family destabilisation, such as considered by the first instance judge in Re H above, were outweighed by the legitimate aim of the child's need to know the truth (as identified by Lord Justice Ward).

This approach is in itself because of (i) the psychological evidence that a child's identity requires this knowledge and, at the same time, partly because of this reason and partly because of changed concepts of morality, and (ii) the change in attitude to adultery and sexual intercourse outside marriage which (unless sufficiently aggravated so as to constitute conduct within the meaning of MCA 1973 s 25[53]) no longer affects a woman's right to financial provision on divorce; thus the old rules about directing tests only if they were not secretly required to prove adultery, but genuinely for the purpose of discovering the child's true parentage, no longer apply: see Hodgkiss v Hodgkiss (1985).[54] It is of course essential to note the date of this case, now nearly 30 years ago, during which period much development has taken place in family law.

The present test is directed entirely to the child's welfare, although the interests of adults (and the human rights of both) are weighed by the court. In theory now whether a child is the child of married, cohabiting or civil partner parents, or of some more atypical relationship, is no longer

---

50 [1972] AC 24; [1970] 3 All ER 107, HL.
51 [2001] 2 FLR 65.
52 [2001] 2 FLR 1190.
53 See Chapter 6.
54 [1985] Fam Law 87.

seen as any kind of slur on the child, as the only question is whether it is or is not in the interests and for the welfare of that child to know the true position: see further below at 13.11 as there are some exceptions evident in the case law.

This attitude has also coincided with the principle that parents should be responsible for their children's maintenance, rather than throwing that obligation on to the state (so that the Child Support Acts provide for testing of a putative father to establish paternity and thus to establish liability to maintain the child). Similarly the principle that the child ordinarily benefits from (a) some involvement with both parents and (b) to be brought up by its natural parents has been restated in case law, so that fathers may in any case need to obtain confirmation of paternity in order to apply for an order under the Children Act 1989.

As a result, although the historic presumption of legitimacy is in theory hard to dislodge, the availability of a virtually 100 per cent accurate DNA test can rebut even that presumption and little weight is now accorded to ideas of embarrassment in relation to birth out of wedlock: see *Re H and A (Paternity: Blood Tests)* (2002).[55]

❖ CASE EXAMPLE

In *Re H and A* (2002) the Court of Appeal specifically considered the question of possible embarrassment or disruption of the mother's family in an appeal by a putative father of twins born to a married woman, and determined that

(i) this was outweighed by the desirability of establishing the truth, and
(ii) in modern times the best scientific evidence was required rather than reliance on unsatisfactory presumptions and inferences used at a time when blood tests could not be so easily ordered, so that results in those days could only show probabilities.

However, these cases involved young children and when older children are concerned, and the child, while not yet *Gillick* competent, is approaching the age when he might become so, and in any case deserved to have his intelligent views taken into account, ordering tests is not always so straightforward. Such a case was *Re D (Paternity)* (2006)[56] (see the panel below). Tests have also been refused in the child's best interests where it would destabilise the child: *Re F (A Minor) (Blood Tests: Parental Rights)* (1993),[57] *Re K (Specific Issue Order)*(1999)[58] and *Re J (Paternity: Welfare of Child)* (2006).[59]

Professor Jane Fortin has strong views on this issue as she considers there are real risks involved despite the theoretical benefit of the child knowing the truth, which she does not consider an absolute right and that it is not necessarily in a child's interests to know his or her true parentage.[60] She claims that the court is 'extending the child's right to know beyond its appropriate boundaries'.

This seems to call into question the court's apparent principles, yet in fact *Re D* shows that the court is balancing the respective rights of both adults and children, and is considering the welfare

---

55 [2002] EWCA Civ 283; [2001] 2 FLR 1195; [2002] 1 FLR 1145.
56 [2006] EWHC 3545.
57 [1993] 1 FLR 98.
58 [1999] 2 FLR 280.
59 [2006] EWHC 2837 Fam; [2007] 1 FLR 1064. Although it is nearly 15 years old the article by Sharp, 'Paternity Testing – Time to Update the Law?' [2000] Fam Law 560 is still worth reading.
60 See her article [2009] CFLQ 336.

of the child in the round. There has been considerable progress in this area in the last ten years, and in general terms Blunkett v Quinn (2004)[61] makes it clear that it is in the child's best interests to have paternity determined at the earliest opportunity once the issue has been raised, even where there may be some undesirable media coverage especially where any of the parties involved is a public figure, as in that case.

❖ CASE EXAMPLES

In *Re D* (2006) the child was an 11-year-old boy who was opposed to testing. This boy had believed that a particular man was his father and had spent his childhood with a woman who was supposed to be his paternal grandmother. On his tenth birthday another man was presented as his father, with whom he wanted no relationship. The judge neverthe-less held that, while it would be in the child's best interests to know the truth, it would not be advisable to press the matter in view of his opposition. The order was therefore made for the sample to be taken, but then its implementation stayed *sine die* to leave open the possibility of doing the test later if the boy agreed.

However, compare *Re K (Specific Issue Order)* (1999), where the mother had an obses-sional hatred of the putative father and the truth would disrupt the child emotionally, so the test was not ordered.

In *Re F (A Minor) (Blood Tests: Parental Rights)* (1993) the test would have destabilised the child so it was not ordered.

In *Re J (Paternity: Welfare of Child)* (2006) the truth would have caused an adverse impact on the child's mother and family upon whom the child was dependent (and this outweighed the value of the child knowing his true parentage).

However, compare again *Blunkett v Quinn* (2004),[62] where the child was not as old as the boy D and the order was made for tests despite the married mother's request to postpone them as she was again pregnant and the putative father was a public figure so that much publicity had been generated (a similar situation to that in Bodey J's 2001 case, *Re T* above, where suspicions about the child's paternity had already been raised).

Thus it seems that parentage and parenting is a two-way process: once a child is old enough to make its own decisions the child may as much not welcome the biological father, preferring to adhere to social parenting relationships, as the biological father may wish to establish a delayed link through their biological connection and shared genetic background, sometimes leaving judges with a difficult decision to make – which appears sometimes to have to be an *ad hoc* decision, depending on its own facts as well as the infrastructure of principles.

In other words, while medical science has made wonderful advances for some parents, its extended capabilities are not always in the interests of children.

---

61 [2004] EWHC 2816.
62 [2004] EWHC 3545.

13.11 Directing tests

The FLRA 1969 ss 20–25 govern the procedure for testing; in s 20(1) there is provision for (a) determination of whether a person is the mother or father of a child and (b) taking of bodily samples from the child and the putative parents.

By s 25 this means bodily fluids or bodily tissue, and either can be used in DNA testing. The test must be carried out by an accredited body: s. 20(1A), and the result reported to the court: s 20(2). Inference can still be drawn by the court from a refusal or failure to take the test: s 23(1).

Any direction must be made, and specify that this is so, under the Act: *Re F (Children: DNA Evidence)* (2007),[63] and not under any other statutory provision or under the inherent jurisdiction.[64]

Adults and children 16 or over must give their consent, when no other consent is necessary: s 21(1) and 21(2). If a child is under 16 the person having care and control of the child must give consent, but if this is not forthcoming the court can now do so: s 21(3).

This addresses the court's previous lack of jurisdiction to compel an uncooperative mother with sole care and control to agree to taking of samples: see *O and J (Children)* (2000).[65] Although Hale J (as she then was) found a way round this problem before the **Child Support, Pensions and Social Security Act 2000** subsequently made the appropriate amendment to s 20 of the 1969 Act (by requiring the Official Solicitor to consent as guardian *ad litem* on behalf of the child) this was criticised at the time, hence no doubt the amendment.

The CSA 1991 s 6(1) required the mother of a child to cooperate with the CSA and its successors in the establishment of paternity in a case where action has had to be taken to recover payments which were the father's liability unless there was a likelihood of danger to her and the child in domestic violence cases, but see Chapter 21 for the present position.

The FLRA 1987 s 1 would have given the unmarried father status as a parent in all cases where paternity was accepted or proved, including in all statutes where the word 'parent' would otherwise include him if he were married to the mother, but this was never brought into force.

13.12 Current debates

Ideas for research on these current discussion questions can be found on the companion website updates.

- Has HAR now gone too far? The judges are obviously not sure where the bundle of HAR, gender recognition, civil partnership legislation and now same-sex marriage is leading in relation to traditional family structures.
- What may the family be like in 2030? Watch for the Family Policy Institute's publications, reported on Jordan's *Newswatch*, for delivery of which direct to a student's mailbox it is simple to sign up by emailing information@familylaw.co.uk.
- To what extent is DNA testing to establish biological parentage a sound concept? Is Professor Fortin right about this?

---

63 [2007] EWHC 3235 Fam; [2008] 1 FLR 348.
64 See Chapter 15 for the powers under the inherent jurisdiction.
65 [2000] 1 FLR 418; [2000] 2 All ER 29.

13.13 Summary of Chapter 13

Regulation of HAR

- All the various forms of HAR are regulated by the HFEA 2008 (or, where it still applies, the HFEA 1990) and the SAA 1985.

  ○ These define a child's mother, father or parents.
  ○ No longer any need for 'father' or 'mother' as such if facts as dictated by statute determine otherwise: can be two male or female parents, or mother + an unrelated social father.
  ○ Statutory parentage scheme, originally generated by the Warnock committee in response to the birth of 'Baby Cotton' in the mid-1980s), has been developed to create non-traditional family units.
  ○ Appears to be largely accepted by the public.
  ○ But judiciary makes clear in reported cases obvious awkwardness about family terminology in terms of traditional names some children cannot now use for their families, e.g. where there are two mothers as in Re D and a biological father who has donated sperm and then claimed PR.

Surrogacy

- Such arrangements not enforceable by either party in English law – different in some other jurisdictions.
- May not be entered into commercially or advertised, also different in some jurisdictions.
- Commissioning parents can also become legal as well as social parents through a parental order.
- Re G has recognised:

  ○ importance of the biological link between parent, especially mother, and child;
  ○ potential for quality in same-sex parenting.

Consents

- Consent an essential element of HAR:

  ○ e.g. if a husband does not consent to his wife's treatment he will not usually be considered the father of the consequential child unless the presumption of legitimacy applies: presumably same presumption in same-sex marriage;
  ○ consent required for the use of stored embryos, even if partners stored them as part of treatment together, or they must be destroyed;
  ○ but no consent of biological father required for abortion, as a foetus (like an embryo) has no separate existence until after birth as a living child.

13.14 Further reading

Diduck, A, ' "If only we can find the appropriate terms to use the issue will be solved": law, identity and parenthood', [2007] CFLQ 458.
Fortin, J, 'Children's rights to know their origins – too far, too fast?', [2009] CFLQ 336.

Golombok, S, 'What Really Matters for the Psychological Well Being of Children', in Thorpe, M and Singer, S (eds), *Integrating Diversity: the Collected Papers of the 2007 Interdisciplinery Conference at Dartington Hall*, Bristol, Hayward, 2008.

Golombok, S, 'New Family Forms', in Clarke-Stewart, A and Dunn, J (eds), *Families Count: Effects on Child and Adolescent Development*, London, Cambridge University Press, 2006.

Herring, J, *Medical Law and Ethics*, Oxford, OUP, 2010.

Lind, C, '*Evans v United Kingdom*: judgment of Solomon: power, gender and procreation', [2006] CFLQ 576.

McCandless, J and Sheldon, S, 'The Human Fertilisation and Embryology Act 2008 and the Tenacity of the Sexual Family Form', (2010) *Modern Law Review* 68: 175.

Moyal, D and Shelley, C, 'Future Children's Rights in New Reproductive Technology: Thinking Outside the Tube and Maintaining the Connections', (2010) *Family Court Review* 48: 431.

Sheldon, S, '*Evans v Amicus Healthcare; Hadley v Midland Fertility Services*: Revealing cracks in the twin pillars', [2004] CFLQ 437.

Smith, L, 'Clashing cymbals? Reconciling support for fathers and fatherless families after the Human Fertilisation and Embryology Act 2008', [2010] CFLQ 46.

Chapter 14

Children's Rights, Autonomy and Medical Treatment

Chapter Contents

Learning outcomes for this chapter

An understanding of the tension between children's rights and parental duties including:

(i) An overview of the underlying theory and practical impact of children's rights in English law.
(ii) An appreciation of the demands of judicial management of children's rights in medical cases.
(iii) An awareness of the complex role of the court when it assumes the parental mantle in wardship or under the inherent jurisdiction of the High Court.
(iv) An ability to analyse the practical impact of the UN Convention on the Rights of the Child (UNCRC) and the ECHR on English Child law.

14.1 Introduction

It is often stated that the concept of parental responsibility (PR) and the philosophies entrenched in the CA 1989 s 1 negate the growing importance of children's rights.

The usual answer to this is that in England and Wales children are perceived as having first of all a right to a childhood and therefore a right *not* to concern themselves with those matters addressed by the concepts of parental responsibility (PR), i.e. welfare, non-intervention in the family by the State and prompt disposal of disputes about their upbringing.

There are, however, one or two areas where consideration is needed of the theory behind the jurisprudence that has developed over the past quarter-century, because clearly there is a tension between observance of the Bromley list[1] of parental duties engaged by the status of PR and the concept of the growing autonomy of the contemporary child, which has quite different drivers.

Broadly, although children's rights have a longer history, in modern times the concept was articulated by a combination of the 1986 Gillick case,[2] the **Children Act (CA) 1989** (which is, to some extent, the catalyst through which English law acknowledges the **UN Convention on the Rights of the Child**, also dating from 1989), and the academic commentary.

The last of these proliferated in the 1990s, and academe was active in this area as the intellectual concept of children's autonomy met the practical task of how best to protect children from their right to self-determination, i.e. to make their own mistakes – but only making those mistakes up to a point; and that point was *not* to the extent that the Court allowed them to die as a result of mistaken medical decisions for which it was thought they had insufficient *experience* in order to deploy the recognisable maturity which they might have in less life-threatening contexts.

This, inherently worthy, but otherwise protective, paternalistic approach is another example of the growing interference of the State in the family's autonomy, as the court also sometimes interferes in the *parents'* agreed stance by deciding that the parents' choice (where it has been made on behalf of the child) is wrong.

The theory behind this also does not sit very well behind the FJR's principle that parents should be encouraged to make their own agreements about their children's post-parental separation life, to which the tenor of the FJR reports is that parents should be given every support to achieve such agreement. However, it is hardly logical that if when the parents make an agreement the court should reverse it – in effect taking away with one hand the autonomy which the other has insistently given them in the recent modernisation of family law (whether that was given for valid ideological reasons or – as some members of both legal profession and the lay public both suspect and regularly articulate! – for the government's cost cutting).

---

1 See Chapter 12 at 12.3.
2 *Gillick v West Norfolk and Wisbech Health Authority* [1986] AC 112.

The concept of children's *rights* in English law has thus most commonly arisen in practice (in a reactive rather than proactive manner) in connection with a child's right to determine his or her own medical treatment, whether pursuant to FLRA 1969 s 8 – which gives 16–17-year-olds the right to consent to their own medical treatment – or to the *Gillick* competence of a child under 16,[3] who if competent according to that rule is accorded the same right.

Specific issues also arise from time to time, such as that of corporal punishment, ended in state schools by the **Education (No 2) Act 1986** and in children's homes by the CA 1989; some cases have been taken to the ECtHR on this point though with the exception of *A v UK (Human Rights: Punishment of Child)* (1998),[4] involving a caning by the child's stepfather, the punishment in question has mostly been found to be generally insufficiently severe to be so degrading as contrary to the child's best interests within the meaning of the Convention's Art 5 (the right not to be subject to torture or to inhuman or degrading treatment), since the Convention requires those welfare interests to be the primary consideration.

Another context in which the minor child might have a right to self-determination is in connection with publicity, of what some adults call the 'undesirable' sort.

However, the **UN Convention on the Rights of the Child (UNCRC)** does not have the force of law in England and Wales, despite some of its concepts being enshrined in the CA 1989. Its status thus differs from that of the **Convention on Human Rights**, which is incorporated into English law by the HRA 1998.

The operation of the UNCRC is therefore only monitored by the UK in its capacity as a signatory, and this duty is now allocated to the Children's Commissioners in England and Wales, although it is also monitored by the UN, which has set up its own Committee to monitor abuses in countries where the Convention has been adopted. The various articles guarantee such basic rights as that to

- life (Article 6);
- freedom of expression (Article 13);
- association and peaceful assembly (Article 15);
- protection of privacy and family life (Article 16);
- thought, conscience and religion (Article 14);
- contact with parents (Article 9);
- protection from drugs, exploitation and torture (Articles 33, 34 and 37);
- education, rest and leisure (Articles 28 and 30);
- an adequate standard of living, health and medical care and protection from work interfering with education or development (Articles 24, 27 and 33).

There is also an obligation on the part of the State under Art 5 to respect the rights and duties of parents to guide the child appropriately to his or her developing capacities.

So there is a tension between parental rights and duties and children's rights in the Convention itself, although McCall Smith[5] argues that there are two types of such rights, parent centred and child centred: the latter include those obviously for the benefit of the child, such as clothing, food and other rights which the parent has in order to fulfil the duty to ensure the health of the child. The former include those where the parent brings the child up in the manner which that parent

---

3 See Chapter 12, particularly at 12.3 where this case and the concept of *Gillick* competence is explained. The case appears in Gilmore, Herring and Probert's *Landmark Cases in Family Law*, Oxford, Hart, 2011, at Chapter 11, p 199, where it is analysed by Professor Jane Fortin.

4 [1998] 2 FLR 959.

5 McCall Smith, A, 'Is anything left of parental rights', in Sutherland, E and McCall Smith, A (eds), *Family Rights, Family Law and Medical Ethics*, Edinburgh, Edinburgh University Press, 1990.

thinks is for the child's benefit, for example in choosing the religion the child shall be brought up to follow. Such a right, although parent centred, may promote the child's welfare but cannot (usually) be shown to harm the child.

However, Bainham has found fault with this distinction between the two types of rights, because, first, it is often difficult to decide whether a right is parent or child centred; second, because even an apparently child-centred right can be parent centred, for instance in choice of food if the parent is, for example, a vegetarian and therefore allows the child to eat only vegetarian food.[6] Thus Herring[7] concludes that the State does not interfere unless necessary, but will override a parent's wishes where required, as in the case of the conjoined twins, *Re A (Conjoined Twins: Medical Treatment)*(2000).[8]

14.2 The theory of children's rights

As a result of the limited concept of children's rights generated by the protective provisions of the CA 1989, which most commentators agree is not overly reflective of the UNCRC, the jurisprudential theory of children's rights has not received much attention in English law.

Eekelaar's[9] 1986 identification of a triple concept of basic, developmental and autonomy rights was pubished in the same year as *Gillick* reached the House of Lords and the CA 1989 was being drafted at the Law Commission, although Eekelaar calls them not rights but interests, i.e.:

- basic (food, clothing etc. which the parent should provide, and of which the State should take over this duty if the parent cannot meet it);
- developmental (education, maximising the resources available to them, which again the State should take on if the parent does not provide sufficiently);
- autonomy (i.e. the freedom for children to make their own decisions about their lives).

In 1986, this analysis was a timely commentary that influenced the development of children's rights to express their wishes, now reflected in the CA 1989 s 1(3)(a), and this has been taken up by other commentators, notably Bainham and Fortin.[10]

Nevertheless, the law as such remains primarily protective towards childhood rather than positively empowering of children. The *Gillick* case drew attention to the fact that we had moved on from the absolute rights of the father in *Re Agar-Ellis*(1883),[11] through the recognition of the modern reality of diminishing parental influence in *Hewer v Bryant* (1970).[12]

This was a watershed case to which may be traced the beginning of recognition of the modern position on children's developing autonomy, leading directly to the contemporary approach of giving effect to the appropriate decision-making potential of the child who is approaching adulthood. Nevertheless, limitations remain, which have led some commentators to the conclusion that any theory of even limited empowerment is entirely hypocritical because where the child's life is threatened the court always overrules the decision of even a *Gillick* competent child, as is seen in the medical treatment cases which come to the inherent jurisdiction of the High Court for decision.

Moreover, it is by no means certain where in some respects the law now stands post-*Gillick*: there is some tension between the House of Lords decision in that case and the **Sexual Offences**

6 Bainham, A, 'Non-Intervention and Judicial Paternalism', in Birks, P (ed), *Frontiers of Liability*, Oxford, OUP, 1994.
7 Herring, J, *Family Law*, 6th edition, Harlow, Pearson Longman, 2013.
8 [2000] FCR 577, CA.
9 Eekelaar, J, 'The Emergence of Children's Rights', (1986) 6 OJLS 161.
10 See Fortin, J, *Children's Rights and the Developing Law*, 3rd edition, Cambridge, CUP, 2009.
11 (1883) 24 Ch D 317, CA.
12 [1970] 1 QB 357.

Act 2003, which deals with the age of consent, since this is a statute much more honoured in the breach than almost any other. As a result Booth considers[13] that while underage sex may not be legal as it remains a criminal activity, children and young people of Gillick competence – an age concept which has now apparently left the teens and invaded ever further and faster into the sub-teens – must be entitled to confidential advice on their health, including sexual activity.

14.3 Medical treatment

However, Gillick does not give the child absolute rights. While the case confirmed the Gillick competent child's right to consent to treatment, the courts have steadfastly reiterated that such a child cannot claim, pursuant to s 8(3) of the FLRA 1969, to refuse life-saving treatment. This distinction remains and was originally established in two landmark cases: Re R (A Minor) (Wardship: Medical Treatment) (1991)[14] and ReW (A Minor) (Consent to Medical Treatment) (1993).[15] The position has relatively recently been reconsidered in the Queen's Bench Division of the High Court in a judicial review case R (On the application of Axon) v Secretary of State for Health (Family Planning Association intervening) (2006),[16] also generating academic comment to the effect that it may now be time to reconsider the interface between consent and refusal.

❖ CASE EXAMPLES

In *Re R* (1991) the court authorised the administration of anti-psychotic drugs to a 15-year-old (Lord Donaldson using the analogy of a keyholder – the competent child or the parent – unlocking the door to treatment and the consent providing a flak jacket to protect the doctor from suit for assault if no such valid consent was given).[17]

In *Re W* (1993) it was held that while the view of the competent child in refusing treatment for anorexia nervosa was theoretically important, there came a life-threatening stage where the court was not bound by it, not least because anorexia nervosa is known to destroy the ability to make an informed choice.

In *Axon* (2006), which, it has been suggested, might be called '*Gillick Part II*', Mrs Axon applied for judicial review of Department of Health guidance similar to that to which Mrs Gillick had objected, this time advising that medical professionals could not only give advice to under 16-year-olds on sexual matters, but including on abortion. Silber J followed *Gillick*, ruling that there was a duty of confidence to young people and that there was no need to inform their parents, otherwise he feared that they would not seek such advice, with detrimental consequences. He rejected the claim that parents had a right to be informed under the ECHR Art 8 if their children did not want them to have that right.

However, he added a certain gloss to *Gillick* by specifically listing five criteria of which a doctor would have to be satisfied before treating an under 16-year-old confidentially:

---

13 [2004] Fam Law 480.
14 [1991] 4 All ER 177.
15 [1993] 1 FLR 1.
16 [2006] 1 FCR 175. See also Taylor, R, 'Reversing the retreat from Gillick: R (Axon) v Secretary of State for Health', (2007) 19 CFLQ 81.
17 See Huxtable, R, 'Re M (Medical Treatment: Consent) – time to remove the flak jacket', [2000] CFLQ 83, which suggests that it is time to move on from this decision of Lord Donaldson.

- the child must understand all elements of the advice;
- the child must have declined to be persuaded to inform his/her parents;
- the child must be likely to have sexual intercourse if the matter was one of contraception;
- the child's physical or mental health might suffer if the advice was not given;
- it must be in the child's best interests to receive the advice.

However, although *Gillick* in the House of Lords remained an authority which the judge was obliged to follow, these points raise others which indicate that neither *Gillick* nor *Axon* answer all the issues in relation to competence and consent. For these see the section on current debates below.

It should also be noted[18] that *Paton v BPAS* (1978)[19] establishes that only the mother (and not the father, or impliedly any other person) is to make the decision in relation to a lawful termination of pregnancy as in theory only the mother has standing unless the court intervenes.

This issue of consent to medical treatment for children was discussed by Michael Nicholls of the Official Solicitor's Office in an article addressing Lord Donaldson's analogy, 'Keyholders and flak jackets – consent to medical treatment for children',[20] and has been the subject of further comment, following the later case of *Re L (Medical Treatment: Gillick Competency)* (1998).[21]

❖ CASE EXAMPLE

In *Re L* (1998) the court considered the case of a 14-year-old who had signed a 'no blood' card and was declared not *Gillick* competent. She had needed a blood transfusion following serious burns and refused it: due to the sheltered life she had led, the surgeons had not thought it right to explain the full consequences of the failure to agree to a transfusion, as it would have been too distressing for her; as a result she had not been *Gillick* competent to take such a decision because she was not fully informed.

This in turn generated an article by McCafferty[22] entitled 'Won't consent? Can't consent! Refusal of medical treatment', in which the author points out that there are no reported decisions in England and Wales in which the court has allowed a Jehovah's Witness child to refuse a blood transfusion, or to have parents do so on the child's behalf. McCafferty took the view that it was better to follow the reasoning in *Re E* (1993).[23]

It appears that there really is some lack of theoretical and logical infrastructure to the underlying thought in relation to children's autonomy in taking medical decisions when they are

---

18 See Chapter 13 at 13.7.
19 [1978] 2 All ER 987.
20 [1994] Fam Law 10. Michael Nicholls now practises in Australia and continues to speak at conferences and write widely on Child Law.
21 [1998] 2 FLR 810.
22 [1999] Fam Law 335.
23 [1993] 1 FLR 386.

notionally competent to do so and that revisiting this whole concept would be beneficial. On the other hand, perhaps, as in so many areas of English law where the apparent theory does not always fit the circumstances, perhaps the answers in these very difficult cases do often lie, not in addressing and finally articulating the apparently conflicting theory in the court's approach to the competency of maturing children, but in some other competing principles – such as the overriding discretion of the court in protecting children by deciding what is for their welfare. Indeed, this alternative to wrestling with the mutual inconsistency of the court's approach to the validity of the autonomous child's respective powers of consent and refusal appears to be behind the basic decision driving judicial reluctance not to allow a child to martyr itself, in which Lord Justice Ward (recently retired from the Court of Appeal, in which he has contributed significant practical thought to this debate) has been in the forefront of what might be called the 'anti-martyr' movement, finding tactful ways to decline to allow life-saving treatment to be refused.

❖ CASE EXAMPLE

In *Re E* (1993) (an earlier case heard by Ward LJ) the judge had held that the boy concerned was *not* competent (but that that was nothing to do with his maturity, or lack of it) but because in refusing a blood transfusion he had not fully understood the horrendous way in which he would die if he did not have the transfusion: in other words linking this not to his essential autonomy but to his inadequate life *experience*.

McCafferty preferred this factual approach to the boy's understanding of the consequences of refusal of a transfusion rather than that taken in the later case of *Re L*, where the doctors had not given the girl in that case the information she needed in order to appreciate what would happen if she did not have her transfusion and had taken an arbitrary decision on her behalf.

Herring also appears to agree with this evaluation, considering it unfair that the child L, who was 14, was found to be *Gillick* non-competent on the basis of the doctors' arbitrary decision that she did not have the capacity to cope with the truth about her condition and its consequences if untreated, when she had not even been given the correct information which would at least have given her the opportunity to make a decision of her own.

This view was supported by Downie in the next article to join the debate, 'Consent to medical treatment – whose view of welfare?',[24] which notes that it is clear that any assessment of the child's competence is almost a pretence as the court will base its decision on its view of the child's welfare.

Nevertheless, the court has had the opportunity to revisit the underlying principles in this debate on a child's competence to consent to treatment versus non-competence in refusals and did order the detention of a teenager in the context of a less threatening environment than the emergency of a life-threatening illness where time may be of the essence in taking a decision, for example in *Re C (Interim Care Order: Residential Assessment)* (1997),[25] where in accordance with the CA 1989 s 38(6) and (7) the teenager C could have *refused* the assessment which the detention to which it applied facilitated.

---

24 [1999] Fam Law 818.
25 [1997] AC 489; [1997] 1 FLR 1.

❖ CASE EXAMPLE

In the case of *Re C* the issue concerned an application in relation to a statutory power of a child of sufficient understanding to refuse a medical or similar assessment in relation to whether a child protection order should be made, and was therefore a direct appeal to the court to make some effective ruling about the child's competence in such a context.

However, when the case arrived in the House of Lords their Lordships neatly sidestepped that decision and held that it turned on another point, holding that the CA 1989 s 38(6) and (7) should be construed *purposively* (a nod to the ECtHR?) since the purpose of the sub-sections was to enable the court to obtain the information needed to make a final decision; in other words in that instance it was part of the process for assessing whether a care or supervision order should be made, which is a different procedure altogether, involving such considerations as proportionality in making the lesser order possible in terms of state intervention in the family.[26]

However, in fact the practical focus of the Court in the case of *Re C*, as in any case whenever a residential assessment is ordered, was on the expense to the local authority of conducting the assessment, so that it was the local authority's wishes which were primarily taken into account on this point.

The relevant statutory extract is as follows:

(6) Where the court makes an interim care order, or interim supervision order, it may give such directions (if any) as it considers appropriate with regard to the medical or psychiatric or other assessment of the child: but if the child is of sufficient under-standing to make an informed decision he may refuse to submit to the examination or other assessment.

(7) A direction under sub-section (6) may be to the effect that there is to be –

  (a) no such examination or assessment; or
  (b) no such examination or assessment unless the court directs otherwise.

This case is, nevertheless, interesting since while it is not one of a direct application to authorising or refusing medical treatment to preserve life, as is more normally the situation in urgent medical cases, Lord Browne-Wilkinson did say that the assessment, despite the necessity to take account of the cost to the local authority, was part of the information-gathering process, and was thus an opportunity lost to consider at relative leisure, and without the pressures of an emergency medical decision where experts are usually advocating urgent treatment, the precise capability of the child in a child protec-tion context to refuse the medical or other assessment which the statutory provision relating to such an assessment apparently gave the right to refuse, and which should shed some light by analogy on those concerning life-saving treatment.

---

26 See Chapters 19 and 20 for the public law orders for child protection and the principles on which they are made.

There may, of course, be some justification for the court's approach, and for the overall approach of English law, in *generally* guarding what they see as the right of children to a childhood in which they should be entitled to have someone else overrule a decision which may be unwise, which is precisely what the reported cases indicate that the court does, only in some cases, such as *Re L* above, finding other credible pegs on which to hang the determination, rather than the more simplistic approach of allowing apparently *Gillick* competent children to consent to treatment but, as the reports show, routinely overruling any refusal of life-saving treatment; although sometimes the opportunity was taken in the judgments to give extended reasons, such as in *Re M (Medical Treatment: Consent)* (1999),[27] where the court, based on their right to override a child's veto as identified in *Re W*, above, predictably intervened in such circumstances, this time when the child's mother consented to treatment.

❖ CASE EXAMPLE

In *Re M* (1999) the court gave consent to a heart transplant for a 15-year-old, who had refused it. Her mother had consented but the girl had refused as she had thought having someone else's heart would make her a different person. Additionally, she had been unwilling to face a lifetime of anti-rejection drugs. However, she later told the media that she was glad that the court had intervened.

Johnson J, who decided *Re M*, took the opportunity in that case to set out the balancing test that the court goes through when making a decision, referring back to *Re W* and identifying the basic principles as twofold:

(a) in a case likely to lead to death or permanent injury, the court does first try to see the situation from the minor's point of view; but then

(b) if necessary, the court must choose the course of action which promotes the child's best interests, even if that goes against the child's wishes.

In later cases, judges dealing with pro-refusal submissions on the basis of a prognosis of poor quality of life have pointed out that if a child is allowed to die owing to such refusal, quality of life would of course be academic.

There may, naturally, be appropriate cases where the court might allow a child to die where it was appropriate to withdraw medical treatment, just as in the case of severely damaged babies who cannot take a decision one way or the other and would not be competent to do so even if undamaged.

See, for example, *Re C (A Baby)* (1996),[28] where artificial ventilation of a warded brain-damaged child who was blind, deaf and in distress was switched off by order of the court. However, these cases are unlikely to come before the court on the issue of a competent child's right to consent, since in the nature of the facts a child of whatever age in such circumstances is unlikely to be competent.

---

27 [1999] Fam Law 753.
28 [1996] 2 FLR 43

Medical treatment cases, due to their urgency and importance, are not usually decided under the provisions of the CA 1989, where there may be a substantial wait for a hearing, but under the court's inherent jurisdiction, or in wardship where the urgency can be catered for.[29]

Under the inherent jurisdiction, however, the court will make a one-off determination in the usual manner, and is unable to continue supervision where that might be necessary (see further below at 14.3.1).

14.3.1 Procedure in medical treatment cases

Medical cases are subject to a Practice Note[30] which facilitates the urgency and importance of an early decision. Sterilisation and other disputed surgical procedure cases are particularly well dealt with by wardship, as in Re D (1976).[31] For this reason the periodic suggestion that there is no further use for wardship is hard to comprehend. The real benefit of wardship is both its immediate effect when there is often no time to take proceedings under the Children Act, which will take some time to be listed, and its ongoing supervisory function where required, so that the court can if necessary assume the parental role at once and continue to discharge that role if the case requires ongoing attention. Applications under the inherent jurisdiction are similarly useful in the first respect but not the second since under that jurisdiction only a one-off decision is made: see further Chapter 19.

❖ CASE EXAMPLES

In *Re D* (1976) the case concerned a mentally and physically handicapped girl whose parents wanted her sterilised at the age of 11, because they were worried about the likelihood of her getting pregnant and being unable to look after either herself or a child in view of her obvious disabilities.

However, the local authority's child psychologist opposed the operation and applied to the court under the inherent jurisdiction for a decision. It was decided that the case would not be decided immediately under the inherent jurisdiction but that it was more suitable for wardship and that the wardship would be continued. The operation was then *not* carried out, although in a similar case a 17-year-old *was* sterilised.

The thinking of the court in this case appears to have been a 'wait and see' approach, so that in assuming the parental role in wardship and taking on the role of the child's parents – which is the role the court assumes in such a case – they were enabled to make a decision in the future if at any time that appeared appropriate.

In *Re B* (1981)[32] the local authority wanted a life-saving operation for a Down's syndrome child which the parents opposed as they wished the child to be left to die, but in that case the court *authorised* the operation.

---

29 For how wardship works see Chapter 19: this jurisdiction traditionally has much wider applications than in medical cases, and is distinguished from inherent jurisdiction cases as there is potential under the wardship process for the court to exercise a continuing function.
30 [1990] Fam Law 375.
31 [1976] 1 All ER 326; [1976] Fam 185.
32 [1981] 1 WLR 1421.

It should, however, be noted that if the issue to be decided is purely a medical one the authority could, and in theory should, be using either the CA 1989 s 8 specific issue/prohibited steps order route or a declaration under the inherent jurisdiction rather than wardship, since CA 1989 s 100 in fact prohibits the use of wardship by local authorities, because it is mutually exclusive with the care order and similar protection orders that are designed for their use. For the useful operation of these practical distinctions between the inherent jurisdiction and wardship see Chapter 19.

14.3.2 Some advantages of the inherent jurisdictions of the High Court

Since the well-known cases of Re W (A Minor: Medical Treatment: Court's Jurisdiction) (1981)[33] and Re R (A Minor) (Blood Transfusion) (1992)[34] (see above at 14.3) it has been established that complex medical cases are usually best dealt with through the expertise of the High Court in its inherent jurisdiction.

As a result, there have been a number of high-profile cases which have examined the principle that a Gillick competent minor who has power to consent to treatment, pursuant to the FLRA 1969 s 8, does not also have the right to refuse it, and why there is such a distinction.

The inherent jurisdiction is particularly useful for decisions of this sort in respect of 'troubled teenagers', a topic which is dealt with in connection with children's rights in both medical treatment and wardship.

The approach of the English court, fairly pragmatically, is that the child should not really have the burden of such 'rights', especially in respect of acute decisions on medical treatment when they may either:

(i)   not fully understand the matter in detail; and/or
(ii)   not actually be well enough to make an informed decision which is in their long term interests;

but that in so far as it can any court will attempt to see the matter from the point of view of a Gillick competent child and only in the case of likelihood of serious harm, such as death or long-term damage, overrule the child in question.

For discussion of this topic, in which it has been suggested that the law is uncertain, and the explanation of Johnson J of the court's balancing act in Re M, see above.

It should also be noted that this was a case where the child who was overruled eventually not only saw the Court's point of view but also acknowledged that she was glad, with the benefit of hindsight, that the Court had taken the decision that it did. This should not therefore be seen as a paternalistic jurisdiction but one capable of relating to the Gillick or near-Gillick competent child.

In practice the issue appears not to be that the law is uncertain, because it is clear that the court can, and does, appropriately overrule a child's refusal of medical intervention, and for good reason. The question is whether this is compatible with the concept of 'children's rights', which it is fair to say still do not have much articulated existence in English law, despite the international conventions to which the UK is a signatory and some obligations imposed on others to consider the child's ascertainable wishes and feelings, as in the CA 1989 s 1(3)(a).

The short point would appear to be that, owing to the rights and duties of parental responsibility (and, in theory, assuming a competent medical practitioner was willing to act as a matter of clinical judgement), a valid consent to medical intervention could probably be given in many cases by a parent notwithstanding the opposition of a Gillick competent child. However, it is clear that in

---

33   [1992] 4 All ER 627, CA; [1993] Fam 64.
34   [1993] 2 FLR 757.

practice the jurisdiction of the court *should* be invoked, when the best interests tests can be applied and the wishes of the child given appropriate weight, and further that this should be seen by the child to be done.

In practice, most of the reported cases on adolescents involve authorising treatment in situations which are life threatening, and where it has been possible in one way or another to hold that the child is not competent. Thus Johnson J's explanation of the 'balancing act' is tactfully illuminating.

It should further be noted that, in accordance with contemporary litigation practice, efforts should be made to resolve this sort of conflict between parent and child by means which do not exacerbate conflict or damage their long-term relationship. Thus exhausted parents simply going along with a child's decision, if that might not be in the child's best interests, might be grounds for the local authority to seek a care order as the CA 1989 s 31 criteria for such an order would probably be satisfied.[35]

For a case where a child wanted an abortion and the parent opposed it, see *Re B (Wardship: Abortion)* (1991).[36]

As already mentioned this area of the law is going to lead to a prime clash of principle and practice under the FJR's recommendations since their policy supports parental agreement ('PAs' as referred to in their final report) and CAFA 2014 and the amended FR 2010 provide for these, but in the case of much medical treatment of young people the decided cases are full of parents agreeing who are then overruled by the judge. Thus while the parents are being strongly encouraged to agree between themselves and not to waste the court's scarce resources by litigating, the thrust of the decided cases is that the judge frequently decides against the parents' agreed stance.

It is due to the inherent jurisdiction, therefore, that there are, for example, no reported decisions in England and Wales in which the court has allowed a Jehovah's Witness child to refuse a blood transfusion, or where parents have been allowed to do so on the child's behalf.

This fact is important to note, as it impacts on the much wider field of pre-April 2014 residence and contact orders, now subsumed into the new CAOs[37] where routine decisions as to where a child will live (and with whom s/he will 'spend time' or 'have contact' and when) often include concern about emergency medical treatment when a child is with a Jehovah's Witness parent who will obviously not normally be willing to consent to a transfusion. The High Court's known stance on this issue can, in an appropriate case, therefore frame such orders to include a condition under the CA 1989 s 11 attached to an order to permit the other (non-Jehovah's Witness) parent or another relative with PR to give such consent.

14.4 Current debates

Ideas for research on these current discussion questions can be found on the companion website updates.

● How in practice are doctors and the court to assess children's competence following the *Gillick–Axon* decisions? Herring[38] suggests the following questions must be asked:

○ Does the child understand the nature of their medical condition and treatment?

○ Does the child understand the moral and family issues involved?

---

35 See Chapter 20 for care orders and the CA 1989 s 31 criteria.
36 [1991] 2 FLR 426.
37 See Chapter 16.
38 *Family Law*, 6th edition, Harlow, Pearson Longman, 2013, p 466.

- ○ How much experience of life does the child have?
- ○ Is the child in a fluctuating mental state?
- ○ Is the child capable of weighing the information appropriately to be able to make a decision?

- There are obviously a number of sub-questions:
  - ○ When can the doctor rely on the parents' consent?
  - ○ Can the doctor be forced to treat the child?
  - ○ Can the parents be criminally liable for failure to arrange medical care for the child?[39]
  - ○ Are there any medical treatments which cannot be carried out on children?
  - ○ Are 'children's rights' relevant in other contexts? E.g. free speech? Munby J (as he then was) in *Re Roddy (A Child) (Identification: Restriction on Publication)* (2003)[40] has held, referring to Gillick, that it can when the 16-year-old in that case wanted to publish her story about having a baby at 12 in a national newspaper, waiving her right to privacy under Article 8, as she had a right to make her own choice.
  - ○ But Lord Nicholls and Baroness Hale, in R *(On the Application of Begum) v Headteacher and Governors of Denbigh High School* (2006),[41] did not uphold the right to freedom of religion of a Muslim girl under Art 9 when the school would not allow her to wear a more extreme form of Muslim dress instead of the school uniform which permitted shalwar kameez; although Lady Hale and Lord Nicholls did not agree with the majority of the House who held that her right had not been breached, they found that the breach was proportionate and justifiable as the school had thought out their uniform policy so as not to cause offence to the religious beliefs of Muslim children and their families.

14.5 Summary of Chapter 14

- Children do not have formal rights in English law, despite the UK being a signatory to the UN Convention on the Rights of the Child.
- The concept of Parental Responsibility acknowledges that the child's relationship with parents and State is one in which the child has some rights and parents and the State have more duties and obligations than rights, especially in relation to Gillick-competent children.
- Nevertheless, the court retains a right to intervene in the decisions of such children where in refusing medical treatment such decisions pose a threat to those children's lives.
- This is usually explained as challenging the child's competence because it is affected by the illness in question.
- There has been much adverse comment by academics who consider there is a presumption that any life-threatening refusal of treatment will be overturned and that the court's examining of the child's competence is not genuine.

14.6 Further reading

Bainham, A, *Children: The Modern Law*, 4th edition, Bristol, Jordan's Family Law, 2013.
Bridgeman, J, *Parental Responsibility, Young Children and Healthcare Law*, Cambridge, CUP, 2007.

---

39 See Chapter 20.
40 [2003] EWHC 2927 (Fam); [2004] 2 FLR 949.
41 [2006] UKHL 15.

Bridgeman, J, Keating, H and Lind, C (eds), *Responsibility, Law and the Family*, Aldershot, Ashgate, 2008.

Fortin, J, 'Accommodating Children's Rights in a Post Human Rights Act Era', (2006) MLR 69: 299.

Fortin, J, 'Children's Rights, Substance or Spin', (2006) Fam Law 36: 759.

Freeman, M, 'Why it remains important to take children's rights seriously', (2007) *International Journal of Children's Rights*, 5.

Huxtable, R, '*Re A (Children) (Conjoined Twins: Surgical Separation)*: Commentary', in Hunter, McGlynn and Rackley (eds), *Feminist Judgments From Theory to Practice*, Oxford, Hart, 2011, Chapter 8, p 134.

Lyons, B, 'Dying to be responsible: adolescence, autonomy and responsibility', (2010) *Legal Studies* 30: 257.

Roberts, L, 'Teenage Jehovah's Witness refuses blood transfusion and dies', *Daily Telegraph*, 18 May 2010.

Williams, J, 'Incorporating children's rights: the divergence in law and policy', (2007) *Legal Studies* 27: 261.

Chapter 15

The Child's Welfare

Chapter Contents

Learning outcomes for this chapter

An understanding of the concept of the child's welfare as a key principle of the CA 1989, including:

(i)   An appreciation of how the judiciary applies, s 1(1).[1]
(ii) An awareness of the methodology of the judicial discretion in interpreting the detailed heads of the s 1(3) checklist.[2]
(iii) An ability to apply the welfare principle through reference to the checklist without the aid of binding precedents which are only of persuasive authority in decisions involving s 1(1).[3]

15.1 Introduction

Of all the broad principles of the Act, the checklist is the key tool for resolution of private law disputes about children, since it is the closest partner of the s 1(1) principle that the welfare of the child is paramount.

Without the checklist it is not easy to determine what is for the welfare of the child, which otherwise depends on the discretion of the individual judge hearing each case. It is also interesting to analyse the manner in which different judges use the checklist, some as an *aide memoire*, some literally to make sure they have not omitted any point of consideration, some homing in instantly on the heads which apply to the fact pattern before them. It is true that nowhere in the Act is a judge required to 'tick off' the paragraphs (a) to (g) of the sub-section. Nevertheless the provisions in s 1(4) making its consideration mandatory in contested cases means that the judge who is not to be appealed must be sure to take all relevant factors into account in reaching a decision, whatever his or her methodology for considering its content.

How this works, and how the no delay and no order principles impact on decisions, may be seen from the decided cases grouped around each head of the list. Nevertheless it should be remembered that the doctrine of precedent does not apply in the usual way to decisions under s 1(1) and 1(3), so that previous decisions are technically only of persuasive (not binding) authority, since each such decision must be made individually on each case's own facts.

However, the FJR Final Report proposed a slightly different approach to the application of the welfare principle and the detailed heads of s 1(3):

(i)   the Report presses for a future targeted towards a self-administered parental agreement ('PA') on the basis of the s 1 principles rather than their application by a judge, alternatively;
(ii) a new 'child arrangements order' (CAO), incorporating both the former CA 1989 s 8 residence and contact orders into one privately ordered document, *either* made by consent, having been thus crafted by the parents without further formality *or* submitted in writing to become a formal order of the court, *or*, if the PA stage has been unsuccessful, decided by the court following the usual hearing process.

There are two distinct points here:

---

1 See Chapter 12 at 12.2.1.
2 See Chapter 12 at 12.2.3.
3 See Chapter 12 at 12.2 1 for the precise circumstances in which s 1(1) applies, i.e. in cases involving a decision as to the child's upbringing or administration of the child's property or income; *not* therefore in applications to the courts for leave to make any application, e.g. for PR under s 4 or under s 10(9) for any person to apply for a residence order under s 8 (now CAO pursuant to CAFA 2014), including under s 10(8) for the child personally to be a party to an action: see Chapter 12 at 12.3.3 and Chapter 16.

- stage (i) is clearly preferred in the new Child Arrangements Programme ('CAP') produced by the working party led by Cobb J, and implemented upon the inauguration of the new unified Family Court in April 2014;
- stage (ii) is articulated in the new CAP Practice Direction as a completely adversarial process, starting with completion of a new form on which the application and certification that a MIAM has taken place are combined (so it will no longer be possible for anyone trying to omit the MIAM stage to start proceedings without completing the *whole* of the new form, including the MIAM certificate, as was possible when they were separate forms). Moreover, stage (ii) does not provide specifically for any fast-track consent order[4] to be made on the basis of the FJR's PA that might have been achieved outside court, through mediation or otherwise, although it is made clear at paragraph 14 of the PD[5] and in the annex[6] to it that if the court is presented with a written agreement the judge *may* be inclined to issue an order in those terms, although the content will be scrutinised.

In view of the fact that the CAO is the replacement for CA 1989 s 8 residence and contact orders, provision was made for conversion to happen automatically to *existing* orders on the day when the new Family Court opened its doors for business on 22 April 2014,[7] so that there are no 'old' orders. Implementation of the new scheme will also not in theory make a great deal of difference either to converted s 8 residence and contact orders of which variation may be sought nor to how new living and contact arrangements are achieved in new CAOs, except to attempt to take the family out of the adversarial litigation process – litigation having been noted by the President of the Family Division to be stressful and damaging to children, although it is not suggested by anyone that such litigation is not stressful also to parents. However, the post April 2014 arrangements for children will be *evidenced* differently where the court is not involved at all because there will be only a PA or at most a consent order.[8] Indeed if such a successful result could be achieved in practice by this particular piece of modernisation it would not only save scarce court resources, and thus substantial costs to the Ministry of Justice, but would be a positive step in reducing conflict in family law cases. The question is, can it do this?

While enthusing over shared PR, the FJR Final Report in no way favoured shared residence, although many recent cases have tended towards this as a starting point, so this is neither incorporated into CAFA 2014, which implements the key recommendations, nor into the amended FPR 2010 CAP. The FJR does, however, recommend self-determination as well as shared PR, both of which have been incorporated into the 2014 Act.[9] Thus it is still open to the parties to adopt a shared residence approach (whether necessarily involving equal time with each parent or not) if they wished to do so, and if the self-determination principle is adhered to in theory no judge making a CAO should realistically oppose such an agreed order unless there are serious inherent risks to the child.

15.2 Welfare and the exercise of judicial discretion

As there is no definition of welfare in s 1(1) of the Act the welfare checklist in s 1(3) is the only means of ascertaining in each case what 'welfare' means. The rule in s 1(4)(a) and s 1(4)(b)

---

4 As under MCA 1973 s 33A in the case of financial provision which is agreed out of court: see Chapter 7.
5 FPR 2010, Practice Direction 12B.
6 Ibid.
7 CAFA 2014 (Transitional Provisions) Order, paragraph 6.
8 Perhaps most similarly to the collaborative law process, although a difference from that is that most parties will not be likely to be advised by lawyers or other professionals before making a private agreement or submitting it for a consent order of the court: see Chapter 6.
9 CAFA 2014 ss 10 and 11.

that the checklist must be worked through when making, varying or discharging any of the s 8 orders which are contested, or any contested special guardianship, care or supervision order,[10] is clearly intended to lend some structure to the judicial approach to these orders. This means to both private and public law orders, other than to *emergency protection orders*: the reason for that exclusion is because the EPO is the public law order designed to provide emergency action where appropriate, so that it is logical that it should not be constrained by any principles other than emergency protection.

Despite the apparent codification of earlier principles in s 1(3), the checklist is not exclusive but indicative, as other factors may be relevant in some cases. Moreover, nowhere in CA 1989 is the list actually referred to as a 'checklist'. Thus, although working through the checklist is a primary duty, a judge is not obliged to refer to its provisions in order, and a decision is not flawed because it does not refer to one particular paragraph of the sub-section. Staughton LJ[11] and Holman J[12] have emphasised that the list need not be traversed comprehensively and sequentially, although Holman J did say in B v B that it was 'an extremely useful and important discipline' to make sure nothing was left out, and this 'memory aid' approach has been echoed by Waite LJ[13] and by Baroness Hale,[14] who considered it helpful to go through each item in a difficult case. Moreover, sitting with Baroness Hale in the same case, another leading family jurist, Lord Nicholls of Birkenhead,[15] underlined its usefulness in the same terms as Holman J, but also flagged up that such a comprehensive exercise assisted in assessing the respective weights of the factors so as to see that none received more than 'it should properly bear'. Ignoring this issue of relative weight could be a ground of appeal where reference to the checklist had been 'perfunctory',[16] although in the case in which he made that comment Thorpe LJ conceded the apparent apathy of the judge below towards the list, but still found her not 'plainly wrong'.

Therefore it does seem that although no one factor is prioritised, and it is not necessary to hold a formal roll call of the sub-paragraphs of the sub-section, it is necessary for there to be a judicial quest for the crux of the matter and to give appropriate weight to the most significant.

15.3 The welfare checklist: CA 1989 s 1(3)

Although the CA 1989 for the first time reduces to statutory form the various matters to be found in the checklist, older decisions show that the courts have always taken these various headings into account when making orders in relation to children, although the case law from which the new checklist was derived may still afford guidelines as to how the court interprets that checklist. There is no order of priority within the following:

---

10 For the impact on these public law orders see Chapter 20.
11 H v H (Residence Order: Leave to Remove from the Jurisdiction) [1995] 1 FLR 529.
12 B v B (Residence Order: Reasons for Decision) [1997] 2 FLR 602.
13 Southwood LBC v B [1993] 2 FLR 559 at p 573.
14 Re G (Children) (Residence: Same-Sex Partner) [2006] UKHL 43 at para 43.
15 Re G (Children) (Residence: Same-Sex Partner) [2006] UKHL 43, [2006] 2 FLR 639.
16 Re S and Others (Residence) [2008] EWCA Civ; [2008] 2 FLR 629.

STATUTORY EXTRACT

's.1(3 . . . the court shall have regard in particular to

(a)   the ascertainable wishes and feelings of the child concerned;

(b)   the child's physical, emotional and educational needs;

(c)   the likely effect on the child of any change in his or her circumstances;

(d)   the child's age, sex, background and any characteristics of his or hers which the court considers relevant;

(e)   any harm which the child has suffered or is at risk of suffering;

(f)   how capable each of the child's parents, and any other person in relation to whom the court considers the question to be relevant, is of meeting the child's needs; and

(g)   the range of powers available to the court under the CA 1989 in the proceedings in question.'

In the almost quarter century of its regular use, the checklist has seemed to be a useful innovation. Since there is no definition of 'welfare' in the Act, it provides a formula to decide whether a particular action is or is not for the child's welfare, which in practical terms is probably more useful than an express definition (as thankfully identified by Wilson J, as he then was, in the context of the implacable hostility syndrome which emerged in the later 1990s and has still beset contact cases in recent years[17]).

The old case law is thus still of guiding importance, although it has to be read in the light of modern conditions; for example children of every class now in fact appear to mature earlier, besides which our contemporary attitudes to children are less paternalistic than before.

Thus children's views generally tend to be taken into consideration more than previously, not only before the middle of the twentieth century but even in the more recent past, where (while they were no longer expected to be seen and not heard, and above all to do what their parents told them) some semblance of parental authority remained at least until the traditional 'terrible teens'. Now children well below the immediate sub-teens expect to have their views taken into account, and judges are criticised for not obtaining them.

There was, however, for a time prolonged discussion as to whether, and at what age, their actual views should be considered. Now the default position is almost the other way, in that the short question seems to be that, given it is accepted that their s 1(3)(a) wishes and feelings should be taken into account, the essential question is 'is the child too young for his/her views to be sought?'

This greater amenability to the consideration of the child's point of view has manifested itself not only in a semi-formal channel in the first head of the checklist under s 1(3)(a) (where their ascertainable wishes and feelings are to be considered) but also in the recognition in s 10(8) of the capability of children of sufficient age and understanding to make their own s 8 applications.[18]

What is clear is that each of the seven heads of the checklist remains of relevance. However, while the meaning of each head was broadly settled in the 1990s soon after CA 1989 was implemented (so that little has changed in relation to some of the apparently simpler concepts) both the impact of social change and also the fact that the doctrine of precedent does not apply in the usual way must be remembered, because each case must be decided on its own facts and merits. Thus

---

17 See Chapters 16 and 17.
18 See Chapter 16.

previous decisions are of persuasive authority, but not precedents as such. This brings the judicial interpretation of the checklist closer to the way in which a continental judge would interpret the Civil Codes in use in many European jurisdictions (which are widely drafted in the first place so as to obviate the necessity for frequent amendment).

15.3.1 The ascertainable wishes and feelings of the child concerned in the light of his age and understanding: CA 1989 s 1(3)(a)

Obviously the *wishes* of a very young child will not be a serious consideration, especially if contrary to the child's long-term interests, but the *feelings* of such a child, in the sense of profound attachment to the parent to whom he or she is used and with whom he or she feels loved, secure and comfortable, is always relevant. Thus, in *Brixey v Lynas* (1996),[19] the House of Lords acknowledged that though there is no legal presumption that a young child should be with his or her mother, there was a 'widely held belief based on practical experience' that this is appropriate. This former assumption about mothers as primary carers, once thought a presumption, now needs in any case to be examined in the context of the vastly expanded role of the father in child care and belated recognition of male parenting capability.

The child's prime communication channel in this respect is the *welfare* officer, now a social worker provided by Cafcass, the Child and Family Advisory and Support Service,[20] established under the **Criminal Justice and Court Services Act 2000** s 11, since in a contested s 8 application a welfare report will (usually) have been ordered, although it is clear that in many cases judges are managing without, owing to the long wait for reports.

By s 12(1) Cafcass is supposed to safeguard the welfare and protection of children in family proceedings, to provide representation for children, and information, advice and support for children and their families. The welfare officer will have seen the child alone as well as with the parent with whom he or she lives, and possibly with the other parent too. The concept is that the reporting officer is in a position both to ask expressly if a child of suitable age has views, and to judge independently from the child's body language and demeanour (alone and in the company of one or other or both parents) whether someone has coached the child in rehearsed responses.

Alternatively, or in addition, the judge (but not the magistrates if the case is at magistrates' level) may interview a child over the age of about seven, in order to discover at first hand the child's views or feelings; anecdotally it seems that judges are resorting more to this option in the absence of reports. Obviously, the older the child the more likely the judge is to want to know his or her view and then if appropriate to take expressed wishes into account. It seems to have become the practice in England and Wales for children younger than seven to be included in a judicial interview if the family contains older children who will see the judge, although the practice in other common law countries differs as judges interview children less in such other jurisdictions.

There are some milestone cases which should be noted along the way to this result. As already seen, *Gillick v West Norfolk and Wisbech Area Health Authority* (1986)[21] established the right of teenage girls approaching age 16 to obtain medical advice without parental knowledge or consent, while in *Hewer v Bryant* (1969)[22] it had been realised that the parental duty to care for and have control of the child will ultimately end in nothing more than a right to give advice as soon as the child matures.

---

19 [1996] 2 FLR 499.
20 The detailed future of Cafcass is probably still uncertain: it has been described as being in 'meltdown' and it seems universally agreed that the service is not working in its present form. However, the FJR recommended that it should become a part of the Ministry of Justice and that recommendation has now been adopted.
21 [1986] AC 112; [1985] 3 All ER 402.
22 [1969] 3 WLR 425; [1969] 3 All ER 402.

Age is always important, and although there is some room for degrees of maturity to be considered, an older child will obviously have more influence on the court than a younger one, although the age of maturity has been dropping rapidly as the years have gone by, as is illustrated by the pre- and post-CA 1989 case law.

❖ CASE EXAMPLES

In *Stewart v Stewart* (1973)[23] (well before the Children Act 1979) a 15-year-old girl wanted to live with her mother and the court took her wishes into account, considering that she was old enough to express a wish sensibly in her long-term interest, rather than making a decision for childish reasons.

However, in *M v M* (1977),[24] only four years later, a six-year-old girl wanted to stay with her father and her wishes were treated with caution. It is fair to say that fathers had perhaps not yet established their sole parenting skills at this date.

In *B(M) v B(R)* (1981)[25] the wishes of a seven-and-a-half-year-old girl were similarly cautiously treated, showing the slow development of the later position in the case of younger children.

In *Marsh v Marsh* (1978)[26] two girls wanted to live with their mother when they were eight and five years old, but at that stage the court took no account of their views; however, when they were twelve and nine years old, and the mother reapplied, the court did listen to them and, although there was nothing wrong with their father's care in the intervening years, agreed to a move. This seems to suggest that even in the late 1970s children aged from about ten to twelve could have a say in their future against even apparently strong principles such as the importance of the established situation (traditionally known in this context as the 'status quo').

In *M v M* (1987)[27] the court had to decide whether to split children if their views differed widely on where they should live. In that case there was a girl of twelve and a boy of nine; the girl wanted to stay with her father and refused to return with her brother to their mother, and the court upheld her wish to remain with the father.

In *Re S (Infants)* (1967)[28] (a very old case in both time and social change terms) the court had to decide what to do when there was suspicion of coaching by a parent of a thirteen-year-old boy who had expressed his 'view'; this was, however, ignored because it was not genuinely his own view, and was in any case contrary to his long-term interests. Irrespective of the age debate (and the age of supposed maturity and intelligence has come down significantly since 1967 in relation to taking children's wishes into account) there does seem to be a principle running through many years of case law that the child's own wishes are what matters if *not* contrary to his or her long-term interests.

---

23 [1973] 3 Fam Law 107.
24 [1977] 7 Fam Law 17.
25 [1981] 1 WLR 1182.
26 [1978] 8 Fam Law 103.
27 [1987] 1 WLR 404.
28 [1967] 1 WLR 396; [1967] 1 All ER 202.

In *Re R (Residence Order)* (2009)[29] it was held by a majority of the Court of Appeal that a judge was wrong not to give real effect to the wishes of a child aged nine. It is now regarded as the *duty* of the court to have regard to the wishes and views of older children, especially if they are sensible, mature and intelligent, though the court will wish to check the factual accuracy of their beliefs in case their views are unrealistic.

In some countries (e.g. Finland) children over twelve can even veto the court's decision.

Article 8 of the UNCRC requires the court to give due weight to the child's views in accordance with age and maturity. Baroness Hale, well known for her view that women judges think in a way different from their judicial brethren,[30] has explained this in terms of the fact that it is the child who has to live with the court's decision and who may have a completely different point of view from those of adults.[31] Recent reported cases over the last five years do indicate that teenage and often much younger children's wishes are now being taken into account, with the exceptions of those cases where it has been apparent that the children's wishes have been flawed in some way, by direct or indirect parental coaching or other wrong influence.

15.3.2 The child's physical, emotional and educational needs: CA 1989 s 1(3)(b)

There are six sub-points to consider here which are conveniently posed as questions:

- Do mothers any longer obtain care of young children and/or girls?
- Do fathers obtain the care of older boys?
- Do living conditions score highly?
- Will the court separate siblings?
- Does education play a significant part?
- Will religious and/or racial and cultural differences be a significant factor?

Question 1: Do mothers any longer obtain care of young children and/or girls?

It was once thought that this was a *presumption*; now it seems it is not even necessarily a practice, and the development of the position is best seen through case law.

❖ CASE EXAMPLES

In *Re W (A Minor) (Residence Order)* (1992)[32] the Court of Appeal held that there was a rebuttable presumption that a tiny baby should be in the care of its mother, but except in such an extreme case it is generally now regarded, if at all, rather as a *practice*, for obvious reasons; *if* it is any longer even a practice, since despite the continuing complaints of fathers' groups that the court is biased against them, fathers who demonstrate appropriate skills and commitment do obtain orders for their children to live with them.

---

29 [2009] EWCA Civ 445.
30 See her introduction to Hunter, McGlynn and Rackley's *Feminist Judgments From Theory to Practice*, Oxford, Hart, 2010.
31 *Re D (A Child) (Abduction: Rights of Custody)* UKHL [2006] 51 para 5.
32 [1992] 2 FLR 332.

Fathers' parenting skills have clearly advanced considerably in the judicial as well as public perception, although this may have originally emerged from the watershed of practical consideration as to which parent should remain at home with the children when unemployment struck and some women more easily found work than some men: see *Greer v Greer* below.

In *Re A (A Minor) (Custody)* (1991)[33] and *Re S (A Minor) (Custody)* (1991)[34] the court specifically held that there was no general rule of any sort that mothers had to have children of any age or sex living with them. However, especially now both custody and residence are no longer contemporary concepts (the modern ideas being centred on PR, 'living with' and 'spending time' or 'having contact' with a child's parents, obviously the good mother in the right circumstances will always have a better chance of having babies and young children 'living with' her (as in *Re W (A Minor)* above). Indeed, there is a long line of cases showing the court's apparent preference for the mother's care in such cases which must have something to do with practical rather than legal concepts.

In *Greer v Greer* (1974)[35] (well before the CA 1989) two girls aged eight and five were returned to the mother after they had been separated from her for some time subsequent to her departure from the matrimonial home. This was despite the fact that it was even said that she had never taken much interest in them while the marriage had subsisted, preferring her career to either home or children. However, after she left she had kept in touch with them and was later successful in her custody application.

It is doubtful whether this result would endure now that there is increased recognition of the parenting and domestic capabilities of fathers, and especially where an apathetic mother was countered by an involved father, although some extremist groups have had to go to great lengths to get this noticed. It is only in the last few years that the tide has turned to some extent in favour of paternal primary care in appropriate cases.

This change seems to be owing to a combination of fathers' pressure groups resorting to less extreme and more dignified measures to press their case for equal treatment, and many unemployed and housebound fathers showing their childcare talents. It is also perhaps owing to the appointment of a younger generation of judges, who were familiar with dual parenting models, that earlier decisions have been turned round, where the court was patently unhappy about a man being out of work on a long-term basis and barely stopped short of saying that he really ought to get back into regular employment!

❖ CASE EXAMPLE

In *B v B* (1985)[36] just such a positive result was achieved on the particular facts even though the case did not look promising to start with in the light of the contemporary decisions mentioned above. The father in *B v B* was left with an eleven-month-old child whom he assiduously looked after for two years before the mother sought custody, by which time the child was strongly attached to him and it was felt that the change might

---

33 [1991] 1 FLR 394.
34 [1991] 2 FLR 388.
35 [1974] 4 Fam Law 187.
36 [1985] Fam Law 29.

harm her. This fact obviously had something to do with the decision (see the checklist *status quo* (s 1(3)(c)), 15.3.3 below), but what *really* tipped the balance it seems was that the father *was* unemployed and could stay with the child all day so had the edge on continuity of care, and the court grudgingly made the order in his favour.

Re H (1990),[37] CA, shows that a mother (or indeed either parent in view of contemporary absolute equality principles[38]) who leaves the child for a prolonged period may definitely now be regarded as at risk of the *status quo* operating against the absent parent (although the *status quo* itself has a long and respectable history, see e.g. *J v C* in 1969[39] and will have its own part to play in such a context). In *Re H* a boy came to England from India to reside with an aunt and uncle, who neglected to send home any news of him, as did the father, while the mother did not keep in touch. By the time she arrived in England to divorce the father, the boy had settled with his relatives, with whom he had thrived, and the mother lost custody to them. The logical contemporary conclusion 20 years later, where fathers' commitment is taken very seriously by the judiciary, is that if mothers behave in this way, only some extraneous circumstance will now save them from losing the child.

In *Re W* (1990)[40] such circumstances did come to the rescue in a similar absent mother case where the mother was young (18) and the father (47) was not of an age to relate as well to the child. But that was 20 years ago and in view of the contemporary respectability of Families Need Fathers and Fathers 4 Justice might not be repeated today.

Question 2: Do fathers obtain the care of older boys?

This has never been a presumption in the way that girls and younger children living with mothers was once thought to be, and even as a practice was never as strongly established. There are some older cases which seem to show a principle that fathers should have older boys with them (i.e. boys older than about eight, when upper and middle-class English boys traditionally went to preparatory school as boarders).

However, even as a practice it is far more shadowy in the case law than the mother principle in respect of girls and younger children. Even in the contemporary context of the father as capable carer parent, another factor, such as the *status quo*, will need to be introduced into the equation for this point to be conclusive in favour of the father, unless the mother simply does not score under one of the other s 1(3) heads.

Moreover, contemporary trends should always be borne in mind and there is currently a significant and continuing statistical drop in boarding school numbers which may be traced to a social trend of preferring to keep children, even male children, at home during their formative years, so that they may be in touch with their families and not isolated in a single-sex environment away from home: this could certainly operate against any already possibly outdated gender-driven practice in relation to residence orders.

Nevertheless it should be noted that in mixed marriages involving some Arab and Latin cultures, the influence of the father on boys appears still to be thought important, and in a situation where a father is once more living in his home culture it is far more likely that there

---

37 [1990] 1 FLR 51.
38 See the EU Gender Directive 2004 and the consequent ECtHR equality decision on car insurance, *The Times*, 2 March 2011.
39 [1970] AC 668.
40 [1990] Fam Law 261.

will be pressure for the father to wish to take boys, and to press this solution on the court in a contested case.

However, in relation to both questions, as to whether mother or father has a better claim to the care of children of either gender, it seems far more likely that in most cases in the contemporary context this will have no more influence than that of whether the natural parent presumption trumps other claims, as this apparent presumption as applied in cases such as Re M (1996)[41] has generated a good deal of doubt and debate, which only goes to underline the fact that, first, social change needs to be taken into account when applying the check list and, second, such presumptions as may still exist, may not be relevant at all in the context of any particular case.

Question 3: Do living conditions score highly?

Obviously, good living conditions will be superior to bad ones, but there is no argument for materialism as such. All other things being equal, good accommodation will always have the edge, but not where this factor is not even a potential tie-breaker, where for example the father's relative affluence contrasts to the mother's somewhat more basic but nevertheless adequate living conditions, but where she is in fact the best person on other grounds to bring up the particular child. This is because any such material imbalance can always be corrected by financial orders (and nowadays this will cut both ways, where a father is not as well off as a mother). There will be equality dimensions to be considered in relation to contact, as in the Supreme Court case of Radmacher v Granatino (2010),[42] where the father was a relatively low-paid academic (albeit a formerly high-earning hedge fund manager) and the mother a millionairess.

The standard of day-to-day care rather than the accommodation itself is likely to be more important to the court in forming a view about the best environment for the child. The court is not interested in acrimonious squabbles between the parents about minor matters, since incompatibility between the parents and their approaches to many things is likely to have been a factor in the relationship ending in the first place, but they will begin to take notice if one parent regularly allows the children to be dirty, ragged, ill mannered and undisciplined.

Obviously a parent who is undertaking the child's care personally will always have an edge over the parent who is not able to be at home full time, but if there has to be substitute care, the quality of that provision will obviously also be part of the overall environment provided by the one home as opposed to the other. In this context the age of the child will be crucial: older children have their own pursuits and married parents may not see much of them, so this is where the divorced working parent need be no worse off. A common-sense approach is what is required.

Where primary care is contested, and accommodation is positively and unarguably substandard, then the parent in question can usually only be advised to make strenuous and preferably successful efforts to change it, since otherwise such a negative factor is bound to be a handicap in s 1(3). However, this too can be addressed by financial orders.

If a move is proposed (obviously involving a child in moving schools, making new friends, settling in a new area, etc.), the parent who is in the awkward position of having to disclose these plans to the court (because it will impact on the status quo) will need at least to have clear and demonstrably workable plans for the child's future (just as in a relocation application where such detailed plans are crucial).[43] As a minimum, an attempt would have to be made to supply particulars of the sort of house that the parent could afford in the new area, particulars of schools and if possible some plans for continuity of care, preferably from a relative rather than from paid help, so that something will remain unchanged in the children's lives.

---

41 [1996] 2 FLR 441.
42 [2010] UKSC 42.
43 See Chapter 18.

Similarly, if council accommodation were to be depended upon, a letter would need to be sought from the local authority specifying what accommodation would be available and when.

From this it will be clear that the results of applications subject to consideration of the s 1(3) checklist are much dependent on the skill of the advocates presenting them, and the level of practical preparation that has been undertaken by the parties, since sadly the state of the law is such that, in a divorce situation, it is well known that parents who are cooperating have always been able to obtain a decree on the basis of a perfunctory statement of arrangements aimed at approval under MCA 1973 s 41 (see Chapter 5) and to postpone their child arguments until a later stage where further careful scheming may enable a cunning parent to manipulate the court's decision, without there remaining any sanction through delay in the grant of a decree because it will already have been granted. Now that s 41 has been repealed the divorce decree may be long past before any argument about the children surfaces. The *status quo* and financial provision for the family which enables that to remain steady is therefore now likely to be the key to retaining primary care of children by whichever parent was previously in that role on separation, and it will probably be harder work to dislodge such a situation which is satisfactory.

Question 4: Will the court separate siblings?

The court has never liked to do this (Re P (Custody of Children: Split Custody Order) (1997)[44] (an early post-CA 1989 case) for the obvious reason that a divorce is upsetting enough for children without disrupting their ties with siblings as well as with their parents as a married couple, but it is sometimes necessary for one reason or another.

There has been a debate as to whether if the children in a family are split between the parents, this can be compensated for by generous and frequent contact. At first the answer was thought to be in the affirmative.

❖ CASE EXAMPLES

In *Re P* (1967)[45] the problem was thought to be completely solved by the children meeting in the holidays, but this dates from a completely different culture where the old-fashioned boarding-school regime meant that many children were separated during term time from siblings as well as parents.

In *C v C* (1988),[46] this idea was strenuously attacked on the basis that meeting frequently was not the same for the children as being brought up together. The four-year-old son was sent to live with his mother along with the seven-year-old daughter as the court said the children would be a mutual support to each other. However, this result could be equally explained by the fact that the boy was only four, so it might not in practice be a strong guideline.

In *B v T* (1989)[47] there was also an issue about the mother's inferior accommodation in a tower block, as opposed to the father's with a suburban garden. While the tower block flat versus the semi-detached home with a garden did not prove decisive, the Court of Appeal

---

44 [1991] 1 FLR 337.
45 [1967] 1 WLR 818; [1967] 2 All ER 229.
46 [1988] 2 FLR 291.
47 [1989] 2 FLR 31.

obviously had difficulty themselves in solving the problem of whether or not to separate a boy of three years and a girl of fifteen months.

The magistrates had initially given both children to the father, whereas on appeal the High Court gave both to the mother. The Court of Appeal's usually keen analytical powers obviously temporarily defeated, they sent the case back to the magistrates with instructions that the whole matter was to be gone into in depth and that the bench should consider the only solution so far not tried of giving the parents one child each. The result is not recorded. The answer to this sort of situation is clearly that other factors in the checklist must be used to flesh out the picture so as to indicate the right solution, which is the contemporary approach to conflicts.

Question 5: Does education play a significant part?

Education is now unlikely to be as important as it once was, other than in relation to the *status quo* under s 1(3)(c) where, if the dispute goes to court, the judge will obviously prefer to see a child kept at the same school if possible, especially if the current stage of education is a crucial one, such as that during a GCSE or A level course or examination year.

Where educational preferences of the parents might play a part is in the classic situation where one considers academic achievement to be important and the other does not, as in *May v May* (1985),[48] where the father was insistent on a good education, and the mother and her cohabitant were not concerned about such matters.

The court's decision was in favour of the father, though this will often be the result where the father is willing to pay school fees. If the parties cannot ultimately agree on education, however, and are otherwise not genuinely disputing where the child shall live, the post-CA 1989 solution is a specific issue order to decide where the child should go to school rather than a contest for primary care. Since custody as such has now successively been replaced by the individual concepts of parental responsibility, residence and contact orders, and now by child arrangement orders, it is usually possible to contain the dispute within limited bounds by using the specific issue order so as to keep the area of dispute in isolation from the broader basis of the child's upbringing.

Question 6: Will religion and/or racial and cultural differences be a significant factor?

Any one of these factors can be of importance. The reported cases indicate that both religious and racial and cultural differences can be of significant importance, particularly within the minority ethnic communities. It is rare for religion to be a significant issue in a decision involving an indigenous Christian context, where one of the most recent was the case of J v C (1969),[49] in which despite being unable, because of the ten-year delay, to return the child to Spain the House of Lords was able to lay down a condition that he should continue to be brought up as a Catholic in the Protestant family in which he would also continue to live. The court of course still has the power to add such conditions to any s 8 order, under s 11 of the Act, in order to safeguard a child's religious observance no matter to whom primary care is granted.

However, for non-Christian denominations religion is still very much a live issue, especially where culture and lifestyle are really part and parcel of the religion. For example, amongst the major world religions both Islamic and Jewish families, and to a lesser extent Hindus, feature in the

---

48 [1985] Fam Law 106.
49 See Chapter 12 at 12.2 and above under Question 1.

decided cases, which pose greater problems for the judiciary where there is an attendant cultural practice which is no longer supported by the spouse, who either belongs to another religion or at least no longer tolerates that of the other parent, although this may not have been an issue when the family was together. In addition to the well-known case of *Re J* (1999)[50] the Court of Appeal has had some particularly difficult cases.

❖ CASE EXAMPLES

In *Re S (Change of Name: Cultural Factors)* (2001)[51] Wilson J had to decide a case where the father was a Sikh and the mother a Muslim, and where the father was suggesting that the boy should be brought up in both religions. The judge declined to agree to this although, having decided that the mother should have the residence order, he did suggest that the child should be brought up to respect the Sikh religion (nevertheless commenting that he was aware that in this case it was inevitable that he would become integrated into the Muslim community of which she was part).

In another case of the same name, *Re S (Specific Issue Order: Religion; Circumcision)* (2004),[52] involving a Muslim mother and a Jain Hindu father, the mother wanted to circumcise the eight-year-old boy, who had been brought up a Hindu, while this was completely contrary to the Jain Hindu religion, culture and teaching. The Court decided that the boy should not be circumcised, though also that he could later decide to have this done when he was older if he then wished; and further held that children of mixed heritage should be allowed to decide for themselves which to follow when they were old enough to do so.

Alternatively, religion may be a significant factor where the religion is regarded by some judges as supporting principles which are in conflict with key tenets of English law, such as in the case of Scientologists, the Exclusive Brethren, the Mormons, Jehovah's Witnesses and similar sects, especially where the sects' principles involve segregation from outsiders so that the child's opportunities to grow up with balanced views might be inhibited. There is a body of case law on this religious/cultural influence.

While it is true that such judgments show a judicial wariness about such sects, it appears that the real concern in allowing children to remain under the influence of sectarian carers is the adverse influence on young people due to actual incidents which have shown how dangerous this can be: these have ranged from mere isolation from other people (which militates against any balance which might otherwise counteract a sect's extremism) to actual psychological damage and disturbance. The court is also anxious about young people losing their property through unwisely giving it away to the movement. There have been a number of decisions in which the court has focused on these various concerns, usually either not approving an application which raised such concerns or finding a practical way round the difficulty.

---

50 [1999] 2 FLR 678, a case decided by Wall J, an experienced family judge, later President of the Family Division. See Chapter 12 at 12.3. In that case the father was a Muslim, pressing for circumcision on the grounds of the child's Muslim male identity, and the mother of another religion, which resisted circumcision.
51 [2001] 3 FCE 68.
52 [2004] EWHC 1282 (Fam).

❖ **CASE EXAMPLES**

In *Re L* (1974)[53] the court focused on the psychological damage done to a child who is uprooted from a familiar culture and language with further consequential damage to his or her identity and education of which they could not approve.

In *Re B and G* (1985)[54] the father and stepmother, who were Scientologists, had had the children living with them for five years, but the court decided that the adverse influence of the sect was such that a residence order was made in favour of the other parent, who had left the sect (the usual practical solution in this type of case).

In *Hewison v Hewison* (1977)[55] the court was concerned that absence of normal social contact is also a negative aspect of the Exclusive Brethren, whose beliefs expressly limit such contact, which is not thought to be good for children, and which they were therefore not able to approve.

It should be noted that there is a similar problem with Jehovah's Witnesses in not permitting house-to-house visiting (which is again thought to endanger children's social development), although this sect also believes that some medical treatment is wrong, so a Jehovah's Witness with care of a child would not be able to consent to any life-saving emergency procedure such as a blood transfusion.

In this context the negative social aspect can be dealt with by ensuring regular contact with the child's other parent who does not belong to the sect, so that in this way it has always been possible to get round the medical treatment embargo by giving shared residence to the parents, or generous contact to the non-primary carer so that that the non-sect-member parent could consent to any urgent treatment such as a blood transfusion or other surgical intervention. Under the new CAOs, this can no doubt be replicated by the 'living with' and 'spending time with' concepts of sharing residence, without actually using the word 'shared', which the Australian experience has shown might cause problems.

Nevertheless this will only work in practical terms provided the parent who is not a Jehovah's Witness genuinely keeps in regular touch by seeing that s/he does 'spend time' with the child, is likely to be told of an emergency if the child is with the other parent at the time it arises and is therefore able to intervene – thus preserving the right of that other parent to belong to such a sect if he or she wishes to do so. This solution can also assist in the cases of religions which prefer not to have contact with outsiders, as the child will then have that contact when with the non-sect member.

15.3.3 The likely effect on the child of any change in his circumstances: CA 1989 s 1(3)(c)

There are two separate questions hidden in this sub-section:

(1)   Will there be a change in the *status quo*? – which it will clearly be desirable to maintain if at all possible; and

(2)   Will there be continuity of care? – which really concerns the child's quality of life.

---

53   [1974] 1 All ER 913.
54   [1985] FLR 493.
55   [1977] 7 Fam Law 207.

This has already been partly considered under s 1(3)(b), above, and which after divorce is the most likely to suffer necessary logistical changes anyway. For example, the mother may go out to work even if that were not formerly the case, in which case she would have to employ child care help, so that if the father, who will presumably continue to work in the occupation which he followed prior to the divorce, wants to make a bid for the children, he might at that point succeed if it is a straight contest between working mother and working father. However, he probably would not succeed if his arrangements involve a more complex chain of carers, however worthy, rather than the mother with some help. Obviously, in this situation, the mother who is at home and able to offer satisfactory full-time care, or who works only part-time, has the edge over the father and even a highly trained nanny. Each case has to be taken on its particular facts, as the cases show.

Question 1: Will there be a change in the *status quo*?

The *status quo* has always been important, as the tragic result of J v C showed in 1969, even though it was the very adherence to the *status quo* principle which had produced the unjust result owing to the delay in proceeding expeditiously with adjourned hearings in that case. This belatedly inspired the express statutory 'no delay' principle now in s 1(2) of the CA 1989. Where *existing care* is *satisfactory*, it is difficult to get the court to change arrangements because of some *potential* but *untried* alternative. The better remedy in this sort of case has usually been generous contact, or perhaps a shared residence order, not an outright residence order in favour of the parent seeking a change of basic living arrangements for the child, as is shown by the case law. This may be one situation where the potentially more flexible format of the CAO may benefit the child as the freehand nature of the order that could be made obviously enables 'living with', 'spending time with' and 'having contact with' in various permutations.

❖ CASE EXAMPLES

In *S(BD) v S(DJ)* (1977)[56] a father had remarried and wanted to obtain custody of two children, a boy aged eight and a girl aged six, but the court did not think it was a good idea to move them from the mother and into a strange home and a strange area.

In *D v M* (1982),[57] already considered under s 1(3)(b), above (where the father's relatively affluent living conditions did not triumph over the mother's more basic but adequate lifestyle) the attempt was to move a one-and-a-half-year-old illegitimate boy from the mother, with whom he had lived all his life, to the father's home, following the father's marriage (as a result of which he felt he could offer the child a better life). However, the court felt it inadvisable to disturb the *status quo*.

This was also the decision in *B v T* (1989),[58] the case of the tower block flat versus the suburban semi-detached house with a garden already considered at 15.3.2 above. This concerned a 15-month-old girl who had lived all her life with her mother, where again the court felt it inadvisable to disturb the *status quo*.

In *Re H* (1990)[59] (also considered at 15.3.2. above), the case of the Indian boy left for an extended period by his mother with an aunt and uncle in England, following which the

---

56 [1977] 2 WLR 44; [1977] 1 All ER 656.
57 [1982] 3 WLR 891; [1982] 3 All ER 897.
58 [1989] 2 FLR 31.
59 [1990] 1 FLR 51.

court decided that he should remain with them, the mother *did* obtain generous access despite losing primary care. This is an interesting decision since it fell within the short period between the new legislation in the CA 1989 and its implementation a couple of years later; moreover it is one of the earliest cases of the quasi-shared residence with which the courts experimented during the 1990s when considering whether shared residence or a residence order with generous contact was more appropriate where both parents were keen to be closely involved with the child or children.

The point to be extracted from these s 1(3)(c) cases is that, where a parent (particularly a mother) is going to leave children in the care of the other parent or even of other relatives, it is absolutely essential to keep in touch with the children or a *status quo* will develop which it may be hard to reverse.

However, where lines of communication have been established and kept open, the case law shows that it is possible to convince the court that what looks like a new *status quo* which has perforce developed for good reasons, and which should therefore in theory be valued as such, is really only a temporary arrangement from which such a temporarily absent parent may retrieve the children when able.

There is one situation where a case may appear to be about the *status quo* but the real point is really some objection to a parent's new partner. This has been manifesting itself again in a number of private law cases where domestic violence has been alleged, which has resulted in a Practice Direction being issued requiring fact finding to establish the precise situation.[60]

❖ CASE EXAMPLE

In *Stephenson v Stephenson* (1985), CA,[61] the mother, who had kept in touch, had not seen the child very often during the two years during which she had left her daughter, then at the age of only seven months, with the father and his cohabitant. She had then set up house with a new cohabitant herself and had seen the child only six times. The new cohabitant, however, was violent and had a criminal record. The court's decision made clear its dislike of the home circumstances into which it was invited to send the child but perhaps tactfully gave as its reason for declining to return the child to the mother the cohabitant's criminal record.

In *R (A Child) (Fact-Finding Hearing* (2009)[62] the earlier 'fudging' in *Stephenson* was in stark contrast with the impact of the formal Practice Direction now in place, which was made clear when a judge made an early decision in an uncompleted fact-finding hearing that the father had no case to answer. The finding was because of discrepancies in the mother's evidence which could have been because of the fact that the parties were of Indian origin and there was a dispute as to whether an interpreter had been present when she made her statement. The judge had terminated the trial, but the mother won her appeal for a retrial. Thorpe LJ said that this should 'never' be done 'without hearing all available violence . . . the judge has the obligation to hear the case out'.

---

60 Practice Direction (Residence and Contact Orders: Domestic Violence and Harm) [2008] 2 FLR 103.
61 [1985] FLR 1140.
62 [2009] EWCA Civ 1619.

In *Z (Children) (Unsupervised Contact: Allegations of Domestic Violence)* (2009)[63] the judge in the fact-finding hearing again made a precipitate decision in favour of unsupervised contact to the Algerian father against whom was alleged serious violence and the potential to abduct the children (aged six, three and two) to Algeria. The judge's decision was made after hearing only the mother's evidence with no cross-examination of the father. The decision was apparently generated by a report to the judge on the second day of an incident outside the court in which the father's cohabitant was injured. The mother successfully appealed for a retrial in which the appeal judge (Wall LJ) stated that the Practice Direction was there to be obeyed, as there was no equivalent of a finding of 'no case to answer' in children proceedings so that the process could not be short circuited.

There are, however, changes to be detected in the court's approach to the *status quo*. In *Re F (Shared Residence Order)* (2009)[64] the Court of Appeal held that it was best to address the factors in the welfare checklist rather than to rely on presumptions of fact that might arise from a mere *status quo* at the time an order is made.

This is because clearly the primary carer can then radically change that *status quo* by moving house. Unless such a move away from the area where the primary carer lived at the time of the order engages s 13(1), which would require leave of the court to remove from the jurisdiction,[65] the court cannot easily do anything about it except to hear a new contact – or residence – application if the parent without primary care objects to changes in the child's home or lifestyle and decides to make another application. Cases have, however, continued to be decided on the basis of the *status quo*, although these are likely to be cases where the *status quo* is not the only positive factor in deciding the result.

❖ CASE EXAMPLES

In *Re B (Residence Order: Status Quo)* (1998)[66] a father had cared for an eight-year-old child since the age of two, so the *status quo* was maintained. The court decided accordingly.

In *V v T sub nom Re C (Residence)* (2008)[67] a child had spent his entire life with his mother and had a strong and beneficial bond with her, so the *status quo* was maintained. The court again decided accordingly.

Question 2: Will there be continuity of care?

The cases unfalteringly go in favour of the parent who can provide personal care.

---

63 [2009] EWCA Civ 430.
64 [2009] EWCA Civ 313.
65 See Chapter 16.
66 [1998] 1 FLR 368.
67 [2007] EWHC 2312; [2008] 1 FLR 826.

❖ **CASE EXAMPLES**

In *Re K* (1988)[68] the father was a clergyman (who had made clear his sense of outrage at his wife's adultery as the basis of his desire to remove the children from her care). He had assembled a team of worthy people to take care of the children while he worked, but the court lost no time in deciding that a child would prefer its own mother who was available for full-time care.

This was therefore a similar result to the full-time mothers who succeeded in *D v M* (1982) and *S(BD) v S(DJ)* (1977) (already considered above), where in both cases the mother was unemployed and the father and his new wife were both working, and so offered a similar chain of helpers to the clergyman's. In the latter case the facts also indicated that father's new wife would clearly have been overstretched in trying to take in extra children on top of what she already had to.

In *S v S* (1990)[69] the father was a builder who worked very long hours, and although he had a willing and suitable mother to provide a grandmother's care, they could not compete with a mother offering full-time care.

In *Riley v Riley* (1986)[70] one parent was always on the move and the other led a settled life. In these circumstances, too, the latter was obviously preferable to the court.

Sometimes the help of relatives in the extended family rates highly in the continuity of care equation (as in the case of the Indian boy who settled happily and thrived with his paternal aunt and uncle).

However, this will not usually succeed where the contest is a mother's full-time care against a father's care helped even by his mother, even though she, as the child's grandmother, clearly has something to contribute to the general family picture which is usually for the child's actual benefit. (Where the mother also works, the balance of power is of course immediately evened up.)

Sometimes the court has resolved such a competition by giving a residence order to the person offering continuity of care and generous contact to the other[71] and, as mentioned above, this can no doubt be replicated in the new CAO.

15.3.4 The child's age, sex, background and any characteristics of his which the court considers relevant: CA 1989 s 1(3)(d)

This is really an extension of earlier categories already examined under s 1(3)(b), and of course s 1(3)(c), and the cases mentioned in relation to them both give sufficient illustration of the problems which arise and the principles involved in resolving them, and of the skill required by the judge in taking into account all the overlapping factors; for example, traditionally, if parents are really going to litigate about contact, Christmas is often the catalyst because of the religious and/or cultural importance of that time of year and the key role in family life that it is supposed to assume

---

68 [1988] 1 All ER 214.
69 [1990] 2 FLR 341.
70 [1986] 2 FLR 429.
71 See further Chapter 16.

in childhood, and certainly statistics show that applications to the court escalate at that time of year. There is a similar rise in applications around the end of the summer term when the school holidays, including annual family summer holidays, are imminent.

Thus, at Christmas, background and religion may occasionally be more important than usual and, due to the prevalence of intercultural marriages and divorces, arrangements may have to be made, whatever the normal residence situation, for a Christian child to spend that period with the Christian relatives rather than with those from whom he has obtained the other half of his genetic and cultural heritage.

15.3.5 Any harm that the child has suffered or is at risk of suffering: CA 1989 s 1(3)(e)

This means harm in its widest sense (i.e. psychological as well as physical harm). Since the amendment of the definition of 'harm' in s 31 of the Act (see Chapter 20) the harm a child suffers from 'hearing or seeing the ill treatment of another', i.e. in the context of witnessing domestic violence, usually between the child's parents, is included under this sub-section.

The court's change of attitude towards contact where such harm is established has already been discussed above in relation to the leading case of Re L, Re V, Re M, Re H (2000),[72] in the context of the influence of social change on the exercise of judicial discretion in applying the welfare principle: see Chapter 12. Basically, the court's rationale is to keep the child from influences that a good parent would protect children from (e.g. violence, overt sex, crime and drugs), and any parent with a cohabitant who might bring such influences into the child's life will be a handicap to the parent seeking any order, especially if it is a primary care order, as has already been seen in Stephenson v Stephenson (see 15.3.3, above).

> ❖ **CASE EXAMPLE**
>
> In Scott v Scott (1986)[73] (a similar case to Stephenson) the mother's new partner had a record of violence and indecency, and as in the former case this lost her the residence order she sought.

Where a child is not able to see both parents, as where one parent opposes contact with the other, this may be considered to be harm, as in Re S (1990)[74] (and see under s 1(3)(f), below). This sort of situation may arise where there are cross-cultural marriages or partnerships, particularly in the case of the more extreme religious sects, such as the Exclusive Brethren and the Scientologists, where (as the case law shows at 15.3.3 above) the personalities of the parties are often not the main factor, but the principles of the cult itself.

---

72 [2000] 2 FLR 334, CA.
73 [1986] Fam Law 301.
74 [1990] 2 FLR 166.

❖ **CASE EXAMPLES**

In *Re B and G (Minors) (Custody)* (1985)[75] the Court described the views of the Scientologists as 'obnoxious and immoral' and refused primary care of the children to the father and stepmother in favour of the mother and stepfather, who had left the church.

(However, refusing an order in favour of a parent on account of religious beliefs may now be a breach of the ECHR, which has been imported into English Law by the **Human Rights Act 1998**. More recently, the ECtHR appears to be uncertain about this.)

Compare the case of *Palau-Martinez v France* (2004),[76] in which that court upheld a claim of discrimination in respect of a refusal to grant residence to a Jehovah's Witness mother as a breach of her Art 8 rights to family life which also discriminated against her under Art 14, whereas in *Ismailova v Russia* (2008)[77] they upheld the Russian court which took children away from a mother because of the effect of her religion on the children.

15.3.6 How capable each of the child's parents, and any other person in relation to whom the court considers the question to be relevant, is of meeting the child's needs: CA 1989 s 1(3)(f)

There are four questions to consider here: the parent's conduct, the parent's new partner, attitudes to contact of both the parents, and same-sex relationships.

Question 1: Is the parents' conduct appropriate?

The court is not concerned with moral judgements, and while it may regret the apparent injustice of having to decide against 'good' parents, will always consider the interest of the child first and the parent qua parent rather than qua conduct (although where the parent's new partner is completely unsuitable as a surrogate parent – such as in the cases of the new relationships of Mrs Scott and Mrs Stephenson, above – these adverse factors inevitably enter the equation despite the parent's ill choice not precisely being 'conduct' within the meaning of the term).

Conversely, the 'good' parent who loses the children to a 'bad' spouse because of care arrangements being inferior to full-time parenting does not do so *regardless* of his or her conduct as such, but because the *interests of the children demand good parenting*, irrespective of personal shortcomings in relation to the marriage. The Reverend K, already considered above, had perseveringly attempted a reconciliation with the children's adulterous mother, who had left him, despite the fact that he had done his best to provide a Christian home for the children, and had taken pains to provide what in other circumstances might have been totally adequate childcare, but Mrs K nevertheless received the residence order for the reasons already explained.

Mrs S in *S(BD) v S(DJ)* was also definitely not an unimpeachable parent, as she had been serially unfaithful in three affairs, and still obtained the residence order sought. However, these results are inevitable if it is only the availability of full-time parenting, as against other carers, which is in issue.

Obviously a parent's health is relevant to ability to care for a child, but if physical health is poor this will not affect such ability provided there is both adequate domestic help and the parent will

---

75 [1985] FLR 493.
76 [2004] 2 FLR 210.
77 [2008] 1 FLR 533.

be present and not, for example, absent for prolonged periods in hospital. As far as mental health goes, this will be relevant only in so far as it may affect the child adversely. A little instability, especially if drug controlled, may not matter, whereas full-blown schizophrenia obviously would. In either case, comprehensive medical reports would be advisable if a s 8 application is to be made or defended.

Question 2: What is the relevance of the parent's new partner?

The *Scott* and *Stephenson* cases have already provided a sufficient illustration of this point (see 15.3.3 and 15.3.5, above).

Question 3: Are attitudes to contact significant?

D v M (see 15.3.3 above) was further influenced by the father's attitude to contact, which he was reluctant to allow. The court regarded this as a very serious matter and did not want to grant him a residence order as a result.

Antipathy to contact is now a distinctly adverse influence in any s 8 application: the court has more recently become increasingly exasperated when confronted by such circumstances (long formally known as 'parental alienation syndrome' and 'implacable hostility', i.e. where one parent has so affected the child in the child's perception of the other parent that the child thinks that s/he does not want contact). After many years of apparent inability to find a solution to frustrated contact orders which did not damage the child even more than the carer parent's recalcitrance over facilitating contact, the implementation of the contact enforcement provisions of the **Children and Adoption Act 2006** in 2007 has enabled judges to relax their former reluctance to apply any significant sanction. Three cases since 2007 have confirmed that judges are now even willing to change the child's residence away from the primary carer who does not cooperate as the harm done to children has been known for at least 20 years. See further Chapter 16 and also Chapter 1.

❖ CASE EXAMPLE

In *Re S* (1990)[78] (only shortly after the CA 1989 was passed, and when it was not yet in force), where lack of contact with one parent was already considered to be potential *harm* within the meaning of s 1(3)(f), there were two boys: one went to live with each parent and the wife would not allow the husband any access to the one in her care. This deprived that child of the society of his brother as well as of contact with the father. The court felt that the wife might have to lose the boy she had living with her unless she proved less recalcitrant, but in practice no sanctions were applied at that time as the judiciary had understandable concerns about the only obvious ones, which would take the mother away from both the children if they imprisoned her for contempt, or changed their order so that the boys both resided with the father.

Question 4: Are same-sex relationships a bar to primary care orders?

The short answer now has to be 'not any more'! English law now includes a **Marriage (Same-Sex Couples) Act 2013** and considerable case law on same-sex relationships so that a court upholding an objection, even by a heterosexual parent, to a child residing with a parent in a same-sex relationship seems very unlikely.

---

78 [1990] 2 FLR 166.

That is not how it was for many years, however, and this was not a matter to which the court had become much accustomed until recently, despite the general change in attitudes of the public.

A decade ago cases on the subject still seemed to suggest that the court did not want to allow a child to live in a same-sex household if that could possibly be avoided. This was because of problems the judiciary foresaw as the child grew up, at school and with friends, etc. Where it was the only alternative, this left the court in some difficulty, as they neither wished to make a residence order permitting children to live in a same-sex household nor to articulate such an aversion. As a result they sought other excuses such as the criminal record or other unsuitable quality in the gay parent's new partner. However, this sort of case would now be unlikely to arise in view of the sweeping changes made by the **Human Fertilisation and Embryology Act 2008** and the research indicating that children suffer no harm from living in a lesbian household: see further Chapter 13.

15.3.7 The range of powers available to the court: CA 1989 s 1(3)(g)

The court always has power to make any suitable CA 1989 order(s) in a case before it, irrespective of whether any application has in fact been made for those orders. The court has always been able, for example, by s 10(1)(b), to make a residence order in favour of some non-party, such as a grandparent or other relative, if it becomes obvious that that would be preferable and the non-party is willing, and no doubt the same can still be done when making a CAO.

The court can also bring an end to any particular saga by prohibiting any further CA 1989 applications without leave: s 91(14). The court's powers also include the power to order investigation by the local authority: s 37(1), which in itself may lead to any of the public law orders contained in Sections III–V inclusive of the CA 1989 being made in respect of the child or children.

Parties seeking s 8 orders (and the PSOs and SIOs can still be made despite the abolition of residence and contact orders) should be aware of the potential impact of these public law orders (see Chapter 20), especially in view of the power of the court under s 37(1) to refer a case to the local authority for investigation (see below).

The range of powers has also often been used to soften the blow of refusal of primary care to one of the parents where, in a contested case where they both seek the same thing, one will inevitably lose. Despite judicial statements to the effect that the range of orders, including the contemporary trend towards shared residence[79] is 'not a consolation prize for disappointed adults', this potential can still keep the peace in a family, in the way that the old custody, care and control choices often merely inflamed the atmosphere.

15.3.8 Power of the court to order investigation by the local authority: CA 1989 s 37(1)

Such an order may be made in any 'family proceedings' as defined by s 8(3), and where the court decides to give such a direction the local authority must carry out the appropriate inquiries and consider whether it should:

- apply for a care or supervision order;
- provide any services or assistance for the child or the family; or
- take any other action in respect of the child: s 37(2).

Where the local authority decides not to take any action, it must within eight weeks inform the court of the decision and of why that decision has been made, together with information as to any

---

79 See Chapter 16.

other action they have taken or propose to take in respect of that child: s 37(3). They must also consider whether they should:

- review the decision at a later date; and
- if so, when: s 37(6).

Unfortunately, the court can do little if the local authority decides not to comply with the court's direction, although the former President of the Family Division (Sir Stephen Brown P) considered the local authority would then lay itself open to judicial review. Formerly, the court could have simply made a wardship order, but could still make an interim care or supervision order (if the threshold criteria were satisfied: see Chapter 20) if the local authority cooperates; if it does not, it could simply, of course, apply for such an order to be discharged though it cannot just send the child home: CA 1989, ss 38 and 39).

15.4 Current debates

Ideas for research on these current discussion questions can be found on the companion website updates.

- Have we now closed the debate on sexual orientation in relation to children's welfare?
- Should shared residence in some form be the norm? Will the new CAO be likely to effect an improvement in disputes over children?
- Is mediation really a better way of resolving conflicts over children than in court?
- The Past President of the Family Division (Lord Justice Wall) has said that middle-class parents disputing such matters over children is harming children: is the welfare checklist out of date?
- How to balance the interests where the welfare of more than one child is involved in an application under the Act but are the interests adverse to each other?

15.5 Summary of Chapter 15

- Use of the checklist is mandatory in all contested s 8 order and public law applications other than emergency protection orders.
- The checklist content is not new but encapsulates principles developed but not necessarily formally articulated or codified previously.
- An important addition is s 1(3)(g), the range of the court's powers, which has the potential to create better family harmony as well as to offer the best range of options for the welfare of the child even if its family is no longer an intact one.
- It is uncertain how the FJR envisages a child's parents using the checklist and the principles in CA 1989 s 1 in reaching their self determined parenting agreements and to what extent a judge making a CAO on the basis of the parents' agreement will approve their PA while exercising the established judicial discretion to make an order for the child's welfare and in the child's best interests.

15.6 Further reading

Collier, R, 'Fathers 4 Justice, law and the new politics of fatherhood', [2005] *Child and Family Law Quarterly*, 17: 511.

Fortin, J, Richie, C and Buchanan, A, 'Young adults' perceptions of court ordered contact', [2006] CFLQ 18: 211.

Gilmore, S, 'Contact/shared residence and child well-being', [2006] *International Journal of Law, Policy and the Family*, 20: 344.

Hunt, J, Masson, J, and Trinder, L, 'Shared Parenting, the law, the evidence and guidance from Families Need Fathers', [2009] Fam Law 131.

Johnson, S, 'Shared residence orders: for and against', [2009] Fam Law 131.

Maclean, M (ed), *Parenting After Partnering*, Oxford, Hart, 2007.

Murch, M, with Keenan, G, *The Voice of the Child in Private Family Law Proceedings*, Bristol, Family Law, 2003.

Smart, C et al, *Family Fragments*, Cambridge, Polity Press, 1999.

Trinder, L and Kellet, J, 'Fairness, efficiency and effectiveness in court based dispute resolution schemes in England', [2007] *International Journal of Law, Policy and the Family*, 21: 22.

Chapter 16

Section 8 and the CAO

Learning outcomes for this chapter

A deeper understanding of the once radical philosophy of the portfolio of orders in Part II of the CA 1989, introduced in Chapter 12, including:

(i) Replacement of the 1989 residence and contact orders by the CAO recommended by the Final Report of the FJR.
(ii) An overview of the court's practical approach to the range of its powers, enabling delivery of decisions in accordance with the s 1(1) welfare principle, the s 1(3) checklist and the no delay and no order principles.
(iii) An awareness of the developing law and practice relating to enforcement of contact, following many years of unsuccessful initiatives, and the recommendations of the Final Report of the FJR.
(iv) An ability to analyse a fact pattern and to apply the law and practice balancing the rights of the child and its parents or other relations in the extended family – as separating parents will now have to do in preparing their shared PR plan in accordance with the recommendations of the Final Report of the FJR.

16.1 Introduction

The first part of this chapter looks at the system of s 8 orders as devised by the CA 1989, two of which (residence and contact orders) were replaced on 22 April 2014 by a new Child Arrangements Order (CAO) when most provisions of CAFA 2014 came into force on the inauguration of the new unified Family Court. The second part, and Chapter 17, then consider how this change, recommended by the Final Report of the FJR, may – or may not – work to reduce parents' adversarial litigation over children which the immediate Past President of the Family Division of the High Court (Sir Nicholas Wall) identified as damaging to those children.

The significant change, in summary, replaces the two separate s 8 orders, for residence and contact, with the new single CAO in which where (and with whom) a child should 'live', with whom 'spend time' and with whom 'have contact' are not only included in one order, but parents are now encouraged to work out these arrangements for themselves and record them in a self-drafted parenting agreement called in the FJR Report a 'PA', only going to the court if a formal order is required.

The CA 1989 s 8 provides for the court to make an order in the course of any 'family proceedings' whether or not that particular order has been applied for. The term 'family proceedings' is defined in s 8(3) Part IV of the FLA 1996 at s 63.

STATUTORY EXTRACT
The definition in the Family Law Act 1996 s 63(1) states:

'"family proceedings" means any proceedings –

(a) under the inherent jurisdiction of the High Court in relation to children; or
(b) under the enactments mentioned in sub-section (2)'.

Section 63(2) then states:

'The enactments referred to in the definition of "family proceedings" are –

(a)   Part II;[1]
(b)   this Part;[2]
(ba) Part 4A;[3]
(c)   the Matrimonial Causes Act 1973;
(d)   the Adoption Act 1976;
(e)   the Domestic Proceedings and Magistrates Courts Act 1978;
(f)   Part III of the Matrimonial and Family Proceedings Act 1984;
(g)   Parts I, II and IV of the Children Act 1989;
(h)   Section 54 of the Human Fertilisation and Embryology Act 2008;
(i)   the Adoption and Children Act 2002;
(j)   Schedules 5 to 7 of the Civil Partnership Act 2004.'

Orders may be made for a specified period, impose conditions on those affected by the order and contain directions as to how the order is to be effected, including in relation to any 'incidental, consequential or supplementary' matters: CA 1989 s 11(7). Orders normally continue in force until discharged by the court, or otherwise until the child attains the age of 16: s 91(10). The court may make an order for a child over the age of 16 (since anyone under 18 is technically still a child) or make an order to continue beyond the age of 16 provided the circumstances are 'exceptional': s 9(6) and s 9(7). But the order will, in any event, be discharged at the age of 18: s 91(11).

These provisions are made because although a person under 18 is technically still a 'child', the school leaving age is 16, and children may then go out to work and in any case leave home, so there would be little point in the court's making an order against which the child could vote with its feet. The likely exceptional circumstances referred to would be if the child was disabled or for some reason needing a s 8 order to be made regardless of the usual cut-off age of 16 having been reached.

Existing residence and contact orders as at 22 April 2014 will automatically have become CAOs on that date so there is no significant change for existing orders since all the impact of the 2014 Act is in the manner in which they will have been effected, i.e. following a court process culminating in a formal order (not a consent order as technically these were not available under pre-April 2014 law[4]): whereas post-April 2014 such a consent order is in theory available,[5] preferably through the 'PA' private ordering agreement between the parents rather than through an adversarial court process, although it seems that pursuant to the new 'CAP' private law outline drawn up by Cobb, J's working group any agreement made between the parents after proceedings have started may now be evidenced in a consent order made by the judge (unlike under the old s 8 residence or contact order process).

Apart from the usual age termination, other circumstances will automatically discharge an order: (1) if the child's parents live together for a period of more than six months this will automatically discharge an order made in relation to where the child will live and with whom:

---

1 I.e. of the FLA 1996, not the CA 1989.
2 I.e. Part IV of the FLA 1996, not the CA 1989.
3 I.e. of the FLA 1996, not the CA 1989.
4 See the no order principle in Chapter 12, at 12.2.4.
5 See 'consent order' in the alphabetically listed annex to the Child Arrangements Programme, FPR 2010 Practice Direction 12B: 'When you have reached agreement with the other parent, which resolves the dispute, the judge may agree to make that agreement into an order called a consent order.'

s 11(5); (2) if a care order[6] is made this will discharge any s 8 order, and vice versa, i.e. if a new CAO is made in respect of a child in care that will discharge the care order. The reason for this is that s 8 orders are part of the private law[7] applying to children and their parents, and a care order is part of the portfolio of public law[8] designed to provide a code of child protection effecting intervention by the state where necessary, so that the two types of order are theoretically (and in practice) incompatible.

(It should be noted that a residence order was the only type of s 8 order that could be made in respect of a child in care, and presumably a CAO can still perform this function: the rationale behind this is that it may be a perfectly valid step to remove a child from care to go to live with someone outside the care regime rather than simply discharging the care order because that has come to an end of its use.)

16.2 The portfolio of orders under s 8

There were up to April 2014 four s 8 orders:

- residence order;
- contact order;
- prohibited steps order; and
- specific issue order.

Now there are only three: a CAO, plus the prohibited steps (PSO) and specific issue (SIO) orders. In other words the residence and contact orders are now united in the new CAO.

It should be noted that, since owing to the non-interventionist principle in the CA 1989 s 1(5), none of these orders can technically be made 'by consent',[9] but the CAO is envisaged as a potential consent order, and it is presumed that the principle in s 1(5) is not breached where a judge decides to make a consent order as envisaged at 16.1 above, because (clearly) if the parties feel an order is necessary and ask the judge to make it as set out in PD12B of the CAP, then it must be better for the child that a formal order is made for clarity in the situation than that none is made. It is possible that PD12B has left this matter deliberately non-specific to allow for flexibility.

However, it is also recommended that the parents should go to mediation if they cannot at first agree, and only then to the court. Accordingly it is odd that both the Report and the PD are silent as to whether this is intended to achieve an agreement which is free standing without requiring further formalisation or whether it must then be formalised in a CAO or some other form of record of the agreement, since in other cases of parental agreement (e.g. agreed PR for an unmarried father) there is a standard form which must be witnessed and registered. It appears that little thought has been given to the underlying theory of the Act or to this practical aspect.

16.2.1 The former residence order/new CAO

This is the first of the former orders that the FJR sought to replace with the CAO, and which was effected by CAFA 2014.

---

6   See Chapters 19 and 20.
7   See Chapter 12 at 12.2.
8   See Chapter 12 at 12.1 for the distinction. The CAP having now been implemented, Cobb J's working group has now moved on to redesign the proposed new 'MAP' (Money Arrangements Programme) which will streamline the divorcing family's financial arrangements, and which delivered its first report on 15 August 2014. These continuing processes may be followed in the 'Views From the President's Chambers'; see Chapter 1, n 16.
9   See Chapter 12 at 12.2.

Pursuant to the ethos of PR, which is designed to generate ongoing practical parenting, this order merely settled where a child should live and no more, although there were some legal consequences in the CA 1989 s 13(1), which prohibited change of the child's surname or the child's removal from the jurisdiction of England and Wales once a residence order was in place.[10]

The reason for this was *because*, unlike the pre-1989 custody orders, the residence order only settled with whom the child should live and did not permit any other significant action which the carer parent might have taken if an old-style custody order had been in place: under the residence order, all such significant issues were designed still to be decided by the court if the carer parent and the non-resident parent could not agree.[11] This was because parents would still share PR even if one obtained a residence order, and even if a non-parent obtained a residence order (which would give that person PR also) the parents would still each retain individual PR, so both still needed to be involved in major decisions.

Section 13(1) of the CA 1989 thus flagged up the two such major decisions most likely to cause argument when parents were separated and perhaps divorced. It was recognised when s 13(1) was enacted that the major step of separation and/or divorce often produced a desire on the part of the woman to revert to her pre-marriage surname, or to assume another if she planned to or had already remarried, and also to give that surname to her children, so that they should be a new family unit without the other parent. Sometimes this 'spring cleaning' approach was also accompanied by a desire to return 'home' if either parent came from a foreign jurisdiction, leading to the disruptive contemporary syndrome of international child abduction.

Thus the CA 1989 specifically provided that, for the avoidance of doubt, the grant of a residence order did not permit either parent to take such a step without agreement of the other, or an order of the court. Similar restrictions were put in place on consenting or refusing to consent to other major steps in a child's life in relation to a parent who has PR only because s/he had a residence order under CA 1989 s 12(1) or (2), for instance s 12(3) prevented a unilateral decision about consent, or refusal of consent, to adoption.

Although under the residence and contact order system the decided cases indicated that the court always preferred children to have one settled home, it was recognised that there might be (in appropriate established circumstances or where such a routine was likely to work) an order in favour of more than one person. This was, at different stages, variously called a 'split' or a 'joint' residence order. The opposite terms ought to mean distinct orders, but seem to have been different ways of expressing the same idea, namely that the child could have a settled home with each parent and, since the parties are (obviously) not living together, the order could detail the periods to be spent at each house, as CA 1989 s 11(4) expressly permitted.

However, the contemporary term then seems to have changed to that of a 'shared' residence order, which then appeared to be developing towards a normative starting point. Cases where such orders have been made from early in the implementation of the 1989 Act included *Re H (A Minor) (Shared Residence)* (1993)[12] and *G v G (Joint Residence Order)* (1993).[13] Much of this old case law can now be disregarded, as both the law and practice then seem to have moved towards the term 'shared residence', and indeed that term did seem (particularly in the last decade) to be moving towards a position where 'shared residence' might be seen as the formal starting point for consideration of whether a residence order should be granted, and if so what type that order should be.

---

10 See below at 16.7.1 and 2.
11 See Chapter 12 at 12.1.1 and 12.3.
12 [1993] Fam 463.
13 [1993] Fam Law 615.

❖ CASE EXAMPLE

In *Re W (A Child) (Shared Residence Order)* (2009)[14] it was settled that 'unusual circumstances' were no longer required for a shared residence order so that the contemporary overriding concern was whether such an order was for the child's welfare and best interest. Lack of consensus or harmony between the parents was not a reason for not making such an order, and it was particularly appropriate where one parent was trying to marginalise the other as this would be better than no order in that case, and the periods in the respective parent's care need not be equal or even nearly so.

A spate of international relocation cases[15] seems to be what disrupted this apparently orderly progress towards shared residence, in logic thus phasing out formal contact, resulting in 2014 with the end of residence and contact orders and the arrival of the CAO. Reported cases since 2009 seemed to turn towards whether it was right to allow relocation out of the jurisdiction[16] when this would clearly disrupt the shared residence to some extent, which coincided with that debate being overtaken by the FJR's decision to support 'shared PR' rather than shared residence; and indeed not to support the orders for 'residence' and 'contact' at all, but to replace them with a new 'child arrangements order'. In many ways this is a pity since this change of direction now distracts from the shared residence debate, since in practice genuinely sharing children's care is a trend that has been developing for many years, whatever labels it went by and however weakly it has been followed up from time to time. The suspicion is that the CAO may be apt to confuse parenting further.

The catalyst for dropping the 'shared residence' tag is anecdotally said to be the adverse Australian experience of a formal recognition of shared residence there, which has, however, been followed up by news of similar problems in England and Wales where there were reported misunderstandings of the parent not resident with the children that shared residence meant that that parent should have an equal share of the child's time rather than any genuinely equal sharing of the parenting involved in bringing up the child (which of course need not be defined by the time spent actually in the child's company). As usual, it seems these misunderstandings were generated by the media and fathers' pressure groups, unfortunately another example of the mishandling of the current modernisation of family justice, which has not been well managed by appropriate release of clear information before misunderstandings could occur.

This confusion between *time spent with a child* and *quality* of parenting unfortunately early confused the debate in Parliament over clause 11 of the Children and Families Bill, now implemented in CAFA 2014 s 11, resulting in both government and legislature somewhat sheepishly changing the original title of that clause (which was 'shared parenting'), replacing it with 'parental involvement'; and the wording of the section also being changed to indicate that this intended involvement of both parents in a child's life was meant to state that the presumption was that 'involvement in *some way*' was for the child's welfare.

The actual Australian research which impacted adversely in England and Wales, having itself been widely misunderstood, is discussed by Professor Joan Hunt in an article in the Collected Papers of the 2014 Dartington Hall Family Justice Interdisciplinary Conference, *Family Justice*

---

14 [2009] EWCA Civ 370.
15 See Chapter 18.
16 For which CA 1989 s 13(1) would require a court application if the parents could not agree that this should take place, since it would clearly be likely to disrupt either shared residence or contact.

Redefined.[17] This Australian experience, which in fact turns out not to be all bad,[18] is therefore the watershed for the amendments to the CA 1989 s 8 replacing residence and contact orders with the CAO in which the different activities of 'living with', 'spending time with' and 'having contact with' the child's parents are now to be more prosaically spelt out in each individual case than in the former 'residence' and 'contact' terms: that is, in those cases in which an order is actually *made* by the court, since the accompanying encouragement of other changes in family justice mean that *most* parents are not going to have an *order* at all, unless they either ask the court to make a consent order or start proceedings from which such an order will be likely to be made.

16.2.2 The new Child Arrangements Order (CAO)

Whether this new CAO system will prove to be a positive factor or not is another matter. It may be that it is only a change of wording which parents will see through, and therefore still fight over the child's time as if their child were a piece of property, possession of which is still regarded as a matter of loss of face if it is not won. Alternatively, if parents think the change means they have equal rights to the child this may promote more international child abduction, not less.[19] As Hunt says in her article, 'professionals in the family justice system may well be faced with demands for equal or near equal parenting time, particularly since most [parents] will now not have been legally advised'.[20] On the other hand it is just possible that the newly 'fudged' wording may be made by the profession to operate well in the same way that they have cleverly created consensual divorce out of the precise wording of the MCA 1973 s 1(2)(a) and s 1(2)(b).

Early in the history of the CA 1989 the potential for splitting the child's time between the parents, and masking the fact that neither parent wanted to be seen as the parent without primary care of the child, through some sort of 'joint' order was seen as an important palliative for family argument. There then developed a trend for judges to say that the Act was not there for such face-saving remedies to be applied; however, it is clear from many reported decisions of the 1990s that that was precisely what it was being used for if it could be said that the child was genuinely spending significant time in each household and the arrangement was working. One judge who picked up on this point was Wilson, J (as he then was) and it can certainly be seen in some reported cases that s 1(3)(g) of the welfare checklist was either explicitly or impliedly in the back of the judge's mind when making a residence order of the 'split', 'joint' or 'shared' variety in order to keep the peace in a warring family, which may well have been for the welfare of the child in question, and which simply could *not* be effected under the pre-CA 1989 law, where similar attempts were sometimes made by granting 'joint custody', sometimes with 'no order for care and control'.[21]

Residence orders have often been used to give some standing to step-parents and this practice appeared to be on the increase since step-parents (whether spouses or civil partners) can now in any case obtain PR.[22] It would seem to be a retrograde step to lose this important tool in achieving as much family harmony as possible in sometimes awkward situations where the original family has been reconstituted, but it is unclear whether the step-parent will still be able to be included in the new 'PA's that are encouraged and in such orders as are made in the new 'freehand' style of the CAO, the terms of which do appear to be able to be adapted as required. Possibly a practice will

---

17 Hunt, J, 'Shared parenting time: messages from research', [2014] Fam Law 44: 676.
18 Cashmore, J, Parkinson, P et al, *Shared Care Parenting Arrangements since the 2006 Family Law Reforms: Report to the Australian Government Attorney-General's Department*, Social Policy Research Centre, University of New South Wales, 2010. The research concluded that there was no connection between shared residence, time spent and positive outcomes for children, but that the 'robust evidence' for positive outcomes was 'relationship and parenting quality'.
19 See Chapter 18.
20 Hunt, op. cit.
21 See Chapter 12 at 12.1.1 for the sometimes problematic background to the Act.
22 See Chapter 12 at 12.3.1.

develop of always including the step-parent in such arrangements and orders, much as the apparently seamless practice grew up sometime in the 1970s or 1980s of married couples owning their matrimonial home jointly, in contrast to the single ownership of the husband which had been the norm up to the 1970s.

> ❖ **CASE EXAMPLE**
>
> In *Re H* (1995)[23] the residence order was in respect of a son and a stepson since the two boys saw themselves as both equally 'sons'. This was easily done in a residence order.

It may obviously be more awkward to achieve the same result under the proposed new CAO scheme, especially in an agreement made through mediation without an order at all: there is nothing in the CAP's PD12B about enforcement of these bare agreements without an order. It may be that the detail of the scheme may in due course make specific arrangements for such atypical situations but its present absence also indicates that there will be more to achieving the new 'child arrangements' that the FJR considers a simplification, but which could in fact exacerbate difficulties following parental separation. It does not appear that the FJR committee has considered that the reason the parents of a child may be separating in the first place is that they cannot cooperate, so that to lose the flexibility of separate residence and contact orders in favour of the universal CAO may be unwise.

> ❖ **CASE EXAMPLE**
>
> In *Re F (Shared Residence Order)* (2003)[24] it was suggested that a shared residence order was only 'a label' but Wilson J said that labels could be very important.
>
> This is a most perceptive comment of an experienced family law judge, now Lord Wilson of Culworth, and in the Supreme Court, since it cannot be denied that such 'labels' have contributed to ending separated and divorced parents' pre-1989 possessory attitudes towards children, even if some have still fought over who should have primary care, and done so in a manner which has attracted criticism of their selfishness from the immediate Past President of the Family Division and others; see further below.

Shared residence has more recently received more encouragement as the previous President of the Family Division, Lord Justice Wall, was in favour of it for some years and during his short tenure as President, which was sadly ended by ill health, commented adversely on parents upsetting children by arguing over them as well as positively on shared residence orders. Wall LJ was the judge in one of the early leading cases supporting the concept of shared residence[25] where the parents apparently

---

23 [1995] 2 FLR 883.
24 [2003] EWCA Civ 592; [2003] 2 FLR 397.
25 *A v A (Shared Residence)* [2004] EWCA 142; [2004] 1 FLR 1195.

could not get on. However, the children had been spending 50 per cent of their time in each home and the judge said a shared residence order would 'reflect that fact and that the parents are equal in the eyes of the law and have equal duties and responsibilities towards their children'.

Thus the lack of cooperation between parents does not seem a bar to shared residence, although geographical distance between the parents' homes, as discussed in Wilson J's case *Re F*, might be, especially if the parents have little contact.

In another case, B v B *(Residence) (Condition Limiting Geographical Area)* (2004)[26] the mother and child were actually required to live within a certain geographical area to facilitate contact as the mother had made two applications to remove the child to Australia and her prime reason for moving from the south to the north of England was to get away from the father! Another of Wall LJ's cases also pointed the way to a greater likelihood of shared residence orders in the future: *Re M (Residence Order)* (2008),[27] which he said was a 'paradigm case' for a shared residence order. The children needed to be kept together, they wanted to be together and with the parents, who lived close to each other and were sufficiently cooperative.

16.2.3 The former contact order

This is the second of the s 8 orders of which the FJR recommended abolition and which the CAFA 2014 has duly replaced, with provision in the CAO dealing with an overarching shared PR plan for the future care of the child which addresses both the child's residence and contact with the other parent.

The former s 8 order required the person with whom the child lived (who might or might not have a formal residence order) to allow the child to visit or stay with a named person (generally called 'staying contact') or for that person and the child to have contact with each other in some other manner. The extent of such contact might either be left unspecified or alternatively be more precisely stated as *reasonable contact*, or even *defined contact* if the parents could not agree a programme and preferred the court to order it in detail for them.

This was a complete change from the former pre-1989 system of 'access', as the residence order was from the former 'custody' and/or 'care and control', which could only be undertaken by physical presence. From 1989 the court might order that letters and telephone calls were to be exchanged between the child and the recipient of the order, or sometimes (e.g. where the child is too young to write or telephone personally) to a limited extent between the latter and the parent with care, although it was not generally possible to order the parent with whom the child resides actually to perform more extensive tasks (e.g. personally to take any positive action in writing progress reports to or communicating news to the other parent if children did not do so themselves or could not do so, e.g., if they are too young to write or even to speak on the telephone).

In theory the CAO now replacing the former contact order is capable of defining contact with the parent with whom the child does not live most of the time, but one must question whether such an unstructured arrangement will in fact work in practice, or whether it will instead lead to further dispute, and more rather than fewer applications to court with LIPs conducting cases which will no longer be legally aided. Moreover, the encouragement of the contemporary modernisation is that parents should not get an actual order at all, unless they want to ask the court for a consent order, but rely on the private ordering of their own 'PA', which is however referred to in the CAP PD 12B paragraphs 2.4 to 2.7, as a Parenting Plan, where at paragraph 2.7 parents are signposted towards the Cafcass website[28] for help in creating one.

---

26 [2004] 2 FLR 979.
27 [2008] EWCA Civ 66; [2008] 1 FLR 1087.
28 www.cafcass.gov.uk/media/190788/parenting_plan_final_web.pdf.

Although the Report claims that 49 per cent of respondents to their consultation questions were in favour of the proposal for these 'PA's', the response to the consultation for replacement of the present residence and contact orders was 'more mixed'; and the Report admits that this 'broad support' was 'tempered' by arguments that the 'PA's' 'must not be seen as a panacea and were not appropriate in all cases'.

The account in Annex G to the FJR Final Report which gives some description of the implementation in Australia of their Shared Parental Responsibility Act 2006 is not encouraging. The Australian evaluations appear to show that the law had become 'overly complex' as a result, that legal practitioners had found it 'difficult to apply' and the key principles were 'difficult for lay people to understand' while it has been difficult for the court 'to evaluate the parties' parenting performance'. It is also suggested that the Australian Act has not helped lawyers, who must advise on the law, and DR professionals, who 'draw on their required knowledge of child development to advise parents' to cooperate so as to assist parents to make their parenting agreements.

Australian surveys had revealed that the Act had increased difficulties in parents making child-focused agreements and that fathers in particular had negotiated 'from a parental rights perspective rather than a child-focused stance'. It appears from Annex E to the report that the FJR committee recognised that there was a great deal of work to do to establish sufficient data to be confident that such a radical change in England and Wales would be worth the associated upheaval, as this annex lists the data gaps then recognised.

The Report does in fact explicitly admit that arguments were raised that the proposed changes might make matters worse 'by increasing confusion and doubt over what exactly was at stake'. Academics – and mothers – it seems were 'the most strongly opposed'. As one of the 'guiding principles' – rather than terms of reference – under which the committee's work was to be done was 'conflict between individuals should be minimised as far as possible' it is discouraging that the resulting Report seriously proposed changes which were already flagged up as troublesome to implement (and which might lead to increased cost, not reduction in that area) and in fact promoted more dissension than they obviated, and of course that these changes were accepted by the government and Parliament which legislated for the amendments to an Act which has been on the whole more successful than unsuccessful.

It would have been helpful to see some evidence of supporting specialist theory for changing principles of the CA 1989, which – even where the operation of some the detailed sections have attracted criticism – have on the whole not worked sufficiently badly to justify such fundamental change.

The Report ends with a very weak, general, non-specific paragraph on proposed implementation. The Law Society was amongst those who pressed for careful planning and implementation, calling the plans 'ambitious' and sounding a resources warning, while the Association of Directors for Children's Services articulated concern about both the culture change required and the 'willingness or skills to take things forward' in the relevant workforces. Clearly much more detail was required to generate confidence that the proposals could work in conjunction with s 1(1), namely to ensure that the welfare of the child is paramount.

It might, for instance, have been worth a trial period in which more formal input from parents in settling future arrangements for their children was more proactively supported by DR professionals, and some data collected in relation to conversion rates for such agreements into orders of the court (where that was felt to be necessary to give confidence to the family, as often happens now where the parties do not entirely trust to the 'no order principle'); following which some useful assessment might have been made as to whether the CAO could satisfactorily replace the two complementary s 8 orders. The Ancillary Relief Pilot Scheme of 2000 (initially tried out regionally before adoption nationally as the standard scheme) might well have provided a helpful precedent.

One positive suggestion of the FJR Final Report seems to be that 'ADR' should be rebranded

'Dispute Resolution Services' to send the message that the service is not alternative but central to the process of resolving differences, only one other limb of which is the court, and this has been taken up by the President with his own term of 'Non-Court' DR, or N-CDR, in his twelfth 'View from the President's Chambers'.

In the circumstances it might in fact have been much more worthwhile to attempt to develop a system in which parents were sure of what precisely they were expected to do in relation to facilitating contact with the parent who did not have primary care of the child or children. A look at some decided cases is enough to illustrate this point.

❖ CASE EXAMPLES

In *Re M (A Minor) (Contact: Conditions)* (1994)[29] an attempt was made to impose extensive conditions on a contact order which in effect was close to ordering contact between the parents rather than contact for the child with the non-resident parent, and the court took the view that such an order imposing more extensive tasks on the carer parent than to allow the child to have contact with the other parent could not be made, although it was deemed that a carer parent could be ordered to *keep the other parent informed* of the child's whereabouts, so that contact could actually take place.

However, in *Re O (A Minor) (Contact)* (1995)[30] the court did approve a mother being asked to send photographs, medical reports and nursery school reports, to inform the other parent of serious illness of the child and accept delivery of presents and cards for the child, which clearly only really involves the ordinary civilised behaviour which might be expected of a carer parent towards the other with whom the child does not reside. Lord Bingham also used the opportunity to spell out to the carer parent the responsibilities to allow and promote contact with the other parent which some parents still ignore, and hinted that as contact with both parents was so important to the child any obstruction was at a carer parent's peril since the court could take appropriate action.

Technically, any conditions which are acceptable so as to achieve indirect contact where direct contact is for some reason impossible may be attached pursuant to CA 1989 s 11(7), which permits conditions to be attached to all s 8 orders, so that presumably these will continue with the CAO. This power must be read in the light of the concept (new following the CA 1989) of promoting indirect contact as an alternative to the non-resident parent's actually seeing the child. However, reported decisions have been at pains to emphasise that this power should not be carried to extremes which require so much of that parent that the concept of contact with the child is distorted into a back-door requirement for contact with the carer parent, which was clearly not the intention of the statute.

Contact will usually always be granted in the case of biological parent–child relationships, even though there is no statutory presumption to that effect, on the basic principle that it is for the good of the child living with one parent to remain in contact with the other parent.

---

29 [1994] 1 FLR 272.
30 [1995] 2 FLR 124, CA.

❖ CASE EXAMPLES

In *Re W (A Minor) (Contact)* (1994)[31] the Court of Appeal made an order for contact despite a mother's hostility to the applicant (as she had remarried and was teaching the child to regard her new husband as the natural father). They allowed an appeal against the judge below who had not made an order, *inter alia* because the mother had said she would disobey it if it were made, so that judge had understandably thought that to make an order in that climate would only destabilise the child and not be in any child's interests. However, the Court of Appeal said he had abdicated his responsibility, not least as the child had a right to contact.

In *Re H (Minors: Access)* (1992)[32] it was held that there must be cogent reasons why a child should be denied the opportunity of contact with his or her natural father.

This must therefore be taken to be the contemporary trend, and that in the absence of complications, such as violence or sufficiently implacable hostility of either the custodial parent or of the children themselves to raise a query as to whether contact is or is not for the child's welfare or is potentially actual harm within the meaning of s 1(3)(e) of the checklist, there is in practice a basic presumption of some sort of a right to contact, with quite a body of *dicta* to that effect in some of the reported decisions, although the theory is that there is no such presumption but only a presumption that in general terms it is good for children to know and have a relationship with both parents. This can and will, however, be displaced by expressly showing (in the words of the text now adapted by the Court of Appeal in 'implacable hostility' cases and with reference to the statutory welfare checklist) that the:

> fundamental emotional need of every child to have an enduring relationship with both its parents' – as contemplated by s 1(3)(b) – is outweighed by the depth of harm which in the light, *inter alia* of the child's wishes and feelings – under s 1(3)(a) of the checklist – the child would be at risk of suffering – i.e. within the meaning of s 1(3)(e) – by virtue of the contact order.

Contact is therefore likely to be refused if that is absolutely necessary and in the child's interests (*Re B (Minors: Access)* (1992)[33]), especially if the child personally opposes it and is of an age when his or her ascertainable wishes and feelings, within the meaning of the statutory checklist, are taken into account (*Re F (Minors) (Denial of Contact)* (1993)[34]). Even indirect contact could be refused if that was in the child's best interests, although reported examples of this are rare owing to the normal assumption that it is highly desirable that, if there can be no direct contact, indirect contact should be established (see *Re C (Contact: No Order for Contact)* (2000)[35]).

Whether an order should be made is less obvious where the hurdle is the *resident carer parent's* implacable hostility to the contact for the child, making the child potentially at serious risk of emotional harm if contact is compelled because it will have such a bad effect on the objecting

---

31 [1994] 2 FLR 441, CA.
32 [1992] 1 FLR 148.
33 [1992] 1 FLR 140.
34 [1993] 2 FLR 677.
35 [2000] Fam Law 699.

parent (see *Re D (A Minor) (Contact: Mother's Hostility)* (1993);[36] *Re F (Minors) (Contact: Mother's Anxiety)* (1993);[37] *Re J (A Minor) (Contact)* (1994)[38]).

This is a very complex subject which has for years bedevilled the judiciary's attempts to enforce contact orders effectively because of the difficulty of imposing any acceptable sanction on the mother. However, since the implementation of the **Adoption and Children Act (ACA) 2006** some new progress has been made and it remains to be seen whether this will act as a deterrent to deliberately uncooperative parents. As indicated in *Re O*, above, courts disapprove of parents being obstructive about contact and in the past have indicated that a parent's attitude to contact might influence them to make an order for residence in favour of the other parent.[39]

❖ CASE EXAMPLES

In *D v M* (1982)[40] the father was reluctant for the mother to have contact and as a result the court was reluctant to let him have a residence order for the children.

In *Re S* (1990)[41] there was a similar situation where the children (two boys) each lived with one parent, and the court said that if the mother did not allow the boy in her care to visit the father and the other child she might have to give up the boy unless she became less recalcitrant, as she was depriving the boys of *each other's* company as well as the father of the company of the boy in her care.

It has of course been stressed that changing residence was usually an empty threat, since in theory the grant of an order must be in accordance with the s 1(3) criteria, reference to which is mandatory in contested cases. However, by s 1(3), the welfare of the child is paramount, thus attitude to contact has always been very important in any application relating to where a child should live after parental separation, because the court can always hang its decision on one or more of the s 1(3) pegs (e.g. the child's emotional needs or the harm to the child if contact with one parent is lost or fundamentally reduced).

Recently, however, the court has taken more decisive steps to give weight to the *actual* fears of children and carer parents where there has been such violence and traumatisation that there is some evidence that contact is resisted for that reason, usually by the mother where it is the father who has been violent.

This issue was initially raised by the Children Act Sub-Committee of the Lord Chancellor's Advisory Board on Family Law, whose report indicated that the earlier position, whereby the court's view that violence was not of itself a bar to contact had prevailed, might not always be a suitable stance; for example in *Re M (Violent Parent)* (1999)[42] Wall J suggested that instead of requiring mothers to arrange contact regardless, the violent father might have to show that he was fit to have contact before it would be ordered. In another case the court actually found that the mother's

---

36 [1993] 2 FLR 1.
37 [1993] 2 FLR 830.
38 [1994] Fam Law 316.
39 See Chapter 17.
40 [1982] 3 WLR 891; [1982] 3 All ER 897.
41 [1990] 2 FLR 166.
42 [1999] Fam Law 527.

traumatisation by the father's behaviour was such that it would inevitably impact upon the child, causing emotional harm, if contact were insisted upon.

The Court of Appeal then reviewed the matter in four conjoined cases: see *Re L (Contact: Domestic Violence)* (2000).[43] Their judgment indicated that there is no presumption either way, for or against contact orders, but that a balancing exercise must be undertaken to determine what is best for the child's welfare by using the s 1(3) checklist in the usual way but looking particularly at the past and present contact of the parties, the effect on the child and the carer and the motivation of the non-resident parent. This is obviously going to be continued in respect of the contact element of the CAO, as the new Practice Direction 12J – Child Arrangements and Contact Order: Domestic Violence and Harm added to the FPR 2010 is subtitled 'This Practice Direction supplements FPR Part 12 and supersedes the President's Guidance in Relation to Split Hearings (May 2010) as it applies to proceedings for child arrangement orders.'

Orders for contact do not confer PR so, like a step-parent without PR, a person with a contact order (now contact provision in a CAO) and no PR can do anything which safeguards and promotes the child's welfare during the contact but should not exceed that duty by doing anything which would be appropriate in a person exercising PR. It should be remembered that, apart from the case of parents with automatic PR, the key to other relations and associates of the child having PR is not the relationship as such but whether that person has an order which does confer PR.[44]

It should be noted that contact has been traditionally the right of the child and that the non-resident parent, having no 'right' to it, could not be compelled to exercise any right or duty to have contact with a child if s/he does not want that. However, after the HRA 1998 came into force European jurisprudence started to develop in relation to the non-resident parent's right to family life and therefore contact. Nevertheless the English court has adopted a robust view based on the assumption of a duty to balance competing human rights, which, inevitably, has followed the child's welfare (see, e.g., in child abduction and relocation cases[45]) and although attempts have been made to encourage contact there is no specific mandatory contact order than can be made although conditions can be attached to any such order.[46]

16.2.4 A prohibited steps order (PSO)

Neither this order nor the specific issue order has been abolished despite the emphasis on the 'shared PR' concept which should underpin all decisions to be taken by parents in respect of the child – if the 'shared responsibility' concept in fact works. Nevertheless the FPR 2010 rule 3A and associated protocol will of course strongly encourage the use of mediation through the MIAM process to preclude litigation over any disagreement that might be settled by a PSO, which could only be in the interests of the child or children involved.

This order is one which can prohibit a parent from taking any step which could be taken in meeting that parent's parental responsibility towards the child. The order is not intended to prevent parents doing anything else which does not amount to a step in meeting their PR, as is shown by *Croydon Borough Council v A* (1992),[47] where the local authority had removed children from their home under an emergency protection order and placed them with foster parents because the father had sexually abused one of them. When the authority applied to the magistrates for an interim care order, the court refused that order and instead for some reason made two PSOs, the first preventing

---

43 [2000] 2 FLR 334, CA.
44 See Chapter 12 at 12.3.
45 See below at 16.7.2.
46 See further Chapter 17.
47 [1992] 136 (LB) 69 (FS).

the father from seeing the children and the second prohibiting him from having contact with the mother. On appeal the second order was overturned because it did not fall within the statutory definition of a parent taking a step in meeting his PR, and the authority duly obtained their interim care order.

Similarly, in *Re H (Prohibited Steps Order)* (1995)[48] a judge made a PSO to forbid contact between a mother's former cohabitant and her children who were living with her, and over whom the local authority had supervision orders because the children had been sexually abused by the former cohabitant. The judge also attached no contact conditions to the supervision orders. On appeal, the Court of Appeal held that the PSO was wrong because it contravened CA 1989 s 9(5)(a), which specifically forbids a court to make a PSO as a back-door means of achieving a desired result which could, and properly should, be effected by a residence or contact order, and that although conditions could be attached to the authority's supervision order (such as for medical or psychiatric examination) a condition for no contact could not be so attached, although the supervisor has other means under CA 1989 Schedule 3 of achieving the same result.

Common use of the PSO is to prevent the two important steps prohibited by s 13(1) of the Act (i.e. change of a child's surname or removal from the jurisdiction[49]).

16.2.5 A specific issue order (SIO)

This order, too, has not been abolished by the CAO and, as the name suggests, it enables the court to give directions to decide a dispute as to any major decision to be taken in relation to a child's future (e.g. a change of surname, school or religion, or whether a child should or should not have a particular medical treatment, such as a blood transfusion, where one or even both of the parents are against it for religious or other reasons, or sterilisation or abortion, e.g. where the child is advised not to have children for some sufficient medical reason).

Sometimes several issues are combined, resulting in a specific issue and a PSO on one and possibly no order, under the s 1(5) principle, on another, as in *Re J (Specific Issue Order: Circumcision)* (1999).[50]

> ### ❖ CASE EXAMPLE
>
> *Re J* is a very good example of the use of the potential of the PSO and SIO. In this case the court first refused the Muslim father's application for a specific issue order that his son be circumcised as the boy's non-Muslim mother had vetoed this (and the court said this was a powerful welfare consideration) and also because it was not suggested by the father that the boy should attend the mosque or receive religious instruction. Second the court made a PSO to stop the father from arranging the circumcision himself. In respect of the child's religion, they did not consider that an order should be made to require the child to be brought up by the mother in his father's religion, since the father had made no proposals for such religious observance, so that the boy's religious instruction should fall within his contact with his father.

---

48 [1995] 1 FLR 638.
49 See below at 16.7.
50 [1999] 2 FLR 678.

The court can either take the decision itself, as in the above case, or direct that a particular person should take it, for example where treatment is directed by a specified doctor as the doctor deems appropriate. Such orders may be sought by non-parents (e.g. a local authority concerned for the child's welfare).

In general the court now tends to order modern diagnostic treatment against parents' wishes, on the basis that the child him- or herself is entitled to the benefits of science unless there is genuine scope for debate.[51]

The same restrictions apply to these orders as for PSOs.

16.3 Interim orders

All s 8 orders may be made as interim orders and, as well as permitting conditions to be attached (s 11(3) and (7)), also allow the court to delay implementation or to restrict the effect of the order to a certain period; which presumably also applies to CAOs, which might have even greater reasons than others for being suitable for interim force.

Tactically, obtaining an interim order is usually in the applicant's interests, because of the *status quo* element in the statutory checklist.[52] The additional value of an interim residence or contact element of a CAO is that it may cement relationships, thus strengthening other statutory checklist points in the applicant's favour (e.g. the child's ascertainable wishes and feelings in favour of remaining with the applicant if temporary arrangements are working out well).

16.4 Enforcement of orders

Enforcement has always been a problem in relation to contact orders and this is considered separately in Chapter 17.

16.5 Who may apply for s 8 orders?

The power of the court to entertain applications for s 8 orders including CAOs, whether formal applications are made or deemed to be made where appropriate of the court's own motion, lies in s 10(1) of the Act. There is an 'open door' policy where persons are already in permitted categories: s 10(7), otherwise leave must be sought where that is required.

Certain persons are entitled to apply as of right:

- any parent or guardian of the child: s 10(4);
- anyone who has a residence order in respect of the child: s 10(4);
- any person with an old style custody, care and control or access order, called an 'existing order' (Schedule 14).

A father who is not married to the mother will usually be classed as a parent, and will not require leave, but only if he can show that he is the father. Alternatively he may have resided with the child for three years (see below) and thus not need leave for that reason.

The following were entitled to apply for residence and contact orders only and remain eligible to apply for CAOs:

---

51 See, e.g., Re C (1999) BMLR 283, which concerned an HIV test on a five-month-old child, which the parents had resisted.
52 See Chapter 15.

(a) any party to a marriage (whether or not the marriage is still subsisting) in which the child was a child of the family as defined in s 105(1);

(b) any person with the consent of all those with residence orders, now CAO with a residence term (or 'existing orders'), or PR in respect of the child;

(c) any person who has the consent of a local authority which has a care order; and

(d) any person with whom the child has resided for three years (not necessarily continuously, but beginning not more than five years before the application is made).

Rules of court may extend this list: s 10(7).

Other persons can still apply but will need leave of the court (e.g. grandparents or any other relatives with whom the child has not established a three-year residence qualification). The test for success is whether there is a good arguable case (*Re M (Care: Contact: Grandmother's Application for Leave)* (1995)[53]) and s 10(9) sets out the criteria the court will take into account, i.e. who the applicant is in relation to the child, why the order is sought, whether any harm will occur, such as disruption to the child's life, if the application is allowed, the wishes and feelings of the child's parents, and the wishes and plans, if any, of the local authority for the child. Where there is a contest between parents and other relatives, weight is given to natural parenthood (*Re D (Care: Natural Parent Presumption)* (1999)[54]; *Re D (Residence Order: Natural Parent)* (1999)[55]). The FJR supports the involvement of grandparents with their grandchildren but did not propose any changes in the present arrangements for their obtaining permission to make an application for which they do not at present have standing to apply.

The child itself may apply if of sufficient understanding: s 10(8), and a number of such applications by teenage and sub-teenage girls have succeeded. A solicitor may accept instructions from such a child and obtain public funding in order to pursue his or her application. It was clear, when in the 1990s children picked up the idea of 'divorcing their parents', that this might be a practice growth area but it has not become an epidemic as once feared.

Acting for children has become a specialism in itself for some family lawyers and, owing to the potential complexities, all such s 8 applications must be heard in the Family Division of the High Court.[56] There is a growing corpus of authority on this area of law and practice which indicates the caution involved, in view of the fact that such an application can have a detrimental effect on parent–child relations. The obvious query is as to whether the formality of an order is necessary or whether informal resolution is preferable. This is another initiative in which the new President has indicated that he feels strongly that DR is more useful. It is uncertain whether the HRA 1998 gives increased scope for leave for children to participate in court proceedings. Not surprisingly, in view of all these doubts, Resolution also issues its own *Guide to Good Practice for Solicitors Acting for Children*.

It is incidentally, of course, despite all media misconceptions, *impossible* for a child to divorce his or her parents, since PR is for life or at least until adulthood or adoption of the child, though the child may naturally obtain an order to go to *live* with other relatives, or with anyone suitable, and maintenance may be obtained from the natural parent(s) to enable this to happen.[57] Since the mid-1990s, when a child first succeeded in making her own application in her parents' s 8 proceedings,[58] such initiatives by children have been accepted as appropriate in certain cases, but are by no means common.

---

53 [1995] 2 FLR 86.
54 [1999] 1 FLR 134.
55 [1999] Fam Law 755.
56 See *Practice Direction* [1993] 1 All ER 820.
57 See Chapter 21.
58 *Re C (Child's Application for Leave)* [1995] 1 FLR 927.

If permission to apply is required the court will be likely to require the adult(s) with whom the child wishes to live to make an application and base its decision on the s 10(9) criteria as set out above.

Applications are often made in the course of a divorce, but this is in no way necessary, since application may be made at any time on a completely freestanding basis. To emphasise the lack of connection between divorce and other dissolution proceedings the same form is now used for s 8 orders irrespective of whether there is a divorce in process, and this is obviously sensible in view of the repeal of MCA 1973 s 41 by the CAFA 2014.

The court will have jurisdiction if the child is either habitually resident in England and Wales or present and not habitually resident elsewhere on the date of application or hearing. Jurisdiction is excluded if there are matrimonial proceedings elsewhere in the UK unless the other court has waived its jurisdiction, or stayed proceedings so that the matter might be heard in England and Wales: FLA 1986, s 3. However, if the court thinks that the matter would be better determined outside England and Wales (i.e. in any other jurisdiction) it has the power to direct that no order be made: FLA 1986, s 2(4).

16.6 The family assistance order: s 16

This is a short-term alternative to a s 8 order, though it may be used for many purposes, such as even when a s 8 order has already been made and the parents need extra support. It is retained by the CAP, where it is described as 'an order of the Court which allows Cafcass or local authorities to provide social-work support to establish contact arrangements which might otherwise fail'. In fact it tends to have much wider application.

The order was introduced by the CA 1989 and is specifically designed to help at times of matrimonial breakdown. Such an order was in the past only made in the most exceptional circumstances, as it merely enables a social worker to give general advice and assistance. Everyone involved except the child has until recently had to consent to the order: s 16(3) and (7).

However, recent amendments have strengthened the potential of the order, as in the past there has not been great use of the FAO, though it has had a role where it was held that a s 11(7) condition of supervision of contact could not be attached to contact orders.[59]

16.7 Change of name or removal from the jurisdiction: s 13(1)

The prohibition of these two acts by s 13(1) provides a common example of the use of the PSO to stop a parent misusing PR. Taking either of these obvious steps (with which objectively the other parent is unlikely to agree if unilateral action is taken instead of agreement sought) is inadvisable as the court cannot be relied upon to support the unilateral action. Where an order with a residence provision is already in force (i.e. where the parents have already had recourse to the court for one reason or another), the section prohibits:

- changing the child's surname; and
- taking a child out of the jurisdiction;

in either case without the written consent of every person with PR or the leave of the court. The reasons for this are obvious. (It should be noted that if there is no restricting order in force, the

---

59 See *Leeds County Council v C* [1993] 1 FLR 269, where Booth J used a family assistance order to achieve supervised contact.

correct procedure to stop the removal or change of name is to apply for a PSO under s 8 as s 13(1) is not engaged. Equally if the parents are not in agreement and both have PR unilateral action is not appropriate. Even if the father does not have PR there is ample authority to indicate that application to the court should be made before either step is taken.)

16.7.1 Change of surname

Both formal change by deed poll or informal change (e.g. by instructing a school that a child is to be known by a certain name) is equally forbidden by the section, and if the other parent will not consent application must to be made to the court. However, the court does not usually insist on changing a name back again where the change has been informally made some time previously, as it has been held that that is not in the child's best interests any more than changing it in the first place: Re C (Change of Surname) (1998).[60] In practice the court cannot do much to control an informal change of name by which a child is known on a daily basis, but only to deal with formal documents.

The court tends to resist consenting where application is made, because of the importance of preserving the formal link with the absent father and of the importance of his name as part of the child's identity regardless of the mother's new associations. The children's own wishes count exceptionally little in this situation, and much less than they might in other contexts *because* of the importance placed by the court on the continuing connection with the father, as shown by cases such as W v W (1981),[61] where the family were all emigrating to Australia and the twelve- and thirteen-year-olds wanted to take their mother's new name, which was that of their new step-father. The court has said in more than one case that there is no longer any opprobrium 'for a child to have a different surname from that of adults in the household': Re B (Change of Surname) (1996).[62]

The court appears to take the view that as long as statistics show a tendency towards serial monogamy and cohabitation, embarrassment at having a different name (or even several different names in the reconstructed family) is now unlikely to be felt by the children, and therefore this will not be given weight by the court. Thus the chances of the court's agreeing to a change appear slimmer than ever. The older cases where some judges did agree are now probably out of date and no longer even a guideline (except perhaps in the case of a *fait accompli*). In particular, as in L v F (1978),[63] where the father is a person of stature and able to make a positive contribution to the children's lives, the court is unlikely to approve the loss of his name, especially as contemporary psychiatric evidence shows that children need to know and acknowledge their biological origins. Conversely, a parent's best chance of success might be if the father were for some reason notorious (as was successful in one well-known case in the USA). There was a similar case in England in Re W, Re A, Re B (Change of Name) (1999),[64] where the father was in prison and unlikely to have a meaningful relationship with the child, so the change of name was allowed.

However, these cases do often involve rejection of the wishes of Gillick competent children and have generated many pages of appellate judgments. Some recent decisions have both re-emphasised the importance of the link with the father for the reasons stated above and also held to the principle that *changing* a surname by which a child is already known is a significant step which places a heavy burden on the party seeking to make the change to show it is in the child's interests. See for example Re S (Change of Name) Cultural Factors (2001).[65]

---

60 [1998] 2 FLR 656.
61 [1981] 1 All ER 100; [1981] Fam 14.
62 [1996] 1 FLR 791.
63 (1978) The Times, 1 August.
64 Reported at [2000] 2 FLR 930.
65 [2001] 2 FLR 1005.

Indeed, the court now appears to be saying that if any change is to be made, even where the mother alone has PR, because the parents have never been married, good practice indicates that this should be approved by the court. This is doubtless in accordance with the contemporary social context, where neither married nor unmarried relationships are supposed to impact upon child status. However, it does in theory conflict with the continuing position of sole PR for the mother, unless the unmarried father has obtained PR in one of the usual ways, and Baroness Hale (then Hale LJ) on the contrary indicated in 2002 that a father without PR did not need to be consulted about a proposed change, but could challenge the change in court. In the same case it was suggested that consideration could be given to the use of both parents' names, as in Spain, and that perhaps they could be hyphenated.

❖ CASE EXAMPLES

In *Re C (Minors)* (1997),[66] the children had taken the mother's maiden name as their parents had never been married. When she subsequently married another man and their father, with whom they lived, obtained a residence order, the court held that their name should be changed to his, since there was no useful purpose in retaining their mother's maiden name, which she herself no longer used.

In *Dawson v Wearmouth* (1999),[67] however, the House of Lords upheld the Court of Appeal in supporting the decision of the mother of an illegitimate child, who had registered the child's name at birth under her own surname, which was that of her former husband, and not of the actual father. They restated the principle that, pursuant to the paramountcy principle, clear circumstances were required to justify changing a child's surname.

In *Re T (Change of Surname)* (1998),[68] between the Court of Appeal and House of Lords' hearings of *Dawson v Wearmouth*, the Court of Appeal laid down some guidelines which acknowledged the right of a father with a parental responsibility order, but no residence order, to object to change of a child's surname. They articulated the principle that names are important to the issue of welfare, so that in any dispute either consent of the other parent or leave of the court is required, particularly where both parents have parental responsibility. It seems, therefore, that s 13 has in no way changed the common law position that neither parent of a legitimate child could change the child's surname without the agreement of the other, and that where the child is not legitimate (so that historically the mother was the only one with parental responsibility) it is now considered at the very least good practice to refer any dispute about name change to the court. This was despite the *obiter* remarks to the contrary in *Re PC (Change of Surname)* (1997).[69] It thus appears that the position is now that the old system, whereby the mother of an illegitimate child was its only parent, is completely dead, because at any moment the unmarried father can apply for parental responsibility (if he has not already obtained it) and in the absence of negative contribution to the child's life is likely to be given at least the status of a father.

---

66 (1997) *The Times*, 8 December.
67 [1999] 1 FLR 1167.
68 [1998] 2 FLR 620.
69 [1997] 2 FLR 730.

In *Re S* (1999)[70] a 15-year-old *Gillick* competent child won an appeal against refusal to allow her to change her name to that of her maternal family on the ground that the judge had failed to give sufficient weight to her wishes, feelings, needs and objectives, to the views of the guardian *ad litem* and to the real motives of her father in objecting. Pursuant to s 10(8), a child of sufficient understanding can alternatively make his or her own application to the court to seek or prevent a change of surname This may indicate a significant trend since only three years earlier the court had said that s 1(3)(a) of the checklist was not to be given as much weight in specific issue cases about change of name, no doubt due to the importance that has always been given to retaining some traditional links with the father: dropping his name – the situation in most change of name cases – obviously severs. Moreover, in 2005, in another case[71] where the children were only seven and nine, the Court of Appeal criticised a judge for failing to place sufficient weight on their views.

16.7.2 Removal from the jurisdiction

If only one parent has PR there will be no offence under the **Child Abduction Act 1984** if the child is taken out of the jurisdiction. If both have PR then consent of the court to removal of the child from the jurisdiction is essential. However, even where there is a CAO with a residence term in place the person with that order may in fact take the child out of the UK for a holiday of up to one month *without leave*. If leave is required for longer it is likely to be given by the court if the other parent will not consent, provided the holiday is not obviously intended as cover for permanent removal beyond the reach of the court's authority. Moreover, a parent who has totally unreasonably withheld consent might find that he or she has to pay the costs of a court application.

The way in which this restriction may be dealt with in practice is to have in place either a general direction attached to the primary carer's order to enable removal of the child whenever convenient subject to a return to the jurisdiction whenever required, or a general undertaking may be given to the court by the parent wishing to remove the child (e.g. a father living abroad whom the child visits regularly).

Permanent removal is more difficult, as this might in practice cut off all contact for the other parent. However, the court is aware of the difficulties that may arise if the parent with primary care is thwarted in attempting to emigrate, with consequent unhappiness for the whole family, as is shown by the accumulated case law.

Historically, the court's generally cautious stance is shown by cases which indicate that, while if the move is in the child's interests and is well worked out the court may consent, precedent has no role in the decision as each case must be approached on its own facts and merits. More recent decisions have indicated the reconfirmation of the long-standing presumption set out in *Poel v Poel* (1970)[72] in favour of requiring a well-worked-out plan for emigration by the carer parent, in which case there is likely to be consent to leave unless that would be plainly contrary to the child's welfare.

Among a number of recent cases, possibly generated by the HRA 1998, there was an unsuccessful challenge to this position by a father who opposed the return of a child and her mother to the mother's home jurisdiction of New Zealand, on the basis that it breached his human right to family life pursuant to the ECHR Article 8, but the Court of Appeal confirmed that the paramountcy of the welfare of the child meant that adult rights in conflict must give way and rejected the

---

70 [1999] 1 FLR 79,
71 *Re R (Residence: Shared Care; Children's Views)* [2005] EWCA Civ 542, CA.
72 [1970] 1 WLR 1469.

submissions that social change in the position of fathers within the family since 1970 indicated that leave to remove should be refused because it disrupted or destroyed appropriate contact with the child for the left-behind parent, usually the father.[73] It is fair to say that there has been some movement towards a change in this position indicated at three specialist conferences in 2009 and 2010, all involving Lord Justice Thorpe, Head of International Family Justice, and also in the judgment of Mr Justice Mostyn in Re AR (2010).[74] However, the position is complex and must be considered further in connection with other contact problems: see Chapters 17 and 18.

16.8 Current debates

Ideas for research on these current discussion questions can be found on the companion website updates.

- Since, despite the previous definable trend towards shared residence when parents part, there is now no formal connection between shared residence and restrictions on relocation of the carer parent with whom the child principally resides, does the FJR's concentration on 'shared parental responsibility' impact on this debate at all?
- Does the right to family life under the ECHR support the view that a non-carer parent should have a right to contact with a child following parental separation? Or should the child have the sole right to contact?
- Should there be some mutuality between the obligations of PR and a corresponding right to contact with the child?
- Is the new CAO likely to make any difference to any of these debates?

16.9 Summary of Chapter 16
The portfolio of orders

- There were four s 8 orders: to decide on residence, contact, specific issues and prohibited steps. There are now only three, since residence and contact orders have been replaced by the CAO. The CAFA 2014 enacted this recommendation of the FJR.
- The contact element of a CAO may be defined or undefined, and provide for direct or indirect contact. There is usually a presumption of contact between a child and its biological parents, on the basis of the blood tie, but contact may be refused, regulated or postponed if there is likely to be harm to the child (e.g. if there is a history of violence). The FJR recommended a new shared PR culture generating parental agreements ('PA's') facilitated by 'ADR' (which they recommended renaming 'Dispute Resolution Services').
- Specific issue orders determine matters outside the CAO residence and contact elements (e.g. education and religion).
- Prohibited steps orders determine whether a parent shall or shall not do any act in performance of his or her PR (e.g. consent to medical treatment on behalf of the child or to remove the child from the jurisdiction).
- There is an alternative to s 8 orders in the s 16 family assistance order, a temporary order designed to provide skilled social worker help for families at a time of relationship breakdown. This sometimes obviates the need for orders and facilitates contact.

---

73 *Payne v Payne* [2001] Fam Law 346.
74 [2010] 10 June.

Who may apply for s 8 orders?

● A parent may apply as of right, other persons, including the child, with leave. The court decides leave applications in accordance with specific criteria, including the motive for applying for the order in question.

Change of surname and removal from the jurisdictions

● These are discrete issues regulated by CA 1989 s 13(1).
● In principle, it is now thought inappropriate in practice to *change* a child's surname without the consent of the child's other parent or leave of the court, possibly even regardless of whether the single mother alone has sole PR for the child.
● In summary, there is a burden on the parent wishing to change the name to justify doing so and the presumption in favour of the *status quo* is very strong.
● No parent may remove a child from the jurisdiction without consent of the other parent or leave of the court.

 16.10 Further reading

Freeman, M (Marilyn), 'Relocation: the **reunite** report', www reunite.org.
Geekie, C, 'Relocation and Shared Residence: one route or two?', [2008] Fam Law 446.
Gilmore, S, 'The Nature, Scope and Use of the Specific Issue Order', [2004] CFLQ 367.
Gilmore, S, 'Court decision making in shared residence cases: a critical examination', [2006] CFLQ 478.
Gilmore, S, 'The Assumption That Contact is Beneficial: Challenging the Secure Foundation', [2008] Fam Law 1226.
Hayes, M, 'Relocation cases: Is the Court of Appeal Applying the Correct Principles?', [2006] CFLQ 19: 351.
Kielty, S, 'Similarities and differences in the experiences of non-resident fathers and non-resident mothers', [2006] *International Journal of Law, Policy and the Family*, 20: 74.
Kirkonel, A, 'Removing Children From the Jurisdiction', [1999] Fam Law 332.
May, V and Smart, C, 'The parenting contest: problems of ongoing conflict over children', in Maclean, M (ed), *Parenting after Partnering*, Oxford, Hart, 2007.
McCallum, M, 'Shared Residence – Just a Label?', [2004] Fam Law 528.
McCallum, M, 'Shared Parenting in Practice', [2005] Fam Law 411.
Perry, A and Rainey, B, 'Supervised, supported and indirect contact orders: research findings', [2007] *International Journal of Law, Policy and the Family*, 21: 21.
Smyth, B, 'Parent–child contact in Australia: Exploring five different post-separation patterns of parenting', [2005] *International Journal of Law, Policy and the Family*, 19: 1.
Spon-Smith, R, 'Relocation Revisited', [2004] Fam Law 190.
Trinder, L and Kellett, J, 'Fairness, Efficiency and Effectiveness in Court-based Dispute Resolution Schemes in England', [2007] *International Journal of Law, Policy and the Family*, 27: 322.
Trinder, L, Beek, M and Connolly, J, *Making Contact: How Parents and Children Negotiate and Experience Contact After Divorce*, York, Joseph Rowntree Foundation, 2002.
Worwood, A, 'International Relocation – the Debate', [2005] Fam Law 621.

Chapter 17

Making Contact Orders Work

Chapter Contents

Learning outcomes for this chapter

A sound understanding of the historic problems in enforcing contact orders including:

(i)   A perception of the background timeline to the present context and the development of the socio-legal principles which have driven initiatives to make contact work.

(ii) An ability to analyse the judicial thinking behind the development of the concept of shared residence and shared parenting.

(iii) An appreciation of the socio-legal issues involved in the currently available sanctions.

(iv) An awareness that unresolved contact problems may lead to worse complexity: i.e. international abduction and/or applications for leave to remove the child to another jurisdiction, threatening contact even further.

(v)   A critical approach to the recommendations of the FJR in the light of the principles of the CA 1989.

17.1 Introduction

This chapter looks at one of the most significant problems in child law, if not perhaps the most significant: how to enforce contact orders made under the CA 1989, whether as the former individual order, or the contact element of CAO, and draws together some possible solutions.

However, none of these is likely to be an absolute panacea: when parents separate it is optimistic to expect them, or even a majority, suddenly to agree about their children's future living arrangements, including arrangements for children to see their non-resident parent. Thus the new CAO already carries within its philosophy the seeds of failure, since the new CAP of the Family Court, established in April 2014, emphasises private ordering through the 'PAs' encouraged by the FJR and based on a Parenting Plan facilitated by Cafcass and/or mediation – which can still be funded even though most private child law cases can obtain legal advice and/or representation only if one of the exceptions to LASPO 2012 cuts is established. This in turn relies heavily on:

(i)   the cooperation of the parents concerned in both the philosophy of private ordering; and

(ii) agreement between separated spouses or ex-partners (who possibly are already also divorced, perhaps with some acrimony, if they were married), and in either case following a separation because they could not get on! The take-up of mediation in the 18 months since LASPO was implemented in April 2013 tells its own story about the likelihood of this initiative succeeding, since these figures have fallen dramatically – according to Christina Blacklaws they have 'fallen off a cliff'[1] – whereas numbers of LIPs have swollen, paralysing the court process, as parties have apparently thought it better to take their chances before a judge. Possibly, at least numbers of mediations undertaken may now begin to rise, following the government's announcement in August 2014 that there will be further financial help for an initial mediation session, but naturally this does not address the potential lack of parental cooperation.

At first glance, the FJR's recommendation that to resolve the contact problem required abolishing residence and contact orders plus any idea of 'shared residence' is not an obvious solution. Shared residence was in fact having some success, since it was naturally in logic impossible, as the Court of Appeal identified in Re W (Shared Residence Order) (2009),[2] to make a contact order at all if the parents had a shared residence order since that would be a contradiction in terms. The idea instead

---

1 Blacklaws, C, 'The impact of LASPO changes to date in private family law and mediation', [2014] Fam Law 44: 626.
2 [2009] EWCA 370; [2009] 2 FLR 436.

to emphasise 'shared parental responsibility' (PR) and to 'make it work properly' initially looks more promising, but their strategy for shared PR and 'making it work properly' appears to rely solely on their philosophy of parents' PAs, facilitated by mediation or other forms of DR – which according to the MOJ figures during 2013–14 has apparently not so far been happening.

While it is true that it has proved equally impossible to facilitate many peaceful shared residence orders, despite the various shared parenting initiatives which have been tried on the basis that PR remains with a parent for life or at least till the child is 18, it is also true that some such orders have worked well, or at least in some cases the parties do not seem to have returned to court.

Moreover, some sort of a presumption of shared residence did seem to be taking root as a starting point (unless obviously unsuitable) when most orders were made, at least as a contemporary theme even if not necessarily granting equal time, although some decisions have denied that there was ever any such presumption, and that the disposal of a residence application was always at the court's discretion and governed by the child's best interests and welfare.

Accordingly this apparent trend towards shared residence where the logistics permitted might perhaps have been allowed to come to fuller fruition before the recent amendment of the CA 1989 replacing residence and contact orders as such, but since no alternative was apparently considered, perhaps the best-kept secret may be that the format of the new CAO does still in fact permit the former solution to many ongoing parental squabbles, i.e. a primary carer with generous contact for the non-resident parent. It is certainly true that fashions come and go, in child law as in other walks of life, and it may be that shared residence was already on the way out of fashion as quickly as it came in, before the FJR proposed their solution of shared PR.

It is, nevertheless, very disappointing to have another major upheaval in family law without clear prognosis of success. The fact remains that when the CA 1989 was passed it was hoped that the new system (and terminology) of 'residence', 'contact' and 'specific issue' or 'prohibited steps' orders under s 8[3] would encourage separated parents to facilitate ongoing contact for children with both of their parents; but this has not been a universal panacea for the embittered feelings of some separated and divorced parents.

One reason for this optimism was the new concept and terminology of 'parental responsibility'[4] – and its 'catchy' abbreviation 'PR' – and also the absence of the formerly emotive terms of 'custody', 'care and control' and 'access', which had long created ill feeling, owing to the suggestive language, which indicated that winning the right to have the child living with the parent to whom custody was awarded was some sort of endorsement of that parent's superiority over the other.

Indeed in practical terms, the old custody order did in fact confer an actual, as well as an unsatisfactory appearance of, superiority, since the parent with custody was able to dictate, or veto, all significant decisions in the child's upbringing: the only way in which the other parent without formal custody could challenge such decisions by the custodial parent was to mount that parent's own full-blown custody application, seeking to have custody transferred away from the other parent to that applicant. This generally caused considerable disruption to the entire family and the child or children, whatever the result, and is certainly well gone.

In theory the new system should, therefore, have worked to revolutionise the experience of parental separation and divorce for children, and looking at the historic timeline indeed overall it has, despite not being universally successful, and, notoriously, causing Wall LJ to comment that it was undesirable for parents to fight over their children in s 8 applications, wasting costs and taking up the courts' time – particularly singling out the middle classes as at fault in this respect, and indicating that he hoped that greater recourse would be had to mediation and other DR methods to preclude this undesirable syndrome.

---

3 See Chapter 16.
4 See Chapter 12 at 12.3.

However, the fact that the original CA 1989 scheme has not worked perfectly does not seem a good reason to abandon it for one which seems to have much less certain chances of success and without any pilot process or preparatory information for the public, suggesting that the real basis of the change was a desire by the government simply to cut costs and at the same time decimate litigation by making it very difficult for parents to go to court through withdrawing legal aid without any alternative provision or even adequate signposting to the DR services that were to be used instead. Many commentators, too numerous to mention, have already made this point.

The question must therefore be asked: 'Is there any sound theoretical background to the abolition of residence and contact orders, other than cost saving?'

It is fair to say that there have been continual problems in enforcing contact orders even from the earliest implementation of the CA 1989. Throughout the decade from 1990 to 2000 successive remedies were discussed and tried, but none was genuinely effective. Threats were made by judges to send obstructive carer parents – who were usually mothers – to prison for contempt, but this was obviously unsatisfactory, since if the carer was in prison the child would either have to live with another relative or go into the care of the local authority; a fine was no better as a sanction since it simply reduced the resources available to the child.

It was held that although the child's welfare was not paramount in deciding whether to make such an order it was clearly a consideration: *A v N (Committal: Refusal of Contact)* (1997).[5] Moreover, one parent imprisoned for refusing to allow contact with the other was hardly a positive influence on the child. Judges spoke of not allowing a 'selfish parent's' charter,[6] suggested handing children over in neutral venues or through a third party where parents would not go to each others' homes. A network of nationwide contact centres grew up; interestingly, this national organisation is expressly referred to as a contact facilitator in the new CAP Practice Direction.[7]

Where 'implacable hostility' was evidenced, often with a domestic violence background which made the carer parent – and sometimes the child – unwilling to see the other parent, supervised contact was suggested; this too is offered by contact centres, and it definitely works although it is unsurprisingly resource limited, and there is usually a wait for places even if there were a centre near every family needing them, which is certainly not the case.

Militant fathers' groups[8] were set up with the expressed aim of 'fighting for' contact with their children in such circumstances, claiming that there was discrimination against fathers, and this sometimes led to extreme public demonstrations. The courts have denied any such discrimination.[9] The suggestion is nevertheless certainly one of the strongest reasons for the initiative of the present President of the Family Division of the High Court for transparency in Family Court decisions (including a presumption of publication of judgments) since such greater transparency will perhaps bring a more accurate perception of family justice by the otherwise largely uninformed public using the Family Court's services.

It is certainly true that if there is a more complex situation for separated and divorced parents in which to find potentially insoluble problems it is in the often inevitable result of problematical enforcement of contact orders, i.e. the resulting international child abduction and applications for relocation out of the jurisdiction, which is the subject of Chapter 18. Contact problems are frequently the first layer of the infrastructure to abduction and relocation syndromes, so that even

---

5 [1997] 1 FLR 533.
6 Per Baroness Butler-Sloss, when, as Butler-Sloss LJ, she was President of the Family Division of the High Court, and inevitably heard some of the worst cases on appeal.
7 The National Association of Contact Centres, www.naccc.org.uk.
8 Such as 'Fathers 4 Justice' and 'Families Need Fathers'. Sir Bob Geldof supported such groups; see Geldof, B (2003) 'The Real Love That Dare Not Speak its Name' in Bainham, A, Lindley, B, Richards, M and Trinder, L (eds) *Children and Their Families*, Oxford, Hart.
9 Per Lord Justice Wall, later President of the Family Division, in *Re O (A Child) (Contact:Withdrawal of Application)* [2003] EWHC (Fam) at para 3.

'usually' is probably not too strong a word. Post-separation contact thus presents important issues for resolution at the earliest opportunity if at all possible.

17.2 Addressing contact problems

More recent attempts to address these problems include (1) judicial emphasis on the importance of contact for the child, (2) initiatives by government, Resolution and contact centres to encourage parents to organise their lives to facilitate contact, (3) specific contact enforcement orders,[10] (4) at least three change of residence orders where all else has failed following the **Children and Abduction Act 2006** (which was implemented in 2008), (5) shared residence orders, (6) the new CAP Practice Direction 12B at paras 2.4–7 (Parenting Plans) and 21 (Enforcement and Separated Parents' Information Plans, 'SPIPs' – available nationally for both parents and grandparents) and (7) settlement of proceedings.

17.2.1 Judicial emphasis on the importance of contact

Of course a parent cannot be forced to have contact with a child if the parent simply refuses to do so. This was specifically considered by Thorpe LJ in the case of *Re L (A Child) (Contact: Domestic Violence)* (2000)[11] when it was held that contact could not be ordered in the face of parental determination not to engage with the child, although some writers have considered whether this is a parental duty.

Nevertheless, there is much judicial emphasis on the importance of contact. This no doubt comes from an increasing emphasis on 'attachment theory' and also on the generally beneficial nature of a child's contact with both parents reported by psychologists.[12] Baroness Hale has stated: 'Making contact happen, and, even more importantly, making contact work, is one of the most difficult and continuous challenges in the whole of family law.'[13]

Most judges and Bainham consider that there is a right to contact on the part of the child[14] and distinguish between the opposition of some mothers with good reason, for example where there has been severe or prolonged domestic violence which might lead to a mother's nervous breakdown if she was obliged to agree to contact (*Re H (Children) (Contact Order) (No 2)* (2001)[15]) and where there is no such good reason, for instance where the opposition is identified as simply 'emotional'. It has usually been difficult to convince the court of good reason to deny contact unless there has been some background of domestic violence, but where that could be shown the court often had no option but to acquiesce in refusing or ending contact.[16] However, there have been some cases where contact has been ended because of the effect on the mother and/or the child.

---

10 Inserting sections 11A to 11P into the Children Act 1989.
11 [2000] 2 FCR 404 at para 43, but see Fortin, J, Ritchie, C and Buchanan, A, 'Young Adults' Perceptions of Court Ordered Contact', (2006) *Child and Family Law Quarterly*, 18: 211. Bainham also considers that there is a duty on the parent to have contact with a child, even if that is unenforceable: Bainham, A, 'Contact as a right and obligation', in Bainham, A, Lindley, B, Richards, M and Trinder, L (eds) *Children and Their Families*, Oxford, Hart, 2003; Eekelaar, J, 'Contact – Over the Limit', (2002) Fam Law 32: 271 casts doubt on the benefits; Gilmore, S, 'The Assumption That Contact is Beneficial', (2008) Fam Law 1226, and 'Disputing Contact: Challenging Some Assumptions', (2008) *Child and Family Law Quarterly*, 20: 285.
12 There is a substantial professional literature on this subject: Shaffer, R, *Making Decisions About Children: Psychological Questions and Answers*, Oxford, Blackwell, 1998; Schofield, G, 'Making Sense of the Ascertainable Wishes and Feelings of Insecurely Attached Children', (1998) *Child and Family Law Quarterly*, 10: 63.
13 *Re G (Children) (Residence: Same Sex Partner)* [2006] EWHL 43 at para 41.
14 See Gilmore's articles at n 11.
15 [2001] 3 FCR, 385, another case of Lord Justice Wall's.
16 See Herring, J, *Family Law*, 6th edition, Harlow, Pearson Longman, 2013, p 558 et seq.

> ❖ **CASE EXAMPLE**
>
> In *Re JA (A Minor) (Contact)* (1994)[17] it was felt by the court that the only solution was for contact with the father to cease because of the mother's implacable hostility, which was also having an adverse effect on the child. This was typical of many such cases.

17.2.2 Initiatives by government, contact centres and others

Initial attempts were made in the 1990s and early in the following decade to educate parents towards organising their lives to facilitate contact. Resolution was active in this project, including introducing, with the courts and social workers, printed Parenting Plans encouraging parents to agree written contact arrangements. These had some success but lately appear to have been partially discontinued, possibly for economic reasons, although they are now expressly referred to in the CAP Practice Direction 12B. However, Resolution has also introduced similar commercially produced stationery for their members' clients. There was also a group of studies on contact centres[18] where a social worker or volunteer could facilitate neutral venue contact, also with limited success, largely because early studies showed that the non-resident parent found them patronising or even sometimes unsafe. The latter comment is now unlikely, following the safeguarding initiatives after the CA 2004, as a result of which safeguarding at such centres appears to be taken very seriously.

17.2.3 Contact enforcement orders

This raft of new orders was provided by the **Children and Adoption Act 2006**, which was specifically 'An Act to make provision as regards contact with children; to make provision as regards family assistance orders . . .'. It was generated by pressure from groups such as Fathers 4 Justice. The Act received Royal Assent on 21 June 2006 but was not brought into force immediately; (the few) cases so far reported do not indicate that it has been much used.

What may have resulted is that heightened awareness of the importance placed by Parliament on ensuring contact has encouraged the courts, which have now been using the draconian change of residence option (which is not new, as it was first suggested in *V-P v V-P (Access to Child)* (1978),[19] and then resurfaced as a 'remedy' in the 1990s, but has always been regarded as the last resort, since clearly a change of residence of the child should be driven by the welfare principle, i.e. that residence with that parent is for the child's benefit on welfare grounds defined by the welfare checklist). However, at least three cases have been identified involving implacable hostility since the 2006 Act was brought into force in 2007: *Re S and Others* (2008),[20] *Re R (A Child)* (2008)[21] and a third in February 2010 (unreported) where residence was changed, in this last case although the child in question, a boy of 10, 'hated' his father.

---

17 [1994] 2 FLR 776.
18 For example, Aries, R, Harrison, C and Humphreys, C, *Safety and Child Contact*, London, LCD, 2002.
19 [1978] 1 FLR 336.
20 [2008] EWCA Civ 653.
21 [2009] EWCA Civ 1316.

❖ **CASE EXAMPLE**

In *Re S and Others (Residence)* the court held that the emotional harm being caused to the children by denial of contact outweighed the disruption that would be caused by the move.

The 2004 Act deals with the (still relatively new) concept of 'contact activity directions': s 1 inserts new s 11A–G after CA 1989 s 11; s 2 deals with monitoring contact and inserts s 11H after CA 1989 s 11G; s 3 deals with contact orders' warning notices and inserts s 11I after CA 1989 s 11H; s 4 deals with enforcement and inserts s 11J–N after CA 1989 s 11I; s 5 deals with compensation for financial loss and inserts s 11O–P after CA 1989 s 11N; s 6 amends s 16 of the CA 1989 in order to strengthen s 16 with regard to contact orders, by CA 1989 s 16(4A) requiring an officer to see what s/he can do to help in 'establishing, improving and maintaining' contact.

In order to understand the potential of these orders it is essential to have a full text copy of these CA 1989 sections, and this is another example (as in the case of HAR) where the student will be completely lost without the actual text. The amended sections are too lengthy to include here but they have also not been much used so are not particularly familiar. This may change under the new CAP PD if an all-out effort is going to be made in the new Family Court, as seems likely, to enforce contact elements of the new CAO.

In summary the range of enforcement powers permits the court to make a contact enforce-ment order if satisfied beyond reasonable doubt that a parent has not complied with a contact order, and these orders can include ordering financial compensation for financial loss (e.g. travelling expenses to contact which does not take place) or to order attendance at relevant classes (i.e. parenting education or other activities which would promote contact). A psychiatric or medical assessment cannot be ordered under these provisions but the court can already direct, and has in the past directed, a psychiatric assessment of the family to report on whether there are prospects for contact to be achieved.[22] However, it is fair to say that no one has been very enthusiastic about these provisions. Professor Michael Freeman has been somewhat scathing about the unpaid work provision, commenting that perhaps the government had not noticed that mothers routinely did significant unpaid work![23]

The child's welfare is not paramount in considering whether to make any of the orders, although it must be taken into account, and this power to order unpaid work and the power to order compensation do not seem to advance the matter further than the concerns of the 1990s that reducing the financial resources available to the child or removing the child's mother at times when she is required to look after the child, such as at weekends, is not a positive step. The Cardiff Law School Family Research Law Project[24] concludes that these provisions will be ineffective if the sanc-tions are not imposed often enough owing to the financial constraints likely to be imposed on parents.[25]

Enforcement is also specifically dealt with in the new CAP programme PD, which suggests these provisions are likely to be used.

---

22 *Contact (Promoting Relationship with Absent Parent)* [2004] 1 FLR 249.
23 Freeman, M, *Understanding Family Law*, London, Sweet & Maxwell, 2007, p 238.
24 'Enforcement of Contact Between Children and Non-Resident Parent'.
25 Dyer, C, McCrum, S, Thomas, R, Ward, R and Wookey, S, 'Enforcement of Contact Between Children and Non-Resident Parents', www.law.cf.ac.uk/alumni/studentproject.pdf. See also Dyer et al [2008] Fam Law 1237.

17.2.4 Change of residence

The only conclusion that may be drawn from the small number of change of residence orders since the implementation of the 2006 Act is that it is possibly better to use the amended CA 1989 provisions for resolution of the underlying problems, such as a contact activity direction as provided by s 11A(3) 'which promotes contact with the child concerned' rather than to change the child's residence arrangements except in most extreme circumstances.

Further, the use of the strengthened FAO may also succeed as the amendment to the former CA 1989 s 16 (inserting a new s 16A) removes the former requirement for exceptional circumstances for such an order to be made. This now requires only the consent of every person involved other than the child and can last up to 12 months. By s 16(6) the court officer assigned to advise and assist can be required to report to the court on the progress of the contact arrangements, which is also probably a positive factor. There was, for instance, an immediate increase in the number of FAOs made in 2007–8 (from 351 to 563). Even with such a small sample some qualitative follow-up research might be worth it, because the general experience of psychiatrists working in the field of child contact has indicated that even the most antagonistic attitude of the (often 'brainwashed') child is capable of being turned round to enjoyable contact with the non-resident parent.

This suggests that it might be more worthwhile to follow up that sort of initiative within the contact activity direction menu rather than to change the child's living arrangements, although perhaps it would do no harm for intractable parents to know that the sanction is still there as a last resort if they do not cooperate. The potential impact of the 2006 Act, particularly in relation to the last resort change of residence sanction, has also been reviewed by Silver in 2010.[26]

It should be remembered that the final report of the FJR, linked to the Green Paper *Support for All*,[27] apparently deliberately avoids any of these potential aids by electing to be focused on persuading individuals to avoid court and to use DR (renamed by them Dispute Resolution Services) for resolving difficulties, i.e. avoiding the adversarial court model, even by way of consent order if possible, and using a more inquisitorial approach where courts are used, while also removing work to administrative bodies, reviewing the roles of agencies and professionals in the family justice system, and also attempting to ensure that individuals take responsibility for the consequences of family breakdown. It aims to minimise conflict, use mediation as much as possible and simplify the resolution of family disputes.

It is fair to say that, worthy as these aims are, they have a familiar (repetitive) ring and some scepticism may be in order. The FJR report was not expected until 2012 but was delivered in November 2011, and could perhaps have benefited from a further gestation period in order to flesh out some of the questions that are inevitably generated by the lack of detail as to how the 'shared PR' ideal is supposed to work any better following the FJR than it has during the years following the implementation of and slow familiarisation with the CA 1989. Parents have ignored Parenting Plans before and may well not take to the methodology that is now proposed. So far, since the introduction of the new Family Court in April 2014 and the consequent amendments to the FPR 2010, there is no indication that parents have changed their stripes!

17.2.5 Shared residence

It has often been said that shared residence would be the ultimate solution to contact problems, not least because it has mutual advantages to the parents (who then have secure child care arrangements

---

26 Silver, S, 'Contact Orders', *Family Law and Practice*, (2010) 1 FLP 54. This online journal is no longer published but the complete archive, 2010–2013, may be found at www.frburton.com, and its successor, *International Family Law, Policy and Practice*, at www.famlawandpractice.com.

27 Cm 7787 TSO, available at http://webarchive.nationalarchives.gov.uk/20130401151715/http://www.education.gov.uk/publications/eOrderingDownload/00148-2010BKT-EN.pdf.

when the children are at the other parent) but also because a contact order is incompatible with shared residence, thus there is instant potential to reduce disputes and the acrimony which is often easily generated when it is said that a child 'lives with' one parent (which is what the CAO proposes to state, while it then records the child will 'spend time' or 'have contact' with the other parent). This seems a potential recipe for disaster if the serially argumentative non-resident parent elects to take advantage of the opportunity to continue arguments, however generous the contact with that non-resident parent.

Moreover, such a shared residence arrangement can significantly facilitate shared parenting where parents do live near one another, where both work (either employed or self-employed) and both are willing to help each other with child care, particularly when money is short. It is well known that this also works well where there are siblings, who are company and support for one another in the unfamiliar context of their parents' separation and usually divorce.

The concept of the child's mere 'residence' as a fact rather than a source of power was introduced by the CA 1989 but early case law was hostile to the idea of a child having more than one 'real', 'settled' 'home'. This is strange, given the frequency of cases about shared residence which were before the courts at the time (in the 1990s) that these conservative judicial ideas were formed.

It was also a time when it is clear from reading reports that many families whose child disputes were first decided under s 8 had actually kept two homes before the parental separation – one in London or some other metropolis and another in the country or even abroad (the 'weekend and holiday cottage' syndrome which was very common in the early 1990s at the time that the CA 1989 was first in force) so that middle-class children already routinely moved between homes.

The question may be asked whether a shared parenting regime could now work better (when many parents are short of money owing to the economic downturn, unemployment and benefit cuts, and might also be glad to have free childcare – otherwise now an enormous expense in any budget) when a shared timetable would mean that there would be definable periods when there was no responsibility for children who were at their other parent's home.

The old 'custody–care and control–access' regime did have an option for 'joint custody' with 'no order for care and control' in the hope that parents would work out a regime for themselves. However, the subsequent case law, and more recent judicial comment about parents harming their children with their acrimonious disputes, is testimony to the triumph of hope over experience in that context. Nevertheless, as time went on in the first decade after the CA 1989 came into force it appeared that the influence of American writers and anecdotal experience, showing that the sky did not necessarily fall in after all if the child moved freely between two (or more) homes, gradually developed a changed attitude, and indeed some virtue was seen in the child's not having to be said to 'live' with one parent and have generous contact with the other – which (contrary to earlier perspectives) was then said to cause a potential confusion in the child's perception which (all agreed) should be that both parents were equal in the eyes of the law: a favourite tenet of Sir Nicholas Wall, an influential family judge before he was President of the Family Division.

It seems that it was around 2001 that shared residence became a viable order, in a case called D v D (2001).[28]

---

28 [2001] 1 FLR 495.

❖ CASE EXAMPLES

In *D v D* (2001) the children were spending slightly less than equal time with each parent, 38 per cent with the father and the rest of their time with the mother. Previous case law to the effect that 'exceptional circumstances' were needed to obtain a residence order was overruled, and it was ruled that mathematical equality of time in each household was not necessary.

This was followed in *Re A (Children) (Shared Residence Order)* (2003),[29] where Lord Justice Thorpe accepted that where 'substantial amounts of time' were spent in each house this gave judges a new flexibility to consider shared residence.

This in turn was followed up by Wilson J (as he then was) in *Re F (Shared Residence Order)* (2003),[30] where he compared the options of shared residence and a residence order with a corresponding generous contact order and concluded that it might amount only to 'a label' but then went on to consider that a label could itself be 'very important' in perceptions.

In *A v A* (2004)[31] Wall J (as he then was) decided a case which readily illustrates the arguments for shared residence in embittered family struggles. The father complained that the mother made unilateral decisions and excluded him from the children's lives. She in turn made allegations against him, including that he frightened one of the children and had sexually abused that child. Wall J said that a shared residence order best reflected the parents' equal status in the eyes of the law and in their responsibilities towards the children, and that a sole residence order to one of them would be misinterpreted. He said the family did not need 'control' but what they needed was 'cooperation'.

Since 2004 judges have been choosing shared or sole residence orders as circumstances within the context of the case before them dictated, but since about 2007 it appears that there has been a greater willingness to grant shared residence orders and in *Re W (Shared Residence Order)* (2009)[32] this seemed to have become a routine tool for use in pursuit of the aim of reinforcing shared parenting. It did seem that the best solution had not only been found in n *Re W*, when it was held that it was manifestly wrong to make an order for contact where there was a shared residence order in force, but that this could be the silver bullet that could finally slay the bitter arguments.

Taken with the strong words of Wall LJ, in earlier cases long before he was briefly President of the Family Division and in a position to state policy, and also taking into account his rebukes to warring parents who fight over children and harm them in the process by such battles, it might have been supposed that the shared residence order would be likely to have a secure future in finding favour wherever surrounding circumstances permit.

This seemed likely to be owing to the combined influence of the principles which have already emerged from the cases, the problems over enforcing contact and the economic circumstances

---

29 [2003] 3 FCR 656.
30 [2003] 2FLR 397.
31 *A v A (Shared Residence)* [2004] 1 FLR 1195.
32 [2009] EWCA Civ 370; [2009] 2 FLR 436.

(which have removed almost all public funding from private law family cases and imposed instead a requirement to use mediation where possible).

Indeed it seemed that shared residence was more than likely to be accepted as the way forward when LASPO 2012 was finally implemented, despite pleas for the government to think again about cutting legal aid so deeply out of family law cases, and despite amendments to the FPR 2010 having already at that stage been drafted and published for referral to mediation before the litigation process could be accessed.[33]

Accordingly, the government's initial drafting of Clause 11 of the Children and Families Bill 2013 to make 'shared parenting' formally a presumption was perhaps unwise[34] (because of the knowledge already available in 2010 of the Australian fathers' rights-based approach to equal time in shared residence, whereas there had never been such an 'equal time' assumption by the judiciary in England and Wales). However, clearly this did not necessitate complete abandonment of the shared residence concept in favour of an apparently blind acceptance of the FJR's unparticularised shared PR and 'making it work' – an idea not at all bad in itself, but which was much more likely to be productive if the shared residence option had been expressly retained, and then articulated for public consumption in a manner which could not be misunderstood; and indeed as shared residence could have been properly presented in the manner in which it has been by several high-profile family judges in the years since it was accepted as a useful tool in resettling the fractured family.

Nevertheless, perhaps all is not lost; a practical approach to, rather than a presumption of, shared residence, could still be utilised in the drafting of such CAOs as actually come before the courts, except perhaps where domestic violence has been documented.

Indeed the case for retention of the option of shared residence seems very strong since, where circumstances favour genuinely shared childcare, it does present as likely to be one of the most important of the ways that separated parents could manage their post separation and/or post-divorce lives on a tightened budget (since they will already be faced with financing two houses, and in a context where their initial arguments may well have been about money when they had to finance only one house and the employment situation was not as bleak as it now is and there was no shadow cast by ultimate interest rate rises impacting on such home financing).

The potential of such financial help from shared residence orders was in fact suggested in early judgments of Mostyn J, a relatively recently appointed family judge, whose reaction is the more interesting since at the Bar he was a property and finance expert, not a child law specialist, but bringing his long experience of family finance packages to bear in the new context.

Taken with that other escalating syndrome, the relocation dispute (which usually occurs when the unhappy primary carer mother wants to return 'home', whether in this country or abroad, thus potentially impacting on contact relied on by the non-resident parent), effective shared parenting through shared residence for children might well be the one factor that tipped the balance against the alternative of uprooting them so she could be nearer her extended family support that is often found in her original location.

Fortunately the silver lining to this so far mismanaged opportunity in the current modernisation is that there is in fact no obstacle to such orders being made within the new CAO, the wording of which permits delineation of not only the persons with whom the child shall 'live' and 'spend time' but also any further detail of how and when this shall happen: that is, in the case of such orders as are made by the courts.

However, since others of the FJR's recommendations have thrown those parents onto their own resources in drafting their agreements, with or without mediation, and without legal advice or

---

33 FPR 2010 r 3A and Protocol.
34 Criticised by many as inept, including Hunt, J in 'Shared parenting time: messages from research', her paper at the 2014 Family Justice Interdisciplinary Conference at Dartington Hall, reprinted in [2014] Fam Law 44: 676.

assistance, achieving a suitable shared residence agreement is unfortunately likely to encounter problems. It is a pity that no one thought deeply enough about this earlier, either the FJR itself at the time of making the recommendations in their Final Report, nor anyone at the time that the government accepted those recommendations when the drafting of the Children and Families Bill Clause 11 might still have presented a late opportunity to salvage the too precipitately abandoned concept of shared residence.

17.2.6 The new CAP PD 12B

This relied heavily on the Parenting Plans[35] and Separated Parents Information Programmes – 'SPIP'[36] – which appear to spearhead the PD's Enforcement of *orders* actually made; however, both may obviously also assist in making private agreements, both helping an agreement to come together in the first place and also to make it work once in place. The CAP process also encourages settlement even where CA 1989 proceedings are actually started.

It should be noted that this encouragement has always been present, at least from the early initiatives in the Bristol conciliation projects which pre-dated the CA 1989 and were taken up by many other courts,[37] but it is possible that current efforts will now enjoy further success in view of the heavy discouragement of taking proceedings at all which is embodied in the CAP, thus possibly giving judges more time to encourage settlement in cases before them. The CA 1989 procedure has always had certain features in theory increasing potential for settlement, as may be seen by an examination of the 1991 design process.

17.3 CA 1989 procedure

Assuming there *are* to be proceedings, instead of the PAs now encouraged, this has always been so different from that prior to the CA 1989 that it is worth detailing it to some extent, since it reinforces the ethos of the Act, the philosophical impact of which cannot be exaggerated, and on which improvements in later Acts are really only a gloss. In theory the new CAP process and CAO should assist PAs even if brokered by the judge in court rather than between the parents alone or in mediation, since the CAP process aims to encourage agreement at every stage, even when the case is before the court. Moreover, human nature being as it is, the parties are more likely to observe an order they have themselves participated in creating than one which is imposed, even if that does not start until the other side of the door of the court.

At least a minimal overview of procedure is important fully to understand how the substantive law works, and how the private and public law aspects of a case impact on each other. It is only when this is appreciated that the full sophistication of the legislation is understood.

Nevertheless, the FJR has had many more criticisms of existing procedure than already detailed above, which are not worth adding here since some changes they envisaged as necessary may either never happen, if not already included in recent legislation or FPR amendments for the Family Court, or not soon. Suffice it to say that while everyone agrees improvements were necessary, there was some disagreement on precisely which ones, in order to deliver the philosophy of the CA 1989, since without effective delivery the ethos is of no effect. The FLBA broadly accepts and supports the FJR recommendations, particularly about reducing delay, however that may be achieved.

---

35 Paragraphs 2.4 to 2.7.
36 Paragraph 21.
37 Including the Principal Registry of the Family Division (PRFD) in London.

17.3.1 The Family Court

Procedure is broadly the same in both private and public law cases, although the two types generally proceed separately. Nevertheless there are cases where, owing to the facts, one area of law impacts on the other: the big change here is that there is no longer the triple tier of courts but one unified Family Court, thus the only transfers are likely to be geographical – now extremely convenient for family justice as the unified structure of functions of High Court, county court and magistrates' courts for children cases all in one building greatly assists continuity of proceedings, which is the signal benefit which has been achieved by the **Crimes and Courts Act 2013** in legislating to create the Family Court.

Moreover the FPR 2010, as amended for the new Court, has built on 20 years of experience of the CA 1989 to present new clarity in a comprehensive set of regulations for the conduct of cases. Whereas not every judge in each tier was able to deal with every case, cases can now be assigned on application to the appropriate level and moved within the Court as required: circuit judges and magistrates all sit in the Family Court and High Court judges are available as required without a High Court transfer. The services of the former three classes of county court are available in the new Court: that is to say those of the

- divorce county courts (not all county courts formerly qualified or did the full range of dissolutions including civil partnerships);
- family hearing centres (not all former divorce county courts qualified); and
- care centres.

Thus it is no longer the case that where a CA 1989 s 8 order was to be obtained in divorce proceedings, the petition had to be filed in a divorce county court which was a family hearing centre (FHC) to avoid the necessity to transfer, nor if there was a likely public law impact at a centre which was a Care Centre as well so as to be a practical way of keeping the entire case under one roof, sometimes with significant benefit to the parties.

It cannot be overemphasised that the various parts of the CA 1989 never existed in a vacuum and neither did the practical implications of resolving problems, so the impact of the new Court's positioning everything under one roof cannot be exaggerated either.

The CA 1989 was conceived as a whole, after much work at the Law Commission involving specialist Family Law Commissioners (including Baroness Hale, then Professor Brenda Hoggett), and the resulting statutory code contains far fewer flaws of conception or realisation than most. The Act, the rules made under it and the court in which they are both applied can therefore be most effectively used to advantage by the new system, in which knowledgeable practitioners can better achieve results which respect the conceptual spirit as well as the letter of the legislation.

There were rules indicating decisive criteria for the choice of venue and allocation of business between the courts when there was a triple tier. The principle that delay is prejudicial dictated the factors to be taken into account, and relevant factors were the length, importance and complexity of the case; urgency of the case; and need to consolidate the case with other pending proceedings – but the fact that delays built up to the extent identified by the FJR speaks for itself despite the flexibility of allocation developed by the judges which enabled, for example, a case to be transferred to a district judge in a county court that would otherwise go to the magistrates for several days (which would be logistically difficult to arrange as all magistrates in their various towns usually did not sit as an FPC on consecutive days). The practicality of the new Family Court is thus self evident.

As one example of the new potential for efficiency, it should be noted that if divorce proceedings are dismissed, a s 8 order can still be made unless the court determines that the matter would better be dealt with outside England and Wales: FLA1986, s 2(4) – how much simpler to arrange now there is a unified Family Court and the repeal of MCA 1973 s 41 means all child disputes are now to be dealt with under the CA 1989.

17.3.2 A form-based application

Unlike the pre-CA 1989 affidavit-based procedure, proceedings have since 1991 begun on prescribed forms, with which no affidavit is filed, and evidence, which is strictly controlled, is given in the form of statements. The forms have been updated for use from April 2014 in the new Court.

The original reason behind developing a form-based culture in 1991 was said to be because of the *then* unification of the triple tier of family courts (High Court, county court and FPC), since the magistrates in the FPC then created were not used to affidavits. Irrespective of their type or the person applying, all applications were then sensibly arranged to be made on the same form.

The latest April 2014 reform makes a further practical change – the form on which applications are made for private law orders is now amalgamated with the former form for certification of a MIAM or exemption from it – so it will now *not* be possible for applicants to sidestep the MIAM as has been happening previously in some cases, thus creating regional inconsistency and even sometimes inconsistency between courts and judges which should now be avoided.[38]

It should also be remembered that in *divorce proceedings*[39] the DJ has now been relieved of the obligation to consider any arrangements for the children owing to the repeal of MCA 1973 s 41, so any s 8 application will go straight to the appropriate Family Court judge for hearing.

Whether in connection with divorce or free standing, the applicant, if hoping for public funding, is likely to find this unavailable unless domestic violence is involved.

Parties to be made respondents to the application are set out in the rules and they are:

(a)   every person with PR for the child;
(b)   every person with PR prior to a care order, if such an order is in place; and
(c)   where the application is to extend, vary or discharge an order, the parties to the order in respect of which the application is made.

However, any person may make a written request to be joined as a party or that that person cease to be a party, and anyone with parental responsibility is entitled as of right to be joined.

The form then needs to be served and the respondent must lodge an acknowledgment so there is no possibility of a case being decided by default judgment as in civil proceedings.

Unlike in former custody proceedings, CA 1989 applications cannot be 'settled' by a consent order or even withdrawn without leave although court conciliation may attempt to persuade the parents or other parties to agree on the child's future and to observe the spirit and philosophy of the Act by having no order, in which case the application may be withdrawn with leave. Moreover, even to get this far, the parties will first have been signposted through the new CAP process to Cafcass or another conciliation process, and to a MIAM, which will encourage the 'PA' encouraged by the FJR, and there may be no order, neither the new CAO, nor other s 8 order, at all.

While this is criticised as more a cost-cutting policy than for the benefit of families, at least in England and Wales there are still *hearings* where required. In some progressive jurisdictions[40] the shared parenting ethos is such a strong presumption that contact has moved to paper-based applications accessed by a call centre. English law is not yet reduced to this level of service.

17.3.3 Directions (and the impact of the 'no delay' principle)

The no delay principle will require a directions appointment to be held forthwith, and either this may be the only one or the first of several: this is set out in great detail in the new CAP process

---

38 See Chapters 1 and 5 for the provisions of the CAFA 2014, which has reinforced the MIAMs procedure.
39 See Chapter 5.
40 For example Denmark.

attached to the associated PD 12B. Notice is normally required for a directions hearing, which may be on request of the parties or one of them or of the court's own motion, though there can be oral application without notice to be made with permission. At the directions hearing there will be a thorough stocktaking of the case. First, a timetable will be drawn up, and adhered to, for the proceedings: CA 1989, s 11(1). The following will also be considered:

(a) variation of time limits, which is only permitted by direction of the court;
(b) service of documents (only those served may be relied on and none may be served without leave of the court, a provision designed to prevent written statements potentially inflaming the situation);
(c) joinder of parties;
(d) preparation of welfare reports and attendance of the court welfare officer preparing them to give evidence;
(e) service of written evidence, in advance, including any experts' reports (no experts' or assessors' reports are allowed without written leave of the court, another distinction from ordinary civil litigation and there is further control of experts in the amended FPR);
(f) attendance of the child, unless excused;
(g) transfer of the case to another level of court; and
(h) consolidation of the case with other proceedings.

All persons who have notice of a directions appointment must attend, including the child if of appropriate age, unless the court directs otherwise, though the court can decide that the proceedings can take place in the child's absence if that is in the child's interests (e.g. due to the nature of the evidence to be given, or if the child is represented by a solicitor).

The respondent who has been served but does not appear may still find that the court has proceeded despite his or her absence. However, they are more likely to refuse the application in such a situation unless they have sufficient evidence to dispense with the respondent's presence.

Obviously if neither party appears the court will refuse the application.

The no delay principle also requires that any adjournment of such directions appointments must include a new date for resumption of the appointment. This is the CA 1989's direct legacy from the 1969 case of J v C (1969).[41]

Alternatively, proceedings can be and in theory commonly will be transferred horizontally or vertically, for example, not only to avoid delay but if there is complex evidence and a higher court is needed. Some applications must go to the High Court (e.g. an application made by the child personally).

Technically, a s 8 order can only be made in 'family proceedings' as defined in s 8(3) and (4), but this covers all the types of proceedings one would expect, and the court may also make an order of its own motion despite no application actually having been made for that order: s 10(1)(b). Directions appointments are in chambers or in private before the magistrates.

17.3.4 Evidence

A major change brought about by the CA 1989 is the restriction on evidence that can be given and how it should be presented. Affidavits did not in fact entirely disappear in the intervening years since 1991, except in the FPC where they never were beforehand, as a judge, in the High Court or county court, could still order them (and some older judges did, since they felt affidavits 'tell the story' in a way in which the form-based procedure did not). However, the statements which have

---

41 [1970] AC 668.

supplanted the traditional affidavit, although not sworn, have always had to contain a statement that the maker believes in their truth and understands that the statement will be placed before the court.

Evidence generally

Advance disclosure was the other principal 1991 innovation, as without permission of the court *nothing* might from that point be adduced in evidence, not even orally, which was not written down and served on the other side. By the same principle *nothing* but the *prescribed* documents (i.e. as required or authorised by the rules) was allowed to be served without permission of the court. For the careful drafting required of statements, especially the parties' witness statements, see below.

Evidence has always been needed from any persons who have much to do with the care of the child concerned (e.g. nannies, childminders, grandparents and other relatives). If no advance notice had been given in the case of someone new or who had been missed out in the advance disclosure stage, such evidence could always be the subject of an oral application with permission of the court at the hearing. Limited hearsay evidence has always been permitted.

Welfare reports

These have normally routinely been prepared by the court welfare officers who work for the court welfare service, most recently called Cafcass, which took over from the old court welfare officers and other court services when the Cafcass service was set up in 2002. The welfare officers have since been officially called Child and Family Reporters, although the former term has sometimes persisted, not least for its comparative brevity and accuracy of description.

By CA 1989 s 7, the court has an extended power to call for such reports, and these may be provided by the local authority: s 7(5). Alternatively they may be by someone delegated to do so by the authority: s 7(1).

Normally a welfare report is ordered automatically at the directions hearing, either requested by one of the parties or ordered of the court's own motion, as it is quite impossible to deal satisfactorily with either public law or s 8 applications without one. Parents are therefore usually warned of the necessity to make a good impression on the welfare officer, since although the court is not bound by their recommendations, it is unusual that their very experienced views are not taken significantly into account and in practice they are generally followed. The report should be filed before the hearing unless a different time limit has been prescribed, and of course all parties will have a copy so as to be able to deal with the contents, although unfortunately it has for some time been the case that the reporters are so busy that frequently the report is very late or not available at all so judges have been obliged to manage without.

Welfare officers' reports are therefore traditionally phrased in a tactful manner since the welfare officer is independent of the Court, the local authority or any other agency, and it is a key element of the system that the report should be seen as professional and not 'taking sides' if this can be avoided; sometimes of course it cannot as the welfare officer has a statutory duty to present the correct information to the court and will not want to be seen as biased by any party. Reports have nevertheless historically managed to convey the recommendations in the most palatable terms for the party whose aspirations and hopes are to be dashed. However, it was a recommendation of the FJR that Cafcass should be subsumed by the MOJ, and it has already been announced that this is shortly to happen, so that whether they will now be seen as independent of the state is another matter.

Expert evidence

Any expert reports have since 1991 always needed permission of the court and any obtained *without* such leave in the first place then needed permission of the court to be used. This embargo has covered *every type* of such reports, even educational psychologists' reports, although a routine ISCO (Independent Schools Career Organisation) type test done automatically at secondary school level (e.g. at most public schools in the fifth form, or Year 11) was probably acceptable if not prepared *specifically* for the proceedings.

Stricter rules on evidence have been introduced by the amended FPR.

The statement in support of a s 8 application

In the absence of affidavits, with both the constraints on evidence to be given at s 8 hearings and the increasing specialism in child work by practitioners, drafting of the witness statements, particularly those of the parties, became skilled work. As such, this has usually been allocated to counsel who was to conduct the application. Just as counsel used to draft old-style custody, care and control and access affidavits, it was thought that counsel should draft these witness statements, if counsel was to conduct the hearing, since they are as much an exercise in advocacy, in which counsel is a recognised specialist as in drafting.

The idea originally was that the statement acted as notice to the other side and to the court of what was to be given orally in evidence, but the mere replacement of an affidavit by an apparently more informal 'statement' of course did not change the reality that even a statement also affords an opportunity to engage the court's attention and sympathy for that party's side of the story. As child applications became an increasingly highly specialised business both at the Bar and for family solicitors, this opportunity has not usually been thrown away in case the position could be recovered at the actual hearing – since the experienced practitioner is well aware that it often cannot. At the very least, failure to take advantage of the opportunity for good written advocacy in advance gives the advocate at the hearing a more uphill task than necessary. For this reason, anything complex has normally gone straight to specialist counsel, and little has been achieved by the so-called post-1991 informalisation of the procedure. Nevertheless this is a small criticism of an otherwise successful overhaul of procedure so that it has largely matched the philosophy of the 1989 Act.

Moreover, while permission was required to withdraw a CA 1989 application once made, obviously there were usually attempts to settle the matter without a hearing, if necessary with the aid of the court conciliation process or that of other mediators. In this connection the sight of strong witness statements, not in one side's favour, was often instrumental in reducing that party's recalcitrance, which was often all that stood between one side and the other. This might then quickly crumble once the relative hopelessness of a particular approach was spelled out in the opponent's formal statement and a trained mediator was involved who might be able to halt what was obviously otherwise going to be a painful disaster for the loser.

Such statements have usually covered the following matters, cross-referenced to the CA 1989 s 1(3)(a) criteria:

(1) *Background information.* This would be a *brief* history of the marriage, beginning with the date of the ceremony and detailing the births of the children, with dates, and some indication of when and how the marriage went wrong, but not a blow-by-blow account, which was neither required by the procedure nor advisable, however aggrieved the applicant might feel.

(2) *The dispute before the court,* for which the post-CA 1989 style called for dispassionate, good written advocacy setting out the facts.

(3) *Current family living arrangements.* This included any new relationship into which the applicant had entered, similar to the Statement of Arrangements up to April 2014 which was filed with a divorce petition, and conveyed the same sort of stability and concern for the child's welfare.

(4) *Any health matters to be noted in connection with the child.* This included any reports mentioned and filed. If there were any such reports which had not been mentioned before or filed, the court was then able to order their disclosure if they came to its notice, despite legal professional privilege and despite any unwillingness on the part of the commissioning party to agree. This was because in theory child proceedings were not seen as adversarial and it was the best result for the child which was being sought.

(5) *Applicant's concerns*, i.e. any *genuine, non-trivial* worries about the other party's care of the child or children, but not an opportunity to enter again into the history of the unhappy marriage or a lengthy disquisition on the other party's deficiencies, since such an approach was, post 1989, categorised by the court as *mud slinging*, was deprecated and discouraged, since in the spirit of shared parenting it was not well received by the judiciary as it did not reflect the ongoing search for the best solutions for welfare of the child as set out in the Act.

(6) *Proposals.* These included the child's wishes, if they had actually been expressed, because of the relevance of s 1(3)(a), plus the attitude to contact of the party making the statement and comments on the other party's statement if it had already been served.

A statement of truth was then required in all post-CA 1989 proceedings.

17.3.5 The hearing

Procedure at CA 1989 hearings was originally governed by the FPR 1991 (which replaced the former Rules of the Supreme Court – RSC – which dealt with both Civil and Family cases) and then by the new FPR 2010 from April 2011, and was deliberately on the informal side, a significant change from the pre-1991 process. Amendments for the introduction of the Family Court in April 2014 have followed this style, with a trend towards the increased efficiency and new-style process facilitated by the unified Family Court.

Unless the court directs otherwise, the applicant's evidence has always been first, then the main respondent, and any other party with PR for the child, then other respondents, and finally the guardian (i.e. the former guardian *ad litem*) if there is one and the child if the child is a party and there is no guardian.

While hearsay evidence is admissible, the weight to be given to it will be in the discretion of the judge.

The no delay principle requires that the decision must be made 'as soon as practicable' and any finding of fact and the reasons for the court's decision must be stated. If a s 8 order is made it must be entered on the appropriate form for the purpose and a copy served as soon as possible on the parties and any person with whom the child is living.

A hearing may be only for an interim application, since by CA 1989 s 11(3) the court is empowered to grant such an order at any time when it is not yet in a position to dispose of the matter finally. This may be a tactical move, since the operation of the *status quo* means that the longer any party is out of touch with the child or children, the worse that party's chances are of retrieving the situation, provided of course that the other parent does not make any mistakes and invoke the operation of some other rule or principle against that parent's interests. It is therefore advisable for any parent seeking, for example, an order for the child to live with that parent, to obtain an interim order at least for contact or, in the parlance of the new CAO, 'spending time', and to make the fullest possible use of it in the time it takes to set up the substantive hearing for the order which is really desired.

Appeals are possible against all such orders and the procedure is set out in the FPR 2010.

Accordingly, procedure in the new Family Court is not much different from that instituted in 1991, except for the much-improved allocation process generated by all levels of judge being available in one building, stricter controls on evidence, and a greater emphasis on the impact of delay on the child and therefore of efficiency. However the new impact that *may* prove to be beneficial in achieving the FJR's aim of making contact work is in their focus being shifted away from contact as such towards *making shared PR work*; and in aiming to achieve this both in promoting PAs so as, if possible, to avoid court proceedings in the first place, and then to encourage settlement at any stage of those proceedings. Only time – to enable these processes to bed down in the new Family Court for longer than the short months since implementation – will tell.

17.4 Current debates

Ideas for research on these current discussions can be found on the companion website updates.

- Should there be a starting point of considering shared residence in most cases that are not manifestly unsuitable owing to domestic violence or other cause?
- Would this be likely to make a major contribution to the problems of enforcing contact? Including those caused by parental alienation syndrome?
- Should cases involving domestic violence be dealt with differently?
- Are the contact enforcement provisions inserted into the CA 1989 by the Children and Adoption Act 2006 an improved sanction?
- Is change of residence (now living arrangements under the CAO) a sensible sanction for refusal of contact by the carer parent?
- Has educating parents about their responsibilities failed or are the new initiatives likely to succeed this time?

17.5 Summary of Chapter 17

- Contact has always been the most troublesome s 8 order to enforce.
- Various methods have been tried and have failed or been of limited success.
- The most recent formal initiative is the provision of contact enforcement orders in the Children and Adoption Act 2006, which has inserted new sections into the CA 1989 after s 11 of that Act.
- This has now been overtaken by the introduction of the new CAO replacing residence and contact orders, and by parental agreements brokered by the parents in pursuit of their 'shared parental responsibility', if necessary with the support of mediators, with the aim of avoiding the necessity of adversarial litigation (i.e. either without an order at all or followed by a consent order).
- Judicial emphasis on the importance of contact for the child continues to be mentioned at the highest levels (e.g. Baroness Hale and the previous President of the Family Division, Wall LJ).
- There has also been an impetus for shared residence which (when such an order has been made) obviated the need for a contact order as the two orders were clearly incompatible, but this has apparently been discouraged by reports of adverse results of introducing presumed shared residence in Australia; however, it seems that the CAO could still cater for this option, which has not necessarily had such an adverse history in English law.
- The new CAP Practice Direction 12B relies heavily on Parenting Plans and SPIPs for enforcement.
- The new CAP process continues the informality of proceedings instituted by the FPR 1991 upon implementation of the CA 1989 for those disputes which are not settled by the 'PAs' recommended by the FJR with further opportunities for settlement of the dispute during proceedings.

 ## 17.6 Further reading

Children Act Sub-Committee's Report *Making Contact Work*, Lord Chancellor's Department, 2002.
Clarkson, H and Clarkson, D, 'Confusion and Controversy in Parental Alienation', (2007) *Journal of Social Welfare and Family Law*, 29: 265.
Craig, P, 'Everybody's business: applications for contact orders by consent', [2007] 37 Fam Law 26.

FJC, *Report to the President of the Family Division on the approach to be adopted in court when asked to make a contact order by consent, where domestic violence has been an issue in the case*, available at www.womensaid.org.uk.

Gardner, R, Sauber, R and Lorandos, D, *The International Handbook of Parental Alienation Syndrome*, New York, Haworth Press, 2005.

Harris, O, 'What's in a Name: A discussion of shared residence orders', *Family Law and Practice*, (2010) 1 FLP 48 (this online journal is no longer published but the complete archive may be found at www.frburton.com and its successor, *International Family Law and Practice*, at www.famlawandpractice.com).

Herring, J and Taylor, R, 'Relocating Relocation', (2006) CFLQ, 18: 517.

Kaganas, F and Piper, C, 'Shared Parenting – a 70% solution', [2002] CFLQ 14: 365.

Morrison, F, *After Domestic Abuse: Children's Perspectives on Contact with Fathers*, Edinburgh, CRFR, 2009.

Reece, H, 'UK Womens Groups Child Contact Campaign: "so long as it is safe" ', [2006] CFLQ 18: 538.

Wall, LJ, 'Making Contact Work', [2009] Fam Law 39: 590.

www.familyandchildcaretrust.org (a merger of the Family and Parenting Institute and the Childcare Trust).

www.sharedparenting.org.uk (Association for Shared Parenting).

Chapter 18

International Child Abduction and Relocation

Chapter Contents

Learning outcomes from this chapter

An introduction to the problems generated by international child abduction and relocation including:

(i) An overview of the origins of the international child abduction syndrome:

    (a) its contemporary management;

    (b) the judiciary's challenges in deciding relocation cases justly and expeditiously.

(ii) An understanding of the links between child abduction and post parental separation contact.

(iii) An appreciation of the unresolved issues in relation to relocation cases.

(iv) An awareness of the different principles currently applied in relocation cases in relation to:

    (a) shared parenting and shared residence;

    (b) applications for relocation of the carer parent outside the jurisdiction.

(v) An ability to analyse and assess arguments in the debate on the impact on continuing contact in relocation cases.

18.1 Introduction

The two topics examined in this chapter together comprise the most serious extension of the problems which have routinely arisen in connection with enforcement of s 8 orders, and in particular with the major challenge of making contact work. Child abduction and relocation are not unconnected with this underlying issue of problematical post-separation contact.

Child abduction is now a significant international problem, generated (as in the case of other contact problems) both by the high incidence of divorce or other relationship breakdown, and by the increasingly adverse impact on the family unit of the failure of mixed marriages involving different nationalities, cultures and jurisdictions.

These interlinked problems are especially awkward for maintaining the child's contact with both parents where initial clashes, and eventual exasperation with disruptive family life, are exacerbated by long geographical distances between the family origins of the parties.

Such marriages or unmarried partnerships are usually themselves the result of cross-jurisdictional relationships formed through greater international mobility, whether through employment or more generally.

Thus such cross-border scenarios may already require subtle diplomacy so that each party can remain in touch with extended family members overseas even at the start of the relationship, when the new family unit comprises only the two people most concerned; however, the addition of children instantly multiplies the potential for discord, and as soon as the relationship is under strain, particularly where one party becomes sufficiently homesick to consider relocation, the situation may simply become another statistic waiting to happen.

Accordingly, when such a marriage (or unmarried relationship) with children breaks down, it is often in circumstances which cause such extreme reactions that litigation is the only recourse, since it is generally the case that it is only at that stage that it is discovered that neither party has considered (as they both might have done at the start of the relationship, and certainly before the birth of children) what would happen if their union foundered and one or other wanted to 'go home', particularly since in the case of the carer parent this would obviously include taking any offspring too, especially as it is now common for both parents to have PR whether they are married or not.

The international child abduction charity, **reunite**,[1] has had some success with its mediation initiative[2] but abductions remain widespread, in some cases in view of incorrect advice given to the abducting parent that returning to that parent's original habitual residence and retaining children there is entirely permissible; whereas of course it is not, especially if the other parent has PR and does not wish to lose contact with the child.

These two topics are not included in all family law syllabuses but some working knowledge of both child abduction and relocation is essential for a proper understanding of cross-border contact and residence issues.

Obviously, in this context, the replacement of residence and contact orders with the new CAO will do nothing to solve the inter-parental disputes that are likely to characterise a separation in the type of 'cross-border' family that is already affected by difficult residence and contact issues and where abductions are prevalent, despite the existence of the specialist **reunite** mediation services.

Of the two issues, it is hard to say which causes the most problems, the trauma of abduction when it happens or the tensions of relocation, since in the absence of parental agreement court proceedings are inevitable before children can be removed from the jurisdiction.[3] An examination of a cross-section of the cases shows that the resulting uncertainty, and possibly unfavourable result, may be more damaging to the stability of the family when relocation is contemplated even than an incident of abduction: this is despite the fact that research into the outcomes of abduction has also shown clearly that abductions also have long-term adverse consequences.[4]

Such relocations may be generated from routine change of employment of a carer parent or sometimes a postgraduate educational opportunity, either of which might have been taken in the family's stride before the relationship breakdown, but either of which can alone cause significant family stress when it is no longer a unit.

Where the relocation is for more complex lifestyle reasons (routinely post-separation or divorce, homesickness of the carer parent and exasperation with an unsupported single parent lifestyle often made hideous by conflict with the other parent) this can be even more stressful, particularly if the projected move arises from a desire to put distance between the reconstituted family (of carer parent and the child or children) and the other parent who will be 'left behind'; this is particularly the case where, regardless of the reason for the proposed move, bitterness has been such that it is the other, 'left behind', parent who is seen as the root of the problem from which escape is desired.

It is easy to see how such bitterness between separated and divorced parents over disputed new living arrangements and contact problems then escalates in the contentious atmosphere that frequently results, often eventually leading to retention of the child or children in the foreign jurisdiction after a permitted visit 'home', which the carer parent mistakenly thinks is a preferable legitimate (and simpler) step than the disagreeable experience of returning to the jurisdiction of England and Wales for relocation proceedings; it is not, of course, since this is the form of 'abduction' called 'wrongful retention'.

This is a specialist area of law which is still developing and is not much understood outside its niche area of practice even in the legal profession, but it is of increasing importance in view of the number of mixed marriages and cross-border divorces.

---

1 The leading charitable organisation working in this field.
2 See the **reunite** website, www.reunite.org.
3 Under s 13(1) which prohibits removal without specific consents, or s 8 (for a specific issue or prohibited steps order). See Chapters 12 and 16.
4 See Freeman, M (Marilyn), **reunite** research, at www.reunite.org. Publication of Professor Freeman's current research, on the long-term effects of abduction and with a Foreword by Baroness Hale, Deputy President of the Supreme Court, was published in December 2014; see update on the book's supporting website.

Attempts to address the abduction syndrome have been made: nationally, in the **Child Abduction Act (CAA) 1984**, which makes abduction a crime; and internationally, by the **Hague Convention on International Child Abduction** ('the Hague Convention') and the **European Convention on the Recognition and Enforcement of Decisions Concerning Custody of Children** ('the European Convention'). The UK is a signatory to both Conventions, which are incorporated into English law by the **Child Abduction and Custody Act (CACA) 1985**. The European harmonisation instrument 'Brussels II Revised' ('BIIR')[5] also makes child orders enforceable internationally within the EU. The UNCRC 1989 states that parties to that Convention shall take measures to 'combat the illicit transfer and non-return of children abroad' and these are the facilitating agreements.

Further assistance in the case of domestic child abduction is afforded by the FLA 1986, which not only made child orders in one part of the UK enforceable in others (e.g. Scottish orders in England and Wales), but also facilitates the child's discovery and return. By FLA 1986 s 33, the court has an express power in s 8 proceedings to require information as to a child's whereabouts from any person, and publicity is permitted where necessary, enabling the judge to lift reporting restrictions, including the publication of a photograph or other identifying information.[6]

Internationally, the operation of the Conventions depends on the concept of judicial comity, and the concept that the child's future is best served by allowing the judges of the child's habitual residence to determine disputes about upbringing.

This works in slightly different ways under each of the two Conventions. The Hague Convention provides a summary remedy to return the child to the jurisdiction of habitual residence for further proceedings, and not to impose English ideas of welfare or to judge or interfere in the merits of the case.[7] The European Convention enforces and engages respect for existing orders; there is also more scope under this Convention for English concepts, such as settlement in England, to be taken into account as a welfare issue unlike under the Hague Convention where the concept of the summary return of the Hague Convention remedy usually ignores such settlement unless a defence is engaged.

Two completely different types of proceedings must thus be distinguished: (1) the welfare aspects of applications to remove children from the jurisdiction under CA 1989 s 13(1) or s 8; and (2) seeking or resisting the summary Hague Convention remedy for a child's return from overseas, although there is a connection as losing s 8 or s 13 proceedings is the trigger for abduction by the frustrated parent.

❖ CASE EXAMPLE

In the case of *Re C (Leave to Remove from Jurisdiction)* (2000)[8] Thorpe LJ, dissenting, commented adversely on the failure of his brethren and of the judge below to reflect on the consequences for the child (C) of the decision to prevent the mother taking C to Singapore where her new husband had relocated to work. In this case the mother had clearly said that this would be likely to break up her marriage as she would not leave the child in the UK to follow her husband, precisely the sort of situation which creates intolerable pressures leading to abduction.[9]

---

5 Already mentioned in connection with jurisdiction in divorce. See Chapter 4.
6 See *Re R(N) (A Minor)* [1975] 2 All ER 749; [1975] Fam 89 and *Practice Note* [1980] 2 All ER 806.
7 Although the European Court has not always respected this principle, leading to adverse academic commentary. See e.g. Silberman, L, 'The Hague Convention on Child Abduction and Unilateral Relocation by Custodial Parents: Has the European Court of Justice Overstepped Its Bounds?', [2014] 4 *Family Law and Practice* 26. This online journal is no longer published but the complete archive may be found at www.frburton.com and its successor, *International Family Law, Policy and Practice*, at www. famlawandpractice.com.
8 [2000] 2 FLR 457.
9 For the operation of s 13, see Chapter 16 at 16.7 and below at 18.8.

It is probably much more important, therefore, not to rely on retrieval of a child abducted from England and Wales, especially in cases where frustration may run high, but to attempt to prevent abduction, since in practice neither the criminal sanction of the CAA 1984 nor the summary remedy of the Hague Convention may be 100 per cent successful – prevention is easier than cure.

Sometimes the courts will grant leave to remove, whether temporarily or more permanently if sanctions are in place, for example deposit of a substantial sum of money (Re S (1999)[10]), swearing a solemn oath on a holy book (e.g. on the Koran before a Sharia court: Re A (1999)[11]), or a mirror order applied for in foreign courts (the purpose of the deposit in Re S was to secure such an order); applications where a mirror order may be needed can be heard orally in the High Court, permitting assessment of the reliability of witnesses.

The next stage, if required, is then prevention of the issue of a passport, or deposit of an existing one, obtaining an order (e.g. a s 8 CAO, SIO or PSO, or wardship if more urgent than the s 8 process allows), then use of the Port Alert System, as in practice the child may also have a foreign passport which cannot realistically be confiscated, even though there is technically jurisdiction[12] unless it is feared that this may lead to an international incident. Any court – even the magistrates in the new Family Court – can order the surrender of a British passport or prohibit such a passport being issued: FLA 1986, s 37.[13] Since under FLA 1986 s 33 a court may require disclosure of information about a child's whereabouts, there is now an equivalent in international proceedings under the two Conventions, and orders can be made for disclosure against any person having knowledge.[14]

An unmarried father should urgently obtain PR for his child if abduction is suspected (possibly also with a SIO or PSO, or seek a CAO quickly, which by CA 1989 s 12(1) will also confer PR.[15] Unless this is done he may find that he has no Hague Convention standing as he may be unable to show that he has 'rights of custody'.[16] These s 8 orders could be made even if the child was already abducted, but if the child is already outside the country the new Family Court may be unwilling to make them because of enforcement concerns.

Alternatively, a wardship order may, in emergency, be obtained immediately on no notice to the other party and will automatically restrict the ward from leaving the country.[17]

These now well-tried tools are so effective that they really make the case on their own for not acceding to the clamour of inexperienced commentators that wardship is out of date and should be both abolished as a remedy and no longer inflicted on students in first-degree syllabuses. It is equally clear that the abolition of the residence order, as recommended by the FJR in favour of the new CAO (or simply PA[18]) is also by no means a universally good idea since, in attempts to recover a child or prevent its abduction across borders a clear and direct 'Residence Order' with the court's seal on it is much more likely to command instant respect and cooperation from foreign border or other authorities, including judiciary, than the PA, even one backed up by a CAO by consent which the Family Court can make, but LIPs are discouraged from involving the court.

---

10 [1999] 1 FLR 850.
11 [1999] 2 FLR 1.
12 See Re A (Return of Passport) [1997] 2 FLR 137.
13 See Practice Direction [1986] 1 WLR 475; [1986] 1 All ER 983.
14 See Re H (Abduction: Whereabouts Order to Solicitors) [2000] 1 FLR 766.
15 See Richardson v Richardson [1989] Fam 85.
16 This is potentially a grey area under the new CAO as the new order is not as clear as the former residence and contact orders since its terms include 'living with', 'spending time with' and 'having contact with' a child, and which of these confer 'rights of custody' may be arguable.
17 See Chapter 19.
18 See Chapter 16 at 16.2.

18.2 The Child Abduction Act (CAA) 1984

This Act was a pre-CA 1989 attempt to regulate the removal of children from the jurisdiction without having to use wardship, or prosecution for kidnapping under the common law, for which the consent of the DPP was required for a prosecution. The CAA 1984 tends to be of little practical importance since a parent who is determined to remove a child is unlikely to be deterred by any statute, even one imposing criminal liability, despite the fact that the sanction for breach is six months' imprisonment or a fine if convicted by the magistrates, or seven years' imprisonment on indictment.

STATUTORY EXTRACT

The CAA 1984 states

'1. **Offence of abduction of child by parent etc.**

(1) Subject to sub-sections (5) and (8) below, a person connected with a child under the age of sixteen commits an offence is he takes or send the child out of the United Kingdom without the appropriate consent.

(2) A person is connected with a child for the purposes of this section if –

(a) he is a parent of the child; or

(b) in the case of a child whose parents were not married to each other at the time of his birth, there are reasonable grounds for believing he is the father of the child;

(c) he is a guardian of the child; or

(ca) he is a special guardian of the child; or

(d) he is a person in whose favour a residence order is in force with respect to the child; or

(e) he has custody of the child.

(3) In this section 'the appropriate consent', in relation to a child, means –

(a) the consent of each of the following-

(i) the child's mother;

(ii) the child's father, if he has parental responsibility for him;

(iii) any guardian of the child;

(iiia) any special guardian of the child;

(iv) any person in whose favour a residence order is in force with respect to the child;

(v) any person who has custody of the child; or

(b) the leave of the court granted under or by virtue of any provision of Part II of the Children Act 1989; or

(c) if any person has custody of the child, the leave of the court which awarded custody to him.'

The offence is not committed by any person having a residence order (or CAO)[19] who takes or sends the child out of the country for less than one month for a holiday (or if the person

---

19 Which will have been converted automatically into a new CAO on 22 April 2014 when the CAFA 2014 came into force on the inauguration of the new Family Court, so there are now technically no residence orders as such.

is a special guardian for less than three months) unless done in breach of an order under the CA 1989 (s 1(4)).

By s 1(5)(a), the offence is not committed if done technically without consent if there is a belief that:

(a) (i) consent has been given; or
     (ii) consent would be given if the person in question were aware of all the relevant circumstances; or
(b) all reasonable steps have been taken to communicate with the other person; or
(c) consent has been unreasonably refused.

The s 1(5)(c) defence does not apply if the person who refused consent is a person who has a residence order/CAO; or is a special guardian, or who has custody of the child; or the departure is in breach of a UK court order.

By s 2, the same connected persons are prohibited from taking or detaining a child under 16 so as

(a) to remove him or her from the lawful control of a person having lawful control of him or her; and
(b) keep him or her out of such control.

It is also an offence for a person 'unconnected' with the child to do this, i.e. someone who is not a parent or guardian and has no order permitting taking or detaining, without lawful authority or reasonable excuse, a child under the age of 16 out of the lawful control of any person having, or entitled to, lawful control of him or her.

It is a defence to show that the person believed the child was at least 16; and/or in the case of an illegitimate child, on reasonable grounds that he was the child's father.

As the statute, and the Hague Convention, only applies to under 16s, it is still possible to fall back on the common law offence of kidnapping for over 16s.

18.3 Dealing with abduction if prevention fails

The prime remedy is the Hague Convention, which establishes a network of international support for the recovery of abducted children, administered through the 'Central Authority' in each signatory state. By Article 7, such authorities must cooperate with one another to find the child, return him or her promptly (if possible, voluntarily), eliminate any obstacles to the proper working of the Convention and meanwhile protect the child from harm by taking provisional measures, which include all necessary judicial or administrative procedures.

In order to invoke this protection the child must be habitually resident in the contracting State requesting his or her return. In the recent case In the matter of LC (2014)[20] the Supreme Court accepted the state of mind of a (mature) child as relevant to determine in which country she should live. The Central Authority for England and Wales is the MOJ, which acts through the International Child Abduction and Contact Unit (within the Official Solicitor's Department). Public funding is available: Art 26, and the service is comprehensive. The Department takes over the entire task of instructing and paying lawyers, and it must act expeditiously: Art 11.

---

20 [2014] UKSC 1.

The process is one of summary proceedings, so that there will be no automatic right to give oral evidence. Normally evidence is given on affidavit and in any case consists largely of legal argument. In England, applications are heard by the High Court, which is empowered to make a declaration of wrongful retention or removal in contravention of Art 3. If the child is already 16, the case can still be considered under the High Court's inherent jurisdiction rather than the Act or Convention (*Re H (Abduction: Child of 16)* (2000)[21]).

18.3.1 The Hague Convention

The objects of the Convention are to:

(a)   secure the prompt return of children wrongfully removed; and
(b)   ensure that rights of custody and of access under the law of one contracting State are effectively respected in the other contracting States (Article 1).

The Convention applies to any child under 16 who was habitually resident in a contracting State immediately before any breach of custody or access rights (Article 4).

The central concept is also to deter abductions, as Baroness Hale has said, to send a message to potential abductors that 'there are no safe havens within contracting states' – the ultimate goal being to return the child promptly to the courts of its habitual residence for determination of the disputed issues because delay is prejudicial: six weeks is the aim for the entire process of return unless there are exceptional circumstances. Thus the court dealing with the summary request for return is not to usurp the function of those courts by considering broader welfare issues.

Contracting states are required to take all appropriate measures to secure within their territories the implementation of the object of the Convention, and (in an echo of the no delay principle of the CA 1989[22]) are to use the most expeditious procedures available for the purpose: Art 2.

Removal or retention of a child is wrongful where:

(1)   it breaches 'rights of custody' (which is not the same as the old-style pre-CA 1989 'custody' in English law but has a wider meaning[23]). Those rights of custody may be attributed to any person, institution or other body, jointly or alone, under the law of the state where the child was habitually resident immediately before the removal or retention. Thus the court can have a right of custody relating to a ward and abduction is a breach of it as the court is an institution.[24] The same is true of any court whenever an application is served in respect of the child, so this right is not restricted to High Court wards;[25] and
(2)   at the time of removal or retention those rights were actually being exercised, either jointly or alone, or would have been so exercised but for the removal or retention: Art 3.

Rights of custody in this sense may arise either by operation of law or from a judicial or administrative decision, or through an agreement with legal effect under the law of the relevant State.[26] Rights of custody include:

---

21   [2000] 2 FLR 51.
22   See Chapter 12.
23   This meaning specific to the Convention has included most types of the equivalent of contact as well as residence, and need not involve a formal court order, though there have been fine distinctions; see further below.
24   *Re J* [1990] 1 FLR 276.
25   *Re H (Abduction: Rights of Custody)* [2000] 1 FLR 374.
26   A PA could be such a document but a CAO would no doubt be better in practical terms.

(a) rights relating to the care of the person of the child, particularly the right to determine the child's place of residence, which includes having '*de facto*' custody; and

(b) 'rights of access', which broadly means the right to take the child for a limited time to a place other than the child's habitual residence (i.e. this term does equate with our understanding of old-style pre-1989 'access', now called 'contact', and is confusingly a species of 'rights of custody' under the Convention).

Some cases may make this clearer.

❖ CASE EXAMPLES

In *Re B (A Minor) (Abduction)* (1994)[27] the unmarried father had no legal rights but used to care for the child and was therefore held to have de facto rights within the meaning of the Convention (the term '*de facto* rights' is technical, but that is to say 'rights in practice'). But this broad view has not always been taken.

In *Re C (A Child) (Custody Rights: Unmarried Fathers)* (2002)[28] Munby J refused to make such a declaration of custody rights under CACA 1989 because in that case the mother had been the primary carer, distinguishing it from the case above where it seems the father had done more than merely have contact.

In *Re J (Abduction: Acquiring Custody Rights by Caring for Child)* (2005)[29] the court said that despite the 'purposive interpretation' of custody rights an unmarried father would not necessarily have custody rights for the purposes of the Convention even if he had shared care for a considerable time. This seems to indicate an evolving analysis over time of what precisely are custody rights, which is likely to have to be looked at again following the introduction of the CAO and the abandonment of residence orders, including shared residence orders, and the separate contact order.

In *B v UK* (2004)[30] the ECtHR held that it was not discriminatory under Art 14 and Art 8 (the right to family life) of the Convention on Human Rights for a court to hold that such a father does not have custody rights for the purposes of the Hague Convention, because there was an objective and reasonable justification for treating a father without PR from other fathers, i.e. he did *not* have PR when an unmarried father can usually, with effort, obtain that status.

Beevers[31] has commented that the result in B v UK might have been different if the father had cared for the child more significantly than only during the early part of its life.

It seems the emerging point is that the more a father provides care which edges towards some perspective of 'shared parenting' the more likely he is to have 'custody rights' when the abduction emergency arises; probably not much comfort to left-behind parents when their children are

---

27 [1994] 2 FLR 249.
28 [2002] EWHC 2219; [2003] 1 FLR 252.
29 [2005] 2 FLR 791.
30 [2000] 1 FLR 1.
31 Beevers, C, [2006] CFLQ 499.

abducted, but it does seem to be an argument towards a theory of shared parenting which it would be useful to have firmly located somewhere within the law,[32] since the impact of the existing (rather weak and unarticulated) concept of PR within the 1989 and 2014 Acts does give some support to the FJR's recommendation that effective 'shared PR' would be a positive step.

While lawyers know what 'PR' is supposed to encompass, the average member of the public clearly does not, or there would not be an army of separated fathers who have not necessarily established a track record of shared parenting while their relationships with the mother subsisted, but then join fathers' pressure groups complaining about of lack of contact after their separation.

The burden of proof is always on the applicant to prove that the removal or retention was wrongful, but there is a heavy burden on the central authority of the contracting states involved to make the Convention work.

By Art 10, it is mandatory for the requested state to return the child during the first 12 months after abduction or retention, unless a defence applies, and although this duty becomes discretionary after 12 months have passed, as Art 11 obliges judges to act expeditiously this time limit is not to be ignored. The ECtHR has held that it is a breach of Art 8 for a contracting State not to secure the return of a child in cases against Spain (2005) and Portugal (2004).

18.3.2 Habitual residence

This term is not defined in any statute but regarded as primarily a question of fact determined by all the circumstances of the case (see per Lord Brandon in *Re J (A Minor) (Abduction: Custody Rights)* (1990);[33] *sub nom C v S (A Minor) (Abduction: Illegitimate Child)* (1990)[34]). It is an important jurisdictional point, without which the child will not be within the Convention (Art 4), and so there can be no wrongful retention or removal without this point being decided in the applicant's favour. Again this is best demonstrated by looking at the core facts of and principles evidenced by some cases.

> ❖ **CASE EXAMPLES**
>
> In *Re J* the unmarried mother of the child left Australia, thus giving up her habitual residence and that of the child, and came with the child to live in the UK. The Australian courts gave the father sole custody and guardianship of the child, but the English court would not order the child's return as the father had no rights of custody at the time the mother and child left, i.e. when they gave up their habitual residence, although he had cared for the child. This case should be contrasted with *Re B*, above, where the unmarried father was successful as it was held that he had *de facto* custody rights.
>
> It seems the father in this case of *Re J* was unlucky since in another case of *Re C (A Minor) (Abduction)* (1989),[35] the court treated the father's right of objection to the removal of his child, again from Australia, as supporting the necessary custody rights and held that Art 5 (defining custody rights) had to be read into Art 3 so that the court could extend the meaning of 'custody rights' beyond our domestic understanding of it.

---

32 I.e. not merely in the watered down version of 'involvement in some way' in the Children and Families Act 2014.
33 [1990] 2 AC 562.
34 [1990] 2 All ER 961.
35 [1989] 1 FLR 403.

Moreover, in the later case of *Re B (A Minor) (Abduction)* (1994)[36] (above) on very similar facts the Australian court found the father had custody rights! The decision seems a little hard on the father in *Re J*, who could not have cared for the child as he did without some *de facto* right to do so, so that the removal of mother and child thus giving up their habitual residence should not have made any difference.

Moreover, although the mother had *given up* her habitual residence in a single day, as she was held to be entitled to do, it has been held in many subsequent cases that a period of time is required to *establish* a new habitual residence (e.g. not a three-week holiday in Greece – see *Re A* (1998)[37] – although in *Re S (Habitual Residence)* (2009)[38] seven or eight weeks' residence plus intention to reside there was sufficient and in *Re H-K (Habitual Residence)* (2011)[39] the CA allowed an appeal where the judge below had looked for greater permanence than a 'temporary' move (a year in that case). But it is usually necessary for a child to be at some stage physically present in the UK rather than to take its habitual residence from the mother as in *ZA and PA v NA (Abduction: Habitual Residence)* (2012).[40]

18.3.3 'Wrongful' removal or retention

This is sometimes a difficult concept to grasp since either can occur in the absence of any order, provided the general law of the country permits removal. However, some common sense needs to be applied here.

What is required to establish wrongful removal or retention is *some* rights of custody recognised by the Hague Convention which are in fact being exercised. The way the court should go about this is to establish whether there are rights of custody under the law of the requesting jurisdiction and then to decide if they are rights of custody under the Hague Convention.

Interpretation of the Convention is to be 'purposive'. By analogy, clearly the removal of a ward is wrong as the court is in *loco parentis* (i.e. having assumed the parental role in relation to the child), so that the High Court in such a case could invoke the Hague Convention if the child was abducted from England and Wales as it has rights of custody.[41] Moreover, in 2008 Bodey J also held that there was no problem about such custodial rights existing in a court and made a declaration under CACA 1985 to that effect.[42] There is a Practice Direction[43] on the point of wrongful removal and retention and rights of custody.

Naturally 'wrongful removal' and 'wrongful retention' are mutually exclusive, since one means taking the child without consent and the other failing to return the child at the end of an agreed period of contact. There remains the query as to whether there can be wrongful retention before the end of a period of agreed contact, when the wrongful retention is already decided upon.

If there is any doubt about the matter of whether there has been a wrongful removal, a declaration that the removal was wrongful may be required, by the requested State, to be obtained in the requesting State, before a child is returned (Art 15).

---

36 [1994] 2 FLR 249.
37 [1998] 1 FLR 497.
38 [2009] EWCA Civ 1021.
39 [2011] EWCA Civ 1100; [2012] 1 FLR 436.
40 [2012] EWCA Civ 1396.
41 Re S (Brussels II Revised: Enforcement of Contact Order) [2008] 2 FLR 1358.
42 A v B (Abduction: Rights of Custody: Declaration of Wrongful Removal) [2008] EWCA 2524.
43 [1998] Fam Law 224.

18.3.4 Exercising rights of access

Rights of access may also be enforced: Art 7. Article 7 (f) requires central authorities to facilitate this, by receiving an application for rights of access in the same way as an application for return of a child: Art 21, although the Convention does not give the Central Authority any powers to enforce access rights. There is a *Practice Note (Child Abduction Unit: Lord Chancellor's Department)* (1993).[44] Clearly, in view of decisions that there are sometimes not rights of custody the query remains as to whether rights of access can amount to rights of custody and enforcing access may be an alternative remedy. If a foreign access order is in place it may be enforced in England and Wales either under the European Convention or under BIIR if an EU order is concerned.

18.4 Defences

While the court is mandatorily obliged to return the child 'forthwith' if the application is brought within one year of removal: Art 12, the child should still be returned if more than one year has elapsed, unless it is demonstrated that it is now settled in its environment, but this is within the court's discretion.

This therefore begins the exceptions to the usual rule that the merits of the case will not be explored since the Convention presents a summary remedy to enable the child's return for determination of its future in the courts of its habitual residence.

This basic ethos of the Convention is based on the theory that all courts are equally competent to determine a child's future and that the merits are therefore not to be explored as to do so would not comply with the central concept. However, although for many years English courts have not returned children where there was a defence, especially where they objected under Art 13 as well, there have been a few recent cases where even children established in their new environment have been returned.

❖ CASE EXAMPLES

In *Re M (Abduction: Zimbabwe)* (2007)[45] two girls aged 10 and 13, of Zimbabwean parents, and born in Zimbabwe, were removed secretly to the UK by their mother, where they failed to obtain asylum but became settled in their school and church. Eventually the father found out where they were but did not ask for their return for two years. First, Wood J said they should be returned, stating that only exceptionally would the court apply their discretion to override the principle of summary return, which was upheld in the Court of Appeal. However, in the House of Lords, Baroness Hale, giving the lead judgment, held that there was no need for the gloss of 'exceptionality', and allowed the mother's appeal, so they were not returned.

In *F v M and N (Abduction: Acquiescence: Settlement)* (2008)[46] Black J did exercise the discretion and ordered a child's return to Poland despite her settlement in England.

44 [1993] 1 FLR 804.
45 [2007] EWHL 55, sub nom *Re M and Another (Minors)* [2008] 1 FLR 251.
46 [2008] EWHC 1525 (Fam).

By Article 13, return of a child can be refused if

(a)   a person, institution or body having the care of the person of the child was not actually exercising the custody rights at the time of removal or retention, or had consented or subsequently acquiesced in the removal or retention; or

(b)   there is a grave risk that the child's return would expose him or her to physical or psychological harm or otherwise place him or her in an intolerable situation.

Quite separately from these two situations, return may be refused under Art 13 if the child objects to being returned and has attained an appropriate age and degree of maturity for account to be taken of such views.

In considering the circumstances under this Article, the judicial and administrative authorities must take account of the child's social background provided by the competent authority of the child's habitual residence. 'Acquiescence' and the s 13(b) 'harm' can best be understood from reported decisions.

❖ CASE EXAMPLES

In *Re H (Abduction: Acquiescence)* (1998),[47] 13(a) acquiescence was held to be a question of fact and that attempts to reach a voluntary settlement are not acquiescence. The family were Orthodox Jews, the mother took the children to England without the father's consent and he contacted his local Beth Din religious court, which made an order to return the children; six months later he started Hague proceedings, which the mother argued was too late, so he had accepted their removal

The Court of Appeal at first overruled the High Court's order that the children should be returned, relying on their own 1992 decision, which had held that a single act could indicate acceptance. However, the House of Lords reinstated the High Court order, as they considered the earlier Court of Appeal decision wrong.

Lord Browne-Wilkinson held that acquiescence was a question of fact depending on the subjective state of mind of the wronged parent, and the burden of proof in disturbing such evidence was on the abducting parent. He said the only exception was where the wronged parent had unequivocally allowed the abducting parent to believe that he was not going to assert his rights.

In *Re S (Acquiescence)* (1998)[48] and *Re D (Abduction: Acquiescence)* (1998),[49] making long-term plans for contact or actually consenting to residence orders was held to be acquiescence.

In *Re D (Article 13b: Non-Return)* (2006)[50] return of the children to Venezuela was refused as there was evidence of serious violence, including shooting of the mother by a hired gunman suspected of being the father's agent.

---

47 [1998] AC 72; [1997] 1 FLR 87.
48 [1998] 2 FLR 115.
49 [1998] 1 FLR 686.
50 [2006] EWCA Civ 146.

But in similar cases (Greece, 2007, *Klentzeris v Klentzeris*; South Africa, 2004, *Re W*; New Zealand, 2001, *TB v JB*; and Israel, 2000 and 2002, *Re S* and *Re S*)[51] the mothers had all argued that violence, abuse, terrorism and/or discrimination against women would all make their lives intolerable and impact on the children, but only in the New Zealand case did the Court of Appeal (Hale LJ dissenting) even hesitate to return the children, and in that case not acceding to Lady Justice Hale's view.

In *AF v M-BF (Abduction: Rights of Custody)* (2008)[52] Sir Mark Potter P summarised the earlier case law and considered that the following were relevant: whether the case had been made out for the child's objections to returning, the child's age and maturity, any undue influence of the abducting parent; and all the countervailing matters which might affect weight given to the child's objections, and affect the duty to respect policy and judicial processes. He declined to return the two children involved to Poland since they strongly objected.

It is clear from other recent decisions in 2007 and 2008 that each case turns on its own facts. Maturity of the child is not always a trump card (an 11-year-old was returned to Lithuania by Black J for investigation of the welfare issues as the main objection was to living with the father and his new wife).

However, Charles J refused return of three children (separately represented) to Argentina as their objection was similarly to their father, whom they said took no notice of their wishes.

Potter P, Wilson LJ and Rix LJ declined to return a girl to Serbia owing to her traumatisation by the experience of having drugs planted on her mother – of which her father was suspected, in persistent attempts to incriminate the mother.

It seems that more children are being allowed separate representation in these cases where their objection to return is the issue.

18.4.1 Grave risk of harm

It is extremely difficult to come within the Art 13(b) defence, since this undermines the whole concept of the Convention, and the combination of mirror orders, state benefits and the presumption of judicial competence overseas combine to reinforce the presumption that a child should normally be returned. See for example *Re D (Abduction: Discretionary Return)* (2000),[53] where Wilson J ordered the children's return to France although they were settled in England, as the French court was seised of the case and it was a better forum to decide their future.

If the defence is made out, the court has a discretion not to return the child, but generally a child will be returned unless a very high degree of intolerability is established; even if the required level is made out, the child may still be returned.

---

51 [2007] EWCA Civ 533; [2004] EWHC 1247; [2001] 2FLR 515; [2000] 1 FLR 454 and [2002] EWCA Civ 908.
52 [2008] EWHC 272 (Fam).
53 [2000] 1 FLR 24.

❖ **CASE EXAMPLES**

In *N v N (Abduction: Article 13 Defence)* (1995)[54] the parents of three children lived in Australia and the father suffered from depression. There was possible sexual interference with the eight-year-old daughter. The mother brought the children to England for an extended holiday with the father's consent, but then changed her address and prevented telephone contact. The father issued a summons under the Hague Convention which the mother resisted, claiming there would be grave psychological harm to the children and that she would not be able to return with them. The children were still returned, Thorpe J saying that parents could not be allowed to manipulate the Convention.

On the other hand, in *Re G (Abduction: Psychological Harm)* (1995)[55] the mother, in similar circumstances, succeeded, and three children under the age of four were not returned, as it was held that serious deterioration in the mother if she was forced to return would impact on the children.

There was a similar result in *Re F (Child Abduction: Risk if Returned)*[56] because the child had been present at acts of violence where the father had threatened to kill the mother.

18.4.2 Where the child objects

The situation is different where it is the child who objects to being returned. This is a question of fact, and while the court still retains a discretion and will not hear oral evidence, it will inquire, through the court welfare officer, into why the child objects. No child over about the age of seven is too young to be listened to here, but children are often still returned despite this. Butler-Sloss LJ, when President of the Family Division, more than once said it was important to find out why a child objected, but in that decade (the 1990s) the court often decided to return the children, including on one occasion a seven-year-old (to the USA), despite supporting psychiatric evidence. Recent decisions seem to take more account of the child's objections.

18.4.3 Consent and acquiescence compared

This is a question of fact in each case and is sometimes complicated by the fact that negotiations at the start of a separation are encouraged, as for example in the leading House of Lords case *Re H* above.[57]

Consent is no breach of Art 3 but must be real, positive and clear, though it can be inferred from conduct.

Acquiescence is an Art 13(a) defence commonly argued but seldom successful, and even if it is established the court retains a discretion to return. The effect of alleging consent successfully is that there has been no wrongful removal or retention. Sometimes a parent will say consent is vitiated by duress or deceit.

Acquiescence is slightly different in that it is *a defence to an admitted breach*, although the same principles apply to disposal of the case.

---

54 [1995] 1 FLR 107.
55 [1995] 1 FLR 64.
56 [1995] 2 FLR 31.
57 [1998] AC 72.

18.5 The European Convention

The European Convention is a Council of Europe treaty and, like the Hague Convention, is given force in English law by CACA 1985. By Art 7 it makes the orders of one signatory state enforceable within the jurisdiction of the others. However, it is now not much used as it has mostly been superseded by BIIR (except for Denmark) when EU states are involved, and also by Hague.

The European Convention has the same central authority structure as Hague, but operates on the basis of 'wrongful removal' of a child, which under Art 4 triggers the right of a person holding a custody order in one State to apply for enforcement in another to which the child has been taken.

By Art 12, it does not matter when the order was made (i.e. whether before or after movement of the child across a qualifying international border). Qualification to apply to use the Convention is similar to 'rights of custody' under the Hague Convention, and includes rights of access and rights to determine the child's place of residence: Art 1(c).

Enforcement involving access can involve the same problems as under Hague as access rights may not always qualify as custody rights. Nevertheless, access rights can also be enforced as such, as an alternative to their being recognised as a right of custody, in which case the State addressed can decide to what extent to afford access, taking all the circumstances into account (e.g. undertakings: see Art 11).

Also, if enforcement of a custody order is refused, the central authority of the refusing State can ask its own courts to decide about access at the request of the applicant.[58] In Re A (1996), for example, a French access order was recognised and enforced in England and Wales. In contemporary UK society, with mobility via the Channel Tunnel and Channel ports making northern France closer for many in the south of England than the border with Scotland, this obviously has great practical importance.

In England and Wales, any custody order to be enforced under the Convention must first be registered: **Child Abduction and Custody Act 1985**, s 16. Application is to the High Court, which can refuse on certain grounds (see below) or where there is a Hague application pending, but cannot review the substance of the order.

Refusal of recognition and enforcement is covered by Arts 9 and 10. Broadly, Art 9 addresses situations where there has been no legal representation or a lack of natural justice in providing an opportunity for a fair hearing involving the applicant or representing lawyer, or where the decision does not involve the habitual residence of the family or is incompatible with a decision of the requested state. Article 10 additionally permits the requested state to review whether the decision is still in the interests of the child's welfare owing to a change of circumstances other than the simple removal to the territory of that State, a substantial difference from Hague. See for example Re L (*Abduction: European Convention: Access*) (1999),[59] where grandparents did not succeed in enforcing a French order in England as there had been a change of circumstances. By Art 15, the child's wishes can be taken into account.

18.6 Non-Convention cases

Non-convention country abductions pose more difficulties. It used to be the policy that the Hague principles, including the Art 13 defences, should apply to these cases as if the countries concerned

---

58 See Art 11(a) and Re A (*Foreign Access Order: Enforcement*) [1996] 1 FLR 561.
59 [1999] 2 FLR 1089.

were signatories to the Convention, since the same summary return and reliance on judicial comity was thought to be appropriate.

However, it was then realised that the child's welfare should be at the forefront of the court's duty, particularly as in some jurisdictions the child's welfare is not paramount, thus displacing any strict application of Hague principles.

Such jurisdictions can apply in England and Wales for return of children abducted to our jurisdiction: see for instance in an abduction from Mozambique in Re F (*Abduction: Removal Outside Jurisdiction*) (2008).[60] Alternatively a s 8 order can be sought, or a wardship order. In some cases the English court may not have jurisdiction to hear the case; in others there will be a choice between summary return and hearing the merits.

Nevertheless, in practice it is still regarded as usually best for a child to go back to the country of its habitual residence for any decision about its upbringing unless there are any indications to the contrary such as would make out a defence under Art 13.

The problem remains that many countries are not signatories to the Hague Convention, and although there has been a House of Commons working party on international child abduction (set up in 1990) which made some recommendations, including appointing a Children's Commissioner to take up cases with foreign governments, and various consultation papers, it is really only the 'rapid accession to the rule of law by all nations', as suggested by Balcombe LJ in Re F (*Minor: Abduction: Jurisdiction*) (1991),[61] which is likely to solve the ongoing problem.

A recent concern has been an epidemic of abductions of British-born teenagers from the UK with the intention of compelling them to contract forced marriages in their country of ethnic origin, a syndrome which is currently being addressed by the government departments which together run the FMU. Abduction in these circumstances is as difficult to combat as other abductions for the rather different reason that it is not always one parent alone who effects the abduction, and it is usually resisted by younger Westernised siblings, rather than by the other parent.

At present the governing principles in non-Convention cases depend on the lead judgment of Baroness Hale in Re J (*A Child*) (*Child Returned Abroad: Convention Rights*) (2005).[62]

❖ CASE EXAMPLE

In *Re J* the mother took the child from Saudi Arabia without the father's consent. The father applied for an SIO for return of the child. The trial judge refused the application and the Court of Appeal allowed it. The mother's appeal to the House of Lords was then allowed and the order of the trial judge restored.

Baroness Hale laid down some principles about such cases: that the welfare of the child is paramount, each case depends on its facts and the Hague Convention should not necessarily be applied to non-Convention-country cases.

In the particular case it was also necessary to take into account that there was no jurisdiction in the home country to deal with the mother's wish to bring the child to England without the father's consent, which provided the opportunity for Lady Hale's further guidance to the effect that in some cases it would be best for the child's future to be decided

---

60 [2008] EWCA Civ 842; [2008] 2 FLR 1649.
61 [1991] Fam 25.
62 [2005] UKHL 40; [2005] 2 FLR 802.

by its home jurisdiction, but in other cases not, so that in some cases summary return would be best and in others the opposite. She considered that the child's connection with the UK and its culture was important so that no harm would be done while his future was decided here, although in others a swift return would be better, because it could not be said that our concepts of welfare were necessarily better than others since the two were often different, especially as English law was capable of taking cultural and religious factors into account.

18.7 Which Convention?

This is a decision which is not often necessary to take, since for the European Convention to apply there must already be a decision or order to enforce. In the absence of a decision or order, it will not be possible to access the sometimes superior benefit of the European Convention, which permits change of circumstances to be taken into account, thus Hague will apply, under which peremptory return is more likely. In the exceptional case of there being qualification under both Conventions, clearly the tactical advantages must be weighed up, in which case the European Convention may afford a better chance of keeping a child in the requested jurisdiction, and equally will be a worse choice for an applicant wishing to secure the return of the child.

18.8 Relocation

The necessity for parental agreement or applications for permission to remove a child from the jurisdiction of England and Wales have already been considered in relation to PR in Chapter 12 and Chapter 16 at 16.7. If there is a residence provision in place an application must be made to the court under CA 1989 s 13(1), or if no order is in force proceedings for a prohibited steps or a specific issue order brought by either parent will be appropriate. If both parents have PR and cannot agree, a decision of the court is essential, although if only the mother has PR in theory the mother could act alone. However, as the father can usually obtain PR, in practice the lack of consensus will mean proceedings are inevitable, and the court will apply the welfare principle.

The leading case is still *Poel v Poel* (1970)[63] and this approach, allowing a reasonable and well-thought-out application to succeed unless incompatible with the child's welfare, was undisturbed, despite much effort on the part of counsel for the father in *Payne v Payne* (2001).[64]

More recent cases[65] have continued to push the *Payne* objections that *Poel* is out of date and out of step with dramatic social change since 1970, but it is more or less accepted that there is nothing to be done but to follow the existing case law without changing the law, until a suitable new case reaches the Supreme Court when the matter can be considered afresh with all issues at large.

The context of *Payne* needs to be understood in order to understand what the problems are as it is a very typical long-haul relocation case with strong links for the relocator at least 11,000 miles away from the jurisdiction of England and Wales – and the other, left-behind, parent.

---

63 [1970] 1 WLR 1469.
64 [2001] EWCA Civ 1166; [2001] 1 FLR 1052.
65 At least three in 2011 which are detailed in the Freeman and Taylor article in the 'Further reading' section of this chapter.

❖ CASE EXAMPLE

In *Payne v Payne* the mother wanted to take a four-year-old girl to New Zealand, which would disturb the contact not only with the father but also the exceptionally good staying contact enjoyed with the paternal grandmother. The Court nevertheless allowed the mother to leave.

The father's appeal was dismissed by the Court of Appeal although his appeal had been made on the grounds that the decision was inconsistent with the CA 1989 and with the HRA 1998. The Court held that the 1998 Act did not require a revision of the principles in the *Poel* case and that in any case the mother had a right to mobility under Art 2 of Protocol 4 of the ECHR. Lord Justice Thorpe proposed a discipline in such cases on the basis that

> refusing the primary carer's reasonable proposals for the relocation of her family life is likely to impact detrimentally on the welfare of her dependent children. Therefore her application to relocate will be granted unless the court concludes that it will be incompatible with the welfare of the children.

He set out the key questions to be posed:

(a) Is the mother's application genuine . . . realistic? . . . founded on practical proposals both well researched and investigated? If not refusal will follow.
(b) If the application passes these tests, appraisal of the father's opposition is required. Is it motivated by genuine concern or by ulterior motive? What would be the extent of the detriment to him and his future relationship with the child were the application granted? To what extent would that be offset by extension of the child's relationships with the maternal relations and homeland?
(c) What would be the impact on the mother, either as a single parent or as a new wife, of refusal of her realistic proposal?
(d) The outcome of the second and third appraisals must then be brought into an overriding review of the child's welfare as the paramount consideration, directed by the statutory checklist where appropriate.

These principles were endorsed by the Court of Appeal in *Re G (Leave to Remove)* (2007)[66] where a father, attempting to appeal against permission given to the mother to relocate to Germany, said that some judges were misunderstanding and misapplying the principles and disregarding contemporary views on the importance of co-parenting. Thorpe LJ strongly disagreed although he recognised that these particular decisions were very finely balanced and difficult for judges to make.

This approach was repeated in other cases and the psychological impact of refusal on the carer parent was given great weight. Concern has, however, been expressed by academics and others, for example Sir Bob Geldof.[67]

---

66 [2007] EWCA Civ 222; [2007] 2 FLR 317.
67 See www.thecustodyminefield.com; Hayes, M, 'Relocation Cases: Is the Court of Appeal Applying the Correct Principles?',
   (2006) CFLQ 19: 351; Gilmore, S, 'The nature, scope and use of the specific issue order', (2004) CFLQ 16: 367.

It has certainly proved to be the case that a shared residence order is not a trump card in the relocation debate: Re T (A Child).[68]

Spon Smith (2004)[69] says that the Court's approach is at odds with the American research[70] which shows that children do not necessarily benefit from such relocations distant from the other parent; Herring and Taylor (2006)[71] say that the Court's approach takes insufficient account of human rights; Geekie (2008)[72] says that the approach is at odds with the approach to shared residence where the Court has been shaking off 'the shackles of a dated approach to shared parenting'; Pressdee (2006)[73] says that Lord Justice Thorpe's approach is too inflexible. Mary Hayes says the 'discipline' is putting a gloss on the welfare principle and is biased in favour of the carer parent, who is nearly always the mother. The only slight sign of elasticity in the court's approach has been in the approach to temporary removal (where hard decisions have been made in the past because it would disrupt contact) as in the case of Re T (Temporary Removal from Jurisdiction) (2004).[74]

❖ CASE EXAMPLE

In Re T (Temporary Removal) (2004) the unmarried mother wanted to go to South Africa for two years when the child was two to work on a PhD, after which she would be well placed for employment as a lecturer in her home town in England. The court held that the same principles did not apply as to permanent removal, and the more temporary the removal the less they would apply. Clear concentration would therefore need to be addressed to practical ways of mitigating the impact on contact with the father (who had PR) as the separation would otherwise be a deficit for the child.

The matter has been moved forward by the Windsor conference of August 2009, the Washington Declaration of March 2010 and the Inaugural Conference of the Centre for Family Law and Practice at London Metropolitan University on 'International Child Abduction, Forced Marriage and Relocation' in July 2010 which assembled a further collection of conclusions and recommendations in which Lord Justice Thorpe participated, as did the Deputy Chief Justice of the Family Court of Australia, the Principal Family Judge of New Zealand, the Deputy Chief Justice of Egypt, Lady Justice Black, Lord Justice Munby of the English Court of Appeal and Mr Justice Singer of the English High Court Family Division. This conference closely followed the case of Re AR (2010)[75] in which Mostyn J, newly appointed to the Family Division, commented that the present law needed revisiting (while, on the authorities, not permitting relocation of the applicant and child to France). Within the UK such relocations no further than some parts of France are meanwhile not restricted at all unless there are exceptional circumstances, such as a malign intention on the part of the carer parent which impacts on the child's welfare.

---

68 [2009] EWCA Civ 20.
69 'Relocation Revisited', [2004] Fam Law 191.
70 Braver et al, 'Relocation of children after divorce and children's best interests: new evidence and legal considerations', (2003) 17(2) Journal of Family Psychology 206.
71 'Relocating Relocation', [2006] CFLQ 517.
72 'Relocation and Shared Residence: one route or two?', [2008] Fam Law 446.
73 'Relocation, relocation, relocation: rigorous scrutiny revisited', [2008] Fam Law 220.
74 [2004] EWCA Civ 1587.
75 [2010] EWHC 1346.

While the present dichotomy between shared residence and shared parenting on the one hand and easy relocation out of the jurisdiction[76] on the other persists there clearly will be difficulties with contact arrangements although the court has acknowledged that this is now much easier given contemporary technology.

This is, however, one area where the new CAO is unlikely to have any impact as the sole issue in English law is the best interests of the child, unrestricted by any of the parameters of the Hague or European Conventions.

18.9 Current debates

Ideas for research on these current discussions can be found on the companion website updates.

- Should the principle of shared parenting and/or the potential for shared residence be a major influence in decisions on relocation?
- Should human rights principles be balanced in such decisions which affect both parents and the child?
- If so, how can this be compatible with the welfare principle?
- Is the welfare principle being misunderstood and misapplied by judges in relocation decisions?
- Is there a role for improved cross-border indirect contact, and if so how could this be managed?

18.10 Summary of Chapter 18

- Both Abduction and Relocation impact adversely on ongoing contact of the child with the non-resident parent.

Child abduction

- Prevention is better than cure.

Resources to address child abduction

- The CAA 1984, FLA 1986 and Hague and European Conventions all combine to discourage domestic and international child abduction. These provisions apply to children under 16, above which age abduction will still fall under the common law offence of kidnapping.
- The CAA 1984 makes child abduction a criminal offence, and the FLA 1986 enables custody orders obtained in one part of the UK to be enforced in others, and also increases the chances of finding lost children, with the assistance of publicity and a judicial power to require information.

---

76 Which is not replicated in many other jurisdictions, e.g. New Zealand where the approach is more restrictive. See George, R, *Relocation Disputes: Law and Practice in England and New Zealand*, Oxford, Hart, 2014, which contains his doctoral research evaluating the law in England and New Zealand and making some suggestions for reform.

- The two Conventions set up a regime by which central authorities in signatory countries cooperate to secure the return of children under 16 for decisions about their future to be determined by the courts of their habitual residence.
- This doctrine depends on a theory of judicial comity which assumes a fair trial of the issues in jurisdictions other than our own.

The Hague Convention

- Provides a summary remedy in which the merits of the case are not examined and the child is mandatorily returned, unless one of the Article 13 defences to an application is exceptionally made out.
- The remedy operates on the basis of a wrongful removal of a child from the jurisdiction of its habitual residence, or his or her wrongful retention outside that jurisdiction after a period of lawful contact elsewhere. An applicant must show that he or she was exercising 'custody rights', which may be less than the formal status of parental responsibility or a residence order which we associate with the concept of physical 'custody'.
- A right to contact which is exercised can be sufficient for *de facto* custody rights, commonly claimed by unmarried fathers, but this depends on individual circumstances.
- The defences under Art 13 are that the applicant was not exercising custody rights as required for jurisdiction, that the child objects to returning, that the applicant has acquiesced in the removal or retention, or that the child risks suffering grave harm (including psychological harm).
- Similarly, if the applicant has allegedly consented beforehand (rather than acquiesced afterwards) to the removal or retention, there will be no wrongful removal or retention in the first place.

The European Convention

- Slightly different, in that the removal of a child across an international border of signatories to the Convention must be in contravention of an actual decision or order in relation to the child's custody or access to the child.
- But changed circumstances taken into account unlike under Hague.

Relocation

- Impacts on ongoing contact with the child by the 'left-behind' parent.
- The leading cases remain *Poel v Poel* and *Payne v Payne* (respectively 1970 and 2001).
- Much academic criticism suggests that it is time for a reappraisal.
- Temporary removal from the jurisdiction is not decided entirely by the dated principles of these cases.
- There has been some international consultation and three separate collections of principles on which such cases should, in the opinion of the specialist lawyers and judges working in the field, be decided.

18.11 Further reading

Beevers, C, 'Child Abduction, inchoate rights of custody and the unmarried father', [2006] CFLQ 18: 499.

Collier, R, 'Fathers4Justice, law and the new politics of fatherhood', [2005] CFLQ 17: 511.

Freeman, M and Taylor, N, 'The reign of *Payne*', (2011) 2 FLP 2: 20. (This online journal is no longer published but the complete archive may be found at www.frburton.com, and its successor, *International Family Law, Policy and Practice*, at www.famlawandpractice.com.)

Freeman, M and Taylor, N, 'International Research Evidence on Relocation: Past, Present and Future', [2010] *Family Law Quarterly*, 44: 3, 317.

Freeman, M and Taylor, N, 'Relocation: The Research: Where Are We Now?', [2011] IFL 131.

Freeman, M, 'Is it all normal once the child returns home?', [2011] IFL 31.

Freeman, M and Taylor, N, 'The Gender Agenda in Relocation Disputes', [2012] IFL 184.

Freeman, M and Taylor, N, 'International Family Mobility, Relocation and Abduction: Links and Lessons', [2013] IFL 41.

Gilmore, S, 'Contact/Shared residence and child well-being: Research evidence and its implications for legal decision making', [2006] *International Journal of Law, Policy and the Family* 20: 344.

Gilmore, S, 'The *Payne* Saga: Precedent and Family Law cases', [2011] Fam Law 41: 970.

Lamont, R, 'The EU: Protecting Children's Rights in Child Abduction', [2008] IFL 110.

McLeavy, P, 'Evaluating the Views of Abducted Children: trends in appellate case law', [2008] CFLQ 230.

Schuz, R, 'Guidance from Luxembourg: First ECJ judgment clarifying the relationship between the 1980 Hague Child Abduction Convention and Brussels II Revised', [2008] IFL 221.

Scott, T, '*Mk v CK*: The Retreat from *Payne*', http://documents.jdsupra.com/d1c62d88-413f-408f-872b-f67259b8a028.pdf.

Thorpe LJ, 'The Search for Common Principles', (2010) 1 FLP 35. (This online journal is no longer published but the complete archive may be found at www.frburton.com, and its successor, *International Family Law, Policy and Practice*, at www.famlawandpractice.com.)

https://www.gov.uk/government/publications/international-parental-child-abduction.

www.hcch.net: Hague Conference Website.

www.reunite.org.

Chapter 19

Child Protection: Wardship, the Inherent Jurisdiction and the CA 1989

Chapter Contents

Learning outcomes for this chapter

A sound understanding of the underlying theory of access to the law for child protection including

(i) An appreciation of the relationship between the inherent jurisdiction, wardship and the statutory code of the CA 1989 in both private and public law.
(ii) A working knowledge of the enhanced framework of public law protection of children provided by the Children Act 2004 following the Laming Report 2003.
(iii) An awareness of the policy of non-intervention by the state in the autonomy of the family.
(iv) An ability to analyse the appropriate remedies where children are at risk of harm in either public or private law contexts.

19.1 Introduction

Prior to the CA 1989 local authorities did not have the comprehensive public law powers for child protection given to them by CA 1989 Parts IV and V. Instead they used the special powers of the High Court to protect children (and other vulnerable persons such as the elderly), and especially to take children into care and keep them there. In 1989 two-thirds of wardship cases were brought by local authorities for this purpose.

But the comprehensive code at which the CA 1989 aimed owed its major inspiration to wardship, though the intention was that it should replace most of wardship's former functions, not supplement them. For example, there were prophecies that wardship would wither away, then disappear when CA 1989 took over those of its remedial functions which could be transferred to statutory provision.

Nevertheless there were at least two functions which could not conveniently be included within the statutory framework – the speed of effective High Court application to access either wardship or the inherent jurisdiction (particularly wardship) and the ongoing supervisory role that the court in wardship assumes over a child for whom ongoing decisions are required.

Wardship was thus retained. Subsequent history has shown the wisdom of that decision, especially for international child abduction and urgent medical decisions.

Thus the two parallel remedies – the portfolio of cheaper, more universally accessible CA 1989 orders alongside wardship – are so usefully complementary that they have co-existed harmoniously for three decades without problems. The 'double act' is in fact beneficial since the most appropriate remedy can be chosen for particular circumstances: the element of choice is often fortuitous.

19.1.1 Changes made by the CA 1989

Following the implementation of the 1989 Act there were changes.

First, local authorities could no longer use wardship for the former purposes since CA 1989 had a codified portfolio of statutory remedies, which were also cheaper, as the High Court remedy of wardship always cost more than a CA 1989 application. Thus ending the High Court's power to commit a child to care under the wardship jurisdiction, effected by the CA 1989 s 100(1), economised, since local authority applications then moved to the more cost-effective CA 1989 s 31.

Second, local authority access to the High Court inherent jurisdiction (of which wardship is a particular species[1]) was also restricted by CA 1989 s 100(2), so local authorities could no longer use that to place a child in care, to supervise it or to accommodate it, since they also had new statutory powers under CA 1989 ss 31, 35 and 20 for those functions.

---

1 See below.

Third, if an authority wanted to use the High Court inherent jurisdiction for some purpose, by s 100(3) and (4) they had to obtain permission and satisfy conditions, namely to show that this was necessary or the child would suffer harm, and that no other remedy would suit instead, for example where a care order was sought for a child aged 17 – which is not available for a child of that age under the scheme of the CA 1989.

This meant in practice that the authority would have to satisfy the same conditions as for a care order under CA 1989 s 31, even though they did not want to obtain PR, which a s 31 order would give them.

These changes combined to take a raft of work away from the High Court, leaving the Family Division judges free to do what had then become the core work of the wardship and inherent jurisdictions: i.e. cases requiring speedy one-off decisions of high-level importance, which tended to go to a specialist judge in those jurisdictions, and those also requiring speed and ongoing supervision, which was the particular speciality of wardship and which could be obtained by no other means.

This use of the inherent jurisdiction by local authorities is thus now mostly used for urgent one-off decisions in serious medical treatment cases,[2] although, owing to its unique specialist role, wardship can also be used in different types of cases where an element of ongoing supervision is required; for all else there is the CA 1989 portfolio of child protection orders.[3] The rationale is that the statutory code is supposed to restrict the state's intervention into the life of the family by providing precise parameters.

A case example illustrates this choice of remedies:

❖ CASE EXAMPLE

The case of *Wyatt v Portsmouth NHS* (2005)[4] highlights the distinction between the inherent jurisdiction (where a one-off decision on a discrete issue is made by the court) and the ongoing supervision character of wardship (where, because the court will assume the role of the child's parents, the court then takes every ongoing decision in their place).

The case concerned aggressive treatment to prolong the life of a seriously ill one-year-old which was potentially not in her best interests despite the parents' wish that it should continue (as it could have done, *if* it had been decided that that was the way forward, since the court had assumed the role of the child's parents).

The issue was therefore whether the parents or the local NHS Trust was right about the treatment, and if the decision was that treatment continued the court in its wardship jurisdiction could undertake the supervision of that ongoing treatment, taking any necessary decisions as they presented themselves.

As Wall LJ said at paragraph 112 of the judgment, 'In the overwhelming majority of cases in which the inherent jurisdiction of the court over children . . . is invoked, the "best interests" decision of the court determines the issue once and for all' – but in wardship the story does not end there.

---

2 As explained in Chapter 14.
3 See Chapter 20.
4 [2005] EWCA Civ 1181.

It should be noted that another distinction between the inherent jurisdiction and wardship is that the former can be used in the case of vulnerable adults, whereas wardship, which is in effect guardianship of children, cannot, because adults are not children (i.e. are not under 18) even if vulnerable. A medical case involving an older 'child' will therefore be dealt with under the inherent jurisdiction.

19.2 Wardship, the inherent jurisdiction and the CA 1989

Because it is sometimes found confusing to have these separate jurisdictions available, both alongside each other and in apparent competition with the CA 1989, the relationship between them all is sometimes confusing. Wardship and the inherent jurisdiction are like two layers of a Russian doll: wardship is the inner layer which fits *inside* the larger shell of the inherent jurisdiction, and the two nest together in the High Court jurisdiction, but sit *side by side* with the CA 1989, which has largely removed the need for the other two jurisdictions in the Family Court by providing a flexible statutory framework for resolving a wide range of issues about the upbringing of children; this code was based on the wardship concept, but has not altogether removed the need either for wardship in particular, or the inherent jurisdiction in general.

In consequence, where there is a *statutory vehicle* for achieving the desired result, neither wardship nor the inherent jurisdiction is used; this is also true where *alternative statutes* provide a regime to regulate other fields in which children may be involved, such as immigration, where the High Court has refused to hear applications for wardship in cases where this would impact upon the powers of the Secretary of State under the Immigration Act;[5] and domestic violence, where there is a menu of remedies under the FLA 1996 Part IV that should be used in family violence cases, rather than seeking an injunction under the High Court inherent jurisdiction, attached to some other suit.[6] This is logical legal theory: if there is a statutory code it should be used rather than the common law unless there is good reason not to.

Waite LJ spelled this out in the case of *Re T (a minor) (child representation)* (1994)[7] when he said that (apart from those in CA 1989, s 100) there were no specific restrictions as such, but that the courts discouraged unnecessary use of the pre-1989 remedies; and that while there was an

> undoubted discretion to allow wardship in a suitable case, this was subject to the courts' clear duty, in loyalty to the scheme and purpose of the CA 1989, to permit recourse to wardship only when it becomes apparent to the judge in any particular case that the question which the court is determining . . . cannot be resolved under the statutory procedures . . . in a way that secures the best interests of the child . . .

Confusingly, wardship is now itself based in statute, the **Senior Courts Act 1981**.[8]

Nevertheless, wardship was originally of ancient origin, stemming from the fact that the king's court was an umbrella jurisdiction in which to protect children and the vulnerable, the king having originally been perceived in feudal times as the *parens patriae* (literally 'the father of the nation') and protector of the weak.

Thus wardship is a means of making the court the modern representative of the medieval king, *in loco parentis* (literally in the place of a parent) to the child.

---

5 See *Re F (A Minor) (Immigration: Wardship)* [1990] Fam 125; *R v Secretary of State for the Home Department ex p T* [1995] 1 FLR 293.
6 See Chapter 10.
7 [1994] Fam 49.
8 Originally called the Supreme Court Act 1981, the name of which was changed to the Senior Courts Act 1981 when the new Supreme Court was created to replace the appellate jurisdiction of the House of Lords. This statutory re-formatting of a common law remedy occurs periodically when common law principles are sometimes codified for convenience.

On the other hand, the inherent jurisdiction (of which wardship was once only one special-ised part, albeit now in statutory form) is as the name suggests not regulated by statute but comes directly from the (inherent) power of the courts of common law, which means that when the inherent jurisdiction is invoked the court has all its hereditary powers plus those created by statute.

Thus, as wardship is 'family proceedings' within the meaning of the CA 1989, the court can use any CA 1989 orders except for those it is prohibited from making by the Act, for example not using wardship to send children into care.[9] Wardship has proved an endlessly useful tool, accessible at any time unless it undermines a statutory power, particularly because once a child is warded no new applications need be made (unlike repeated applications necessary for any SIO or PSO[10]). Even when a first application is made its flexibility and immediate protection from harm can be activated at short notice.

Only an outline knowledge of wardship is therefore likely to be required in practice since the CA 1989 is often the more common procedure, not least because it costs less.

Nevertheless, the subject area remains of interest to both academics and practitioners since it is

(i)   the watershed from which the CA 1989 concepts sprang, and sometimes
(ii)   still of unique practical use for cases which are not conveniently settled through the CA 1989 jurisdiction (e.g. any case requiring urgent action and ongoing supervision, which are not well catered for by the CA 1989's s 8 orders for the reasons mentioned).

As wardship is only one specialised part of the court's inherent jurisdiction, with special suitability for emergencies and those requiring supervision, it is logical that the inherent jurisdiction is used to decide complex cases referred to the High Court, for instance where a decision is required to investigate overriding that of a *Gillick* competent child who has vetoed life-saving medical treat-ment[11] or to decide disputes between parents and other interested parties about the proper clinical treatment of a child.

Some such cases are therefore brought not technically in wardship as such (i.e. where there is no ongoing supervisory element required which would need that feature), but under the inherent jurisdiction of the court, which will then be used to make the necessary one-off decision (e.g. whether there should be treatment of a life-threatening condition, when such treatment has been refused by the minor, or where there is disagreement as to whether it should be carried out, which has generated a dispute between responsible parties having an interest in the welfare of the minor, i.e. parents and the local authority, doctor or other care professional).

The real distinction between wardship and the inherent jurisdiction is that wardship not only confers PR on the court, which a decision under the inherent jurisdiction does not, but that the court's PR is wider than the common sort enjoyed by natural persons. This is because, unlike the PR of natural parents, which is generated by the birth of their children, the court's version derives from the Crown, which assumed the corporate mantle of the king when his personal attendance at his courts of justice became delegated to his judiciary and he no longer personally participated. This has not stopped modern judges referring back to the origin of wardship and stressing the parental role of the court.

---

9   As explained at 19.1 above.
10 See Chapter 16.
11 See Chapter 14.

❖ **CASE EXAMPLES**

In *Re E(SA) (A Minor)* (1984)[12] see per Lord Scarman, where he expressly refers to the court becoming the child's parent.

In *Re S (Infants)* (1967)[13] see per Cross J, where he refers to the fact that in these circumstances every major decision must be taken by the court, just as would normally be the case on the part of a natural parent.

In *Re D (A Minor) (Justices' Decision: Review)* (1977)[14] see per Dunn LJ, where he speaks of wardship as the 'golden thread' in complex child disputes for which wardship may be regarded as an appropriate forum.

In *Re A (Children)* (2001),[15] the case of the conjoined twins, the court gave its consent for the twins to be separated despite the parents' opposition, and although this would inevitably lead to the death of the weaker (but would correspondingly preserve the life of the stronger who might otherwise have died).[16]

19.2.1 Wardship or CA 1989?

It was suggested when the CA 1989 was drafted that wardship should be abolished when that legislation was passed, rather than waiting for it to die of natural causes. However, recognising the value of the separate High Court remedy, it was instead expressly preserved, to work alongside the new range of s 8 private law orders as well as those required for public law child protection, since it was appreciated that wardship could sometimes achieve results which the CA 1989 could not.

Nevertheless, it is fair to say that in taking the decision to retain wardship it was anticipated that the flexibility of the orders which the court could then grant under the CA 1989 – in particular SIOs and PSOs – would mean that s 8 orders would be applied for in preference to wardship, and this has mostly proved to be the case. Yet it is clear that the remedy of wardship can still add to the range of s 8 orders, as there are occasionally reasons for the preference of wardship which have justified its separate existence, such as where:

(a) it is convenient to bypass the CA 1989, e.g. if the applicant does not have status under the Act;
(b) there is a genuine need for the court's continuing supervision (which, once s 8 orders have been granted, cannot be achieved under the CA 1989 without a new application as the court's function is complete on issue of its order, but the opposite is the case in wardship owing to its supervisory role which is what makes it so expensive).

---

12 [1984] 1 All ER 289, p 290.
13 [1967] 1 All ER 202.
14 [1977] Fam 158.
15 [2001] Fam 147, CA.
16 It should be noted that there is an analysis of this case in Hunter, R, McGlynn, C and Rackley, E (eds), *Feminist Judgments*, Oxford, Hart, 2011, Chapter 8, at p 134.

Re W (Wardship: Discharge: Publicity) (1995)[17] is a clear instance of the supervisory use of wardship in protecting children, where the supervising role of parental care was the essential element of the order.

The case concerned two boys, aged 10 and 15, who became wards when their parents' marriage broke down; the boys grew hostile towards their mother and care and control was eventually awarded to the father. Litigation continued over a variety of matters in dispute between the parents and the boys became identifiable in stories in the press in which they spoke of their dislike of their mother and of their dissatisfaction with being represented by the Official Solicitor.

An injunction was issued prohibiting the father from giving the press any further information about the issues in the wardship proceedings; he applied to discharge the wardship, but the court held that it should be continued, since wardship offered protection for the children which could not be achieved by orders under the CA 1989 where a PSO could not be framed to anticipate every possible way in which the father might act. The father had shown that he was not able to consider the boys' best interests objectively, which the court in wardship could do on an ongoing basis.

There are some essential restrictions to the use of wardship besides those explained above[18] in relation to the local authority. Wardship cannot be used to stop abortions because a foetus *in utero* (i.e. in the womb) is not 'a child' so cannot be a ward of court.[19] However, wardship can be used to deal with:

● kidnapping;
● medical treatment cases;
● adoptions;
● undesirable associations.

Thus, for example, a liberal construction of s 100 *does* permit a local authority to use wardship where a care order would be inappropriate and where a supervision order would not achieve the desired end.

In *Devon County Council v S* (1995)[20] the object was to protect the younger children in a family where the eldest was married to a person convicted of sexual offences. Wardship permitted supervision of his visits to the family without interfering in the mother's other-wise unobjectionable care of the younger children.

---

17 [1995] 2 FLR 466.
18 At 19.1.
19 *Re F (In Utero)* [1988] 2 WLR 1297; [1988] Fam. 122.
20 [1995] 1 All ER 243.

Kidnapping

The use of wardship to prevent kidnapping has to some extent been reduced in importance because of the CAA 1984 and the Port Alert System, which may be activated by the police if they are themselves alerted by any person to the fact that a minor is about to be abducted overseas. Nevertheless, given that the police and immigration services do need to be involved to activate the latter, their aid is much more easily invoked if there is an order in force, and wardship is an obvious candidate for such an emergency where the CA 1989's lengthier procedures would be useless. It may also now achieve a new function in backing up the 'PAs' recommended by the FJR and encouraged by the CAP processes in place of a CAO; although it would certainly be a prime example of an unintended consequence if the saving of the costs of a cheaper CA 1989 s 8 CAO by use of the FJR's informal PA in practice must be supported by a more expensive High Court wardship order in order to obtain the assistance of public agencies to prevent an abduction! Now wardship has a statutory origin and there are High Court judges sitting in the unified Family Court perhaps a new fast-track form-based procedure is required to maximise the use of wardship and minimise its costs in this context).

The CAA 1984 s1(1) does make it an offence for a 'connected person' (i.e. a child's parent, guardian or person with a CAO in respect of the child) to take or send a child overseas without the appropriate consent[21] but there are defences, unless inter alia the departure is in breach of a court order, and some parents are not deterred by a statute creating criminal liability. Thus sometimes a wardship order, in assisting in activating the Port Alert System, can make the difference between preventing a child being abducted or not.

It is easy to see why wardship orders have such a useful role in this respect. The Port Alert System is the subject of a Practice Direction[22] and is a 24-hour service operated in conjunction with immigration officers at all ports including airports. To use it, applicants must show that there is real and imminent danger of removal of a child. Help cannot be sought as 'insurance', so 'real' means there must be some evidence and 'imminent' is interpreted as meaning within the next 24 to 48 hours. Application should in theory be made to the local police station, but in emergency to any police station. This will result in the child's name being entered on the 'stop' list at all ports for four weeks, after which it will be removed, unless fresh application is made.

Details are required for effective help:

(a) a photograph of the child or at least a very good description, including of any accompanying person(s) who will probably be more easily recognised than the child, especially if the child is young;
(b) the likely port of departure and destination;
(c) details of the proposed route as departures of this type are seldom direct.

So while strictly there is no need to have any order in force, in practice this will usually assist in engaging the police's attention in order to invoke the system. A wardship order in particular not only commands respect but can be quickly obtained.

Medical treatment cases

These are also subject to a Practice Note.[23] While sterilisation and other disputed surgical procedure cases are particularly well dealt with by wardship,[24] if a local authority is concerned, and if the issue to be decided is purely a one-off medical decision, the authority could, and perhaps should, be using the s 8 SIO/PSO route or a declaration under the inherent jurisdiction rather than wardship.

---

21 See Chapter 18.
22 [1986] 1 WLR 475; [1986] 1 All ER 983.
23 [1990] Fam Law 375.
24 See Chapter 14.

Adoption

The most usual role for wardship in this type of case is that the court can investigate fully where there is some issue such as a condition to be attached to the adoption, for instance where there is a dispute as to whether the natural mother will continue to see or care for the child, as in *Re O* (1978)[25] and similar cases.

❖ CASE EXAMPLES

In *Re O* (1978), ongoing contact was initially agreed and then the adopter tried to back out. The court held that the matter must be fully investigated within the wardship procedure.

In *Re E* (1963)[26] the adopters, whose application to adopt had failed, tried to retain care of the child in its best interests. In this type of case, the court will follow only the child's best interests, so if the application is a last-ditch attempt to prevent a page turning in the child's life, the application will be dismissed immediately, but if there is an issue which requires investigation the court can investigate it fully.

In *Re K* (1997)[27] it was held that if the court revokes or declines to make an adoption order, it can allow wardship to continue and leave the child with the proposed adopters rather than make a CAO with residence element.

Undesirable associations

The court can prevent unsuitable marriages or unmarried associations, or joining an undesirable religious or other sect, especially where a sect has a reputation for taking advantage of impressionable young people.

19.2.2 How wardship works

No particular relationship is required to take out an application, which is one of the great advantages of wardship as a remedy, though a genuine interest in bringing the proceedings must now be shown. The child can apply by a litigation friend. However, this flexibility must not be abused – as it has been for ulterior motives.

❖ CASE EXAMPLE

In *Re Dunhill* (1967)[28] a nightclub owner warded a 20-year-old model for publicity purposes, and the application was struck out as frivolous, vexatious and an abuse of the process of the court, on top of which the applicant had to pay all the costs! (This is, of course, an old case preceding the change of the age of majority from 21 to 18.)

---

25 [1978] 2 All ER 27; [1978] Fam 196.
26 [1963] 3 All ER 874.
27 [1997] FCR 387.
28 (1967) 111 SJ 113.

The application is made directly to the High Court. Public funding is in theory still available in appropriate cases. Applications can be made *ex parte* (i.e. without notice). Wardship is then immediately effective (which is why it is so useful in kidnapping cases) but lapses if not pursued by obtaining a hearing date within 21 days. The defendant must acknowledge service and furnish an address and also the address of the minor, noting any changes.

The first appointment will be before the DJ for directions. The full hearing, before a High Court judge in chambers, will not be for many months. There is power to adjourn to open court (e.g. where the ward is missing and publicity is desired). The court will then confirm or discharge the wardship. If confirmed, 'care and control' (i.e. similar to the former s 8 residence order or the 'living with' provision of a CAO) will be entrusted to an individual, and a wardship application can, if desired, be coupled with any s 8 applications or a CAO; the court can then make those orders instead if the wardship is not granted.

Once a wardship order is made, no important step can be taken in the child's life without the consent of the court; for example, permission is needed even for a short holiday outside the jurisdiction – technically in wardship even to go to Scotland, which is not within the jurisdiction of England and Wales – but a certificate can be issued to show to immigration officials to obviate the need to apply every time. Permission is also required to marry or to emigrate, in which case the wardship is likely to be discontinued as the court may not want to supervise the ward at a distance. Alternatively, the applicant can be required to give an undertaking to return the ward to the jurisdiction if ever asked to do so. What the court considers here is whether the ward will in fact be returned if return is asked for and therefore whether it is in the ward's interests to go at all.[29]

19.2.3 The inherent jurisdiction

As explained above, this is the jurisdiction often used by local authorities to settle an issue about a child in care as they cannot usually use wardship. For the types of medical case in which this jurisdiction is used, see Chapter 14.

19.3 State intervention

The basic standpoint of non-intervention is one of the key changes in the public law child protection effected by the CA 1989. As Lord Mackay[30] said in his Joseph Jackson Memorial Lecture in 1989:

> The integrity and independence of the family is the basic building block of a free and democratic society and the need to defend it should be clearly perceivable in the law. Accordingly, unless there is evidence that a child is being or is likely to be positively harmed because of a failure in the family, the state, whether in the guise of the local authority or a court, should not interfere.

The basic premise is, therefore, that parents have primary responsibility for their children, not the state. This is also recognised by the **European Convention on Human Rights**' Art 8 right to family life. Intervention must therefore be a proportionate response to a legitimate aim.

Thus social services in any local authority need to exhaust their support functions before removing a child from its home.[31]

---

29 *Re F* [1988] 2 FLR 116.
30 Lord Chancellor under the Conservative governments up to 1997.
31 See Chapter 20 for the CA 1989 public law child protection provision at the disposal of the local authority which acts for the state in this respect.

Similarly there must be procedural fairness, to avoid a potential breach of Art 6 (right to a fair and timely hearing) if parents are not fully involved in the decision-making process. The UNCRC 1989 also contains various Articles relevant to child protection.

> ## ❖ CASE EXAMPLE
>
> In *Re L (Care: Assessment: Fair Trial)* (2002)[32] the mother of a child was not attending multidisciplinary meetings which were critical of her. It was held that she must be told of the meetings and given an opportunity to improve.

However, the state must intervene where parents cannot, or will not, take proper care of their children.

Social services departments of local authorities have primary responsibility for making provision for children in need and dealing with children who suffer, or are at risk of suffering, significant harm.

This is a fine balance which has to be struck: intervening too readily and they are criticised, not intervening soon enough and the criticisms still flow.

This is apparent from a reading of the Report of the Inquiry into Child Abuse in Cleveland in 1987[33] where social workers were criticised for being overzealous in their interventions when more than 100 children were taken away from their homes on suspicion of being sexually abused, on the evidence of two paediatricians without other agencies being consulted.

The Report mentioned, amongst other things, the desirability of better inter-agency cooperation to protect children and better safeguards for parents and children where intervention was necessary.

This theory of better inter-agency cooperation was taken up in the **Children Act 2004** following the 2003 Laming Report (which followed the Victoria Climbié case) but the impact is not seen in the results since there continue to be similarly shocking child deaths where social services have long been involved and yet did not prevent them, for example that of 'Baby P'. Better safeguards for parents have received no such direct attention, other than in, perhaps, the failure of an attempt to use the opportunity of the CAFA 2014 to amend the threshold criteria in CA 1989 s 31[34] for taking children into care, following academic argument over a series of cases in the Supreme Court on the subject of potential future harm from a possible perpetrator, in which Baroness Hale has pointed out the obvious concerns about inappropriate intervention in such cases.[35]

Despite the extensive recommendations of the FJR (incorporated into CAFA 2014 and the amended FPR 2010 for the introduction of the Family Court in April 2014) the main Act governing the law of child protection remains the CA 1989, which has been further amended by CAFA 2014 (as it was by the CA 2004 after Lord Laming's post-Climbié inquiry). The policy objectives remain that parents should have primary responsibility for their children, who should be kept in their families unless this is against their best interests. Non-intervention is the cornerstone of CA 1989 and, if anything, this is strengthened by the FJR recommendations, which have really focused on the delay in determining child cases, which is addressed both in CAFA 2014 and in the FPR 2010

---

32 [2002] EWHC 1379 (Fam); [2002] 2 FLR 730.
33 (1987) Cm 412.
34 See Chapter 20 at 20.4.
35 This is discussed in Chapter 20 at 20.4.

by the requirement normally to complete all child cases within 26 weeks unless there is some justification for not doing so.

As Johnson J said in B v B (*A Minor*) (*Residence Order*) (1992):[36]

> It is inherent to the philosophy underlying the Children Act 1989 that Parliament has decreed that the State, whether in the guise of the local authority or the court, shall not intervene in the life of children and their families unless it is necessary to do so.

This principle is reinforced by CA 1989 s 1(5).[37] Additionally, an order is required to remove a child from its parents, an action which is taken very seriously so specific grounds must be satisfied to do so.

Local authorities are also required to work in partnership with parents as fully as possible in order to promote the presumption that children are best kept with their families.[38] Inter-agency cooperation is provided for in CA 1989 ss 27 and 47.[39]

19.3.1 Children Act 2004

The main provisions of this further legislation were a response to the death of Victoria Climbié, aged eight, from malnutrition and ill treatment, notwithstanding contact with social workers and other agencies. There was an Inquiry chaired by Lord Laming which found grave errors on the part of social services for failing to intervene.[40] The Report found the CA 1989 to be fundamentally sound but with gaps in the implementation and practice of child protection. The statute also created Children's Commissioners in each devolved area of the UK as well as in England.[41]

In response the government published the Green Paper *Every Child Matters*,[42] which proposed a range of measures to reform and improve children's care. There were five *Every Child Matters* ('ECM') outcomes:

- be healthy;
- stay safe;
- enjoy and achieve;
- make a positive contribution;
- achieve economic well-being.

A series of guidance documents was published to support local authorities and their partners in implementing the new statutory duties, including an overview of the 'ECM' programme.

The duty to cooperate between agencies is in CA 2004 s 10, which provides the underpinning framework for 'children's trusts', which were designed to bring together all services for children and young persons in a local authority area, supported by the s 10 duty to cooperate so as to focus on improving outcomes for all children and young people.

This was supposed to help all those who work every day with children, young people and their families to deliver better outcomes, so that children and young people experienced more integrated

---

36 [1992] 2 FLR 327.
37 See Chapter 12 at 12.2.4.
38 See the paper *Working Together to Safeguard Children*.
39 Absence of this was the problem in Re L above.
40 See the Laming Report, *Inquiry Into the Death of Victoria Climbié*, Cm 5730, January 2003.
41 The Children and Families Act 2014 also further strengthens their roles. They are supposed, for example, reactively to monitor UK compliance with the UNCRC and also proactively to look out for children's interests in law and practice.
42 HMSO 2003.

and responsive services, with specialist support embedded in the framework which was to be accessed through these universal services.

The concept was that people involved in the field would work together in effective multi-disciplinary teams, to be trained jointly to tackle cultural and professional divides, to use a multi-professional model where many different disciplines were involved, and to be co-located, often in extended schools or children's centres.

The conclusion must presumably be reached that this scheme neither delivered, nor seemed in future likely to deliver improved services, since there have still been scandalous child deaths reaching the popular as well as the legal press,[43] finally becoming a prime focus of the FJR, whose Final Report majored in recommendations to tackle the child protection area of family justice. This may well be because amongst the 'grave errors' found by the 2003 Laming Inquiry were organisational and management problems, which would not necessarily be touched by the interdisciplinary training requiring the police, NHS, the new Safeguarding Authority, the Sure Start teams, Cafcass, and those concerned with youth offender work to cooperate, since it appears that one reason for missing children at risk is under-resourcing, which is now likely to be even worse affected everywhere following subsequent nationwide cuts in both central and local government funding.

It may thus be that the child protection provisions of CA 1989[44] will still be the strongest shelter from harm for children after all, even if the last resort, since it seems that the framework conceived by the 2004 Act was not in practice sustainable without adequate resourcing, which was not forthcoming owing to economic restraints and ongoing reductions in public services[45] – as Lord Laming expressly stated in his second report in 2009, *Protection of Children in England: A Progress Report*,[46] that not enough had been done to make his 2003 reforming recommendations a reality.

Meanwhile the FJR has recommended better, and faster, processing of court applications when social services do intervene, and there is a new Public Law Outline, coinciding with the inauguration of the unified Family Court launched in April 2014, which aims to achieve a routine 26-week completion for all such cases unless they are in some way exceptional.[47]

19.4 Current debates

Ideas for research on these current discussions may be found on the companion website updates.

- Was it worth keeping wardship?
- Have CA 2004 and CAFA 2014 now significantly improved public law child protection?
- To what extent should state intervention in families happen at all?

19.5 Summary of Chapter 19
Wardship, the inherent jurisdiction and the CA 1989

- These three jurisdictions conveniently co-exist and in practice remain useful for their respective purposes despite the consolidation of most child law in the CA 1989.

---

43 E.g. the ongoing saga of the death of Baby P despite many apparent alerts which social services failed to act on, and the subsequently long drawn out disciplinary process in the social services of the relevant London Borough.
44 See Chapter 20.
45 A statute book for perusal of the precise provisions of Parts 1 to 4 is essential for an understanding of the ambitious nature of this framework.
46 Available from the Stationery Office.
47 See Chapter 20 at 20.1 and 20.7.1 where it is more convenient to deal with this topic in further detail.

- The statute provides a flexible framework for most orders, was inspired by the wardship jurisdiction, but delivers its remedies at a more cost-effective level, especially since orders are now obtained in the unified Family Court.
- Wardship is simply a sub-division of the non-statutory High Court inherent jurisdiction derived from the common law, and both wardship and the inherent jurisdiction's more general powers may be used when no convenient statutory framework is applicable.
- Wardship, although derived from the inherent jurisdiction, is now in fact statutory pursuant to the Senior Courts Act 1985 (formerly the Supreme Court Act 1981).

Wardship or the CA 1989?

- Normally the CA 1989 is used where possible, but some cases are more suitable to wardship, e.g. kidnapping, adoption, preventing undesirable associations, emergencies, and where ongoing supervision is required.
- Local authorities can use wardship (even if they cannot obtain a care order) if requiring the supervisory aspect of wardship.

The inherent jurisdiction

- This is very suitable for medical cases, especially if urgent or complex (e.g. the conjoined twins, Re A (Children) (2001).[48]
- It can also be used by the local authority when wardship is not available pursuant to CA 1989 s 100.

State intervention

- The policy is non-intervention by the state unless a child will come to harm without it.
- The 2003 Laming Report recommendations (enacted in CA 2004 to address continued failings leading to unnecessary child deaths owing to social service shortcomings) generated the strengthened child protection function of local authorities and other agencies; however, the 2009 Laming Report identified insufficient resources to make his reforms a reality.

19.6 Further reading

Bailey-Harris, R and Harris, M, 'Local authorities and child protection: the mosaic of accountability', (2002) CFLQ 14: 117.

Bridge, C, 'Religion, culture and conviction: the medical treatment of young children', (1999) CFLQ 11: 1.

Brophy, J, 'Child maltreatment and diverse households', (2008) *Journal of Law and Society* 35: 75.

Fortin, J, *Children's Rights and the Developing Law*, London, Butterworths, 2009.

Masson, J et al, *Protecting Powers: Emergency Intervention for Children's Protection*, Oxford, John Wiley & Sons, 2007.

Mitchell, J, 'Whatever Happened to Wardship?', [2001] 21 Fam Law 355.

---

48 [2001] Fam 147, CA.

Seymour, J, *Childbirth and the Law*, Oxford, OUP, 2000.
Welstead, M and Edwards, S, *Family Law*, Oxford, OUP, 2013.
www.childrenscommissioner.gov.uk, Children's Commissioner for England.
https://www.gov.uk/government/organisations/department-for-education
www.every-child-matters.org.uk

Chapter 20

Care, Supervision and Protection Orders

Chapter Contents

Learning outcomes for this chapter

A sound understanding of the operation of child protection under the CA 1989 including:

(i)   An appreciation of

    (a) the tension and dividing line between the mutually exclusive principles of family autonomy and state intervention;

    (b) the philosophy of the partnership of local authority and parents underpinning Part III of the Act.

(ii)   An awareness of the minimalist approach to the range of remedies in Parts IV and V.

(iii)   An ability to apply

    (a) the 31 criteria in circumstances which may dictate a care or supervision order;

    (b) the welfare checklist to decide whether such an order, and if so which, should be granted;

    (c) the local authority's guidance on when a child assessment or emergency protection order should be applied for and if so which.

(iv)   An awareness of the difference between family proceedings in child law and other civil litigation.

20.1 Introduction

Under Part III of the CA 1989 local authorities were placed under a duty to provide support for children in need and their families. The aim of these provisions, highly innovative in 1989, was to obviate the need for care or supervision proceedings at all unless essential. This ethos is an integral feature of the statute because of the accepted undesirability of state interference in the family's personal autonomy – otherwise unavoidable in such proceedings. However, as this must be balanced with the necessity for state-provided child protection, there is inevitably a tension between the two principles of such protection and non-intervention.

Thus this is an area of law and practice where the CA 1989 Part III has effected major changes, although they naturally do not seem so novel now a quarter of a century later – nevertheless, they did at the time, in contrast to the former approach of the law which was towards aggressively proactive removal of children from parents perceived as inadequate.

The key sections of the Part III 'non-intervention' provisions[1] are found in CA 1989 ss 17, 20 and 22–23, together with ss 27 and 47 which require inter-agency cooperation in furtherance of the underlying principle of Part III to provide services and support for families where possible. One of the first major changes made by the CA 1989 was introducing the concept of a working partnership between the local authority and the child's parents to promote the child's welfare – instead of (as formerly) the local authority's simply taking into care every child not being properly looked after (and usually resisting the return of that child to its apparently inadequate parents).

As a result, the local authority is now statutorily compelled by CA 1989 s 17(1) 'to safeguard and promote the welfare of children within its area who are in need', and (so far as it is consistent with that general duty) to 'promote the upbringing of children by their families, by providing a range and level of services appropriate to those children's needs'. It should be noted that the provision of services is discretionary only and will depend on local authority policy and resources.

---

1 Mostly in Part III, although s 47 is not, since it belongs with the protection powers of the state, which are in Parts IV and V.

It should also, of course, be noted that these high ideals have not worked to provide the necessary protection and that one reason that has been advanced is that the various responsible agencies which need to contribute to holistic child protection have not managed to work together in a cooperative manner;[2] as a result the local authority has sometimes been unable to work satisfactorily with parents, and children have still died unnecessarily, sometimes in terrible circumstances.

The CA 2004 sought to address these deficiencies following the (first) Laming Report,[3] but nevertheless it appears that this was still not enough to stop the deaths of children where the family *was* in touch with various social workers.

It should, however, be noted that despite the horrific aspects of these incidents there is routinely a large number of cases where local authority intervention *does* achieve good or satisfactory results,[4] so that it appears that the system is not entirely inherently deficient and that failures have probably been rightly blamed on human error and resources.

Nevertheless, the statutory framework means there remains, every day, a difficult decision for a local authority to make: to interfere or not to interfere, including how long to continue to hope to educate and train parents rather than to use the more powerful statutory provisions to remove children from them.[5] This is what s 47 is for: the provision for the authority to hold a holistic multi-agency investigation to determine whether intervention should take place.[6]

'Family' is defined in CA 1989 s 17(10) as including any person who has PR for the child and any other person with whom he has been living. Services for such families can only be provided with a view to safeguarding or promoting the welfare of a child in need: s 17(3). A 'child in need' may be one of three types defined in s 17(10):

STATUTORY EXTRACT

CA 1989 s 17(10) states:

'(a) he is unlikely to achieve or to maintain, or to have the opportunity of achieving or maintaining, a reasonable standard of health or development without the provision for him of services by the local authority under this Part;

(b) his health or development is likely to be significantly impaired, or further impaired, without the provision for him of such services; or

(c) he is disabled.'

And

' "family", in relation to such a child, includes any person who has parental responsibility for the child and any other person with whom he has been living.'

For the purposes of s 17 a child is disabled if he is blind, deaf or dumb, suffers from any kind of mental disorder or is substantially and permanently handicapped by illness, injury or congenital

---

2 Some such agencies confessed as much to Lord Laming when he worked on his 2009 second report, *Protection of Children in England*, to which his response as reported to the media was 'Then do it now.'
3 See Chapter 19.
4 The FJR notes that for these children 'care works', *Final Report* para 3.24.
5 Professor Peter de Cruz examines this difficult dividing line in De Cruz, P, 'The Conundrum of Child Abuse Investigation: Will we ever get it right?', (2011) 2 FLP 2: 5. This online journal is no longer published but the entire archive is available at www.frburton.com, and its successor, *International Family Law, Policy and Practice*, at www.famlawandpractice.com.
6 See further 20.6.3 below.

deformity: s 17(11) states that 'development' includes physical, intellectual, emotional, social or behavioural development and 'health' includes both mental and physical health.

The general duty in s 17 is fleshed out by further responsibilities set out in CA 1989 Schedule 2.

The range of services includes a duty under s 20 to provide temporary accommodation, as an alternative to the former duty of provision of care or supervision under a formal order.

This significant shift of emphasis underlines the change in the character of the local authority, which is thus transformed by the CA 1989, in theory at least, from ogre to fairy godmother.

This softer and more creative approach to child protection had its origins in the government White Paper, *The Law on Child Care and Family Services*.[7]

Clearly there are times when a family may need help, such as when a parent dies or cannot care for a child for some reason which falls short of justification for a care or other more intrusive order.

Section s 17(6) of CA 1989 is thus the source of a *power* to provide accommodation for a child in need while s 20(1) sets out certain circumstances in which the local authority *must* provide accommodation for the child: namely where no one has PR for him, where he is lost or abandoned, or where the person who has been caring for him is unable to provide appropriate accommodation or care (whether permanently or not) but both are Part III, supporting, not Parts IV to V, protective control.

Therefore whenever the local authority accommodates a child in this way – in the absence of a care order engaging different statutory provisions – the arrangement is voluntary so that the local authority must comply with the wishes of all those with PR, unless the child is suffering significant harm, in which case the local authority should seek a care or supervision order.

The CA 1989 also abolished the former status of voluntary *care*, together with the former power to assume 'parental rights' over the child in voluntary care by administrative resolution, and saving post-1989 'care' for the ss 31–32 protective control.

Children in voluntary s 20 accommodation, or informally in the authority's care for more than 24 hours, have thus since the implementation of CA 1989 been referred to as 'looked after': s 22(1) and s 105(4).

Moreover, by s 20(6), before providing accommodation a local authority must ascertain the wishes of the child (if he is old enough). This provision foreshadowed a major upgrading of the importance of the 'voice of the child' in all contemporary child law and practice, which (although it appeared in the UNCRC) owes its current high-profile significance to the ongoing development of the once novel approach of the CA 1989.

20.2 The approach of Parts III to V of the CA 1989

While this once novel approach was obviously overall a significant change, there are clearly circumstances in which all the authority's help and assistance does not work in practical terms.

If it does not look as though there will be any improvement before the child suffers actual *harm*, inadequate parents can still expect either to lose control of the child through formal care proceedings under ss 31–32, or possibly initially through an emergency protection order (EPO) under s 44.

Alternatively, they may at least suffer the imposition of a s 35 supervision order, which, while not bestowing PR on the local authority (and therefore perhaps less interventionist than a care order and for that reason often chosen in preference by the court) will still usually enable the local authority to help the child, effectively by placing the limits around decisions in relation to the child which the parents have manifestly failed to do.

---

7 Cm 62, 1987, para 21.

To facilitate decisions in this respect, the CA 1989 created a new child assessment order under s 43 (CAO but distinct from the new private law s 8 order[8]) which enables the local authority to obtain possession of the child for assessment purposes when parents will not cooperate. However, the philosophy of the statute is that these stages should only be reached after other methods have failed. Parents whose children's 'need' is noticed by the local authority are thus always advised to cooperate, since the authority's powers are subject to its obligations; if parents can demonstrate that any child care inadequacies are not deliberate but result from ignorance or poor resources, and above all lack of awareness of the actual or potential harm caused, care orders should be avoided at least temporarily and the onus thrown onto the local authority to honour its obligation to help.

20.3 The local authority's duty to accommodate: s 20

This s 20 duty is significantly different from formal 'care' and arises where s 20(1)(a) to (c) applies, i.e. where there is no one with PR for the child, or the child is lost or abandoned, or temporarily without care from his family.

A local authority which 'looks after' a child in these circumstances is under a general duty, set out in s 22(3):

(a)   to safeguard and promote his welfare; and
(b)   to make such use of services available for children cared for by their own parents as appears to the authority to be reasonable in his case.

Under s 23 they have more extensive duties:

- to maintain the child in other respects as well as accommodating him: s 23(1)(b);
- to do so by placing him with his family or a relative or any other suitable person on such terms as they may determine; or
- maintaining him in a children's home: s 23(2)(a) and (aa).

If he is placed with any person rather than a parent, person with PR or someone who previously had a residence order or CAO under s 23(2)(a) that will be with a local authority foster parent: s 23(3).

A child so accommodated can be removed by any person with PR at any time without formality, including without giving any notice: s 20(8).

There are two exceptions:

(1)   where a person with a CAO or old-style care and control order made in the exercise of the High Court's inherent jurisdiction (i.e. what is technically called in the statute 'an existing order') agrees to the child being looked after by the local authority: s 20(9), though if there is more than one such person all of them must agree: s 20(10); and
(2)   where a child over age 16 agrees personally: s 20(11).

20.3.1 Retaining an 'accommodated' child

If the local authority objects to removal of a child informally accommodated it has two choices, and must apply to the court for:

---

8 See Chapter 16.

- a formal care order – then satisfying the statutory grounds under s 31; or
- an EPO, which is for when the case is urgent: s 44(1).

The local authority must consider the child's wishes (or such wishes as they are able to ascertain, having regard to the child's age and understanding) wherever possible before providing the child with accommodation: s 20(6).

If the child is over 16, any decision to accept accommodation from the local authority lies with the child:

- regardless of the child's parents' wishes: s 20(11); and
- regardless of whether the local authority can accommodate the child: s 20(4).

There are thus now two distinct categories of children:

- those with a formal care order; and
- those voluntarily in local authority accommodation for more than 24 hours.

The local authority which accommodates a child informally must act as a good parent, taking account of the child's wishes as well as those of its parents and anyone else with PR, *before* taking any decisions about the child: s 22.

They must also take account of the child's religion, racial origin and cultural and linguistic background.

By s 24(1), the authority also has a duty to 'advise, assist and befriend' the child, with a view to promoting its welfare when s/he ceases to be looked after by the authority. There is a statutory presumption that the authority must if possible make arrangements to enable the child to live with one of the following:

(a) a parent;
(b) any person with PR, or who had it immediately before a formal care order was made; or
(c) a relative, friend or person connected with the child, unless none of these solutions would be reasonably practical or consistent with its welfare: s 23(6).

20.3.2 The authority's duties: welfare, reviews and contact

It should also be noted that there is a general duty on the authority to safeguard and promote the child's welfare and to make such use of services available for children cared for by their own parents as appears to the authority reasonable in any particular child's case.

Moreover, the statute requires the authority to conduct a general review at regular intervals of the progress of each child, so that the whole emphasis is on keeping children in their own families wherever possible.

If this is impossible, there is a duty to promote contact, so far as is practicable, and consistent with the child's welfare, between the child and its parents, or those with PR, or with any person with whom the child is 'connected'.[9] By s 34(1), where the child is subject to a care order, there is a presumption that the child should have contact with such persons, though other persons (e.g. grandparents, and brothers and sisters) must obtain leave to apply to be named in any contact order, which can be made at the same time as the making of a full care order or later: s 34(10).

---

9 See Schedules 4 and 2 respectively.

Obviously, sometimes contact will be inadvisable (e.g. in cases of sexual abuse), in which case either contact can be on conditions: s 34(7), or the authority (but only the authority) can apply for such contact to be prohibited: s 34(4). Contact can, where appropriate, also be refused altogether as a matter of urgency and for no more than seven days: s 34(1). All such orders would of course be discharged when the formal care order was discharged, whereupon an ordinary s 8 order, for example a CAO giving residence to some named person, might be made instead: s 10.

Where the child is not subject to a care order the local authority has limited powers to restrict contact, in which case s 3(5) may be its only power, i.e. to do what is reasonable as in the case of any person without PR who has care of a child.

20.3.3 Challenging the authority's accommodation decisions

The local authority's duty 'to accommodate' under this section does not normally extend as far as re-housing a family, but in an early judicial review case the authority's decision simply to adapt the existing accommodation of a severely disabled child rather than to re-house him together with his mother and brother was criticised for asking the wrong questions and not obtaining enough information to reach a reasonable decision: Re C (1999)[10] (unreported). There is always the possibility of judicial review of the authority's decisions.

❖ **CASE EXAMPLES**

In Re T (1995)[11] it was held that a decision not to accommodate could be challenged by judicial review.

In R v Thameside Borough Council ex p H (1999)[12] it was held that the authority should not have moved a severely disabled 13-year-old from accommodation near her parents to a foster home much further away, despite their objections, as this 'trespassed into the area of PR'.

In R (G) v Barnet London Borough Council, R(W) v Lambeth London Borough Council and R(A) v Lambeth London Borough Council (2003)[13] the House of Lords considered the scope of the duty in s 17(1) and raised questions of whether social services departments were obliged to provide accommodation for children in need and their families when the local housing authority could not house them. The House dismissed all three appeals and held that housing was a function of the local housing authority and they did not have to provide it if they did not have resources.

Thus the informal status of a child 'looked after' by the local authority is entirely distinct from a formal care order and the 'looked after' status cannot slide imperceptibly into the formal 'care' status. Local authorities who try to effect that are pulled up sharply by the judiciary.

---

10 Unreported, 30 November 1999.
11 [1995] 1 FLR 159.
12 (1999) The Times, 22 October.
13 [2003] UKHL 57; [2004] 1 FLR 454.

❖ **CASE EXAMPLE**

In *R(G) v Nottingham City Council* (2008)[14] (a very clear example of such a 'no snatch' case) Munby, J, as he then was,[15] on judicial review, returned a newborn child to the 18-year-old drug-abusing (also alcoholic and self-harming) mother where no order had been made to justify the medical team peremptorily taking the child away, because no judicial order had been made.

Despite the mother's obvious unsuitability to care for the child the judge held that the only time when such an action might be justified was when the child was otherwise going to suffer immediate harm from violence from the parent or another person. This was despite the fact that in due course an interim care order was made later that same day (which was upheld by the Court of Appeal).

Later still the child was again returned to its family by placing it in foster care with the mother – the local authority of course retaining PR alongside the mother pursuant to the interim care order – but as this did not ultimately work a further order for no contact for a limited period was then made.

Nevertheless the judge had made his point: a judicial order is required for social workers to remove a child.

20.4 Formal care orders: CA 1989, ss 31 and 33

Where the stage is reached that the optimum outcome of the local authority voluntarily working in partnership with parents under Part III is not working, the local authority may finally have to intervene and have recourse to the Part IV care or supervision order and/or the Part V emergency orders, for example an EPO. Care and supervision orders are not the same although both have to satisfy the same criteria, articulated in s 31 in terms of 'harm'.

Where a formal care order is applied for, there is a two-stage process: first, the local authority must satisfy the statutory criteria in s 31, and then the welfare principle must be applied.

In stage 1, the threshold criteria, the court must be satisfied that both:

(a)   the child is suffering, or is likely to suffer, significant harm; and
(b)   the harm, or the likelihood of harm, is attributable to:

- the care being given to the child, or likely to be given to the child if the order is not made;
- not being what it would be reasonable to expect a parent to give the child; or
- the child's being beyond parental control.

---

14 [2008] EWHC 152; [2008] 1 FLR 1660.
15 Now Munby P, President of the Family Division, and currently promoting the programme of transparency in Family Court decisions detailed in his recent 'Views from the President's Chambers' and in the resulting PD referred to in Chapter 1, an initiative well known to have been generated by his dislike of the media's misinterpretation of some family judges' decisions, whereas in fact the family judiciary has always been quick to make clear to social workers that their powers of state intervention, however well meant as protective of children, are not unlimited without judicial sanction.

These criteria in (a) and (b) are cumulative and must both be satisfied.

'Harm' means ill treatment or impairment of health and development: s 31(9).

The definition of 'ill treatment' includes both sexual abuse and non-physical ill treatment. Since the ACA 2002 s 120 came into force on 31 January 2005, clarifying the definition of harm in s 31(9), this now also means impairment of health and development as a result of witnessing the ill treatment of another person, as in domestic violence.

'Impairment' is not defined in the 1989 or 2002 Acts but should carry its normal meaning of damage or weakening. Development means the whole range of physical, intellectual, emotional, social or behavioural development.

The meaning of 'significant' harm is not laid down in CA 1989 or any other statute, but has been the subject of some consideration in case law.

❖ CASE EXAMPLES

In *Re MA (Children) (Care Proceedings: Threshold Criteria)* (2009)[16] the Court of Appeal considered that the dividing line must be where the harm was such that it could be said that state intervention was justified, disturbing the autonomy of the parents to bring up the child as they chose, so as to enable the court to make a care or supervision order if the welfare of the child required that.

They considered that Article 8 of the ECHR (the right to family life) also informed the meaning, but Wall LJ preferred the ordinary dictionary meaning, i.e. 'considerable, noteworthy or important'.

The court's problem in this case was that they acknowledged that the distinction was a fine one and that as it happened the decision as to the nature of the harm could, as in many ordinary family cases, have gone either way, so that (per Hallett LJ) it was 'a classic case for trusting the judgment of the trial judge'.

For this reason it is usually difficult to disturb the discretion of the judge who sees the parties and forms a view in the case before him, which cannot usually be replicated by an appellate court, at some distance from the initial hearing.

In *Re L (Care: Threshold Criteria)* (2007)[17] Hedley J held that it was not the task of the state to protect children from the consequences of all defective parenting, so 'significant harm' must be something out of the ordinary, more than commonplace human failure or inadequacy.

The meaning of 'likely' has also come under scrutiny.[18]

The harm is that which is suffered immediately before the authority was involved, so that an abandoned newborn baby who is rescued is likely to have suffered significant harm within the meaning of the section immediately before rescue and older children who are then taken into foster care will also have suffered such harm immediately before their removal: see the House of Lords

---

16 [2009] EWCA Civ 853.
17 [2007] 1 FLR 20.
18 See below in connection with *Re H* [1996] AC 563 80, HL.

discussion in *Re M (A Minor) (Care Order)* (1994),[19] where the father had murdered the mother in front of the children and the argument was that as the children had immediately been taken into the protection of the local authority they could not be suffering harm by the time the care hearing came up. Lord Mackay rejected this reading of the circumstances and decided that the harm had occurred at the date at which the local authority had initiated the protective procedure.[20]

It does not matter if it cannot be established which of two parents is responsible for harm if that cannot be decided, provided the court is satisfied that both parents are a danger to the child. It has been held in some cases that this should be considered at the welfare stage on the basis that any of the possible perpetrators could be responsible, but in *Re S-B* (2009)[21] it was held that if it is not clear who was responsible a simple balance of probabilities test should be applied, although the court should not strain to identify the perpetrator if they know who is in the pool of likely culprits.

❖ CASE EXAMPLE

In *Re B and W* (1992),[22] B, a seven-month-old, was twice in hospital with shaking injuries which could have been caused by either parent or by the childminder. At first instance the judge could not decide who had caused the injuries. On appeal the court decided it was not necessary to determine which part of the care network had broken down, but since unsatisfactory care was established on the part of B's parents, this was sufficient for s 31. However, a care order for the childminder's child, W, was refused as there was insufficient causal connection between the facts of B's case and the likelihood of harm to W, since it was uncertain whether W's mother had injured B or not.

In stage 2 the court must then consider:

- s 1(1) welfare;
- s 1(3) checklist;
- s 1(2) delay; and
- s 1(5) non-interventionist policy.[23]

It will thus be seen that obtaining a new-style care order is a demanding task for the local authority, although if the basis for an order is there, hairs will not be split, for instance over whether a truanting child is beyond parental control or that the parents did not give the child reasonable care.[24]

The standard of proof of the threshold criteria was earlier said to be not as high as on a balance of probabilities because the court is dealing with predictions (i.e. a significant likelihood or 'real possibility', and not mere suspicion) – this is the suggested yardstick since the court is dealing with the protection of a child: *Re H (Minors) (Child Abuse: Threshold Conditions)* (1996),[25] in which it was held

---

19 [1994] 2 FLR 577.
20 See Grand, A, 'Working together after *Re M*', (1995) Fam Law 26, which criticises this case, pointing out the wide implications.
21 See below. This case is one of those which led to an attempt to amend the s 31 criteria because of the ramifications of assessing the likelihood of harm from potential perpetrators in reconstituted families.
22 [1992] 2 FLR 833.
23 See Chapter 12.
24 See *Re O* [1992] 1 WLR 912.
25 [1996] AC 563, HL.

that suspicion was not enough and, if the harm was projected in the future rather than in the present, it must be really likely, 'a real possibility': per Lord Nicholls in that case. Unfortunately, a later comment hinting at a possibly higher standard of proof has confused readers about this decision, leading later judges to comment that Lord Nicholls, in explaining his 'real possibility', had been misinterpreted as there was only one standard of proof regardless of the seriousness of allegations.

This 1996 explanation was criticised and not followed (but not overruled in the case of Re B (Children) (Sexual Abuse: Standard of Proof) (2008),[26] where the House of Lords held that in relation to past facts the standard was 'the simple balance of probabilities, neither more nor less', with no gloss. This slightly modified approach to Lord Nicholls' 'real possibility' was not surprisingly upheld by Baroness Hale in Re S-B (Children) (2009),[27] when she said 'the law has drawn a clear distinction between probability as it applies to past facts and probability as it applies to future predictions ... so that future facts need only be based on the degree of likelihood that they will happen which is sufficient to justify preventive action', and that there must therefore be a 'pressing need' to remove children, since it was she who, in Re B, had led the House's declaration 'loud and clear' that the standard of proof in s 31(2) was the ordinary civil standard (i.e. balance of probabilities), and that this applied to the welfare stage considerations as well as to s 31(2) itself.

These two cases and Re J (2013),[28] which followed, were, however, the cause of the academic comment[29] which led to the attempt to amend s 31 to make it more explicit in relation to the likelihood of future harm from possible perpetrators where suspicions had not been substantiated in an earlier similar context. The three cases were similar in that nothing was proved against the possible perpetrators. In Re B Baroness Hale explained that it was unacceptable for children or parents to risk state intervention on the basis of unproved suspicions about possible past perpetration of harm. Action taken on suspicion alone would mean those suspected needed to prove that abuse had not happened! In Re J the local authority issued care proceedings in respect of three children only on the basis of suspicion that one adult in the household might have been the earlier perpetrator of harm to another child, and in any case there was no logical link between possible past perpetration and future likelihood of harm.

Nevertheless, even satisfying the threshold criteria under the existing s 31(2) is insufficient, as the local authority must also satisfy four sub-sections of s 1 listed above – particularly the welfare principle and the checklist which includes as the final head 'the range of the court's powers'.[30]

❖ CASE EXAMPLE

In Re FS (1996)[31] the judge weighed the risk of further sexual abuse in a case where the father's conduct had already satisfied the s 31 criteria against the emotional harm to the other children if the father were removed. He originally therefore made a supervision order but this was replaced on appeal by a sole residence order in favour of the mother, coupled with an undertaking by the father not to visit the home without the mother's written consent.

---

26 [2008] UKHL 35; [2008] 2 FLR 141.
27 [2009] UKSC 17.
28 Re J (Care Proceedings: Possible Perpetrators) [2013] UKSC9.
29 See Gilmore, S, Re J (Care Proceedings: Past Possible Perpetrators in a New Family Unit) [2013] UKSC9: 'Bulwarks and logic – the blood that runs through the veins of law – but how much will be spilled in future?', [2013] CFLQ 215; Hayes, M, 'The Supreme Court's failure to protect vulnerable children: Re J (Children)', [2013] Fam Law 1015.
30 See Chapters 12 and 15.
31 [1996] 2 FLR 158.

If necessary, an interim order will be made pending investigation or further consideration, and this is common as it enables the court to maintain the *status quo* pending the final hearing while further inquiries are made. This is obviously a useful 'holding' step, although the order can only be made for eight weeks: s 38(4)(a). Care of the child passes to the local authority as soon as the interim order is made and conditions under s 38(6) and (7) may be imposed. This includes imposing duties on a local authority to fund a residential assessment of the parents and child, thus compelling the authority to allocate resources where an assessment has been identified by the local authority as being appropriate in a case.

A care order operates like a private law former residence order or new CAO under s 13(1) to prevent change of the child's surname or removal from the jurisdiction for more than a month: s 33. This also enables the authority to decide to what extent the parents shall exercise their PR, as the parents will retain this although the local authority also obtains it with their care order.

The authority will also have to produce a s 34(1) care plan, which they must keep under review, although the court can still make an order (even a final order) even if there is no care plan, and the new Public Law Outline has amended the extent to which the court must now consider the care plan and in particular which parts of it they should consider and which may be omitted, laying more emphasis on the core parts and less on those which are of a more ancillary nature. Often the plan can place the child with the extended family.

The court must then consider contact which is dealt with under s 34(11). Reasonable contact is presumed by s 34(1) to be likely with parents, anyone else with PR, any guardian and anyone who had a prior residence order or CAO, although this can be denied for up to seven days, if necessary as a matter of urgency to promote or safeguard the child's welfare: s 34(6). The local authority needs to take some care when refusing contact, however, if relying on the safeguarding ground. The effect of a care order is set out in s 33.

❖ CASE EXAMPLES

In *R v Cannings* (2004)[32] three of the defendant's four children had died in early infancy. There was serious disagreement between the experts about the cause of death. The Court of Appeal Criminal Division quashed the defendant's conviction and stated that where deaths continued to be unexplained and there was nothing to demonstrate a deliberate infliction of harm in the criminal process concerned, 'the deaths could not properly be treated as cause by unlawful violence'.

In *Re U (Serious Injury: Standard of Proof)* and *Re B* (2004)[33] (two cases heard sequentially) there were general issues involved about the standard of proof to be applied in care proceedings based on allegations of serious harm in view of the impact of the decision in *R v Cannings*.

It was held that the standard of proof in cases under the CA 1989 was that articulated by Lord Nicholls in *Re H* (i.e. that the burden of proof was on the applicant – the local authority – and that the parents were not to be at risk of having the child taken away on the basis of suspicion, whether of the judge, local authority or anyone else).

---

32 [2004] EWCA Crim 1; [2004] 1 All ER 725.
33 [2004] EWCA Civ 567.

It was further held that the basis of the authority's responsibilities had not changed since the *Cannings* case, so that the local authority's case should be prepared upon the civil standard as set out in *Re H*. (Now, of course, *Re S-B* and *Re B* should be factored in to this principle, in that Lord Nicholls' suggestion of the existence of a higher civil standard of proof is not now relevant, and indeed Baroness Hale has clarified this further in *Re J* (2013).)

An alternative to a care order, if the court does not think that the stage 2 welfare considerations support such an order, is a s 35 supervision order. This requires the same statutory grounds to be made out but is less intrusive.

It usually lasts for a year, unless extended. An extension can be made by the court but cannot prolong the order beyond three years from the date it was first made. Thus a fresh application will need to be made if the order is to continue. The supervising officer does not acquire PR as the purpose of the order is only to provide a degree of supervision, including specifying living arrangements, activities to be engaged in, and some positive help in the form of the requirement to 'advise, assist and befriend': s 35(1).

However, as a further alternative, a care order can always be varied or discharged and this is governed by s 39(1), otherwise the order will remain in force until the child is 18 unless determined earlier: s 91(12).

20.5 Supervision order: s 35

As the same criteria must be satisfied for the imposition of both care and supervision orders, the local authority will have to justify the imposition of the more draconian care order where a supervision order would suffice.

The court can decide which is appropriate regardless of which was applied for, and is most likely to be influenced by the crucial differences (e.g. whether it is necessary for the local authority to have PR for the child), since supervision, while sitting well with the non-interventionist principle, will not carry PR which the authority might want for control.

The court must also decide whether it is necessary for the order to last for the child's remaining minority, since a supervision order has a limited life, even with renewal, of three years, after which there would have to be another application.[34] Proportionality is usually the key to the decision.

❖ CASE EXAMPLES

In *Re O (Supervision Order)* (2001)[35] the court ordered the children to remain at home under a supervision order rather than the care order made at first instance, and said the order must be proportionate to the legitimate aim.

In *Re C and Re B (Care Order: Future Harm)* (2001)[36] the court balanced the risks of future harm to two of the four children involved against the local authority's duty to support and

---

34 See per Hale LJ in Oxfordshire County Council v L [1998] 1 FLR 70.
35 [2001] 1 FLR 923, CA.
36 [2001] 1 FLR 611.

attempt to reunite the family unless the risks were so high that there was no alternative to a care order, especially as Art 8 of the ECHR emphasises that intervention must be proportionate to a legitimate aim.

In *Re T (Care Order)* (2009)[37] the Court of Appeal recognised that the two reasons for preferring a care order were usually that it carried PR for the local authority and also permitted the authority to plan for the long term, although the latter could also be done through the application of the authority's obligation to provide services, so that it was not a reason alone for the more draconian order. In this case the authority did not want a care order and the Court of Appeal upheld their view that the stronger order was not necessary, not least as this was supported by all parties including the children's guardian.

In *Re H (A Child)* (2008)[38] a supervision and residence order was substituted for a care order as the child's wish to be with her mother, and her distress at separation, had not been given sufficient weight by the trial judge, who had not given enough consideration to the aim of retaining the child in her family if at all possible.

A further distinction from a care order is that a supervision order cannot have conditions imposed because they do not fit into the supervision order framework, but a supervision order may nevertheless be more appropriate in a case where there is a need to develop a working relationship with the parents and that is already going well.

Both care and supervision orders are 'family proceedings' for the purposes of CA 1989 s 8(3) so that the court can make any other family proceedings order regardless of what has originally been applied for, even of its own motion.

20.6 Emergency orders: ss 43 and 44

The principal orders in this category are the CAO: s 43, and the EPO: s 44.

20.6.1 Child assessment order: s 43

The child assessment order (CAO[39]) is designed to enable the authority to obtain physical access to the child whom it suspects is being abused or neglected. This is in order to establish what protection steps are necessary, and is used where the parents refuse to cooperate (e.g. by not making the child available for a medical assessment). Application has to be on full notice and the court must be satisfied that:

(a) the applicant has reasonable cause to suspect that the child is suffering, or is likely to suffer, significant harm;

(b) an assessment of the state of the child's health or development, or of the way in which he or she is being treated, is required to enable the applicant to establish whether or not he or she is suffering, or is likely to suffer, significant harm; and

---

37 [2009] EWCA Civ 121; [2009] 2 FLR 574.
38 [2008] EWCA Civ 1245; [2009] 2 FLR 55.
39 But note this acronym CAO has also been adopted for the new Child Arrangements Order which has now replaced the former separate orders for residence and contact, so that the context should show which one (s 8 private law order or s 43 public law order) is referred to in the particular instance.

(c)   it is unlikely that the assessment will be made, or be satisfactory, without a Child Assessment Order.

As usual the court must have regard to s 1(1), 1(2), 1(3) and s 1(5).

The maximum time for assessment is seven days: s 43(5). The order has no effect on PR. It merely requires production of the child for assessment and requires the person in a position to produce the child to comply with any other terms of the order. The order makes provision for contact between the child and the persons connected with the child: s 43(9) and (10), although it may not be necessary to remove the child from its home.

It should be noted that if the child is of an age to do so, he or she personally may refuse to consent. Both the child and the parents or those with PR may always apply for the order to be varied or discharged.

20.6.2 Emergency protection order: s 44

The emergency protection order (EPO) is for really serious urgent circumstances where the local authority and/or the NSPCC is investigating a child's significantly worrying circumstances, their enquiries are being frustrated and they believe that access to the child is needed as a matter of urgency. The court can direct any person in a position to do so to comply with any request to produce the child to the applicant: s 44(4)(a). The court can also authorise removal of him or her from any hospital or other place where the child is being accommodated immediately prior to the order: s 44(4)(b).

Anyone having this order has PR, but contact can be directed by the court and the applicant is under the general duty to allow contact with the usual person(s) who should be allowed to see the child. The maximum duration of the order is eight days: s 45(1). However, the order can be challenged by the child, or the child's parents, or those with PR: s 45(8). However, this cannot be done before the expiry of 72 hours from the time the order was made, nor if the challenger had notice of the hearing and was present at it: s 45(11).

Other than this, there is no appeal against the grant or refusal of an EPO: s 45(10). If the applicant returns the child because it appears to be safe to do so and then suffers a change of mind, the child may be removed again as long as the original order is still running, i.e. its validity is still within the initial eight days or the permissible seven days of extension: s 44(10) and (12) and s 45(1) and (6). A court can make an immediate care order when the EPO comes to an end, if the 'cogency of the evidence is commensurate with the gravity of the allegations'.[40]

20.6.3 Addressing the deficiencies of the system

This account is of necessity brief, providing an outline only of the principles involved. This is because, besides much case law in this subject area, which is often the province of specialist practitioners on the Law Society Child Panels and specialist counsel at the Family Bar, there is an enormous amount of detail involved in public child law which is excessive for this book.

There are also other orders apart from the two main remedies when immediate protection is required: for example the police protection order under s 46, or the s 50 recovery order. These respectively permit the police to take ad hoc charge of a child for a limited period in appropriate circumstances, in which they have an obligation to notify the local authority and the parents: s 46, and under s 50 enable the retrieval of a child who has been unlawfully removed from police protection or from a place where the child should be pursuant to an EPO.

---

40 Re P [1996] 1 FLR 482.

Further detail of these orders may be obtained from a specialist practitioner text.[41] The above outline account of the impact of the public law sections of the statute which sometimes affect private law provisions is, however, important so as to flag up and understand the potential problems parents may face if they do not cooperate with the local authority in appropriate circumstances.

In general terms, especially if parents were not aware of any ill treatment (e.g. by a relative acting as childminder who appeared to be treating the child well), it is highly unlikely that any steps would be taken other than gentle informal supervision, provided that the parents then cooperated fully and took swift and decisive action to prevent the situation continuing, once it had been brought to their notice.

However, as precedent strictly has no application in family law other than as a guide to previous decisions in similar cases, it is always open to the court to make its own decision as to whether the local authority's view should be biased towards its duty to care and provide services for children and their families or towards its protective role.

One disadvantage of the legislation is that there is no power in the court to require the local authority to apply for orders, but only to direct it to investigate the child's circumstances under s 37 of the Act. But this is underpinned by the authority's obligations under s 47, formally setting out the local authority's duty to investigate where it is informed or discovers that there is a child in its area which is 'in need' and may[42] require protection. If the authority's internal inquiries under s 47 reveal that to be the case the authority is then obliged (1) to initiate protection proceedings, or (2) if it is revealed that the child and the family should instead be supported with services, to provide them, or (3) if there is no need for intervention at all because all is well, to do nothing.

Where the local authority has not initiated any s 47 inquiries already, s 37 provides a further potential safety net. The court may intervene if it is noticed that there may be a situation which requires such investigation: s 37 provides a formal power of the court to direct an investigation. Thus the two sections are complementary in effect although they provide different processes, neither of which involves any court application, although s 37 obliges the local authority to report its findings to the court, including whether it intends to take any proceedings, and, if not, if and when intends to review the case.

However, the main problem in the delivery of what appears on the face of it to be a creative and reasonably appropriate system of child protection is not necessarily the difficulty of deciding whether there should be state intervention or not in any particular case as this affects a minority of families and children: the real problem is the delay in the system in delivering appropriate decisions, i.e. in processing cases through the courts, when action does need to be taken.

Clearly delay of the magnitude that has been occurring, which has been ascribed to 'meltdown' in the family justice system, is in effect a denial of appropriate remedies. The FJR addressed this as a very serious defect. The Final Report accepts that 'the protection system is under great and increasing pressure' because of greatly increased case volumes and cases which have recently been taking increasingly longer (an average of 61 weeks in care centres and 48 weeks in FPCs, with an increase even in the six months between the Interim and Final Reports, and with 20,000 children at that time waiting for a public law decision).

The two FJR Reports do identify local authorities waiting too long before deciding to make an application to court to intervene, but also inconsistent quality of evidence, lack of confidence in local authority work, difficulties of providing court social work by Cafcass, multiple time-

---

41 Such as Hershman and Macfarlane (4 volumes) or the specialist academic text Bainham, A and Gilmore, S, Children: The Modern Law, Bristol, Jordan Publishing, 2013.

42 This seems to be where the local authority is falling down: once they have concerns or suspicions it seems to be time for a s 47 multi-party and multi-agency investigation, on which they should identify one of the three outcomes above; they have had enough guidance on how this should be done – though this may be one of the resource issues identified by Lord Laming.

consuming reports from expert witnesses, case management being ignored or not applied robustly by courts, and lack of capacity in 'all parts of the system'. They also emphasised the damage done by delay,[43] commenting that delay has become 'habitual', and further stressed concern about the cost to the state of public law cases (nearly £1.1 billion in 2009/10, the year before the Final Report of November 2011).

The FJR proposals to address these problems, which have been adopted by the government and implemented in the CAFA 2014 and the amended Public Law Outline (PLO) in the FPR 2010, include less involvement of the courts in the care plan for a child going into care. Although Art 6(1) and Art 8 of the ECHR require a fair hearing in this situation – because this is interference with family life so that proportionality is required – it has nevertheless been provided in CAFA 2014 that the court should no longer scrutinise the *entire* care plan as has been done previously as this causes so much delay.

The CA 1989 and the updated FPR 2010 now provide that the court should look at the threshold considerations, the 'no order' principle and the benefit to the child but not normally at the fine detail, other than such aspects as the planned return to the family (if relevant), placing with family or friends and contact with the birth family.[44]

This slimming down of one of the major pieces of child protection documentation was supported by John Eekelaar of the Oxford Centre for Family Law and Policy and a number of others consulted during work on the public child law system.

The Final Report also called for more leadership and systemisation in the family justice system, more dialogue between the courts and the local authorities and some procedural reform to cater for the 'Timetable for the Child', owing to FJR emphasis that the present waiting times are too long for children's perception of time. The FJR also criticised experts' reports, which have now been made the subject of even more stringent rules (although experts are always a perennial concern of procedural reviews, so that this may still not be the final position on this subject).

With regard to leadership, as the President of the Family Division has acknowledged, the contribution of Lord Justice Ryder, who has been in charge of modernisation based on the FJR, has been invaluable, but the leadership of the President himself, Lord Justice Munby, should not be undervalued: his hands-on involvement has been crucial to delivery of the new processes required by CAFA 2014, the amendment of the FPR 2010 and the implementation of the new Family Court at a time when the profession has been much discouraged by both cuts in court resources as well as in legal aid, and the consequent swell in the numbers of LIPs with whom judges have had to deal.

The Final Report further contains detailed proposals for improvement of the Public Law Outline (PLO: the main procedural guide for public law child cases in the courts) which appear to be supported by the profession. The Report stresses an aim to complete public law child cases within six months (specifically supported by the President of the Family Division), which has now been incorporated into both the CAFA 2014 and amendments to the FPR 2010, of which the PLO has been an important part for some years, and within which it has been undergoing extensive and ongoing improvements since its first introduction in 2008. However, while upon the inauguration of the Family Court in April 2014 it was said to have reached its ultimate version, time will doubtless tell whether this is finally so once the new Court has been in operation a little longer than the few weeks of a first summer to bed down all its new procedures.

The Final Report also supports the work of Professor Eileen Munro on child protection.[45]

---

43 First identified in the 1969 case of J v C and already formally addressed in s 1(2) of the CA 1989.

44 One further recommendation of the FJR Final Report is that there should be a government consultation on whether there should be contact with siblings, amending s 34 of the Act in relation to contact with children in care.

45 For recommendations in 'The Child's Journey' and suggestions of numerous reforms, see *The Munro Review of Child Protection*, 10 February 2011, downloadable from www.safeguardingchildrenea.co.uk.

20.7 CA 1989 procedure

Public child law procedure is not substantially different from private law proceedings and after 1991 has always been so distinct from that prior to the CA 1989 that it is worth repeating that it reinforces the ethos of the CA 1989 Act in exactly the same way as in private law cases: i.e. the same best interests of the child as set out in s 1(1) and s 1(3), and the same s 1(2) and 1(5) principles apply.

The only real difference between private and public law proceedings is that in the latter the applicant is always the local authority, acting in the interests of state intervention when that is appropriate and unavoidable, and that the major criticism of the FJR about delay in child law cases is of public law proceedings, including child protection and adoption: it is in respect of that failure that the CAFA 2014[46] has enacted the new 26-week time limit for conclusion of cases save where there are exceptional reasons to exceed that period, and other timetable-tightening changes have been made as well as reducing judicial scrutiny of less crucial parts of care plans.

Public law cases are governed by the PLO in the FPR 2010; the private law equivalent is also in the FPR.

20.8 Current debates

Ideas for research on these current discussions may be found on the companion website updates.

- Has the CA 2004 now created the right framework for child protection to succeed in preventing fatal child abuse?
- Is the balance between family autonomy and state intervention now correctly struck?
- Is the standard of proof in child abuse cases now settled after *Re B*, *Re S-B* and *Re J*?

20.9 Summary of Chapter 20

The CA 1989: public law orders – a major shift of emphasis

- The CA 1989 effected a significant change of approach in child protection, creating a duty on the authority both to protect children in need in its area and if possible to promote the upbringing of children in their home and family: s 17, by providing a range and level of services appropriate to children's needs, although the statute has had to be supplemented by a further CA 2004 addressing the first Laming Report.
- The CA 1989 includes a duty to accommodate children temporarily where necessary, and to do this without seeking a formal care order unless the criteria for such an order are met: ss 20 and 31(2). The relevant definitions are contained in s 17.
- There remain formal protection orders for use in appropriate circumstances, care or supervision orders: EPO: s 44, and CAO: s 43, by which the authority may, in order to assess whether a protective order is necessary, obtain possession of a child where parents will not cooperate.

Care and supervision orders

- A care order gives the local authority PR to be shared with the parent(s), although the order limits the extent to which parents may exercise their concurrent PR.

---

46 See CAFA 2014 ss 13 and 14.

- The local authority has a duty to promote contact with the child's parents or those with PR: s 34, and must act as a good parent while the child is in care.
- The court takes a restrictive view towards the draconian nature of a care order where a supervision order would suffice, and decides which order is appropriate, depending mostly on whether it is essential that the local authority should have PR for the child or whether the order should last until the child is an adult, as supervision orders are limited in time to a maximum of three years after which fresh application is needed.
- The FJR recommended a less time-consuming scrutiny of care plans by judges to reduce delay in decisions being issued: this was implemented by CAFA 2014.

Other orders

- CAOs: s 43, EPOs: s 44, PPOs: s 46 and recovery orders: s 50 also support the local authority child protection work.

Procedure and evidence

- Procedure significantly changed when the CA 1989 was implemented in 1991 to reflect the philosophy of the statute: the Family Court now continues that informal style with some recent further improvements from April 2014, including a 26-week time limit if a case is not exceptional, more tightly controlled evidence and a time-saving reduction in judicial scrutiny of care plans supporting other delay avoidance strategies.
- The new Family Court continues to make public and private law orders within the philosophy of the CA 1989 in accordance with amendments made by CAFA 2014: procedure is similar in both types of case but the local authority is the public law applicant.
- The FJR recommended numerous procedural and system reforms to improve the delivery of public child law some of which have been incorporated into the latest PLO.

 ## 20.10 Further reading

Brophy, J, *Research Review: Child care proceedings under the Children Act 1989*, London, DCA, 2006.

Hayes, M, 'Farewell to the cogent evidence test, *Re B*', [2008] Fam Law 859.

Keating, H, 'Suspicions, sitting on the fence and standards of proof', [2009] CFLQ 21: 230.

Masson, J, 'Reforming Care Proceedings – Time for a Review', [2007] CFLQ 19: 411.

Masson, J, 'The state as parent: Reluctant parent? The problems of parents of last resort', [2008] *Journal of Law and Society*, 35: 52.

Masson, J, 'Controlling Costs and Maintaining Services – the reform of legal aid fees for care proceedings', [2008] CFLQ 20: 425.

Masson, J et al, *Protecting Powers: Emergency Intervention for Children's Protection*, Oxford, John Wiley & Sons, 2007.

Ryder, Hon Mr Justice, 'The risk fallacy: a tale of two thresholds', [2008] Fam Law 30.

Working Together to Safeguard Children, 2006.

Chapter 21

Financial Provision for Children

Chapter Contents

Learning outcomes for this chapter

An understanding of financial provision for children including:

(i) An awareness of the historic jurisdiction of the courts up to the creation of the Child Support Agency and the Child Support Act 1991 which came into force on 5 April 1993.

(ii) An overview of the current child support system in place since 1993.

(iii) An appreciation of the contemporary options of CSA/CMS awards, court orders and private agreements (and of the CA 1989 s 15 and Schedule 1 awards where the child's parents are unmarried).

(iv) An ability to synthesise these options in the context of the financial provision orders following divorce, nullity, dissolution of civil partnership or end of cohabitation.[1]

21.1 Introduction

One of the definable aspects of PR[2] is the obligation to support a child financially. This has resulted over the past quarter century in the separation of child maintenance from support and financial provision for the spouse, whether on divorce or within marriage, and in the creation of a uniform regime for child support, regardless of whether the child's parents are married or not – so that all children, marital and non-marital, can theoretically be treated equally for this purpose.[3]

The original **Child Support Act (CSA) 1991** was also seen as an essential reform as it met the requirements of the **UNCRC** Article 27(3), namely that:

'State Parties shall take all appropriate measures to secure the recovery of maintenance for the child from the parents.'

The magic vehicle was supposed to be the Child Support Agency (also abbreviated to CSA), set up to implement the CSA 1991, the context showing which 'CSA' was meant. Unfortunately the subsequent history of the project since its implementation in 1993 can only be described as appalling, but happily the agency has finally been taken over by the Department of Work and Pensions, a practical step since the DWP also administers benefits and pensions and is already making significant improvements in introducing a new system with every sign that it will at last work, although some 1993 regime cases still remain.

In theory the initial scheme was a positive idea, as many individual family law theories have undoubtedly been. In practice it has proved to be more disastrous than most, offering one of the most obvious examples of the real necessity to treat family law holistically, rather than as the sum of its independent parts, in order to avoid unexpected knock-on effects in other areas of the law. Both the original concept and later history of the subsequent comedy of errors has attracted adverse

---

1 See Chapters 6 and 9.
2 See Chapter 12.
3 In practice the scheme does not work entirely equally: while the child of divorced parents will have somewhere to live, as the court will put the children first in deciding financial provision, which will mean the carer parent and the children will have a home until the child is no longer dependent and this will be treated under the MCA 1973 as a priority, the child of unmarried parents will only have a roof with a carer parent (unless that parent has independent means), if a home is awarded under the CA 1989. Moreover such a home will usually revert to the non-resident parent who has been obliged to supply it when the child becomes independent, usually now regarded as after tertiary education. There are also other distinctions where the relevant jurisdictions for the two different situations come from different statutes.

academic comment, although worse was certainly delivered by the popular press which reported every blunder.

The fault does not appear to have been in the concept of child support itself – although the substantive law and practice as originally set up was certainly unnecessarily complicated, and suffered from an ongoing rash of equally complex (and sometimes even muddled) amendments – but in the administrative disaster of the government agency, by whichever name it has been known. In this connection, moving the work to the DWP, which has not been tainted by past mistakes, can only be a step forward.

The original, apparently accident-prone, agency immediately caught the attention of the media, which recorded with glee the ongoing story of the fatally flawed and implacably rigid calculations which produced astronomical sums said to be owing by quite ordinary people, and drove some children's non-resident parents to suicide in despair of ever stopping the computers which endlessly churned out such frightening demands.

Moreover, the agency seemed always to pursue those who were already paying for their children (although according to the computerised calculations they were not paying enough), but never seemed to catch those who were paying nothing. Indeed, through a series of embarrassing errors the system sometimes broke up marriages when in cases of mistaken identity they targeted the wrong person as allegedly the absent parent of a child. The unfortunate victim was sometimes completely unable to convince a wife, who took the assessment at face value, that the husband who had received one of these demands was not, and could not be, the father of the child for whom the agency was pursuing support.

Additionally, there were cases of assessments so large that attentive fathers who had kept in touch with their children, and would have liked to continue to do so, were unable to afford the costs of contact as well as being stretched to pay the new assessment. In particular, capital given to their families at the time of divorce (including obligations under loans sometimes taken out by absent fathers on their families' behalf to provide both necessities and luxuries) were disregarded as the assessment regime made no allowance for such items.

Moreover, no allowance was originally made for obvious costs, such as travel to work to earn the money out of which the assessment would have to be paid, nor for the expenses of a subsequent family to which the father had concurrent obligations. This was despite the recognition of the importance of such obligations in court decisions which acknowledged such relevant contemporary issues, for example *Delaney v Delaney* (1990),[4] in which a father's aspirations for a life after divorce were expressly recognised by the court.

Of course, the previous situation was scandalous, in which many absent fathers paid minuscule child maintenance (and then often had to be let off by the court when they built up arrears and could not pay them). Baroness Thatcher is credited, when first Prime Minister, with vowing to reverse this unsatisfactory state of affairs, and the implementation of the scheme in the hands of a government agency was in character with the philosophy of her era.

However, while other agencies were more successful, it seemed that the CSA was doomed from the start and a series of 1990s resignations identified it to those likely to be appointed to replace its unhappy leadership as a poisoned chalice particularly important to be avoided. Parents, too, fled from its intervention wherever they could, which the Child Support (Written Agreements) Order 1993 enabled them to do, as long as they were not on welfare benefits. Those unlucky enough not to be able to avail themselves of this escape were therefore trapped within the apparently unstoppably catastrophic CSA system. Moreover there were 'silly' cases, for example where a millionaire father could not be assessed for payments as he had no assessable income, which should not have been an insuperable problem when drafting the regulations in the first place, since tariff income

---

4 [1990] 2 FLR 457.

from capital has always been included in the welfare benefits regime and could have been similarly included in the CSA's system.

Since the original legislation in 1991, as significantly amended by the second dedicated statute in 1995, then again by the **Child Support, Pensions and Social Security Act 2000** and the **Child Maintenance and Other Payments Act (CMOP) 2008**, there have been at least two cosmetic and substantive 'makeovers' for the agency, including one change of name and one consignment to the bonfire of unwanted 'quangos' – from which there was a last-minute rescue – until, since October 2008, the system has returned to the 1993 position, where it was possible to contract out of the statutory regime, except that now this self-help and voluntary agreement alternative is no longer controlled but positively encouraged, as it fits with current government economic policy which is to save public expenditure.

This dovetails well with the recommendation of the Final Report of the FJR that separating and/or divorcing parents should agree arrangements for their children themselves, if necessary with the support of mediation or other DR services; so if they want the CSA to calculate their maintenance, and/or to enforce it, fees now have to be paid. This encouragement of private ordering has since seen two further positive changes:

(i)   initially the retrieval of the unpopular and unsuccessful CSA name for the agency, but only temporarily and eventually to be supplanted by a new Child Maintenance Service (CMS), when the arrears of the sorry past are addressed, then also dropping the unpopular name;

(ii) control of the entire system passed to the DWP, whether operated as to the 1993 regime as the CSA or, as to new applications under the CMOP 2000 regime, as the CMS.

21.2 The dual CSA–court application system

Application to the court for child maintenance to be included in consent orders under the MCA 1973 has already been discussed;[5] those made pre-1993 can continue and be varied unless there is a CSA assessment. This chapter therefore looks mainly at the statutory arrangements for child support under the CSA 1991–5 and other associated statutes, and also under the CA 1989 (which provides much the same supplementary financial orders for children of unmarried parents as the MCA 1973 does for those of parents who have been married and are divorcing) and at the interface between the CSA and the court.

However, unless agreed between the parents (as now encouraged), statutory child maintenance is now obtained through assessments under the CSA 1991–95, as amended, although the Family Court has residual powers.

It is worth mentioning the messy trail of unsatisfactory CSA 'rescues' which have had to be mounted – and then discarded – since 1995, as this conveys some idea of the shambles in which these important family law provisions have been so ineptly handled and the extent of the CMOP 2008 and DWP improvements.

The first major post millennium 'reform' was by the **Child Support, Pensions and Social Security Act 2000**, passed on 28 July 2000, and supposed to be progressively operational from 2002 – which did not in fact occur as it proved too difficult to implement. There was expected to be a gradual phasing in of new provisions, probably up to 2009, but by 2009 there was a further new statute making more significant changes – the CMOP 2008 – which in turn has also already suffered some further change; for example it created a Child Maintenance and Enforcement Commission (CMEC), which, although having its origins in that 2008 Act, and intended to take

---

5 See Chapter 6.

over from the accident-prone CSA, was itself then abolished on 1 August 2012, an early victim of the 2010 Coalition Government cuts.

Since that date, the DWP has been implementing the new 2008 system, which eventually involves the (final?) demise of the original agency name and transfer of all cases to a new Child Maintenance Service (CMS) which meanwhile is already taking new cases while the CSA deals with the (shocking) backlog.[6]

The 1991–95 system, as successively amended, is therefore currently still in use and for a while there will be two systems, as the CSA is still able to deal with cases under the pre-1995 system, and there is also the DWP's reformed system for which the current version of the leading practitioner software, *Child's Pay*, caters so that calculations can be made under both systems.

The new DWP dedicated website is also much improved: LIPs, struggling with other family law concepts without lawyers, should be able to use it easily; it explains the dual CSA/CMS systems clearly and states that the agency staff will inform the inquirer which of the CSA/CMS systems their case is allocated to. Suddenly, it seems, parents are 'customers', not miscreants to be bullied through a rigid system by a mandarin-driven administration; the atmosphere has completely changed.

As the entire framework of child support, both old and new, is quite complex, but nevertheless forms an integral part of many undergraduate syllabuses because of its underlying theory that parents should be responsible for the maintenance of their children rather than throwing that responsibility onto the state, probably the best way for students to grasp the complexities is to access the website[7] which (unusually in the current modernisation of family justice) provides clear information and a calculator, in a format entirely reasonable to expect the average member of the public to use.[8] Alternatively, those undergraduates whose universities offer vocational law courses, and are therefore likely to have *Child's Pay* in their electronic resources, could use the software to find out for themselves in making the calculations how the assessments work: this is a classic case where 'learning by doing' is superior to learning second hand through textbooks.

Accessing the system in this way quickly provides a view of whether the various reforms on which the contemporary assessments are based are, in fact, effective or not.

21.2.1 The Child Support, Pensions and Social Security Act 2000

Some account is necessary of the enactment of these abortive 2000 reforms as, despite being over-taken by events before much could be introduced, they followed a Green Paper, *Children Come First*,[9] which generated significant academic and practitioner comment.[10]

---

6 2008 data at www.childmaintenance.org (reflecting the position when the CMOP 2008 was enacted) are no longer available since the DWP has taken over the CSA websites, but in summary the CSA is still attempting to collect substantial arrears and new cases are being dealt with by the new CMS (Child Maintenance Service) which charges both payer and payee for its services in calculation and enforcement, although family-based arrangements effected by the parties themselves are free even if the website is used for advice and the online calculator service.

7 www.cmoptions.org. If parents elect to use the website to obtain information and/or to calculate and agree their own likely liability, there is no charge, but if an application is made to the CSA/CMS the applicant now pays £20 and the payer also pays a fee if enforcement is required.

8 The confused LIPs who have been left to struggle through court processes alone would have been well served if they had had information of similar quality when the LASPO 2012 cuts in April 2013 removed their access to legal advice and representation. See Chapters 1 and 5.

9 Cmnd 3992 (1998).

10 See e.g. Barton, C, 'Third time lucky for child support?', [1998] Fam Law 668. Professor Barton, who has a long-standing interest in child support, also writes regularly on this subject and others in *The Times* legal pages. Also Mostyn, N, 'The Green Paper and child support – children first: a new approach to child support', [1999] Fam Law 95. Nicholas Mostyn QC (now Mostyn J) was one of the innovative co-authors of the software *Child's Pay*, and when at the Bar a leading financial provision advocate and family finance expert. Their commentary is therefore particularly valuable since they have devoted many years of commitment to analysing the subject with some intellectual rigour.

Unfortunately, child support had, within a short time of its introduction, become so complex that it generated a specialist series of reports which have for some years recorded decisions on both substantive law and procedure. Their appeals are now decided by judges of the relatively recently unified Tribunals Service into which the Child Support Appeal Tribunal and the Child Support Commissioners have been subsumed. In other words, child support has grown into a significant specialist area of family law, although the government's contemporary encouragement to the public is quite the opposite, i.e. that it is simple and a suitable DIY area for parents to manage their child support payments.

21.2.2 The court's residual jurisdiction

Alongside the CSA/CMS system the residual powers of the court can make orders outside the CSA framework for lump sums and property adjustment, plus 'top up' maintenance orders for children who qualify (formerly in either the county court or the FPC, now in the Family Court – as the CSA deals only in periodical payments up to its limit).

For these jurisdictions the children concerned must be one or more of the following:

(a) over age 19, or still under 19 but have finished their non-advanced (i.e. secondary) education (as they are then not 'children' as far as the CSA/CMS is concerned);

(b) 'non-qualifying children' within the meaning of the CSA 1991–95, i.e. there is no natural 'absent parent' (since 2000, now called the 'non-resident' parent) who can be assessed, so that the CSA/CMS can make no assessment but the court can make an order against a step-parent if a child is a 'child of the family' pursuant to MCA 1973 s 52;

(c) overseas residents or where one or both parents are not resident in the jurisdiction, so that the CSA/CMS can make no assessment but the court, if it has jurisdiction in divorce, nullity or JS, may make a court order for child maintenance;

(d) applicants for top up payments, e.g. for disability, school fees or other educational expenses in addition to the CSA/CMS computerised calculation of the maintenance requirement which does not include such expenses.

The other statutory sources of financial orders for children, apart from financial provision under the MCA 1973, which supplement the CSA, will be either

- *instead of* the CSA/CMS assessment in the relevant cases mentioned above; or
- *to top up* the CSA/CMS assessment when that has reached the limit of its remit (as the CSA can only assess incomes of up to its limit, now £3,000 per week).

The statutes under which the court can entertain such applications are:

- DPMCA 1978;[11]
- MCA 1973 s 27;
- CA 1989 s 15 and Schedule 1 (see below).

Generally the last named will be used by the unmarried, since married parents can secure the same or better provision under one of the other statutes.

---

11 See Chapters 6 and 9.

21.3 The CSA 1991–95 as amended

The language of the original statute was distinctive (although subtle tactful changes in terminology were made by the 2000 reforms which *were* implemented in the CSA 1991–95 as amended before the 2000 legislation was overtaken). The actors in the drama as described at various times comprised:

(a) The *qualifying child* (i.e. the child who needs the maintenance), who is a child one or both of whose parents is in relation to him an *absent* parent, now called the 'non-resident' parent or 'NRP': s 3(1). An adopted child or a child born by artificial insemination by a donor is included as a qualifying child unless in the latter case the husband/partner of the mother treated is proved not to have consented to the treatment: HFEA 1990 s 28(2) and HFEA 2008 s 35.[12] But a child who is or ever has been married is excluded from the operation of the CSA 1991: s 55(2).

(b) The *absent parent* (any parent who is not living with the child where the child has a home with someone else who has care of that child) for the pursuit of whom the CSA was created, now called the 'non-resident' parent 'NRP': s 3(2).

(c) The *person with care* or 'PWC' (the person with whom the child has a home who provides day-to-day care for that child, whether exclusively or in conjunction with any other person), sometimes also called the *carer parent*, but the acronym 'PWC' seems to have established itself more widely: s 3(3).

The local authority does not appear anywhere in this cast of actors as the CA 1989 provides alternative means of their recovering the cost of caring for children when appropriate.

The CSA/CMS operates on the basis of the statutory duty to maintain a qualifying child, which is set out in CSA 1991 s 1(1) and makes each parent equally responsible, but by s 1(3) it is the *absent* ('non-resident') parent ('NRP' in contemporary parlance) who has the duty of making the payments under a CSA assessment. The CSA then uses a computer-based formula to make assessments, as to the operation of which see below.

21.3.1 The CSA/CMS, benefit cases and the CMOP 2008

Where a carer parent is in receipt of specified state benefits, it used to be a requirement that the Secretary of State be authorised to take action to recover the amount paid out for the child, in maintenance from the absent parent: CSA 1991, s 6(1), and by s 46 benefit might be reduced if cooperation was not forthcoming from the carer parent, either in refusing authorisation or in refusing essential information (e.g. the identity of the natural father).

Nevertheless, in an appropriate case the carer parent could decline to do this without losing benefit, provided the child support officer accepted that if the carer parent were to cooperate there would be adverse consequences of some kind. Since the officer had a discretion, this normally meant showing a likelihood of violence to the carer or child though regard also had to be had to 'the welfare of any child likely to be affected by his decision': CSA 1991, s 2.

However, ss 6 and 46 were repealed by the CMOP 2008, which also provided a £20 maintenance disregard if a carer was on benefits. The object of this was the radical new philosophy of the CMOP 2008, in which the text stated clearly in its opening sections that the object was to promote child support through a new institution created by the statute, i.e. the now defunct CMEC, which was 'to maximise the number of those children who live apart from one or both of their parents for whom effective maintenance arrangements are in place'. Nevertheless this new agency was one

---

12 See Chapter 13 for HAR and the HFEA 1990 and 2008 generally.

of the key casualties which overtook CMOP 2008 before its particular scheme could be brought into force as CMEC was promptly abolished by the Coalition Government in August 2012 as part of their 'bonfire of the quangos' just as the new name had registered on the public consciousness!

The original idea was that CMEC would take over from the CSA, which had had a bad press (whether entirely deserved or not), but the opposite has in fact been the case as CMEC still appeared tarred with the old brush. Thus although all the public relations efforts between 2008 and 2012 were directed towards a new system being administered by a new organisation, in the end the CSA remained officially and temporarily the agency while the DWP took over and concentrated on promoting the encouragement of private agreements – the really key part of the 2008 Act reforms – on dealing with the baggage of the old CSA arrears and moving towards the new CMS; which is where the system is now.

21.3.2 Review of assessments

There is provision for review of assessments, originally every two years, but now to be annual: CSA 1991 s 16 as amended. Either the absent ('non-resident' 'NRP') or the carer can apply at any time for a review if there has been a change of circumstances: s 17.

Although there is no room for discretion in making assessments (and if the figures fed into the computerised system are right the result should also be correct) any assessment which is thought to be wrong should be appealed within 28 days. Further appeal is possible, formerly to the Child Support Appeal Tribunal, then to the Child Support Appeal Commissioner on point of law, and subsequently to the Court of Appeal and House of Lords in the normal way, but now the initial appeal goes to the successors to the Child Support Appeal Tribunal within the new unified Tribunals Service.

Collection and enforcement are also provided for by the Act. When the original Act was passed it was ultimately intended that the CSA would take over the assessment, enforcement and collection of all child maintenance, although this was progressively postponed as the CSA clearly found its existing workload onerous and complex.

It remains to be seen what will happen under the latest post-2008 reforms. Meanwhile the usual methods of enforcement can be used, but additionally the regime offers the administrative procedure of a deduction of earnings order for which no court order is needed and there are also liability orders obtainable from the magistrates, and the options of confiscation of passport and/or driving licence, or even a prison term. Interest is available on arrears in excess of 28 days old.

21.3.3 The effect of clean break settlements

Originally any capital given to the carer parent at the time of divorce had no effect on liability for a CSA assessment under the non discretionary rules (causing much hardship), but subsequent amendments by statutory instrument have since April 1995 enabled past capital settlements[13] to be taken into account. However, although these provided some relief where before there was none, the effect was hardly dramatic. The maximum deduction was £60 per week if the value of the transfer made under the capital settlement exceeded £25,000, and if it was less than £5,000 it did not count at all. Up to £10,000, the absent parent got £20 per week off maintenance and up to £25,000 it was £40 per week.

The capital settlement must have been made by court order or written agreement prior to 5 April 1993 (i.e. when the 1991 Act came into force), and must otherwise have satisfied the normal conditions of a clean break capital settlement, in that while the parties were separated

---

13 See Chapters 6 and 7 for financial settlements on divorce and similar decrees and orders, which will affect child support.

(though divorce was not necessary) an outright transfer of property or payment of capital must have been made by the absent parent to the carer in circumstances other than to buy out the carer parent's share of an asset.

While this might have been some help for people caught up in the maelstrom behind earlier settlements before the CSA was introduced, this was a further incentive to parties to clean break settlements to take warning and attempt to deal with matters in a manner which benefited the family overall by agreement while they could, and the new encouragement to private agreements will be a simplification of these former problems.

21.3.4 The parties affected by the legislation

The Child Support Acts affect all NRP natural parents of qualifying children, whether they were ever married to the carer PWC parent of the child or not.

21.3.5 The assessment formula: how maintenance was assessed under the original CSA framework

Both parents completed detailed forms to give the agency full information about their financial position. Maintenance was then assessed, not on the basis of any discretion, but by applying a rigid computer-based formula which was aimed to achieve consistency in assessments and to provide a realistic sum which recognised the true costs of child caring and rearing. Unlike in the case of the old court-assessed orders, which were usually tacked on to a substantive order for the custodial parent, this was supposed to provide a realistic amount towards the real costs of bringing up a child, and this was generally the case even where the custodial parent was no longer being maintained (e.g. because of remarriage).

Under the court system, the child would have been left with an uneconomic order, frequently too low actually to provide food and clothing let alone contribute to the cost of keeping a roof over the child's head. Thus, if the CSA assessments (even under the original regime) have done anything, they have helped remarried parents and step-parents, since the natural father would usually have to pay something closer to the true cost of bringing up the child, removing some financial strain from step-parents and also from step-parents' first families, who often suffered under the former system.

The formula for calculating the child's maintenance used to be extremely complicated, and was related to other social security benefits, mainly income support. The formula had four parts and it was not only the complexity which annoyed both parents but also that it had some unfair latent incidents.

The original components of the calculation were:

(1)   the child's maintenance requirement (based on income support levels + an allowance for the carer);

(2)   the assessable income of each parent after deducting certain allowances, though the *actual* living expenses were irrelevant;

(3)   the basic deduction rate (which was the income of both parents added together and if this was equal to or less than the maintenance requirement each parent was liable to pay up to half their assessable income in child support); and

(4)   the additional amount, which meant that where there was more income than was necessary to satisfy the maintenance requirement a further amount of child support was payable.

This system was disliked for the following reasons.

The allowance for the carer under element (1) meant that some NRPs were indirectly maintaining the child's carer, usually the mother, through the carer's personal allowance, even though this was a small percentage of the total award. It was an irritant to some fathers who did not want to maintain the mother anyway, either because there had been a clean break settlement[14] after divorce or because they had never been married to her, so there had never been an obligation to maintain the mother as such; having to pay through the CSA was the last straw! Thus this was obviously a situation where an agreed solution outside the CSA framework would have been demonstrably better, and is one reason to welcome the new encouragement to private ordering.

Second, the treatment of the assessable income under (2) was another irritant to NRPs who, if they were, for example, buying a car or TV or other household appliance under hire purchase, would find these regular payments did not count for the assessment! Thus if the mother and child now wanted such an item it was another encouragement to contract out under the reformed system.

Third, NRPs complained that the figure assessed under the basic deduction rate in element (3) was hard enough to find (while PWCs complained that it was wrong to take their income into account) and under (4) the additional element was found so onerous and NRPs complained so bitterly that it took away further sums from their income that they could not spare if they were also to meet the costs of keeping in touch with their children on contact visits that in April 1995 the maximum amount that they had to pay was halved.

However, there have been further and much more practical amendments under the reformed system.

21.4 Reform of the CSA regime

The result of the ongoing tinkering with the 1991–95 Acts (whereby the 1991 Act remains in force subject to the changes made by the 1995 Act, in which were reflected any further amendments made by subsequent statutes) had been a large number of gates to a 'departures' order where parents were obliged to be within the CSA system and yet had special circumstances which morally required consideration within the CSA assessment, but these were initially excluded by the computerised framework. This in turn generated a wholesale exodus to agreed orders pursuant to s 8(5) because of the complex formulae adopted. Attempts to try to provide fair assessments within the rigid computer-driven scheme, so that there were 'safety nets' for low earners, became too complicated, especially because of the concepts of siphoning off certain sums: first, a basic element of 50 per cent of the payer's assessable income up to the threshold of £75–£110 per week, followed by, second, a stepped 'additional element' depending on the number of children – 15 per cent for one child, 20 per cent for two, 25 per cent for three or more up to a ceiling (calculated by another formula) of about £55 per child.

The CSA 2000 scheme therefore adopted a simpler approach. This was based on:

- the children who were the subject of the assessment; and
- the circumstances of the payer (after 2000 called the 'non-resident' 'NRP' rather than the insulting 'absent parent');
- 'departures' were simplified as 'variations'.

21.4.1 The 2000 reforms

Under the six-point framework of the 2000 reforms the circumstances of the resident parent, the PWC, were completely ignored, and also the non-resident parent's (NRP) housing costs, both of

---

14 See Chapter 6 for clean break settlements.

which were allowed under the previous scheme. Children's overnight stays with their NRP, as before brought down the NRP's liability, but instead of the pre-2000 reduction for more than 104 nights per annum, 52 nights operated as a reduction by one-seventh, moving up a further reductions scale to 175 nights which cut the liability by 50 per cent.

The NRP's circumstances included his or her (but usually his) income, pension contributions (after 2000 100 per cent as against only 50 per cent formerly allowed) and all the children in his household, including step-children, whether of a legal marriage or unmarried partnership (to qualify in this respect the NRP would have to show receipt of child benefit by himself or his partner). Professor Barton was concerned about this, as in his view it was a clear invitation to the unmarried man to obtain potentially undeserved relief from obligations to women and children in a series of relationships.

Perhaps the most significant reform in the 2000 Act was that it created a straight line rather than a stepped formula from the start so that the NRP simply handed over 15, 20 or 25 per cent of his entire assessable income, up to a ceiling of £2,000 per week, depending on the number of children to be supported. This meant that the maximum assessment was £15,600 for one child, £20,800 for two and £26,000 for three or more. Top-ups were retained, so that it would still be possible to go to court for more where appropriate, though there was a ceiling on CSA payments per week and top-ups only operate when the CSA assessment ceiling of income of £2,000 per week was reached. There were also four simpler rates used for calculating child support maintenance which vastly improved on the original highly complex regime:

(1)   the basic rate (for most people, where the NRP's income was at least £200 per week, when the figures above would apply);

(2)   the reduced rate (where the NRP's income was between £100 and £200 per week, when the NRP would pay a flat rate of £5 on the first £100 and then a higher percentage – 25, 35 or 45 per cent – of any income over £100);

(3)   the flat rate (where the NRP's income is £5 to £100, or s/he has a partner, when the flat rate is halved, or is on certain benefits both partners on benefits would pay £2.50 each);

(4)   the nil rate (where the NRP has a weekly income of less than £5 – students, those under 16, or in hospital, a care home or prison).

There was, however, a complex system for protection of parents at the lower end of the scale, which was intended to specify who pays what. Moreover, the CSA was for the first time able to assess NRPs working overseas for UK and UK-based companies or for government employees such as the armed services or diplomatic service. Departures were retained but renamed 'variations' (conveniently the same term as for court order variations).

Further changes made it easier for the CSA to operate. It became a crime to give false information. The CSA found it easier to fix paternity after the 2000 legislation, as if the father was married at some time between the conception and the birth a presumption of paternity arose, as was also inferred from registration of the birth showing the name of the father. This obviously linked to the then Lord Chancellor's Department initiative to give PR to those unmarried fathers who lived with the mothers of their children at the time of the birth and registration, eventually becoming law when CA 1989 s 4[15] was finally amended to provide this route to PR despite amendments generated by earlier initiatives having been lost in the failure of previous Bills. Enforcement was also stepped up. Instead of getting a liability order from the magistrates and then going for distress, or any of the usual forms of civil enforcement, even committal if complex rules are followed, the CSA could after 2000 get the defaulter disqualified from driving for up to two years, and/or imprisoned much

---

15 See Chapter 12.

more easily. Equally, instead of the complex penalty and interest provisions under the earlier statutes, the CSA had the power, like the Inland Revenue (now HMRC) of issuing penalties. Commentators thought that the driving disqualification was a brainwave!

At first in 2000 the likely positive result was thought to be that the exodus to court would be stemmed, as a new provision enabled either parent to approach the CSA on two months' notice even if there had been an agreed court order, once the court order had been in force for a year. This was designed, however, to apply only to new orders obtained after 2002; earlier orders were to remain with the courts for variation as previously, unless a parent went onto benefits. This provided extensive drafting potential for family lawyers who struggled to keep their clients' child maintenance in the hands of the court. It was thought that there would have to be regulations made under the CSA 1991 s 45 to deal with the potential for ongoing conflict between the court and CSA variation applications, as it was felt that this could be a key area in which the law was temporarily uncertain, especially if courts took a robust view of their ongoing jurisdiction as happened when the CSA 1991 was implemented in 1993.

Non-resident parents on welfare benefits still had to pay some Child Support – formerly £5.10 per week, and under the 2000 reforms a flat rate of £5 per week, avoided if the child had 52 nights of staying contact – and there was a power to assign an NRP a notional income for assessment purposes.

21.5 The future settlement of child maintenance

While the 2000 statute must now be seen as the watershed of the current CMOPA 2008 reformed system, which seems likely to work better than its predecessors, there has been a good deal of transitional muddle, which has been exploited by the better off using the system inter alia for tax planning, rather than particularly assisting the poorer parents for whom adequate child maintenance was the original goal. One of the few good things that could be said about the 2000 statute was that it confirmed recognition of the growing trend for parents to share child care by giving credit for nights of staying contact with the NRP, a rare nod to family law core principles which naturally encouraged contact.

All new applications from 2002 were set by the 2000 Act to be either via the agency or to the court if the parties agreed, but after one year of the order being in force either party could apply to the agency on two months' notice, when the court's power to vary would be lost for ever.

Thus, those parents who wanted to fund a child by joint parenting agreements had to rely on the skill of practitioners in drafting their agreements, which might or might not be able to protect them from CSA intervention (e.g. by a consent order including a chargeback where the CSA was relied upon following an agreed financial settlement). The FLBA had been piloting this since well before the 1991 regime was implemented, with mixed success, but in that case tended to be aided and abetted by robust judges who hung on to the court's power to vary even when the CSA was claiming that they had no jurisdiction to do so; at that time the CSA's teething troubles much assisted this outcome.

After the 2000 reforms the general view was that it remained to be seen whether the implementation of the new regime in new cases in the first pilot year (whenever it actually started) was more successful and less controversial, so that radical changes did not have to be made as had happened on the previous occasion that reforms had been generated. One idea being floated in the *Child's Pay Bulletin* at the time was that an annual order, lasting for a minute less than a year, expiring on Christmas Day (so no one would be able to make an application to the CSA that day!) and automatically reviving the next day, would mean that no order had ever lasted for the qualifying year!

By CSA 1991 s 9(4), any provision in an agreement *not to apply* to the CSA was void and this still remains; further the existence of an agreement will still not prevent access to the CSA: s 9(3).

However, there were often good reasons why there should not be an assessment, for example if there was to be a nominal maintenance order for the child because it was more convenient to make provision out of capital, and wealthier parents' lawyers made use of this. The underlying rationale was that it could sometimes be extremely effective for inheritance tax planning purposes because such payments would usually be exempt if pursuant to a court order, either as a disposition for family maintenance or as not intended for gratuitous benefit.[16] Thus if a nominal order was made in favour of each of the children of the family and capital provision also made for them (e.g. to capitalise school fees) this enabled capital to be passed to them free of tax and then the court could subsequently vary the nominal order upwards as required.

This was always the normal route for obtaining an increased level of provision from the court to provide for children, but would be precluded by a CSA assessment, as pointed out by Wilson J in a case incidentally of some importance in relation to the children of unmarried millionaire fathers, where this plan would work in reverse to prevent their escaping making provision for their children through the CSA. This was because, regardless of how wealthy they were in capital terms, the CSA could not make an order as if they had no income as such since an assessable income was essential for the CSA's regime to operate on – so the mother's only recourse was then to apply for provision under the CA 1989 where capital orders could be made so as to access their substantial assets![17]

Some decided cases on these points give an indication of the vicissitudes of parents involved in the more recondite backwaters of child support, where ingenuity has been used by parents, both to avoid paying child support and to navigate round the complex conditions so as to obtain provision; it would be worth students reading the full reports of the following cases so as to appreciate how they worked.

❖ CASE EXAMPLES

In *V v V (Ancillary Relief: Power to Order Child Maintenance)* (2001)[18] Wilson J was dealing with such an application by both parties to determine child provision in which he distinguished *Philips v Pearce* (1996),[19] which had been just such an attempt indirectly to challenge a nil CSA assessment of a millionaire father with no assessable income for CSA purposes, so that recourse to capital was the *only* means of obtaining provision from him for the child – an entirely different process from the parties both inviting the court to determine child provision in the most tax-efficient way for the benefit of the family as a whole.

In *Phillips v Pearce* the CSA could only make a nil assessment as the father had hidden all his wealth in various companies, but he did live in a £2.6 million house. In 1996 a very substantial property could be obtained for that sum so this was some indication of means. Unable to get any child support from the CSA, as the father notionally had no income, the mother applied under the CA 1989 Schedule 1 but could still get no income order as the nil assessment also applied in the court where normally 'top-up' orders could be obtained where the CSA powers to make a sufficient income order were subject to their usual ceiling. Under the court's jurisdiction she was, however, able to obtain a lump sum for a house and furniture, although this was held to be a 'once for all' payment so she was

---

16   Inheritance Tax Act 1984, ss 10 and 11.
17   See below for Children Act financial provision.
18   [2001] 2 FLR 657.
19   [1996] 2 FLR 230.

unable to return for another lump sum. Herring thinks that this was wrong in respect of cash lump sums, because the statute does not say in s 1(5)(b) that only one order can be made except in relation to a settlement of property under s 1(2)(d) or (e), and a child might need a further lump sum under s 1(2)(c) during his or her childhood.

It is unsurprising that it has been suggested that the CSA regime may be contrary to the welfare of the child; however the CSA 1991 s 2, requires that when any step is taken under the statute the agency shall 'have regard to the welfare of any child likely to be affected by the decision'. In the past this has been interpreted as meaning that if the NRP's payments were so high that it affected contact this would not be for the child's welfare; however, the greater flexibility afforded by the post-2008 system, especially since it encourages private agreements, may now counter this.

Additionally, under the original system there were strong pressures following the 2000 reforms on both the NRP and the resident parent to evade the CSA (since any changes in child support inevitably impacted on other financial provision orders, e.g. pension sharing and clean breaks by Duxbury lump sum; this too was obviously not for the child's welfare, as it made settlement of any financial provision package in the case of a high earner NRP difficult until the impact of the CSA figures was known.

Thus an umbrella figure, including child maintenance, had to be agreed for spouse and children in any negotiated private settlement. Indeed, it meant that, following the 2000 reforms, the law in this area was somewhat uncertain for a period, although perhaps no more uncertain than because the law of financial provision was also 'work in progress' following *White v White* (2001),[20] which threw any certainty in financial provision into some disorder in the same 12 months as the 2000 Act, another failure to link child support to other principles of family law.

While reform of the post-*White* financial provision system remains work in progress, the reforms effected by CMOPA 2008, on the basis of which the DWP has been working, do chime with the FJR Final Report, which recommends that all issues facing separating or divorcing parents should be the subject of parental agreement, which may well be more beneficial than CSA assessments, since nothing has in the meantime occurred to make the agency more efficient or quicker in processing applications; anecdotally it appears that they are even slower than before, possibly due to ongoing cuts.

There is also another change to the maintenance calculation, now to be based on the NRP's *gross* rather than *net* income. Under this system the NRP is liable to pay 12 per cent of weekly gross income for one child, 16 per cent for two and 19 per cent for three or more. If the NRP's income exceeds £800 per week, the lower figures of 9, 12 or 15 per cent will apply to the excess amount over £800. Another change is fixed annual awards so that no change will take place (unless a major one, such as a change in the NRP's income) until the annual review.

In view of the ongoing changes still to work through from the CMOPA 2008, and the fact that the CSA/CMS has been operating a dual system with the intention of the CMS eventually taking over completely, students should watch the academic journals, in particular *Family Law* and *Child and Family Law Quarterly*, for articles about the new regime as commentary on it develops; also the CSA website, which regularly upgrades its downloadable leaflets, some of which are currently updated roughly to the present time. The website also explains many of the agency's processes, including DNA testing for parentage, leading to declarations of non-parentage where appropriate, and default rate decisions, where adequate information cannot be obtained promptly.

---

20 [2001] AC 596, HL.

21.6 Child maintenance and provision under the CA 1989

The provisions in CA 1989 s 15 and Schedule 1 provide for the Family Court to make orders against the child's parents which can still usefully supplement other jurisdictions, in particular in the case of lump sum and property transfer orders which are outside the remit of the CSA/CMS. The criteria are similar to those governing the DPMCA 1978 and the MCA 1973.

Any person may apply for such an order who has an order for a child to live with that applicant, such as relatives of the child with whom the child prefers to live than with the parents, a common situation involving children who think this is a way of 'divorcing their parents' (otherwise legally impossible because of the enduring nature of PR). This does allow such relatives who are willing for an order to be made in their favour to obtain support which they would not qualify for from the CSA/CMS. Similarly, a guardian, adoptive or step-parent, will qualify under the Schedule, as will an adult child over age 18 in education, providing that the child's parents are not living together.

Most commonly this route is convenient to obtain a property transfer in favour of the parent of a child with whom the child is residing, and who was not married to the child's other parent and is therefore unable to use the MCA 1973 to secure a home for the child's minority. Such a transfer is usually expressed to be for the benefit of the child until independence, which is now recognised to be more likely to be age 21 than 18, owing to the lack of public support for undergraduate degrees, an argument which originated with Baroness Hale, who has brought a new perspective to many decisions such as this. The property will usually then revert to the transferor: T v S (1994).[21]

This provision is able to address the otherwise possible gross disparity between the father's circumstances and those of the mother and the child by the advancement of capital for the mother and child's housing needs.

This problem was examined in detail, again by Baroness Hale, then Hale J, in J v C (1999),[22] when she concluded that the relevant criteria, although not expressly included in CA 1989 Schedule 1, paragraph 4, must include the child's welfare while a minor, part of which should include entitlement 'to be brought up in circumstances which bear some sort of relationship with the father's present standard of living'. In this case the father had won £1.4 million in the lottery.

It seems the father does not, however, have a right to dictate where the property in question should be, or its type, and this would appear to be confirmed by the **European Convention on Human Rights** Art 8, unless the court's interference was for some reason legitimate, necessary and in proportion to the restriction proposed, since it was established, per Johnson J in *Philips v Pearce* (see above), that it is not for the court to decide where the parties should live, although this may be a part of the factual decision-making process in granting any CA 1989 order.

On the other hand, the father's financial investment can be properly protected by trust deed.[23]

The court, including the magistrates under the DPMCA 1978, can also make these s 15 and Schedule 1 orders of its own motion when making, discharging or varying a CAO.[24]

The criteria applied when the court is considering awarding orders to or for the benefit of children under this jurisdiction are the same as for child orders in financial provision on decree of divorce or similar order,

---

21 [1994] 2 FLR 883.
22 [1999] 1 FLR 1989.
23 See Spon Smith R, [1999] Fam Law 763.
24 See Chapter 6.

21.7 Current debates

Ideas for research on these current discussions may be found on the companion website updates.

- Where is statutory child support now and is the latest reform likely to be more successful than previous attempts?
- Should child support fall on the state or the parents? Is this a matter of children's rights as perceived by the UNCRC?
- What level should support be?
- Is the approach to child support following the CMOPA 2008 – a mix of private agreement, CSA/CMS orders and court top-up orders – the right one?

21.8 Summary of Chapter 21

PR and child support

- The background to the current regime of child support is in the concept of PR and the obligation to support a child which falls on all natural parents of that child, whether the parents are married or not.
- This is now formalised in a regime of statutory child support under the CSA 1991–95 as amended, and is supplemented by provisions for child maintenance in the MCA 1973 and CA 1989.
- Under the MCA 1973, where parents are agreed on maintenance provisions, their arrangements can be included in the consent order formalising their own financial provision on divorce. otherwise contested cases must be assessed by the CSA/CMS under the CSA 1991–95, unless the arrangements are in respect of a child outside the CSA/CMS remit (i.e. step-children whose natural parent cannot be found, children outside the age and other qualifying limits, and children requiring capital, property and/or top-up orders).
- The CA 1989 provides for similar capital etc. orders to be made in the case of unmarried parents who are not able to use the MCA 1973.
- The earlier regimes of child support are being further reformed pursuant to the CMOPA 2008.

CSA 1991–95

- These statutes created a framework of 'qualifying child', 'carer parent' ('PWC') and 'absent' ('non-resident' – 'NRP') parent'.
- The CSA assesses the qualifying child's maintenance requirement on the basis of financial disclosure of the NRP, and the child's needs which are linked to welfare benefit rates.
- Reforms in 1995 created 'departures' to recognise more fairly than before the payer's other obligations (e.g. costs of contact and travel to work, and also capital paid over on divorce clean breaks), but this system became so complicated, without delivering increased fairness, that departures were completely reformed and renamed 'variations' in 2000, and the entire scheme simplified and further reformed, by the CMOP 2008.

Reform of the CSA regime

- The 2000 legislation created a flat rate of child support depending on the number of children: thus 15, 20 or 25 per cent of the payer's assessable income was paid depending on whether there were one, two or three or more children. There was an allowance introduced for payers with 'step-children', whether those were children of a formal marriage or informal cohabitation.

- The CSA was enabled to assess British parents resident overseas and enforceability was improved.
- There was also an increased likelihood of application to the CSA after an initially agreed court order, since as soon as such an order has been in force for one year either party could apply to the CSA, rather than the order remaining with the court for variation. This has been displaced by a new approach encouraging private ordering under CMOPA 2008, under the new management of the DWP, and again changing the basic percentages to be paid to 12, 16 and 19 per cent.

CA 1989

- The CA 1989 provides for capital and property orders to be made in favour of children who do not have access to such orders through their parents' divorce under the MCA 1973, i.e. mostly for children of unmarried parents, and also for maintenance orders in favour of non-parents with whom a child lives (e.g. relations other than the parents with whom the child prefers to live).

 ## 21.9 Further reading

Children Come First, Cm 1264, 1990.
Improving Child Support, Cm 2745, 1995.
Children First: A New Approach to Child Support, Cm 3992, 1998.
A New Contract for Welfare: Children's Rights and Parents' Responsibilities, Cm 4349, 1999.
Henshaw, D, *Recovering Child Support: Routes to Responsibility*, Cm 6894, DWP, 2006.
A Fresh Start: Child Support Redesign, Cm 6895, DWP, 2006.
A New System of Child Maintenance, Cm 6979, DWP, 2006.
Public Consultation. Supporting separated families; securing children's futures, Cm 8399, DWP, 2012.
Tod, J, 'Schedule 1 and the need for reform: *N v D*', [2008] Fam Law 751.
Wikely, N, *Child Support: Law and Policy*, Oxford, Hart, 2006.
Wikely, N, 'Child support reform – throwing the baby out with the bathwater?', [2007] CFLQ 434.
Wikely, N, 'Financial support for children after parental separation: Parental responsibility and responsible parenting', in Probert, R, Gilmore, S and Herring, J (eds), *Responsible Parents and Parental Responsibility*, Oxford, Hart, 2009.

Chapter 22

Adoption

Chapter Contents

Learning outcomes for this chapter

An understanding of the radical changes in adoption law and practice brought about by the Adoption and Children Act (ACA) 2002 including:

(i)   An appreciation of the philosophy of promoting adoption as a route out of care for more children.
(ii) An awareness of the political motives for promoting PR and the tensions between those practical motives and the welfare of the child.
(iii) An ability to analyse and assess which of the possible orders of adoption, CAO or special guardianship would best suit a child depending on the context of the child's life within its extended family, if any.
(iv) A critical approach to the most recent policy statements, legislation and practice on the perceived need for a further relaxation in the criteria for matching potential parents and children waiting to be adopted.

22.1 Introduction

English adoption law is entirely statutory having had its origins only in 1926, since when family law and the social context which influences it have moved on apace. This is particularly true of the period between 1976 and 1989, so that reform was seriously overdue when the **Adoption and Children Act (ACA) 2002** was passed and even more so when it was fully implemented in December 2005, since it replaced the **Adoption Act (AA) 1976**, which only came into force in 1988 and then almost immediately received much criticism. The long interval and implementation history from 1976 to 1988 and then to 2002 indicates the hesitation in finally articulating new legislation, introducing a number and variety of changes which had been suggested by reform groups, including updating the pre-2002 welfare test in adoption, which did not reflect that of the CA 1989.

The ACA 2002 was originally supported by the **Family Procedure (Adoption) Rules 2005** and the President of the Family Division's Practice Direction, *President's Guidance (Adoption: the New Law and Procedure)*[1] (needed then owing to the significant changes made by the ACA 2002), but adoption is now included in the FPR 2010 Part 12. There was also an Independent Reviewing Mechanism established under the 2002 Act, which was designed to increase public confidence in the current system by offering prospective adopters who were turned down by an adoption agency a right of review. It might be said that adoption had now been more integrated into family law than previously.

Various government circulars regulate the practice of adoption, which is clearly driven by policy, but the latest legislation is perhaps more fundamental than previously, although during the past four decades the role of adoption in England has dramatically changed like much in family law. The latest changes have been made in the CAFA 2014, Part I, ss 1–7 and 9, and Schedule 1, which together amend the CA 1989 and the ACA 2002 to facilitate and speed up adoptions, by allowing a local authority to foster children earmarked for adoption with parents already approved as potential adopters and to reduce the impact of a child's ethnicity, religion and culture in matching them to families, provided the 2002 welfare test is not thus diluted. These changes reflect government policy to facilitate adoption so as not only to improve the adoption system, which has been much criticised owing to an apparent mismatch between numerous children in long-term care

---

1   [2006] 1 FLR 1234.

without adopters and numerous families apparently fruitlessly seeking children to adopt, but also to address problems in the care system: too many children in long-term care and general over-whelming of the local authority child protection processes, not least as the local authorities also run adoption agencies.

In particular, some childless parents have sought children to adopt from overseas owing to restrictive adoption practices at home. At the same time others adopted from Third World and Eastern European countries out of compassion, while in both cases UK-based children have remained unplaced; while yet other potential adopters, such as same-sex couples, have resorted to surrogacy to obtain children with whom they have a genetic link.

In the same period, while step-families have proliferated, new attitudes have developed towards what at one stage appeared the desirable norm of simple step-parental adoption, i.e. the Victorian and early twentieth-century model of reconstituting the family by social parenthood, which is now regarded as better achieved by other means, such as by giving step-parents PR with the natural parent with whom there is a marriage bond, as this does not remove PR from the other natural parent while still supporting the new step-family.

Since divorce, remarriage and other re-partnering is no longer rare and alternative contem-porary family formats have now been developed by HAR, government policy has thus now moved on from in the earlier period of English adoption law where the step-parent was seen as the natural missing piece in the family jigsaw and into the contemporary position where in a multicultural society government policy is to meet the need to find families for children in long-term care by matching the desire for children of those childless parents who cannot or do not access HAR with those children who need to leave local authority care for a new life in a family context.

It is fair to say that the picture of social parenting in step-families as presented in Victorian literature has long been outmoded. It was discouraged after the 1972 Houghton Report[2] saw dis-advantages and dangers for the child in thus formalising the reconstituted family because of distort-ing existing family relationships and thus damaging the child. Subsequently step-parent adoptions fell dramatically,[3] the suitability of step-parent adoptions was again queried in the review of adop-tion law[4] in 1992 and the creation of the status of special guardianship (by insertion of ss 14A–14G into the CA 1989 and the implementation of the 2002 Act[5]) was designed (and expected) to reduce these numbers further.

The factual basis for this expectation was that, while the 2002 Act did not prohibit step-parent adoption as such, in fact for the first time it also permitted a *single* person, thus including a step-parent, to make a sole application for adoption, whereas previously a step-parent had to apply with the child's parent to whom s/he was married – which was logically and philosophically odd as it also resulted in the child's *parent*, to whom the step-parent was married, adopting his/her own child.

However, even this form of full step-parent inclusion in the reconstituted family has been over-taken by further social change and corresponding law reform: special guardianship was at first thought to be the logical route by which adoption would be phased out in the step-family context, since special guardianship gave status but did not sever former family ties, but in fact the greater change arrived when the ACA 2002 s 112 amended the CA 1989 s 4 to enable step-parents to obtain PR, either by agreement or court order (or by obtaining a residence order – now a CAO – which automatically conferred PR), which after the Houghton Report was seen as more suitable

---

2 Cmnd 5107.
3 From 10,751 in 1971 to 1,107 in 2004; however, adoption numbers generally have fallen, from 21,495 in 1971 to only 4,000–5,000 a year in the present decade. There were 4,734 in 2012, an increase of 6 per cent over the previous figures, with a slight increase in numbers from unmarried families.
4 *Adoption Law Review: Consultation Document*, 1992.
5 ACA 2002 s 1(2); see below at 22.9.

than adoption and was obviously more convenient than special guardianship[6] in the case of step-parents.

However, more recently the Court of Appeal, in considering adoption versus special guardianship in this context, has said that the question of whether there is distortion of family relationships by step-parent adoption should not be overplayed.[7] It has been emphasised that there are some situations in which an adoption order is better for a child than special guardianship, for instance where the child is older and does not want any of the alternatives to adoption[8] or where a child maintains regular and good contact with the father.[9]

Both these trends are addressed by ACA 2002: ss 83–91 deal with adoption with a foreign element, restricting movement into and out of the country by ss 83 and 85, giving PR prior to adoption abroad s 84, and power to make further controlling regulations by subordinate legislation.

Reform has, however, been long in coming so it is not surprising that large numbers have built up of both discontented potential adopters and children waiting to be adopted. The first step was the interdepartmental working party on the review of adoption law, which published the consultation document in October 1992 referred to above. This was followed by a White Paper in November 1993[10] and a second consultation document.[11]

In March 1996 there was yet another consultation paper, *Adoption: A Service for Children*, which contained the draft Adoption Bill which was the forerunner of the new Act. This introduced a 'placement order' to replace the former flawed process of 'freeing for adoption', new grounds for dispensing with consent of the natural parent(s) and a new welfare test, which have subsequently been refined over the period in which the initial draft Bill went through at least two separate incarnations.

The ultimate influences on the 2002 legislation were the *Prime Minister's Review: Adoption*, from the Performance and Innovation Unit, in July 2000, and the December 2000 White Paper *Adoption – A New Approach*,[12] from the Department of Health, which set out the government's plan to promote greater use of adoption, to improve the performance of the adoption service and to make it child centred. It was a policy of the late 1990s New Labour government to support adoption reform because it could potentially reduce the numbers of children in care. This was partly driven by the Waterhouse Report.[13]

There are in fact fewer adoptions now than in previous decades: for example, the figure for 1974 was 22,500; this dropped to 6,326 over the 20 years to 1994. Numbers have currently been steady annually since 2007 at about 3,300 each year, but the Coalition Government statement in February 2011 that policy should change to permit more adoptions, followed up by the CAFA 2014 amendments which should now begin to generate an increase in numbers once the policy of prohibiting mixed-race placements in particular, and also excluding certain potential adopters in general on grounds of weight or other less desirable factors in their personal profiles, is updated to take account of the fact that it is recognised as more important that children waiting to be adopted have a loving home as soon as possible. Many more older and foreign children are now adopted, and a Hague Convention on Inter-country Adoption was produced in 1993 in an attempt to regulate this latter, potentially dangerous, development. Open adoption with both direct and indirect

---

6 Which has its own formal administrative processes which must be addressed; see below at 22.9.
7 *Re AJ (Adoption Order or Special Guardianship Order)* [2007] 1 FLR 507.
8 *Re M (Adoption or Residence Order)* [1998] 1 FLR 570.
9 *Re B (Adoption Order)* [2001] EWCA Civ 347; [2001] 2 FLR 26.
10 Cm 2288.
11 *Placement for Adoption – A Consultation Document*, Department of Health, 1994.
12 Cm 5107.
13 *Lost in Care – Report of the Tribunal of Inquiry into the Abuse of Children in Care in the former counties of Gwynedd and Clwyd* (2000).

contact between the child and his or her birth family has also developed,[14] a practice which would have been unthinkable 30 years ago, and it is accepted that same-sex couples can now adopt. A look at some of the cases gives some indication of the step-by-step social development which has driven the contemporary approach over the period between the two 1976 and 2002 statutes and since the latter's implementation in 2005.

❖ **CASE EXAMPLES**

In *Re W (Homosexual Adopter)* (1997)[15] it was held that AA 1976 s 15, which referred to the 'application of one person', did not stop the court making an order in favour of a homo-sexual woman living with her partner, as the statute need not be interpreted 'in a narrow or discriminatory way', which was logical as although that other common contemporary family unit, the unmarried opposite-sex couple, could not adopt under the 1976 Act, an order could be made in favour of one partner, with a joint residence order in favour of both.

In *Re AB (Joint Residence Order)* (1996)[16] an application was made by an unmarried couple whose stable relationship had lasted for 20 years – the adoption order was made in favour of the man with the joint residence order being made in favour of both, thus prior to the 2002 Act achieving the *practical* result they desired.

The ACA 2002 of course now formally permits adoption by unmarried couples; ss 49 and 50; a definition of unmarried couples (restricted to the Act) appears in s 144 and includes same-sex couples.

22.2 General provisions of adoption law

An adoption order under the AA 1976 gave PR for the child to the adopters, and the child ceased to be a member of its birth family: AA 1976 s 12(1) as amended by the CA 1989, Schedule 10. Now ACA 2002 s 46 has the same effect except where the adoption is by a step-parent who is married to one of the child's parents and the other parent has PR. The AA 1976 s 12(3) adoption, however, extinguished any CA 1989 order in force and the same occurs under ACA 2002 s 46. This differs from some other systems, such as Islamic law, where there is no family *severance* but adoption provides an alternative care mechanism. It seems English Law is the only system which does sever all family connection even in non-consensual adoption.[17]

The domicile of the child is highly relevant: AA 1976 s 55 permitted adoption of children abroad under foreign law, and this gave PR to adopters in England. The ACA 2002, in providing additional restrictions on bringing children into the UK for adoption, aims to ensure that British residents follow the appropriate procedures whether they adopt overseas or bring a child to the UK for adoption. Adoption in England (or overseas by British citizens) will confer both PR and British citizenship, although a British child adopted by a foreigner will not lose British citizenship.

---

14 See CAFA 2014 s 9.
15 [1997] 2 FLR 406.
16 [1996] 1 FLR 27.
17 I.e. when a child is adopted out of care under ACA 2002; see 22.10 below.

Any adoption will extinguish the PR of any person who had it previously in respect of the child in question.

Adoptions are 'family proceedings', so orders under CA 1989 s 8 can be made of the court's own volition where appropriate. Such an order, for example a CAO, may be better than an adoption order in some cases (e.g. where a step-parent is the applicant), since the s 8 order will not cut the child off from the former family as an adoption order inevitably does, but this alternative may now be overtaken by the power to give PR to a step-parent (see also further below).

The welfare test in adoption law under the AA 1976 was not the same as that in the CA 1989. Thus the two earlier Acts were out of step with one another for 15 years but this has been changed by the 2002 Act. There has been ongoing argument as to whether harmonisation was necessary or desirable, since different considerations apply in adoption from those affecting children generally, i.e. in adoption there are the interests of the birth parents to consider, as well as the impact on the child of cutting biological ties.

STATUTORY EXTRACTS

The AA 1976 s 6 provided:

> 'In reaching any decision relating to the adoption of a child a court or adoption agency shall have regard to all the circumstances, first consideration being given to the need to safeguard and promote the welfare of the child throughout his childhood, and shall so far as is practical ascertain the wishes and feelings of the child regarding the decision and give due consideration to them, having regard to his age and understanding.'

The ACA 2002 s 1(2) provides:

> 'The paramount consideration of the court or adoption agency must be the child's welfare throughout his life.'

Thus the matter has now been settled by the ACA 2002.

The ACA 2002 s 1(4)(a)–(f) uses a welfare checklist which is similar to the welfare checklist of the CA 1989 s 1(3):[18]

(a)   the child's wishes and feelings;
(b)   the child's needs;
(c)   the likely effect (throughout his life) of having ceased to be a member of the original family and become an adopted person;
(d)   the child's age, sex, background and characteristics;
(e)   any harm (within the meaning of the Children Act 1989) which has been suffered or there is a risk of the child suffering;
(f)   the relationship the child has with relatives and with any other person the court considers relevant including:

    (i)   the likelihood of any such relationship continuing and the value to the child of its doing so;

---

18 See Chapter 15.

(ii) the ability and willingness of any of the child's relatives, or of any such person, to provide the child with a secure environment in which the child can develop, and otherwise to meet the child's needs;

(iii) the wishes and feelings of any of the child's relatives or of any such person.

'Relationships' in s 1(4) does not include only legal relatives, but does also include, amongst others, the child's mother and father: s 1(8)(b). The court needs to read s 1(2) and 1(4)(c) carefully in view of the requirement to consider the child 'throughout his life' as this may include inheritance. The child's religion, race, culture and linguistic background must still be considered pursuant to s 1(5) although it is no longer determinative if it conflicts with the general welfare test;[19] however, the requirement to maintain his religion is not as strong as in the CA 1989, nor in some cases such as J v C (1990) where the Catholic religion was non-negotiable for the child C in a Protestant English household[20] but only one of the items the court must now consider.

By s 1(3) and s 1(6) they must also observe minimum intervention and no delay principles which have become settled in decisions under the CA 1989 although they are phrased slightly differently in the ACA 2002. They must also consider their other powers, i.e. s 8 orders, PR and special guardianship. By ACA 2002 s 47 the court must also be satisfied that whoever needs to consent to the child being placed for adoption (that process replacing the awkward system of 'freeing for adoption' under the AA 1976) duly has the opportunity to fulfil that role.

22.3 Who can adopt and be adopted

Only a single person or a married couple over the age of 21 could adopt under the AA 1976 – unless one spouse was a parent of the child, when it was sufficient if that parent was at least 18 and the other 21: ss 14(1) and 15(1), and this is retained by the ACA 2002 s 50 – but since the ACA 2002 unmarried couples are included.

If an applicant was married it was never possible[21] for that person to adopt as a single person unless the spouse could not be found, or was incapable owing to physical or mental ill health, or the parties were separated permanently, and this too was retained by the ACA 2002 s 51(3).

As step-parent adoptions were discouraged by the 1972 Houghton Report (although they still constituted half the adoptions in 1994) the draft Adoption Bill 1996 sought to introduce instead a PR agreement for step-parents that would result in shared PR with both the natural parents, and this provision was finally enacted in the ACA 2002 s 112. Accordingly it seems that step-parent adoptions are still likely to be discouraged, despite, or perhaps because of, the increasing numbers of step-families. See, for example, Re G (Adoption Order) (1999).[22] The potential for awkwardness in this context is illustrated by this case in which the interrelationships were considered by the judge.

---

19 See CAFA 2014 s 3.
20 See Chapter 15.
21 AA 1976 s 15(1).
22 [1999] 1 FLR 400.

> ### ❖ CASE EXAMPLE
>
> In, *Re G* (1999) the mother remarried and the new couple applied to adopt the mother's child of an earlier unmarried relationship where the father had had contact, which terminated on the mother's remarriage. The guardian *ad litem*, i.e. the person now called the children's guardian, supported the adoption on the basis that the family needed the order for their sense of security as a family, but on appeal the adoption order was made with limited contact for the father. The judge said that such an order should not be made simply to give the new step-family identity and 'the sense of security it craves' and that in this case the father should undoubtedly have obtained PR and should therefore have had a right to have his agreement to the adoption sought. Basically, this approach reinforces the court's long-held view in change of name applications that the father has some role to play in most children's lives and that links with him, even if tenuous, should usually be maintained if he wants them and they would benefit the child.

It was never possible to adopt a child who was or had been married: AA 1976 s 12(5), though a child could be adopted more than once: AA 1976 s 12(7). A child has always had to be a person under 18 when the adoption was commenced but could be over 18 when the order was finally made. This remains in ACA 2002 Act ss 47 and 49.

The definition section of the AA 1976 is s 72(1) and of the ACA 2002 s 2 (providing 'basic definitions'), s 144 ('general interpretation'), and s 147 and Schedule 6 ('glossary').

22.4 Arranging adoptions

Generally, adoptions are arranged through local authority agencies: AA 1976 s 1, and ACA 2002 s 3, unless the child was a relative of the adopters: AA 1976 s 11, and ACA 2002 ss 92 and 93 continue this restriction. There is no bar, however, on a relative of the child, other than the mother, making arrangements with an agency, especially where the mother is unable to do it herself.[23]

The ACA 2002 does not change the scope for non-agency adoptions: s 44 requires notice of intended adoption to be given to the local authority, not more than two years nor less than three months prior to the application. The local authority must then carry out all the usual investigations as if the adoption had been arranged through them.

The 2002 Act provides new restrictions on advertising children for adoption or for children to be adopted and creates a criminal sanction for breach: ss 123 and 124. However, by s 125 *et seq*, an official register is provided to match children and adopters.[24]

The 2002 Act places a duty on every local authority to establish and run an agency, setting up an Adoption Panel to screen adopters and supervise placements. Adopters must be in good health and, as under the AA 1976 process, within certain age limits. The result has been that although adoption is seen as a service to children, many children remain unadopted because of the criteria, although this was intended to change under the ACA 2002, which provided a new right to an assessment of needs for adoption support services under s 4 with detailed regulations and local authorities having to prepare plans: s 5, and s 12 provided a right to ministerial review of any determination

---

23 *Re W* (*Arrangements to Place for Adoption*) [1995] 1 FLR 163.
24 This is expanded in the CAFA 2014 s 7 to include children whom the authority is considering making available for adoption.

under the new arrangements. However, CAFA 2014 s 3, which permits the Secretary of State to make new regulations about agencies selecting potential adopters, and other CAFA 2014 changes may improve results. But no second-time applications are entertained under any provision unless there has been a change of circumstances, and no payments may be made or received, other than for certain adoption agency and medical expenses and fees: ACA 2002 s 11 (as under AA 1976 s 57).

This raises the question of surrogacy and payment of expenses.[25] By ACA 2002 s 95 payments are prohibited but it seems that the court can retrospectively authorise them as in the case of the 1976 Act. In *Re Adoption Application (Surrogacy)* (1987),[26] £10,000 for loss of earnings of a surrogate mother was acceptable and presumably this will remain possible. Nevertheless, sometimes orders are still made where there has been a payment and/or a private placement.

22.4.1 Adoption agencies

The local authority agency is an 'adoption service' and AA 1976 ss 1(4) and 72(1), and ACA 2002 s 2 define agencies further. Such agencies must operate within the 2002 welfare test, which under the 1976 Act put the child's welfare 'first' and did not make it 'paramount' as in the CA 1989, but by ACA 2002 s 1(2) aligns the test with the CA 1989. This still means that some regard can be paid to the interests of adult family members, but it does end long confusion as old cases under the 1976 Act show.

❖ CASE EXAMPLES

In *Re W (A Minor) (Adoption)* (1984)[27] (decided at a time when the child's welfare was first but not paramount) Cumming-Bruce J decided that it was not in the interests of the child's *welfare* to be adopted by the step-father applicant, where the father had paid maintenance and had contact. At first instance the judge had decided that 'fairness' to the natural parents was irrelevant, which under the criteria of the 1976 Act was not strictly true since the obligation was to give the child's welfare first consideration. However, the decision could still be based on first consideration being given to the child's welfare and the interests of parents still considered.

In *Re D (An Infant) (Adoption: Parents' Consent)* (1977)[28] the child's welfare was properly defined as 'first' but 'not paramount' over the interests of the child's parents, though in this case the adoption was allowed as the natural father was a practising homosexual and the mother and step-father could offer an environment which protected the child from homosexual contacts (still an issue at the date of this case).

The draft 1996 Bill would also have brought the welfare test into line with that of CA 1989 s 1(1) and despite debate up to the very time the 2002 statute was passed, ACA 2002 finally ended the long-running argument. The court must now consider the child's welfare 'throughout his life'. However, in an age of post-adoption contact, the irreversibility of adoption[29] and children's human rights interest in knowing their origins this can be a difficult task.

---

25 See Chapter 13.
26 [1987] 2 All ER 826.
27 [1984] FLR 402.
28 [1977] AC 602, HL, p 638.
29 Even in the case of erroneous evidence: see *Webster v Norfolk CC* [2009] EWCA Civ 59; see below at 22.5.

22.4.2 Procedure for making orders

This was governed by the AA 1976 s 13, and a similar process remains except that the detailed probationary periods of residence of the child with the prospective adopters are different and the former 'freeing for adoption' step is now replaced by a placement order before the adoption process begins. Whether the child is placed by an agency or with relatives, the process is laid down in the ACA 2002 ss 42, 43 and 47. Under the ACA 2002 the child must have spent the appropriate period with the prospective adopters, depending on whether the adoption is a step-parent application, or by other relatives, or is an agency adoption: at least ten weeks if placed by an agency or the court with the prospective adopters (or for longer periods of six to 12 months if the application is by a partner of a parent of the child or by foster parents) or three years in any other case unless the court abridges these periods.

The court will appoint a children's guardian in a contested case, or an independent social worker where the application is not opposed, and in both cases this will usually be a Cafcass officer, who also has the task of witnessing that the pre-court consent to the placement order is freely given.

22.4.3 Adoption by relatives

A relative was defined by the AA 1976 s 72(1) as including the following:

> '. . . grandparent, brother, sister, uncle and aunt whether of the full blood or half blood or by affinity and includes, where the child is illegitimate, the father of the child and any person who could be a relative within the meaning of this definition if the child were the legitimate child of his mother and father'.

Great uncles and aunts were not relatives for this purpose. The ACA 2002 Act adopts a similar list.

It was often within the relative context that the relevance of CA 1989 s 8 orders was seen, as, for example, in adoption applications by grandparents to which it has usually been thought a s 8 order might be preferable.[30]

The approach of the ACA 2002 has built on this attitude by making no special provisions for adoption by relatives and instead introducing the new PR provision for step-parents,[31] which is intended to cater for the most common past relative adoption applications.

The ACA 2002 also builds on the status of 'special guardian' to cater for those children for whom adoption is not thought appropriate. Children being cared for by the wider family were thought to be the core beneficiaries of such a concept, since there were many in this category who could not return to their natural parents but who would benefit from greater security without losing their legal relationship with their parents. Some ethnic or religious groups also prefer such a solution.

It is curious that this contemporary provision now gives legal force to a status commonly found in practice in both history and literature (where 'guardians' appear in many eighteenth- and nineteenth-century classics) and yet it has taken 30 years of clumsy attempts to address the fallout from the disintegration of the traditional nuclear and extended family to reach the obvious conclusion that adoption is not the best solution in every case.

A special guardian takes all the day-to-day decisions about a child and although the birth parents cannot exercise it in an unrestricted manner, they do not completely lose their PR but remain legally the child's parents. Moreover the special guardianship order is not finite: it can be discharged, unlike adoption, which is the only child order which can never be reversed.

---

30 See e.g. Re W (A Minor) (Adoption by Grandparents) [1980] 2 FLR 161.
31 See 22.1, above.

22.4.4 Notice to local authority in non-agency placements

This made a child a 'protected child' under the AA 1976 ss 22(1) and 32. The child had to wait at least three months in such cases to be adopted. By s 36, certain information had to be given in relation to a protected child. By the ACA 2002 the s 44 notice to adopt triggers an investigation at least as thorough as the local authority's own adoption agency would have conducted had it arranged the adoption itself, and also requires such a local authority to give notice to any other local authority in whose area the applicant(s) resided immediately beforehand, thus maximising the chances that all factors relating to the suitability of the proposed adopter(s) will come to light.

22.5 Parental agreement to adoption

Agreement could never be given within the first six weeks after the birth: AA 1976 s 16; ACA 2002 s 52(3) repeats this. An order used to be made 'freeing the child for adoption', giving the agency PR: AA 1976 s 18, and in effect gave the child to an agency at an early stage so that the parents could not then change their minds so easily; however, many did, sometimes leading to distressing proceedings, although if the child was not then adopted after 12 months had elapsed, the order could be revoked.

The ACA 2002 ss 18–29 provides a new system of placement by consent to placement orders. Consent to a placement now in effect includes advance consent to adoption, unless there has been a change of circumstances: s 47(7), when the court can give permission for the natural parent(s) to oppose the making of an adoption order: s 47(5). When deciding whether to allow the adoption order to be opposed if change of circumstances is established, the court must then consider the welfare test in s 1. This means that although the natural parents' consent can be withdrawn at any time before the adoption application is made: s 20(3), once an adoption application is made it is much more difficult for the natural parents to take it back, the aim being to take this fundamental decision as to whether adoption is the way forward earlier in the adoption process, which is why by ACA 2002 s 141 a placement order cannot be made unless the court is satisfied that the natural parents have been notified or at least every effort has been made to notify them.

Once an adoption order is made there is virtually no chance that it will be reversed, as once lawfully made it is not considered right that they should be disturbed as has been shown in some cases which have attracted media attention.

❖ CASE EXAMPLE

In *Webster v Norfolk County Council* (2009)[32] the parents failed to have adoption orders set aside when three of their children had been adopted following a wrong diagnosis of non-accidental injury, since time had passed, the adoption process had been correctly followed and the court decided the circumstances were not exceptional.

---

32 [2009] EWCA Civ 59; [2009] 1 FLR 1378.

22.5.1 Dispensing with parental consent

A parent is defined by AA 1976 s 72 as any person who has PR for the child under the CA 1989, and the definition is repeated by the ACA 2002 s 52(6) subject to two minor exceptions under s 52(9) and (10). An unmarried father, therefore, does not fall into this category unless he has a PR agreement with the mother or a PR order from the court. However, the court has been increasingly unwilling to proceed without efforts being made to contact the unmarried father because of the potential breach of his human rights, and in practice the judge usually gives directions for him to be notified if possible.

The position is different if the father is not known, the conception of the child was not in an established relationship and the mother opposes efforts to identify the father. The Court of Appeal has applied the s 1(4) checklist and ordered that the local authority should not look for a father in a case of a 'one-night stand' where the mother was young and did not want the father identified.[33] This is a context clearly distinguishable from the average 'unmarried father' case but it has been criticised[34] on the grounds that the Court of Appeal took too narrow a view of welfare and gave too much weight to the wishes of the child's mother.

The child's agreement is not required.

22.5.2 Grounds for dispensing with parental agreement

There were six grounds in the AA 1976 s 16(2), that:

- the parent or guardian cannot be found or is incapable of giving agreement;
- the parent or guardian is withholding consent unreasonably;
- the parent or guardian has persistently failed without reasonable cause to discharge his parental responsibility for the child;
- the parent or guardian has abandoned or neglected the child;
- the parent or guardian has persistently ill treated the child;
- the parent or guardian has seriously ill treated the child.

By ACA 2002 s 52, the court must be satisfied that it should dispense with parental consent on one of only two grounds, that:

(a)   the parent or guardian cannot be found or is incapable of giving consent; or
(b)   the welfare of the child requires consent to be dispensed with.

The whole process of consent to *adoption* has been accelerated by the *placement for adoption* process which has replaced 'freeing for adoption',[35] so that placement under the ACA 2002 is the stage at which parental consent is often given to *adoption* as well. While s 52 still permits a parent a change of mind with all the attendant problems that arose in the 1976 Act case law, under the new ACA 2002 s 1(2) welfare test, adoption order hearings are less protracted because it will almost always be that the adoption is for the child's welfare.

---

33 *Re C (A Child) (Adoption: Duty of Local Authority)* [2007] Civ 1206; *Re C (A Child) v XYZ County Council* [2008] 1 FLR 1294.
34 Sloan, B, '*Re C (A Child) (Adoption: Duty of Local Authority)*, Welfare and the rights of the birth family in "fast track" adoption cases', CFLQ 87 (2009).
35 See 22.6, below.

22.6 The placement order replacing 'freeing for adoption'

By AA 1976 s 18(2), the parent(s) had to consent to the application or the child must already have been in the agency's care under a formal care order. If this was not the case, the agency could not apply to free the child for adoption. By s 18(1), the court had to be satisfied that the parents had freely and with understanding consented to the freeing for adoption, or that the consent was dispensed with on a s 16(2) ground, but the court could not dispense with agreement unless the child was already placed or a placement was likely.

If parents disagreed the agency could seek to dispense with their consent. If the order was made the parents lost PR and the agency acquired it. By s 18(7), the court had to be satisfied that an unmarried father had not applied for PR and was not likely to. There was provision in s 20 for revocation of s 18 orders, or this could be done under the inherent jurisdiction of the High Court, but this was a discretionary order. The general principle was that unmarried fathers had rights: their views had to be sought if they planned to seek PR.

By ACA 2002 s 18, an agency may place a child for adoption when it considers that that is appropriate for the child, but needs either (1) parental consent or (2) a placement order from the court to do so, unless there is a care order in place or in process: s 19. By s 20 a parent may also give advance consent to an adoption order, which may be revoked under s 20(3). While, as already explained, a placement order may also be contested and revoked 'on the application of any person': s 24(1), only the child or the local authority will not have to show change of circumstances to obtain leave to do so: s 24(3).

Various organisations, including the Family Rights Group and the Women's Interest Group of the Society of Labour Lawyers, have been concerned about how these provisions could work in practice to the detriment of natural parents, and in particular what could happen if parents precipitately give their consent to a placement, and then change their minds, and the court was not minded to give permission for them to contest the adoption. Commentators have queried to what extent the court will always be prepared to give such permission, and the LAA to fund hearings especially now such funding is provided, if at all, under the secondary legislation of the Funding Code. There is a concern that parents can elect not to be told of the date when the adoption application is to be heard: s 20(4), and if they do this clearly they will lose the protection given by s 143 of the right of knowing when they could change their minds and to contest the adoption with permission of the court if there was a change of circumstances. The fate of the Websters in their attempts to reverse their children's adoption in the tragic case where their children were misdiagnosed and adopted because the parents had been presumed to have harmed them[36] shows how averse the court is to reversing adoption orders, so that the process can clearly be very risky for natural parents who avail themselves of the option of giving early consent.

22.7 Adoption orders with conditions

By AA 1976 s 12(6), an adoption order could contain 'such terms as the court sees fit', including, for example, contact. The same is true under ACA 2002 s 26, where an application for contact can be heard at the same time as an adoption order application. Any CA 1989 s 8 order including contact, and an order under CA 1989 s 34 for a child in care, is discharged by an adoption order, as will any contact activity direction under CA 1989 s 11A. As it is a proactive policy of the ACA 2002 to promote adoption of children in care, it is not infrequently that post-adoption contact may

---

36 See above at 22.5.

be ordered for older children with siblings or other members of their original families, although the court may be unwilling if there is any friction between the families or especially if the adopters do not want it. Post-adoption contact was possible even under the 1976 Act, and it was not unusual for it to be accepted by the time that Act was implemented.

❖ CASE EXAMPLES

In *Re C (A Minor) (Adoption: Conditions)* (1988),[37] the contact order was to enable a girl to see her brother. This type of sibling contact order is more common than such conditions allowing contact to a mother, although that could be ordered in appropriate cases. Some contact does seem to be accepted now, perhaps through familiarisation, for example because of some celebrity adoptions.

In *Re O (Transracial Adoption)* (1995)[38] a contact order was made in favour of the birth mother although her consent to the adoption had been dispensed with.

However, while under the 2002 Act it may be more usual for such orders to be made, it is important that the natural parents make their application before the adoption order is made: once that has happened they will have lost their right to apply under the CA 1989 s 8 and will have to apply to the court for permission to apply for contact under ACA 2002, which the court might not want to grant in case it destabilised the child or the adopters. On the other hand, before the adoption order is made, ACA 2002 s 1(4) and the welfare checklist require the court to consider the full range of its powers, which will include whether there should be a contact order, and by s 46(6) is further required to consider whether any person should have contact. Thus at that stage the natural parents are much more likely to be pushing against an open door than if they leave their application until later.

22.8 Effects of adoption

Adopters always obtained PR, and anyone who had it before the adoption order lost it under AA 1976 s 12(2). Natural parents had no right to keep in touch (unless a contact order has been made, which was possible under the CA 1989 s 8[39]) and they had no obligation to maintain the child. An adopted child was never illegitimate, even if adopted by a natural parent: AA 1976 s 39(4). Broadly, these effects of the order remain the same although post-adoption contact may now be easier to obtain.

There was also a separate adopted children's register not open to the general public except by court order: AA 1976 s 50. This is continued by ACA 2002 ss 77–79.

Children who are adopted could under the 1976 statute discover their origins once they were 18 years old: AA 1976 s 51. The ACA 2002 ss 80–81 continues this. There is an adoption contact register through which relatives can make contact subject to safeguards: their enquiries are transmitted to the adopted person.

---

37 [1988] 1 All ER 705.
38 [1995] 2 FLR 597.
39 As explained above at 22.7.

There has been much criticism during the long period of proposals for reform of the apparent lack of support for disadvantaged natural parents in a framework which was thought to be meant to balance the interests of both children who might benefit from a fresh start and of their birth families. However, the government appears always to have seen adoption more as a service to children and childless families than to any other parties in the story.[40]

The ACA 2002 attempted to address some long-standing criticisms, changing the law to make the welfare of the child the paramount consideration in all adoption decisions. It also tried to bring adoption law more closely into line with the CA 1989, for example in allowing courts to set timetables to cut delays, improving the adoption process itself, including establishing a review process for prospective adopters turned down for adoption, and providing better post-adoption support. In the summer of 2001, the Lord Chancellor's Department also issued new guidance to courts on speeding up the adoption process and making it more efficient, since which from 2010 the Coalition Government has continued to promote reform.[41]

Nevertheless, adoption law and practice has continued to generate criticism, not least because of the large numbers of children still in care who would benefit from placements which would give them a new start and a stable home from which they could develop from a better base than in local authority care or fostering.

The most recent review of adoption policy[42] recommended that some of the criteria which have hindered such a result should be relaxed as it is more important that otherwise disadvantaged children should have permanent 'loving homes' where they can obtain a new start in life than that the cultural match between them and the families into which they might move should be exact and perfect. The government immediately announced that guidance on adoptions, including on mixed-race placements, would be updated, to which has now been added the CAFA 2014 s 3 (on disregarding ethnicity) and s 4 (new regulations for choosing adopters). It remains to be seen whether statistics change.

The detailed working of provisions which appear to be likely to disadvantage the birth parents remains to be assessed in practical terms. However, adoption is probably an area of the law where it is impossible to serve two mutually exclusive sets of interests, and the Act has apparently come down on the side of the presumed interests of the child to find a non institutional home in secure circumstances. Whatever the controversy, the special guardianship seems to be an inspired idea for the older child who has always faced most difficulties in finding an exit from care.

22.9 Special guardianship

The following persons can apply for this order under CA 1989 s 14A:

- guardians;
- persons with residence orders;
- persons who have the consent of all persons with residence orders;
- persons with whom the child has lived for three out of five years, provided all the consents mentioned are obtained;

---

40 See the White Paper on *Adoption: The Future*, Cm 2288, 1993, introduced into the House of Commons in 1993 by the then Secretary of State for Health; the comment in [1994] Fam Law 1 by Deborah Cullen, Secretary to the Legal Group, British Agencies for Adoption and Fostering; and in the same issue the article by Jolly and Sandiland of Nottingham University, 'Political correctness and the Adoption White Paper' at p 30.
41 The government published two papers in 2012: *Contact Arrangements for Children: A Call for Views* and *Placing Children in Sibling Groups for Adoption: A Call for Views*, both Department for Education, 2012.
42 By Barnado's, www.barnados.org.uk, followed by the announcement by Education Secretary Michael Gove in February 2011 that policy guidance would be updated.

- any other person who has those consents;
- a local authority foster parent with whom the child has lived for one year;
- anyone else with permission of the court;
- the child if of sufficient understanding and with permission of the court.

The court considers the matter of permission to apply in the same way as considering permission to apply for an order under the CA 1989 s 8: s 14(12), and can make a special guardianship order of its own motion in any family proceedings (in which adoption is included). The local authority has to make a report about the suitability of the proposed special guardian, in the same way as they must report on an adoption application. The court applies its discretion in the same way as it would apply the welfare checklist and other principles in s 1 in an adoption. The result of a special guardianship order is that the special guardian obtains PR for the child, and is entitled to services from the local authority including financial support. The order discharges all other orders.

The court has favourably considered orders in favour of grandparents, where children have lived with them for a substantial period, and found this more suitable than adoption, which would disrupt family relationships, but rejected such an application from an aunt and uncle for whom adoption would, in the court's view, be better as the aunt and uncle would then have some protection from the importunities of litigious parents. On the other hand, sometimes such relatives have not received an adoption order because of the potential to skew family relationships and because of the relatives' discordant relationship with the child's mother. Each case turns on its own facts.

22.10 Current debates

Ideas for research on these current discussions may be found on the companion website updates.

- Does the ACA 2002 give adequate consideration to the human rights of the birth parents?
- Does special guardianship really serve a need for children who could otherwise reside with relatives or other persons under a CA 1989 s 8 CAO?
- Is post-adoption contact in 'open adoption' really appropriate?

22.11 Summary of Chapter 22
Background to adoption

- Adoption law is entirely statutory and was long in need of reform after several abortive attempts to update it since 1976. This has been effected by the ACA 2002 implemented in 2005, with further amendments in 2014.

Effect of adoption

- The effect of an adoption is to transfer PR from the birth parents to the adopters.
- An adoption made abroad under foreign law will be recognised in the UK.
- The AA 1976 welfare test in adoption law was not the same as under the CA 1989; ACA 2002 s 1(1) was drafted to bring adoption and the CA 1989 welfare tests closer together.
- The AA 1976 test permitted some regard to be had to the interests of the parents and family of the child to be adopted but this is much weakened under ACA 2002 where the ongoing link with the birth family is seen only in the context of the child's interests.

The adoption process

- Either a single person or a married couple can adopt, provided the applicant(s)' age is over 21, or 18 if one of a couple is the parent of the child and the other is at least age 21.
- Step-parent adoptions are discouraged, but same-sex adopters, or adopters in partnership with others of the same sex, are acceptable and ACA 2002 permits unmarried couples to adopt.
- Adoptions are arranged through local authority agencies, which provide a service to children; no payments may be made or received except for expenses. Private placements are outlawed except between relatives.
- A child must be at least ten weeks old and have been placed for a qualifying period with the adopters. There is a court-appointed children's guardian in a contested case.
- Parents must agree to an adoption but consent may be dispensed with on various grounds.
- Under AA 1976 consent could be dispensed with if the mother or parents had ill treated, neglected or abandoned the child, or withheld consent unreasonably.
- The 2002 Act reduces the grounds for dispensing with consent of a parent as a principled welfare decision which should streamline such hearings, especially because of the introduction of a placement order system instead of 'freeing for adoption' under AA 1976.
- The ACA 2002 frontloads consent to adoption to an earlier stage.
- An unmarried father not applying for PR does not need his consent sought.
- Conditions may be attached to orders, including for post-adoption contact, but this is more usual for siblings than parents, unless the adopters agree.
- There is an adoption contact register for adopted children to contact parents if they wish when they are 18.

 ## 22.12 Further reading

Choudry, S, 'The Adoption and Children Act 2002, the welfare principle and the Human Rights Act – a missed opportunity', [2003] CFLQ 119.

Cullen, D, 'Adoption – a (fairly) new approach', [2005] CFLQ 475.

Curry-Sumner, I, '*EB v France*: a missed opportunity', [2009] CFLQ 365.

Hall, A, 'Special guardianship and permanency planning: unforeseen consequences and missed opportunities', [2008] CFLQ 359.

Hall, A, 'Special guardianship: a missed opportunity: findings from research', [2008] Fam Law 148.

Ray, P, 'Placement for adoption or legal limbo?', [2012] Fam Law 979.

Webb, A, 'Leave to oppose an adoption: unhelpful legislation', [2012] Fam Law 1119.

Implementing Special Guardianship, Department for Children, Schools and Families, 2009.

www.baaf.org.uk, British Association for Adoption and Fostering.

https://www.gov.uk/government/organisations/department-for-education

www.every-child-matters.org.uk

Index